READING
THE WOMEN
OF THE BIBLE

ALSO BY TIKVA FRYMER-KENSKY

Motherprayer

In the Wake of the Goddesses

READING
THE WOMEN
OF THE BIBLE

Tikva Frymer-Kensky

SCHOCKEN BOOKS   NEW YORK

A cataloging-in-publication record has been prepared for
Reading the Women of the Bible by the Library of Congress.

ISBN 0-8052-4121-3

www.schocken.com
Book design by Anthea Lingeman
Printed in the United States of America
First Edition
2   4   6   8   9   7   5   3   1

Dedicated to Professor Yohanan Muffs,

beloved teacher of my youth,

who gave me the gift of Torah,

sharing with me his love of this fascinating book

and the joys of its study.

CONTENTS

Part IV. Voice

Part V. Reading the Women of the Bible

ACKNOWLEDGMENTS

I have spent many years working on this project. Like many women my age, I grew up translating myself into the men of the Bible. In my imagination I was Abraham, not Sarah; David, not one of his wives. My feminist sensibilities were directed at gaining access to the world of study, not in transforming the curriculum. But in the 1970s, inspired by the women's movement, I realized what I—what all of us—had been missing. I began to study and teach Women in Religion, and I was immediately struck by the complexity and sheer abundance of the stories about women in the Hebrew Bible. My first project, *In the Wake of the Goddesses,* was not about the women in the Bible. Trained as an assyriologist, I decided to begin at the beginning, with the females in Mesopotamian literature, the goddesses, and the book that resulted is a study of the role these goddesses played in the ancient religious imagination, and an exploration of the impact on Biblical thought of the elimination of goddesses from Israel's religious life and imagination. Clearly, at least one of the functions of goddesses—thinking about gender—was carried on in the Bible through the stories about human women, and so I began my intense study of the stories about women in the Bible. I included my study of the gender attitudes of these stories, or rather, of the surprising lack of specific gender differentiation in Biblical thought in *In the Wake of the Goddesses,* but I realized that the stories were not primarily about gender. Ever since, I have been studying these stories.

During this time, I moved from Ann Arbor to Philadelphia to teach at the Reconstructionist Rabbinical College, spent a wonderful year in residence at the Center for Jewish Studies in Philadelphia, came to Chicago to teach at the Divinity School of the University of Chicago, and spent another wonderful year at the Center.

These were superb places to work, with supportive colleagues eager to encourage each other to keep learning. The Center for Jewish Studies is a scholar's paradise, a garden of knowledge in which no labor is required other than tending the books of the garden and eating their fruit. I am deeply grateful for my time there. But my two teaching institutions, the RRC and the Divinity School, have also been excellent places to work, with an interested administration, collegial faculty, and—above all—phenomenal students. Many of the analyses in this book were done in coordination with the courses on Women in the Bible that I taught several times at each place, and once at an adult women's education program in Philadelphia. Much of the careful word analysis was done in anticipation of and in answer to the demands of my students that I prove my points; many of the discoveries came as part of the searching interactions and wonderful conversations that took place in these classes. The Rabbinical students' search for relevance kept me from ascending ivory towers, the life experience of the adult women kept me aware that these stories have always resonated with the personal experiences of women's lives, and my graduate students gave me the gift of demanding that I show the same scholarly meticulousness and intellectual rigor that I demand from them. Much as I sometimes long to spend more time in the uninterrupted contemplative atmosphere of a research institute, I know that my work would not be the same without the stimulation of my students, and I am grateful to them.

No matter how many years one spends working on a book, the last year is always a mad rush to fill in blanks and complete postponed tasks. I have benefited during these years from the able assistance of my secretary, Nathelda McGee, who made sure that things got sent to their appropriate places, and my student assistants Sharon Mattila, who tracked down publication dates and other bibliographic details, Holly Bland, who keeps me in a steady supply of Xeroxed articles to mark and devour, and Sally Stamper, who made sure that other things didn't get abandoned while I concentrated on this manuscript. I would also like to thank two students, Sharon Albert and Laura Lieber, who were kind enough to step in and give me a crash course in contemporary ways to transliterate Hebrew so that this book would not have to use Hebrew symbols.

Above all, I would like to acknowledge my husband's support. I typed my own manuscript, but he provided needed encouragement to keep working on this book whenever the administrative and pastoral details of an academic position threatened to derail me or my periodic illnesses exhausted me. Often, in recent years, this encouragement had to come by telephone, and I am thankful for the patience and support that he has given so freely.

I give thanks to all of these, God's agents, by which God sustained me and brought me to this moment. *Berûkîm tiheyû,* Blessed be!

Tikva Frymer-Kensky
Chicago, April 2002

INTRODUCTION: READING THE
WOMEN OF THE BIBLE

The women of ancient Israel have carved a place for themselves in our consciousness. Sarah, Rebekkah, Rachel, and Leah are the mothers of Israel; the biblical Eve is our mother in myth, now joined by "mitochondrial Eve" as our mother in genes. Bathsheba and Delilah: their very names conjure up scenes in our imagination, nights of ancient sex and betrayal. Children walk around today bearing the names of Miriam and Deborah, ancient leaders, poets, and prophets, and the names of Abigail, Yael, Ruth, Naomi, and Esther, heroines and queens of the Hebrew Bible. Faced with the memory of so many prominent women, a visitor from a distant planet might justifiably conclude that ancient Israel was a feminist paradise.

But the visitor would be wrong. Ancient Israel, like all other great historical civilizations, was a patriarchy. Men owned almost all the land, which was passed on from father to son. The legal tribunals consisted of men: the judges at the central courts and the elders in their local councils. The army was composed of men, as was the administrative bureaucracy. Men also dominated public religious life, serving as officiants in local and national rituals and holding all the positions in the temple hierarchy. Women, while not physically confined to the home, expended most of their energies there. Economically dependent on the head of their households, they had a limited ability to determine events beyond their own families, and even within the family they ultimately had to conform to the wishes of the father or husband.

Our visitor from a distant planet might not be troubled by this discovery, but readers from the late twentieth century are often startled. The Bible, after all, has informed and continues to inform much of our own moral thinking. How can a book that teaches the common divine origin of all humanity and the sacred nature of each human being reflect a social order in which women are systematically disadvantaged and subordinated? This question creates a whole range of answers among contemporary readers. At one end of the spectrum is the leadership of the Southern Baptists, who embrace the biblical system and mandate that today's women suppress their demand for equality and be subordinate to their husbands. Other readers, at the opposite pole of the spectrum, find the patriarchy of the Bible a reason to abandon the monotheist religions based on it. They suspect that the Bible itself led to patriarchy. These readers argue that since Israel had only one god, and this god is referred to as "He," this male "Lord" provides a divine model for males as master. After all, as Mary Daley said concerning contemporary religion, "If God is a man, than a man is god." Monotheism, then (according to this argument), created patriarchy.

Like the visitor from a distant planet, these twentieth-century theorists are drawing logical conclusions, but they are simply wrong. History shows that patriarchy was well entrenched fifteen hundred years before Israel first came into being. As we trace our written records from the beginning of writing in ancient Sumer through the ensuing centuries and millennia in the ancient world, we can trace the *intensification* of patriarchy as time goes on. But even the first written records reflect a social system in which males were predominant. Male-dominated social systems were (and are) very widespread, encompassing geographically distant societies with very different religious and sociopolitical systems. Biblical Israel did not invent patriarchy. It was not even the most intense or thorough patriarchy in the ancient world. Other classical societies, like Assyria and Athens, show a much greater degree of domination of women. The worship of Ishtar in Assyria and Athena in Athens did not lessen male control over real women. The male Lord did not create patriarchy. The truth is just the opposite: patriarchal thought required that the one Lord of all be conceived as a male and portrayed in a masculine grammar.

It is important to get the facts straight; though patriarchy preexisted the Bible, the Bible was not written to construct it. Readers can accept the Bible's moral stature without conforming to the patriarchal social structure within it. At the same time, there is no ignoring the fact that even though the Bible did not create patriarchy, it also did not eliminate it. The Bible did not question the patriarchy in the social structure it shared with the rest of the ancient world, just as it did not question another glaring social inequity, slavery. Biblical thinkers, so radical in their transformation of ideas about God and about the relationship of humanity to the cosmos, never conceived of a radical transformation of society. They were very aware of social problems, trying to ameliorate the suffering of the downtrodden, curtailing abuses, helping runaway slaves stay free, redeeming those sold into slavery, and calling for a limit to capitalist aggrandizement. Despite such concerns, the Bible did not eradicate slavery, it did not eliminate patriarchy, it did not eradicate economic oppression.

However, the Bible also does not defend the status quo, for the idea of social revolution is integral to biblical thought. God is a god of change, for God elevates the lowly, brings the marginalized to the center, and raises high the socially inferior. In this way, power and privilege are necessarily impermanent. But reversing position does not create a more egalitarian world any more than ameliorating suffering does: it only changes the fortunes of individual people. Biblical thinkers never conceived of a social order without hierarchy.

The Bible, a product of this patriarchal society, is shaped by the concerns of the men of Israel who were involved in public life. As such, it is a public book, concerned with matters of government, law, ritual, and social behavior. But why, then, does this clearly androcentric text from a patriarchal society have so many stories that revolve around women? And why are there so many memorable women in the Bible? The sheer number of their stories demands an explanation: What are they doing here? Why were they written? Why were they included in this compact text?

One possible answer soon occurred to me: could the biblical stories about women have been written because of the desire of Israelite men to explore the nature of women and their role and to understand the question of gender? To explore this possibility, I analyzed the biblical stories from the perspective of gender questions: What, according to these stories, do women want? What are they like? How do they achieve their goals? The results, documented in *In the Wake of the Goddesses*, were unexpected. Contrary to all assumptions—my own included—the Hebrew Bible, unlike other ancient literature, does not present any ideas about women as the "Other." The role of woman is clearly subordinate, but the Hebrew Bible does not "explain" or justify this subordination by portraying women as different or inferior. The stories do not reflect any differences in goals and desires between men and women. Nor do they point out any strategies or methods used by women that are different from those used by men who are not in positions of authority. There are no personality traits or psychological characteristics that are unique to women, and the familiar Western notions of "feminine wiles," "the battle between the sexes," "sisterly solidarity," and "sex as weapon" are all absent, as are any discussions of the nature of women. There are also no negative statements and stereotypes about women, no gynophobic ("woman-fearing") discourse. The only misogynist statement in the Bible comes very late in biblical development, in the book of Ecclesiastes, and shows the introduction of the classical Greek denigration of women into Israel.

The Bible's lack of ideas about female otherness does not make it a feminist paradise any more than the presence of memorable women does. Women were still socially disadvantaged and excluded from public power. But the Bible does not add insult to this disadvantage, does not claim that women need to be controlled because they are wild, or need to be led because they are foolish, or need to be directed because they are passive, or any of the other justifications for male domination that have been prevalent in Western culture.

The Bible's lack of justification for social inequity can be interpreted in two radically different ways. Reading with a hermeneutic of suspicion, we might speculate that the Bible did not need to justify patriarchy, because patriarchy was so firmly entrenched, and that the Bible's lack of stereotypes about women is simply a gender blindness that totally ignores everyone but economically advantaged males. If, however, we follow the hermeneutic of suspicion with a hermeneutic of grace, we might conclude that even though the Bible failed to eradicate or even notice patriarchy, it created a vision of humanity that is gender neutral. Biblical thinkers treated social structure as a historical given: they sought to regulare social behavior, but not to explain or justify the social structure itself.

The Bible's view of gender sets up a dramatic clash between theory and reality. On the one hand, women occupied a socially subordinate position. On the other hand, the Bible did not label them as inferior. This gap between ideology and social structure has a major disadvantage: it did not explain people's lives, did not give people a way to understand why women had no access to public decision making. Such dissonance could not last forever: one of the two had to give, and the Bible's vision of a gender-neutral humanity ultimately gave way in the face of ongoing patriarchy. At the same time, the biblical vision had the enormous advantage of not adding prejudice to powerlessness. The biblical view understood that women were powerless and subordinate without being inferior. This insight had enormous implications for the way Israel viewed itself. Israel was always small and vulnerable in comparison to the empires surrounding it. As time went on, this vulnerability gave way to defeat, and Israel was conquered by more powerful nations. The Bible's view of women became central to Israel's thinking, for it provided a paradigm for understanding powerlessness and subordination without recourse to prejudicial ideas. Israel was subject to the power and authority of others on an international level just as women were subordinate within Israelite society, and the Bible's own image of women enabled its thinkers to accept this powerlessness without translating it into a sense of inferiority or worthlessness. In this way, the Bible's image of women was an essential element in its self-image and its understanding of Israel's destiny.

The Women-stories

The stories, then, were not written in order to make statements about women. To understand why they were written, we have to look at each story intently, with all the techniques described below, and also consider them collectively, as a group, reading them in relation to one another instead of confining them to the context in which they occur individually. When we do this, patterns begin to emerge, not only type-scenes and parallel plotlines, but also recognizable themes with which these stories are concerned. I have identified four categories of stories, four "discourses" to which these stories address themselves. With my fondness for alliteration, I label these "woman as victor," "woman as victim," "woman as virgin (bride-to-be)," and "woman as voice (of God)."

The "woman as victor" stories are tales about heroic women who become saviors. These women, both Israelites and foreigners, help Israel survive and defeat its enemies. The stories about these women appear in the book of Exodus, during the time of the redemption from Egypt, in the books of Joshua and Judges from the days of the settlement, in the books of Samuel from the early days of the monarchy. And then they disappear, to appear again in the days after the death of the kingdom, during the Persian exile. The absence of victor stories from the four hundred years of the kingdoms of Israel and Judah is no accident. When there is no centralized power, when political action takes place in the household or village, then women can rise to public prominence. When times are peaceful, they may be leaders and counselors; in times of danger, they can become heroic figures of resistance. When war brings action into the homes of women, they may act with what until recently would have been considered "manly" courage and aggression. They can also be masters of indirection, knowing the techniques and skills upon which people not in positions of power have to rely. When a strong central government is established, a pyramid of power extends from the top down through the various hierarchies and bureaucracies. At such a time, women in Israel were frozen out of the positions of power, and relegated to the private domain. They may have been heroines in their own families, but they left no trace in the public record.

Not all women fared well, as the second category of stories—"women as victims"—illustrates. These are the "texts of terror," tales of women who suffer at the hands of the men in power. At first glance, one might assume that these stories are a form of gender propaganda, demonstrating to women the dire events that could befall them. If this were indeed their purpose, the Bible authors would be expressing a concealed but malignant misogyny. But the placement of these stories is a clue to revealing their purpose. They all appear in two of the historical books of the Bible, Judges and Second Samuel, which relate the initial settlement of Israel and the consolidation of the Davidic monarchy. The "historian," the composer of the great sequence of historical books from Joshua through Kings, tells these "texts of terror" in a symmetrical way that indicts and condemns the political systems under which these abuses occurred. The tragedies of the daughter of Jephthah and the concubine in Gibeah mark the progressive deterioration of society in the time of the judges. In so doing, they dramatize the flaws in the sociopolitical structure that allows the victimization of vulnerable women. In the absence of a centralized power structure, women are under the unsupervised control of the men of their families. Sometimes, when the men act well toward their women, individual women can rise to prominence. But when the men act violently, there is no one to restrain them. By the end of the book of Judges, the reader, stunned by the story of the destructive spiral of violence that first killed a concubine in Gibeah and then almost consumed Israel, is ready to accept monarchy. But once David has consolidated the monarchy, the historian presents two more stories, of Bathsheba and of Tamar. Together they show that the Davidic monarchy contains the same basic flaw as the premonarchic system. Because of this flaw (which we now understand is patriarchy itself), the monarchy could not succeed. These stories about victims, far from supporting oppressive social systems, indict them.

The third group of stories, which we can call "voices," is also placed artfully within the historical books. The placement of these stories conveyed an important message. The first "voice" story appears at the very beginning of the book of Joshua, as Rahab announces that God has given Israel the land. The last "voice" story is at the end of Kings, when the prophet Huldah announces that Israel will be sent into exile. These two female oracles form a literary bracket that encloses Israel in Canaan. Throughout these books, women appear as oracles to announce each stage in the history of Israel. Rahab and Deborah bracket the conquest of Canaan; Hannah and the witch of Endor surround the kingship of Saul; Abigail and Huldah support the Davidic monarchy. These women are very different from one another, coming from a wide range of social locations to appear as oracles of Israel's destiny at significant junctions of its history. The choice of women as the voice of God's decisions makes a powerful statement about how the marginalized can be chosen to convey the word.

These three categories of stories about women—as victors, victims, and voices—are quite distinct from one another. The stories of victims and victors are about issues of polity and control, while the stories of the oracles involve prophecy and destiny. But whether they deal with power or Providence, all these stories have something in common: the women are all viewed positively. The victims are an index of Israel's social justice, the victors are agents of Israel's destiny, and the oracles are the medium of God's word. There is nothing dark or threatening about any of them. Even the few female villains of the Bible are uncomplicated: they are simply on the wrong side, enemies of the state, agents of foreign kings or foreign gods. But the fourth category of stories, the tales of "virgins," presents a more varied picture. These stories concern questions of marriage, intermarriage, ethnicity, and boundaries with non-Israelites. These boundary issues play a significant role in the development of a national identity; the permeability of boundaries to marital partners determines the ethnic character of the group. The dilemmas of this issue are highlighted by the story of Dinah, but most of these stories concern women brought into Israel as brides. The Bible does not speak with one voice on this issue, does not have one single attitude toward such marital alliances. The stories range from the extreme negative pole of Cozbi and Jezebel to the heroic positive figures of Rahab and Ruth. They offer a whole spectrum of opinions about the complex issues of identity and survival. These stories, and the attitudes they express, are an important window into the soul of Israel.

Women in the Mind of Israel

The identification of these four discourses helps refine the question of "why" with which we began, enabling us to look closely at these four types of women, the victors and victims, the virgins and voices, in order to see what it is about these images that so resonated with the thinkers of ancient Israel.

It is easiest to see why Israel preserves stories about virgins, about women being "taken" in marriage (to use the biblical idiom). The contracting of marriages is a vital occasion in a group's history. At this moment, there can be no doubt that the personal is political. The marital alliances formed by individuals determine the makeup of the community's future. Any group concerned about its future has to give serious thought to whom its members will marry. Since the general pattern of marriage in biblical Israel had the man "taking" a woman in marriage and bringing her into his household, the issue of "whom do we marry?" was usually formulated in terms of "which women could the men of Israel marry?" Telling stories about foreign women was the Bible's way of conducting a public discussion of this issue so vital to national survival.

National survival is also the concern of the stories about victors. The tales of marginalized women who acted without governmental authority, military training, or superhuman physical strength to become figures of salvation are not only memories of heroines of the past. They also convey a powerful message to people who are feeling (and probably are) weak, small, and vulnerable. These women are paradigms for individuals, groups, and nations who find themselves in such disadvantaged situations, a dramatic representation of how they can nevertheless rise to redeem themselves and others. Like these women, the people of Israel can persevere to preserve their destiny. The gifts of faith, persuasion, persistence, and cunning can allow the nation of Israel to be victorious when surrounded by, besieged by, and even conquered by more powerful nations.

The identification of Israel with vulnerable and marginal women is also at the heart of the stories about women as victims. At one level, the tragedies of these victims indict their societies and show the inability of Israel's successive forms of government to ensure the well-being of the vulnerable, and the demonstration of this failure helps explain the disappearance of these governments. But on a more profound level, there was a reason that the biblical writers chose the tragedies of women as their social barometer, the same reason they told stories about heroines victorious against all odds: Israel identified with marginalized vulnerable women in their tragedies and in their triumphs. Israel's sense of self as a woman is explicit in the poetic metaphor of "maiden Israel," "maiden Zion," and "maiden-folk" that Israel's classical prophets Amos, Hosea, and Jeremiah use to express their sorrow over the suffering of Israel and Jerusalem. The pathos of the tragic victim encapsulates the people of Israel battered by her enemies.

This underlying metaphorical understanding of Israel as a woman also explains why the historians bracketed Israel's history with the appearance of female oracles who carried the voice of God. After all, Israel was vitally concerned with the voice of God. The Pentateuch revolves around the central revelation at Sinai; the classical prophets derive the force and authority of their critique of Israel from their position as voice of God; and the historical books present a scenario in which prophets come to advise or indict kings throughout Israel's history. But despite all these prophets running around, the historians tell tales in which God chooses female prostitutes, mediums, housewives, and "professional" prophets in order to announce the turning points in Israel's history. Just as these women, not politically powerful themselves, are privileged to know the will of God, so too Israel, small and marginal between the great empires of the world, is nevertheless the bearer of God's word.

Virgins "taken" in marriage define the borders of Israel. Women as victors and victims parallel Israel's role in the world through her vulnerability and oppression and in her victory over oppression, and the women as the voice of God demonstrate Israel's ultimate significance despite her size. All these tales are important, for the individual stories they tell, the issues that they discuss, and their underlying metaphorical significance for Israel's self-understanding.

This biblical metaphor of Israel as a woman is made possible by its unique gender ideology, and by the dissonance between this gender-neutral ideology and the Bible's patriarchal social structure. The Bible's view that women were socially disadvantaged without being essentially inferior provided a paradigm through which biblical Israel did not have to equate its own powerlessness with inferiority. The subordination of women in Israelite society provided a way to understand national subordination and ultimate captivity without prejudice, so that the telling and preservation of these stories illuminated the role of Israel in the world. The role of these stories in Israel's understanding of its own history, its "metanarrative," accounts for their abundance in the Bible.

How to Read Biblical Stories

Understanding these issues can come only from in-depth study of the biblical stories themselves, each one studied by itself, and then groups of them examined collectively and "intertextually," with reference to one another. The minute analyses of these stories form the heart of this book. At first sight, reading laws and stories seems much easier than reading the poetry of biblical prophecy or wisdom. The language is relatively simple, and students can begin to read narrative selections fairly early in their studies of biblical Hebrew. But biblical stories are artfully crafted documents that open up deep levels of meaning in response to careful study. Underneath the simple Sunday school tales taught by faith traditions lie complex, deeply ambiguous narratives that require the reader to take an active part in their exposition. Serious study begins with the effort to remove the traditional interpretations and read the stories in their richly enigmatic artistry. To do this, the contemporary reader can make use of a whole range of modern techniques that serve as optical lenses. Zoom camera lenses and microscopes let us focus ever more deeply on the minutiae of grammar and rhetoric; wide-angle lenses let us see the story in its structural integrity and, beyond that, in its relation to biblical literature, biblical law, and biblical social context; telescopes let us see an even larger canvas of the ancient world and global culture.

The multiple process of reading starts with subtraction: taking away the veils of tradition and stripping the story of the layers of interpretive midrash that have been incorporated in it. This is not as easy as it might seem. In fact, it is a task worthy of Hercules, a kind of cultural cleaning of the Augean stables. Some interpretations have become so intertwined with the text that they are very difficult to see. The only way to make them visible is through a slow, close reading, informed by all the classic techniques of philological analysis. In this close reading, the reader carefully checks both traditional interpretations and her own personal presuppositions with the written text. It is almost axiomatic that there is no "pure text" untainted by assumptions, and the reader always has some degree of participation in the creation of a meaningful story. Careful disciplined reading highlights those passages where earlier readers made choices and allows us to go beyond our received traditions. This fundamental close reading is not only the first stage: it is an ongoing process that has to be repeated many times after each method of interpretation is applied. The biblical text itself always has to control the reading process.

Close reading is not esoteric. There is a certain level that every reader can reach, learning to read slowly, word by word, to check translations against each other, to see if conclusions are based on the words or on the white space around the words where interpretations have found their home. Professional biblicists have the advantage of being able to penetrate below the level of translation. Every translation, after all, is an interpretation. Every translator must make choices, and the more gapped or ambiguous the text, the more choices the translator has to make. For this reason, all the translations of the stories in this book are my own. When I diverge from the more common English translations, I indicate the reason in my notes.

The next stage in reading biblical stories is to "go small," to look beyond the actual words to understand the literary nature and structure of the text. Recently developed techniques of rhetorical criticism, literary analysis, and narratology help us to understand the art of the storyteller. They also pinpoint the narrative techniques of ambiguity by which the narrator provides the moments in which readers determine the meaning.

Going small can also involve going back into the prehistory of the text. Most stories were part of Israel's cultural life for hundreds of years before they were written in their present form. Through dramatic storytelling and earlier written versions, many voices transmitted the story through generations, and sometimes left their traces. "Higher literary criticism" seeks to unravel the layers of tradition in a text; "tradition criticism" or "redaction criticism" tries to trace the development of the text. A "holistic" or "final form" study of the story focuses on the creative decisions and crafting of the redactor, the last hand to treat the story before its form was frozen in the canon. The studies in this book are all final form studies, but they try to be conscious of historical development.

Another perspective uses wide-angle lenses: Stories have a literary context. They are embedded in a larger narrative, which influences the impression that the story creates in its readers. Biblical authors also connect stories to others that appear in different biblical books by using techniques of allusions, key words and phrases, or parallel structure.

These intertextual techniques add a deeper dimension to the story that may be vital to the storytellers' ideological agenda. They create clusters of stories about women that comprise the discourses I present in this book.

Even wider lenses encompass the cultural context of the stories. Biblical stories take form against a background of customs and behavior. Often, the study of biblical law helps illuminate points of the story that literary reading might not reveal. Biblical laws consider problematic situations and present a way of dealing with them. Reading the stories intertextually with laws can often illuminate some of the deep social concerns that motivate both. Wider and wider lenses, from farther and farther away, take in the cultures surrounding Israel. We need to back away and look at larger sections of the map, seeing Israel as part of the "fertile crescent" with ancient Mesopotamia, Canaan, and, at certain periods, Egypt. Stories and laws assume the type of informal cultural knowledge that people who live together often share, but modern readers, not having this background, may miss many of the nuances of an ancient text. The study of ancient Near Eastern literature and law is often a very important tool to fill in some of the gaps in our knowledge. The many texts from Mesopotamia, Egypt, and Ugarit prove invaluable as we reconstruct the cultural heritage of ancient Israel and the traditions that biblical Israel inherited, adopted, and transformed. Knowing the heritage that Israel received from the ancient world and the cultures with which it was in contact enables us to "read with ancient eyes," often helping us fill in the unexpressed background of the readers of ancient Israel. We then also need to adjust our telescope to the eastern Mediterranean world to see the Bible together with Hittite and ancient Greek ideas. The stories in the book of Judges, including the ones presented in this book, are often illuminated by classical studies. And sometimes nothing less than the long-distance view of a spy satellite or the Hubble telescope will do, and we turn to anthropological, sociological, and ethnographic studies to provide information that clarifies further nuances in the biblical story.

The many techniques and disciplines that biblical scholars use provide new perspectives and reveal many facets of the stories. Putting them together builds a composite picture that can shed new light on these deceptively simple-looking narratives that have long been oversimplified into morality tales and children's stories.

The Active Reader

The photographer looking at a scene through the various prisms on the camera is also looking through the lens of her own eye. Our own values and ideologies create a philosophical filter through which we read biblical stories. This filter is always there, and even when we are striving to be totally objective, our values inform the questions that we bring to the Bible. For a long time, readers believed that they could read the story objectively, determining with ever greater precision what the original author said. But everyone reads with presuppositions. The misogynistic and gynophobic assumptions of traditional readers transformed the biblical stories in ways that then reinforced the *a priori* beliefs of these readers. This process of deformation was invisible because the readers who shaped the tradition all shared the same patriarchal beliefs. Modern readers, confronted with these traditional stories, had to make a choice. They could "accept" the Bible as a faith document despite the patriarchal slant of these stories, or they could "reject" the Bible as not appropriate for people who believe in the full humanity of women. It was only when people, notably women, who did not share patriarchal assumptions began to read and analyze the Bible that they saw how patriarchal readers had transformed biblical texts into patriarchal stories. They then began the work of "depatriarchalizing" the biblical material.

Removing the traditional patriarchal lenses does not create a "value-free" reading. There is no such thing as a value-free reading. It is easy to see how other people's assumptions influence their reading, much harder to see how the same process operates in our own reading. All readers have both assumptions and goals in pursuit of which they devote the time and the effort to understanding this ancient and sometimes difficult book. These combine with our particular combination of skills and methods to create a personal hermeneutic. This has always been the case; the difference in contemporary reading is that we have become more aware of this philosophical filter, more self-conscious as we make interpretive choices, more willing to expose the filter, make it visible, and reveal the principles on which we operate.

My own readings, like everyone else's, are informed by who I am. I have the advantage of being a biblical scholar. I bring to my readings knowledge of biblical Hebrew, of grammar, and of history. As a scholar, I pay close attention to the text and attempt meticulousness and discipline in my analysis. I also look at how these stories relate to biblical ideas about society, and try to make my interpretations consonant with the totality of what I know about biblical culture. I am particularly interested in intellectual and cultural history, the development of ideas and institutions in religion and law. To understand how biblical ideas developed, I became an Assyriologist, studying Akkadian and Sumerian precisely for the purpose of understanding the development of ideas from the Babylonian world into the Bible. Conscious of the processes of interpretation and development, I attempt to trace the life of ideas and institutions within the Bible itself and then on into the post-biblical world of Midrash and exegesis.

I am also a feminist. My first principle, which may be called my feminist philosophy, is that men and women are created equal, and it is hard for me to imagine how and why "feminist" is such a provocative term. It seems to me self-evident that women are full characters in the world. I was not always cognizant of feminism. Gradually, like other people, I became aware of androcentricity and patriarchy and how they affect all elements of life. I began to see how patriarchy has distorted monotheism itself, how it has impoverished our religious traditions and perverted biblical ideas. My feminism combined with my love of the Bible determine my interpretative choices. They cause me to combine a hermeneutic of suspicion with a hermeneutic of grace, not assuming evil intent on the part of the biblical authors, but not ignoring the patriarchal difficulties. The combination creates an actively liberationist stance. When my scholarship presents alternative readings, I choose those readings that I believe will prove most beneficial to people.

The Path Not Taken

This book is not a comprehensive encyclopedia of all the women in the Bible or even a tour of its greatest women. In fact, this may be the only book ever written about women in the Bible that does not include Eve and Miriam. This is not because they are not important. Miriam was one of the great triumvirate who led Israel out of Egypt, and the traces of her story in the Pentateuch barely hint at her original prominence. Eve is the much misunderstood and much maligned mother of all who began the transformation of humanity from natural creatures to people of culture and knowledge. Her story is the key to the biblical conceptions of humanity, and I presented my reading of the so-called fall in *In the Wake of the Goddesses*. But the lives of great women do not always illuminate the lives of others, and the enormous shadow of individual great women can block other women from the limelight. These special women may grow so great that other women suffer in comparison, until one can say (as was said of the Virgin Mary) "alone of all her sex she found favor." In the same way, the stories about Eve, the matriarchs, and Miriam often obscure the stories of other women and may block the impact of the total picture.

Instead of focusing on individual woman-figures, this book looks to the meaning of the women-stories as a group and to the concept of "woman" in the Bible. It does so by examining these stories in reference to one another, by analyzing their composition and their purpose. The groundwork for such an analysis has been laid during the thirty years since contemporary feminist study of women in the Bible began. There is now a large body of scholarly literature that informs and enriches my own scholarship. In acknowledgment of my debt to this scholarship, and to help guide other readers through this ever growing scholarly literature, I include a discussion of this literature in the notes to each chapter. But this book goes beyond these individual studies to create a picture of the composition of the women-stories and of the way these function in the Bible as a whole. This synthesis of the whole fabric of these tales then enables us to go beyond scholarship to consider what they might mean to us in our own culture today, when the lives of most women are dramatically different from the lives of the biblical figures who have so fascinated us throughout the millennia.

Part One

VICTORS

THE VICTORS are the great women of the Bible. Some are women who have been remembered through the centuries as figures of power and influence. Their names and their stories have influenced countless generations. And some of the great women have been ignored and are only now gradually being rediscovered. Most of the great women were heroines; a few have been remembered as villains. Most of them were Israelites, but some of Israel's heroines were originally foreigners. The women came from different niches in society. Some of them occupied the stereotypical roles of mother, wife, midwife, and prostitute; others were extraordinary in stepping forward as fighters or possessing political power as judge, wise woman, and queen. They are united by the fact that they appear on the scene to act powerfully to affect Israel's destiny.

The Hand That Rocks the Cradle
The Rivka Stories

AT THE BEGINNING of the Bible is a book of beginnings, the beginning of the world and the beginning of Israel. Ancestor stories trace Israel's development from one couple, Abraham and Sarah. The stories are preoccupied with family, with generation and transmission. They reveal the structure of Israel's ancestral family: a patriarchy, like other ancient families, in which decision-making authority rested in the hands of the father. They also reveal the important role that women could play even in patriarchal families. The matriarchs worked to direct, shape, and secure the destiny of the family. First Sarah and then Rivka (who was married to Sarah's son Isaac) show how significant the character and actions of a woman could be to the future of the family.

Both of the two original mothers, Sarah and Rivka, set the pattern of female involvement. Like Abraham, they each undertook the decisive journey from Mesopotamia to Canaan that marked Israel's destiny. It is easy to overlook Sarah, who was already married to Abraham when she made the journey. Abraham himself did not realize her importance. God had to inform him that God's promise to Abraham had also been given to Sarah (Gen. 17:21) and that Abraham should pay attention to Sarah's desires (Gen. 21:12). Rivka (Rebecca) is not so easily overlooked, for she receives the fullest treatment of any matriarch. Rivka is the only woman of the Bible whose birth is recorded. Her birth notice interrupts the action, coming right after the binding of Isaac. After saving Isaac, God reiterated God's promise to Abraham of multitudinous progeny (Gen. 22:15–19). The narrator then changes focus.

◇ *Prologue. Birth: Intimation of Destiny (Gen. 22:20–24)**

> It happened after these matters.
> Thus was told to Abraham: "Look! Milkah has also borne sons,
>> to Nahor your brother:

---

*All chapter and verse citations follow the Hebrew Bible.

> Utz his firstborn and Buz his brother and Kemuel the father of
> Aram.
> And Keshed and Hazo and Pildash and Yidlaph and Bethuel.
> Bethuel gave birth to Rivka.
> These are the eight whom Milkah bore for Nahor the brother of
> Abraham.
> His concubine—her name was Reuma—also gave birth, to
> Tebah, Goham, Tehash, and Ma'akah.

A new matter is beginning: **It happened after these matters.** The narrator lists Nahor's descendants, presenting first the sons of Nahor's wife Milkah and then the sons of his concubine. The form is typical for genealogies, except that after listing Milkah's sons, before stating there were eight sons, the narrator jumps to the next generation to include the son's daughter: **Bethuel gave birth to Rivka.** The placement of this birth notice is important. Isaac has been saved, the promise has been repeated. The genealogy informs Abraham that his own birth family, the lineage of Terah, has not really been left behind. Through Isaac and this birth it will again be connected to God's promise to Abraham. Isaac will carry on the promise, and the baby Rivka will be the child of destiny, the agent of this promise. Another aspect of the placement of her birth notice illuminates her destiny. Her birth is mentioned just before Sarah's death: Rivka will carry on Sarah's role. Moreover, the birth announcement appears just after Abraham has been promised that his descendants will inherit their enemies' gates (Gen. 22:17). Re-readers of the story may catch the intertextual allusion, for this is the very blessing that Rivka's family bestows upon her as she leaves to marry Isaac (24:60). The one who will succeed Abraham in this role has just been born.

◇ Act I. The Marriage of Rivka

Rivka's destiny comes into closer view when Abraham is ready to find a wife for his son.

Scene 1. The charge of destiny (Gen. 24:1–9)

> Abraham was old, advanced in years, and YHWH blessed Abraham with everything.
> Abraham said to his servant, the elder of his house who ruled over all he had: "Put your hand under my thigh, and I will adjure you by YHWH the God of heaven and the God of

earth that you should not take any wife for my son from the daughters of the Canaanite in whose midst I am living. Rather, you shall go to my land, my homeland, and take a wife for my son Isaac."

The servant said to him, "Perhaps the woman will not be willing to come after me to this land—should I bring your son back to the land from which you came?"

Abraham said to him, "Be careful not to return my son to there. YHWH the God of heaven, who took me from my father's house and my homeland and who spoke to me and who swore to me thus, 'To your seed I give this land'—he will send his angel before you and you shall take a wife for my son from there. And if the woman is not willing to come after you, you are free of your oath. Just do not bring my son there."

The servant placed his hand under Abraham's thigh and swore to him about this matter.

Abraham, too old to go himself, sends his chief steward. The charge is clear: bring back a girl from the homeland. The alternative is also clear: Isaac is not to go there. If the girl will not come, the steward is discharged from his oath. God's promise connected Abraham and Sarah's progeny with the land. And so everything hinges on whether the woman that the servant finds is willing to come to Canaan.

Scene 2. Seeking serendipity (Gen. 24:10–14)

The servant took ten of his master's camels and went with all the bounty of his master in his hand.

He arose and went to Aram-Naharaim to the city of Nahor.

He parked his camels outside the town at a well toward evening, at the time that the girls who draw water come out.

He said, "YHWH, God of my master Abraham, make it happen for me today and act benevolently with my master Abraham. Look! I am standing by the water spring and the daughters of the men of the city are coming out to draw water. Let it be that the girl to whom I say 'Incline your jug to me that I may drink' and she says 'Drink, and I will also water your camels'—her you will have brought for your servant Isaac and through her I will know that you have acted benevolently with my master."

The servant asks for a serendipitous "happenstance," that the right girl would chance to come his way that very evening. He wants the hand of Providence to be clear, and asks for a sign. The sign is not random: it will also show that the girl has a willing heart. Abraham has described the characteristics of an ideal woman for his son: she must be from the homeland and be willing to come. The servant wants more: she must be hospitable and strong. The sign that she is truly the destined one is that she not only agrees to give him drink but volunteers to water his camels too. Like the mighty wife of Proverbs 31, she must be both caring and industrious. Moreover, as everyone knows, "A good wife comes from God" (Prov. 19:14).

Scene 3. Providence (Gen. 24:15–27)

> It happened that before he finished speaking, look! Rivka is coming out, she who was born to Bethuel son of Milkah the wife of Nahor the brother of Abraham, and her jug was on her shoulder.
>
> The girl was very beautiful, a young maiden whom no man had known.
>
> She came down to the spring and filled her jug and came up.
>
> The servant ran toward her and said, "Draw for me please a little water from your jug."
>
> She said, "Drink, my lord!" and hurried to lower her jug to her hand and give him drink.
>
> She finished giving him drink and said, "For your camels also I will draw water until they have finished drinking." The girl hurried and emptied her jug into the trough and ran again to the well to draw, and drew for his camels.
>
> The man, astonished at her, was keeping quiet to know if YHWH had made him succeed or not.
>
> And it happened when the camels finished drinking, the man took a gold nose ring whose weight was a half-shekel and two bracelets on her arms, ten shekels their weight.
>
> He said, "Whose daughter are you? Tell me please, does your father's house have room for us to spend the night?"
>
> She said to him, "I am the daughter of Bethuel the son of Milkah whom she bore to Nahor."
>
> And she said to him, "We have both straw and plentiful food and also a place to spend the night."
>
> The man bowed down and prostrated himself to YHWH.

He said, "Blessed is YHWH the God of my master Abraham
who has not abandoned his deeds of benevolence and his fidelity from my lord. As for me, YHWH led me on the way
to the house of my lord's brothers."

The emissary's prayer is answered immediately, and in a way far more
providential than he ever imagined. First, **the girl was very beautiful,**
always a desirable trait in a wife and, in the Bible, a mark of divine favor.
Second, she is a *betûlah,* a girl of marriageable age. Third, she is a virgin.
Unless virgins wore identifying clothing, how would the servant know?
And even if virgins wore identifying clothing, one would assume that all
unmarried girls would wear that clothing, so again, how would the servant know? But the narrator knows everything, and clearly, the narrator
cares that she is a virgin. Chastity is an important value in the Bible; the
chastity of young girls not only makes them "pure," it also shows that
they are well disciplined and faithful to their family's control. A girl who
stays chaste while unmarried is most likely to stay faithful as a wife. Finally, the girl goes even further than the servant imagined. She not only
offers to draw water for his camels, she offers to water them **until they
have finished drinking.** Camels can hold a lot of water, and after they
have traveled such a long distance, they will be ready to drink a great
amount. Rivka is very generous. She is also very strong. Ancient Near
Eastern wells were not vertical shafts through which buckets are low-
ered by rope. They were inclined slopes that the girl **went down** and
came up. To water ten camels after a long journey, Rivka had to go
down and come up many times. It is no wonder that the servant watching her was astonished!

The servant has asked for two logical signs, one more meaningful
than the other, that would indicate the girl's suitability: she must give
him something to drink and offer to water the camels. Not all women
would be thoughtful enough to consider the camels. If girls had come
and failed one of these tests before Rivka arrived, there would be no reason to conclude that the choice of Rivka indicated anything more than a
clever envoy. It is the fact that she arrived immediately, before the servant even finished his prayer, that shows the hand of Providence at
work. So the servant is ready to take the next step. He offers her gold,
possibly to assure her of his generosity as a guest. He has brought ten
camels of goods for wedding gifts and bride-price, but it is premature to
offer them yet. She has met his criteria for a good wife, but not yet Abraham's. For that he asks two questions: Who is she? And will her family

offer him hospitality? When he hears that Providence has brought him to Abraham's close kin, he immediately offers blessing and thanks to God. God has truly led him on the path of success to find this exemplary young woman from Abraham's own lineage. But there are still two hurdles before he can be successful: Will her family agree to the marriage? And will she come?

The envoy must meet the family. Rivka runs home to her mother's house, a sign perhaps that she realizes marriage may be discussed.

Scene 4. The family of destiny (Gen. 28–52)

> The girl ran home and told her mother's house about these matters.
>
> Rivka had a brother named Laban.
>
> Laban ran outside to the spring.
>
> It happened that when he saw the nose ring and the bracelets on his sister's arm and when he heard the words of his sister Rivka, "thus the man said," he came to the man and look! He was standing with his camels at the spring.
>
> He said to him, "Blessed be YHWH—why do you stand outside and I have cleared the house and a place for the camels?"
>
> The man came to the house and settled the camels and gave straw and feed to the camels and water to wash his feet and the feet of the men who were with him.
>
> Food was placed before him, but he said, "I will not eat until I have spoken my matter," and he said, "Speak!"
>
> He said, "I am the servant of Abraham. YHWH blessed my lord greatly and he grew great, and he gave him sheep and cattle and silver and gold and man- and maid-servants and camels and asses. Sarah, my lord's wife, bore a son for my lord after she had grown old and he gave him everything he had.
>
> "My lord adjured me thus, 'You shall not take a wife for my son from the daughters of the Canaanite in whose land I dwell. You must go to my father's house and take a wife for my son.'
>
> "I said to my master, 'Perhaps the woman will not come after me.' He said to me, 'YHWH before whom I have walked will send his angel with you and make your way successful and you will take a wife for my son from my family, from my father's house. Then you will be clear from my oath. If

you come to my family and they do not give her to you, you will be clear from my oath.'

"I came to the spring today and said, 'O YHWH, God of my lord Abraham, if you will please make successful the way upon which I am going—Look, I am standing by the water spring, and the maiden who comes out to draw and I say to her, "Give me a little water to drink from your jug" and she will say to me, "You drink, and I will draw also for your camels"—let her be the woman whom YHWH has decreed for my lord's son.' "

"And before I finished thinking this, look! Rivka was coming out with her jug on her shoulder. She went down to the spring and drew, and I said to her, 'Give me a little to drink.' She quickly took her jug down and said, 'Drink and I will water your camels,' and I drank and she watered the camels too. I asked her thus, 'Whose daughter are you?' and she said, 'The daughter of Bethuel son of Nahor whom Milkah bore for him,' and I placed the nose ring on her nose and the bracelets on her arms. And I bowed and prostrated myself to YHWH. And I blessed YHWH, the God of my lord Abraham, who directed me on the true way to take my lord's brother's daughter to his son.

"And now, if you will act benevolently and faithfully to my lord, tell me, and if not—tell me and I will go left or right."

Laban and Bethuel spoke up and said, "The matter is from YHWH. We cannot say to you bad or good. Look, Rivka is before you. Take her and go and let her be a wife to your lord's son, as YHWH has spoken."

When Abraham's servant heard their words, he prostrated himself before YHWH.

Abraham's emissary is very smart in the way he retells his story. He places a slight "spin" on the matter that emphasizes the family association and highlights Bethuel and Laban's household. Abraham, who is not a great family man, said nothing about his father's house. The envoy himself had not prayed that God bring him a Terahite, only a willing, hospitable wife. But now he "relates" Abraham's desire for his father's family and his concern that the family will agree to the marriage. He also emphasizes how important this particular family is by reporting that he first found out who Rivka was and only thereafter placed the gifts on her nose and arms. The steward would not give gifts to *any* girl, no matter how virtuous. Only a girl from this family will do! In this way the steward also intensifies the providential nature of the meeting: God not only found the right woman for Isaac; he has guided the servant to the family of destiny. Faced with this recounting of the story, the family has only one possible response: since God has singled them out, they must agree.

Despite the fact that this focus on the family is the servant's spin, the narrator makes it clear that God did arrange this providential meeting with Rivka, and that it is indeed very important that she be Bethuel and Milkah's daughter rather than someone else. There are three reasons for this: the facts that the family worships Yahweh, that Rivka's father is descended from Terah, and that Rivka's mother is also descended from Terah. The family's devotion to YHWH is immediately apparent. Laban's first words to the emissary are **"Blessed be YHWH,"** and Bethuel and Laban's response to the servant's story is **"The matter is from YHWH"** and that they will do **"as YHWH has spoken."** This God language is not simply verbiage to suit the servant. YHWH is also Laban's God, and much later, when Laban makes a treaty with Jacob, he takes an oath by "The God of Nahor and the God of Abraham, their father's God" (Gen. 31:53). The worship of YHWH may be the reason that Terah first left Mesopotamia to head for Canaan.

Terah's lineage is very important. In Genesis 20, Abraham says of Sarah, "She is really my sister, the daughter of my father but not the daughter of my mother." If so, Isaac would be doubly descended from Terah, through his father Abraham and through his mother's father. Bethuel's lineage is also doubly Terahite, through his father Nahor, son of Terah, and through his mother, Milkah, who was the daughter of Nahor's brother Haran. Rivka, like Isaac, is doubly Terahite. A marriage between them will keep the lineage as pure as possible. The genealogy of the mothers is important to preserve the intensity of this same lineage. The genealogies repeatedly mention Milkah's name, and God reminds Abraham that Abraham's covenant must come through a child of Sarah (Gen. 17:15–19). In the same way, Rivka is destined to be the one to bear a child to Isaac, who will inherit YHWH's covenanted promise.

But the marriage is not a fait accompli. Rivka must agree. Abraham had mentioned the possibility that the girl might not agree to go. We do not often hear of the consent of children in an arranged marriage. Abraham and his servant do not consult Isaac before the servant tenders his offer. But Rivka has to move far away, cut her ties to her birth family and go out to what is essentially a pioneer country.

Scene 5. Embracing destiny (Gen. 53–62)

> The servant brought out silver vessels and gold vessels and garments and gave them to Rivka.
>
> He gave gifts to her brother and her mother.
>
> They ate and drank, he and the men who were with him, and they stayed the night.
>
> He said, "Send me off to my master!"
>
> Her brother and mother said, "Let the girl stay with us a few days or ten; after, she may go."
>
> He said to them, "Do not make me stay later when YHWH has made my way successful. Send me off and I will go to my master."
>
> They said, "We will call the girl and ask her."
>
> They called Rivka and said to her, "Will you go with this man?"
>
> She said, "I will go."
>
> They sent off Rivka their sister with her nursemaid and Abraham's servant and his men.
>
> They blessed Rivka and said to her, "Our sister, may you become a thousand myriads, and may your seed inherit its enemies' gates!"
>
> Rivka arose, and her handmaidens, and they got up on the camels and they followed after the man.
>
> The servant took Rivka and went.

The family may be reluctant, and may wish to delay matters. But the girl shows no such hesitation, and answers simply, **"I will go."** Not knowing either Abraham or Isaac, whose name is not even mentioned, she declares her willingness to go. At that moment, it becomes clear that Rivka is the counterpart to both Abraham and Sarah. Like Sarah, she is the instrument of the promise, the agent through whom Isaac will become the father of a nation. She is also a second Abraham, who, like him, voluntarily chooses to leave Mesopotamia for Canaan. Her **"I will go"** answers the four times the issue of going has been raised in the story (in vv. 4, 7, 38, and 40) and echoes God's command to Abraham to "Go!" in Gen. 12:1. The voyage from Mesopotamia to Israel was the one

qualification that Abraham sought in a daughter-in-law, and her willingness to do so establishes her credentials.

Rivka is very much like Abraham. They are both models of hospitality, and the narrator of her story highlights her similarity to him by describing her actions toward the emissary in the same language that
describes Abraham's actions toward his angel visitors (Gen. 18:1–8). Both
of them are eager to perform their hospitable acts. Abraham "ran" to
meet the three stranger-angels and "ran" to the flock; Rivka "ran" to the
well. Abraham "hurried" to cook for them, Rivka "hurried" to lower her
jug and "hurried" to empty her jug. They also both show a greater generosity than hospitality codes require, Abraham giving the strangers
meat and Rivka watering ten camels to their fill.

Like Abraham, Rivka is the bearer of a promise. The promise is bestowed in her family's blessing: many children, a progeny that "inherits
its enemies' gates." "Inheritance" (yaraš) is an essential theme of Genesis, and indeed of every family history. When Abraham had no children,
he complained that someone from his household would "inherit" him
(Gen. 15:3). After the binding of Isaac, God promised Abraham, "Your
seed will inherit its enemies' gate" (Gen. 22:17). Rivka's family offers her
the same blessing; later, Jacob is told that he will inherit the land in
which he lives (Gen. 28:4). Isaac is promised the land and progeny (Gen.
26:3–4), but "inheriting" is too active a word for him. "Inheriting" goes
from Abraham to Rivka to Jacob and to the people of Israel. Her deci-
siveness, her strong will, and her embrace of her destiny make her a
strong active link between Abraham and Jacob.

First, Rivka must become a wife.

Scene 6. Rivka, the wife of Isaac (Gen. 24:62–67)

> Isaac was coming from the way to Beer Lahai-Roi,
> He was living in the Negeb.
> Isaac went out to converse in the field before evening.
> He raised his eyes and look! Camels are coming.
> Rivka lifted her eyes and saw Isaac.
> She slipped off the camel.
> She said to the servant, "Who is that man, the one who is walk-
>   ing toward us in the field?"
> The servant said, "He is my master."
> She took a scarf and veiled herself.
> The servant related to Isaac all the things that he had done.
> Isaac brought her into the tent of Sarah his mother.

He took Rivka and she became a wife to him and he loved her.
Isaac was consoled over his mother.

Abraham's servant, who represented him in the negotiations, now
continues to play that role in the presentation. Abraham is not involved.
The servant does not change his role: he acts in the Negeb as he acted in
Mesopotamia. But Rivka changes. She who was so assertive and decisive
in her meeting with the servant and in her discussions at home now
turns into a wife. She who left Mesopotamia as an autonomous person
turned into a betrothed woman "taken" by the servant and is now
"taken" into her husband's domain. As soon as Isaac enters the scene,
she veils herself. Veiling may have been required. The Assyrian laws require married women to be veiled. The fact that Jacob marries Leah
thinking she is Rachel seems to indicate that such a custom also applied
to betrothed women. But the veiling is also symbolic: all of Rivka's attributes, not only her beauty, will be less visible as a wife. In marriage,
women, even the active Rivka, become the object of action: Isaac takes
her. But her qualities do not remain hidden to him, for he loves her. She
not only takes Sarah's place in the tent, she takes her place in his heart.
The biblical ideal of marriage may consider the husband the dominant
partner, but it nevertheless envisions a love relationship. Modern commentators assume a mismatch between a strong Rivka and a passive
Isaac, but the story tells us that **he loved her.**

Isaac's love for Rivka did not prevent him from imitating his father
and pretending that Rivka was his sister when they went to Gerar (Gen.
26:6–11). Marriage was patriarchal, and even a beloved wife could be disposable when the man's life was at stake. But his love for her may have
prevented his ruse from succeeding, for Abimelech king of Gerar saw
Isaac "playing," *meṣaḥḥēq,* with Rivka and realized that they were married (v. 8). The marriage of Isaac and Rivka, even though arranged, was a
love relationship.

The reader has been given two clues that God has a special interest in
Rivka. Both the announcement of her birth and the providential nature
of her marriage indicate that she is a woman of destiny with a divinely
ordained role to play. But first, she must become a mother. And this is
neither easy nor ordinary. Like Sarah before her, and Rachel after her,
Rivka has to undergo a period of infertility.

◇ *Act II. Motherhood: Giving Birth (Gen. 25:20–26)*

> Isaac was forty years old when he took Rivka daughter of
> Bethuel the Aramean from Padan-Aram, the sister of Laban
> the Aramean, as his wife.
>
> Isaac entreated YHWH in the presence of his wife, for she was
> infertile.
>
> YHWH was successfully entreated by him and Rivka his wife
> became pregnant.
>
> Inside her, the children moved around tumultuously.
>
> Rivka said, "If this is the way it is, what do I need this for?"
>
> She went to inquire of YHWH.
>
> YHWH said to her:
>
>> "Two peoples are in your belly,
>>
>> Two nations from your loins will divide.
>>
>> Nation over nation will be strong,
>>
>> And the older the younger will work."
>
> Her days till birth were complete, and look! There were twins in
> her belly.
>
> The first one came out, red, and all of him like a mantle of hair,
> and they called his name Esau.
>
> Afterward, his brother came out, his hand holding Esau's heel.
> They called his name Jacob.
>
> Isaac was sixty years old when she gave birth to them.

Since God has promised Isaac numerous progeny, Isaac entreats. But
Rivka does not always turn to Isaac to mediate between her and God.
When her pregnancy distresses her, she does not involve Isaac; she goes
directly to inquire of YHWH. There is no need for intercession. And
Rivka gets her answer; the struggles in her womb are just the beginning.
In oracular poetry, she is told that she has twins in her womb who are
destined to become two separate nations. Twins, of course, heighten
the problem of sibling rivalry, which is such a prominent issue in the ancestral stories. Rivka is given a clue as to how the struggles are destined
to be resolved. "The elder will work (for) the younger," says the oracle.
Or does it say "the elder, the younger will work (for)?" Oracles may be
informative, but they are never clear. The events that happen later enable the petitioner to interpret the oracle. The birth of the twins seems
to provide such a clue. Jacob coming close on Esau's heel seems to bear

out the idea that the younger son will not be content to be the lesser and that the elder will someday work for the younger.

Oracles are expected to lead to action. If the oracle predicts evil to come, the petitioner is expected to try to avert it. Some Mesopotamian collections of oracles even contain the "solution," the ritual to perform to avert the doom. In Assyria, an evil astral omen might even cause the king to descend temporarily from his throne and appoint a substitute king. In the same way, a petitioner will try to ensure that nothing will prevent the predicted good fortune. Rivka takes a prominent role in fulfilling her birth oracle, acting to guarantee that her younger son will achieve his destiny as the preeminent heir. That moment comes as it is time to transfer the family heritage from Isaac to the next generation.

◇ *Act III. Motherhood: Fulfilling the Destiny (Gen. 27)*
Rivka's Plan (27:1–13)

> It happened that Isaac was old, and his eyes were too dim to see.
> He called Esau his elder son and said to him, "My son!" and he said, "Here!"
> He said to him, "Look! I have gotten old. I do not know the day of my death. And now, please take your tools, your bow and arrow and go out to the field. Catch game and make me a delicacy such as I love and bring it to me, and I will eat so that my soul can bless you before I die."
> Rivka was listening while Isaac was speaking to Esau.
> Esau went to the field to hunt game to bring back.
> Rivka said to Jacob her son thus, "Look, I have heard your father speaking to your brother Esau thus, 'Bring me game and make me a delicacy and I will bless you before YHWH before I die.' And now, my son, listen to me, to what I am commanding you! Go, please, to the flock and take two fine goats and I will make them into delicacies for your father such as he loves. And you will bring it to your father and he will eat so that he will bless you before he dies."
> Jacob said to Rivka his mother, "But Esau my brother is a hairy man and I am a smooth man. Perhaps my father will feel me, and I will be a liar in his eyes and bring a curse upon myself and not a blessing."
> His mother said to him, "May your curse be upon me, my son. Just listen to me and go get it for me."

Rivka is faced with a problem. In the world of the ancestors, a father could determine who was going to be his "firstborn," his chief heir, and could change his mind even on his deathbed. Family documents from the Syrian city of Nuzi, from around 1600 B.C.E., include several documents in which a man promises another that he will be the firstborn. Nevertheless, one of the documents shows that the man's family came to him on his deathbed to tell him to designate his firstborn. Esau had sold the prerogatives of firstborn to Jacob, but despite the arrangement that they once had made, Isaac's blessing in anticipation of death can determine their future relationship. Rivka knows that Isaac has always favored Esau the hunter and wants to give him the blessing. If she is going to ensure that the omen of Jacob's destiny will be fulfilled, she must act. Her motives may be pure, to carry out God's will. She may also be influenced by the fact that she favors the more domestic Jacob. She may believe that he is more likely to care for her in her old age. Motives are rarely unmixed. Moreover, even people who operate purely from selfish reasons may unwittingly be carrying out God's plan, like the brothers who sell Joseph into Egypt or Potiphar's wife, who gets him into the dungeon where he can come to the attention of Pharaoh. Actions have consequences whatever their motives. And whether or not Rivka is thinking of the oracle at this particular moment, the oracle has shown her and the reader what God's plan is. Isaac must bless Jacob. Only he has the right to bestow the blessing. Rivka knows that he has made his decision and she will not be able to persuade Isaac to change his mind. And so she decides to trick him, and turns to persuade Jacob of her plan.

Rivka's plan is straightforward, based on an intimate knowledge of sheep breeding. Shepherds try to match up orphaned lambs with ewes who have lost their lambs. But ewes nurse only their own lambs. In order to convince a ewe to suckle an orphaned lamb, shepherds will flay the dead lamb and wrap the orphan in its skin. In the same way, Rivka will wrap a goat around the smooth-skinned Jacob. But Jacob is not enthusiastic about Rivka's plan to disguise him as Esau. He is worried that his father will brand him as a "trickster" (which he certainly is) and will utter a curse instead of a blessing. Rivka knows that once uttered, a curse cannot be easily removed, but it can be deflected, and Rivka offers to take the consequences of the curse upon herself. She is the first woman to do so, but not the last. Women who ask men to do something need to allay the fears of those men; both Abigail and the Wise Woman of Tekoa will offer to take upon themselves the consequences of the acts that they ask David to do. This is a very persuasive technique, and it works. Jacob puts on the goat skins and goes to trick his father into giving him the blessing he plans for Esau.

The deception of the blind elderly Isaac is a bizarre episode, verging on both the tragic and the burlesque. It rests on a premise alien to contemporary thinking, that a blessing unwittingly bestowed is still a blessing. And it assumes that trickery is not automatically immoral. Many heroes of the Bible, including Moses and David, use trickery when frontal assaults will not work, and the Jacob cycle has quite a few trickster stories. Isaac himself is a trickster, having tried the wife-sister trick on Abimelech. Jacob takes Isaac's place in the next generation, as well as Rivka's, being both a trickster and bearer of the promise. Rivka will use whatever means are in the tool kit of those without authority to make decisions.

The story never tells us that Rivka must use deception because she is powerless, and later readers have often accused her of improper and immoral behavior. But the biblical world valued cunning in the underdog. Only the powerful value honesty at all costs. The powerless know that trickery may save their lives. Early interpreters, both Jewish and Christian, praised Rivka, as did medieval and reformation writers. The censure did not begin until the end of the nineteenth century, when male biblical scholars began to condemn her as a Lady Macbeth. The pendulum is beginning to swing again as we learn more about how the disadvantaged make their way in the world and how women negotiate through patriarchy. To some contemporary eyes, the ingenuity and cunning of Rivka's plan is itself a mark of divine guidance and her role as divine helper.

The story also does not tell us that the purpose of her action was to fulfill the oracle. But the oracle provides an interpretive prologue to these events, and a divine authority for action that supersedes Isaac's male authority. Moreover, Isaac's blessing refers back to the language of the oracle. First, Isaac blesses Jacob with prosperity (a blessing he was able to repeat with Esau). Then comes the crucial sentence (v. 29):

> Many peoples will serve you,
> many nations will submit to you.
> Be a magnate to your brothers,
> The sons of your mother will submit to you.
> Cursed are those who curse you
> and blessed are those who bless you.

Like the words of the oracle, the blessing is in poetry. Moreover, it uses the same key terms. The oracle had spoken of two nations, *le'ummîm,* separating from Rivka's womb: Isaac refers to the nation, *le'ummîm,* who will submit to Jacob. The oracle spoke of the older serving, *ya'abôd,* the younger; Isaac says that "peoples will serve you," *ya'abdûka,* and tells Jacob to "be a magnate over your brother." This is the dramatic moment. The oracle was enigmatic, with language that allowed either one to serve the other. The birth story lent credence to the idea that Jacob would be prominent, as did the sale of the birthright. But not until the blessing of Isaac does it become clear and unambiguous: the one Isaac speaks to will "be magnate over your brother." And Rivka has guaranteed that Jacob will be the son standing there at that moment.

Did Isaac know? Some commentators believe that he realized what was happening but went along with it. He is certainly suspicious, asking, "Who are you, my son?" (Gen. 27:18); asking to feel Jacob so that he could see "Are you my son Esau or not?" (v. 21). He expresses doubt, for "The voice is the voice of Jacob and the hands are the hands of Esau" (v. 22), and he asks yet a third time, "Are you my son Esau?" (v. 24). He asks Jacob to come close and kiss him, and finally identifies him as Esau because his smell is "as the smell of the field" (v. 27). Does a goat smell like the field? And would an old man trust his sense of smell over his hearing? Or is the storyteller hinting that Isaac realized what was happening, while at the same time casting aspersion on Esau and the Edomites that they smell like goats? Rivka's plan and Jacob's execution of it may have brought Isaac to realize that, come what may, Jacob would be superior over Esau. Or not, and Isaac was simply tricked.

Rivka has one more role to play in Jacob's life. Having heard that Esau wants someday to take his revenge, Rivka wishes to spirit Jacob out of town. At the same time, like Abraham before her, she desires her designated heir to find a wife from Mesopotamia. Esau's anger is her opportunity to send Jacob to Mesopotamia. But she cannot send him, or arrange a marriage for him. Jacob must want to go, and his father must send him. So Rivka sets out to persuade the two men to follow her plan.

◇ *Epilogue. Assuring the Future (Gen. 27:42–28:5)*

Rivka was told the words of Esau her son.

She called Jacob her younger son and she said to him, "Look! Esau your brother is consoling himself to kill you. And now, my son, listen to my voice. Get up and run away to my brother Laban, to Haran. Live with him awhile until your brother's anger subsides. Until your brother's anger turns away from you and he forgets what you have done to him, and I send and take you from there. Why should I be bereft of both of you on one day?"

Rivka said to Isaac, "I am almost dying because of the daughters of Het. If Jacob took one of these daughters of Het, one of the girls of the land for a wife—why should I live?"

Isaac called Jacob and blessed him. He commanded him and said to him, "Do not take a wife from the daughters of Canaan. Arise and go to Padan-Aram to the house of Bethuel, your mother's father, and take a wife from there, from the daughters of Laban, your mother's brother. And El Shaddai will bless you and make you fertile and numerous and you will become a national community. He will give you the blessing of Abraham, and to your seed with you, to inherit the land in which you live, which God gave to Abraham."

Isaac sent Jacob off and he went to Padan-Aram to Laban, son of Bethuel the Aramean, the brother of Rivka, the mother of Jacob and Esau.

Rivka says nothing to Jacob about marrying a woman in Haran. Marriage is not on Jacob's mind, and he would not be convinced that this was the appropriate thing to do right at the moment that he has alienated his brother. Rivka uses the one argument that would work with him, sending him temporarily for refuge. She reminds him that his brother's rage is murderous, if temporary, and subtly convinces him that he should be careful of his life for her sake if not for his: **Why should I be bereft of both of you?** If Esau killed Jacob, he himself would have to be executed, and Rivka would lose both her children. To prevent this, Jacob must flee, and her brother's house, she intimates, would be sanctuary.

Isaac, however, is another story. Talking to him about the danger to Jacob would bring up the topic of the trickery. It might anger Isaac. Even if it did not, Isaac might not wish to send Jacob away. He might wish to resolve the issue between his sons by discussing matters with them, or even by sending Esau to one of his in-laws. Or else he might send Jacob to Abimelech king of Gerar, with whom he had treaty relations, or to his uncle Ishmael. Both would keep him safe, and both are much closer than Haran. Isaac, the only patriarch never to leave the land of Canaan, might not think to send his son back to Mesopotamia. But Rivka wants to get Jacob to Haran. She therefore brings up the subject of Esau's wives, who, the narrator told us just before Isaac announced his desire to bestow the blessing, were "bitterness" for Isaac and Rivka (Gen. 26:35). Like other petitioners in the Bible, she speaks forcefully, using a guilt-producing rhetoric. But in this death-invoking hyperbole is a truth: the life of a mother involves assuring the life of her children. Rivka, moreover, has devoted her life to the promise. To her, the future of her son is bound up with the promise. The promise brought Abraham from Mesopotamia, and her after him. Rivka wants her own successor to make the same journey. Through her initiative, Isaac duplicates Abraham's charge that his son should not marry a local woman, and repeats the promise that God gave him. In this way, Rivka assures that Jacob's future will imitate Isaac's and that the girl he marries will be like her. Then, having secured for Jacob both the blessing and the charge to marry within the line of Terah, Rivka disappears from the Bible's view.

The portrait of Rivka is more extensive than that of Sarah, but they are not different in any fundamental way. Both play a determinative role in deciding the future of their children. The narratives make sure that we know that both mothers are acting only to ensure the future that ought to happen. They are acting as God's partner and agent, working to bring about God's will. God explicitly tells Abraham to do as Sarah wishes (Gen. 21:12). In the case of Rivka, the storyteller relates the oracle to legitimate Rivka's actions, to make sure that readers understand that tricky as they might be, they are in accord with the word of God.

The two first matriarchs are notable for determining the success of their sons, often against their husbands' inclinations. The assertiveness of these Genesis mothers should not surprise us. Recent anthropological fieldwork in contemporary rural Greece and Turkey, both unabashed self-proclaimed patriarchies, shows that wives and mothers can be to all appearances subordinate women, and nevertheless exercise enormous real power within their households and villages. In the case of Sarah and Rivka, their own preferences are made more powerful with divine charge and divine knowledge. These women temper paternal authority to bring about God's will.

The third generation does not pass as smoothly into the fourth. It begins much the same, as Jacob finds Rachel as a young woman at a well, beautiful as Rivka was beautiful. And he loves her, as Isaac loved Rivka. A younger child favored over the older, Rachel is a kind of echo of Jacob himself. She is ambitious and attached to the teraphim of her father's household, symbols of both authority and family. Taking this symbol (much as Jacob took Isaac's blessing), she then (again like Jacob) tricks her father so that he cannot find the teraphim. But, unlike Jacob, she cannot separate from her sister. She does not have the autonomy or the means to decide that she would not like to spend her life trying to best her sister. When her father, Laban, decides that Jacob must marry both Rachel and Leah, the two sisters become co-wives, rivals for the same husband. And then, like so many women, Rachel dies in childbirth.

Rachel's premature death has great consequences for Jacob's family. She is not there to guide her young son Joseph as the children grow up, or to mediate between him and his brothers. Leah does not fill Sarah's or Rivka's position in the family. Either she is too busy managing a household with thirteen children, or she also dies at some point. Without Rachel's presence, Jacob cannot ensure their transition to the next generation. As the stories of Genesis show, nobody orchestrates their marital contracts, and the stresses between Jacob and his grown sons and among the brothers threaten to destroy the family. When nobody rocks the cradle, nobody rules the world.

Saviors of the Exodus

OUR FOCUS now shifts to the period after the end of the book of Genesis. The question is no longer "Who will inherit the mantle of this ancestry?" It is "What will become of the descendants of these ancestors?" Some things have not changed since the days of Genesis. The descendants live in families and center their political organization and power in the family. As a result, women continue to demonstrate considerable ability to influence events. But with the national emphasis of the book of Exodus, it becomes clear that choices made by women in the course of their domestic lives determine the destiny of the entire people. Acting in their routine roles as midwives, mothers, daughters, and wives, women become the saviors of early Israel and bring on the redemption from Egypt.

The book of Exodus opens as the new king expresses fear at the ever multiplying alien group in his land. Having enslaved them, he then commands the midwives to kill the boy children they help deliver.

◇ *Act I. The Midwives (Exod. 1:15–22)*

> The Pharaoh said to the Hebrew midwives, one of whose name was Shifrah and the other's name was Pu'ah;
> He said, "When you birth the Hebrew women, you will look on the birthstones. If it is a boy, you shall kill it; if a girl, she shall live."
> The midwives feared God and did not do as the king of Egypt had instructed them.
> They let the boy children live.
> The king of Egypt called for the midwives.
> He said to them, "Why have you done this thing, that you let the boy children live?"
> The midwives said to Pharaoh, "Because the Hebrew women are not like Egyptian women. They are animals. Before the midwife can get to them, they have given birth."

> God was good to the midwives, and the people grew greatly numerous.
>
> And it happened that because the midwives feared God, God made them houses.
>
> Pharaoh commanded all his people thus: "Every son that is born—cast him into the Nile. Every girl you can let live."

Pharaoh's injunction seems strange. To kill a population, one surely should kill the future birth-givers. But Pharaoh is worried only about the boys. From his perspective, the girls are insignificant. Without men, they are not even Israel. Their wombs have not yet been claimed and branded. If married by Egyptians, they will produce Egyptian children. The boys, however, may grow to be men who will fight against Egypt. Within his limited perspective, Pharaoh is no fool.

The narrator relates Pharaoh's intensely male-oriented perspective and then shows how the women begin to act. The midwives are not so easily persuaded to murder Hebrew boy babies. They themselves might be Israelite women. The Hebrew *lmyldt h'bryt* is ambiguous: it could mean "to the Hebrew midwives" or "to the midwives who serve the Hebrew women." The Masoretic vowels *lammeyalledôt ha'ibriyyôt* opt for the former, the Septuagint leaves the question open, and Josephus relates that they were Egyptian (Antiquities II, 206–7). The women were most probably Hebrews, for midwives usually come from the community they serve. Their names can have meaning in Hebrew, Shifrah from "beautiful" and Pu'ah from "pant," or Pu'ah can be related to Ugaritic *pġt*, "young woman." These would be meanings appropriate to midwives. On the other hand, the names are not the usual form of Hebrew names. They may have come from another subject people. Now, however, they cast their lot with Israel and defy Pharaoh's orders to kill.

The midwives make an independent moral decision. Fearing God, they refuse to obey immoral orders and do not murder the boy children. Called on the carpet, they do not declare their defiance in what would have been both a futile and fatal act of frontal resistance. Instead, they trick Pharaoh, belittling the Israelite women as "animals" who give birth so quickly that they need no midwives. The word *ḥayyôt*, "animals," is too often softened in translation to "lively." But the midwives would certainly not compliment the Hebrews over the Egyptian women! Instead, building on the fact that Pharaoh sees Israel as "other," they make an ethnic slur belittling these "others." In this way, they demonstrate to Pharaoh that they are not in favor of Hebrews. Not seeing the power of these women to defy him, Pharaoh is all too willing to hear something negative about Hebrews and falls for their trick. The midwives have failed to kill the male children and have pulled the wool over Pharaoh's eyes in a way that shows his own denigration of Israel is ludicrous. The humor in their answer to Pharaoh is compounded by God's response. God rewards them for their uprightness by making them very successful. More successful midwives means that fewer children die at birth, and as a result, Israel grows even more numerous.

But Pharaoh is not yet done trying to destroy Israel. He corrects one mistake he made, no longer appointing individuals to be the killers, but commanding the whole people to take part in this murder. But he repeats his more fundamental mistake. He commands everyone to throw the boy children into the Nile. But he tells them to let the daughters live. The next to defy Pharaoh will be the daughters.

⬦ *Act II. The Daughters (Exod. 2:1–10)*

Part 1. Three daughters (Exod. 2:1–6)

> A man from the house of Levi went and took a daughter of Levi.
> The woman became pregnant and gave birth to a son.
> She saw that he was good and she hid him three months.
> She couldn't hide him anymore and took an ark of reeds and tarred it with pitch and tar.
> She put the boy in it and placed it in the reeds at the banks of the Nile.
> His sister stood by at a distance to see what would happen to him.
> The daughter of Pharaoh came down to bathe in the Nile.
> Her maids were walking by the side of the Nile,
> She saw the ark among the reeds and sent forth her arm and took it.
> She opened it and saw him, the boy child.
> Look! The lad was crying and she had pity on it.
> She said, "This is one of the boys of the Hebrews."

Pharaoh has a problem. Just as he took no heed of daughters, daughters take no heed of him. Immediately, two *daughters* defy Pharaoh's command and act to preserve the life of a boy child. A daughter of Levi gives birth to a son. As long as Israelite women are still alive, they will continue to give birth to children, and sons will continue to be born. And, like the midwives before her, the daughter of Levi will not kill at Pharaoh's command. Instead of throwing her son in the river, she hides her son for three months. Then, unable to hide him anymore, she sets the baby adrift in an ark on the river where he will at least have a chance for survival. The word "ark" (*teibah*) appears only twice in the Bible: here and Gen. chapters 6–9. Noah didn't drown because God placed him in an ark; Moses didn't drown because his mother did the same. There is another allusion here: she seals the baby in the ark as God closed the ark for Noah.

Moses' mother subverts Pharaoh's order. She does indeed place the boy child in the Nile, but in a way that will give him a chance. In this, she does not act alone, for her own daughter, the child's sister, goes to keep watch.

Yet another daughter—Pharaoh's daughter—finds the baby. She has compassion for the crying infant, but she knows right away that this is a Hebrew child. She has a decision to make. On the one hand, as Pharaoh's daughter, she should obey the royal decree and throw the boy into the Nile. On the other side—**she has pity.** Her motivation is not quite the same as that of the midwives: they acted on moral grounds, she acted on compassionate grounds. They decided in the abstract: **the midwives feared God** and concluded it was wrong to kill babies. Pharaoh's daughter made no such previous judgment; she may have considered the whole affair her father's business. But: **the lad was crying and she had pity on it.** At this moment, the baby's sister crystallizes the issue and precipitates the moment of decision.

Part 2. A conspiracy of women (Exod. 2:7–10)

> His sister said to the daughter of Pharaoh, "Should I go and call a nursemaid woman from the Hebrews for you, and she will nurse the child?"
>
> The daughter of Pharaoh said to her, "Go!"
>
> The young girl went and called the boy's mother.
>
> The daughter of Pharaoh said to her, "Take this boy and nurse him for me and I will pay you your wages."
>
> The woman took the boy and nursed him.
>
> The boy grew and she brought him to the daughter of Pharaoh and he became her son.
>
> She called his name Moshe as she said, "For from the water I drew him out."

The three women now enter a conspiracy to save the child. The daughter of Pharaoh restores him to his own mother to nurse—but with a difference: **nurse him for me.** To all appearances, Moses' mother will simply be a wage-earning nurse, and the boy will be safe in his mother's arms. The fate of the child is coming full circle, as the story emphasizes by repeating "(she) **took.**" The mother of Moses *took* an ark for him, the daughter of Pharaoh *took* him, and the mother of Moses *took* him back and nursed him. Then, after he was weaned, she brought him to the daughter of Pharaoh and **he became her son.** And since he was now hers, Pharaoh's daughter named him. Like so many names in the Bible, "Moses" is a play on words. Moshe/Moses comes from a standard Egyptian word *mes* for "son," as in Tutmoses (son of Tut). At the same time, his name, like the names of Jacob's children, is ostensibly related to his birth circumstances, **for from the water I drew him out.** But the form *mōšeh* is an active participle of the verb "the one who draws out," and the one who "draws out" from the waters is Pharaoh's daughter, not Moses, who is only the one drawn out (*māsûy*). The narrator and the listeners know that the real meaning of the name refers to Moses' life, not his birth. For Moshe will be the one who "draws out" (*mōšeh*) the people of Israel from Egypt as their savior (*môšîʿa*). The "drawing out" of Moses from the waters saves the one who will "draw out" Israel from Egypt.

And so Moses is born, and saved to be reborn, by the collaboration of this triad of daughters, who begin the redemption of Israel. The Bible records the name of Moses' mother, Yochebed, and his sister Miriam, and midrash adds the name "Bithya" for the daughter of Pharaoh. But none of them is named in this story, for like the anonymous daughters of the book of Judges, they are archetypal. They are *daughters,* women, the very ones overlooked by both Pharaoh and the tradition that remembered the names of only the men who came to Egypt. Three subversive daughters have foiled the plans of men and shaped the destiny of the world.

But Moses must first grow up, and then he must become a savior. Nursed by his birth mother and tended by his finder-mother, he experiences transformation in two traumatic crises. First he kills an oppressive slave master, flees Egypt, and meets his future wife, Zipporah, marries her and has two sons. Then one day, Moses is confronted by God in the burning bush, who sends him back to Egypt to lead the redemption of the Israelites. And then comes the second crisis, for on his way back to Egypt, God, the One mightier than Pharaoh, attacks him.

Once again, Moses is saved by a woman.

◇ *Act III. The Wife (Exod. 4:24–26)*

> On the way to the night lodging, God confronted Moshe and
>   sought to kill him.
> Zipporah took a flint and cut off her son's foreskin.
> She touched it to his feet.
> She said, "For you are a bridegroom in blood to me."
> He let him be.
> Then she said, "A bridegroom in blood" about the circumcision.

In this bizarre and incomprehensible episode, this much is certain: God attacks in a lethal way, and the child had not yet been circumcised. The story does not tell us which son. It does not even tell us whom God attacked: we assume it was Moses. The object of the attack could have been the son, for the story says just "him." It was probably Moses, for "seeking to kill" has been a leitmotiv in his life. He fled to Midian because Pharoah sought to kill him (Exod. 2:15), and God assured him that it was safe to go back because those who were seeking his life were dead (Exod. 4:19). Now suddenly God apparently attacks and seeks to kill him; the narrator leaves this ambiguous to further heighten the enigmatic nature of this episode.

The narrator also does not give any indication why God attacked. Was the noncircumcision of his son the reason that Moses (or the son) got into danger? This is the suggestion of the Targumim and midrashim, but God knew that the son was not circumcised when God commissioned Moses. God may have attacked Moses or the uncircumcised son so that Zipporah would save with blood, thus foreshadowing the way Israel would save their firstborn children in Egypt with the blood of the lamb. Certainly in both stories the Israelites are saved because blood is "touched" to its object, and both stories use the verb *ngʿ* to describe the "touching" (Exod. 12:22). The narrator alerts the reader to the parallel to the Exodus by mentioning the death of the firstborn in Egypt just before the story begins (Exod. 4:23). Early readers noted the parallels between the two blood stories, and the Septuagint and the Targums heighten the parallels by having the attacker be not God but an angel, which it calls "the destroyer," the same name Exodus 12 calls the killer of the firstborn.

There are other possible explanations for God's attack. Some scholars have suggested that God is angry at Moses for first refusing to go to Egypt. This does not seem likely, for prophets are expected to refuse their call initially, and it would make no sense for God to attack someone who had "repented" and was now doing God's bidding. But Moses carries a different kind of guilt, the bloodguilt (*dāmîm*), on his head for having killed the Egyptian. Perhaps this bloodguilt might imperil him as he leaves on his mission, and the blood serves as atonement. Or perhaps Moses has done nothing wrong, and God attacks for the same reason that the angel attacked Jacob at the Jabbok River in Genesis 32 (and perhaps Balaam in Num. 22:22–35) in some kind of dangerous ordeal from which he will emerge transformed before he goes to complete his destiny. The text leaves the cause mysterious.

Zipporah doesn't hesitate or ask why. She quickly takes a flint and circumcises their son, and by circumcising him, she averts doom. Nothing else is clear. Did circumcision rescue Moses or his son by sanctifying them? Or was it the blood that averted the doom? Does blood always have mystical protective properties, or is it only the blood of the firstborn or a foreshadowing of the blood of the Paschal Lamb? There is something almost homeopathic about the saving use of blood: a few drops of bloodshed avert the spilling of a person's blood, which is the life. Perhaps circumcision contains this "hair of the dog" aspect: a small act of ritual violence to keep away other, more dangerous acts of violence. The narrator does not tell us, and perhaps does not know.

Zipporah knows. She takes a flint and circumcises her son. The story is set long after the Stone Age, long after people got into the habit of using metal implements. Zipporah may have used flint because it was readily available on the ground. Flint may also have been the appropriate material for circumcision, as Joshua circumcised Israel with flint knives when they entered Canaan (Josh. 5:2–3). Traditional rituals are often highly conservative, and circumcisers may have used flint long after sharp metal knives were available. The Bible associates metal implements with warfare. No metal was to be used to build an altar (Deut. 27:5) or the temple (1 Kings 6:7), and it would make sense to avoid metal for circumcision.

Zipporah then touches the bloody foreskin at *his feet*. Whose feet? Her son's? Moses'? God's? And is it really "feet" that she touched, or is it genitalia? And then Zipporah cries, **"You are a bridegroom in blood for me."** To whom is Zipporah talking, who is the "bridegroom," and is she referring to a "bridegroom"? *Ḥatan* often means "father-in-law" rather than "groom," so the "you" may be God, and Zipporah may indicate that she has entered into a special relationship with God through this ceremony. The "you" may also be Moses, but even then there are questions about the meaning of her statement. By calling Moses her bride-groom, Zipporah may mean that this ritual has now united them in a blood-sealed covenant stronger than normal marriage. But ḥatan can also be "son-in-law." Zipporah may be suggesting that she herself has become the virtual father-in-law of Moses by becoming the circumciser of the family. She has assumed her own father's role in the family, becoming a surrogate for Jethro even as she leaves his household. Circumcision often has to be performed before marriage, and Israel may have known customs in which the prospective father of the bride circumcised his son-in-law-to-be, symbolically exposing and preparing the boy's genitalia.

The little story abounds in wordplays, some with words that do not even appear in the text. The "trouble," ṣar, (which does not appear), is averted by Zipporah, ṣprh, with her flint, ṣûr. The ḥatan is saved by circumcising, which in Arabic is khatana (as khatan, it means "son-in-law"), either because circumcision was performed by the bride's family or by coincidence of sound. There are other wordplays involved in this very short story. **God confronted Moses** (pgš) and **tried** (bqš) to kill him, and the story starts and ends with two words that sound alike, mālôn, "the lodging," and mûlōt, a word that is otherwise unknown but is translated "circumcision" because it sounds like mîlah. In the face of so many wordplays, even the word the narrator uses for "bloody," dāmîm, may not mean just "bloody" (which could be simply dām) but may be an allusion either to the bloodguilt Moses may carry (dāmîm) or to the multiple deaths in the tenth plague.

Moses cannot act. He is either under attack, deathly ill, or paralyzed by a "dark night" of the soul. He needs another savior, and another woman steps up. Zipporah may know about the protective value of circumcision or of blood from Moses or her own traditions. Circumcision was wisely practiced in the ancient world, and may have had an apotropaic aspect in her tradition. She draws on ritual for dispelling the overwhelming power of deity, and on almost incantatory words to accompany her act. Above all, she acts with whatever methods she knows to protect her young. It is not hard to see why the Bible associates such protection with women. There are ferocious females in the divine world: Ishtar acts as "mother" particularly when she protects in war; Anat protects her brother by defeating his enemy Mot; Isis protected her brother Osiris, guarded his dead body, and milked it to bring him back to life through his child Horus. These goddesses are related to the animal kingdom. Ishtar is mistress of lions and protects as a lioness protects her cubs. Anat is a winged deity, and Isis is often represented as a hawk hovering over Osiris. No creatures are more protective of their own than the great eagles and hawks. It is no accident that Zipporah means "bird."

The story, the language used to relate it, and its themes are highly cryptic, and even in biblical times this story was not understood, for the narrator of the last line is trying to puzzle it out, identifying Zipporah's statement with *mulôt*, most probably circumcision. But within the enigma, the figure of Zipporah is decisive and clear. She understands what is happening, knows what to do, averts the doom, and rescues Moses.

Zipporah acts to prevent a killing. In this experience of the frightening aspect of divine power, Moses' wife grows into a savior. She becomes a surrogate parent, protecting Moses as well as her children. Moses' Israelite "biological" mother and his Egyptian "foster" mother are now joined in a triad of saviors by this Midianite "ritual" mother. Now Moses will turn from being the rescued to the rescuer, from the saved to the savior.

The stories of the great women of the Exodus show the true meaning of the Midrashic proverb "Because of the righteous women of that generation, Israel was redeemed from Egypt." These women were proactive and assertive even while the men were passive, reactive, or absent. They continued to function strongly and decisively even in conditions of dire oppression. And they stood up to overwhelming power. Political power, paternal power, even divine power all failed to deter these women. What enabled them to act in the face of overwhelming odds? Ironically, the empowering element may be their habitual disempowerment. Women have usually (if not always) been in subordinate positions, subservient to and sometimes even subjugated by the men in their lives. As a result, external oppression did not change their lives in fundamental ways. Certainly oppression intensified their suffering, but it did not turn their experience of reality upside down. Because women have rarely had autonomy, negotiating with authority has been their normal mode of existence. Women are used to ignoring outside events and regulations, used to maneuvering through the system to follow personal imperatives: helping their husbands, protecting their children, and being loyal to their God. When people who are used to authority are denied it, they may collapse, but those who have never had it know how to react. Women have learned how to acquire some power and autonomy in households where legal authority belongs to men. They have learned skills of indirection, wits, and deception—skills well adapted to conditions of subjugation. Such experience can be very useful when the household itself comes under outside rule in conditions of capture or slavery.

There is another way in which the experience of oppression may not have been as debilitating to women as to men. Men have defined themselves by their ability to run their households. Proper control over members of their families has been an important ingredient in their self-esteem, in the "honor" of the household that they see themselves as protecting. Under conditions of capture and oppression, men may be debilitated by the loss of their "natural" role. But the culturally defined personal imperatives of women to help their husbands and protect their children do not disappear. In fact, they may become even more important when external oppression magnifies the dangers facing their families. Women in such dire circumstances feel the importance of using the skills of the powerless to succeed as protectors of life.

The Guardian at the Door
Rahab

ISRAEL ENTERS Canaan in families organized around their men. But the pattern set in the days of Egypt reasserts itself: the men who act for Israel are saved by women. Male generals, first Joshua and then Barak, lead the troops. Nevertheless, female saviors mark both the beginning and the end of the war with the Canaanites. The women are not all members of Israel: Rahab is a Canaanite and Yael a Kenite. But from their marginal position, they move center stage to initiate and terminate the conquest of Canaan.

The story begins as the people of Israel, having wandered forty years in the desert, are poised on the edge of the land. Years earlier they were not ready to conquer it. Are they now strong and determined enough to do so? In the first story of the historical books, Joshua, chapter 2, a Canaanite prostitute provides the answer to this question.

◇ *The Heroine Harlot (Josh. 2:1–7)*

> Joshua ben Nun sent out from Shittim two men, spies.
>
> He said, "Go! See the land and Jericho."
>
> They went and came to the house of a prostitute whose name was Rahab.
>
> They slept there.
>
> Thus was said to the king of Jericho, "Look! Men have come this night from the Israelites to scout out the land."
>
> The king of Jericho sent to Rahab, saying thus: "Bring out the men who come to you, who have come to your house, for they have come to scout out the land."
>
> The woman took the two men and hid him.
>
> She said, "Yes, the men came to me but I did not know where they were from. The gate was about to close at dark and the men went out. I do not know where the men went. Chase after them quickly, for you may overtake them!"

> She had taken them up on her roof and hidden them in the flax
>   that was spread out for her on the roof.
> The men chased after them by way of the crossing of the
>   Jordan.
> The gate was closed after the pursuers went out.

Rahab is a familiar anti-type in folklore, the prostitute with the heart
of gold. She has faith in God's might, adopts the Israelites as her own,
and rescues them. But at the beginning, Rahab is a triply marginalized
woman. From Israel's point of view, she is an outsider; from Canaan's
point of view, she is a woman; and even from the Canaanite woman's
point of view, she is a prostitute, outside normal family life. Rahab is
smart, proactive, tricky, and unafraid to disobey and deceive her king.
Her allegiance to God and Israel make her one of Israel's early saviors.

The reconnaissance mission recalls the time forty years earlier when
Moses sent twelve choice men, great men of Israel whose names are
recorded. He gave them a specific charge: "See whether the people living
there are weak or strong, few or numerous; whether this land is good or
not good and whether the cities are open or fortified; whether the land is
fat or thin, has wood or not, and you shall be strong and bring back fruit"
(Num. 13:18–20). But their mission was a terrible failure. Only two of the
twelve, Joshua and Caleb, trusted that Israel could conquer the land. The
others, men of noble office and pedigree, did not feel powerful enough
to conquer. They reported that the nations were strong, that the land
could be lethal, and that there were giants in the land, compared to
whom the Israelites looked and felt like grasshoppers (Num. 13:27–33).
Seeing the anxiety of the people, God decided that the entire generation
had to stay in the wilderness until death overtook them. Now it is time
to try again. But this time, Joshua sends two ordinary men to Jericho and
does not tell them what they should report.

The men go directly to the house of Rahab. The narrator doesn't tell
us why. Perhaps they went there because a prostitute's establishment is a
good place to blend in unobserved and listen to people. Or, perhaps,
men who had been out in the wilderness all their lives headed for a bor-
dello with soft beds and soft women. Whatever their reason, the king
finds out and sends envoys to demand that Rahab hand over the two
men. This message is a direct, explicit order. It covers all circumstances
and leaves no room for ambiguity: whether the men have come **"to
you"** (which could mean sexually) or have only **"come to your house,"**
the king wants them. There is no room for Rahab to fudge or misunder-

stand. This is her moment of truth: she must choose whether to be loyal to her king or to protect the men. And, like the midwives in Egypt, she chooses Israel. Like them, she tries to avoid a frontal attack. Like them, she can deceive the king. Rather than say "No, I won't," she declares her total ignorance: **"the men came to me, but I did not know from where . . . The gate was about to close at dark and the men went out. I do not know where . . ."**

It is not surprising to find Rahab acting as the "midwife" of the embryonic Israel. The book of Joshua tells the tale of the entry into Canaan as a mirror image of the Exodus from Egypt, filling the account of the events of the entry with allusions to the Exodus. God promises to be with Joshua as with Moses (Josh. 1:5); flint knives are used in circumcisions (Josh. 5:2–3); Joshua and Moses—and only they—are told to remove their shoes because they stand on holy ground (Josh. 5:15); and the people cross the Jordan on dry land as they had crossed the Red Sea. The narrator heightens the parallel between Rahab and the Exodus story by using a relatively rare word for "hide," ṣpn, when she conceals the two Israelites under the flax. The form of the verb, the third-person imperfect feminine, wattiṣpenô, "she hid him," is even rarer. Moreover, it has a strange suffix: him? There are two men under the flax. The incongruous use of the singular suffix draws attention to the only other time the verb occurs in the third-person feminine imperfect. When Moses' mother saves Moses "she hid him," wattiṣpenehû. Rahab hides the Israelites spies just as Moses' mother hid her baby. The women of the Exodus have met their successor.

The heart of Rahab's story is the dialogue between her and the spies after the soldiers leave.

◇ Faith and Hesed (Josh. 2:8–14)

> They had barely lain down when she came up to them on the roof.
>
> She said to the men, "I know that YHWH has given you this land and that dread has fallen upon us, and that all the inhabitants of the land have melted before you. For we have heard that YHWH dried up the waters of the Reed Sea before you when you left Egypt, and what you did to the two Amorite kings across the Jordan, to Sihon and to Og, that you utterly destroyed them. We heard and our hearts melted, and there is no spirit left in anyone because of you,

> for YHWH your god is God in heaven above and on the
> earth below.
> "And now, swear to me by YHWH: Inasmuch as I have acted
> benevolently toward you, you will in turn act benevolently
> toward my father's household, and you will give me a truth-
> ful sign. May you grant life to my father and my mother and
> my brothers and my sisters and everyone that is theirs! May
> you rescue our lives from death!"
> The men said to her, "May our lives die instead of yours, pro-
> vided you do not tell about this matter of ours. And it will
> be when YHWH gives us this land, we will act benevolently
> and faithfully toward you."

Rahab begins by declaring her faith in God's intentions and might, **I know that YHWH has given you this land.** With this statement, the would-be savior acknowledges God and becomes the oracle of Israel's occupation of Canaan, the first of the female oracles who appear throughout the historical books (and are discussed in "Voice," pp. 297–330). Rahab is also the first of the inhabitants of the land to declare her allegiance to God, and she is the first to join Israel.

Rahab's speech has a considerable amount of hyperbole: if no one has the spirit to stand against Israel, what are the king of Jericho and his soldiers doing chasing these envoys? But it is an important message, and it is the sum content of the favorable report that the men brought back to Joshua.

Rahab's speech is couched in language familiar to readers in ancient Israel. She uses special terms, *'eimah*, "dread," and *namag*, "melt away," from the vocabulary of Israel's holy war to conquer Canaan. These phrases allude to the great song of Israel's sacred history, the Song of the Sea: "All the dwellers of Canaan are aghast, terror and dread descend upon them" (Exod. 15:15–16). The prediction made by the Song is indeed coming true, the process of conquest has truly started. Her speech also contains all the essential elements of the classic Deuteronomic form of covenants. Her acknowledgment of God's greatness forms the *preamble* and the *prologue;* her request for her family's salvation and for a sign of assurance are her *stipulations;* the Israelites' demand for silence and stay-ing within the house are their *stipulations;* their promise of salvation or death are their *sanctions.* She requests the *oath* that they give, and in the next section they offer the scarlet cord as the physical *sign* of the treaty.

By all these official treaty elements, the narrator conveys the standard nature of the arrangement by which Rahab allies herself with Israel.

Rahab ends with a request. In return for her demonstration of loyalty in saving the spies, Rahab asks for benevolent action, *ḥesed*, from Israel. She wants a particular beneficence, that she and her family be spared in the destruction. Israel offers this same *ḥesed* in the very short story of the Israelite conquest of Bethel (Judg. 1:22–26), a story that is in many ways a "narrative analogy" to the story of Rahab. The Josephite scouts see a man coming out from Bethel and offer him *ḥesed* if he reveals the entrance to his city; when they defeat the city, they spare him. Rahab's benevolence will enable Israel to spare her life. Abimelech king of Gerar requested reciprocal *ḥesed* from Abraham: "Do with me according to the *ḥesed* that I did to you" (Gen. 21:23). Abimelech proposes a treaty with Abraham, Rahab seeks a similar arrangement with Israel, and both Rahab and Abimelech use legal language to reflect the juridical importance of this treaty transaction. Even though *ḥesed* means action beyond any legal requirements, it can form the basis for a new formal arrangement.

◇   *The Scarlet Cord (Josh. 2:15–24)*

> She let them down through the window by a rope, for her house
>   was in the fortification wall and she lived in the fortification.
> She said to them, "Go to the hills, lest the pursuers encounter
>   you. Hide there three days until the pursuers return and
>   then go on your way."
> The men say to her, "We are quit of this oath that you made us
>   swear. Look! We are coming to the land. Tie this scarlet
>   cord in the window through which you have let us down,
>   and gather into your house your father and your mother
>   and your brothers and all your father's house. And it will be
>   that whoever goes out of your doors to the outside—his
>   blood is on his head and we are clear. And all who will be
>   with you in the house—his blood is on our heads if anyone
>   touches him. And if you tell about this matter—we are clear
>   from the oath that you have had us swear."
> She said, "It is according to your words."
> She sent them off, and they went.
> She tied the scarlet cord in the window.
>
> They went and came to the hills and stayed there three days, un-
>   til the pursuers went back.

> The pursuers searched the whole path and didn't find (the men).
>
> The two men turned back and came down from the hills and crossed over.
>
> They came to Joshua ben Nun and related to him all the things that confronted them.
>
> They said to Joshua, "Indeed YHWH has given the whole land into our hands and the inhabitants of the land are melting away before us."

When Rahab lowers the men outside her window, she makes a seemingly extraneous remark, **"Go to the hills."** This is good advice, but why include it in the story? Like so much in this story, the purpose is allusive. A similar phrase appears in the story of the destruction of Sodom and Gomorrah, where the angels tell Lot to "escape to the hills" (Gen. 19:18). By including this phrase, the narrator draws attention to the many similarities between these apparently different stories. They have a similar plot sequence: two strangers lodge in a city, their host defies a demand to "bring out the men," the city is destroyed, the inhabitant who lodged them is saved, and his descendants are identified. There are further parallels. In both stories, the host is marginal to the city's social structure, Lot as an outsider from elsewhere, Rahab as a prostitute. And both stories take place in the Jordanian plain, and may have originated as local legends. The narrator emphasizes the intertextual similarities by using a similar vocabulary, by including the escape to the hills, and by a giveaway lexical allusion in which the narrator reports that Rahab hid the "envoys," *hammal'akîm* (Josh. 6:25), the word for the angels in Sodom. The narrator accomplishes two important goals by writing the story in this fashion: he/she can highlight the assertiveness and proactivity of Rahab in comparison to the hesitant and tentative Lot. And he/she can underscore the evilness of the Canaanite city of Jericho and the fact that it, like Sodom, deserved to be destroyed.

The response of the men is equally allusive. Absolving themselves of their original oath, they add an additional stipulation before recommitting themselves. They give her a *tiqwat ḥûṭ haššānî,* a scarlet thread, and tell her to place it on her house. A scarlet cord is known from the legend of Peretz, David's ancestor. When Peretz was born, the midwife wrapped the scarlet cord around Zerah's wrist to show that he was the first twin to emerge, but his brother Peretz (the barrier-break) actually came through first. The scarlet cord brings Rahab into the august company of the barrier-breakers of David's ancestry. Moreover, the Israelite men explain, the scarlet cord is to be used in a special way. Rahab is to gather her family into her house. During the fighting, only those who stay inside the house marked with the scarlet cord will be safe from the devastation. Once again, the alert reader, ancient or modern, may catch the reference. On the night of the slaying of the firstborn of Egypt, the Israelites marked their doors with lamb's blood and stayed inside. Rahab's family, inside the house marked in red, is to be rescued from Jericho as the Israelites were from Egypt.

When the Israelites conquered Jericho, Joshua remembered the promise the spies had made.

◇   *In the Midst of Israel (Josh. 6:21–25)*

> They utterly destroyed everything in the city, male and female,
>   young and old, ox and lamb, and ass, (all) by the sword.
> To the two men who spied out the land, Joshua said, "Come to
>   the house of the prostitute and take out from there the
>   woman and all that is hers, as you swore to her."
> The spy-lads went and took out Rahab and her father and her
>   mother and her brothers and everything she had.
> They took her whole family and placed them outside Israel's
>   camp.
> They burnt by fire the city and all in it.
> One exception: they took the silver and the gold and the bronze
>   and copper implements into the treasury of YHWH's
>   house.
> Joshua granted life to Rahab the prostitute and all her father's
>   house and everything she had.
> She dwells in the midst of Israel until this very day, for she hid
>   the envoys whom Joshua sent to spy out Jericho.

Joshua sent the two men to Rahab's house, they brought her and her family out, and she lives **in the midst of Israel,** *beqereb yisrael,* **until this very day.** The family of Rahab reenacts the drama of Israel, and this resourceful outsider, Rahab the trickster, is a new Israel. All has ended happily: Israel has been enriched by the family of a heroine, and the conquest has begun.

But is this the way the conquest is supposed to proceed? According to Deuteronomy, the inhabitants of the land ought to be destroyed: "You must doom them to destruction, make no pacts with them, grant them no quarter" (Deut. 7:2). Ḥerem, total war, is an important motif in the story of the conquest of Jericho. Chapter 6 uses eleven variations of the verb *ḥrm*, summarizing the conquest with the statement **"They utterly destroyed everything in the city."** Right after this record of total destruction, Joshua sends the spies in to get Rahab, and **"The spy-lads went and took out Rahab and her father and her mother and her brothers and everything she had."** In the light of *ḥerem*, it seems strange to see Rahab and *her whole family* joining Israel, and one might conclude that the first thing the Israelites did on entering Canaan was break the rule of the *ḥerem*.

The saving of Rahab seems even more problematic when it is seen in juxtaposition to the next chapter in Joshua, which tells how the Israelites were defeated at Ai because of a violation of the *ḥerem* at Jericho. God instructs Joshua to call the people to an oracular procedure to determine who took the *ḥerem*.

Ḥerem in your midst (Josh. 7:13)

> Arise, sanctify the people and say, "Sanctify yourselves for tomorrow, for thus says YHWH, 'There is *ḥerem* in your midst, Israel! You will not be able to stand before your enemies until you take away the *ḥerem* from your midst.' "

The oracular process narrows down to Achan, who confesses that he took a beautiful Sumerian cloak, two hundred silver shekels, and a gold tongue, all of which are found buried in his tent and brought out. As a result, Achan, the loot, his children, his animals, and his goods are taken to the valley, burned with fire, and stoned. At that place, they set up a large heap of stones as a marker, which is there "until this day."

Parallel phrases point out the contrasts between Rahab's story and Achan's. Israel must take away the **"ḥerem in your midst,"** but Rahab is **in the midst of Israel;** Achan's whole household is stoned and Rahab's whole household is saved. The mound of stones that marks the violation stands **until this day** and Rahab lives in Israel **until this day.** Rahab is saved despite the *ḥerem*. If the purpose of the *ḥerem* is to prevent contamination by foreign ideas, it would seem that saving *people* from the *ḥerem* is a more serious violation than saving a cloak, and the reader might begin to suspect that there is a dark side to the Rahab story. And yet the book of Joshua does not present it that way. The two stories contain a discourse on the nature of obedience to the *ḥerem*. God punishes Achan's "liberation" of the cloak by a defeat at Ai, but follows the men's promise to Rahab by a glorious conquest of Jericho, a victory achieved

by God's miraculous intervention in felling the walls. Israel has clearly
not angered God by agreeing to save Rahab. When Achan ignored the
ḥerem for selfish reasons, all of Israel was punished and could not conquer Ai until he was found and executed; when the men of Israel ignored the ḥerem as an act of ḥesed to repay ḥesed, then God reacted by
miraculously conquering Jericho. The juxtaposition of the stories implies that the ḥerem is not an absolute, and is superseded by issues of justice and mercy.

The application of the ḥerem is also at issue in the next group of stories in the book of Joshua. Chapter 9 presents the Gibeonites, who pretend to be a faraway nation.

◈ *Gibeon's Approach (Josh. 9:6–11)*

> They went to Joshua, to the camp at Gilgal.
> They said to him, "To the man of Israel, we have come from a
> far land. And now, cut a treaty with us."
> The man of Israel said to the Hivite, "Perhaps you live in my
> midst—how could I cut a treaty with you?"
> They said to Joshua, "We are your servants."
> Joshua said, "Who are you and where have you come from?"
> They said to him, "From a very far-off land, your servants come
> for the sake of YHWH your God. For we have heard his rep-
> utation, everything he did in Egypt, and everything he did
> to the two Amorite kings who are over the Jordan, to Sihon
> king of Heshbon and to Og king of Bashan in Ashtaroth.
> Our elders and all the inhabitants of the land said, 'Take
> provisions and go meet them and tell them, "We are your
> servants." ' Now cut a treaty with us."

Like Rahab, they seek alliance, **"For we have heard."** And as with Rahab, what they have heard is the story of Egypt and the destruction of
Sihon and Og. The name of YHWH has grown great, the report has
gone out. The kings of the Amorites gather to fight, but the Gibeonites
are moved by this report to try to ally themselves with Israel. The Israelites know that they should not make an alliance if **"you live in my
midst."** Since the Gibeonites know this in advance (for they, like Rahab,
seem to have studied Deuteronomy), they trick Israel into believing that
they come from far away, and Joshua grants them their treaty. Once
again, a smart outsider has escaped the ḥerem and joined Israel. And once
again, God shows approval by coming to the aid of Israel with a miracle.

When Israel comes to rescue the Gibeonites from the Amorites, God makes the sun stand still.

Rahab and the Gibeonites refer to Egypt and to Sihon and Og. In each case, God "hardened the heart" of the kings. Exodus tells us that Pharoah first hardened his own heart; then God hardened it. Possibly, this was true also of Sihon and Og: since Sihon and Og wanted to fight Israel, God made their resolve even firmer. The Rahab and Gibeon stories may represent an old tradition that remembered the conquest as a process during which many inhabitants of the land survived, became aligned with Israel, and ultimately joined it. According to this tradition, ḥerem applied only to those nations or kings who actively opposed Israel. The battles of conquest were "defensive." These stories show that there was an alternative to resisting the Israelites; those who were convinced by the reports of God's might were assimilated rather than destroyed. Such a view of the amalgamation and incorporation of local inhabitants is strikingly like the account of the settlement of Israel that is currently accepted by archaeologists and historians.

The book of Joshua is part of the Deuteronomistic history, and Deuteronomy does not trust foreign alliances and foreign women. To Deuteronomy, the very purpose of the ḥerem is to prevent the introduction of "foreign" ideas into Israel, and the nations that remain are sources of danger. From this point of view, the rescue of Rahab would look like Israel's first act of apostasy, committed immediately upon Israel's entry into the land. The Deuteronomist does not make any direct negative statements, but the repeated use of the verb ḥerem in Joshua insinuates the suspicion that saving Rahab contains the first seeds of the nation's destruction.

The very first words of the Rahab story may hint at Deuteronomic disapproval. The narrator informs us that when Joshua sent out the spies, he was at Shittim, the place where Israel angered God in the incident of Baʻal-Peʻor. When Zimri brought the Midianite princess Cozbi into the Israelite camp, Phineas the priest stabbed them both. As we juxtapose these two Shittim stories, Rahab's position, profession, and name take on new significance. Rahab is a prostitute, *zônah,* and the word for Israel's faithlessness at Shittim is *zanah.* The names of the two women show the different attitudes of the two stories. Cozbi's name means "deception," and she was killed immediately. Phineas gave her no chance to profess her loyalty to God or to Israel. To Phineas, the sight of a foreign woman was such a danger that she must be eradicated immediately, she and the man who brought her. Had this same Phineas been in charge at

Jericho, Rahab too might have been killed. By contrast, Rahab's name means "wide, broad." She is the "broad of Jericho." Her name is emblematic of the permeable boundaries of Israel. She is the wide-open woman who is the wide-open door to Canaan, or maybe (in the negative view) the wide-open door to apostasy. To Phineas and Deuteronomy, open boundaries are dangerous; others can see them as presenting an opportunity.

In the Rahab story, the negativity implied sotto voce by the mention of Shittim and the reminders of the ḥerem is more than counterbalanced by the positive images that the story projects. Rahab's persona has many of Israel's classic hero themes. She is a female savior, like the mothers of the Exodus. She is a trickster outsider, like Jacob in Laban's house, one who survives by her wits and comes to God by her faith. Rahab the whore is also the outsider's outsider, the most marginal of the marginal. She is the quintessential downtrodden with whom Israel identifies. Just as her pious behavior reverses expectations of how prostitutes act, so her elevation is a reversal of the normal expectations for a prostitute's future. YHWH interrupts normative societal expectations by exalting the prostitute just as YHWH interrupted expectations by choosing the younger sons and freeing the slaves. The saving of Rahab is part of and an example of God's nature and Israel's mission.

Warriors by Weapon and Word
Deborah and Yael

ISRAEL, CROSSING into Canaan, changes its role. It is a time of conquest, a time of war. The Israelites have become fighters, and the saviors of Israel—women as well as men—have to be aggressors. The times call for warriors, and two warrior women appear in the decisive defeat of the Canaanites. One, Deborah, initiates the battle, calling the troops to action and declaring the start of hostilities. The other, Yael, delivers the coup de grâce that completes the defeat of Canaan.

These women are remembered in both story and song. The story is in Judges 4, and the song is in Judges 5. The Song of Deborah is a very ancient poem, one of the earliest writings that the Bible preserves: it was most probably written in the eleventh century, soon after the events it records. The story reached its present shape much later in Israel's history. The two literary creations have subtly different attitudes, and in placing them side by side, the historian of the book of Judges encourages the reader to read them together as well as separately.

Deborah (Judg. 4:4–16; Judg. 5:1–31)

Deborah was very different from the savior women we have already encountered. They were private women; she was a recognized public figure. They lived ordinary lives until the politico-military world intruded into their realm; Deborah was active in the public arena as part of her normal everyday life. Her role as leader began sometime before the events related in the narratives by which she is remembered, but how she became a leader is one of the many facets of her life that went unrecorded.

◇ *Deborah, Prophet and Judge (Judg. 4:4–5)*

> Deborah the prophetess-woman, Lapidot-woman—she judged Israel at that time.

> She would sit under "Deborah's Palm Tree" between Ramah
> and Beth-El on Mount Ephraim, and the Israelites went up
> to her for judgment.

The record begins as Israel is oppressed by Yabin king of Hazor. Deborah is a prophet-woman, someone who speaks with divine authority, and she is *Lapidot-woman*. ʾĒšet lapidôt could be translated "wife of Lapidot," but it also means "woman of torches." *Lappîdôt*, "torches," comes where we would ordinarily expect a husband's name, but it is a strange-sounding name for a man and, moreover, does not have the standard patronymic "son of." The reader must decide whether to translate *lapidôt* as a name or a noun. Translating it "wife of Lapidot" has the advantage of emphasizing that a prophet could be married and that a married woman could have another role. On the other hand, "woman of torches" or "fiery woman" fits the image of Deborah and would fit the story in the manner of biblical names. "Torch-Lady" provides a significant wordplay, for it is Deborah, not her husband, who is the torch that sets the general Barak (whose name means "lightning") on fire. Moreover, in Mesopotamian mythology, the torch and the lightning (ṣullat and haniš) are the heralds of the storm god. In the same way, "Torch-Lady" and "Lightning" are fit agents for the God of Israel who defeats Sisera by creating a river of mud to incapacitate his chariots.

The story also tells us that Deborah judged Israel. The "judges" were Israel's charismatic leaders in the days before the monarchy. These leaders usually acquired their political authority after they saved Israel through battle. The first such judge, Othniel ben Kenaz, set the pattern: the oppressed people cried out to God, "the spirit of YHWH came upon him (Othniel), he judged Israel and went out to battle, and YHWH gave Cushan Rishatayim king of Aram into his hand" (Judg. 3:10). Did Deborah become a judge in the same way, by leading a group in battle? Or perhaps she acquired her authority by offering sage advice that led to a victory, or by predicting an important matter that came true. The story never tells us.

The Song of Deborah is no more interested in Deborah's biography than the story is, but it may give a hint of how Deborah rose to importance. In the Song, Deborah describes a total breakdown of order in Israel. Wayfarers had to go by roundabout ways to avoid danger; in those days there was no rescue "Until I arose, Deborah, until I arose, a mother in Israel" (Judg. 5:7). Somehow Deborah imposed order on Israel. How this happened, neither the poem nor the story records. Their silence on such important matters is a reminder that neither the story nor the Song was framed as a record of Deborah's life. The biblical story is not a biography: it is a memory of Israel's defeat of Canaan, a defeat in which Deborah played an important role. Only this role is remembered, and when the action begins, Deborah is already in mid-career. The rest of her legend is unrecorded and unpreserved.

One day, Deborah called Barak.

◇ *Summons to Battle (Judg. 4:6–10)*

> She sent and called for Barak ben Abinoam from Qedesh-Naftali.
>
> She said to him, "Did not YHWH God of Israel command: 'Go and pull toward Mount Tabor and take with you ten thousand men from the men of Naphtali and Zebulun. I will draw Sisera the head of Yabin's army and his chariotry and masses to Wadi Kishon and I will give him into your hand.' "
>
> Barak said to her, "If you go with me, I will go. If you will not go with me, I will not go."
>
> She said, "I will indeed go with you, especially since you will get no glory on the way you are going, for into the hand of a woman YHWH will deliver Sisera."
>
> Deborah rose and went with Barak to Qedesh.
>
> Barak mustered Zebulun and Naphtali to Qedesh.
>
> Ten thousand men went up at his feet, and Deborah went up with him.

What prompted Deborah to call Barak? Perhaps the people initiated the call. The story tells us that the Israelites went up to her for judgment. This verse describes the way she used to judge Israel, arbitrating disputes between Israelites as once Moses had done, and as a prophet, possibly also being asked for oracular decisions about political and administrative matters. But the narrator introduces a new tense, the imperfect, with the verb **went up to her**, *wayya'alû* (v. 5), so that the phrase may also serve as a bridge between the background information and the initiation of the action. The people not only regularly went to her for decisions, they came to her one day for a particular kind of "judgment." The poem provides a hint as to what they wanted: "Then the people of YHWH went down to the gates: 'Awake, awake, Deborah. Awake, awake, speak a song. Arise, Barak, take your captives, son of Abinoam' "

(Judg. 5:12). This anguished outcry may have impelled Deborah to begin the redemption.

Deborah calls Barak in her role as a prophet, an envoy of God. Such prophetic initiation of battle was known in the ancient Near East; in Assyria it was called a *šir takilti,* a "song of support." The Assyrian records preserve the report of a liver omen that Esarhaddon received before his fight for power in which the divination experts tell him "Go without delay!" Deborah's call to **"Go"** is in this tradition. Moreover, Deborah hints that she is following up on a previous call to Barak: **Did not YHWH God of Israel command?** God has spoken to Barak, and Deborah's call is a second summons. Barak is reluctant to go, like Moses before him, like Gideon and Samuel later in Israel's history, others called by God to be envoys. He seeks assurance that God is really with him and insists that Deborah go with him to the battle staging area where the warriors assemble.

Readers have often been bothered by Barak's reluctance to go without Deborah, declaring that his hesitation makes him "less manly" or tarnishes his glory. But Barak has good reason to be insecure: Yabin, after all, has nine hundred chariots! Moreover, prophets have an important role to play in battle. Letters from the ancient city of Mari show that prophets sent word to King Zimri-Lim to give assurance and advice in battle, and Assyrian inscriptions record omens in which prophets urged the king to take action and promise the presence and protection of the gods. The Esarhaddon oracle cited above continues, "We will go by your side and slay your enemies." Prophets play several roles in battle: they muster and inspire the troops, and also declare the correct, auspicious time to begin. The Septuagint, the Greek translation of the Bible, understands this second role of battle oracles, for it adds to Barak's request the phrase "because I do not know on what day the Lord will send his angel to my side." Prophets are such an important presence in battle that Elijah and Elisha are called "Israel's chariot and cavalry."

Many readers of this story have been particularly troubled by the presence of women in war, believing that they are somehow out of place there and assuming that ancient Israelites would have felt the same way. But one of our earliest literary creations, the Sumerian epic "Enmerkar and the Lords of Aratta," shows the king consulting with a female sage. Most of the Assyrian prophets were women, and reports from both the ancient and more recent Near East show a consistent pattern of the presence of women to inspire the troops and taunt the enemy. There is no reason to think that biblical readers found anything strange about Barak's request to Deborah, in her capacity as either prophet or woman.

◇ *The Battle (Judg. 4:13–16)*

> Sisera mustered all his chariotry, nine hundred iron chariots, and all his people from Harosheth-Hagoyim to Wadi Kishon.
>
> Deborah said to Barak, "Arise, for this is the day that YHWH gives Sisera into your hand. Does not YHWH go out before you?"
>
> Barak quickly descended from Mount Tabor and ten thousand men after him.
>
> YHWH distressed Sisera and all the chariotry and all the camp by the sword before Barak and Sisera descended from his chariot and fled on foot.
>
> Barak chased the chariots and the camp to Harosheth-Hagoyim and fell on Sisera's camp with the sword. Not even one remained.
>
> Sisera fled on foot to the tent of Yael the wife of Heber the Kenite . . .

On Mount Tabor, Deborah the prophet announces the victory, **"God will deliver Sisera."** She announces God's presence, **"Does not God go out before you,"** and sets the battle, **"Arise, for this is the day."** She herself does not go down to the battle. Like Moses, Deborah is not a battle commander. Her role is to inspire, predict, and celebrate in song. Her weapon is the word, and her very name is an anagram of "she spoke" (*dibberah*). The battle itself is not essential. It is important only to remember that God fought: God distressed Sisera. Deborah has announced God's victory, Barak has facilitated it, and God has saved Israel. The Song of Deborah provides a glimpse of how God defeated Canaan: God brought a flash flood that made a bog of sliding mud in which chariots were useless. Barak destroys the Canaanites, but Sisera escapes to meet his destiny.

Both the story and the song emphasize the fact that Deborah is a woman. The story tells us that she was a prophetess-woman, adding the word "woman," *'iššah,* when the female noun "prophetess," *nebî'ah,* already conveys that information. She is called "Lapidot"-woman or Lapidot's woman, again repeating the word "woman," *'ešet.* And the song stresses that Deborah was a "mother in Israel." The femaleness is neither hidden nor incidental: it is an integral part of the story. Deborah is not the typical "mother": she does not stay at home protecting the children and awaiting the return of her husband. If she had children, they played no part in the story. The motherhood of this "mother in Israel" goes beyond biology. It describes her role as counselor during the days before the war, and it indicates her role in preserving the heritage of Israel, in her case by advising in battle.

There is another sense of "mother" in this poem, one very foreign to most modern readers, but well illustrated in an ancient oracle to Ashurbanipal. The oracle took the form of a nocturnal vision in which the goddess Ishtar of Arbela appeared in full battle array. The priest who had the vision reports: "You (Ashurbanipal) were standing in front of her and she spoke to you like a real mother . . . giving the following instructions: 'Wait with the attack, for wherever you intend to go I also am ready to go.'" After Ashurbanipal says he will go with her, the priest continues, "She wrapped you in her lovely baby sling, protecting your entire body. Her face shone like fire. Then [she went out in a frightening way] to defeat your enemies, against Teumman, king of Elam, with whom she was angry." In this vision, Ishtar acts like a mother precisely when she protects the king while defeating his enemies. The Assyrians, like us, rarely thought of women as warriors. Ishtar, whom they called "the one who smites the heads of the enemy," was the great exception. But the observation that mothers protect their young against enemies is a universal one. Deborah, the "mother in Israel," protected the people in time of danger.

Deborah sees herself in juxtaposition with the mother of Sisera. The Canaanite general's mother plays a role more typically assigned to women in times of war. Like Atossa, the mother of Xerxes in Aeschylus' play *Perseus,* Sisera's mother stays at home, imagining the battle and awaiting the return of her son. Deborah's and Sisera's mothers stand in the poem as opposite poles between which the Israelites and Canaanites contest. At first it seems that Deborah is going to sympathize with her, mother to mother. But the first glimpse turns malevolent, for Deborah portrays Sisera's mother eagerly awaiting the defeat of Israel. Nor does Sisera's mother (in Deborah's vision) show any sympathy for Israelite women, for she sits gloating over the many girls her son will bring back as spoils. These mothers do not arc in solidarity over the tragedy of war; on the contrary, each has sympathy only for her own people. As "mother in Israel," Deborah is fiercely protective of her own—she is not a member of some international club of mothers.

The fullest sense of Deborah as mother is revealed in her name, which is not only an anagram of "she spoke"; it is also a noun meaning "bee." This name may hint at the fullest sense of her as "mother in Israel." Like the queen bee, she raises up the swarm for battle, sending out the drones to protect the hive and conquer new territory.

The Coup de Grâce: Yael (Judg. 4:17–21; 5:24–27)

Judges 5 is the victory song that Deborah sang after the defeat of the Canaanites. The language is archaic, and scholars agree that this is a very ancient poem, written soon after the events, and perhaps by Deborah herself. In the Song, Deborah dates the happenings "in the days of Shamgar ben Anat, in the days of Yael" (Judg. 5:6), associating Yael with the victorious Shamgar who smote six hundred Philistines (Judg. 3:31). She depicts the battle and the parts she and Barak played, and pronounces praise for the tribes who participated and curses for those who didn't. Then, abruptly, she changes both tone and topic.

◇ *Yael, the Song (Judg. 5:24–27)*

> Blessed be Yael by women,
> Blessed be the wife of Heber the Kenite by women in the tent.
> He asked for water, she gave him milk;
> In a beautiful beaker she brought the keffir.
> She sent forth her hand to the tent peg,
> her right hand to a workman's striking tool.
> She struck Sisera, she pierced his head,
> she crushed it and pierced the hollow of his head.
> Between her legs he sank to his knees, he fell, he lay.
> Between her legs he sank to his knees and lay.
> Where he sank to his knees, there he lay, destroyed.

Here is the warrior Yael whom Deborah mentioned at the beginning of her song. A woman warrior, perhaps married, **the wife of Heber the Kenite**. And perhaps not, for *ḥeber* means "a group." Instead of **Yael the wife of Heber the Kenite**, the Song may refer to **Yael the woman of a band of Kenites**. Whether mentioned or not, the husbands of Yael and Deborah play no role in the action. But Yael's womanness is important: she is *'iššah*, "woman" (or wife). Deborah calls on women to praise her; translators who are perhaps influenced by the way they read Elizabeth's blessing of Mary ("blessed among women," Luke 1:42) often put it that

Yael is most blessed of women. There is a subtle difference: to translate "most blessed of women" is to imply that Yael is alone among women to be such a heroine; **Blessed be Yael by women** calls for women to claim Yael as their own heroine and even role model. The Hebrew *tebōrak minnāšim yáel* can be understood both ways. The reader must decide: Do all women have this capacity for ferocity and courage? But the translator decides for the reader, who never sees the Hebrew.

Beyond the ambiguity there is clarity: Deborah finds Yael praiseworthy. When the warrior comes to her tent, Yael treats him with dignity. Then, as he stands there, Yael grabs the tools she has on hand and fells him, smashing his skull and piercing it. The more familiar story portrays a sleeping Sisera, but in the Song, he is erect, and sinks to his knees and falls prone as she stands over him.

The Song emphasizes that he lay **between her legs.** Midrash and some modern scholars see sexual allusion here, envisioning a scene in which Yael disarms Sisera through sexual enticement, or even, says a midrash, through exhausting him sexually, once for each "between her legs." But the image of Sisera falling between Yael's legs is not a sexual allusion. It is rather a savage grotesquery of childbirth. Sisera doesn't find sexual release and the *petit mort* ("little death") of orgasm; he finds total death. Rather than being delivered to life, he is delivered to death. The Song delights in this and repeats the phrase "between her legs" twice, for in delivering Sisera to death, Yael helped deliver Israel to life. Just as the "motherhood" of Deborah involved directing battle, this savage "motherhood" of Yael "rebirths" Sisera to his death.

Yael is Sisera's last "mother," and as he lies there, defeated, the scene shifts to Sisera's birth mother. Like Yael, she is at home. But instead of going home to his birth mother, Sisera has come to the home of his death mother. His birth mother imagines that he is late because he is taking women as booty: "a girl, two girls for each man" (Judg. 5:30). Instead, two "girls" have finished him off. One, Deborah, encouraged Barak; the other, Yael, made him a battle casualty. For this act, Yael is a heroine and a role model: **Blessed be Yael by women, blessed be the wife of Heber the Kenite by women in the tents!** Women in their tents may not go out to the battlefield, but they can still be the saviors of Israel.

Yael kills her enemy, an unusual act for a woman. Even the savior women generally save by prolonging the life of their own people, rather than ending the life of the enemy. The saviors of Exodus and Conquest saved Israelites by doing in terrible circumstances exactly what women do in normal times: nurturing and preserving lives. Yael kills. The stories of the women warriors sometimes show unease with their actions, but in this ancient song there is no such ambivalence: **Blessed be Yael.**

How did Yael come to be near the battlefield? Why did she act on behalf of Israel? The Song tells us nothing, but the story answers the first question. As Deborah and Barak go to Kadesh, the story interrupts the preparations for battle to note a new character, Heber the Kenite, "separated from the Kenites, from the children of Hobab, Moses' father-in-law, and pitched his tent at the terebinth tree in Soanim which was by Kadesh" (Judg. 4:11). The narrator then turns to Sisera's preparations. The tent, and Heber's wife, become significant only after the battle.

Yael, the Story (Judg. 4:17–23)

Scene 1. Invitation (Judg. 4:17–18)

> Sisera fled on foot to the tent of Yael the wife of Heber the Kenite, for there was peace between Yabin king of Hazor and the house of Heber the Kenite.
>
> Yael came out to meet Sisera.
>
> She said to him, "Turn aside, my lord, turn aside to me. Don't be afraid!"
>
> He turned in to her, to the tent.
>
> She covered him with a blanket.

The story tells us that Heber had a treaty with the Canaanites. This makes sense: Kenites were often smiths, and Heber may have pitched his tent not too far from the battle in order to service the weaponry. Knowing that Heber worked for Yabin, Sisera may have assumed that Heber's wife would be loyal to her husband's ally. Sisera may have been simply looking for shelter, for Heber is part of the family of Moses' father-in-law, a priest, and a Kenite's tent would represent sanctuary. There are also indications that Kenite women, like Midianite women, had a cultic role, and Sisera could have seen Yael as a priestly functionary.

Yael's invitation to Sisera seems odd. Women do not usually encourage men to enter their tents, and her invitation may be a hint to the reader that all expectations of hospitality are about to be turned upside down. Yael's words may hint that she knows who he is, for her invitation **"turn aside,"** *sûrah,* which she repeats twice, is reminiscent of the name Sisera. At the end, when she sees Barak, she offers to show him "the man whom you seek" (Judg. 4:22). Her invitation to this man whom she recognizes may indicate that she already has a plan to dispatch him. Sisera, however, is not suspicious, for he has no reason to expect that Yael has ulterior motives for inviting him in, and her actions once he is inside do nothing to arouse his suspicions.

Scene 2. Mothering him to death (Judg. 19–23)

> She covered him with a blanket.
>
> He said to her, "Give me a little water to drink, for I am thirsty."
>
> She opened the skein of milk, gave him drink, and covered him.
>
> He said to her, "Stand at the gate of the tent so that if a man comes and questions you and asks, 'Is there a man here?,' then you will say, 'No!' "
>
> Yael the wife of Heber took the tent peg and placed the mallet in her hand.
>
> She came to him quietly and stuck the peg through the hollow of his head and through into the ground.
>
> He was alseep. He was tired and he died.
>
> Look! Barak is chasing after Sisera.
>
> Yael went out to meet him.
>
> She said to him, "Come and I will show you the man that you are seeking."
>
> He came with her and look! Sisera is lying dead and the tent peg is in his head.

At first, Yael seems exactly like all other women. She is at home, not on the battlefield. She welcomes Sisera into her home and begins to nurture him, covering him with a blanket. When he politely asks for water, she gives him fresh milk and covers him again. More than just a hostess, she acts as a mother, and as her mothering enables him to feel secure, he asks her to hide him and lie about his whereabouts. The request seems reasonable, but the tone is not. He had asked politely, even superpolitely, for a little bit of water. Now, revived and confident, he starts to issue orders. His demand that Yael stand at the door is not polite: not only does he not say "please," he curtly uses the masculine command form rather than the proper address for a woman. Yael's nurture is beginning to bring out his habit of command.

Her mothering also makes him feel secure enough to fall asleep. Yael kills him as he lies asleep, and the narrator adds that he had been very tired. The picture of Yael sneaking up on an exhausted Sisera is very different from the Song's portrait of the fierce woman who attacks him. Sisera's death seems ignoble, a death that would humiliate him in the eyes of warriors. In the story (not the Song), Yael's act shames him; Sisera is unmanned as well as killed. It also may shame Barak, who pursues Sisera only to find him already dead. Deborah had foretold that Barak's battle with Canaan would not bring him personal glory, "for into the hand of a woman YHWH will deliver Sisera." And indeed Barak never became a political leader in Israel. And as for the image of women: Yael in the story stands for stealth rather than ferocity.

The Song remembers Yael of Strength; the story Yael of Stealth. Neither presents a Yael of Seduction. That is left to later readers, beginning with the Graeco-Roman period, when many of the biblical stories about women were eroticized. The figure of Yael is often merged with a much later heroine whose story is presented in the Apocryphal book of Judith. Judith's story, written in the Graeco-Roman period, is set at the time of the Assyrian invasion of Israel. The Assyrian general Holofernes besieged Bethulia (Bethel), called for surrender, and announced his intention to mutilate the men of the city. Long before, Nahash the Ammonite besieged Jabesh-Gilead with a similar demand, but Saul had mustered Israel in his first act of kingship and rescued the city (Judg. 11). But the Assyrians put an end to the kingship of the North; no help can be expected from a king, and the elders of the city are ready to surrender. Once again, it is time for an old-fashioned savior, and the spirit of YHWH rests on Judith, a pious widow. In order to save Israel, she removes her widow's garb, clothes herself sumptuously, and has her hair dressed in splendid Hellenistic fashion. The result is that she is so stunningly beautiful that she is able to walk past the guards of a city under siege, past the guards of the Assyrian camp, and reach Holofernes, who invites her to dine. Judith comes to dinner bearing a bag of parched corn (her Kosher food), and sits and eats it while Holofernes drinks more than he ever has before and falls drunk at her feet. She takes his sword, cuts off his head, puts his head in the bag she brought with her, and goes back to her city. The rest of the book is a paean of praise that makes allusion to all the old heroes of Israel, including Yael.

The similarities between Yael and Judith are obvious: both are domestic women who kill the enemy general. But the differences are equally striking. The story portrays Judith in erotic terms and describes both her beauty and the male reaction to it. There is no doubt that her beauty is the weapon by which Judith saves Israel. Yael's appearance, by contrast, is never described, nor does Sisera react to her as anything but a source of help. The difference between Yael and Judith is precisely the difference between biblical ideas and the ideas that came into Israel from the Greek world. In classical biblical works, the beauty of women is never their weapon. It can make them vulnerable to male desires, as with Sarah and Bathsheba, but it does not help them manipulate such desires. It is not until Esther, one of the latest of the biblical books, that the beauty of women is any use to them, and even Esther cannot rely on her beauty to influence Ahasuerus.

Many modern readers feel great discomfort about Yael's actions, accusing her of failing to observe her husband's treaty, violating hospitality, and deceiving her guest. Elizabeth Cady Stanton is perhaps the most extreme (but not by much) when she writes, "the deception and cruelty practiced on Sisra by Jael under the guise of hospitality is Revolting . . . it is more like the work of a fiend than of a woman." But the Bible contains no such condemnation of Yael's actions. The Song has no such qualms and praises Yael. The story may reflect some sense that men should have been able to do the job, but it clearly portrays Yael as acting in accordance with the divine will, and in fulfillment of a divine oracle. The story presents no real shame for Barak, for no one man could have delivered Israel. God has an interest in both saving Israel and having Israel realize that God is the savior. In the Gideon story, God insists that Gideon take only three hundred men to battle so that it will be obvious that God rather than Gideon is the ultimate savior (Judg. 8). In the defeat of Canaan, God carries out the salvation of Israel both directly, through the storm, and by the combination of men and women, each doing part of the deliverance.

Yael confounds all expectations. The tent does not always make the warrior secure. An old Canaanite tale, the Aqhat epic, conveys a similar message. Aqhat angers the fierce goddess Anat. Later he sits alone in a tent, eating, when Anat's servant Yotpan swoops down in the form of a vulture and strikes him in the head so that he dies. A ferocious woman will find you in the tent. Yael reverses Sisera's expectation that she will protect him, an expectation that many readers share in their assumption of what a "hostess" will do. And she completely inverts the common experience of women in war. When a warrior approaches a tent in wartime, we normally fear, not for the warrior but for the woman inside. We brace ourselves for a violent rape in which the warrior brutally penetrates the woman. Instead, it is Yael who penetrates with her weapon. Women in their tents are not always victims.

Yael, the woman of action, never explains her actions. Did she feel the divine call, directly from God or through God's prophet Deborah? Did she fear what might happen when this newly imperious Sisera would awake? Was she loyal to Israel despite her husband's employment by the Canaanites? The Kenites, after all, were normally closely allied with Israel. Or did she reason that those chasing the general might find her hiding him and punish her as his ally? Neither the story nor the Song tell us anything about her: she is the heroine of the moment. Her own motives do not count. She fulfills God's oracle, and whatever she might have been thinking, God delivered Sisera into her hands.

Rahab and Yael have a lot in common. This is not readily apparent, for they seem very different. Rahab is a prostitute and Yael a married woman (at least in the story); Rahab has her own establishment and Yael lives in her husband's tent. But these distinctions are superficial and arbitrary, pernicious oppositions that have nothing to do with the lives of these women but are imposed by our own categorizations of women as "good" (married, in her husband's home) and "bad" (prostitute at large). In truth, they have significant similarities. Both are women marginalized within their own society, Rahab as a prostitute and Yael as a Kenite in Canaan. As a result, neither has a stake in the power structure of Canaan. They are living their normal lives, each in her own house, when political events encroach upon them as the Israelite men come to Rahab's house and Sisera to Yael's tent. Each has a "moment of truth" when her destiny is thrust upon her and she has to demonstrate her loyalties: Rahab to the spies or the king of Jericho, Yael to Sisera or Israel. At that moment, confronted by history and destiny, each woman abandons whatever claims the Canaanites might have to her loyalties, deceives the Canaanite men, and acts for God and Israel.

A Wise Woman of Power

DEBORAH WAS NOT the only woman with political authority in the early days of Israel's history. During the account of a revolt against King David, the story of Sheba ben Bichri, a figure of the revolt, leads us to the town of Abel-bet-Ma'acah, where we find a "wise woman" in charge. Sheba flees to the town with David's general Joab in pursuit.

◈ *The Wise Woman of Abel (2 Sam. 20:15–20)*

The siege (2 Sam. 20:15–17)

> They gathered and came after him.
> They came and laid siege against him in Abel-bet-Ma'acah.
> They cast a ramp against the city and it stood at the rampart.
> All the people with Joab were engaging in destruction in order
>   to topple the wall.
> A wise woman called from the city, "Hear me, hear me! Say to
>   Joab, 'Come close up to here and I will speak to him.'"
> He approached her.

The pursuit turns into a siege. Joab throws a ramp against the town wall and is about to destroy the wall when a woman calls. Hers is the voice of the besieged, who are fellow Israelites. The battle stops; the wise woman asks Joab to approach. Despite her prominence, she is not named; she is called a "wise woman." Women who have names are each totally unique. Rivka is the mother of Israel, Rahab the only Canaanite prostitute to join Israel, Deborah the only woman prophet-judge in Israel's memory. But the namelessness of this woman is an indication that she was not the only "wise woman" in Israel. The Bible remembers another, the Wise Woman of Tekoa, probably because she too played a role in David's story (2 Sam. 14). Their namelessness indicates that there were still others, that "wise woman" indicates a particular role. The

Bible never spells out their role, but as the story continues, it demonstrates that they occupied a position of leadership.

The woman calls to Joab to approach. Coming close to a wall during a siege can be very dangerous. Abimelech the son of Gideon died an ignoble death when he came too near the wall of a besieged city. He was on the verge of winning as he approached the wall, but an unknown woman dropped a millstone on him and cracked his skull (Judg. 9:53). Joab knows this story. He himself mentioned the death of Abimelech when he sent a messenger to inform King David of the battle in which Bathsheba's husband died. Nevertheless, when the woman tells him to approach, he does so. His willingness to risk it is an indication that the "wise woman" who calls him is not simply a woman who happens to be smart. She is an official. As such, she is calling him in her official capacity to a formal parley. Parleys always involve a temporary cease-fire. No one will rain things on Joab's head during a parley, and he can safely draw near to negotiate with her.

The peacemaker (2 Sam. 20:17–22)

> She said, "Are you Joab?" and he said, "I am."
>
> She said, "Listen to the words of your servant."
>
> He said, "I am listening."
>
> She said thus: "They have always spoken thus since early times: 'Let them inquire at Abel and then they will conclude.' I am of the peacemakers of the faithful of Israel. You are seeking to kill a mother city in Israel. Why would you swallow up YHWH's patrimony?"
>
> Joab spoke up and said, "God forbid! God forbid that I should swallow up or destroy. That is not the issue. Rather, a man from Mount Ephraim by the name of Sheba ben Bichri raised his hand against King David. Give him alone and I will go away from the city."
>
> The woman said to Joab, "Look! His head is thrown to you over the wall."
>
> The woman came to all the people in her Wise-Womanhood. They cut off the head of Sheba ben Bichri and threw it to Joab.
>
> He blew the shofar and they dispersed from the city, each to his tent.
>
> Joab went back to Jerusalem to the king.

The Wise Woman knows it is up to her to avert the attack. She must choose her words carefully. Like Abigail in a similar situation not long before, and like the Shunammite as she desperately speaks to convince Elisha to heal her son, the Wise Woman begins with the humility of a supplicant petitioner, calling herself "your servant." At the same time, her "listen to the words" highlights the importance of what she is about to say. And her next words draw upon Israelite custom and knowledge. Abel, she declares, is known in Israel as a place to go to render decisions and settle disputes. **"They have always spoken thus since early times: 'Let them inquire at Abel and then they will conclude.' "** Just as the people came to Deborah's palm tree to be judged, so they have also come to Abel when cases are too complex or politically dangerous for the local legal authorities to decide. In Exodus 18, when Moses first appointed judges, he provided that people would come to him for difficult decisions, and he would take them to God. The laws of Deuteronomy prescribe that "if any legal matter is too difficult for you . . . among the cases disputed in your gates, you should go up to the place that God will choose and come to the Levites and the judge who will be at that time and make inquiry; they will tell you the decision" (Deut. 17:8–9). The elders gave judgments in the local towns, but disputes that were too hard to resolve, or disputes between towns, needed a central arbitration center. In Deuteronomy, the place of the sanctuary is also the place of such judicial appeal, and the Levites serve a judicial function as well as their ritual ones. In addition, someone has been appointed the "judge" in this social location, though Deuteronomy does not indicate who it might be. Near Eastern documents show that the king could render judgment, and both David and Absalom were known to perform this function, as was Solomon. There has to be a place for such decisions and a person responsible. Once the monarchy was fully established, the place was Jerusalem and the highest judge was the king; but our story takes place at the very beginning of monarchy, long before the supreme judicial and religious authority was centralized. Everyone knows, says the Wise Woman, that Abel-bet-Ma'cacah is a center for judgment. **" 'Let them inquire' "** is proverbial: let them send inquiries to Abel for resolution. Abel resolves disputes in Israel as a mother resolves disputes among children, and thus Abel is 'îr va 'ēm, a "mother-city" in Israel.

The city of judgment has to have a judge. Moses in the desert was followed by Deborah under the palm tree. Samuel was a "circuit judge," settling disputes and resolving cases as he traveled between his home at Ramah and the major cities of Beth-El, Gilgal, and Mispah. People lined up to have their cases heard by David, and Absalom set himself up in that role. And Solomon's fame for wisdom grew from his ability to solve an "intractable case," to be "like an angel" in his ability to distinguish right from wrong (1 Kings 3:16–28). The Wise Woman of Abel describes herself as of the peacemakers of the faithful of Israel (šelûmê 'emûnê yisra'el). The "peacemaker" resolves disputes, making decisions that answer the inquiries presented at Abel-bet-Ma'cacah. The "faithful" or "trustworthy" abide by the peacemaker's decisions rather than settle disputes by force.

The Wise Woman's next words show that her role in Abel also includes a considerable amount of political power. When Joab explains that he is only after Sheba ben Bichri, who has committed treason, she confidently promises, **"Look! His head is thrown to you over the wall."** The passive mušlāk "is thrown over," and the deictic "Look!" show that her word has authority. Rather than say, "I will see what I can do and report back tomorrow," she announces that the deed is as good as done. Then she comes to report in her Wise-Womanhood beḥokmātāh. The implication of this term is not simply that she comes to advise wisely; that would be beḥokmah, "with wisdom, wisely." "In her beḥokmātāh" means "in her Wise-Womanhood," in her official capacity as Wise Woman. She has made the decision. The people did as she said, they cut off Sheba's head and threw it to Joab. And so, the siege is lifted, war is averted, and the city is saved.

How does a woman acquire such authority? Unlike Moses, Samuel, and Deborah, the Wise Woman is not called a prophet, and her decisions must rely on her judicial and political authority rather than on divine revelation. The story of the Wise Woman of Tekoa (2 Sam. 14) provides some clues as to how a woman might attain such power. That story also takes place during the reign of King David, some years after Absalom killed Amnon. Absalom is an exile in Geshur, and Joab knows that the king misses him. Joab devises a plan that needs a Wise Woman, and he sends to Tekoa for her. The story does not show her acting in her normal capacity, but perhaps Tekoa, like Abel, was the seat of a Wise Woman. In this story, she acts as an agent of Joab, following his general plan, but at the same time reveals characteristics that may be a component of Wise-Womanhood.

The contours of Joab's plan are similar to Nathan's approach to David after David's affair with Bathsheba. Nathan, who was known to the king, had to present his case as a parable told in the third person. The Tekoite Wise Woman can seem to be talking about herself. She is to come disguised as a petitioner and present a legal case for the king's judgment; afterward she is to reveal that the story she presented is really a parable about the king. Disguised as a woman in mourning, she tells a sad tale: she is a widow whose two sons had a fight in the fields during which one killed the other. Now her family is demanding that she deliver the surviving son to their blood vengeance. If that happens, she explains, her patrimony will be gone and her husband will have no surviving name in Israel. The woman presents David with a dilemma between two very important Israelite principles: the need to avenge the blood of a murdered person and the supreme importance of preserving a man's lineage. The king must decide.

To this point, the plan has been Joab's. Now, when the king reserves judgment, the woman begins to use her own wisdom. She knows that pardoning a murderer can bring bloodguilt upon the one who spares him, and she realizes that the king will be reluctant to take the bloodguilt of the murdered man upon himself. She therefore assures him that she will take any bloodguilt upon her own father's household so that David's throne and David himself will be free. The Tekoite's words are an echo of Rivka's on the two occasions when she persuaded Jacob to do her bidding. When he worried that his father might curse him instead of blessing him, Rivka offered to take the curse upon herself. And when she wanted to convince him to leave for Haran, she asked him to prevent her from being bereft of both her sons in one day. Rivka and the Tekoite are masters of the biblical rhetoric of persuasion.

The king responds to her dilemma, suggesting that she bring to him anyone who bothers her. This is not enough for her ultimate purpose, so she points out that by the time she could bring anyone before the king, the blood avenger already would have killed her son. That prompts the king to take an oath that no one will harm her son. This is what she has been trying to get him to say. Just as Nathan explained his parable as soon as David passed judgment against the rich man (2 Sam 12:5–7), the Wise Woman now reveals the analogy between her fictive son and Absalom: "Why have you done this to the people of God—the king speaks thus while he himself is guilty of not bringing back his abandoned one" (2 Sam. 14:13). Like the prophet Nathan, the Wise Woman has led the king to an understanding that he is in the wrong.

The Tekoite's next statement reveals the basis of her authority as a Wise Woman. Her exceedingly cryptic words mean something like "for we must all die like waters split upon the ground that cannot be gathered, and God will not forgive the one who makes plans without abandoning the abandoned from him" (2 Sam. 14:14). Her words sound as cryptic as an oracle's, but she is not an oracle and claims no divine revelation. Instead, the first part of her statement sounds like a proverb, and the woman sounds like a sage immersed in Israel's wisdom/proverb tradition. Women could be considered "wise" for several reasons. Mother-raised children remember the mother of early childhood as wise and powerful. Moreover, human communities often rely on women to perform tasks that depend on their accumulated knowledge of plant foods and herbs. The many goddesses of wisdom reflect these individual and communal memories, but the Wise Woman represents yet another stream of women's wisdom: the memory of "grandmother's tales" and proverbial sayings. In this respect, the Wise Woman of Tekoa is the personification of "Lady Wisdom."

The parable-telling Wise Woman of Tekoa demonstrates mastery of Israel's common lore. The Wise Woman of Abel's authority to settle disputes and make decisions may also rest on such knowledge, and this authority gives her political power. These two Wise Women figure in stories about the reign of David, but not in later history. In many respects, the reign of David is still "pre-monarchic." The reign of Solomon marks a turning point in Israel's history and completes the change possibly begun when David took a census of Israel. Under Solomon, Israel became a centralized state, with a regular system of bureaucracy that was ultimately responsible to the king. Even the wisdom tradition was co-opted by the monarchy, as "Solomon the Wise" became the patron of wisdom and learning. None of Israel's bureaucracies—the palace, the army, the law courts, even the "Sages"—had any room for women. Once the state was consolidated, women had no role in the pyramid of power; they were not leaders outside the domestic sphere. They could still be wise, but they were no longer Wise Women. From the standpoint of political power, the days before the state were the good old days to women. Once the state was established, they could exercise considerable family power as wives and mothers—but only queens had an impact on the destiny of the nation.

The Shunammite

THE DISAPPEARANCE of women from the public realm (or at least from the public record) does not mean that they all became meek or mild, helpless or victimized. Within their families, women continued to exhibit the same sort of power that the matriarchs demonstrated. Several less than flattering proverbs attest in a negative way to the considerable power of women's speech, particularly the repetitive request: "The nagging of a wife is like the endless dripping of water," says one proverb (Prov. 19:13). Through persuasion, women continued to influence the destiny of their families. A different portrait of a woman emerges in the tale of the Shunammite, a wealthy woman who appears in the Elisha cycle of stories, which take place against a backdrop of harsh rural poverty. In contrast to the near-starving peasantry to which Elisha miraculously supplies food, the "great woman" of Shunem has the means to offer him hospitality.

◇ *Act I. The Prophet and the Woman*

Scene 1. A patron in Shunem (2 Kings 4:8–10)

> It happened one day that Elisha passed through Shunem.
> There was a great woman there and she grabbed him to (make him) eat food.
> And it happened that whenever he passed by, he would turn in there to eat food.
> She said to her husband, "Look! I know that he is a holy man of God. He always comes to us. Let us make him a little chamber on the roof, let us place for him there a bed, a table, a chair, and a lamp, and it will be that when he comes to us he will turn in there."

Like so many women in the Bible, the Shunammite is not remembered by name. In biblical stories, both names and their absence are significant. The Shunammite is a "great woman," and as such she is representative of all "great" or wealthy women. She is not identified as her father's daughter or her husband's wife, for these relationships do not define her destiny or her role in the story. She is identified by the name of her village because her attachment to a particular location will turn out to be important in her life and in her story.

The Shunammite is strikingly free in her dealings with the prophet. She recognizes and acknowledges the fact that he is a prophet and holy man, and becomes his patron and benefactor. She acts on her own, without asking her husband's permission, as she provides food and hospitality to him on his journeys. Her wealth may contribute to her boldness, for wealthy women have greater freedom of action than poor women, and sometimes even more than poor men. But poor women could also be close to the prophets. The prophet Elijah lodged with a poor widow without worrying about gossip, and no one would react badly to the Shunammite's entertaining Elisha. A wife can dispense food without her husband's supervision: another woman of means, Abigail, brought great amounts of food to David without her husband's knowledge. The Shunammite brings her husband into the picture only when she wishes to add an addition to her house.

Prophets are known to repay kindness. Hospitality does not call for reciprocity, offers of which may impugn the honor of the host, but prophets transcend such consideration. Elijah rewarded the poor widow of Zarephat with never-ending food, and Elisha looks for some way to repay his hostess.

Scene 2. The patron's reward (2 Kings 4:11–17)

> It happened one day that he came there and turned in to the upper chamber and slept there.
> He said to his servant Gehazi, "Call this Shunammite."
> He called her and she stood before him.
> He said to him, "Say to her, 'Look! You have exerted yourself for us with all this great effort. What is there to do for you? Is there some matter of which we can speak to the king or general?' "
> She said, "I live among my own people."
> He said, "What is there to do for her?"
> Gehazi said, "Ah, she doesn't have a child and her husband is old."
> He said, "Call her!"
> He called her and she stood in the doorway.

> He said, "At this time, at the life season, you will be holding a
> son."
> She said, "No, my lord, man of God, do not lie to your hand-
> maiden."
> The woman conceived and gave birth to a son at that same time,
> in the life season, just as Elisha spoke to her.

The protocol between Elisha and the Shunammite seems strange: if
she is standing before him, why does he speak to Gehazi as an interlocu-
tor? Elisha is not reticent about speaking to women: in the previous
story, he spoke directly to the widow he was helping. And he is, after all,
no stranger to the Shunammite, with whom he has often dined. But perhaps in this instance he is creating the formal circumstances of a magnate offering largesse. He underscores his ability to grant her request by
increasing the distance between them and using Gehazi as the interlocu-
tor. The Shunammite will have none of such pretense. She ignores Gehazi and speaks directly to Elisha, both when he asks Gehazi what they
can give her, and when he finally addresses her directly.

As Elisha foretells the birth of her child, the narrator adds what looks
like an extraneous detail: the Shunammite woman is standing in the
doorway. Like so many details in biblical stories, the doorway is an allusion to another story: the Shunammite stands in the doorway much as
Sarah stood in the doorway of her tent when the divine guests foretold
the birth of Isaac (Gen. 18:10). The allusion is strengthened as both
Elisha and Abraham's guest use the term "life season," *'ēt ḥayyah,* for
the time of birth.

The Shunammite woman has not asked for a child. Alone among the
childless women in the Bible, she is not actively seeking a child. She is married to an old man, and may or may not be elderly herself. Even faced with
a miracle worker and given the opportunity to make a wish, she never
mentions her childlessness and answers only, **"I live among my own people."** Her answer seems cryptic. It doesn't seem to address the question,
and it contradicts what we know about ancient marriage. We would expect
her to be living among her husband's kinfolk, not her own. But she stays
living in Shunem among her own folk. These two "abnormalities" are
clues, pieces of a puzzle, and are joined by a third clue, the Shunammite's
lack of anxiety about her childlessness. More pieces emerge later in her
story. But at this point, when Elisha is looking for a way to reward her,
Gehazi points out that she is childless, and she is given a child.

The next vignette is several years later, as the child has a crisis.

◇ *Act II. The Prophet, the Mother, and the Child (2 Kings 4:18–41)*

Scene 1. Mother to the rescue (2 Kings 4:18–23)

> The boy grew.
>
> It happened one day that he went out to his father to the harvesters.
>
> He said to his father, "My head, my head!"
>
> He said to the manservant, "Carry him to his mother."
>
> He lifted him and brought him to his mother.
>
> He sat on her knees till noon and died.
>
> She arose and laid him down on the man of God's bed, closed the door, and went out.
>
> She called to her husband and said, "Send me one of the manservants and one of the asses and I will run to the man of God and return."
>
> He said, "Why are you going to him today; it is neither new moon nor Sabbath?"
>
> She said, "Be well!"

The woman may not have been actively seeking a child, but when faced with his death, she acts, and goes to the prophet to intercede. Her husband's question reflects the close connection between prophets and women. On Sabbath and festivals, women would go regularly on pilgrimages. They could also go for help in a crisis, as the wife of Jeroboam went to Ahijah the prophet when her son fell sick (1 Kings 14:1–17). But Jeroboam sent his wife off; the Shunammite does not even inform her husband of the reason she is leaving. When he asks why, she brushes him off with a simple **"be well"** or **"all is well."** His lack of understanding as to why she is going is puzzling, but she can't wait to explain it to him. She has a child to save. Still, her independence is equally puzzling, for normally even a wealthy woman depended on her husband's goodwill for her own economic well-being. Women have power in their own households, but the Shunammite does not show any concern that her husband might get angry or even divorce her. This lack of concern, her lack of desperation for a child, and her living among her own kin are all unusual behaviors that make the Shunammite stand out among women.

She continues her decisive ways as she comes to Elisha.

Scene 2. Confronting the prophet (2 Kings 4:24–30)

> She cinched the ass and said to her manservant, "Guide it and
> walk, and don't stop me from riding unless I tell you."
> She went and came to the man of God at Mount Carmel.
> It happened that when the man of God saw her opposite him,
> he said to his manservant Gehazi, "Here is that Shunam-
> mite. Now please run to meet her and say to her, 'Is all well
> with you? Is all well with your husband? Is all well with your
> son?' "
> She said, "Be well!"
> She came to the man of God on the mountain and grabbed his
> legs.
> Gehazi approached to shoo her away.
> The man of God said, "Leave her alone, for her soul is bitter and
> YHWH has hidden the matter from me and has not told
> me."
> She said, "Did I ask for a son from my lord? Did I not say, 'You
> should not fool me'?"
> He said to Gehazi, "Gird your loins and take my staff in your
> hands and go. If you meet a man on the way, do not bless
> him, and should someone bless you, do not answer him.
> Place my staff upon the boy's face."
> The boy's mother said, "By the life of YHWH and by your life, I
> will not leave you!"
> He arose and went after her.

The Shunammite is a woman with a mission. She is in a hurry. She
has no time to tell her husband where she is going, she has no time to
rest on the way, and she has no time to waste telling Gehazi about the
matter, no time for pleasantries once she gets to the prophet. When Elisha sends Gehazi to ask why she has come, she brushes him aside just as
she brushed off her husband. She goes straight to the prophet himself
and grasps him so that he must listen. Elisha is ready to listen, for unlike
Ahijah, who knew why Mrs. Jeroboam had come to him, he does not
know what has brought the Shunammite. The Shunammite chooses her
words carefully. She has rushed to see him, but she does not rush to tell
him what is wrong. She takes a posture of subservience, but there is no
supplication in her tone. She begins her petition in classic biblical guilt-
producing mode: she has not demanded a son, she even demurred when

offered one. Instead, she challenges him to live up to his responsibility. Her implication is clear: now that the child is in danger, Elisha owes it to her to act.

Elisha asks no questions. As soon as she mentions her son, he realizes that the boy is ill or dead and commands Gehazi to go quickly. Considering all that the Shunammite has done for him, it is strange that the prophet would send his servant. And the Shunammite will have nothing of miracle-by-proxy: she wants Elisha, not his surrogate, and she will not be satisfied until he comes himself. Elisha understands such determination. In the same way, and using the same phrase, he refused to stay behind when Elijah went up to heaven, three times answering Elijah, "By the life of YHWH and by your life, I will not leave you!" (2 Kings 2:2, 4, 6). And so they go off together.

Scene 3. A miracle for mother (2 Kings 4:31–37)

> Gehazi went before him and placed the staff on the boy's face.
> There was no sound and no response.
> He returned toward him and told him thus, "The boy didn't awaken."
> Elisha came to the house and look! The boy was dead, laid out on his bed.
> He came and closed the door on the two of them and he prayed to YHWH.
> He got up and lay down upon the child and placed his mouth on his mouth, his eyes on his eyes, and his palms on his palms, and crouched over him, and the child's flesh warmed.
> He sat up and walked in the house once this way and once that way,
> He got up and crouched over him.
> The child sneezed seven times.
> The child opened his eyes.
> He called Gehazi and said, "Call that Shunammite!"
> He called her, and she came to him, and he said, "Pick up your son!"
> She came and fell upon his feet and prostrated herself to the ground.
> She picked up her son and went out.

The Shunammite was right to demand that Elisha come himself: Gehazi could not revive the child. The power is not in the staff, it is in

Elisha, who uses intercessory prayer and what seems like a combination of artificial respiration and anti-shock treatment. Elisha returns him to his mother. Her imperious manner has worked: nothing has blocked her way as she mobilized the prophet to rescue her son. And as he once told her that she would embrace a son, he now gives her the son again. The Shunammite has convinced Elisha to use his healing powers, and Elisha has proved himself the holy man and miracle worker she always knew him to be. Now that the emergency is over, she can take the time for protocols of respect, and she acknowledges his greatness by prostrating to the ground.

Elisha and the Shunammite continue in relationship. Sometime later, Elisha comes to do her another prophetic favor. He warns her of the coming famine and advises her to leave the land.

◈   *Act III. The Woman, Her Household, and the Land (2 Kings 8:1–6)*
Scene 1. Exodus and famine (2 Kings 8:1–3)
> Elisha spoke to the woman whose child he had revived thus: "Arise and go, you and your household, and live awhile wherever you will live, for YHWH has called a famine and it will come to the land for seven years."
> The woman arose and acted according to the word of the man of God.
> She went, she and her household, and she lived in Philistine land for seven years.

Like Abraham before her, like the family of Jacob at the end of the ancestral period, and like the family of Elimelekh in the time of judges, the Shunammite and her household leave for a place that has food. There is no mention of her husband, and he may not even be alive. The Shunammite is the major figure. She, not he, has been Elisha's patron and his demanding client. She is the one he warns, and she is the one who believes his message, uproots the household, and leaves Israel for seven years.

Scene 2. Mistress of her house (2 Kings 8:3–6)
> It happened at the end of seven years.
> The woman returned from the Philistine land and came out to issue a cry to the king for her house and her field.
> The king was speaking to Gehazi, the man of God's manservant, thus, "Tell me please all the great things that Elisha has done."

And it happened that he was telling the king that he revived the
dead, and look! The woman whose son he revived was crying to the king about her house and her field.

Gehazi said to the king, "This is the woman and this is her son
whom Elisha revived."

The king questioned the woman and she related it to him.

The king gave her a eunuch, saying thus: "Return to her all that
is hers and all the produce of the field from the day she left
the land until now!"

Seven years later, the Shunammite comes back. Somebody else has
been farming her land in her absence, but she "cries" to the king for help
in retrieving her property. Crying to the monarch is a fairly standard legal procedure, and she can expect him to restore the land. But he not
only restores the field to her, he gives her the produce for the period that
she was gone. Near Eastern law indicates that owners can reclaim a field,
but the "usufruct," the produce, should belong to the people who
worked the land. People who plant can expect to reap: not being able to
do so is one of God's dire punishments (Deut. 28:33), and eating the food
someone else has planted is a special mark of divine benevolence (Deut.
6:12). God gave Israel the produce of the land when Israel came into the
land of Canaan. The king presents the Shunammite with the same favor
when she comes back to the land. Perhaps he did so because Gehazi was
(providentially?) in court that day, telling him of Elisha's resurrection of
the Shunammite's son just when she came to claim her land, and he
pointed her out as the person for whom Elisha had worked this miracle.
Her special relationship with Elisha motivates the king's generosity.
Many years earlier Elisha had asked if there was a matter about which
she would wish him to speak to the king. Then there was not, but now
the very fact of their proven close relationship is enough of an "intercession" to allow her to reap the king's largesse.

The Shunammite herself comes to petition. Her husband is not there,
and may be dead. She comes to cry for **her house and her field,** and the
king instructs, **"Return to her all that is hers."** But is the land hers? By
Israelite law, as far as we know, a woman does not inherit the property: it
becomes her son's, and her son has the obligation to let her stay on it. So
why does the story say **"her land"? "Her field"? "All that is hers"?** In a
comparable situation, when Naomi wants to regain possession of and
sell the field that she and Elimelekh left when they too departed Israel to
escape from famine, the field is carefully specified as "the portion of field

that belonged to our brother Elimelekh" (Ruth 4:3), and the property is called "all that was Elimelekh's" (Ruth 4:9). Surely the Shunammite's land is her husband's, if he is still alive, or her son's, if he is not!

The Shunammite's story has four unusual elements that may all be interrelated. The land is hers. She expressed no need for a child and is markedly independent of her husband. These three abnormalities may all relate to the answer that the Shunammite gave when Elisha first asked if he could do something for her: **I live among my own people.** Most women marry outside their kin and go to live with their husband's family. The only women required to marry within their own tribe are the "daughters of Zelophehad." As the book of Numbers relates, the five daughters of Zelophehad approached Moses toward the end of the period in the desert and asked for a change in Israelite inheritance law. Only sons could inherit land, but there were five daughters and there was no son. They petitioned that since their father did not deserve to have his lineage and his name completely die, they should be allowed to inherit his property and perpetuate his name. Upon consultation with God, Moses issued the provision that whenever a man died without sons, his daughters could inherit (Num. 27:1–11). Later, upon petition by the tribal elders not to allow tribal lands to be lost, Moses issued a further decree that the daughters of Zelophehad must marry only within their father's tribe (Num. 36:1–12). From then on, a woman who had no brothers owned her land for her lifetime and married within her father's extended family.

Like a latter-day "daughter of Zelophehad," the Shunammite lives among her own kin, and her land belongs to her. She might very well be an example of a daughter of Zelophehad. Owning her own land, she is not as dependent on men for her livelihood. She can brush off her husband when she has no time for him, knowing that she would still have her property if he divorced her; and she will not have to rely on a son to allow her to live on her husband's land when she is widowed, and support her from her husband's patrimony. This may explain why the woman of Shunem, alone among barren women in the Bible, did not actively seek a child.

Her ownership of land gives her independence from her husband, whose permission she need not ask, either to be Elisha's patron or to seek his aid. The Shunammite may be an example of how women act when the *economic* constraints of patriarchy are removed. This is why she is identified by locale rather than by name or as "Mrs. Somebody." Her location remains her identity in a way that most women's do not. It is *her* village, the village of her father's household and the one where she lives as an adult woman, the site of the land she owns. She is a woman of place and, by contrast, shows how significant the lack of such place is to most women's history. The limitation of women's property rights is the economic linchpin of patriarchal structure; it made women dependent first on their fathers, then on their husbands, and, ultimately, on their sons. Even the humanitarian injunctions of the ancient world to care for widows and the fatherless were an outgrowth of this male monopoly: if widows could inherit land, there would be no need for humanitarian injunctions to care for them. The characteristic determination and boldness of the Shunammite may be a lesson on the freedom that property bestows. It is also a window onto the way at least some women successfully negotiated with prophet and king (the male power structure) despite their lack of official autonomy or authority.

Villains

Potiphar's Wife, Delilah, and Athaliah

NOT ALL the strong women in the Bible are good. A quartet of historical villainesses make their mark: Potiphar's wife, Delilah, Athaliah, and Queen Jezebel, the archvillainess discussed later (pp. 209–14). Potiphar's wife and Queen Jezebel are foreigners. Athaliah is an Israelite princess and Delilah's ethnicity is unknown. But one factor unites them: they are allied with the other side in Israel's national and cosmic battles. For this reason, all of them represent the "Other," the alternative to Israel's destiny and way.

Potiphar's Wife

Not much is told about Potiphar, the man who bought Joseph as a slave, or about his wife. Potiphar is a laissez-faire owner, entrusting the affairs of his house to Joseph.

◆ *A Woman Refused (Gen. 39:5–10)*

> Joseph was very handsome, very lovely.
> It happened after these things
> His master's wife cast her eyes on Joseph and said, "Lie with me!"
> He refused and said to his master's wife, "Look! My master does not pay attention to what is in the house with me, for everything he has, he gave into my hand.
> He is not greater within this house than I, for he has not kept anything from me except for you, since you are his wife, and how would I do this great evil? I would sin against God!"
> It would be as she spoke to Joseph daily that he did not listen to her, to lie with her, to be with her.

Joseph is beautiful, and she wants him. Beauty in the Bible is sometimes a vulnerability, for powerful people go after beautiful objects. Mrs.

Potiphar's desire for Joseph may have another source: Potiphar is called Pharaoh's *sarîs,* a word that ultimately came to mean "officer" but originally meant "eunuch." Ancient kings could demand that their closest officers be eunuchs, both as a foil to their ambitions and to lessen the chances that they would usurp the king's prerogatives in the harem. Is *sarîs* in this story literal? Was Potiphar a eunuch? If so, it certainly adds another dimension to his wife's desire for Joseph. And there is yet another aspect to her desire. Normally, wives are in charge of their households. But in Potiphar's house, Joseph runs the show. There is nothing for Potiphar's wife to do but admire the beautiful young man.

Her approach is direct. She does not try to seduce him, simply issues words of command. He is, after all, her husband's slave, and she expects to be obeyed. Joseph refuses on the grounds of loyalty to Potiphar. A servant should never dishonor his master by cuckolding him. If the roles were reversed, if the slave were female and the master male, there would be no question of saying "No!" He would simply claim the right to her body, and if she angered him by refusing, he could sell her, or worse. But as far as we know, married women did not have the right to sleep with slaves any more than with other men. Potiphar's wife may not have the right to demand sex with Joseph. She certainly does not have the authority to penalize him, and cannot sell him out of her husband's hand. Her commands are empty, for she cannot punish him for refusing. Nevertheless, she is unwilling to accept his refusals, so she asks him daily for quite some time.

Finally a day arrives when they are alone in the house.

◇ *Refusal and Revenge (Gen. 39:11–20)*

> It happened on a particular day that he came to the house to do his work and there was no one from the people of the household there in the house.
>
> She caught him by his garment, saying, "Lie with me!"
>
> He left his garment in her hand and fled, going outside.
>
> It happened that when she saw that he left his garment in her hand and fled outside, she called to the people of her household and spoke to them, saying, "Look! He brought us a Hebrew man to mock us. He came to me to lie with me, and I called in a loud voice. And when he heard that I lifted my voice and called, he left his garment with me, and fled and went outside."
>
> She kept the garment with her until his master came home.

She spoke to him about these matters, saying, "The Hebrew slave came to me, the one you brought to us to mock us. And it happened that when I raised my voice and called, he left his garment with me and fled outside."

When his master heard his wife's speech that she spoke to him, saying, "These things your servant did to me," he was furious.

Joseph's master took him and placed him in the prison, the place where the king's captives were kept. And he stayed there in the prison.

If Potiphar's wife had been a male slaveholder, he might have raped a slave girl who refused him. But men are not readily raped, and Joseph slips easily from her grasp. Now she faces a real problem: Joseph might report her to his master. He has not done so yet, but now she may have gone too far. Even more probable, someone might have seen him as he **fled outside,** a phrase emphasized in the story. Whoever saw him without his clothes might assume that she has slept with him, and she could be publicly branded an adulteress, with all the scandal and peril that it would entail. This she cannot allow, for it would put her very life at risk. She must do something to protect herself.

Potiphar's wife decides on a preemptive, self-protective strike: she will accuse Joseph of trying to rape her. Interestingly, this Egyptian woman decides on a plan known to us from Egyptian literature: in "The Tale of Two Brothers," a woman who has been rejected by her husband's brother accuses that brother of assaulting her. Here, knowing that Joseph might have been seen, and that public scandal might erupt, Potiphar's wife denounces him to the household. She increases the chance that she will be believed by including an ethnic slur: **"A Hebrew man"** has come **"to mock us."** She plays on the emotion of her audience, and then of her husband, by subliminally building on the common fear that foreign men prey on a nation's women. To her husband she also brings up the impudence of **"your servant,"** that he dared to approach the master's woman. Her choice of words is cunning, and her ploy works. Potiphar may be very fond of Joseph, but it is in his best interests to believe that his wife is innocent and to demonstrate this belief publicly. He removes Joseph from his household and throws him in jail.

Potiphar's wife now disappears from the Bible. Her motives have been selfish, her methods injurious, but ironically, she has been the instrument of Joseph's destiny, removing him from his pleasant position to a place from which he can ultimately rise to a much greater one.

Delilah

In the middle of the book of Judges comes a cycle of stories about an extraordinary hero of Israel, Samson. His story begins in the pattern of a biblical hero, when a divine envoy comes to his mother to announce the conception. But within its conformity to this pattern, the annunciation scene differs dramatically, a sign that the child will himself differ dramatically from the usual biblical hero. This annunciation centers on the mother (who is not named) and the relationship she forges with the envoy from God. This angel behaves like other angels, appearing suddenly and prophesying. But he then gives the mother specific instructions. She is to abstain from alcohol during her pregnancy, so that Samson will be consecrated as a Nazirite already in the womb. The Nazirites were especially devoted to God; their status was marked by long hair and abstinence from alcohol. It is not clear what Nazirites were expected to do, but the prophet Amos considers their importance to Israel on a par with that of prophets (Amos 2:11). Samson was a very unusual Nazirite. Other people took vows to become Nazirites and could undo those vows (Num. 6). But Samson's Nazirite state is promised to his mother before he is born, and she knows it is permanent, "from the womb until the day of his death" (Judg. 13:7). Her statement hints that breaking the Nazirite status will lead to Samson's death.

The close connection between the divine envoy and Samson's mother and their parallel roles in determining Samson's fate have made modern readers suspect that the angel also *caused* the pregnancy, either through sexual intercourse or through his speech. The story itself never tells us that Samson had a divine father. It does tell us that his Nazirite status conveyed upon him superstrength. He was remembered as a superhero with a cluster of tales relating his exploits against Israel's enemy, the Philistines. Like Superman, the superhero of the twentieth century, Samson was limited in his abilities. Superman could inflict defeats on the Nazis, but he couldn't overcome them. And Samson inflicted defeats on the Philistines but was barely the "beginner of the liberation" that God's messenger predicted he would be (Judg. 13:5).

The first stories about Samson involve a foreign woman whom he sought to marry. His parents suggested that he would do better to marry an Israelite woman, but the narrator informs us that YHWH had planned this as an occasion for Samson to engage the Philistines (Judg. 14:4). And engage them he did. Samson proposed a riddle for a wedding wager, a riddle his wedding guests could not answer. They then threatened his bride that they would burn her house if she could not find out the answer for them. She began to nag Samson and cry that he didn't love her. On the seventh day of the feast, she persuaded Samson to tell her the answer and she revealed it to her countrymen (Judg. 14:12–17). When they answered the riddle, Samson realized what had happened, and the battle was on. He struck down thirty men to pay the wager and departed (Judg. 14:18–20). When he tried to visit his bride and discovered that she had married the best man, he caught three hundred jackals, tied torches to their tails, and drove them into the fields, burning the entire grain harvest. When the Philistines burned the bride and her household in revenge, Samson effected a tremendous slaughter and left. He would no longer be a friend to Philistines (Judg. 15:1–8). Later, the Philistines came to enact revenge, giving Samson another opportunity to slaughter them and to demonstrate his superstrength (Judg. 15:9–16). Then they tried to capture him when he visited a prostitute in Gaza, but Samson escaped by lifting the locked city gate on his shoulders and carrying it away uphill (Judg. 16:1–3).

Later—still possibly, years later—Samson fell in love with a woman named Delilah.

◇ Act I. A Woman Turned (Judg. 16:4–5)

> It happened after these matters.
> He loved a woman in the valley of Sorek named Delilah.
> The Philistine kings went up to her and said, "Entice him and
>   see what makes his strength great and how we can prevail
>   over him, and we will bind him to degrade him. We will
>   give you one thousand one hundred shekels each."

The story very conspicuously does not call Delilah a Philistine. Samson's first wife was Philistine, but Delilah, whom he loved and with whom he lived, was simply a **woman in the valley**. The valley of Sorek was Danite territory, overrun by Philistines; the population was mixed and traditions may have been exchanged. The Philistines approach her with an offer of an enormous sum—just how much becomes clear in comparison with other biblical acts of betrayal. The brothers sold Joseph for twenty shekels; Judas would betray Jesus for thirty. It would have taken a great heroine to resist fifty-five hundred shekels, and Delilah was no heroine. The promise of a fortune, not her parentage, is the source of her loyalty.

Delilah now becomes a woman with a mission. She is to "entice" Samson into revealing the secret of his strength. The erotic imagination of Western art and literature has created a portrait of sultry seduction. Paintings and retellings have portrayed Delilah as a forerunner of Mata Hari. But the biblical verb *pattî* means to entice through words. Israel entices God (Ps. 78:36), God "sweet-talks" Israel (Hos. 2:16), a prophet has a vision in which God sends a lying spirit to entice Ahab into battle (1 Kings 22:20–23). There are no sexual connotations in these scenarios. The biblical story of Samson and Delilah is also a lot less sexy than later retellings.

◇ *Act II. Nagging Samson*

Scene 1. A failed attempt (Judg. 16:6–9)

> Delilah said to Samson, "Tell me please, with what is your great strength, and how can you be bound to abase you?"
>
> Samson said to her, "If they bind me with seven green cords that have never been dried, then I will become weak and become like any man."
>
> The Philistine kings brought her seven green cords that had never been dried and she bound him with them.
>
> The ambush was sitting in her room.
>
> She said, "The Philistines are upon you, Samson!"
>
> He split the cords as a wick splinters when fire touches it.
>
> And so his (full) strength wasn't (even) discovered.

She asks, he answers, she binds him, the Philistines attack, and Samson splits his bonds. She then accuses him of mocking her and asks again. Samson gives her a second answer, "new ropes," and the charade is played again. And then Samson gets a little closer, mentioning his hair and ironically binding it with a woman's tool, the very symbol of womanhood, and the charade is played yet again.

Scenes 2 and 3. Again and again (Judg. 16:10–14)

> Delilah said to Samson, "You have made mock of me and told me lies. Now, please tell me with what you should be bound."
>
> He said to her, "If they bind me with new ropes that have never been worked, I will become weak and become like any human."

Delilah took new ropes and bound him.

She said to him, "The Philistines are upon you, Samson!"

The Philistines were sitting in the room.

He snapped them from his arms like a thread.

Delilah said to Samson, "Till here you have mocked me. You have spoken falsehoods to me. Tell me with what you can be bound."

He said to her, "If you tie up seven strands of my hair with a loom and it is fixed with a pin."

She said to him, "The Philistines are upon you, Samson!" He awoke from his sleep and tore the pin of the weave and the net.

Matters are coming to a head. Three women have already appeared in Samson's story: his mother, his would-be wife, a prostitute in Gaza, and now Delilah. Three times the Philistines encountered Samson before they approached Delilah, and they are in their fourth encounter; and three times Samson has tricked Delilah. The critical moment has arrived. Until now, Samson has been cunning in the midst of his stupidity, for there is a pattern to his lies. Samson the trickster is riddling riddles. The green cords are natural, never even dried; new ropes have been twisted into ropes, a cultural activity, but applied to raw material. And woven hair is formed by weaving, a cultural activity, but directed onto a material not usually woven. Should Samson not answer Delilah, someone thinking about these clues might notice this pattern of increasing cultural involvement and might conclude that the next stage, material that is usually woven (like goat hair), might weaken Samson. After all, he is a "wild man." He is closer to nature than most people, exhibiting the wild hair of an uncivilized man and the great strength that civilized people often imagine that wild men have. He has mastery over nature, often seeming like a force of nature as he attacks the Philistines with animal jawbones, foxes' tails, and his bare fists. The Samson stories show him in battle with those who represent the culture side of the nature/culture wars that the "wild man" wages, and one might conclude that "culture" is his enemy. In an irony of language, the English word "philistine" evokes a barbaric lack of culture. But the Israelites knew the Philistines as people with a monopoly over iron and could see them as archaeology is now revealing them, a people with a highly developed culture. The Philistines may have shared the later Greek sense of cultural superiority, and the Samson stories send their self-image back at them through this image of the wild man who fights them. They will never guess that his undoing would come not from a cultural artifact but in the removal of his nature-aspect, represented by his long hair. Samson must speak, and Delilah applies emotional blackmail.

◇ *Act III. A Man Undone (Judg. 16:15–21)*

> She said to him, "How can you say 'I love you' when your heart is not with me? You have mocked me three times and have not told me what makes your strength great."
> It happened because she attacked him every day with her words.
> She kept pressing him and his soul was ready to die.
> He told her his whole heart.
> He said, "No razor has ever been on my head, for I have been a Nazirite to God since my mother's womb. If I were to be shaved, my strength would turn from me, and I would grow weak and become like any man."
> Delilah saw that he had told her his whole heart.
> She sent and called for the Philistine kings thus, "Come up this time, for he has told me his whole heart."
> The Philistine kings came up to her and brought the money in her hands.
> She had him sleep upon her knees. She called for a man and shaved his seven layers of hair.
> She began to abase him, and his strength turned away from him.
> She said, "The Philistines are upon you, Samson!"
> He awoke from his sleep and said, "I will go out this time as always and shake out," for he did not know that YHWH had turned away from him.
> The Philistines grabbed him and put out his eyes.
> They took him down to Gaza, bound him with bronze fetters and he was a grinder in the prison.

This was the climactic moment. Delilah recognized that **this time** he told the truth; characteristically, Samson took longer to discover that **this time** was different from the others. He had told Delilah that he should be bound, *'sar*, though defeat was not in something binding him but in something "turning away," *sar*, from him: as soon as she cut his hair, **his strength turned away** and **YHWH had turned away.** His hair was the way God gave him superstrength. There is irony in wordplays. Delilah *saw* what was happening; Samson should have seen what was

going on and his failure to see led to his loss of sight. He who was blind
to Delilah's intent became literally blind.

Delilah defeated Samson by using the weapon that she had at hand,
her tongue. She kept asking him till he couldn't stand it anymore, and by
the power of nagging, she wore him down. Samson has been here before. Both of his women asked him, over and over. And they accused
him of not loving them. Over and over. Samson is susceptible to this
combination of persistence and guilt. It would not be fair to say that he
had great brawn and little brain, but somehow he does not recognize the
tactic and it works again. It is, after all, a very good tactic. According to
Proverbs, it is better to live in the desert or a corner of a roof than with a
contentious wife (Prov. 21:9, 19; 25:24). Delilah may not have been generally vexatious, but on this matter she was relentless, and Samson could
not resist.

This battle between a nagging woman and a susceptible male is also a
contest between a domesticating woman and a "nature man" or "wild
man." Delilah destroys that which made Samson different so that he has
become like any man. The contest between woman as civilizing agent
and half-civilized man is a staple of American history, encoded in the
iconic relationship of the schoolmarm and the cowboy on the American
frontier. This archetypical contest has a very long history, for
Mesopotamian literature also has a wild man, Enkidu, and a woman
who attracts and then domesticates him. In the Gilgamesh Epic, Enkidu
upsets the economy by championing the animals, so the civilized world
sends a courtesan to bring him into the human fold. Her teachings ready
him to fulfill the god's plan to become the companion of King Gilgamesh. But Enkidu is mortally wounded on one of his adventures with
Gilgamesh, and he is ready to curse the courtesan who civilized him.
The god Shamash tells him, and the audience, that even a short civilized
human life is better than an animal existence, and Enkidu dies blessing
the courtesan. American history teaches the same about the impact of
the schoolmarm. Women reenact this archetypical battle over and over
as mothers clothe, toilet-train, and socialize their toddlers. One could
speculate whether the taming of humans would look as benevolent if
the stories were written by Enkidu's animal friends or by two-year-olds.
Nevertheless, there is still an enormous difference between the courtesan and Delilah. The courtesan doesn't destroy Enkidu, and Delilah does
not turn Samson into a Philistine. Perhaps she imagined that the
Philistines would simply leave Samson an ordinary mortal, but instead
they blind and enslave him. Their enmity does not disappear when Sam-

son loses his strength, for this is a battle between a Philistine agent and an Israelite hero, one episode in a contest that continues until death.

The Samson-Delilah story is the closest thing the Bible contains to a "Battle of the Sexes," the wars and contests between males and females so common in Greek mythology. It is significant that this battle story is part of the Samson cycle, a literary creation with so many other similarities to Mediterranean myths. The importance of the wedding riddle is reminiscent of the riddle of the Sphinx. Samson's particular riddle about lions and honey relies on a bee culture familiar more to the Greeks than to anyone else in the Mediterranean. Bees swarming in animal carcasses may also lie behind Virgil's story of Aristeas, who sacrificed oxen to get back a swarm of bees. The very idea of a superhero is unique in the Bible, and the possible hint that the deity did more than announce the birth would fit the pattern of Zeus's many encounters with human women. Even the miraculous hair of Samson finds its parallels in Greek mythology. The gods Dionysus and Apollo had uncut hair, as did the Greek superhero Herakles. Even closer are legends that Apollodorus relates about Nisus, king of Megara, and Pterelaos, king of Teleboa. Nisus's locks made him invincible, Pterelaos's made him immortal. Both kings were undone by their daughters, who were in love with their enemies. Nisus's daughter Scylla cut her father's hair and her beloved, King Minos, captured him (Appolodorus iii 15.8; and Ovid, *Metamorphoses* viii 6–100). Pterelaos's daughter Comaeto shaved his head and caused his downfall (Apollodorus ii 4.7). It may be significant that Herakles was conceived on the very night that Comaeto's beloved Amphitryon defeated Pterelaos, a night Zeus spent with Amphitryon's queen (Apollodorus ii 4.8). The characteristic Greek motif of family betrayal is absent in the Bible: Delilah was not Samson's daughter and she was not in love with a Philistine. But the haircutting cannot be coincidental.

The figure of Samson as a wild man and the nature of his exploits are very unlike that of other biblical heroes. Most notably, Samson has many similarities to Herakles, a fact recognized since late antiquity. Like Samson, Herakles was a man with notably long hair who engaged in feats of strength, and was attached to a woman he could not keep (Megara), who married someone else and was later murdered. And like Samson, Herakles was undone by another woman, Deianeira. The many parallels between Samson and Greek heroes, and between Delilah and the women who cause their downfall, may result from the close contact between Israelites and Philistines (an Aegean people) in the Danite territory, the very valley of the Sorek in which Samson's exploits took place. The diffusion of stories from the Philistines may have colored the memory of the hero who fought against them.

In many respects, Samson is the anti-type of a biblical leader. He is more like Ishmael than like Isaac, more like Esau than Jacob. But he is not simply a hunter or nomad. He is a figure who does not sit readily in civilized society—marginal by his strength, by his hair, and by his dedication to God. Of all biblical characters, he is most like Elijah, who is also a man of hair, and who outran a chariot. Samson, however, is no miracle worker. And Elijah never dies.

Samson is the polar opposite of Moses, who shares the word "liberate" with him. Moses liberated Israel from Egypt: Samson will "begin to liberate" Israel from the Philistines. But Moses is described as "humble" and no paragon of strength. The one time he has to demonstrate unusual physical strength, to hold his arms up while Israel fights Amalek, he cannot do so, and has his arms held by Caleb and Hur. The figure of Moses with his tired arms held up by others could not be more different than the image of Samson carrying away the city gate on his back. And Moses' relationship with women is diametrically the opposite of Samson's. His mother, his foster mother, his sister, his wife, all act as his saviors enabling him to develop his mission. But Samson's women and his behavior toward them get him into trouble; only his mother emerges as a positive character. Samson has much more in common with Greek heroes than with biblical leaders.

No other biblical hero is ever defeated by an Israelite woman. Such a scenario is not part of biblical storytelling, though the Delilah story has sometimes been retold later to serve such purposes. But Delilah is not entirely unlike every other woman of the Bible. The anonymous woman at Thebez killed the attacking general by dropping a millstone on his head (Judg. 9), and Yael caused the death of another strong man, the Canaanite general. Delilah is the "bizarro-universe" image of Yael. Yael uses her position as hostess to nurture Sisera into a sense of well-being and then kills him. Delilah uses her presence in the house to deprive Samson of his liberty. Neither man suspects, possibly because they assume that women are not dangerous. Both women are determined, bold, and very dangerous. But one difference between them makes Yael a heroine and Delilah a villainess: Yael defeats an enemy of Israel, and Delilah destroys one of its heroes.

Athaliah

Like Delilah, Athaliah has often been labeled a foreigner. Once again, this is an assumption that reflects the bias of the readers and has no basis in the text. Athaliah is a member of the royal family of Israel. The Bible calls her "daughter of Omri" and "daughter of Ahab," and her husband, King Jehoram of Judah, is called the "son-in-law" of the house of Ahab. "Daughter of Ahab" can have only one meaning, and in patrilineal Israel the child shared her father's nationality. "Daughter of Omri" might mean that the historians are not sure whether she was the daughter of Ahab or of his father Omri, or it might mean "member of Omri's dynasty." It may also identify her as a northerner, for the Assyrians continued to call the northern kingdom *bit humri*, "House of Omri," long after the Omride kings were dead. Either way, as daughter of Omri or Ahab, she certainly would have been considered an Israelite. Even if she was the daughter of Jezebel—and the Bible never tells us that she was—as Ahab's daughter (or sister), she would still be considered an Israelite woman. After all, King Rehoboam's Ammonite mother did not make him an Ammonite. It is a mark of the vilification that Athaliah receives in history that she is later identified as Jezebel's daughter and, in addition, tagged as a foreigner.

Athaliah was responsible for only one recorded act, but it was enough to make her a villain:

◈ *Act I. Slaughter of the Innocents (2 Kings 11:1–2)*

> Athaliah was the mother of Ahaziah.
> She saw that her son had died, and she arose and killed all the royal seed.
>
> Jehosheba, daughter of King Jehorem, sister of Ahaziah, took Joash son of Ahaziah from among the slain royal sons, and stole him and his wet nurse away into a bedchamber.
> They hid him from Athaliah and he was not killed.

Athaliah's action is very puzzling. What would Athaliah stand to gain from killing the royal children? Her husband had died the year before, and she had been in a position of considerable power as queen-mother. It would make much more sense for her to oversee the appointment of the infant Joash as heir and continue as queen-mother regent, like the famous Sammuramat (Semiramis) of Assyria or Adad-Guppi of Babylon. At most, she might want to dispose of Tsibia, the infant Joash's mother, so that she and not Tsibia would be the regent. But why would she want to destroy the royal line?

In any case, there were very few members of the royal line left for Athaliah to kill. Jehorem's general, Jehu, had not only killed off the Omrides, he had also slain Atahaliah's son Ahaziah, who was visiting the king of North Israel at the time of the coup, and Ahaziah's forty-two brothers. The few members of the royal family that he left alive could not have posed much of a threat to Athaliah.

The bloody, murderous nature of Jehu's revolt and his religious zeal against the Omrides may have contributed to Athaliah's slaughter of the few remaining Davidides. There are three possible scenarios in which this may have been so. Athaliah might have been infected by the reformist zeal that motivated Jehu. The book of Chronicles records that her sons, the Davidide princes, had taken some of the holy materials in the temple to give to Baʿal. Perhaps Athaliah, whom even her enemies never accuse of idolatry, killed these sons in the same religious fervor that fueled Jehu's insurrection. She too might have been acting to rid the country of those who supported Baʿal worship. The other two possible scenarios involve fear rather than zeal. Jehu claimed the word of God as justification for his slaughter of the house of Ahab. The book of Kings relates that a prophetic delegate anointed him to revolt. He also asserted that he was doing God's work by murdering the Omrides. Athaliah might have feared that the remaining Davidides in Judah would be attracted to Jehu's religious message, despite the fact that he had murdered so many Judean princes, and kill her, the daughter or sister of Ahab. Or she might have feared that Jehu would actively try to incite the people to murder her, as she was an Omride. Perhaps she hoped to forestall this, trying to curry favor with Jehu by killing Judean princes.

Whatever Athaliah's reasons, her attempt failed. She was thwarted by Ahaziah's sister Jehosheba, who rescued Ahaziah's infant son as Moses' mother had rescued him. And like Moses, the child who was saved from a murderous decree became a "savior," or at least the symbol of revolt.

◇ *Act II. The Return of the House of David*

Scene 1. Revealing the hidden child (2 Kings 11:3–4)

> He was with her hiding in the temple for six years while
> Athaliah was ruling over the land.

> In the seventh year, Jehoiada sent and took the lieutenants
> of cavalry and infantry and brought them to him into the
> temple.
> He showed them the king's son.

Six years later, the high priest Jehoiada, Jehosheba's husband, revealed
the existence of a royal son and used him to spark an insurrection. In the
next scene, he commanded the army to take battle stations at the temple
and surround the king's son. Then:

Scene 2. Coronation and Conspiracy (2 Kings 11:9–16)

> The lieutenants did what Jehoiada the priest commanded.
> Each took his men, those on duty that week, and those on leave
> that week, and they came to Jehoiada the priest.
> The priest gave the lieutenants King David's spear and quivers,
> which were in the temple.
> The runners stood, each with his weapon in his hand, from the
> right edge of the temple to the left edge, to the altar and the
> house, surrounding the king.
> He brought out the king's son and placed upon him the wreath
> and the insignia.
> They crowned and anointed him, clapped hands and said,
> "Long live the king!"
> Athaliah heard the shouting of the runners of the people.
> She came to the people in the temple.
> She looked and lo! The king was standing on the pillar, as was
> the rule, and the officers and the horns (were) toward the
> king, and the whole people of the land (were) happy and
> blowing horns.
> She tore her clothes and cried, "Conspiracy! Conspiracy!"
> Jehoiada commanded the lieutenants over the army.
> He said to them, "Take her out outside to the columns. Who-
> ever comes after her, kill by sword."
> For the priest said, "Let her not die in YHWH's temple."
> They placed hands on her and she came to the horses' entryway
> to the palace and was killed there.

Modern skepticism might make us question whether this baby was
really a rescued seed of David or a royal imposter. The child was cer-

tainly the major focus of the insurrection that brought down Athaliah, and there is no hint that anyone at the time took him for anything but a descendant of David. The revolt was not a religious revolution. Neither the narrator nor Jehoiada ever indicts Athaliah as a Ba'al worshiper, or ever mentions Asherah. Modern commentators may assume that the queens worshiped female deities, but the Bible does not accuse them of this. Athaliah bears a -*yah* name, a sign of a worshiper of YHWH, as did her son Ahaziah. Unlike Jehu, Jehoiada cannot use any religious pretext or proclaim an anti-idolatry crusade. But he does not have to. He has a royal pretender to the throne, and orchestrates an armed coronation. Using Joash, Jehoiada takes the reins of power, has Athaliah killed, and then rules as the young king's regent.

History does not treat Athaliah well. The book of Kings remembers that she "was ruling over the land" (2 Kings 11:3), but the editors do not give an opening or closing formula to her reign. The book of Chronicles accuses her of being her son Ahaziah's "adviser to make him guilty" (2 Chron. 22:3) and indicts her along with her sons for neglecting the temple and giving sacred objects to Ba'al (2 Chron. 24:7). Chronicles labels Athaliah as 'atalyah hammirša'at, "Athaliah the evil woman" (2 Chron. 24:7), and that is the way she continues to be remembered.

A Note About Villainesses

The villainesses of the Bible are strong, determined, and ferocious, not very different from the savior heroines. Like the victors, villains can be Israelite or foreign. Potiphar's wife and Jezebel are foreign women, as are Zipporah, Rahab, Yael, and Pharaoh's daughter. Athaliah and probably even Delilah are Israelite women, like Yochebed, Miriam, and Deborah, even though readers often assume that they were foreign. The foreignness of Athaliah and Delilah lies not in their origin but in their villainy. As they act as enemies of Israel's institutions, their behavior puts them beyond the pale. Their otherness is circumstantial rather than genetic, existential rather than essential. But as time goes on, this distinction is lost. Just as Jezebel's foreignness led to her lack of faith in Israel's traditions, so by the time of the exile, the prophet Ezekiel attributes Jerusalem's lack of faith to the city's foreign origins. The Deuteronomist declares that foreignness is villainy; later generations make all villainy foreign. In postbiblical traditions up to and including much contemporary scholarship, villains are simply assumed to be foreigners. In the Bible itself, it is the villainous behavior that makes an individual foreign, not the genes.

Part Two

VICTIMS

THE STORIES about the "victors," the "great women" of the Bible, are somewhat misleading. The strength and prominence of these women might lead a reader to believe that ancient Israel was a partially egalitarian society; their influence on Israel's destiny might cause us to think of their era as "the good old days," a time when women had considerable autonomy. They might even induce reveries of halcyon times when matriarchs benevolently ruled their families, and the family was the world. But even as biblical stories portray strong women, they show a patriarchy within which these women had to maneuver, and even as they depict women's power, they show the power of the patriarch to control and even to destroy the women and children in their families.

Biblical Israel, like all other ancient societies, was a patriarchy. Men headed their households and continued their lineage through male descendants. With the lineage went the land, for only sons could inherit. The future existence of the lineage and the memory of its past (what the Bible calls its "name" and its "memory") depended on maintaining the "patrimony," the land inherited from the fathers. Women, who passed from their father's lineage at marriage, did not normally inherit their father's land. And they also did not inherit their husband's land, which went to his sons.

A man had considerable power within his family, essentially reigning as a household monarch, as "king in his castle." His wife, no matter how significant her economic contribution to the household—and in farming economies it could be very significant—was his dependent. She might normally have considerable powers of persuasion, but when her husband wished, he could assert his dominance.

The ancestor stories of Genesis give us an image of Israel's conception of the life of women in ancestral times. This, of course, is not their purpose, which is to depict the beginning and development of a single family for four generations as it grows into the people of Israel. But in order to do so, the narratives concentrate on those events that have an impact on the family's future—the births of children, the finding of wives for growing sons, the transfer of family leadership to the children, and the splitting off of the family from the surrounding peoples—and they often revolve around the actions of the women, the wives and mothers.

The Bible does not show a lot of friction between husbands and wives. In this, it is like other Near Eastern literature. Greek myths often feature the "Battle of the Sexes," but Near Eastern literature concentrates more on the conflict between brothers to inherit from the father. Rage and revenge between husband and wife, if it existed to any great extent, is ignored in Near Eastern mythology and in the Bible. Instead, the conjugal relationship is portrayed as one of love and companionship. The Gilgamesh Epic relates that the gods rewarded the hero Utnapishtim and his wife with immortality for surviving the flood; as a result they live together for eternity, isolated on the island of the living. Conventional Western wisdom would characterize this eternal weddedness as more of a sentence to hell than a reward of paradise; the ancient Babylonians clearly considered it a reward. In a similar vein, Genesis weaves into its story of the creation of humanity the injunction that a man should leave his father and mother and cleave only to his wife.

This vision of conjugal bliss, of course, is seen through male eyes and male-authored text. Close examination of the stories reveals that part of this bliss results from the fact that wives are subordinate to husbands and often vulnerable to their whims. In the final analysis, the man is the autonomous "self" and the wife his important, even beloved, subject whose faithfulness he can command. Several of the stories of Genesis, placed as they are in the days when there was no state and the family was autonomous, show that the proprietary rights of the man of the house could even allow him to sacrifice his wife to his own well-being in extreme situations.

The Disposable Wife

THE EXTENT of the power that husbands possessed is revealed in the bizarre thrice-told wife-sister masquerade, told twice about Abraham and Sarah and once about Isaac and Rivka. The first episode occurs at the beginning of the Abraham cycle of stories, soon after Abram and Sarai come to Canaan. Beset by famine, they leave Canaan to head for Egypt. Abram is afraid that the Egyptians will kill him in order to attain the beautiful Sarai:

◇ *Act I. Share a Wife, Spare a Life (Gen. 12:10–20)*

Scene 1. The bartered bride (Gen. 12:10–16)

> It happened when he drew close to approaching Egypt. Abram said to Sarai his wife, "Look! I know that you are a beautiful woman.
>
> "It can happen that the Egyptians will see you and say, 'that one is his wife' and will kill me and leave you alive. Say, please, that you are my sister so that it will go well for me for you and I will live because of you."
>
> It happened when Abram arrived in Egypt. Pharaoh's officials saw Sarai and praised her to Pharaoh.
>
> The woman was taken into Pharaoh's house.
>
> He was very good to Abram on her account: Abram had sheep and cattle and asses and manservants and maidservants and donkeys and camels.

The story tells us little about this strange plan, for it concentrates only on Abram's perceptions. Sarai, an object of beauty, is certain to be noticed. The Egyptians will balk at taking a married woman but will not hesitate to kill him. He therefore willingly gives her away in order to save his own life. Modern scholars have offered theories to explain how Abraham could have thought up such a plan. One suggestion looks to ethnographic data about a custom called "sexual hospitality" in which a man traveling through foreign territory will barter his wife's favors for safe passage. But no traces of this custom have been found in the texts from the ancient Near East. Nor is it likely that this custom will be found there, given the strong strictures against adultery in the Near Eastern civilizations. Furthermore, if men routinely shared their wives, why would Abram think to pass her off as his sister? Another suggestion has been to look at anthropological evidence that the brother (or uncle) was a woman's chief protector, even more than her husband, and was considered irreplaceable. By passing as her brother, Abram could provide protection against Sarai's violation; they would be less likely to take a woman traveling with her brother than a wife with her husband and, at the very least, would be more likely to negotiate with him rather than kill him. This explanation makes Abram come off noble and self-sacrificing, but if this was the convention of the time, neither the biblical author nor the Egyptians in the story have any knowledge of it, for they take Sarai from her "brother" without any recorded concern. A popular explanation draws on a custom found in cuneiform tablets from Nuzi, a town in central Syria in the sixteenth century B.C.E. whose family archives often contain interesting parallels to the ancestor stories in Genesis. Nuzi marriage contracts sometimes record marriages "into wife-hood and sisterhood," and it has been suggested that "wife-sisterhood" conveyed greater status than ordinary marriage. In calling her his sister, Abram was trying to accord Sarai this higher status so that she would be better treated by the Egyptians. Since this custom was not known to the biblical author, he added his own explanation, that Abram was trying to save his own life. This explanation "saves" Abram's reputation, but more recent research into "wife-sister" marriage has failed to show that "sisterhood" gave any status advantage to wives, and biblical scholars have now abandoned this thesis.

These narratives relate the story as most biblical stories are related, matter-of-factly, without moral judgment. But the choice of words indicates clearly what is going on. **When he drew close . . . when Abram arrived in Egypt.** The story uses the masculine singular of the verbs even though Abram was traveling with Sarai and probably with an entire entourage. This is a story about Abram, focused on Abram and told as if through Abram's eyes. Abram is going, Sarai and the household move **with him** until **the woman was taken into Pharaoh's house.** The very rare passive "was taken" emphasizes that she no longer has independent volition. She is also stripped of her individuality, no longer recognized as a person, for both Abram and Pharaoh treat her as "a woman"—an unspecified generic object of desire. Sarai has been commodified, and nobody in these stories uses her name. No longer Sarai, she is "she" or "wife" or "this one" or "woman," an object being transferred from Abram's household to Pharoah's, there to be a slave-concubine. But God has other plans.

Scene 2. In the matter of Sarai (Gen. 12:17–20)

> YHWH smote Pharaoh with great plagues, and his household, in the matter of Sarai, wife of Abram.
>
> Pharaoh called to Abram and said, "What have you done to me? Why did you not tell me that she is your wife? Why did you say 'she is my sister' and I took her as a wife? And now here is your wife: take her and go!"
>
> Pharaoh commanded men about him and they sent him off, he and his wife and all that he had.

God restores some measure of personhood to Sarai. To God, she is not just any woman: she is Sarai, Abram's wife, and God has plans for her. So God intervenes and all ends well.

The story seems strange even to biblical authors. When a parallel episode is related about Abraham and Sarah in Gerar, the narrator provides a meditation on the reasons for Abraham's behavior.

◇ *Act II. Once More with Feeling (Gen. 20:1–18)*

Scene 1. In rescue of Sarah (Gen. 20:1–8)

> Abraham journeyed from there to the Negeb, settled between Qedesh and Shur and resided in Gerar.
>
> Abraham said of Sarah his wife, "She is my sister." Abimelech king of Gerar sent and took Sarah.
>
> God came to Abimelech in a night dream and said to him, "Look! You are dead because of the woman that you took, and she a married woman!"
>
> Abimelech had not approached her, and he said, "My Lord, will you kill a righteous nation? Did he not say, 'She is my sister' and she also, she said, 'He is my brother'? In innocence of heart and purity of hands I have done this."
>
> God said to him in a dream, "I also know that in your innocent heart you did this, and I, for my part, prevented you from sinning before me, therefore I did not let you touch her.

> And now, return the man's wife, for he is a prophet and he will pray for you and you will live. If you do not return her, know that you will truly die, you and all of yours."
>
> Abimelech arose early in the morning and called his servants. He spoke to them these words and the people feared greatly.

By this time in the Abraham–Sarah stories, Ishmael has been born, God has reminded Abraham that his covenant is through Sarah, has renamed each of them in accord with their special status, and has announced the birth of Isaac. None of this prevents Abraham from being ready to relinquish Sarah yet again in order to save his life. Once more, God considers Sarah central to the divine plan, and intervenes to save her. Perhaps feeling uncomfortable, the narrator adds a new detail: **she also, she said, 'He is my brother':** Sarah has actively participated in the masquerade, at least according to Abimelech. The narrator also adds something else: Abimelech has not touched Sarah. The story in Genesis 12 said nothing about what happened in Pharaoh's household. Later commentators speculated that Pharaoh must not have touched her—otherwise, they reasoned, Abraham would not have taken her back! But this is a later assumption, not necessarily true of biblical attitudes. In the story of the Levite and his concubine (Judg. 19), the Levite is clearly willing to take her back even after he himself sent her out to the mob. The narrator of Genesis 20 cannot rely on assumptions, for the episode with Abimelech is too close to the birth of Isaac. The writer has to offer reassurance that Isaac was Abraham's child, not Abimelech's.

The narrator continues to explain other parts of the story.

Scene 2. In the matter of Sarah (Gen. 20:9–18)

> Abimelech called Abraham and said to him, "What have you done to us? And what have I done wrong to you that you bring such a great sin upon me and upon my kingdom? You have done to me things that should not be done."
>
> And Abimelech said to Abraham, "What did you see that you did this thing?"
>
> Abraham said, "Because I thought that there is no fear of God in this place and they will kill me in the matter of my wife. And, after all, she is my sister. She is the daughter of my father but not the daughter of my mother, and she became my wife.

> "It happened that when God made me turn away from my fa-
> ther's house, I said to her, 'This is the benevolent act that
> you should do for me, to everywhere that we come, say, "he
> is my brother." '"
>
> Abimelech took flocks and cattle and manservants and maidser-
> vants and gave them to Abraham and returned to him his
> wife Sarah.
>
> Abimelech said, "Look, my land is before you. Live wherever
> seems good to you." To Sarah, he said, "Look! I gave a thou-
> sand pieces of silver to your brother, it is for you, an 'eye-
> covering' to all who are with you and all before you."
>
> Abraham prayed to God and God healed Abimelech and his
> wife and his concubines and they gave birth. For YHWH
> had stopped up all the wombs of Abimelech's house in the
> matter of Sarah wife of Abraham.

Abraham's answer to Abimelech, **"after all, she is my sister,"** reveals
something that the genealogy of Abraham in Genesis 11 does not: Sarah,
called Terah's daughter-in-law in Genesis 11, is actually Terah's daughter
by another woman. So, claims Abraham, he wasn't really lying, he was
simply not telling the whole truth. He omitted one small detail: that
Sarah was also his wife. Abraham also adds that he was not plotting
against Abimelech, for he used this strategy everywhere. And Sarah was
certainly not conspiring against Abimelech, for she lied only as an act of
ḥesed toward Abraham, a benevolence toward her husband beyond normal wifely duties.

None of these apologies changes the basic fact. Abraham has once
again given Sarah away, and God has once again restored her because
God considers her important to God's plan. But God does not berate or
castigate Abraham for putting her at risk. According to the social conventions of his time, Abraham has done nothing wrong. As head of the
household, he had the right to do whatever he would with the members
of his family. The stories of Genesis make the right of the paterfamilias
very clear: in Genesis 20, Abraham gives Sarah to Abimelech; in Genesis
21, Abraham sends Ishmael out of his household; in Genesis 22, Abraham is prepared to sacrifice Isaac to God. In all of these stories, the family members and Israel survive because God intervenes to make sure
there is no permanent damage to the family. Without this special divine
supervision, the rights of the father would have led to disaster for those
under his control. Nobody was beyond this power of the patriarch; not

even the powerful ancestral mothers of Israel were secure. In the wife-sister stories, Abraham and Isaac used their wives as shields in times of danger. Other stories from the ancestral period show that a man could send away his wife and son (Hagar); that a wife could lose status in the household by not having children, or not enough children, and might be forced to contend for prominence with a slave-concubine (like Sarah and Hagar) or even with another wife (like Rachel and Leah). A patriarchy is, after all, a patriarchy.

Daddy's Daughters

WIVES ARE IMPORTANT to men: they run the household and they raise the children. The combination of their economic importance and the power of pair-bonding was usually enough to protect wives from the more extreme types of husbandly abuse. But children did not have these advantages. The biblical father could marry them to whomever he pleased and could sell them into slavery to cover his debts. In the early days of Israel, he may have been able to sell them as ordinary slaves or make his daughter a prostitute. There was even a time when a man could kill his children, as Abraham almost killed Isaac.

All children everywhere are vulnerable to the actions of their parents, and girls are even more so than boys. The most vulnerable people in a patriarchal society are daughters. In all families there comes a time when the children are stronger than their parents. At that time, the sons will be at home, working with the father and expected to take care of the parents in their old age, and even to continue to provide for them after their death with funerary services and offerings. The son is the name and remembrance of the father, the father's ticket to immortality and the future of the family. Because of this, sons who are not well treated as children will have their chance at "payback time," and the knowledge that this could happen may have served as a built-in check on excesses of parental behavior. But a daughter has no such check. Ancient agrarian societies expected that a girl would leave her family soon after puberty and join her husband's household. Once married, she was expected to be loyal to her husband and his family, even over her parents. As a result, a daughter was only a temporary member of her family, and would not be with her own parents at the peak of her strength and economic power. The temporary nature of a girl's daughterhood meant there could be no payback time for her and contributed to her vulnerability within the family.

The ancestor stories of Genesis have a positive vector. They concentrate on the development and growth of a family that manages to survive, reproduce, and thrive despite difficulties and dysfunctions (though sometimes only because God saves the day). Most of the women-stories in Genesis reflect this positive vector. They focus on mothers and wives, women of at least some authority in the household and great influence on its destiny. By contrast, the book of Judges is not about thriving. It depicts the same system of family relationships, but in the process of dissolution and decay. It understands Israel's political life as a progressive deterioration from the time of the conquest until the total collapse that preceded the creation of a monarchic state. The book's episodes have a cyclical form: the people stray, God brings an enemy to conquer them, their suffering makes them repent and return to God, God sends a deliverer who rescues them and judges till he dies; then the people stray again and the process repeats. The cycles head downward in a continuing spiral of disintegration. The judges are increasingly ineffectual, civil wars break out, and above all, the most vulnerable members of society become victims. The three stories about daughters in the book of Judges are spaced at strategic points, one at the beginning, one at the middle, and one at the end, and they dramatize this downward spiral. Through the progression of these stories, the book of Judges increasingly horrifies its readers. As a result, the people of Israel (and the readers) put aside their reservations and come to want a strong king to bring an end to these terrible events.

The first story, about Achsah (Judg. 1:11–15), reveals how a daughter became a wife: her father determines whom she would marry, and when. The story begins as the tribe of Judah is encamped before Kiryat-Sefer during the wars of conquest. At that time, Caleb takes a battle vow: "I shall give my daughter Achsah as a wife to whoever attacks and captures Kiryat-Sefer." The victor is Othniel son of Kenaz, and Caleb gives her to him as a wife. To modern readers used to the free choice of mates, Caleb's vow seems autocratic and unfair. Achsah is treated like a spoil of war, bestowed upon the conqueror as a battle trophy. To the biblical audience, this is business as usual. In the biblical world, a father had the right to give his daughter away. He might listen to her wishes or he might not. The decision was his, and Caleb was simply exercising his right in a way that would add extra incentive to the battle for Kiryat-Sefer. Moreover, Achsah is fortunate: her own uncle Othniel conquers the city and marries her.

Achsah now takes matters into her own hands. She is neither pawn nor victim. As soon as Othniel marries her, she convinces him to ask for a field from her father. She slides from her donkey and asks her father to give her a gift. "You have given me away as dry land and now you must give me Gulot-Mayim (water sources)." Achsah's complaint makes sense. A daughter usually benefits from the bridewealth that the groom gives the father. But when the payment has been made by winning a battle, what good does it do the bride?

Caleb, Achsah's father, is a good man. He listens to her, understands her predicament, and gives her a fair marriage settlement: "he gives her upper and lower Gulot." She winds up possessing her own watered land. Achsah is more fortunate even than Israel's matriarchs. Like Achsah, Rachel and Leah married their uncle, and their husband offered service as bridewealth rather than goods or money. But their father, Laban, never shared the value of Jacob's service with them: "He sold us and has used up all our money," they exclaim (Gen. 31:15). Within the workings of the patriarchal family system, Achsah has negotiated the transition from daughter to wife smoothly, and the story has a happy ending.

Father-right Awry
Jephthah and His Daughter

THE STORY of Jephthah's daughter does not end so harmoniously. Like the story of Achsah, it revolves around a battle vow in which a man has promised a prize to the one who brings victory. But neither the man nor his daughter is as fortunate as Caleb and Achsah, and Jephthah winds up sacrificing his daughter to God.

The story begins with the background: the coming of war to Gilead, and the biography of the hero up to that historical moment.

◇ *Act I. Setting the Scene (Judg. 10:17–18; 11:1–3)*
Historical prologue: War!
>   The Ammonites mustered and encamped in Gilead.
>   The Israelites gathered and encamped at Mispah.
>   The people, the leaders of Gilead, said to each other, "Whichever man will begin to fight the Ammonites will be the head of all the inhabitants of Gilead."

Biographical prologue: The outcast boy
>   Now Jephthah the Gileadite was a mighty warrior.
>   He was the son of a prostitute, and Gilead engendered Jephthah.
>   The wife of Gilead gave birth to sons for him.
>   The sons grew and kicked Jephthah out and said to him, "You will not inherit from our patrimony, for you are the son of another woman."
>   Jephthah fled from his brothers and settled in the land of Tob.
>   And there gathered to Jephthah empty men, and they went out with him.

This story starts like an archetypical biblical hagiography of a hero. Jephthah is the son of a marginal woman, a prostitute. He lives in his father's house, but he is vulnerable, and when his father dies, his half brothers eject him. This is not right. In the ancient Near East, prostitutes could be hired as surrogate wombs as well as sexual objects. Laws and contracts regulated the relationship between the child of such a prostitute and children of the first wife. A man could bring the child to live in his house and had to give its mother the same economic support that he would provide for a wife—though he could not bring the prostitute to live in his house as long as his wife was alive—and the child was his legitimate heir. A man could acquire a child in many ways—with his wife, by using a slave as surrogate womb, by marrying a secondary wife, by going to a prostitute, by adopting a foundling. However he acquired a child, once he brought him into his house, he acknowledged him as his son. Even if the primary wife gave birth, the acquired and acknowledged son could not be disinherited after the father's death. Jephthah has been wronged, but he has no recourse. He must leave home. The biblical audience, knowing that his brothers' action was improper, will be sympathetic to Jephthah. They are ready to root for his success.

Jephthah is out but not down. Like the later David when he fled from King Saul, Jephthah becomes the leader of a band of fighters. By the time the Ammonites attack, he has made a name for himself as a mighty warrior.

◇ *Act II. Poor Boy Makes Good (Judg. 11:4–11)*

> Some years later the Ammonites warred against Israel.
>
> When the Ammonites warred against Israel, the elders of Gilead went to take Jephthah from the land of Tob.
>
> They said to Jephthah, "Come and be our captain and we will fight the Ammonites."
>
> Jephthah said to the elders of Gilead, "Didn't you 'hate' me and eject me from my father's house? Why have you come to me now when things are difficult for you?"
>
> The elders of Gilead said to Jephthah, "For this we have returned to you now. You will go with us and you will fight the Ammonites and you will become the chief of all the inhabitants of Gilead."
>
> Jephthah said to the elders of Gilead, "If you bring me back to fight the Ammonites and YHWH gives them before me, I will become your chief."
>
> The elders of Gilead said to Jephthah, "God hears (what is said) between us (and God will punish us) if we do not do exactly as you have said."

> Jephthah went with the elders of Gilead and the people made
> him their chief and captain.
> Jephthah related all his words before YHWH in Mispah.

Times have changed. The "elders of Gilead" are the sons of Gilead grown older. The threat of the Ammonites is so grave that they sue the very brother they wronged for aid. When Jephthah balks, they acknowledge their wrongdoing in the classic biblical language of repentance, *šabnû ʾelêka*, "we have returned to you." Moreover, they elevate their offer; he will not only be *qaṣîn*, a military "captain," he will be *rōʾš*, "chief" over all the inhabitants of Gilead. Jephthah accepts their repentance and the restoration it invites by using the same verbal root, **"if you bring me back,"** *mešîbîm ʾattem ʾōti*. The language of their negotiation is replete with the technical terms found for rejection, ejection, and restoration. When Jephthah says **"if you bring me back,"** the meaning is clear to all concerned: they are to restore him to his rightful inheritance as well as to their company. He also makes the implications of their remarks explicit: **If . . . YHWH gives them before me, I will become your chief**—even after the victory. Military crises have often caused democracies and oligarchies to turn to one strong leader; the ancient Near Eastern gods acquired their kings in this same way. The Babylonian Enuma Elish describes how the threat of the frightful primeval sea Tiamat induced the council of gods to make Marduk king; the Ugaritic Baʾal epic recites much the same scenario about Baʾal's defeat of Yam, and poetic passages in the Psalms and the prophets allude to a similar story in Israel in which YHWH became king by defeating the mighty primordial waters. Jephthah does not intend to be ejected again; if he comes to Gilead and wins, he is here to stay.

Jephthah's response reveals both strength in negotiation and deep piety, as he reminds the elders that victory can come only from God. Perhaps mindful that there are trust issues involved here, they take an oath to do exactly as he has stipulated. Jephthah goes to Mispah, the religious center, and relates *all his words* before God at Mispah. He then tries to negotiate a peace with the king of Ammon.

◇ *Act III. The War with Ammon (Judg. 11:12–33)*

Scene 1. Prelude to a battle (Judg. 11:12–28)

> Jepthah sent messengers to the king of the Ammonites thus:
>   "What issues do we have between us that you have come to
>   fight in my land?"

The king of the Ammonites said to Jephthah's messengers: "Because Israel took my land when it came from Egypt, from the Arnon to the Jabbok to the Jordan. Now return them peacefully."

Jephthah again sent messengers to the king of the Ammonites and he said to him, "Thus says Jephthah: 'Israel did not take the land of Moab or the land of Ammon. For when they came out of Egypt, Israel went in the desert to the Red Sea and came to Kadesh. Israel sent messengers to the king of Edom saying, "Let me cross your land." The king of Edom didn't listen and sent to the king of Moab and he didn't agree and Israel was in Kadesh. Then Israel went in the desert and circled the land of Edom and Moab and came east of Moab and camped across the Arnon and never entered the territory of Moab, for Arnon is the border of Moab."

Israel sent messengers to Sihon king of the Amorites, king of Heshbon, and Israel said to him, "Let me cross your land till my place." But Sihon didn't trust Israel to let him cross his territory. Sihon assembled all his people and they encamped at Yehza and fought Israel. Then God gave Sihon and all his people to Israel and they smote them. Israel inherited all the land of the Amorite who dwelt in that land and they inherited the whole territory of the Amorite from Arnon to Jabbok, from the desert to the Jordan.

"And now: YHWH God of Israel dispossessed the Amorite before Israel, and you will possess it? You should possess that which Chemosh your god gave you to possess, and we will possess what YHWH our god gave us to possess.

"And now: Are you better than Balak, son of S̟ippor king of Moab? Did he quarrel with Israel or fight them? While Israel has been settled in Heshbon and her satellite cities and Aroer and her satellites and all the cities along the Arnon for three hundred years—why didn't you recover them during that time?

"I have done you no wrong and you do evil by fighting me. May YHWH judge today between Israel and the Ammonites!"

The king of the Ammonites did not listen to the words of Jephthah which he sent to him.

Jephthah has a multifold argument: first, Israel never tried to capture this territory and came to occupy it only after Sihon attacked them. Second, the territory had been Amorite, not Ammonite; third, the Amorites should have been like Balak, who didn't attack and whose territory Israel did not take. And finally, the land has not been contested for three hundred years and it is too late now to argue about whether Israel had the right to conquer it back then.

Jephthah is keenly aware of the role of God in Israel's history: YHWH gave Israel the land, and YHWH will decide the present issue. We aren't told how Jephthah expects God to judge; perhaps he would have wished to use lots or the Urim and Thumim. But when Ammon will not listen, the only recourse is to have God determine the result of battle.

Scene 2. The battle-vow (Judg. 11:29–31)

> The spirit of YHWH came upon Jephthah and he crossed the
> Gilead and Manassah and he crossed to Miṣpeh-Gilead and
> from Miṣpeh-Gilead he crossed to the Ammonites.
> Jephthah vowed a vow to YHWH.
> He said, "If you give the Ammonites into my hand, then the one
> who comes out of the doors of my house toward me when
> I return in peace from the Ammonites, that one will be for
> YHWH, I will offer that one for an offering."

Jephthah, infused with the divine spirit, sets out for war. He truly believes what he told the Ammonite king—that the battle itself is a form of divine decision making. And his piety leads him to an action that will eventually bring his ruination. Before the battle, he makes a battle-vow. Both vows and battle-oaths are venerable traditions in Israel. Making a battle-oath is not a sign of disbelief; on the contrary, it demonstrates faith that God can grant victory, and offers, in advance, an expression of gratitude. Such an oath seems entirely in character for Jephthah, who lives with a great awareness of God.

But why did he make such a strange promise: **"the one who comes out of the doors of my house toward me when I return in peace from the Ammonites, that one will be for YHWH, I will offer that one for a sacrifice."** Biblical vows usually have some sort of inner logic, a connection between what is asked for and what is promised. Jacob, who asks God to be with him, offers to build a sanctuary when he gets home (Gen. 28:20–22); Israel, asking to defeat a city, offers to devote that city to

God (Num. 21:2); Hannah, asking for a child, offers to consecrate that child to God (1 Sam. 1:11). A vow can, of course, promise general worship and sacrifice; Absalom, asking to come home, offers to sacrifice to God in Hebron (2 Sam. 15:8). But Jephthah is very specific: **the first to come out of my house.** Did he expect an animal to be the first one out, as a dog runs to meet its master? The Latin Vulgate translates *quicumque,* "whoever," but maybe Jephthah intended an animal. Or perhaps he intended all along to offer a human sacrifice but expected a servant to come out. Or did he know that it might be his daughter?

Strangely enough, Jepthah was not the only hero in the ancient Mediterranean to make this same foolish vow about "the first." King Idomeneus of Crete (Idomeneo in Mozart's opera) was another: encountering a storm on his return from the Trojan wars, he vowed that if he got home safely, he would sacrifice to Poseidon the first one who came out to meet him. General Meander took a similar battle-vow to the Mother of the Gods. Both these vows led to tragedies. The first to greet Idomeneus was his son; and as for Meander, he was greeted by his son Archelos and by his mother and sister. After sacrificing them all, he jumped into the river that bears his name.

There may have been other stories with this tragic but traditional motif. Perhaps they were told to caution people about the danger of vows that are not quite specific enough, for Jephthah's lack of specificity will come to haunt him.

◇ *Act IV. The Tragedy (Judg. 11:32–40)*

Scene 1. Trapped! (Judg. 11:32–34)

> Jephthah crossed over to the Ammonites to fight them and YHWH gave them in his hand.
> He smote them from Aroer as far as Minnith, twenty cities all the way to Abel-Kramim, a very great strike.
> The Ammonites submitted to the Israelites.
> Jephthah came to Mispah, to his house.
> Look! His daughter is coming out to meet him with timbrels and dances.
> She is the only one, his sole child. He has no other issue, son or daughter.

The victory has been won. Most emphatically. At the height of his power, Jephthah comes home. And then is defeated by his daughter's alacrity and his own stupid vow. The text never hints why the girl emerged so quickly. Perhaps it was just daughterly eagerness to see her father, but the fact that she came **with timbrels and dances** suggests yet another reason. Much earlier, after the defeat of the Egyptians at the Red Sea, Miriam led the women of Israel "with timbrels and dances" (Exod. 15:20). And later, the women of each city would come out to greet the victorious David and Saul as they came from defeating the Philistines, "with timbrels and joy" (1 Sam. 18:6–7). Perhaps Jephthah's daughter wants to surprise her father by observing this custom, even though it is a custom for women, *našîm,* and she is only a pubescent girl. Jephthah's wife is conspicuously absent from this story, and the young girl may be trying to do the woman's job. And that, Jephthah couldn't expect.

The Bible adds a twist that is particularly heart-wrenching. Jephthah's daughter is **the only one, his sole child. He has no other issue, son or daughter.** This singularity, this "sole-ness," deepens the father's dilemma. If he sacrifices her, he will have no descendants, and his name will die. Biblical Israel considered the extirpation of a lineage, which it called *karet,* the worst fate that could befall anyone. The biblical investment in the survival of lineage is so intense that, as we have seen, the daughters of Zelophehad relied on it as their trump card when they petitioned to inherit their father's estate. Israel's horror at the prospect of losing one's lineage also motivates the story that the Wise Woman of Tekoa tells David: one of her two sons killed the other, and if she releases her remaining son to the family for execution, "They will extinguish my last ember without giving my (dead) husband a name and remembrance on the earth" (2 Sam. 14:7). David responds to this dread possibility by promising to make sure that no one harms the remaining son. The teller of Jephthah's story knows that his audience will respond with great sympathy to the news that the girl was an only child, and horror *on behalf of the father.*

Scene 2. The heroic daughter (Judg. 11:35–38)

> It happened that as soon as he saw his daughter, he tore his clothes and said, "O woe, my daughter, you have really brought me to my knees, you have become one of those who bring trouble to me, for I, I opened my mouth to YHWH and cannot go back."
>
> She said to him, "My father, you have opened your mouth to YHWH! Do to me as came out of your mouth, now that

YHWH has done avenging deeds against our enemies the
Ammonites."

She said to her father, "Let this thing be done for me: leave me
be for two months and I will go and I will descend upon the
hills and I will cry about my maidenhood, I and my com-
panions."

He said, "Go!"

Jephthah is overwhelmed. He doesn't ask her why she came out. It
isn't like him not to ask. He asked the elders why they came to him
(Judg. 11:7); asked the Ammonite king why no one for three centuries
had tried to recover Gilead (Judg. 11:26); will later ask the men of
Ephraim why they have come to fight him (Judg. 12:3). But he has no reason to question his daughter. Whatever her reasons may have been cannot change the result. Instead, Jephthah's reaction expresses his sense of
horror and tragedy. His cry *ʾahāh*, "woe," sets the tone, and his three key
expressions, *yiqraʿ*, **"he tore his clothes,"** *harēaʿ hikraʿtinî*, **"you have
really brought me to my knees,"** and *beʿōkrāy*, **"you have become one
of those who bring trouble to me,"** each of which has a specialized
meaning, echo one another to produce the sound of a mournful cry.
Tore his clothes is a mourning act: Jephthah is already grieving for his
daughter and his lost future. **"You have brought me to my knees"** is a
war term: what the enemy tried and failed to do, his daughter has done
unintentionally in her desire to honor him. And his next words, **"you
have become one of those who bring trouble to me,"** comes from the
vocabulary of reproach. Reproach? Such a reaction seems both self-
centered and an outrageous shifting of blame. But parents do talk like
this. Shimon and Levi destroyed Shechem, and their father Jacob told
them, "You have brought trouble to me." The daughter of Jephthah has
dealt her father an unavertable blow simply by being the first to greet
him. Like Jacob, Jephthah thinks of himself, not his child.

Jephthah also acknowledges his own part in his disaster, **"for I, I
opened my mouth to YHWH."** This act has defined his entire future. It
even explains his name, "Jephthah," in Hebrew *Yiptaḥ,* for *yiptaḥ* is the
ordinary Hebrew verb for "he has opened." The story uses the more poetic word *paṣîtî,* for "I opened." Jephthah has opened his mouth care-
lessly. His action gives new meaning to the old World War II slogan
"Loose lips sink ships." Words, once spoken, cannot be taken back, and
Jephthah **cannot go back** on his word. He is not a stubborn man; he is

willing to change direction. After all, he went back to his brothers. But there is no way he can go back on his vow. And so he sees only his doom. Jephthah's words crystallize the moment in which he sees that he has become a tragic figure: he is mourning the loss of his only child.

The daughter is now given a voice. She could have shifted the blame back on Jephthah. When King Ahab said to the prophet Elijah, "Are you the one who brings trouble to Israel?," using the same verb 'kr, Elijah turned the reproach back at him: "Not I have brought trouble to Israel, but you and your family have" (1 Kings 18:17–18). Or she could have been like King Saul's son Jonathan. When Jonathan found himself trapped by a battle-oath he had never even heard, he reproached his father without waiting for Saul to accuse him: "My father has troubled the land" (1 Sam. 14:29). But Jephthah's daughter neither argues within him nor weeps. With her opening words, **"you have opened your mouth,"** she both echoes his statement and subtly reminds him of his responsibility for their predicament. With the words that came out of his mouth, he began the tragedy; when she came out of her house, she precipitated it. His words, after all, were to YHWH, and YHWH granted him his victory over the Ammonites. Jephthah, says his daughter, must pay his vow, even though he will pay it with her body. She shares piety as well as tragedy with her father. She is a heroine, worthy of respect and admiration. The audience cannot be indifferent to her fate.

The conversation is conducted on such a high moral plane, and the discussion is so exclusively centered on the issue of fidelity to one's vow, that it is easy to forget that behind this dialogue lurks the horror of child sacrifice. Incredible and repulsive as it may seem to us, this practice was not unknown to the peoples of the ancient eastern Mediterranean. Both early Greece and Phoenicia knew this custom. Philo of Byblos relates that in times of terrible emergency, the Phoenician kings sacrificed their most beloved children. Even the god Kronos, he states, whom the Phoenicians call El, reacted to the great dangers of war by arraying his son Ieoud in royal apparel and sacrificing him.

The most famous of these stories is that of Iphigenia, the daughter of Agamemnon, who bears numerous similarities to Jephthah's daughter, particularly in the play *Iphigenia in Aulis,* by the fifth-century B.C.E. Greek tragedian Euripides. Brought to Aulis in order, so she thought, to be Achilles' bride, Iphigenia ran to be the first to greet her beloved father. Hearing that she was to be sacrificed, she begged Agamemnon to spare her, declaring, "Better live a life of woe than die a death of glory!" However, learning that the goddess Artemis was demanding the sacrifice,

Iphigenia became heroic: "If Artemis is minded to take this body, am I, a weak mortal, to thwart the goddess?" She decreed that there should be no mourning for her, and went to the sacrificial field to die.

These stories are set in the distant past, but child sacrifice was practiced in the full light of history, and many tombstones in the child cemetery of Carthage say *lndr*, "as a vow." The phenomenon seems to have been widespread throughout the Phoenician area.

Israel knew about Canaanite child sacrifice. Deuteronomy and Leviticus list burning children to the gods and the Molech offering (a technical term for child sacrifice) among the abominations that the Canaanites performed. And Israel had direct experience of the local custom. When Mesha, the king of Moab, rebelled against Israelite rule, and the Israelite army attacked his city, Mesha went up on the walls of his city and sacrificed his son, his designated heir. The ploy worked: a great "rage" went out into Israel and they abandoned the siege, leaving Moab independent (2 Kings 3:27). In Israel itself, the book of Kings records that King Ahaz "passed his son through the fire" like the abominations that the nations had performed (2 Kings 16:3, 21:6; 2 Chron. 33:6). Nor was Ahaz the only one to adopt the custom, despite the proscriptions of Deuteronomy (Deut. 12:31). Jeremiah complains that the Israelites built a *tophet* (probably an oven) in the Valley of Hinnom and were passing their children through fire, "which I (God) never commanded and never even imagined." Jephthah, his daughter, and the listeners know very well that the girl might be facing imminent death.

Jephthah's daughter asks only leave to prepare herself. She must mourn her lost future, and she must **"descend upon the hills."** The hills are away from the normal settlements; since she is at Miṣpah, the highest point around, she must go down to them, however strange the expression seems. The essential idea is that she must go away, away from her father's house, and away from the rule of society. She is leaving her father's house: when she returns, she will belong to another world,

Scene 3. Retreat and return (Judg. 11:38–39)

> He sent her for two months.
> She went, she and her companions, and she mourned her maidenhood on the hills.
> It happened that at the end of two months, she went back to her father.
> He did to her as his vow that he had vowed.
> She never knew a man.

The daughter mourns the end of her maiden life, and then, faithful to her own word and to her father's, she **went back to her father.** The words double back on one another. Words came out of his mouth, she came out of her house. He cannot go back on his words, so she goes back to his authority. What happens to her then is shrouded in silence. At the binding of Isaac, we see him lying on the altar, with Abraham standing above him holding a knife. Here we see and hear nothing. The story has no spectacle of violence, no blood and gore. All the action takes place offstage. Jephthah had said that the first one out of his house to greet him **"will be for YHWH and I will offer that one up as an offering."** His daughter said, **"Do to me as came out of your mouth,"** and now the narrator tells us, **He did to her as his vow that he had vowed.** Everything else is unsaid. The term ʿôlah that Jephthah uses for "offering" is also the term for the holocaust offering in the temple, the sacrifice that was totally burnt. The reader can justifiably conclude that Jephthah killed his daughter, but we do not see it happen. Throughout the millennia, readers have suggested that Jephthah never killed her at all, that he made her a servant of God's sanctuary for the rest of her life.

The tales of Iphigenia, Idomeneus, and Isaac are also not clear about the death of the child. Each story has two diffferent endings. The classical historian Servius reports that some say Idomeneus killed his son; others that he attempted to sacrifice his son but could not; in both variations, a plague then hit Crete and Idomeneus was banished. In the biblical story, God rescues Isaac and provides a ram for his sacrifice, but some later versions of the story end with the death of Isaac. And in the earliest version of the Iphigenia story, the Cyprian (seventh to sixth century B.C.E) Artemis, angry at Agamemnon for killing a deer, sends a storm. A seer tells him to sacrifice his daughter. But at the moment of sacrifice, Artemis substitutes a deer and spirits Iphigenia to Taurica. Euripides wrote two plays, *Iphigenia in Tauris* and *Iphigenia at Aulis.* In the first, Artemis carries Iphigenia off to serve in the goddess's sanctuary at Brauron. Some have suggested that in the original version of *Iphigenia at Aulis,* Iphigenia died, but the present version reads: "As the priest struck, and all heard the blow, but Iphigenia vanished, and in her place was a dying hind. The seer who demanded the sacrifice now declares that Artemis has preferred the hind and all exit happily." In the most famous version of the story, the tragic version by Aeschylus, Agamemnon kills Iphigenia before setting out for the Trojan wars.

Such variations may arise because these stories were told as foundation legends for cults that involve animal sacrifice. The result of either version of the telling is the same: an animal is to be sacrificed, not a human. The version in which the child dies sanctifies the substitute for the original human sacrifice: never again! The version in which an animal is substituted highlights the divine warrant for the cult's sacrifice of animals. Each animal sacrifice is a sacred reenactment and memorial of the divinely provided surrogate.

Epilogue: A rule in Israel (Judg. 11:39–40)

> She became a rule in Israel:
> Every year the daughters of Israel went out to chant the daughter of Jephthah, four days a year.

Not only sacrificial cults can be served by these stories. They can also be foundation legends for nonsacrificial rites of sanctuary service and for life cycle rituals. The Iphigenia story may be related to the *arkteia*, a girl's ritual at Brauron that young girls had to perform before they were allowed to marry. Judges 11 gives several indications that the story of Jephthah's daughter was also connected to an annual ritual. *She became a rule in Israel:* **every year, the daughters of Israel went to chant (the story of) the daughter of Jephthah the Gileadite, four days a year.** Her virginal status, **She never knew a man,** suggests a girls' puberty ritual, performed once as a rite of passage or annually between puberty and marriage—though for most girls this might also be only once.

What could such a ritual contain? The text tells us that one component was *letannôt* the daughter of Jephthah. *Letannôt* is often translated as "to mourn," but the same verb in the Song of Deborah clearly indicates celebration and not mourning: *šam yetannû ṣidqôt YHWH*, "there they chanted the great deeds of YHWH" (Judg. 5:11). During their four-day ritual, the daughters of Israel hear a public recitation of the story of the daughter of Jephthah. They may themselves mark the "death" of a girl child, their own prepubescent selves, as they relive her experience. Puberty marks the onset of a major transformation for all girls, a transition from being "daughter of" their birth family to member (wife, daughter-in-law) of their marital household. The "daughter of the father" will disappear as the father first promises and then gives his daughter to her husband/father-in-law. All girls undergo this death-and-transformation when they *die* as girl children and emerge as marriageable young women.

In ancient societies, the advent of puberty must have been terrifying to girls. They knew they were not masters of their own fates. In

wartime, that fate could be dire indeed; the women of a conquered people were raped, enslaved, and killed. It was no different in biblical times.
The mother of the Canaanite general Sisera waits for her victorious son
and gloats about the captive "(womb)girls, two-fold (womb)girls" whom
he will bring home (Judg. 5:30). The Israelites also captured women in
war, and Deuteronomy stipulates the proper behavior toward them
(Deut. 21:10–14). Even a woman on the winning side might become a trophy of war, like Achsah, given as a prize for victory. Peacetime was not
radically different; the fate of women in war is only an intensification of
their normal destiny. Even in peacetime, every girl at puberty knew that
she would be given away to a man of her *father's* choice, who might
abuse and exploit her. Under the best circumstances, her husband would
be good to her; still, half of all women would die in childbirth.

In a society in which women had so few choices, a ritual for girls
would be an opportunity to alleviate the anxiety of puberty, or at least to
help girls endure it by enabling them to share "women's mysteries" and
women's destinies. They would associate themselves with Jephthah's
daughter as their heroine, an association heightened by the fact that she
is remembered not by name but as an archetypal "daughter." She is like
them, yet special. Instead of being given to an ordinary man, she was
given to God. Instead of going passively to her fate, she demonstrated
bravery and power in choosing to honor her father's vow. Thus her story
provided girls at puberty with a heroine they could admire, and possibly
with a role model who could help them return to honor their own father's commitments. Her pious self-sacrifice, her honoring of the vow,
and the glory of her fate all added a sacred element to their own destinies, and perhaps made them easier to anticipate. There is no element
of radicality here: the ritual, which temporarily removed girls from the
male-dominated world, prepared them to return and accept this world.
Jephthah's daughter, a mistress of piety and devotion to God, could inspire them to be the same. They could admire her and, at the same time,
gain comfort from the fact that their fate was not hers.

The fate of Jephthah's nameless daughter is a transcendent (and perhaps worst-case) scenario of the fate of daughters writ large. Anonymity
can have many causes, of which insignificance is only one: it can also
convey a sense of archetype. She is simply the Daughter, vulnerable to
the actions of her father. Post-biblical Jewish writings call her Še'ila, "the
asked-for woman," and Pseudo-Philo's version of the story has Jephthah
telling her, "Your name is Še'ila, for you were born for this." More
recently, Mieke Bal named her Bat, Hebrew for "daughter," a name

adopted by some other readers. Both of these names are really epithets describing her role in the story, as is Jephthah, but they sound like names and so undermine the universality and archetypal nature of her story.

The historian of the book of Judges did not include this story of the daughter of Jephthah as an antiquarian notice about girls' puberty rites, or to present girls with a sacred archetype to glorify their new futures. The reason for inclusion goes to the heart of the biblical ideas about child sacrifice. The Bible knows that the people of Jerusalem who were sacrificing their children in the Valley of Hinnom had the best of intentions. Believing that God wanted them to sacrifice their children, they did so out of sincere piety. They might have believed that their own family tragedy was redeemed by the honor and piety with which Jephthah and his daughter acted, and by the glory of God to whom the sacrifice was made. They might even have considered sacrifice a glorious fate for the daughter of Jephthah. But not so the narrator of the historical books, nor any other biblical author. The prophets are vociferously in opposition. The priests in the Pentateuch consider child sacrifice a great abomination, and provide for the "redemption" of human children by payment of silver and then by dedication of the Levites to God *in place of* ordinary Israelites. The story of the binding of Isaac is told in such a way as to make it the paradigm for the animal sacrifices at the temple. Judges and Genesis portray Abraham and Jephthah as sincere and religious but consider child sacrifice a tragedy. In the story of Jephthah's daughter, the tragedy was intensified by the fact that both the father and the daughter lost their futures.

The horror with which biblical authors react to child sacrifice is the very reason this story is included in the book of Judges, which explains no other rituals. The story has a profoundly disquieting effect. Something seems terribly wrong. Both Jephthah and his daughter are sympathetic heroic characters. Jephthah was a victim who rose to be a hero, and then by his own action turned himself back into a victim. His daughter was a victim's victim with all the faith and fortitude of a heroine. Nobody acts with malice and yet, despite everyone's goodness, events proceed inexorably toward tragedy, the vulnerable heroine is sacrificed, the hero's name is gone. The very ambiguities with which this story is replete heighten the effect. Not knowing why Jephthah took his vow suggests that any misstep could result in tragedy, and not knowing whether she was actually killed prevents any resolution. The reader waits for salvation—why doesn't somebody stop the sacrifice and rescue the daughter? In the more famous story, the binding of Isaac, God intervenes to save the son. Why doesn't God save the daughter? Isaac's heart-wrenching question rings in our ears: "Where is the lamb for the slaughter?"

It will do no good to ask where God is or why God does not answer. The book of Judges takes place in the real world, historical time, in a world in which God will no longer intervene to save individuals. At this time, God is active on a national scale, bringing first conquerors and then redeemers. But God no longer saves private individuals and families. In the days of the ancestors, in Genesis, God saved Sarah from Pharaoh and Abimelech, rescued Lot's daughters from the mob at Shechem, saved Isaac from his father's knife. But the world of the book of Judges is more like the world of the readers, past and present, and neither they nor we can expect God to appear to save family members when we endanger them. In the absence of God's intervention, human beings and their social system must prevent such horrors.

But the social system of judges had no way to prevent the tragedy. The sacrifice of Jephthah's daughter is a sign that something was not right in Israel. Something was rotten in the state of the judges, and things were unraveling. They unravel even further as a civil war breaks out against Jephthah after the daughter's sacrifice. Throughout the Bible, violence against women is a symptom of a basic social flaw and a harbinger of social disintegration, and the very weakness in the social fabric that resulted in violence against Jephthah's daughter also caused the more widespread violence of civil war.

The problem that destroyed Jephthah's daughter will ultimately consume the entire body politic and the whole sociopolitical system of Israel in the time of the judges: Jephthah did to his daughter what he had vowed. He had the authority to do to his daughter what he had vowed. In the world of modern readers, fathers do not have such a right. In an orderly state, fathers may not kill their children. Men who do so are outlaws, and the state will punish them. This was also true of biblical Israel at the time the book of Judges was written, but Jephthah and his daughter lived before there was a monarchy, in a time when Israel was not a unified state. Who in that world would punish him? There had been no one to prevent his brothers from wronging him when he was weak and vulnerable. And now that he is the chief of the Gilead family, there is no one to punish him. The family is its own world. There is no institution over the family, nobody who has authority over the fathers, nobody who can control brothers when the fathers die, nobody who can control fathers when their children are in peril. But this does not create a paradise for the fathers. There is also no one to whom a father can turn for help if he has made a careless vow that compels him to act against his own will and his own self-interest. There is no higher authority to whom the father is answerable except God, who no longer intervenes directly to rescue family members from paternal power.

The story of the pious Jephthah and his heroic daughter is the turning point of the book of Judges. It is the first hint that lack of control over heads of families is a crucial flaw that will ultimately lead to the destruction of the social order. The rest of the book of Judges spirals down through problematic stories until it culminates in the catastrophic implosion of society that begins when the Levite's concubine leaves her husband.

The Bad Old Days
Concubine and Chaos

THE LAST STORY in the book of Judges begins quietly with a girl going home to her father, and escalates into violence that totally breaks down Israel's pre-monarchic order. The story is set when "there was no king in Israel." This is the same historical period, "when the judges judged," in which the book of Ruth takes place. These two contemporaneous stories present radically different views of life at that time. Ruth depicts an orderly society in which everyone behaves well; Judges 19–21 relates a process of implosion and dissolution in which everyone behaves badly. The story set "when the judges judged" has no villains; the story set when "there was no king" has no heroes.

◇ *Act I. The Levite and His Concubine (Judg. 19)*
Prologue (Judg. 19:1–4)
> It happened in those days,
> There was no king in Israel.
> There was a Levite man living on the slopes of Mount Ephraim.
> He took a concubine from Bethlehem in Judah.

In those days, very different from the days of the narrator, **there was no king.** The lack of a national government plays a central role in the story, for as the devastation described in the story unfolds, the reader begins to see that a king could have prevented it. By the time it is all over, when the narrator repeats the phrase **in those days, there was no king in Israel,** readers are ready to embrace monarchy.

The story introduces two characters: the Levite and his *pilegesh*, a lesser form of wife. They are both nameless, a sign that they are important not as individuals but as representatives of society. The Levites are best known as cultic officers who serve at the sanctuaries, though biblical stories reveal other aspects of their image. They were God's "shock troops": zealous, even violent defenders of what they perceived to be correct behavior. Their ancestor Levi (and his brother Simeon) killed the men of Shechem in revenge for the deflowering of Dinah; the Levites stood by Moses at Sinai and killed those who had worshiped the golden calf. The Levites were landless people with no independent means of support, "hired hands" who lived in the household of those who paid for their upkeep, or who depended on the support of the landed population in other ways, such as the tithe of later Israel. They had no fixed place in the tribal system of pre-monarchic Israel: there was no particular geographical area in the land of Israel that was called "Levite." As a result, the Levite was an "outsider" everywhere. He may have been honored, but he did not dwell among his own extended kin, and his loyalties to the people among whom he lived may have been suspect. At the time of the judges, the Levites were itinerant religious experts. The previous story in the book of Judges relates how a Levite from Bethlehem-Judah became a priest in the household of an Ephraimite named Micah, and later absconded with Micah's cultic equipment to join the Danites who came through on their journey to conquer Laish (Judg. 17–18). In the days of our story, the Levite was a figure of both power and danger, centrality and marginality. At the same time, the *pilegesh* ("concubine") had a lesser status than an ordinary wife. When the Levite takes a wife-*pilegesh,* a second-class wife, the power dissymmetry between husband and wife is even more pronounced than in the average patriarchal household, and the relationship of husband to wife is placed in high relief.

The breakdown begins with a small ripple in the domestic scene.

Part 1. Tear and repair (Judg. 19:2–4)
> His concubine was faithless to him.
> She went away from him to her father's house, to Bethlehem-
> Judah.
> She was there for four months.
> Her husband arose and went after her to speak to her heart to
> bring her back.
> His servant was with him and a pair of asses.
> She brought him into her father's house.
> The girl's father saw him and was happy to meet him.
> His father-in-law, the girl's father, took hold of him and he sat
> with him for three days.
> They ate, they drank, and they spent the night there.

The story does not tell us why the girl went home to her father, only that "she was faithless," *wattizneh*. This term, often translated "played the harlot," does not always imply sex. The verb *znh* describes the lack of fidelity, the breach of contract between wife and husband or between Israel and God. Ancient marriage was not an egalitarian relationship. The wife was subordinate to her husband, and if she did not show proper and exclusive fidelity, she acted faithlessly, *znh*. Our story does not imply any particular action, and going home to her father for four months may have been enough to constitute "faithlessness." When it begins to be clear that she will not come back, the Levite goes to get her.

There is no major rupture in the social fabric here, just a minor difficulty. He goes in a conciliatory mood to **speak to her heart to bring her back.** Shechem spoke to Dinah's heart (Gen. 34:3), God will speak to Israel's (Hos. 2:16). The phrase describes the act of a superior who reassures his alienated or anxious subordinate partner. The Levite wants to restore his former situation, and his *pilegesh* doesn't seem to mind. She brings him to her father, who receives him with joy and great hospitality. The Levite could have gone after her in a righteous rage, for *qin'ah*, "jealousy," or righteous indignation, is an appropriate response of the husband/master whose wife has broken trust. Alternatively, the girl and her father could have met him with hostility. But instead we have an amicable scene of good fellowship.

The story makes no mention of coercion. The girl may have been ready to return, and according to law, she has to return. As far as we know, she would not have had the right to divorce the Levite. Bedouin customs suggest that the father could have given her a refuge rather than giving her back to a husband, but Bedouin customs might not apply. The narrator is not interested in these matters, and does not indicate whether any negotiations may have been going on. The story relates only that the visit was in good spirits.

Part 2. Do not spend the night among strangers! (Judg. 19:5–13)

> It happened that on the fourth day, they arose in the morning to go.
>
> The girl's father said to his son-in-law, "Take a morsel of bread for yourself and afterward you can go."
>
> They sat and ate, the two of them together, and they drank.
>
> The girl's father said to the man, "Please stay over, and be gladdened."

The man arose to go, but his father-in-law pressed him and he
returned and stayed there.

He arose early on the fifth day to go and the girl's father said,
"Please, eat to satisfy your heart."
They tarried till the day was high and the two of them ate.
The man got up to leave, he and his concubine and his lad.
His father-in-law said to him, "The day is waning toward
evening. Stay and sleep here. The day is declining. Stay here
and be gladdened. You can get up early in the morning and
be on your way and go home."
The man did not agree to stay over.
He arose and went and came to the area of Jebus, which is
Jerusalem, and he had with him a pair of laden asses and his
concubine was with him.

They were at Jebus and the day was far spent, and his servant
said to his master, "Let us turn in to this Jebusite city and
spend the night in it."
His master said to him, "We will not turn in to a foreign city
where there are no Israelites. We will pass on to Gibeah."
He said to his servant, "Come and we will approach one of the
places and spend the night in Gibeah or in Ramah."

The Levite stays three days and then a fourth, and even tarries on the
fifth day. The girl's father is a gracious host, sharing whatever he has. He
cannot be a rich man, or he would have been able to marry his daughter
off as a full wife rather than as a concubine; nevertheless, he is the very
model of hospitality. He may even go to excess, perhaps to delay his
daughter's departure. The story emphasizes *the two of them together,* the
man and his father-in-law. This is the story of relationships between
men.

On the fifth day, the man leaves too late to reach home by nightfall.
The focus is on the man, and the verbs are all in the masculine. And his
concubine was with him: he has succeeded in his mission to get her
back. The manservant is not mentioned, though he speaks in the next
verse, but the presence of the concubine is significant for what has happened, and for what is yet to happen.

As night begins to fall, the Levite turns down his servant's suggestion that they remain there, for he does not want to spend the night among foreigners. Traveling in ancient times could be dangerous; an individual's safety depended largely on the deterrent power of his family, who would avenge any harm. Peace among strangers was like the Cold War of the twentieth century: it was maintained because all parties were conscious of the dire consequences of breaking the standoff. But the very presence of travelers could arouse suspicion—"What are they doing here?"—and suspicion might generate hostility: "Who needs them here?" And the hostility might lead to aggression: "We'll show them who's boss!" No fear of revenge would check this aggression, so to prevent the eruption of violence against travelers, cultures often develop elaborate codes of hospitality. Through these protocols and conventions, distrust can be alleviated and the traveler safely harbored. But such codes depend on a common sense of trust, and this trust might not exist among different peoples. Kings can ensure the safety of travelers with a letter, much like a rational passport, declaring that the king himself would avenge death or injury to the bearers. But there is no royal authority in Israel, and the Levite doesn't trust the Jebusites to observe the codes of hospitality. With great dramatic irony, the narrator reports the Levite's preference to stay in the Israelite towns of Gibeah or Ramah. There he will be safe!

Part 3. Lodgings in Gibeah (Judg. 19:15–21)

> They passed on and continued walking and the sun was beginning to set near Gibeah, which belonged to Benjamin.
> They turned in there to go in to spend the night in Gibeah.
> He came and sat in the city square.
> Nobody was gathering them home to spend the night.
> And look! An old man came from his work, from the field, in the evening.
> The man was from Ephraim and lived in Gibeah, and the men of the place were Benjaminites.
> He lifted his eyes and saw the man sitting in the town square and nobody gathering him home to spend the night.
> The old man said, "To where are you going and from where are you coming?"
> He said to him, "We are passing from Bethlehem of Judah to the far side of Mount Ephraim. That is where I am from. I went to Bethlehem of Judah, I am on my way to the House of YHWH, but nobody gathers me home. We have straw and

food for our asses. I also have bread and wine for your maidservant and the manservant together with your servants.
We lack nothing."

The old man said, "Peace be to you. I will take care of all your
lack. Just do not spend the night in the square."

He brought him to his house, with fodder for the asses.

They washed their feet and ate and drank.

The man has made his first miscalculation: his trust in the men of
Gibeah is misplaced. He sits in the town square, but no one offers him
hospitality. An old man comes from the fields who is not a native of the
town—he is from Mount Ephraim, where the Levite lives, while the
people of the town are from Benjamin, a different Israelite tribe—and
invites them to stay at his house. Without a doubt, the Benjaminites
who lived in the town should have taken the travelers home, but perhaps
it was not wise for the man from Ephraim to do so? After all, the
Ephraimite himself was an outsider. Could he have had the authority
and trust to offer hospitality to strangers? If the Benjaminites were suspicious of strangers, might they not suspect that the Ephraimite host and
the Levite from Ephraim were in collusion, that the outsider-host was
betraying the town's secrets to spies? But the Levite really has no other
invitation. He is a proud man and assures the Ephraimite that he has
enough provisions for both himself and his maidservant and goes, with
his entourage, to the man's house, where they relax and feast. This may
be his second miscalculation.

Part 4. An outrage in Israel (Judg. 19:22–26)

While they were making merry, look! The men of the city,
worthless men, surrounded the house.

They pounded on the door and said to the owner, the old man,
thus: "Send out the man who came to your house and let us
know him."

The owner of the house went out to them and said to them,
"Don't, my brothers, please don't do evil, for the man has
come to my house. Do not do this outrage. Here are my virgin daughter and his concubine. I will send them out and
you can degrade them and do to them whatever is good
in your eyes. But toward this man—do not do this act of
outrage."

The men did not listen to him.

The man grabbed his concubine and sent her out to them outside.

They knew her and raped her all night till morning and sent her away as the dawn was rising.

The woman came toward morning and fell at the entrance to the man's house where her husband/master was, until light.

The cry **"let us know him"** must have come as a shock to the Levite, who had bypassed Jebus in order to come "home" to Israelite Gibeah. Instead, he now realizes, he has come to Sodom. "Know"? The term suggests carnal knowledge. The word "sodomy" has come to mean homosexuality because the men of Sodom want to "know" their visitors. But there is really no homosexuality or any other kind of sexuality either in the Sodom story or here. Rape is not a sexual act. It is an act of hostility and aggression, not sexual interest. **"Let us know him"** may indeed mean carnal knowledge, but the proposed rape of the traveler is like the rape of newcomers in jail. The purpose of such a rape is neither enjoyment nor love; it is the assertion of dominance and the dishonoring of the man forced to submit.

Sexuality is often tied to power. Rape is violently attached to power, and male rape no less so. Of course, "to know" may not refer to carnal knowledge, and the men may mean that they want to "know what this man is made of." They may want to assault him, to rough him up without raping him. Whether or not the "knowledge" will be carnal, the purpose of it is to emasculate the traveler, strip him of his pride and his honor, and render him submissive and nonthreatening. The townsmen aren't interested in the old man's offer. They have no need to humiliate him or show him who is boss; after all, the text tells us four times, he is old. But when they get their hands on the traveler's concubine, and "know her" sexually, they will assert their "superiority" over the man, too. Controlling women is a mark of manhood in patriarchal societies; failure to protect others from violating her emasculates the man.

Just as Lot in Genesis offered his virgin daughters to assuage the mob, so here the Ephraimite offers his virgin daughter and the traveler's concubine. Like people throughout the ages, both the old man and Lot address the sexual aspect of rape rather than the hostility that fuels it. The host, the ancient code of hospitality, and the storyteller are interested primarily in relations among *men*. To save the guest under his roof, the host will give up the nonessential persons there: the young women. To attack a guest is a *nebalah,* an outrage that flouts social morality. The concubine is not the Ephraimite's guest, she is only part of his guest's entourage, and his obligations are to the Levite himself.

The host betrays his knowledge that the attack is about control and dominance by the language he uses, **"you can degrade them and do to them whatever is good in your eyes."** This phraseology is familiar to the reader of the Bible from a very different context. After Hagar ceased to see Sarai as superior to her, Sarai complained to Abram that her own status had diminished. Abram then handed Hagar back into Sarai's control with the same ironic expression, "Do to her what is good in your eyes." And immediately, the narrative tells us, "Sarai abused her." Those who want to assert their own power over another do so by acting in ways that please them by degrading the other. The host has no illusions that the women will be well treated. Nevertheless, he offers them up in order to save his guest. In turn, the Levite quickly shows his "consideration" for the host and his safety, and sends his concubine out to the mob.

From the viewpoint of wives and daughters, this is a horrifying situation. From the viewpoint of husbands and fathers, it is tragic. Heads of household do not want to have to sacrifice their children and/or their wives. However, they do have the power to do so, and in an extreme situation, they will sacrifice their dependents to save their own lives. Girls are the coin of the realm, the bounty that men exchange as they jockey for power and survival, and sometimes the bloody fields on which men contest for power. The Levite has undertaken a long and arduous journey to retrieve this girl, but when he sees that he has to give her up to save his own life, he does not hesitate.

The situation of the concubine in Gibeah is the same as that of Lot's daughters in Sodom, with one significant difference. In Sodom, the guests were really angels who turned on their luminous wattage to save themselves, Lot, and his daughters. But it is no longer the time of Genesis. The concubine in Gibeah cannot expect God to intervene to rescue her or the men any more than Jephthah's daughter could look to God to save her. The Gibeonites don't want the girls, and pay no attention to the host's offer. Their attention is focused on the stranger, their intention is to assert their own power. But when the girl is cast out to them, they rape her. Raping him might be a more direct way to humiliate the traveler, but gang-raping the girl will also show him who is boss. The assault is graphically clear, even though biblical Hebrew has no word for "rape." Literally the words mean "they knew her and tortured her"; the combined sense is they tortured her by "knowing" her carnally, one short phrase encapsulating a long night of violence. And then they send her away. There is no purpose in keeping her: the man must see that they have humiliated and dishonored him. But the result is her death.

Modern readers cannot but be appalled. From our perspective, such "sacrifice" is a scandalous disregard for the personhood and lives of daughters and wives. We treat each individual as a separate person, not as an appendage of the father/husband. We can find no justification for sacrificing a daughter or a wife to save a man, and are horrified at such biblical stories. Ironically, our contemporary perspective on the individuality of family members owes much to biblical law, which took major steps toward viewing children as separate from their parents. Ancient Near Eastern laws called for children to be punished for the misdeeds of their parents. If, for example, a builder erected a wall that fell on a child and killed him, the laws of Hammurabi (ca. 1760 B.C.E.) provide that the young child of the builder be put to death. Not so Exodus and Deuteronomy, which did not allow such vicarious punishment. Moreover, the millennia of consideration of the biblical concept of the sanctity of human life have contributed to our stated (if not always observed) reluctance to sacrifice children and spouses. So we must ask: were the biblical authors and readers of this story blind to the personhood of these women? Did they consider such actions simply a part of patriarchy, regrettable but necessary? Or did they view Lot's offer and the Levite's sacrifice as an abuse, a rupture in the social order, a tragedy even when "necessary"?

Part 5. The bloody body (Judg. 19:27–30)
> Her husband/master arose in the morning.
> He opened the doors of the house and went out to go on his way.
> And look! The woman, his concubine, was lying at the entrance to the house and her hands were on the threshold.
> He said to her, "Get up and let's go!"
> There was no one to answer.
> He placed her on the ass. And the man arose and went to his place.
> He came to his house and took the knife and took hold of his concubine and cut her through her bones into twelve pieces.
> He sent her throughout the whole territory of Israel.
> And it happened that everyone who saw it said, "Such has never been, has never been seen, since the day the Israelites came

up from Egypt until this very day. Take note of her, take counsel and deliberate."

In the morning, the man seems prepared to leave without his concubine. The affair is over; he has given her away, and she is lost to him. Instead, he sees her stretched out in front of the house, with her hand on the threshold. With her last strength, she has reached out for the "safety" and "protection" of the home. **"Get up and come!"** he says to her. He shows no solicitude for what might have happened to her, no gratitude for having saved his life. A horrible, inhumane monster, we think. But there is another side to this command to **come!** The Levite wants her to accompany him. He does not react like the husbands of women raped by the enemy in today's ethnic wars: he does not disown her, does not react with revulsion at the thought that she might have had sexual relations with another man, and does not act as if her victimization were a source of shame. He will not treat her any differently than he had before. In his eyes, he has done what he had to do to save his life and the life of his host. Like the patriarchs Abraham and Isaac as they traveled in Egypt and in Gerar, the Levite has given his wife to strangers so that they would not harm him: share your wife and spare your life! It is time to go home.

The Levite may not have imagined, might not have let himself imagine, what befell his concubine. He too has been misled by the common conception of rape as an act of sex rather than aggression. When he sent her out to the mob, he realized that they would have sexual relations with her. But he may not have envisaged, or he may have been in denial, of the fact that they would treat her brutally and violently. And now he is in denial of the extent of the calamity that she has suffered. Seeing her lying there, he does not realize that she is not sleeping. And when she does not answer, he slings her on his ass and goes home.

The story does not let us know if she was dead on the doorsill, died on the donkey, or was even still alive when she got home. The Septuagint cannot bear the silence, and tells us that she did not answer him because she was dead. The Hebrew Bible prefers to be silent on this matter, and to let the reader speculate. It does show us the horrible aftermath. The man raises a slaughtering knife, the *ma'akelet,* the same type of knife that Abraham raised over Isaac's head. He hacks her body into twelve parts and distributes them throughout Israel.

What is the Levite doing? This is not the proper treatment of the dead. It is an act that horrifies everyone, for it is an act **Such as has never**

been, has never been seen, since the day the Israelites came up from Egypt until this very day. This, of course, was the man's intention, and the Septuagint makes this intention explicit, reading, He commanded the people he sent thus, "this is what you should say to every man of Israel: 'has there been such a thing from the day the Israelites came out of Egypt until this very day?' " This is a grisly act and carries a serious curse. It is a bizarre and grotesque foreshadowing of King Saul's first kingly act, for Saul would also send out butchered body parts to muster the land. But there is a difference: he sends out pieces of an ox. And he articulates the curse: Whoever does not respond will have his oxen butchered as this ox was butchered (1 Sam. 11:7). The dismemberment of a woman's body rather than that of an ox shows the monstrous nature of the event at Gibeah. Feeling himself abused, the man now abuses his concubine's corpse and uses it to inscribe and dramatize his message. Her torn body is a symbol of the torn shreds of the social fabric: what has been done to her has already been done to the bonds of trust between Israelites.

◇ *Act II. Israel Against Benjamin (Judg. 20)*

Part 1. All Israel gathers (Judg. 20:1–11)

> All the Israelites came out.
>
> The Assembly gathered as one man, from Dan until Be'er Sheba and the land of Gilead to YHWH in Miṣpah.
>
> The whole people, all the tribes of Israel, stood in the assembly of the people of God, four hundred thousand sword-wielding foot soldiers.
>
> The Benjaminites heard that the Israelites came up to Miṣpah. The Israelites said, "Tell us how this evil thing happened!"
>
> The Levite, the murdered woman's husband/master, said, "To Gibeah in Benjamin I came, I and my concubine, to spend the night. The householders of Gibeah came and surrounded me, the house, at night. Me, they intended to kill, and my concubine they abused and she died. I took hold of my concubine and I hacked her up and I sent her throughout the whole field of Israel's patrimony, for they have done a depraved act, an outrage in Israel.
>
> "Look! You are all Israelites. Consider the matter and bring a plan now."
>
> All the people arose as one man, saying, "We will not go to our tents and our houses. This is what we will do to Gibeah. We

> will cast a lot and take ten men out of a hundred from each
> tribe, a hundred from a thousand, a thousand from a myriad
> to bring provisions for the people for their coming to Gibeah
> of Benjamin because of all the outrage it did in Israel."
> Every man of Israel gathered to the city as one man, comrades.

The concubine is gone, but the calamity goes on. The horrendous message works: all of Israel assembles **as one man** waiting to hear what has happened. The Levite relates the event, telling the truth but not the whole truth. He emphasizes the impact of the attack on him: **"the householders . . . surrounded me . . . me they intended to kill, and my concubine they abused and she died."** To the Levite, as to his hearers, the attack on the girl was an attack on him and, by extension, of any Israelite traveling among his fellow Israelites. He also claims that they were going to kill him. Having seen what happened to the concubine when they "knew" her, he realizes what would have happened to him. He dismembered the corpse because they had committed outrage in Israel. Attacking him was an outrage; raping her to death was an outrage. But the Levite omits the role that he himself played in the tragedy; neither he nor the Ephraimite considered that their offer of the girls or even sending the concubine to the mob was an outrage of that magnitude.

The people react as one: they will punish Gibeah for the outrage. Ironically, Israel is now united for the first time since the Israelites came from Egypt. All earlier actions had been local and involved only each area's tribes. Now the whole people, even the tribes from Gilead, is united. But this unity is against one of their own. The tribe of Benjamin has not joined this mustering of all the tribes. They have been invited: the Levite hacked his concubine into twelve pieces and sent them throughout the land. Since there were twelve tribes, he must have also sent a piece to the tribe of Benjamin. Benjamin, however, chose not to join Israel at this point. Once again, the Greek version makes the relationships explicit, for it reads: "The Benjaminites heard that all the Israelites had gone up to Mispah and they refrained from coming among them." And so Israel is united against Benjamin.

Part 2. Refuge in sovereignty (Judg. 20:12–15)

> The tribes of Israel sent men in all the tribes of Benjamin, saying, "What is this evil that occurred among you? Now give us the worthless men in Gibeah. We will kill them and we will excise evil from Israel."

The Benjaminites were not willing to listen to their brothers the
   Israelites.

The Benjaminites assembled from the cities to Gibeah to go out
   to war against the Israelites.

There were mustered from the Benjaminites of the cities
   twenty-six thousand sword-wielders apart from the inhabitants of Gibeah, from which were mustered seven thousand
   select men.

The Israelites demand that the tribe of Benjamin deliver the perpetrators. Israel will purge the evil by punishing the evildoers. They give a
good reason: the men who committed this act are "worthless men," *benê
beliyya 'al,* a judgment the narrator of the story has already made. This is
not accidental language. Deuteronomy provides an example of *benê beliyya 'al,* men who convince their city to worship foreign gods. Israel is to
utterly destroy the city, burn it and make everything in it anathema
(Deut. 13:13–19), such *benê beliya 'al* have to be eradicated from Israel. In
this case, Israel's demand seems very measured; but the Benjaminites refuse and prepare for battle.

At first it seems strange that the Benjaminites would go to war to protect the men of Gibeah. It is unlikely that they had such a different sense
of morality, that they did not find the rape-murder an outrage, that they
approved of the behavior of the Gibeonites. Rather, the Gibeonites find
themselves—in their own eyes—in a situation similar to that in which
the Levite found himself in Gibeah. The Gibeonites surrounded the
house and threatened force against the Levite; the tribes are doing the
same to Benjamin and Gibeah. There is a question of territory here, of
the protection of boundaries. The tribes are invading Benjamin's turf
and jurisdiction, demanding extraterritorial rights to punish an event
that happened within the tribe of Benjamin. In the absence of a nation-
state and supreme ruler, Benjamin is concerned with its own sovereignty.

The Benjaminites may have another reason for refusing to hand over
the men of Gibeah. They themselves may be enmeshed in the very code
of hospitality that the Gibeonites violated. The men of Israel are looking **in all the tribes of Benjamin.** The men of Gibeah are somewhere,
having taken refuge in their tribe. As a result, the men of Benjamin may
be honor-bound not to give them up. The Greek story of Paktyas illustrates the importance of protecting the accused. Paktyas rebelled against
the king of Persia and fled to Kyme. When the king demanded his extra-

dition, the Kymians consulted the Branchidai oracle, who told them to surrender the man. Unbelieving, they consulted the oracle a second and third time, until the oracle told them to give up the man or perish. Instead, they sent him to another city, which did deliver him in return for a large reward. This reward, says Herodotus, began the defeat of the Ionian cities. One must protect the outsider seeking refuge; surely one cannot protect one's own tribesmen any less.

The personal relationship between the Levite and the men of Gibeah is mirrored by the political relationship between the Benjaminites and the rest of Israel. The whole calamity began because the men of Gibeah were suspicious of and inhospitable to a fellow Israelite whom they viewed as an outsider, a stranger to the tribe of Benjamin, a foreigner. The whole tribe of Benjamin now manifests the same view. It sees itself as distinct from the rest of Israel and views the other Israelites as an invasive force. They do not consider "Israel" a national entity with jurisdiction over the tribes. Rather than join the rest of Israel in turning against Gibeah, the men of Benjamin prepare to defend their integrity and independence. In the aftermath of the murder of the concubine, the old tribal confederation cannot hold. With no central authority, the legal system depends on achieving consensus. The distrust and otherness felt by the men of Benjamin prevents such cooperation and becomes a self-fulfilling prophecy. The system breaks down and the men of Israel react to Benjamin's separation and otherness with aggression: they attack Benjamin in a total civil war.

But first the men of Israel turn to the divine oracle for sanction and direction. Before they attack,

Part 3. The war (Judg. 20:17–48)
>   They arose and went up to Bethel and inquired of God.
>   The Israelites said, "Who will go up first in the battle with the
>   men of Benjamin?"
>   YHWH said, "Judah is first."

God acts as the leader of Israel, arbitrating the rivalry among the tribes. When the first battle results in a dreadful defeat for Israel,

>   The Israelites went and cried before YHWH till the evening and
>   inquired of YHWH, "Shall I continue to approach for battle
>   with the Benjaminites my brothers?"
>   YHWH said, "Go up against him."

Then, when the second day of battle also resulted in slaughter for Israel,

> All the Israelites and all the people went up and came to Bethel
> and cried and stayed there before YHWH and fasted on that
> day until the evening and offered burnt offerings and com-
> munion offerings before YHWH.
> The Israelites inquired of YHWH (the ark of the covenant of
> God was there in those days).
> Pinhas son of Elazar the son of Aaron stood before it in those
> days saying, "Should I continue to go out to battle with the
> Benjaminites my brothers, or should I cease?"
> YHWH said, "Go up! For tomorrow I give it into your hand."

On the third day, Benjamin was defeated: **YHWH smote Benjamin
before** Israel. The Israelites slaughtered twenty-five thousand fighting
men. Six hundred men fled to the desert and hid for four months as the
Israelites destroyed all of Benjamin and burned their cities.

There is irony in the telling of this war. Israel has acted as it believed
it should: all serious questions were directed to God, mediated by the
priests. This is the pattern that God prescribed to Moses for Joshua his
successor-leader: "He will stand before Elazar the priest and he will inquire for him by means of the decision of the Urim and Thummim. By
his mouth they will go out, by his mouth they will come in, he and all
the Israelites with him and all the congregation" (Num. 7:1). Israel has
behaved perfectly, inquiring of God through a descendant of Elazar at
each step of the battle. And God has given them victory. Israel has
behaved properly and the system works! There is just one problem:
this battle was not against enemies, it was against one of their
own, and the result is that a tribe of Israel has been almost totally destroyed. Only six hundred Benjaminite men remain. The threatened
death of the Levite, which led to the real death of the concubine, has
now led to the deaths of many, and to the threatened death of a whole
tribe.

The people, who never intended total destruction of Benjamin, are
filled with remorse and agony. They recognize the need to repopulate
the tribe, to put the past hostility behind them and build for the future.
But there are only six hundred male survivors—and no females! What
has happened to the women of Benjamin? We can only speculate that
they were killed or carried away into a captivity from which there is no
return. Such is the fate of the women in war. The second aftermath of

the concubine's rape and murder has been the rape and murder of all the women of the tribe of Benjamin.

◇ *Act III. Murder for Marriage (Judg. 21)*

Part 1. Let not a tribe perish from Israel! (Judg. 21:1–14)

> The men of Israel had taken an oath at Mispah: "No man among us will give his daughter as a wife to Benjamin."
> The people came to Bethel and sat there before God.
> They lifted their voices and cried a great cry.
> They said, "Why, YHWH God of Israel, has this happened in Israel, to muster out of Israel one tribe?"
>
> The next morning, the people arose and built an altar and offered up burnt offerings and communion offerings.
> The Israelites said, "Who was it who did not come up to YHWH in the congregation of all the tribes of Israel?"
> For there was a great oath against whoever did not come up to YHWH at Mispah thus, "He will surely be put to death!"
> The Israelites had remorse toward Benjamin their brother, and they said, "A tribe of Israel has fallen today. What can we do for those who remain for wives, since we have sworn by YHWH not to give them our daughters for wives?"
> They said, "Which one of the tribes of Israel didn't go up to God at Mispah? Look! No one came to the camp from Jabesh-Gilead to the congregation."
> The people took a reckoning and there was no one there from the inhabitants of Jabesh-Gilead.
>
> The congregation sent twelve thousand warriors, commanding them thus: "Go and strike the inhabitants of Jabesh-Gilead by sword, women and children too. This is what you should do: every male and every sexually experienced woman you will totally destroy."
> There were found among the inhabitants of Jabesh-Gilead four hundred virgin daughters who had never known a man sexually.
> They brought them to the camp at Shiloh in the land of Canaan.
>
> The whole congregation sent and spoke to the Benjaminites at the Rock of Rimmon, calling "peace" to them.

> Benjamin returned at that time and was given the women who
> were kept alive from Jabesh-Gilead.
> They didn't find them an exact match.

Now that the war is over, the Israelites no longer want Benjamin to disappear. But matters are not so simple. Their previous desire, expressed in their oath not to give their daughters as wives to Benjamin, now limits their actions. Like Jephthah before them, they have no way to control this oath; there is no one to release them from it or to absolve them from the responsibility of breaking it. As a result, they are controlled and coerced by their own previous will, which they themselves provided with divine authority. They cannot revive Benjamin by marrying their daughters to the survivors.

A solution suggests itself from the curse implicit in the dismembered body of the concubine. Once again, this story contains a reverse mirroring of the coming story of Saul. Saul made the curse explicit when he sent around the dissected pieces of ox: "Whoever does not come, his oxen will be butchered." By his action, Saul was able to rally Israel to rescue Jabesh-Gilead from the Ammonites. But this same curse, implicit in the body of the concubine, only brings further death, for Jabesh-Gilead, the very city that Saul will later rescue, did not come to the convocation of tribes. Like the Benjaminites, they separated themselves from the whole of Israel. And so they incurred the retaliatory butchery symbolized by the concubine's body. With tragic irony, this section of the story uses all the terms of Israel's unity and solidarity: the 'am, "people," 'edah, "congregation," and qahal, "assembly." Israel is acting as one, but because Jabesh-Gilead excluded itself from these, it has become "other."

Jabesh-Gilead was intimately involved in the career of Saul. His first act of kingship was the rescue of Jabesh-Gilead (1 Sam. 11); the people of the city were always faithful to him. They buried him (1 Sam. 31:11–13), and later buried his remaining sons (2 Sam. 21:12–14). The mention of Jabesh-Gilead focuses attention on all the correspondences between this story and the accounts of Saul's career. Saul was from the tribe of Benjamin; his home was in Gibeah and he established his court there (1 Sam. 10:26); and he was crowned at Mispah. The worthless ones, benê beliyya-'al, refused to accept his kingship until he proved himself a leader in the rescue of Jabesh-Gilead (1 Sam. 10:27). He mustered all the tribes of Israel by sending out pieces of a butchered carcass and brought them to save Jabesh-Gilead. Even the detail that six hundred men of Benjamin hid at the Rock of Rimmon resonates with the fact that Saul and

Jonathan's battle against the Philistines began with six hundred encamped under a *rimmon* (pomegranate) tree (1 Sam. 14:2). Finally, Saul overrides his oath in order to spare Jonathan (1 Sam. 14:45). So many correspondences cannot be coincidental. Does this association with the nadir of Israel's history taint Saul's kingship? More probably, it reflects well on it, for Saul's acts are inversions of this story's with much better effect. Saul butchers an ox, not a woman; he saves Jabesh-Gilead rather than destroy it; he is not driven to violence by his own oath. Saul's campaign comes out very well in comparison to this story, and it is most likely that the story is subtly hinting what might have happened here had Saul been king.

There is only one purpose for this war against Jabesh-Gilead: to provide wives for Benjamin. But Israel doesn't want the wives of the men of Jabesh-Gilead, for it now sees the city as "other." The story emphasizes that Israel took **virgin daughters who had never known a man sexually.** The phrase **who had never known a man** specifies that the girls are sexually virgin. The storyteller then adds *lemiškab zakar,* literally "for sexual intercourse," to indicate that these girls are blank slates, they have not had Jabesh-Gilead "stamped" on them through sexual intercourse. Their pristine nature makes them fit to be married off to Benjamin, and the surviving men of Benjamin are called back into Israel and given wives.

When Israel attacks Jabesh-Gilead, it hikes the cycle of violence up yet another notch. The violent rape and death that first came upon the concubine and then befell the women of Benjamin is now visited on a city that was not a party to the war. And the tale is not yet done. There are only four hundred virgins in Jabesh-Gilead, not enough to go around. Two hundred Benjaminites still don't have wives.

Part 2. The rape of the Shiloh women (Judg. 21:15–24)

> The people had remorse for Benjamin, for YHWH had made a breach in the tribes of Israel.
>
> The elders said, "What shall we do for wives for those who remain, for all the women from Benjamin have been destroyed?"
>
> And they said, "Let Benjamin have a surviving inheritance and let not a tribe in Israel be erased. We cannot give them wives from our daughters, for the Israelites took an oath, 'cursed be the one who gives a wife to Benjamin!' "
>
> They said, "Look! There is a festival of YHWH in Shiloh every year, which is from north of Beth-El, east of Mesila, which

goes from Beth-El to Shechem and from the Negev to Le-
vonah."

They commanded the men of Benjamin: "Go and take ambush
in the vineyards. Watch and look! When the girls of Shiloh
come out to dance in circles, you will come out of the vineyards and snatch for yourself each man his wife from the
daughters of Shiloh, and go to the land of Benjamin.

"If their fathers or their brothers come to fight with us, we will
say to them, 'Spare them, for we have not taken for each his
wife in battle. For you are not giving them to them so as to
incur guilt.' "

The men of Benjamin did this and they took wives to the exact
number from the dancing girls that they kidnapped.

They went back to their patrimony and built cities and lived in
them.

The men of Israel went back at that time, each man to his tribe
and to his family, and they went out from there, each man
to his own patrimony.

The men of Israel cannot provide their daughters to the remnant of
Benjamin because they took an oath not to do so. But, they reason, the
fact that they cannot *give* their daughters does not mean their daughters
cannot be *taken*. In normal times, an attack against a daughter was an attack against the family, and the family would retaliate. But now the men
of Israel withdraw the protection that they owe their own daughters.
They collude with the attackers as they provide the opportunity for the
surviving men of Benjamin to attack their daughters in a rape-capture
reminiscent of the rape of the Sabine women in Roman mythology. As
the girls dance at a festival in Shiloh, each man should **"take ambush"**
and **"snatch"** a wife. These are violent terms. At a festival, precisely
when women should be able to dance without fear, the men will attack.
Should their fathers and brothers complain, the elders will explain that
in this way they do not incur the guilt of breaking their oath, and the
Benjaminites get their wives.

The rape-capture of the girls at Shiloh is the final betrayal. Violence
against one woman by guilty men has led to violence against those who
stood by the guilty men (the "Other") to violence against those who
stayed out of it (the neutral "innocent" bystanders) to violence against
the self. The violence turns inward, against the very heart of Israel,
against girls who had not declared themselves apart from Israel either by

attacking Israelites or by refusing to join them in an attack on the "Other." These daughters are not culpable even of associating with the other side: there can be no question of punishment or revenge. They are subjected to a brutalizing experience solely to further the relationship between two groups of men.

We have been here before. The whole story started when the men of Benjamin violated the security of the Levite. To protect his guest, the Ephraimite offered his daughter; to protect his host and himself, the Levite sacrificed his woman. The Levite and the rest of Israel retaliated to punish the outrage and prevent it from happening again, and the catastrophe escalated. Now even the threat of retaliation is gone. The very men who declared Benjamin outside the pale, and used force against these outsiders, now declare them inside and promise not to use their force to protect their own family members. They encourage the men of Benjamin to violate Israelite families and take Israelite daughters with impunity: there will be no retaliation. To Israelite eyes, this is an emergency, and in emergencies, daughters are expendable. All this bloodshed has taught the men of Israel nothing about the need to acknowledge the personhood and lives of daughters and wives. The Levite treated his concubine as his to dispose of, the men of Israel regarded the virgins of Jabesh-Gilead as booty to be captured, and now the men of Israel equally disregard the personhood of Israelite girls: they are to be captured in peacetime as if in war.

All the bloodshed, the deaths of so many men and women and the threatened extinction of a national consciousness, have now come full circle to more violence against the young women of Israel. Horror continues to follow horror.

Epilogue (Judg. 21:25)
>In those days there was no king in Israel.
>Each man did what was right in his eyes.

The narrator caps the story with the message on which he began: **In those days there was no king in Israel. Each man did what was right in his eyes.** Now the reader can fully appreciate the tragic irony in these words, for what was right in the eyes of the people was not right at all. The reader is left anxiously awaiting an end to such abuses. Someone has to limit the authority of heads of household, someone has to prevent the power of men over their women from being carried to such extremes, someone has to direct the congregation of Israel. Someone has to protect society's vulnerable members! By the end of this story, the readers are ready to add their voices to the chorus of Israel's elders who said to Samuel, "Give us a king to rule us" (1 Sam. 8:5). The king will save Israel!

But, as readers of the Bible know, the kings did not save Israel, and the next book of the Bible, Samuel, once again uses stories about women to show the flaws in monarchy and its inability to create a just and holy society.

Kings to the Rescue?

THE STAGE has been set for the advent of a king. The reader is ready for a savior, and the book of Samuel begins quietly with a birth narrative. This literary pattern is used elsewhere in biblical composition and editing. The first chapter of Exodus tells of enslavement, the second relates the birth of Moses the liberator; Judges chapter 10, describes the Ammonite threat, chapter 11 relates the birth of Jephthah the redeemer. Judges 19–21 has demonstrated internal collapse and chaos; the first chapter of Samuel begins with the birth of the man who will oversee the transition to statehood. Somewhat surprisingly, the chapter is not about the birth of Saul, the first king. The naming of the baby, with its puns on the name Saul, hints that the story, or a similar one, may originally have been told about Saul or that it will ultimately lead to Saul. But the search for a savior will not be easy: first Samuel, then Saul, will prove not to be the one. Only the third leader, David, will found the dynasty that consolidates the institution of kingship.

At first, Saul looks like the solution. The story of his rescue of Jabesh-Gilead reverses the gory tale of the concubine and its aftermath. Instead of chaos, there is order. A dissected ox, not a butchered woman, musters the troops; Benjamin produces a king, not miscreants; war is waged against an external invader, not against one of the tribes; instead of the tribes destroying Jabesh-Gilead, they come to its rescue. National unity has replaced tribal infighting; Israel has been saved! But the following chapters begin to reveal Saul's flaws. He is a "democratic" king, sensitive to the desires of the people and responsive to them. Time after time, he acts in response to their needs. When the people are fearful before a battle, Saul stops waiting for Samuel and performs a sacrifice for them. When they want to bring Amalek's cattle home to sacrifice properly to God, Saul once again ignores Samuel's instructions and listens to the people. Today we appreciate such a responsive monarch, but to the biblical writer, people's desires were precisely the danger that required a king. When there was no king, says the end of Judges, "each person went according to the desires of his heart." A king was supposed to control them and bring them back when their inclinations lead them astray. A king responsive to the people's desires cannot prevent them from doing evil.

Saul does solve one of the problems that plagued Israel in the time of the judges. He took a battle vow, as Caleb, Jephthah, and the Israelite men did before him: "Whoever eats before the battle will be put to death" (1 Sam. 14:24). His son Jonathan, not hearing the vow, ate (1 Sam. 14:27). Like Jephthah's vow, Saul's oath has condemned his child to death. But Jonathan is a popular hero who has won the battle that day. The people demand that Jonathan be released, and Saul, ever responsive to their wishes, releases his son from the effect of his vow (1 Sam. 14:41–45). Saul has established a precedent: the king can override a vow. No longer will fathers and their children be trapped by the fathers' words. The tragedy of Jephthah's daughter and the girls at Shiloh will not be repeated. But this royal benefit was not enough. Saul's very action in annulling the vow is motivated by his desire to be sympathetic to the people, so he will not be able to save the Israelites from their own desires.

By this point, the narrator has directed Samuel's (and our) attention to Saul's successor, David, the true king who redeems Israel. David's philosophy of kingship is far different from Saul's. He is a monarch with a sense of power and authority. Saul had no palace or grandiose court. David set his political capital in the "city of David," Jerusalem, which he conquered with his own army. He made the city Israel's religious capital by bringing to it the ark of the Lord, the great religious icon of the Israelite tribes. He led the solemn procession, dancing before the ark while wearing a linen ephod, normally the garb of priests. Ever since the days of Joshua, carrying and guarding the ark had been the responsibility of the priests. David changed that, subverting the tradition by wearing priestly garb and playing a priestly role, dancing in near ecstasy before the ark and offering sacrifices of thanksgiving.

The radical nature of David's action comes out in his conversation with his wife Michal, who was watching from the window. The daughter of Saul shared her father's minimalist approach to kingship and took no part in the celebration of the priest-king. To her, the dignity of the kingly office was connected to reticence. Michal castigates David for behaving like one of the "empty ones"—the propertyless of Israel, which includes Levitical priests as well as those who joined David and Jephthah in the outlaw years. David answers with his certainty of the majesty of his office: God chose him over Saul, and whatever he may do, including acts far worse than Michal has seen, the people will honor him, for he is the divinely appointed king of Israel! With this, David expresses his concept of kingship and his primacy over norms and laws. First he usurped the kingship, now he will assert royal dominance over religious institutions. He claims freedom from worrying about what people will think. David seems to be unstoppable, and the next few chapters show the development of a powerful, imperial, and permanent monarchy.

But Israel's monarchy will not be totally without limits. In the very next story, Nathan, David's court prophet, brings a message from God: David is not to build God's temple. But the same message brings a promise: David's son will rule after him (as Saul's sons did not) and will be so successful that he will build the temple. Nathan's words contain a further message encoded in the very fact that he brings it. God has spoken to Nathan, not to David. David may usurp the prerogative of priests, and even install his sons as priests (2 Sam. 8:18). But the role of prophet is not so easily assured. Nathan is God's intermediary, and David is expected to submit to Nathan's mediating authority. The king is not to be the medium of God's communication with Israel, and David does not have ultimate authority. He has taken over control of the ark, which Joshua did not have; but he cannot be the prophet.

This restriction of David's kingship is accompanied by an enormous gift: his kingship is permanent. God may punish David's misbehaving descendants, but God will not withdraw the kingship from David's line. This is a promise of divine right for David's descendants: no one will be able to claim prophetic or divine support in order to create a revolution or usurp the throne.

In the next chapters (2 Sam. 8–10), David begins to create an empire, secure both within and without. He subdues the Philistines and annexes territory, reversing the strategic retreats of the Saul years. He defeats Israel's neighbors, commanding tribute from Aram and Tot, making vassals out of Edom and Moab. He develops a regularized bureaucracy and becomes the chief judge of Israel. He neutralizes the possibility of divided loyalties within Israel by co-opting Mephibosheth, the lone surviving son of Saul, bringing him to eat at the king's table, granting Saul's lands to him and putting Saul's steward Ziba in charge of them. With one gracious act, David commands the gratitude of those who might have been in the forefront of opposition. David's very genius for the gracious act and his taste for dominance became part of his reputation, and when he sent envoys to Ammon to offer condolences on the king's death, the Ammonites suspected that they were spies, humiliated them, and joined several Aramean states for war against Israel. After a climactic battle, the Arameans sued for peace, and Ammon stood alone.

This strong, unstoppable king seems the answer to the problem posed by the chaos at the end of the book of Judges. He will be able to prevent the people from doing whatever they might want to do. He will control the populace so that they abide by social norms to create a just society. But now, at the pinnacle of David's rise, come two stories about him and women. Together they reveal the flaws in the concept of king as social savior and provide serious indications that the Davidic kingship will not solve Israel's dilemma and will, in fact, become the problem rather than the solution.

"Off with His Head"
David, Uriah, and Bathsheba

IN THE MIDDLE of the story of the Ammonite wars, action slows and the tone of the narrative changes from historical chronicles to story. As chapter 11 of Second Samuel opens, the war retreats to the background of a tale about individuals.

◇ *Historical Prologue: Springtime in Jerusalem (2 Sam. 11:1)*

> It happened at the turn of the year, at the season when the kings
>   go out:
> David sent Joab and his servants and all of Israel.
> They slaughtered the Ammonites and laid siege to Rabbah.
> And David sat in Jerusalem.

The story opens with a typical narrative introduction, **It happened at the turn of the year.** It is spring: the rains have stopped and wars can begin again. **At the season when the kings go out,** continues the verse. Or does it? The actual written letters of the Bible (the *ktib*) read *maĺākîm,* with an aleph, which means "(when) the envoys (go out)." The Masoretes do not read this aleph; *melākîm,* "kings," is the Masoretic reading of the Hebrew text (the *qere*), and all the early translators say "the kings go out." Different philosophies inform the variant readings, different ideas about who should wage war, the king or his deputies. The people of Israel had asked for a king to lead them in battle (2 Sam. 8:20); they had chosen David for his ability as a warrior (2 Sam. 3:17–18). Reading **when the kings go out,** one expects the king to go, and this provides an ironic backdrop to David on his rooftop, perhaps anticipating that he in this story will not live up to our expectations. On the other hand, kings can die on the battlefield. Saul did, and Ahab was later wounded fatally during his attack on Rabbat-Ammon (1 Kings 22:35). David had already sent Joab to fight against the Arameans, only later meeting the Aramean kings on the battlefield. Later in David's life, his own men will beg him not to come to battle, lest his death "extinguish the light of Israel" (2 Sam. 21:15–17). Reading *maḷakim*, "when the envoys go out," encodes the expectation that an established king is needed at home and must leave the fighting to generals. Perhaps David is wise to attend to affairs in Jerusalem and foray out only during the most crucial battles.

In the end, it doesn't matter whether we read "kings" or "envoys," whether the people expect the king to be at home or on the battlefield. David does not go. Whatever his reasons, **David sat in Jerusalem.** We don't know it yet (nor does David), but this is the turning point of his reign. His defeat of the Aramean coalition was the height of his power. Staying in Jerusalem begins his decline, and the decline of our expectations that the Davidic kingship will save Israel.

◇ *Act I. David and Bathsheba (2 Sam. 11:2–6)*

Scene 1. The sight of a woman (2 Sam. 11:2–3)

> It happened toward evening.
> David got up from his couch and went walking on the roof of the king's house.
> He saw a woman bathing on the roof.
> The woman was very beautiful.

The story continues with another introductory **It happened** and a narrower time frame, *toward evening.* The first **"it happened,"** *vayehî,* lets us know we are entering a story and sets David at home in Jerusalem. This second *vayehî* begins the action. David gets up from his afternoon siesta and goes for a walk on the roof of the palace. Nothing unusual—toward evening, a cool breeze rises in Jerusalem. But, as he is walking on the roof, **he saw a woman bathing—the woman was very beautiful.** We join him this classic male gaze, just as we have shared the male gaze at countless odalisques in the history of art. Nothing has happened, but our attention has been arrested: we too look at this woman. We cannot see her, but David alerts and causes us to wonder about her: What does she look like? What is she wearing? Is she naked? Why is she there? Some modern readers have been very suspicious of Bathsheba, questioning her motives for being on her roof and suggesting that she went up to entice the king. But this suspicion is not warranted. If she wanted to bathe, where else would she be? It is spring, when the cisterns and water jugs on the roof stand full of the winter's rain. And when better to bathe but in the cool of late afternoon, after the day's work is done? To say that Bathsheba set out to entice the king is to say that violated women "were asking for it" because they smiled, or wore tight clothes, or went to a club. Bathsheba is enjoying a private moment—she thinks—and we violate it the moment we stop to contemplate her beauty.

The beauty of a woman is often a spur to male action. In the Bible, men like to acquire beautiful things. And beautiful women. Abram said to Sarai, "Indeed I know that you are beautiful" (Gen. 12:11), and this knowledge made him afraid that the Egyptians would want her, as indeed they did. Now, just as the king of Egypt reacted to Sarai's beauty, David, king of Israel, reacts to Bathsheba's. The story is conspicuous for what it does not say. Nowhere do we read "David loved her." David knows about love. Michal loved him in her youth (1 Sam. 18:20), as did Jonathan (1 Sam. 20:17). But David, whose very name probably means "beloved," doesn't love. For him it is enough that she is beautiful.

Scene 2: Affair with Bathsheba (2 Sam. 11:3–5)

> David sent to enquire about the woman.
> And he said, "Isn't that Bathsheba, daughter of Eliam, wife of Uriah the Hittite?"
> David sent envoys and took her.
> She came to him and he lay with her.
> She was purifying herself from impurity;
> And she went home.
> The woman conceived and sent to David. She said, "I am pregnant."

David gets his answer: it is Bathsheba, a married woman, which should be enough to end the story before it begins. A married woman is off limits to other men; even in his worst nightmare, Abram never expected the Egyptians to take his wife without killing him first. And he was right, for when Pharaoh learned that Sarai was Abram's wife, he was horrified and immediately gave her back. When Abimelech king of Gerar took Sarah, he had a vision that he would die for taking a man's wife, and when he told his court, they were all horrified. In the social order of Israel and the ancient world, adultery was a serious transgression. Ancient texts from Ugarit and Egypt call it "the great sin," and the law codes prescribe death for the adulterous parties. But David is not stopped by the knowledge that Bathsheba is married, and does not leave her alone. There have always been kings who considered themselves exempt from strictures against adultery. After all, even though according to ancient patriarchal conceptions the woman might belong to her husband, all subjects belong to the king! And whatever the king desires should be his. So Bathsheba's married state might not make a great difference to the imperial and imperious David, who told Michal that he could do whatever he would.

Bathsheba is not simply any married woman. Both her father, Eliam, and her husband, Uriah, are members of David's trusted inner "circle of thirty." They have been with him since his outlaw days, and Eliam was the son of the counselor Ahitophel (2 Sam. 23:34). To take Bathsheba is to violate the trust of a loyal lieutenant. But none of this matters: **David sent envoys and took her.** The story gives us no explanation for this bizarre action, shows us no motive, no deliberation, and no hesitation. It doesn't even tell us whether David disregards the seriousness of adultery and his long-standing relationship with her husband, or whether these are the factors that made him act. "I could be far less honorable and become base in my own eyes," he had said to Michal, "and I would still be honored by the maids of my servants" (2 Sam. 6:22). The challenge is there: Is there anything a king cannot do? And David, the imperial king, may be testing the limits.

But we do not know for sure. Motives and intentions of the story are left to the readers, who have come up with many versions of this story over the years. The narrator tells only what happened: he sent, he took, she came, he lay with her. The action of the story speeds up. The reader does not learn why David acted in this manner; to the story, it is irrelevant. Nor are we told of Bathsheba's reactions. Was she flattered or frightened? Attracted to David's fame and power or terrorized by them? By the rules of Israelite society, she had no right to consent. But in this new world of powerful kingship, did she have a right to refuse? For whatever reason, the deed was done. One verse of short clauses: he sent, he took, she came; he lay with her—the stark reality of an affair reduced to its essentials. But even these little verbs relate a crucial aspect of this affair: it was not clandestine. David stays in the palace and sends people out and in. He **sent to enquire** who she is; **David sent envoys and took her.** Later, he will send for Uriah and then send him back. The king is not hiding; he does not arrange to have a secret tryst at some inconspicuous place. Like Pharaoh taking Sarai (Gen. 12:15), David took. Bathsheba comes into the palace in sight of those who are bringing her and those who guard the entrance. David does not feel that he has to sneak her in: the king can act and the people will accept.

The focus now shifts to Bathsheba: **She was purifying herself from**

impurity; And she went home. The phrase *wehîʾ mitqaddešet miṭṭum'-ātāh* is often understood as a reference back to her initial bathing, "she had just purified herself after her period." Understood this way, the phrase alerts the reader to the state of her fertility, and sets the scene for David's later dealings with Uriah. Nevertheless, despite the appeal of this interpretation, it is anachronistically based on later rabbinic law, and is improbable for the time of David. It has two major flaws. First is the matter of timing. In rabbinic law, women immerse in a ritual pool, a *mikvah*, before the resumption of marital relations after their menstrual impurity. This immersion takes place one week after the menstrual flow ceases, normally between the twelfth and sixteenth days of their cycle. Sexual relationships after this immersion would quite frequently result in pregnancy. But the biblical period of menstrual impurity is one week long. Sexual relations would resume on the eighth day, a time very unlikely to produce pregnancy. The second flaw in this common understanding is that—in the Bible—women do not seem to wash after menstruation. The phrase "He shall wash his clothes and bathe in water," used regularly in Leviticus for the end of periods of impurity, is conspicuously absent in the passage on menstruation. Menstrual impurity is regular and time-linked, and time itself, rather than water, brings an end to it. The same is true for a woman's impurity after childbirth. She is to wait the appropriate period of the "blood-purification" and then bring a sacrifice and resume attending the temple (Lev. 12). Nothing is said about bathing as a rite of purification for women. Bathsheba's bath on the rooftop was simply that: a bath, and probably had nothing to do with postmenstrual purification.

There is one occasion for which Leviticus prescribes that a woman bathe: "If a man has carnal relations with a woman, they shall bathe in water and they shall be impure until the evening" (Lev. 15:18). When Bathsheba purifies herself, she is washing off the impurity that comes with all sexual relations, even licit ones. In our verse, the phrase does not refer back to the bath that she was taking when she was first introduced, but to postcoital purification. The verbal form (present participle) also implies the sequential arrangement: having purified herself, she returned home. Of course, the use of the term "purification" is another ironic element in the author's narration: she can purify herself from the ordinary pollution of sexual intercourse, but the defilement of illicit sexuality is not so easily washed off.

The mention of Bathsheba's purification, like the verbs that precede it, underline the unhurried, nonsecretive nature of this affair. There is no rush here. David does not send her away abruptly after he has satisfied himself. And she does not hurry off. If Levitical law can be taken as a guide for action in David's time, they may even have waited until evening. Their affair is deliberate, measured, slow, and obvious. And most likely, David didn't give it another thought.

Until Bathsheba sent word that she was pregnant.

◇ *Act II. David and Uriah (2 Sam. 11:5–15)*

Scene 1. Sending for Uriah (2 Sam. 11:5–9)

> David sent to Joab, "Send me Uriah the Hittite!"
> Joab sent Uriah to David,
> Uriah came to him.
> David asked after Joab's welfare and the people's welfare and the welfare (good progress) of the war.
> David said to Uriah, "Go home and wash your feet."
> Uriah went out of the king's palace and behind him was the king's "levy."
> Uriah lay down at the gate of the palace together with all the servants of his master.
> He didn't go down to his house.

Pregnancy changes everything. Even though people might see a woman come to the palace and stay with the king for a day, they could shrug off the evidence and go on with their lives. A baby makes such denial impossible. A wife's pregnancy while her husband is gone is undeniable evidence that she has not been faithful. Bathsheba's situation is very like that of the many daughters of Greece who gave birth to *parthenoi* "children born of a virgin." Their birth provoked a crisis as it disproved society's assumption that their unmarried mothers were chaste. Bathsheba's pregnancy cannot simply be ignored; it indicts her as an adulteress.

Adultery is a capital offense in the Bible, as it is in the rest of the ancient Near East. And the situation is not much different when the husband is away. Both the laws of Hammurabi (ca. 1760 B.C.E.) and the Middle Assyrian laws (ca. 1100 B.C.E.) consider the case of a wife whose man is forced to be away, captured in war, or in the army. If she has provisions to live on, she is expected to wait for her husband. The Middle Assyrian laws place a cap of two years on the time she is expected to remain faithful; the Hammurabi laws do not specify. But neither time frame is relevant here: Uriah has not been gone for years, and there is no hint that Bathsheba is indigent. There do not seem to be any grounds for leniency. The wife who does not wait, say the Hammurabi laws, should be cast in the river. Bathsheba is at risk. However much she might have been intimidated by kingship, she was not forcibly raped, and so common understanding would condemn her as an adulteress. She knows that she cannot stay silent. As David sent for her, now she sends to him—and thereby becomes like the other women who "send" in these historical books (Rahab and Deborah and Delilah and Jezebel), a player in history.

The stakes are not as high for David, who has brazenly acted as if the law of adultery doesn't concern him. He has openly brought Bathsheba to the palace for a liaison, and he should not have any problem riding out whatever scandalous talk her pregnancy would bring. But even though his position may make him invincible, Bathsheba is very vulnerable. Her stark words to David, the only words she says in the story, make it imperative that he do something. And so he takes action. He brings Uriah back to the palace to render a report on the war, and then sends him home for the night.

Uriah's return home would accomplish several things. It would muddy the evidence and make it possible for everyone to presume that the child was his. It would also solidify Bathsheba's relationship to Uriah and remind him of the joys of the marital home. For it is he who holds Bathsheba's fate in his hands. In ancient times, the head of the household had enormous power over the members of his household, power that extended to life and death. No one could stop Abraham from killing Isaac, or Jephthah from killing his daughter. In these early days of King David, the patriarchs may still have had this power, for the state did not become truly centralized until the time of Solomon. If so, Bathsheba will be in danger precisely from her husband, Uriah. When Judah heard that Tamar was pregnant, he ordered her to be burned; Uriah may do something similar to Bathsheba. Even if the monarchy in Israel had already succeeded in taking the power of death from the patriarchs, Bathsheba is still the one at risk. Both an adulterous wife and her lover are to be put to death, but only when they are convicted by witnesses or caught in flagrante. A pregnancy may "prove" the woman's adultery, but it does not indict the father, and public rumor would not be sufficient to convict a man. Once again, it is the woman who is in danger.

There is a way out of this perilous situation. Uriah, even if he no longer has the power of death, may still have the power to give Bathsheba life. Ancient Near Eastern laws, which also prescribed the death penalty for adultery, often allowed a husband to pardon his wife on the proviso that if he spares her, he also spares her lover. The sage's advice in Proverbs hints that Israel also allowed a husband to spare his wife and her lover, at least where there is not enough evidence to convict: "the fury of the husband will be passionate; he will show no pity on his day of vengeance. He will not have regard for any ransom. He will refuse your bribe, however great" (Prov. 6:34–35). The stakes are very high. If Uriah sleeps with his wife, he will assume that the baby was conceived that night. Even if he doesn't sleep with her, the public will assume that the baby is his. There will be no scandal to disgrace Uriah as a cuckold, and he will be able to pardon Bathsheba without dishonoring himself. But in order for Bathsheba to be safe, Uriah must go home.

Uriah does not go home. Instead, he sleeps publicly in the gate of the palace amid all the king's servants. This seems rather odd, and it raises the question of just how unsuspecting he is. It may, of course, be that he simply doesn't like his wife, or that he doesn't want to be tempted to sleep with her and then return to battle in a state of sexual contamination. Or he may suspect David's motives. He is one of the king's inner guard, acquainted with the palace personnel. It is not hard to imagine that someone has told him that the king sent for Bathsheba. Even if he knew nothing before his encounter with the king, he must have started to suspect. David sent for him by letter, and yet asked him only the most general questions about the welfare of the people, questions that could have been answered by letter. This itself might be enough to awaken a man's suspicions. Moreover, David cannot leave well enough alone. He not only sends Uriah, but *maś'at hammelek* went out after him. *Maś'at* is a cryptic term. It comes from the root *nś'*, "to carry, lift." Anything "lifted up" can be called: a levy taken in grain from the poor (Amos 5:3), the special collection for the priests (2 Chron. 24:6–9), or the food Joseph passed to the brothers at their banquet (Gen. 43:34); the smoke signal, *maś'at he-'aśan*, sent up when Gibeah was captured (Judg. 20:38, 40), to alert Israel (Jer. 6:1), and in a letter from the time of the siege of Lachish (letter 4:10). David sent something along with Uriah, perhaps a gift or food for a banquet. Or perhaps David sent someone and *maś'at hammelek*, which went "out" rather than "up," refers to the royal bearers. Josephus relates that the king's weapons-bearers went out after him, and the Qumran manuscript 4Q Sam seems to agree with this version. But why would the king send either people or things to accompany Uriah on a routine visit home? It is too much, and Uriah must have been suspicious.

Scene 2. A man of honor (2 Sam. 11:10–15)

> They told David thus: "Uriah didn't go down to his house."
>
> David said to Uriah, "Haven't you come from the way? Why didn't you go down to your house?"
>
> And Uriah said to David, "The ark and Israel and Judah are living in shacks and my master Joab and my master's servants are camping in the field, and I should go down to my house to eat and drink and lie with my wife? By your very life, I shall not do such a thing."
>
> David said to Uriah, "Stay here also today, and I will send you off tomorrow."
>
> Uriah stayed in Jerusalem that day and the next.
>
> David sent for him and he ate before him and he drank.
>
> He got him drunk and he went out in the evening to lie on his place with David's servants.
>
> And he didn't go down to his house.
>
> In the morning, David wrote a scroll to Joab and he sent it by Uriah's hand.
>
> He wrote in the scroll thus, "Bring Uriah into the very thick of hard battle and turn back behind him, and he will be struck and die."

Matters are not private around a palace, and David is told that Uriah slept at the gate. When David asks him why he did not go home, his answer reveals his sense of principle. "How can I," he exclaims, "eat and drink and enjoy my wife while the soldiers and my general are in the field and the ark lives in a shack?" Uriah is a man of piety. And a man with a strict sense of justice. A man of principle and a man of honor. Such a man can be dangerous. He will not be willing to lie down and play the cuckold, even if there is no public scandal. And just as he is unlikely to go through the motions of claiming paternity, he is unlikely to pardon Bathsheba. He might even feel that he has to avenge himself by committing a grand *crime of honor*, killing Bathsheba and possibly David himself.

Uriah's speech is full of hints that he will not let the majesty of a king override his own sense of honor. He refers to **"My lord Joab and my lord's servants."** In addressing the king, should he not say, "Joab my lord's servant and all my lord's servants"? The king should be "my lord," not the general, and one of his subjects should also make it clear that the fighting men are the king's servants and not "my lord's servants" right after "my lord Joab." Uriah concludes his speech with another subtlety, positioning himself vis-à-vis David: "By your very life," he says, a proper form of oath for kings and gods. But he doesn't add the polite "my lord the king." There is nothing servile about Uriah. He has, after all, been with David a long time. "He knew him when," and he knew him when David himself would have been out in the fields.

David tries again. He has Uriah stay another night, and plies him with liquor. But even inebriated, Uriah does not go home. His sense of honor overcomes even his drunkenness. He is also disregarding his king's direct commands. There is no telling what he will do once he hears publicly that Bathsheba is pregnant. The very next morning, David instructs Joab to send Uriah into the thick of battle so that he dies. What Abraham once feared that Pharaoh would do to him, David will have Joab arrange for Uriah.

◇ *Act III. Aftermath (2 Sam. 11:16–27)*

Scene 1. Away with Uriah (2 Sam. 11:16–25)

> It happened while Joab was guarding the city.
> He gave Uriah into a place in which he knew there were valiant men.
> The men of the city came out and fought with Joab and there were those who fell from among the people and from David's servants.
> Uriah the Hittite also died.
>
> Joab sent and told David all the details of the battle.
> He commanded the messenger thus: "When you finish telling the king all the details of the battle, should the king get angry and ask you, 'Why did you approach the city to fight it? Didn't you know that they would shoot at you from atop the wall? Who struck down Abimelech son of Yeruboshet? Didn't a woman throw a millstone on him from the top of the wall and he died at Thebez? Why did you approach the wall?' Then you shall say to him: 'Uriah the Hittite also died.' "
>
> The messenger went and came and said to David all that Joab had sent.

The messenger said, "The men overcame us and came out to us
in the field, and we were upon them up to the gate. But
there were men on the wall who shot at your servants.
Some of your servants died. Uriah the Hittite also died."

David said to the messenger, "This is what you should say to
Joab: 'Let not this matter be evil in your eyes. For the sword
consumes this and that. Let your battle be strong against
the city. Destroy it and make it strong.' "

And so it happens. "Innocently." **It happened.** Just a tale of war like
any other story. But, of course, things are not that simple. In order to
make sure that Uriah dies, Joab has to conduct the battle stupidly. He has
to "forget" that coming close to a fortified city can be dangerous, that
there can be men with arrows and even women dropping millstones.
And then Joab has to cover himself by subtly reminding David that there
was a reason for his strategic mistake: **Uriah the Hittite also died.**
When David hears the word of Uriah's death, he sends back to Joab that
he should not think the matter ill for **the sword consumes** at will. Another irony, for David and Joab (and the reader) know that the sword did
not consume at *its* will, but at David's. The cover-up is complete.

Scene 2. Bathsheba acquired (2 Sam. 11:26–27)

The wife of Uriah heard that Uriah her husband died.
She mourned her husband.
When the mourning was over, David sent and gathered her into
his house.
She became his wife and she gave birth to a son for him.
And the thing that David did was evil in the eyes of YHWH.

Outwardly everything looks fine. Bathsheba mourns her husband,
and afterward David takes her into the palace as his wife and she gives
birth to a son for him. David has behaved honorably. Rather than leave
Bathsheba to widowhood, he has brought her into the palace. A happy
ending for the happy couple. But, of course, they are not a couple: David
has been in the habit of "gathering" or "harvesting" the wives of other
men. First Ahinoam, who otherwise appears as Saul's wife (1 Sam. 14:50);
then Michal, Saul's daughter whom David first married, then left, then
took from the weeping Paltiel (2 Sam. 3:14–16); then the newly widowed
Abigail, after her husband, Nabal, died of apoplexy (1 Sam. 24:42), and
now the newly widowed Bathsheba. If we accept the cover-up and forget

the little fact that David engineered Uriah's death, then David is behaving with honor. But even if the people may not know, or may overlook, the murder, God knows what David has done. **And the thing that David did was evil in the eyes of YHWH.** There is one last ironic twist on words to end chapter 11. David thought he had laid the matter to rest, telling Joab: **Let not this matter be evil in your eyes.** But the narrator tells us, **And the thing that David did was evil in the eyes of the Lord.** There is, after all, someone who can indict and convict the king.

◈ *Epilogue: Judgment and Retribution (2 Sam. 12)*

Part 1. The parable (2 Sam. 12:1–6)

> The Lord sent Nathan to David.
>
> He said, "There were two men in one city, one rich and one poor.
>
> "The rich man had exceedingly many sheep and cattle; the weak had nothing but one little lamb, which he had bought and sustained. She grew with him and with his children: ate from his bread, drank from his cup, lay in his lap, and was like a daughter to him.
>
> "A traveler came to the rich man. He had too much 'compassion' to take from his own sheep and cattle to prepare for the guest who came to him. But he took the poor man's lamb and prepared her for the man who came to him."
>
> David was greatly incensed at the man.
>
> He said to Nathan, "By the life of YHWH, the man who did this should die. And he will pay fourfold for the lamb because he did this thing and because he did not have compassion."
>
> Nathan said to David, "You are the man."

There is someone besides God who can indict and convict: the king himself. God wants to underscore the lesson, to have David condemn his own act, and so God sends Nathan to tell him the parable. David reacts with indignation. He convicts the rich man on the spot: he should die, and he must pay a fourfold indemnity.

You are the man, says Nathan. There is no doubt that David is the rich man who killed the poor man's lamb. But the rest of the parable is not as transparent: who is the poor man, and who is the lamb, and what has David done that is so wrong? The conventional wisdom has always been that Uriah is the poor man, and Bathsheba the lamb. But David has not killed Uriah's sheep, and he has not killed Uriah's wife. Even if we were to assume that the Bible equates adultery, or "killing the marriage," with killing the lamb, if Uriah is the poor man, then the parable ignores the actual killing, paying no attention to the fact that David killed Uriah by proxy. Nathan specifically condemns David for the murder when he unveils the parable. Nor does the parable ignore the murder, but our own gender stereotyping leads us astray. Bathsheba is the poor man, the one whose husband lies in her lap and eats from her bread until David, who has many wives, has him killed. As a result, says God, the sword will not leave David's house.

Part 2. The punishment (2 Sam. 12:7–13)

> "Thus says YHWH God of Israel, 'I anointed you king over Israel and I saved you from Saul. I gave you your lord's house and your lord's women in your bosom and I gave you the house of Israel and Judah and if that was too little, I added thus and such.
>
> " 'Why have you despised the word of YHWH to do evil in the eyes of YHWH? You have struck Uriah the Hittite with the sword. You have taken his wife as your wife and you have killed him with the sword of Ammon. Now the sword will not depart from your house forever because you have despised me and taken Uriah's wife to be your wife.'
>
> "Thus says YHWH, 'I bring evil to your house and take your wives before you and give them to your neighbor and he will sleep with your wives before this very sun. You acted in secret, but I will do this before all Israel and in the sun.' "
>
> And David said, "I have sinned before YHWH."

Nathan reminds David of all that God has done for him; but what God gave, God can take away. God's punishments are measure for measure, "an eye for an eye," but with the intensification that corresponds to multiple damages. David used the sword of battle to kill Uriah, and the sword will haunt his own house. David took Uriah's wife; God will give David's wives to someone else, publicly to dishonor him. This is no empty threat, for when David's son Absalom took over Jerusalem, he publicly slept with ten wife/concubines that King David had left in the city (2 Sam. 16:20–24). Though unfair to the wives, such measure-for-measure retaliation for male misdeeds is a feature of ancient law, and the Middle Assyrian laws even call for the rape of a married rapist's wife. There is poetic justice here: David stopped to see Bathsheba from the rooftop, and Absalom slept with the women on the roof. And the person who suggested that Absalom do this? It was Ahitophel, David's sage counselor, who sided with Absalom in his revolt against David: Bathsheba's grandfather. To a wise man, revenge is a dish best tasted cold.

By parable and act, God and Nathan have taught David about the limitation of the rights of kings and the accountability of the king to God's law and God's prophet. The death sentence that David pronounced on himself (as the rich man in the parable) was commuted because of his repentance. But there had to be some punishment. The baby conceived in adultery died. God visited the sin of the father on this infant, taking his life in return for the life David had caused to be taken. This allowed David to begin again. Bathsheba bore another son for David whom he named Solomon and Nathan called Yedidyah, "the beloved of God."

It would seem that all will now be well in the reign of David. And yet, in the very next stories, the fourfold indemnity that David decreed comes to pass, as Tamar, raped by Amnon, becomes a "ruin" in Absalom's house; Amnon is killed by Absalom; and Absalom dies in his rebellion. Perhaps the baby, Tamar, Amnon, and Absalom were the four, or perhaps the baby, Amnon, Absalom, and Adonijah, as the Babylonian Talmud counts them (BT Yoma 22b). The biblical authors never hint that YHWH caused any of these problems, and yet the death of so many children does sound like the fourfold penalty that David, unknowingly, imposed on himself. One last irony from our author?

This story reveals the dark side of kingship, an imperfection that will cause ongoing unrest. Only a king could misbehave in precisely this way, and reading the story, one reader begins to suspect that kingship will not solve Israel's problems. This growing disillusion only increases as the story immediately following reveals yet another flaw in both kingship and the king.

Trauma and Tragedy
The Betrayals of Tamar

◈ *Part 1. A Problem (2 Sam. 13:1–2)*

It was after these matters.

Absalom, David's son, had a beautiful sister named Tamar, and Amnon son of David loved her.

Amnon was distraught to the point of being ill over Tamar his sister. For she was a maiden and it seemed to Amnon that it would take a miracle to be able to do anything to her.

A new story is beginning. It has nothing to do with the Ammonite wars that occupied chapters 10–12 of Second Samuel, nothing to do with David, Bathsheba, and Uriah, nothing to do with the death of David's son or (ostensibly) with Nathan's declaration of divine retribution for David's sin, and nothing to do with the birth of Bathsheba's son Solomon and God's approval of him. What happens now is a whole new chain of events. The slate has been wiped clean, and we wait to see what will happen to the kingship of David and, with it, to the Israelite monarchy.

The stage is now set by an introduction of the main characters and their relationship with one another. Absalom is introduced first, even though Amnon is David's eldest son. The narrator wants us to know that the tale we are about to hear is part of the larger story of Absalom. As for Tamar, the center of the story, she is presented as an object: Absalom has a sister. Her story begins with her relationship to Absalom, and ends with this same relationship (2 Sam. 13:22). His brothership to her determines both her destiny and, ultimately, his own.

David has many wives and many children, and another son of David views her as an object: **Amnon son of David loved her.** She is surrounded by the two brothers, trapped between them. Their actions will determine her life.

But at first there is no action. Tamar is a "maiden"; she is ripe for marriage. A man who loves her would want to acquire her as a wife. But she is a princess, and Amnon cannot imagine being able to do anything about his love. As his half sister, she might not be given to him. As David's beautiful daughter, she might be destined for a dynastic marriage. As a princess, she will be well guarded. As Absalom's sister, she will be well protected. How could he even approach her? And so Amnon is lovesick.

Enter another character, Jonadab, with a plan to break the impasse:

◇ *Part 2. A Plan (2 Sam. 13:3–5)*

> Now Amnon had a friend named Jonadab, son of Shimeh, David's brother.
>
> And Jonadab was very smart.
>
> He said to him, "Why are you so weak, O Prince, morning after morning? Won't you tell me?"
>
> Amnon said to him, "I am in love with Tamar, sister of my brother Absalom!"
>
> Jonadab said to him, "Lie on your bed and be sick, and the king will come to see you. Say to him, 'Let Tamar my sister make me healthy with food, let her make the *biryah* before me so that I can see and eat from her hand.' "

This is a strange plan, for it seems so obvious that we cannot imagine David falling for it. Why should Jonadab expect David to send Tamar? Why wouldn't David find Amnon's request suspicious? Surely there were many cooks in the palace! The answer must be in the nature of the *birya* itself. The word comes from the root meaning "fat" or "healthy" and may mean a healing substance. Its semantic development may be similar to that of the Babylonian medicinal prescription, the *bulṭu*, which comes from the verb *balāṭu* ("to live"), with the causative *bulluṭu* ("to heal"). The *birya* is not simply a food, and making it is not simply an act of cooking; it is the preparation of a medicinal concoction. Perhaps, we could speculate, the princesses of the realm were instructed in the creation of healing foods. This speculation accords with the well-known historical connection of women with healing. It also makes sense of Jonadab's plan. If Tamar was instructed in medicinal herbs and rituals, then Amnon's request for her would seem legitimate, and David might be expected to comply without becoming suspicious or alarmed.

And so it happened:

◇ *Part 3. The King Acquiesces (2 Sam. 13:6–7)*

> Amnon lay down and was ill, and the king came to see him.
>
> Amnon said to the king, "Let Tamar my sister come and make two heart cakes before me, so that I may be healed through her hand."
>
> David sent for Tamar at home, saying, "Go, please, to the house of your brother Amnon and perform the *biryah* for him."

The scenario plays out. Performing the *birya* involves making "heart cakes," a cake whose name indicates either its shape (like a Valentine) or its function, to "enhearten" the sick person and make his life force flow. Amnon asks for Tamar, and she is sent on a mission of doom by her unsuspecting father.

◇ *Part 4. The Trapping of Tamar (2 Sam. 13:8–10)*

> Tamar went to the house of Amnon her brother as he was lying down.
>
> She took the dough and kneaded it, and made the heart cakes before him and cooked the heart cakes.
>
> She took the tine and held it before him.
>
> He refused to eat.
>
> Amnon said, "Send everyone out from before me," and everyone went out from before him.
>
> Amnon said to Tamar, "Bring the *biryah* into my room and I will be healed through your hand."
>
> So Tamar took the heart cakes that she had cooked and brought them to Amnon her brother into his room.

The narrator draws Tamar ever so slowly into the spider's web. She has no reason to be suspicious. He is, after all, her brother, and her father has sent her. Her brother's house is like her own, and she acts without concern to perform the *birya*. The narrator details each step of its cooking; in a ceremony of healing, after all, each step in the process is as important as the product itself. And the narrative emphasizes her innocence as she goes about her business in Amnon's house, drawing out the tension of the reader, who knows it is all a trap. And so, like many girls who assume that they are safe in the house of a close relative, Tamar does not suspect anything as Amnon kicks everyone out and then invites her into his bedroom. The trap is ready to be sprung.

◇ *Part 5. The Rape of Tamar (2 Sam. 13:11–14)*

> She held it out to him to eat, and he grabbed hold of her.
>
> He said, "Come lie with me, my sister!"
>
> She said to him, "Don't, my brother! Do not degrade me, for such should not be done in Israel; do not do this outrage. For I, whither would I go with my shame? And you—you will be one of the outrageous boors of Israel. And now—speak, please, to the king, for he will not keep me from you."
>
> But he was not willing to listen to her.
>
> He overpowered her, he degraded her, and he lay with her.

The change is sudden and unexpected. Tamar expects him to take the *birya,* but he wants her. She, who has come on a mission of healing, now suddenly finds herself an object of lust. Unexpectedly, her life has begun to parallel that of Dinah, daughter of Leah. Tamar has not acted like Dinah, who went out of her home compound to the outside, a place about whose danger girls are warned. Tamar stayed at home until she was summoned by the king, her father, and then went ever more inward into the heart of her own family. Dinah went of her own initiative to see the girls of the land; Tamar has come on an authorized errand, sent by her father into her brother's house. Her visit to Amnon's room is both totally innocent and socially approved. Nevertheless, in a scene reminiscent of Potiphar's wife and Joseph, Amnon grabs her and says starkly, **"Come lie with me."** He is used to command, used to being immediately obeyed by his servants. He does not even try to seduce her. And Tamar, who has trusted in her safety, suddenly finds herself in a sexual situation.

Amnon then adds **"my sister."** Readers of Song of Songs will remember "my sister" as a nickname for the beloved, "my sister the bride." The love poetry of Sumer often has Dumuzi refer to his beloved Inanna as "my sister" and she to him as "my brother." These words are frequently the terminology of love, and we almost hear the love poetry in Amnon's caressing "my sister." But Tamar really is Amnon's half sister, and we realize that he is taking advantage of the intimacy of family relationships to demand a sexual encounter that Israel's Levitical laws consider incestuous.

Like Joseph before her, Tamar also tries to speak from the moral high ground. Joseph reacted to Potiphar's wife's imperious "Lie with me" by describing the immorality of his betraying his master's trust. Tamar tries to counter Amnon's imperative **"Come lie with me, my sister!"** with the language of Israel's ethical wisdom. She begins with the classic *'al te-'anneni,* "Do not degrade me," using the key word of Israel's moral vocabulary. Once, when Egypt degraded Israel, they were severely punished. The legal tradition warns that if Israel degrades the poor or the stranger, God will avenge them by punishing Israel. And when Shechem degraded Dinah, he set off a chain of events that culminated in the destruction of his city. **"Do not degrade me"** is the strongest language that Tamar can use. She then adds more of the language of Israel's traditional sexual teachings, **"for such should not be done in Israel; do not do this outrage."** Tamar, who unexpectedly finds herself a double of Dinah, uses the language of *nebalah,* the outrageous act that should not be done. In the Dinah story, the narrator uses this language to inform the audience that her brothers were very angry because of the magnitude of Shechem's act: "for he had committed an outrage in Israel by lying with the daughter of Jacob, for such should not be done" (Gen. 34:7). In Tamar's story, she herself is given the voice to pass this ethical judgment on Amnon's demand. As a daughter of Jacob, an Israelite girl, she is supposed to be chaste. Lying with her is a moral outrage.

Tamar then adds another argument, an appeal to personal consideration. She asks Amnon to consider the consequences of sexual intercourse. **"For I, whither would I go with my shame?"** If she fails to remain chaste, Tamar will be disgraced and shamed. She is not thinking of sin or guilt. *Ḥerpah*—"shame"—is not a question of guilt, and she, after all, has done nothing wrong. But she knows the social importance of remaining a virgin. A sexual act with Amnon will bring disgrace upon her. She asks her question in the same plaintive tone that Reuben used when he found Joseph missing from the pit: "I, whither will I go?" Reuben, the eldest son of Jacob, was not himself guilty of selling Joseph, but he had failed to protect him. As Tamar talks about her possible disgrace, she skillfully insinuates a reminder of the importance of her mission to remain chaste. Then she adds a personal matter for Amnon to consider about himself. He also will be disgraced: **"And you—you will be one of the outrageous boors of Israel."** Only one of the *nebalim* performs such a *nebalah!*

Tamar then tries to talk Amnon into delaying his gratification. **"And now—speak, please, to the king, for he will not keep me from you."** If he wants her, he should do *now* what all men should do: ask her father. She does not mention here that he is her brother or that the union might be incestuous. She is, after all, only a half sister, from a different mother, and possibly the Levitical rules were not yet in force and such a union would not yet have been considered incestuous. Abraham, after all, declares that his wife Sarah was his own half sister; and Jacob married two sisters, a union that Leviticus declares incestuous in the same chapter in which it forbade it. David's appeal to the priest of Nob shows that not all the Levitical regulations were in force in his day, so marriage between nonuterine siblings might have been acceptable. Even if such marriage was not generally accepted, Tamar's use of the term "the king," rather than "my father," may hint that David, being king, could override custom. There were, after all, marriages between sisters and brothers in the Egyptian dynasty; David (she may imply) might be interested in having his heir marry one of his own seed to ensure the purity of the Davidic gene heritage.

And perhaps none of this is true, and Tamar is just trying to deflect Amnon's assault. **But he was not willing to listen to her.** Amnon doesn't care about any of this, not about moral teachings, Tamar's honor, or even his own; and he isn't really interested in a permanent union with her. And suddenly we realize that Tamar is following the wrong script. She is not living Dinah's life, she is living out the story of the Levite's concubine! As we have seen, the Ephraimite host tried to talk the men of Gibeah out of their evil plan against his guest with the same words, "Do not do this outrage" (Judg. 19:23–24). He had an alternative, one that he did not consider a *nebālāh*: he would send out his maiden daughter and the Levite's concubine for their sexual degradation, but "toward this man do not do this act of outrage." We would consider the Ephraimite's plan as outrageous as that of the Gibeonites, but, in any event, "The men were not willing to listen to him. The man grabbed his concubine and sent her outside, to them" (Judg. 19:25). Dinah's story was about love. The rape of the concubine has nothing to do with love; it is about assault and the assertion of dominance. And so is Tamar's.

The time for talk is over. Amnon, who "grabbed hold of her," *wayyeḥezaq bāh*, before he even began to talk to her, now "overpowers her," *ye ḥezaq mimmennāh*, degrades her, and lays with her. In this confrontation between reason and might, might wins. There is no question of seduction here: Amnon has raped her by force. The word *'innah*, "degrade," used before the verb for intercourse rather than after it, indicates rape. It is not strange that a mere change of verb order can denote such a colossally different experience for the woman. After all, in the case of unauthorized sex, the sex itself can be sweet, romantic, and passionate; it is only the fact that the girl has been unchaste that degrades her. In the case of rape, the sex itself is degrading and humiliating, and the degradation begins the moment that force is used, before penetration. For this experience of brutality, the verb "degrade" properly goes first.

Tamar's experience has been one of total degradation. And it is about to become even worse.

◇ *Part 6. The Worm Turns (2 Sam. 13:15–18)*

> Amnon hated her with a very great hatred. Indeed, greater was the hatred with which he hated her than the love that he had loved her.
> Amnon said to her, "Get up! Go!"
> And she said to him, "Don't! Concerning this great evil,—more than the other which you did to me, sending me away."
> But he was not willing to listen to her.
> He called his young man who served him and said, "Send, please, that away from me, outside, and lock the door behind her."
> Now she was wearing a long robe, for that was what the young maiden royal daughters wore as cloaks.
> But his servant took her out and locked the door behind her.

Amnon, possibly appalled at his own violent act, now hates Tamar for being the occasion for it, blaming her as its "cause." He shows none of the tenderness and love that Shechem showed Dinah. This rape was an act of violence, and it is followed by yet another. Amnon looks at Tamar and says, **"Get up! Go!"** A few generations earlier, the concubine's master/husband showed the same lack of consideration: "Get up and let's go," he said to the girl supine on the doorstep (Judg. 19:28). Insensitive to her plight, he wanted life to return automatically and simply to the way it had been before the rape. In the concubine's story, we can say that at least her master/husband didn't reject her, that he had intended to resume his normal life with her. But Amnon doesn't intend even that much. Even more insensitive to what has happened to Tamar, he only wants her gone.

Tamar tries to answer him, but her speech betrays her shock and pain. Before the rape, she had argued eloquently in the familiar language of Israel's moral discourse. It didn't do any good, of course, but for a moment Tamar stood revealed as wise, skilled, and intelligent. But now she cannot speak a grammatical sentence. **"Don't!"** she stammers, and we have to supply the "do this." **"Concerning this great evil"**—we add "it is greater"—**"than the one which you did to me."**—**"Sending me away"** we go back to the verb: "is worse than the other evil that you did by raping me." She expresses partial thoughts, but her meaning is clear. Rape is a horrible act, but it can be a (nasty) way of acquiring wives, as the men of Benjamin acquired the girls dancing at Shiloh. Even Deuteronomy allows a father to give his daughter to a man who has slept with her, and the text is worded in such a way as to suggest it might if one's victim is beyond comprehension and beyond smooth articulation.

"Sending me away," the poignant phrase left dangling at the end of Tamar's speech, appears forty-four times in "the succession narrative" (2 Sam. 9–20) and twenty-two times in the three chapters immediately preceding this story (the tales of the Ammonite war and David and Uriah). It is a power word: the person who "sends" or "sends away" has power over the one sent. In the case of David and Uriah, David has absolute power over his lieutenant's life and death. In Tamar's case, the girl realizes that rape is an act of subjugation, and that by sending her away, Amnon could continue to act out his dominance over her. She pleads with him not to strip her of the last shred of her power. But Amnon, who wouldn't listen to her when she tried to prevent the rape, will not listen to her now. Her words have no power over him, and his next sentence demonstrates how little value she has in his eyes. **"Send, please, *that* away from me,"** he says to his servant. Translations often soften his statement: "send this woman away," but Amnon does not say "woman"; he says **"that."** He has totally dehumanized her. In the same sentence in which he addresses his servant with the gracious "please," he points to her as to something unmentionable that must be purged from his presence: **"outside, and lock the door behind her."** This is hardly a way to treat a princess, and the story reminds us of Tamar's identity by telling us she was wearing the special garment that marks her royal status. But even this does not protect her from the act of ultimate degradation that follows. The servant, more loyal to his master than to the honor of David's daughter, does exactly as Amnon commands. Tamar, the good girl who stayed at home until her father sent for her, is now "outside" in the most devastating of circumstances.

Tamar has only one recourse left.

◇ *Part 7. Betrayal and Tragedy (2 Sam. 13:19–20)*

> Tamar placed ashes on her head, tore the long robe she was
> wearing, placed her hands on her head, and went, walking
> about and crying out.
> And Absalom her brother said to her, "Has Aminon your
> brother been with you? And now, my sister, hush—he is
> your brother. Pay no attention to this matter!"
> So Tamar lived devastated in the house of her brother Absalom.

As the final scene of her tragedy begins, Tamar creates a public spectacle. She draws attention to her own devastation by openly revealing
her plight. Not trying to hide her shame, she performs an act of grief
and lament. She acts as those who see a ruin: "They shall raise their
voices over you and cry out bitterly, they will place dust on their heads
and strew ashes on themselves, they will tear out their hair over you,
making bald spots, and wear sackcloth, weeping a bitter lament and
wailing a dirge" (Ezek. 27:30). To these mourning actions, Tamar adds
another public gesture: she places her hands upon her head to show that
she has been defeated, that she is a victim.

Why would Tamar want to act this way? A Middle Assyrian law may
provide the answer. It concerns a married woman who is tricked into
adulterous sex: the scenario is that a married woman brings another
married woman into her house to have sex with a man who knows she is
married. Should the woman not know what was intended, "If, as soon as
she leaves the house, she should declare that she has been the victim of
fornication, they shall release her, she is clear: they shall kill the fornica-
tor and the female procurer." If the woman does not make that declaration, then she is to be treated as an adulteress: the husband imposes
whatever punishment he wishes. Tamar is not a married woman who
might be suspect of adultery. But she is a *betûlāh*, a young marriageable
girl who owes her father her chastity. She knows that she might not be
able to hide the fact that she is no longer a virgin. Amnon might act to
protect himself by claiming that Tamar seduced him, or, at the very
least, that she was his willing partner. Or her future bridegroom might
find that she is not a virgin. Or she might become pregnant. The rape
could do her even more damage in the future, and Tamar needs to let
the world know she is a victim. The Bible does not condemn the victims
of rape. A girl who cries out when she is attacked is considered innocent

of sexual wrongdoing (Deut. 22:24). Now, after the fact, Tamar needs to cry out so she will be seen as a victim of rape.

So Tamar is "crying out," yelling and making a loud sound. She may be lamenting, "woe to me," and she is probably crying, "rape!" The verb that the narrator uses for her crying, za'aq, indicates yet another purpose for crying out. The author could have said "she cried out" with the common verb qar'ah. This verb would have the advantage of a verbal play with "she tore (qar 'ah) her garment." But the verb za 'aq has a special connotation. In Israel, the one who cries out can expect to be heard. At the very least, God may hear her, for God vindicates the one who cries out from oppression. As God heard Israel's cries in Egypt (Deut. 26:7), God promises to hear and avenge any oppressed stranger or poor person in Israel who cries out (Exod. 22:22). Even more immediately, the king may hear. A petitioner can "cry out" to a king, demanding royal action. Mephibosheth demands nothing else from David: "What else do I have to cry out to the king for?" (2 Kings 19:29), but the Shunammite woman comes to cry out to the king (2 Kings 8:5), as does the cannibal mother (2 Kings 6:26).

So Tamar is walking about, crying out words such as "woe" and "rape," "answer me" and "somebody do something." Her life has been irrevocably changed by the five occurrences of the verb halak ("to go, walk") in her story: First David took her from her home, saying, **"Go, please** to your brother's house," and Tamar **"went"**; **"where would I go with my shame,"** she asked Amnon, but he abruptly told her, "Go," and so now **she is going** on her journey to her final destiny. And her brother Absalom sees her. Perhaps this is one of the "coincidences" by which things happen in the Bible; more probably, he sees her because, in her walking, she has gone back to her mother's compound where she and her brother live, and where she can expect protection.

Absalom her brother sees her and speaks to her. But his first words show her that she can expect no help from him. **"Has Aminon your brother been with you?"** Absalom's use of "Aminon," a form of Amnon that stresses the 'ammi ("my people") and his *"your brother,"* are both reminders of Amnon's place in the family. In the one verse about Absalom's speech, the narrator calls him "her brother" twice, Absalom calls Amnon "your brother" twice, and he calls Tamar "my sister" once. Tamar is enmeshed in family relations. The one who did this to Tamar is not an outsider, and so her outcry implicates a member of her own family. By accusing him, Absalom implies, she will bring public disgrace upon the family.

Absalom does not recognize the enormity of the offense against Tamar, and minimizes what has happened. Amnon, he says, has **"been with you."** By not naming the offense as rape, he belittles Tamar's pain, denies her outrage, and compounds her tragedy. **"Pay no attention to this matter,"** he says to her, as if "this matter" were something trifling that she could forget or ignore. Absalom underscores his message **"And now, my sister, hush—he is your brother."** But for Tamar to hush means that she will forgo any chance that she can be vindicated and her honor restored. She herself will be complicitous in covering up Amnon's crime, and she will be denied the satisfaction of retribution and revenge. Absalom makes her stifle her rage and leave her grief unassuaged. And why? Because Amnon is her brother. Tamar should sacrifice her rights for the "good of the family."

With Absalom's words, he betrays her. Like so many victims of domestic sexual abuse, Tamar is trapped by family. Raped by a close family member, she is denied her right of reaction. She is the victim of both brothers: first by Amnon's rape, then by Absalom's silencing. Nobody looks at her as a person. To Amnon, she was an object of lust and then hate; to Absalom, she is a crisis that has to be contained. Tamar's own feelings do not enter into their calculations.

But why is Tamar herself silent? Why does she listen to Absalom? The girl who tried seriously, if unsuccessfully, to talk Amnon out of raping her says nothing to Absalom as he denies her vindication. Tamar, whose voice has gone from rational argument to stammering supplication to loud outcry, is now silent. She will be heard no more. Like so many other victims of domestic rape, she joins the conspiracy of silence that dooms her. We can imagine her motives, imagine the burden that Absalom places on her by reminding her that she bears the fate of her own brother in her hands. Girls were (are?) always taught that their family honor depends on their actions. They were told that their chastity was the foundation of their family's honor, that their improper behavior would bring scandal and disgrace upon the family. This message conditioned them to accept responsibility for their family's destiny even in cases where they did nothing to offend, but themselves were offended. Tamar will say nothing rather than bring disgrace upon Amnon.

But the price is high: she disappears into Absalom's house and stays there as a *šōmēmā*, a ruined woman. Cities and women can be ruined, left with neither husband nor children. Lamentations tells us how Zion became a *šōmēmā*, faint all day as God rained fire upon her (Lam. 1:13). Someday, at the redemption, Isaiah promises his beloved city-woman

Zion that she will have more children than the married woman (Isa. 54:19). But there is no such redemption for Tamar, who is desolate in both senses of the word: ruined and miserable. She cannot marry, not because nonvirgins cannot marry, for they could, but because her non-virginal state would have to be explained by exposing Amnon. And this is exactly what Absalom has told her not to do.

And the men who should be her protectors?

◇ *Part 8. Nothing (2 Sam. 13:21–22)*

> David the king heard these things and fumed.
> Absalom did not speak to Amnon evil or good, for he hated Amnon because of the fact that he had degraded his sister Tamar.

David . . . fumed. But he did nothing. He did not punish Amnon, he did not vindicate Tamar, he did not rescue her from her desolation. Why not? Did he have no power over his sons? The Greek Septuagint has a phrase that the Hebrew text does not have, "but he didn't trouble the spirit of Amnon his son, for he loved him, for he was his firstborn." Is this phrase part of the original version of the story, or is it added by the Septuagint in order to explain David's inaction? The Qumran manuscript 4Q Sam. has part of this line, "[for he lo]ved him, for he was [his fir]stborn." These ancient versions may explain David's inaction, but they make no difference to the events: David was angry, but he did nothing. Jacob, we may remember, did nothing when he heard about Dinah. But he was only waiting till his sons came home, and then entertained a marriage proposal. David does nothing as two years pass.

David could have pursued several courses of action. If Tamar was right about the possibility of marriage, David could have forced Amnon to marry her. Alternatively, he could have punished Amnon as a rapist. But he does neither. Either action would have required that he acknowledge the reality that Tamar was raped, and perhaps he is afraid of the scandal that might result. It is also David's pattern to do nothing when his sons do wrong. When Adonijah starts pretending to the crown, David does not stop or trouble him (1 Kings 1:6). Like Jacob before him, who didn't act in the face of his sons' envy of Joseph, David does not control the actions of his sons. He will not avenge his daughter at the expense of his sons.

And Absalom, Tamar's other protector/guardian? Brothers are most often the guardians of their sisters' chastity and the punishers of those who violate it. But **Absalom did not speak to Amnon evil or good.** Absalom also does nothing to rescue Tamar. The fact that he ignores Amnon for two years does nothing for her, and may not have presented a problem for Amnon. It is only after two years that Absalom takes bloody vengeance on Amnon. He invites him to a celebration and induces David to let him go, and then has his servants kill Amnon. David's nephew informs the king that Absalom had intended this from the day that Amnon raped Tamar. But does such delayed vengeance vindicate Tamar in public? Does it enable her to resume her life as a princess? Or will the world assume only that Absalom has disposed of the elder brother who stood between him and the crown?

The book of Samuel doesn't tell us. It is a dynastic story, after all, and goes on to relate how Absalom fled and stayed in exile several years, how he was brought back but led a revolt, fought a civil war, and was killed. It does not tell us if Tamar's tragedy has an end. It gives us only one glimpse, but this glimpse suffices to see that "the more things change . . ." Israel now has a king, but in his own family, the vulnerable continue to be victims and the king fails to be their recourse. The king himself shows the same deadly syndrome as the family patriarchs of the period of the judges. They went to war against Benjamin, but they let their own daughters be raped by the surviving Benjaminites. David wages wars of conquest and kills obstacles in his path. But he does not protect the daughter who depends on him.

From the point of view of Tamar, the monarchy has changed nothing. The very names of the characters tell the tragedy with dramatic irony. Their names exemplify the ideal king: a true and trustworthy (Amnon from *'amn*) father who brings well-being (Absalom from *'ab* "father" and *šalom)* "well-being, peace." But together they fail dismally to nourish the palm tree (*tamar*), who is destroyed. In this new monarchy, the weak can still be victimized by the powerful, girls are vulnerable to violence, and violence against them still spreads unchecked until it culminates in civil war. The monarchy does not solve the problem that is its only reason for being: it cannot govern society so that outrage will not occur.

Power and Person
A Problem of Political Life

THE STORIES of Bathsheba and Tamar show that the monarchy of Israel didn't answer the problem of vulnerable women, it simply moved it up to the governing level. The book of Judges shows us daughters controlled by their fathers with increasingly disturbing results. With no one to direct the people in their faith, and no one able to keep people from killing each other and abusing the innocent, society goes increasingly out of control. Kingship comes to fill this need, but kingship fails. When the king will not or cannot control his own family members, nothing will protect the innocent from their power. And no one can control the king. As the story of David, Bathsheba, and Uriah shows, what the king covets, he takes. And what the king doesn't want, he destroys. There is nothing beyond the king's control and his willingness to use it. In some ways, matters have changed only for the worse. Tamar's very obedience to her father led to tragedy. The same David who asserted his power and dominance over Uriah and Bathsheba did not manifest these traits when he failed to avenge his daughter, the most vulnerable member of the household. The reader who might expect protection for the vulnerable under the state now sees that the state cannot control itself.

When the treatment of vulnerable women is the measure of worth, the failure of Israel to live up to the mandate of Sinai is revealed in high relief. Israel never created a system of government that could control violent abuse. Neither the lack of polity of the Genesis ancestors, nor the localized sporadic government of the period of the judges, could prevent such outrages. And neither could kingship. Since Israel is under special obligation to create a fully just society, the Deuteronomistic historian relates these stories of outrages against women as a key indicator of the failure of the social order. Because such things happened, Israel was destroyed.

The ultimate failure of the monarchic state does not mean that it had no impact on the life of women. The subordination of the patriarchal family to the patriarchal state meant that public institutions could act as a check on the heads of household and could protect the more vulnerable members of families (except, of course, within the family of power). The laws of Deuteronomy, which reflect the ideals of the monarchic period, consistently curtail the freedom of the heads of household to do as they will. The right of a father to decide what to do about an unchaste daughter is minimized. Dinah's affair led to a reprisal raid by her brothers. The laws of Exodus (which may date from the period of the settlement of the land) regularize the situation by providing that the girl's father is to receive a virgin's brideprice from her lover and may then decide whether or not to give her to him in marriage. In the laws of Deuteronomy (which were from the monarchic period, written during the monarchy), matters are entirely determined by law and no one has any choice: the lover must pay the brideprice, the father must marry her to him, and he may never divorce her (Deut. 22:28–29). By enforcing such laws, matters were kept in check and not allowed to escalate into violent confrontation.

Another move by the state was to curtail the power of a father to appoint his chief heir, thereby removing a major cause of rivalry between brothers. In ancestral Israel, as elsewhere in the ancient Near East, the preeminent position of "firstborn" did not necessarily go to the first son to be born. So Jacob and Esau jockeyed for this position, and later, Jacob had the right to appoint Joseph, the eldest son of his beloved wife Rachel, as "firstborn." The result was murderous jealousy. In the laws of Deuteronomy, by contrast, whoever is born first to a father is considered the "firstborn" and receives the double portion due to the chief heir (Deut. 21:15–17).

The laws of Deuteronomy also eliminated many of the rights of the patriarch to dispose of the members of his family. For example, Reuben slept with Jacob's concubine Bilhah; Deuteronomy forbids a man from marrying his father's wife (Deut. 23:1). Judah kept Tamar bound to his family even though he didn't provide a levir.* The state also curtailed the parents' authority to determine life or death. The "Law of the Slandered Bride" considers the case in which a man declares that his bride was not a virgin. As in many other cultures, the accusation is tested by examining the bridal sheet, which is brought before the council of elders. If the sheet is bloody, the bridegroom is flogged, must give a hundred shekels

---

*The law of the levirate required a childless widow to cohabit with her dead husband's brother.

to the girl's father, and may never divorce the woman. If the sheets are not bloody, then the girl is stoned by the whole community at the entrance to her father's house, for "she committed an outrage in Israel by being faithless to her father's house" (Deut. 22:13–21). The father can no longer simply order his daughter executed, as Judah once ordered Tamar to be burned. The family is no longer sovereign, and the supervisory council of fathers must decree the girl's death.

A very revealing quirk in the "Law of the Slandered Bride" shows that Deuteronomy actually leaves the father very much in control of his daughter's destiny. When bloody sheets are used cross-culturally as a proof/test of virginity, the groom or his parents take possession of the sheet right after the consummation of the marriage. But in Deuteronomy, the girl's father and mother produce the sheets before the elders. This allows them to decide what to do. If they are angry that she brought them dishonor, they can show unspotted sheets and the girl will be killed. But if they are not angry (or if they knew that the girl was not a virgin but were trying to trick the bridegroom and get the full brideprice), then they could always plant some blood on the sheets before displaying them. In the laws of Deuteronomy, parents no longer have the authority to command life or death, but they still retain the real power to decide whether their daughter lives or dies.

The monarchic state does not want to eliminate parental control, for the Bible considers it essential to the upbringing of children and the prevention of social chaos. The wisdom literature exhorts young men to give heed to the advice of their parents, and honoring of father and mother is encoded in the Ten Commandments. In one respect, Deuteronomic law actually gives the parents more power to control their sons than they had under the old patriarchal system. In the pre-state system reflected in the ancestor stories, a father's ability to control his sons rested on his own powers of persuasion and intimidation. As long as he could threaten them with discipline (and maybe even, in extremis, with his life-or-death power over them), then they would listen to him. But when the sons grew up and were stronger and more numerous than the parents, they might no longer listen and might ignore or intimidate their parents. Jacob could no longer control his sons, who formed alliances and committed acts of violence against outsiders and against a member of their own family. But in Deuteronomy, the ability of parents to control their children no longer depends on their ability to intimidate them physically. Parents can bring a son before the elders and denounce him, and the son will be stoned (Deut. 18–21). The council of elders shores up the ability of parents to control their children, even as it limits the extreme measures they can take.

There were limits to the state's ability to prevent parents from exercising proprietary rights over their children. A devastatingly bizarre story that dramatizes this limit takes place in the Northern Kingdom. The Arameans were besieging the capital, Samaria, and the famine was severe. As the king walked the ramparts,

◇ *Cannibal Mothers (2 Kings 6:24–31)*

> A woman cried out to him thus, "Save me, my lord king!"
> He said, "If God doesn't save you, from where should I save you, from the threshing floor or from the winepress?"
> The king said to her, "What is wrong with you?"
> The woman said, "That woman said to me, 'Give your son and we will eat him today, and my son we will eat tomorrow.' We boiled my son and ate him, and I said to her on the next day, 'Give your son and we will eat him!' and she hid her son."
> It happened that when the king heard the woman's words, he tore his clothes and walked along the wall.
> The people saw that he had sackcloth inside upon his flesh.

The woman appeals to the king to come to her aid. He immediately suspects that she is asking for food, but she relates her story. The other woman doesn't dispute the facts in the case, and the petitioning woman doesn't say what she wants the king to do. What could he do? Should he order the woman to bring forth her son? Should he punish her for breach of promise? There is no right thing to do here, and the king tears his clothes and walks along the wall so that the people can see he is in deep mourning, that he has already been wearing sackcloth under his clothes. Like so many stories in the historical books, this story has a parallel. At the beginning of the truly centralized social order, Solomon sits as the arbiter of disputes among the people. Two prostitutes come before him to fight over a child. Each has given birth, but one child was born dead and each mother claims the living child as her own. Solomon settles their dispute by manifesting "Solomonic wisdom," the angelic ability to discern right from wrong. His judgment is famous: he offers to cut the living child in half, then awards the child to the mother whose love was so great that she renounced her claim to the child rather than see it killed (1 Kings 3). But this king cannot be as wise as Solomon, for there is nothing he can do: the dispute is between cannibals who have already killed a child, and true justice is impossible.

Child cannibalism is a symbol of utter moral collapse in the face of suffering so severe that ordinary ethical considerations cannot be sustained. Assyrian treaties threaten such a horrendous fate for those who break the agreement. A people who eat their children cannot long exist, and the inability of the state to prevent such devastation is the death knell of the Omride dynasty in the north. Much later, in Lamentations, the poet mourns that the disastrous siege of Jerusalem has brought compassionate women to this utter degradation of killing and eating their children.

In a strange way, this black story also shows the success of the state. Even in this horrible extreme situation, adults are not killing one another. Civil order has not broken down, and the people still turn to the king as the arbiter of their disputes. The kings of Israel succeeded in keeping order between households. But they couldn't protect members of a household from one another, and they did not completely eradicate child sexual abuse and child murder from the land. As the stories in the historical books reveal this failure, their retelling presents a critique of kingship, a critique that may have contributed to the end of the institution in Israel, for the monarchy was not restored when the people came back from the Babylonian exile.

Part Three

VIRGINS

THE VIRGINS are brides, women whom (as the Bible would express it) the men of Israel "take" in marriage. How will the children of Israel relate to the peoples around them, how will they arrange treaties and marriages? These theoretical questions pose practical problems in the political arena, as communities have to decide whether to forge alliances or to rigidly avoid foreign entanglements. But, as the Dinah story shows in dramatic fashion, the political is also an issue of personal life: whom should the Israelites marry? Families forge alliances with each other through marriage, and groups seeking to maintain their distinctiveness have to decide whom they will marry. Women usually went to live with their husbands' family and kin, and became members of the group into which they married. But wives who came into the Israelite family joined Israel. All wives must come into the family from the outside, for to marry within the family is to commit incest. But what are the parameters of the outside pool?

The best-known answer to this question is from Ezra, who convinces the new Judeans to reject their wives if they were not returnees from Babylon. But Ezra is only one voice in the Bible, relying on and extending Deuteronomy's injunction against taking wives from the local inhabitants. Other biblical voices have different opinions. Chronicles accepts foreign wives matter-of-factly, and stories express a whole spectrum of opinions, ranging from the advocacy of separation, isolation, and the dangers of taking foreign wives to the assertion of the advantages of openness and the benefits of welcoming new people, such as wives, into Israel.

The Dinah Affair

PATRIARCHY IS about control. The man in power, patriarch or king, can determine the destiny of those under his rule. In special cases, this authority carries with it power over life and death. In more ordinary circumstances, the power takes the form of controlling relationships of the "household" to the outside world. The king decides to go to war or forge an alliance; the patriarch decides with whom to arrange a treaty of marriage. Genesis 34 dramatically illustrates the relationship between "domestic affairs," control over household members, and "external affairs," boundary definition and the relationship with other groups. It involves the intricate connection between the relationship of a girl to her birth family and the relationship of that family to the outside, and between the relationships of individual families to each other and the destiny of the nation as a whole.

The story brings us straight to the action:

◇ *Act I. (Gen. 34:1–5)*

Part 1. The daughter's disgrace (Gen. 34:1–2)
> Out went Dinah the daughter of Leah whom she bore to Jacob, to see the girls of the land.
> Shechem the son of Hamor the Hivite, Prince of the Land, saw her.
> He took her, and lay with her, and degraded her.

Every phrase of that deceptively simple first sentence is fraught with implications for biblical Israel. Dinah, who initiates the action, is identified by her position within her family: she is **the daughter of Leah whom she bore to Jacob.** Her mother is a full-status wife, freeborn and even from the home kin, not a slave woman with a "field promotion" to wife. As the story develops and as each aspect of Dinah's position in the family becomes an occasion for action, she is called "daughter of Jacob" and "sister" of the brothers. Right from the outset, her identification as the daughter of Leah locates her securely within the family. It may also hint that the story will concern marriage in some fashion. Mothers in the ancient Near East were particularly involved in the marrying of their daughters and appear as the chief negotiators in the marriages of the goddesses Ninlil and Inanna. So too in the Bible, at least in the early days: Rivka ran to her mother's house to tell her about Abraham's servant's mission (Gen. 24:28), and then went as a bride into Isaac's mother's tent (Gen. 24:66).

At the moment, marriage is not on Dinah's mind. She is off to **see the girls of the land.** Dinah is not looking for trouble; she is not running away or seeking sexual adventure. On the other hand, she is not out performing a chore for her family, drawing water or shepherding flocks. She is acting on her own initiative, reaching beyond the family, opening the gates to a relationship that goes beyond the confines of her home. She has made a choice: she will go to meet the daughters of the land. The tellers of the story repeat the words **the land** several times, for the people of Israel have a very complicated attitude toward the peoples of the land. Its appearance here in the first sentence is a reminder of this and also a hint that matters will not go simply for Dinah. Meanwhile, seeking to establish connections with them, **Out went Dinah.**

Out went Dinah, the first words of the story, are the only ones in which Dinah acts as the subject of a verb, creator of her destiny. But what words! To a patriarch, "going out" can strike terror. It means leaving the family domain, leaving both the protection and the control of the head of the household. Even today people talk about the vulnerability of girls, their potential victimhood, as a reason that they should stay at home. But they do not often articulate the other side of the issue: when a woman in the patriarchal world goes out, she leaves her family vulnerable. If something bad happens to her, it not only causes her kin sorrow and loss, it also reflects poorly on the patriarch's ability to protect his family. If she does something of which her family or society might not approve, it is a sign that the father/husband cannot control his relatives. The family is dishonored and loses political and economic influence. The honor of the family and its ability to marry off its children advantageously depend on the honor of the father, and he whose daughter has not been chaste is in much the same situation as a man whose wife has committed adultery. Both men lose their honor by being unable to control their women. When women go out, their men become vulnerable to their behavior. A famous phrase in *The Wisdom of Ben Sira* reflects the fear and rigidity that this vulnerability induces: "Daughters are trouble, let there be no window, do not expose her to any male and let her not take counsel among women" (Ben Sira, 42:9–14).

Some cultures have carried their concern over this issue to the point of simply forbidding girls to leave home except under specific, strictly chaperoned occasions. Biblical and ancient Near Eastern societies were not that extreme and did not confine girls to the house. They had responsibilities, such as drawing water, which took them out into the public sphere, but one who left the house without a specific chore was viewed with suspicion and condemnation. The laws of Hammurabi demonstrate this attitude when they consider the case of a woman who wants a divorce. If the local court finds that the woman was a paragon and her husband a profligate, she gets her divorce and takes back her dowry; if, on the other hand, they find that her husband has been a proper spouse, and she has been a gadabout, then she is to be thrown into the river. The word for "gadabout," *waṣitum* (literally "the woman who goes out"), has such a negative connotation that an Old Babylonian word list equates it with *harimtu*, "prostitute." Prostitutes walk the street. Their boundary-breaking divine patron Inanna/Ishtar walks about, and female demons roam the streets. But proper Babylonian women were not streetwalkers. Nor were biblical women: when Judah saw a woman sitting by the roadway, he immediately assumed that she was a prostitute. Attitudes do not change quickly. The great twelfth-century Jewish Bible commentator Rashi calls Dinah a *"yaṣ'anit,"* the Hebrew equivalent of *waṣitum*, "goer-outer," with the same connotation. The Renaissance Christian commentator Tyndale states, "Dinah goeth but forth alone, and how great myscheve and troble followed." Calvin draws an explicit message from this story: "Fathers are taught to keep their daughters under narrow watch." The control of girls is only slowly disappearing in our own culture, and our languages still encode the same message: the word in Yiddish for prostitute, *nafqa*, is actually an Aramaic word meaning "goer-out"; the word "streetwalker" in English means the same. With all this cultural background, **Out went Dinah** is not an innocent statement. It carries a warning that something is going to happen. And what happens is a father's nightmare: Dinah, who went out to see the girls, is seen by a boy.

The story is commonly called "The Rape of Dinah." But the story is not really about Dinah, who never speaks and essentially disappears from the narrative after the third verse. And it never tells us clearly that Shechem raped her. This story piles ambiguity upon enigma by "gap-

ping" (leaving unsaid) vital elements. The significance of the story depends on the way that readers fill in these gaps. If we assume that she
was assaulted, then the story can and has been read and interpreted as a
straightforward narrative of rape and revenge, a classic "morality tale," a
dramatic illustration of society's desire to keep girls under surveillance.
But the story says only: **Shechem the son of Hamor the Hivite, Prince
of the Land, took her, and lay with her, and degraded her.** If we do
not assume that he raped her, the story becomes a fascinating tale of
love, honor, intrigue, and war.

How did Shechem approach her? The story never hints at what happened. Did he speak to her? Did she speak to him? Did he take her by
force, or did he persuade her? Did he act like Prince Charming, or like an
imperious monarch stating his demands? And what about her? Was she
love-struck and happy, defiant and satisfied—or the victim of rape? We
will not know how Dinah feels. Her feelings are not the story's concern;
nor are the events that led up to the sex. Even her consent is not the issue, so the story does not make it absolutely clear whether she consented or not.

A later detail makes it most probable that Shechem did not rape Dinah. While describing the anger of Dinah's brothers, the narrator interjects a direct address to the readers, **for he had done an outrage in
Israel to sleep with the daughter of Jacob, and such should not be
done.** Such biblical asides are commentaries within the text, sermonic
punch lines that underscore the social lessons the author wants the hearers to learn. The most famous such aside appears in the creation story.
After Adam recognizes the newly created woman, the narrator adds the
"lesson" of nuclear marriage, "Therefore a man leaves his father and
mother and cleaves to his wife and they are one flesh" (Gen. 2:24).
Adam's act in the Garden is the paradigm of how a man should behave;
Shechem's act with Dinah is an example of what man should not do, and
the narrator points it out: **for he had done an outrage in Israel by lying
with the daughter of Jacob, and such is not to be done.** The narrator
uses a somewhat anachronistic phrase, "in Israel." It fits, for Jacob is indeed called Israel, and the act was an outrage against him, but this story
otherwise uses the name "Jacob" consistently. By using "Israel," the
aside invites the readers to switch from a concentration on Jacob's problem to their own interests as people of Israel. Using the traditional vocabulary of biblical moral teachings (*nebalah,* "outrage") and its syntax
("should not be done"), this narratorial statement forcefully admonishes
the readers that it is utterly wrong **by lying with a daughter of Israel.**

Nothing is said about forcible rape, for any sexual intercourse with a daughter is a moral outrage that may not be done.

The story focuses on the illicit aspect of Shechem's action: **he degraded her.** *'Innah,* "degrade," is a key word in both the sacred history of Israel and in the story of Sarai and Hagar. It usually has nothing to do with sex, and means to treat people without regard to the proper treatment that their status requires. The one biblical law that is explicitly and unequivocally about rape (Deut. 22:25–26) uses the term "lie with by force"; the word *'innah* does not even appear. In the story of Tamar and Amnon, where the issue is forcible rape, *'innah* is augmented for clarity by the word "overpower" and by the order of the words, "he overpowered her, degraded her and lay with her" (2 Sam. 13:14). Word order counts. In rape, the word *'innah* comes before the words "lay with"; in other forms of illicit sexual intercourse, *'innah* comes after "lay with." There is a reason for this difference in word order. In rape, abuse starts the moment the rapist begins to use force, long before penetration. In other illicit sexual encounters, the act of intercourse may not be abusive. The sex may be sweet and romantic. But the *fact* that the man has intercourse with her degrades her, and so the word *'innah* comes after the words "lay with."

It seems strange that the Dinah story only hints that the act was consensual instead of making it clear. After all, from Dinah's point of view, there is a very big difference if she was willing or forced. Modern readers, particularly women readers, are extremely sensitive to this matter and outraged that Dinah's consent is not mentioned. But the biblical author views things differently. The story is told from the viewpoint of the family and society from which Dinah went out. From their perspective, an unmarried girl's consent does not make sex a permissible act. She has, after all, no right of consent.

Volition and Virginity

In biblical Israel, as in many other societies, the right of consent to a proposal for sex or marriage belonged to the girl's father. It was he who "giveth this woman in marriage," as the English-language wedding ceremony phrases it. The father determined who and when a girl should marry, and she was expected to demonstrate her allegiance to him by remaining a virgin until her marriage. Biblical Hebrew encodes the cultural expectation that unmarried girls be virgins in the word *betûlah,* which can mean "virgin" and can also refer to any girl of marriageable age. The term may mean "virgin" in Levit. 21:14, which states that the High Priest cannot marry a widow, divorcée, profane woman, or prostitute; he can marry only a *betulah* from his people. On the other hand, the word refers to a young bride rather than a virgin in Joel 1:8, "like a *betulah* wearing sackcloth for the husband of her youth." The common pairing of *baḥûr* and *betûlah* means "young man/men and woman/women," and says nothing about their physical characteristics or sexual experience. When sexual inexperience counts, the Bible has to add the phrase "who has not known a man." The ambiguity and variation of the term shows that Israel expected young girls to be virgins, and so viewed all young girls as presumptive virgins. Likewise, the Greek word *parthenos* encodes the same cultural assumption and means both "young girl" and "virgin," and until very recently, the English "maiden" also carried both meanings.

Life does not always conform to social expectation. Girls who have indeed "not known a man" are prized trophies: Lot stresses the desirability of his daughters by announcing their virginal state. Virginity was so prized in Greece that the word *sophrosyne,* "right action," which refers to cautious moderation for men, means absolute chastity for girls. Virginity was also prized in Mesopotamia, where the laws of Lipit-Ishtar (¶33) provide that "If a man claims that another man's virgin daughter has had sexual relations but it is proven that she has not had sexual relations, he shall weigh and deliver 10 shekels of silver."

Western culture has attributed such moral and social importance to the biological *virgina intacta,* the "intact virgin" with the unruptured hymen, that we take such emphasis for granted. We rarely ask "why?" Why should society care that its young women be virgins at marriage? What harm do premarital sexual relations create in society? If the question is asked at all, it is often answered with an a priori assumption that men want their wives to be virgins so that they can be sure any babies are theirs. But that desire, if true, does not demand bridal virginity. Societies could have a convention that any baby born during the first nine months after the marriage belongs to the bride's family—after all, in an agrarian society, there is economic value in the labor of children. Or societies could have a rule such as Sparta is reputed to have had, wherein biological fatherhood was immaterial and only sociological fatherhood (who raised the child) counted.

A second common "explanation" for prizing virginity is that men want the "property" that they acquire to be new and unused. This also doesn't make sense. When sexual pleasure is a concern, experience might help. Delight in a "tight cunt" is ephemeral; only the first time affords the dubious pleasure of opening and penetrating. Women rarely want their bridegrooms to be virgins, and when they do, it is because the culturally transmitted ideological value of "purity" has outweighed the advantages of an experienced lover. Men who want their brides to be virgins may be influenced by their own culture's supervaluation of virginity, particularly female virginity. The advantage of nonvirginal brides is readily apparent. Since one of the main purposes of marriage is the production of children, a society could have a convention that a girl who has already become pregnant—indeed has already birthed a living baby—has demonstrated that she is fertile and therefore has increased her worth. There are a few societies that do not place stock in a girl's premarital chastity, but very few.

Several noteworthy attempts by anthropologists to explain the virginity ideal have not fully solved this puzzle. Some have concentrated on the well-known modern Mediterranean obsession with female chastity without realizing that the same valuation of virginity existed pre-Aristotle, pre-Bible, and around the globe.

There may be psychological elements in the attachment of culture to the virginity of daughters. Even though father-daughter incest is universally prohibited, this "Prime Rule" is all too often broken. The rule itself is evidence of the attraction that girls may feel for their fathers and that their fathers may feel toward them. The culturally decreed necessity to suppress this attraction, the guilt that feeling may generate and the denial and guilt caused by transgression, all may combine to generate an atmosphere of suspicion and jealousy and a determination to control the sexuality that cannot be enjoyed. This adds an edge to the proprietary sense of paternal rights over all children that has also been part of the social fabric.

Chastity and Control

There is a strong connection between chastity codes and the guarding of girls. Maintaining the girl's virginity is the prerogative and the duty of the male members of the family. Girls are carefully guarded and infractions seriously punished, and the chastity of the girl becomes an indicator of the social worth of the family and the men in it. "Real men" have the strength and cunning to protect their women; men whose female relatives have been defiled are judged to lack these qualities. The family becomes vulnerable when a girl hits puberty. Men of a family may trust one another as they join together to safeguard their women, but they will view other men with suspicion as potential seducers or rapists who would drive away legitimate suitors and make evident the father's inability to control his own daughter. A seducer or rapist shames a girl's father into lowering her bride-price. The father's solution is to limit his daughter's freedom and make examples of one who trespasses. Guarding her not only "protects" her against seduction and against accusations of promiscuity, it protects the family against the damage she might do to its standing.

Protocols of Propriety

One way of guarding daughters is to keep them indoors, an option chosen in Athens and to some extent in later Europe. In the ancient Near East, where girls were not so restricted, both laws and narratives deal with the possibility that a man might meet a girl in the street and sleep with her. The proper protocol demands that the man (or his father) approach the girl's parents, and possibly first her mother. A love poem from ancient Sumer demonstrates the way things should happen. The goddess Inanna relates that she was playing in the street before her house when Dumuzi approached her, put his arm around her shoulders, and invited her to come away with him. She answered, "Let me go that I may go home. What stories would I tell my mother?" Dumuzi has an answer: he will teach her the "stories women tell." She should tell her mother that she spent her time listening to music in the square with a girlfriend. "With this story," he says, "confront your mother; as for us— let us be dallying in the moonlight." Inanna is not persuaded, and convinces Dumuzi that he must court her properly by coming to see her mother, Ningal. And so he does, and they are engaged to be married.

Another Sumerian myth, "The Marriage of Sud," also demonstrates the proper protocol. In this tale, the god Enlil is taken with the young goddess Sud. He goes to her mother, Nunbarshegunu, to negotiate a marriage, and Nunbarshegunu accepts his offer to make Sud his queen and let her rule alongside him. Sud is then renamed Ninlil as a token of her new status and goes to marry Enlil.

Breaching the protocols of propriety threatens the entire system until the situation can be rectified. Ancient Near Eastern laws provide for ordinary financial procedures. In Israel the seducer of a virgin must pay the *mōhar habbetûlôt,* the normal bride-price for young girls even if her father refuses to allow him to marry her (Exod. 22:16); in Assyria, the payment is triple the value. But yet another Sumerian myth, "Enlil and Ninlil," shows that matters were not always so easily resolved. This myth is another version of the mating of these two gods, very different from the "Marriage of Sud." In this tale, Ninlil goes to the banks of the holy canal and Enlil accosts her: "Let me make love with you . . . let me kiss you!" She demurs, "If my mother learned about it, she would slap my hand; if my father learned about it, he would grab hold of me." But Enlil pursues the matter, sleeps with her, and inseminates her with the moon god Su'en. When Enlil comes through the town square, the court of the fifty great gods and the seven deciding gods try him and decree, "The sex offender Enlil will leave the town." Enlil is banished. Ninlil loves him, and indeed follows him, but he is cast out nonetheless. The story never says he rapes her, and her willingness to follow him is not the reaction of a rape victim. Nevertheless, his act is too dangerous to the social order to allow him to live in civil society.

Inanna insists that her suitor go to her mother. Ninlil and Dinah do not. But regardless of the willingness of the maidens, the suitors had no right to sleep with them. Even if Dinah was willing, even if she was the aggressor, it would not matter: Shechem is a ravisher. To use the terminology of Roman law, Shechem's act was not *stuprum per vim*, "wrongful intercourse by force," but it was certainly *stuprum*, "wrongful intercourse." In America, below a certain "age of consent" (which varies by state), a girl's willingness is legally meaningless, and intercourse with her can be prosecuted as statutory rape. In ancient times, no unmarried girl or woman, at any age, had the right of consent, and a married woman could not consent to anyone other than her husband. Only widows, divorcées, and prostitutes had any control over their own sexuality. To sleep with a girl before acquiring the consent of her parents was to treat her as if no one was responsible for her sexuality, no one was guarding it, and no one controlled it. A young girl with sexual autonomy could be only a prostitute. As Dinah's brothers say in their defense, "Shall our sister be treated as a prostitute?"

As modern readers, we often feel outrage that Dinah's will is not consulted, her voice not heard. In our society, after all, girls have some amount of control over their destiny, though we often forget how recently such phrases as "Who gives this girl in marriage?" and "asking for your daughter's hand" lost their legal import. The right of fathers to decide their daughter's marital destiny was an unquestioned prerogative, even in the United States, until well within living memory. Anxiety toward a girl's emergent sexuality and outrage at her unlicensed exercise of it still lurk in the parental psyche and the political arena. And when we factor in Dinah's age (she is called a *yaldah,* a little girl), then even today's explicit belief in a girl's self-determination begins to shatter—does a girl of twelve have the right to unregulated sexual freedom? Or are there situations when a girl should be controlled by laws of statutory rape? In the ancient world, there was no "age of consent."

Dinah and Dishonor

Genesis 34 is written from the point of view of the family. Dinah has brought disaster on them. Her consent would not change this; on the contrary, from the family's perspective, matters might even be worse if she had consented than if she had been raped. When a girl is raped, the rapist brings shame on the family. But if she is a willing participant, the shame is compounded. The man has shown the weakness of the family's boundaries, and the girl has revealed its inability to control itself internally. "Out of control," she brings dishonor to her father. In some cultures, such as Saudi Arabia, a father can kill her for this. In the "Law of the Slandered Bride," in Deuteronomy (22:13–21), the father cannot kill his daughter. But if she is found guilty, she will be stoned at the entrance to her father's tent "because she was faithless to her father's house." The word used for "be faithless," *zanah,* describes the action of a nonvirgin daughter, an adulterous wife, and an unfaithful Israel. All of these were required to demonstrate absolute fidelity: Israel to God, a wife or concubine to her husband, a daughter to her father.

But the deed has been done, and what will come next?

Part 2. An offer of reparation (Gen. 34:3–5)

> His heart cleaved to Dinah the daughter of Jacob; he loved the girl and spoke to her heart.
> Shechem said to Hamor his father thus: "Get me this girl for my wife."
> Jacob heard that he had defiled his daughter.
> His sons were with the flocks in the field and Jacob was silent until they would come.

The story hastens to assure the reader of Shechem's true feelings by using special phrases with precise technical meanings. **His heart cleaved.** *Dabaq* is the very word used in Genesis 2, "and shall cleave to his wife." *Dabaq* describes the love of husband for wife (Gen. 2:24), of Ruth for Naomi (Ruth 1:14), of Israel for God (Deut. 4:4 et al.; Ps. 63:9), and of God for Israel (Jer. 13:11). In all these contexts, *dabaq* emphasizes the permanence of the attachment. Shechem is not fickle, and his love is not transitory. And so "he spoke to her heart," *dibber 'el libbah*. This is another special term, which appears only eight times in the Bible. Always, the one "speaking to the heart" has a superior position: Joseph the ruler "speaks to the heart of" his brothers (Gen. 50:21); the Levite to his concubine (Judg. 19:3); Boaz to Ruth the gleaner (Ruth 2:13); God the husband to Israel as wife (Hos. 2:16); kings to their people (2 Sam. 19:8; 2 Chron. 30:22 and 32:6); and the people to Jerusalem (Isa. 40:2). The superior offers loving assurance to his upset, insecure, or alienated partner that he will rectify the other's insecure or alienated status. Eight times, the passages imply that "speaking to the heart" is successful; the positive response of the other party is not even recorded.

The choice of verbs suggests a poignant scene. Dinah is worried and insecure, with good reason. She has broken protocols and realizes, belatedly, what this might entail. Shechem reassures her: everything will be all right, they will be forgiven for "jumping the gun," and their fathers will arrange for them to be married. He lovingly offers commitment, and she stays with him, not because she has been kidnapped or is a captive but because he "spoke to her heart." But the problem will not be easily resolved. Shechem has "done her wrong." He may not have forced her, but the very fact that he has slept with her means that he has degraded her and her family.

But Shechem wants to rectify the situation by asking his father to offer to arrange a marriage. Done right, this should restore the honor of Dinah and her family. But before Dinah or Shechem or Hamor goes to speak to Jacob, Jacob hears that Shechem has defiled his daughter Dinah. People are talking. The deed has become known, and Jacob has been publicly dishonored. Their offense has escalated into scandal.

Jacob decides to keep quiet until his sons come home. This has puzzled many readers, who contrast it with David's fury over Amnon's rape of Tamar, or with Jacob's inconsolable wailing when confronted with Joseph's bloody coat. If Jacob had heard that Dinah had been *raped*, perhaps he would have been furious. But he has heard only that Shechem has slept with Dinah. Jacob is in a predicament. He must figure out the best way to vindicate himself and restore the honor this deed has destroyed. And so he waits for his sons.

The involvement of the brothers might seem surprising: it is Jacob, after all, to whom Dinah owed her fidelity, and the word "daughter" echoes through the lines. Jacob heard that he had **defiled his daughter Dinah;** Shechem committed an outrage by **lying with the daughter of Jacob.** Nevertheless, if the honor of the family is impugned, the sons will suffer. It will be harder for them to protect their interests if society at large considers them unable to safeguard their domestic territory. Moreover, if the family's status falls, they will have a harder time obtaining wives, will have to pay a greater bride-price, and may not be able to marry into high-status families. A girl's chastity is important to her brothers, and it is often they who avenge the "dishonor of their sister" by killing the girl's lover; in contemporary Arab societies, they are likely to kill the girl herself. The brother may not even be conscious of the damage his sister's act can do to his future, but he is aware that the culture considers his own honor at stake, and that he must avenge her violation to restore his violated honor.

The honor of a family may be restored in two ways. One rests with the girl's lover, who can demonstrate that he and his family intend no dishonor to the girl's family by offering a very large bride-price. The other rests with the girl's kinsmen, who can conduct a reprisal raid to show that the men can protect their boundaries and that outsiders encroach upon their territory, property, or personnel at the risk of their own lives. Both methods are represented in the Dinah story: Shechem offers the former, the brothers demand the latter. The scene is set for confrontation and negotiation.

◇   *Act II. (Gen. 34:6–34)*

Part 1. A princely proposal (Gen. 34:6–12)

> Out came Hamor, the father of Shechem, to Jacob to speak to him.
>
> Jacob's sons came from the field as they heard.
>
> The men were sad and very angry, for he had done an outrage in Israel by lying with the daughter of Jacob, and such is not to be done.
>
> Hamor spoke to them thus: "Shechem, my son—his soul desires your daughter. Please give her to him as a wife. Intermarry with us: give us your daughters and take our daughters for yourselves. And live with us. The land will be before you. Settle down or travel about, and take possession of it."
>
> Shechem said to her father and her brothers, "Let me find favor in your eyes and whatever you tell me, I will give."

Shechem knows he must restore Jacob's honor. Normally, as the son of a chief, he would find it easy to acquire a wife. But since he has violated procedure and dishonored the family, he is willing to pay any brideprice that Jacob demands. Negotiations begin when Hamor makes his (from his point of view) magnanimous offer, **"Intermarry with us; give us your daughters and take our daughters for yourselves, and live with us."** He is giving Jacob equivalent status with himself and offering a permanent alliance. To him the personal is indeed political; the marriage of Dinah and Shechem can be a paradigm for the relationship between the peoples, and the first step toward continual intermarriage. This is a most generous offer, and could have stood as a solid offer of marriage. The very eager Shechem, however, shows the same impulsiveness in this "negotiation" that he showed by sleeping with Dinah prematurely. Before Jacob can reply, the young prince rushes in to offer any brideprice Jacob might stipulate, and additional gifts. No demand will be too high. The combined effect of alliance and high brideprice will demonstrate the esteem in which the king's family holds Jacob's family, and thus restore Jacob's honor.

But the sons of Jacob are in no mood to accept this peaceful resolution.

Part 2. A deceitful deal (Gen. 34:13–19)

> Jacob's sons answered Shechem and his father Hamor with deceit. They spoke because he had defiled their sister Dinah.
>
> They said to them, "We cannot do this, give our sister to a man who has a foreskin, for that is a disgrace to us. But in this way it may be agreeable for you. If you will be like us, circumcising all your males, then we will give our daughters to you and take your daughters to ourselves, and we will be with you and be like one people. If you will not listen to us by circumcising, we will take our daughter and leave."
>
> Their words seemed fine to Hamor and Shechem son of Hamor.
>
> The boy didn't delay to do the act, for he wanted the daughter of Jacob.
>
> And he was the most honored of all of his father's house.

The brothers know that their own marriages remain to be worked out, and it is not clear whom they are to marry. Jacob and his father married their kin, the family of Laban. But there is no reason for Jacob's sons to go back to Mesopotamia for wives, for Jacob has cut his ties with his ancestral family. He has also separated from his own brother Esau, and has come to Shechem with no attachments other than to his own children. His children will have to marry outside the family. But exogamous marriage presents a real dilemma for a group wanting to maintain its own identity. By admitting an outside partner, the family opens itself to new blood and new customs, and forms allegiances with other groups. Through the marriage of Shechem and Dinah, the fate of individuals becomes a national issue. Hamor offers to become "one people"; the brothers demand that the Shechemites become more like Israel by adopting their custom of circumcision.

But the brothers' counteroffer is a lie. They are angry. They feel that their honor as men who can protect and control their women has been impugned. Shechem has **defiled their sister Dinah.** This is why they take over the negotiations, which would normally be conducted with Dinah's father. The brothers need to restore their own honor, upon which their virility depends. In their anger, they need to react violently. To do so, they are willing to denigrate an important component of their identity, circumcision, and to sacrifice a significant cultural value that is in itself part of the honor code: keeping their word reached in negotiation. They have no intention of giving Dinah to Shechem.

Not knowing that the brothers are lying, Shechem and Hamor agree to the terms. Shechem acts in his characteristic "act now, think later" fashion, and doesn't delay to be circumcised. He really wants Dinah. He is paying a very high price, though it might not have seemed quite as bizarre to Shechem and his family as it does to us today. Circumcision was and still is widely practiced as a puberty ritual, and many cultures still require it before marriage. In the ancient Near East, the Egyptian upper class was circumcised. Shechem is quite willing to cut off his foreskin in order to have Dinah. The narrator adds a final point to this negotiation: *he was the most honored of all of his father's house.* Shechem is not a nobody. He is not even just a prince. He is the most honored and respected prince. His agreement to marriage and to the brothers' terms restores the honor of Jacob's house.

Part 3. Ratification (Gen. 34:20–24)

> Hamor and his son Shechem came to the gate of their city and
> spoke to the men of their city thus: "These people are at
> peace with us and they live in the land and travel around it.
> The land is very broad before them. Let us take their daugh-

ters for wives and give them our daughters. But only with
this will the men come to us to live with us and be one people: if every male of us is circumcised as they are circumcised. Their cattle and possessions and all their
animals—wouldn't they be ours? Let us accommodate
them and they will live with us."

All those who go out the gate of his city listened to Hamor and
his son Shechem.

And all those who go out the gate of the city were circumcised.

Hamor links the marriage of Dinah and Shechem to the marriage of
the city and Israel. He offered to make their union a paradigm of further
marriages between their groups, and the brothers spoke in the same
terms. They are on the verge of becoming "one people," which is a
diplomatic term meaning total peace and lack of restrictions between
them. But Hamor is no despot. He is not going to "circumcise by the
sword." He goes back to convince his people to ratify the agreement he
negotiated. He speaks to the adult male townspeople. The women, the
ones who are to be given in marriage, are not consulted; their fate will
be determined by their fathers.

Hamor needs to convince the townsmen to agree to circumcision.
But why should they? They are being asked to adopt a marker of identity
that is not theirs: why should they do so? Unlike Shechem, they are not
overwhelmed by love of Dinah. Hamor and Shechem have to show
them that joining with Israel will be to their advantage. So they concentrate on the economic benefits of compliance. We have no reason to suspect that Shechem's protestations of love for Dinah were only a sham to
mask his desire for Israel's property. The story emphasizes that he really
loved and wanted her, and his offer of marriage was not economically
motivated. On the other hand, Hamor's act of linking their union with a
national treaty may have involved economic considerations. The Shechemites would gain a pastoral partner, a market for their agricultural
and urban products, and a steady supplier of meat, wool, leather, and
other pastoral products. Israel would gain a place to settle and a chance
to hold land. Abraham had acquired only the Cave of Machpelah, but Israel could now get real fields. Letters from the city of Mari (ca. 1700
B.C.E.) reveal such a relationship between pastoral tribes and the urban
population. This type of symbiosis also has a social advantage: it enlarges the choice of marital partners for both groups. This could be especially advantageous for Israel, which has no connections outside the

immediate family of Jacob, and needs wives to marry its sons. The advantage of this marriage to Dinah's brothers is so obvious that Hamor has no reason to suspect their offer. At the same time, their demand of the circumcision of a group with which they may have symbiosis could have seemed a fair price to pay for the benefits of connection. The people ratified the negotiated agreement and circumcised themselves, and the matter should have ended there.

But remember, we already know that the brothers' offer was a lie.

◇ *Act III. (Gen. 34:25–31)*

Part 1. Vengeful violence (Gen. 34:25–29)

It happened on the third day, while they were in pain.

Two sons of Jacob, Simeon and Levi, Dinah's brothers, took each his sword.

They came upon the city lying securely and killed all the males.

Hamor and Shechem his son they killed by the sword.

They took Dinah from the house of Shechem and went out.

The sons of Jacob came upon the corpses and despoiled the city that had defiled their sister.

Their sheep and cattle and asses, which were in the city and the fields, they took.

Their staff and their children and their wives they took captive, and they plundered what was in their homes.

Simeon and Levi attack the town in a classic revenge raid. It was easy: the men were debilitated from the circumcision and, not expecting trouble, had posted no guards. Dinah's brothers killed all the males, even Shechem and Hamor. Then **They took Dinah from the house of Shechem and went out.** Dinah has never come home. We are full of questions. Was Dinah still in the palace because she wanted to be Shechem's wife? Or because Shechem and Hamor insisted on keeping her there? What was Dinah's reaction to the raid? Did she consider herself rescued or kidnapped by her brothers? The story never tells us, just as it never told us how or why she slept with Shechem. Such matters are as irrelevant to the storyteller as they were to the brothers. Dinah's destiny cannot be allowed to rest in her hands. The brothers reestablish the control over her that they lost when she slept with Shechem.

The raid accomplishes two purposes at once: it teaches daughters that they cannot push the envelope of their own self-determination, and it teaches the Shechemites (and others) that they cannot violate Israel's boundaries. Their next act underscores this second lesson: **The sons of Jacob** despoiled and plundered the city. Who did the plundering? Most likely Simeon and Levi themselves despoiled the city, but it may be that the other brothers came and plundered after Simeon and Levi killed the males. The sons of Jacob killed the "perpetrators" (in their eyes) and then collectively punished the whole city, **for they defiled Dinah their sister.** The brothers' act and the storyteller's "they defiled" both underscore the same message: the city is liable for the actions of its rulers. For ancient audiences, this was nothing new. Wars were always fought because rulers offended one another or their gods. Moreover, if the brothers had killed only Hamor and Shechem, the townspeople would have been obligated to avenge their death by attacking Israel. The brothers' raid must be a full-scale punitive war, in which they take for themselves all the wealth of Shechem.

Part 2. The horns of the dilemma (Gen. 34:30–31)

> Jacob said to Simeon and Levi, "You have brought trouble upon me, making me stink to all the inhabitants of the land, the Canaanites and the Perizzites.
> "I am few in number, and they may gather against me and strike me and I will be destroyed, I and my house."
> They said, "Shall he treat our sister as a whore?"

Jacob, who has not said a word heretofore, now speaks. He let his sons take over the negotiations, for their future was most immediately endangered by Dinah and Shechem. And he had no objection to the brothers' demand for circumcision. The higher the bride-price, after all, the higher Jacob's status. But he apparently did not know that the proposal was a ploy, and he is dismayed by their actions. They have sacrificed their reputation as honest men, and his along with theirs, and this may make the other peoples hate him and may lead to his destruction.

It is easy to see why Jacob reacts the way he does. Throughout his life he preferred to compromise, maneuver, and accommodate rather than initiate confrontation. The mature head of the household, moreover, has the responsibility to counsel prudence and compromise even while hotheaded young men advocate war. He must tend to both the honor and the safety of the family. In their rush to restore the honor that Dinah's actions have endangered, the brothers have brought a new type of dishonor upon themselves. Their violence and their untrustworthy word have made it unlikely that others would wish to risk a treaty with them. The result can be war.

The brothers have only one answer, **"Shall he treat our sister as a whore?"** A whore is literally "up for grabs." One can deal directly with her, for she has no guardians, no protectors. The brothers want to make sure that everyone knows they are real men who can protect their own.

Did the brothers do wrong by attacking the town? Jacob points to an essential characteristic of Israelite history—Israel is small, few in number, and surrounded by those who could destroy her. If she makes herself hateful, she might disappear. Next to this rational reckoning, the brother's response sounds immature and rash. And yet the brothers' response also conveys a philosophy of protection: if people know that we will violently avenge wrongs that are done to us, then they will hesitate to attack us. Which is the best strategy for survival, accommodation or deterrence? The argument could be lifted out of today's headlines.

Dinah's story ends with her "going out" from Shechem's house. We have no idea what happens to her next. But Israel's story is just beginning. Jacob's instinct that their household can expect attack from the surrounding peoples may be right. In the very next chapter, the Israelites leave Shechem to go to Bethel to rededicate themselves to the God who appeared to Jacob as he left Israel. As they travel, "divine dread [comes over] the cities around them and they do not pursue the sons of Jacob" (Gen. 35:5). Why would they have wanted to pursue them, if not in retaliation for the raid on Shechem, and because the raid has made them consider Israel a dangerous, aggressive group? But they did nothing. What is this "divine dread"? Is it a special dispensation from God to keep Israel safe despite the animosity that the raid aroused? Or is the "divine dread" a result of the raid? Perhaps the brothers' actions have intimidated the local people into leaving them alone. The story doesn't tell.

Jacob maintains his opposition to Simeon and Levi's attack on Shechem. On his deathbed, he once again castigates them for their cruel slaughter and curses their fierce wrath. As a result of their action, Jacob declares, "I will divide them in Jacob, scatter them in Israel" (Gen. 49:5–7). The editors of the book of Genesis also disapprove, placing this story in a line of stories that show the inability of first Reuben and then Simeon and Levi to be the prime heir of Jacob, leaving only Judah and Joseph to contest for that position. History confirms Jacob's deathbed prediction, for the tribes of Simeon and Levi did not acquire and maintain land in Israel. Simeon entirely disappeared, the worst possible disaster of loss of land and lineage. But Levi became cultic functionaries who served God and Israel for their livelihood, and one could argue whether the fate of Levi was as disastrous as that of Simeon. Levi has no land, and to be an officiant at the cult may be economically precarious. But it is a prestigious role, and one wonders whether Levi is punished or rewarded for his zealousness.

The Dinah affair raises the questions of honor and self-defense with high drama, but leaves them unanswered. Who is right—Jacob, who will negotiate the return of his honor, or Simeon and Levi, who fight for it? And the ambiguities do not stop there. Jacob's stated objection is to the brothers' bloodiness. Would he have approved (and should we approve) if the brothers had simply refused the Shechemites' plans for merger, not on the grounds that "they" had defiled Dinah but on grounds similar to Jacob's objection to militancy—that the peoples were many and Israel small and they were afraid that Israel could be destroyed by absorption? Or if they presented a Deuteronomic-type philosophy that foreigners could contaminate Israel's culture? Would the story—the characters, the author, or the readers—approve if the brothers had openly refused to allow Dinah to marry Shechem, a refusal that could have resulted in the same type of war but without the advantage of a surprise raid? On the other side, what if the brothers' offer had been sincere? Would their proposal to merge with the Shechemites after they circumcised themselves have been acceptable if it had been an honest one? If they had merged with a people much larger than they, even if the others joined them by becoming circumcised, could they have remained distinct? And what about allegiance to the God of Israel? The brothers have not demanded, and the Shechemites have not suggested, any formal statement of allegiance. The circumcision is presented not as the prime symbol of Israel's covenant with God but simply as a marker of the in-marrying group.

The story of Dinah and Shechem highlights the dilemma of any small group trying to survive. If it is militant, it courts destruction. But if its boundaries are too permeable, it might be loved to death. The distinctiveness of Israel was and is placed at risk every time it comes into close amicable contact with other peoples. But the price of isolation may be eternal enmity and warfare, a price contrary to Israel's own self-understanding as a nation of peace. Should Israel welcome those of her neighbors in the land who wished to be absorbed, like Gibeonites in the period of the conquest and like Samaritans in the Assyrian period? And during those periods in which Israel had military strength—under David and Solomon and later under the Hasmoneans—should conquered nations become part of the people of Israel? And should they be formally converted? After the biblical period, the Dinah story continued to be the means by which these discussions took place, and the story was retold often in Hellenistic literature with different variations and permutations.

The questions of boundary protection and boundary definition pre-occupy Israel throughout its existence. Like the family of Jacob, Israel dwells apart. This national dilemma plays itself out on a national scene when kingdoms confront one another in war and peace. But it is also ever present on a personal level, whenever a girl goes out to visit the daughters of the land.

To the Barricades
Views Against the Other

THE BOOK OF DEUTERONOMY has no doubt about how to treat the Other: at arm's length! The Other, to Deuteronomy, is a perennial occasion for temptation:

◇ *Make No Covenant (Deut. 7:1–6)*

> When YHWH your God brings you to the land which you are going to inherit,
>
> And He dislodges many peoples before you, the Hittite, the Girgashite, the Amorite, the Canaanite, the Perizzite, the Hivite, and the Jebusite,
>
> Seven nations greater and mightier than you,
>
> And He gives them into your hand,
>
> You shall strike them, and completely destroy them.
>
> You shall make no covenant with them, nor show mercy to them.
>
> You shall not make marriages with them; your daughter you shall not give to his son, nor his daughter shall you take to your son.
>
> For he will turn your son from after me
>
> And they will worship other gods.
>
> YHWH will be very angry with you and destroy you quickly.
>
> Rather, this is what you should do to them: you should tear down their altars, break their worship-pillars, uproot their tree-symbols, and burn their statues in fire.
>
> For you are a holy people to YHWH your God.
>
> You, YHWH has chosen to be his people, a treasure-people from among all the peoples on earth.

The people of Canaan should be avoided. Even better, they should be destroyed. This is urgent, because if the other nations entice Israel to

worship their gods, YHWH will destroy Israel. Self-preservation demands *herem*, total destruction. The *herem* Deuteronomy calls for never
happened. Israel may not even have thought of it until Deuteronomy
was written in the eighth or seventh century B.C.E., long after the
Canaanites had disappeared or merged into Israel. The writers of
Deuteronomy are not facing Canaanites, but they are facing the real possibility of destruction. With disaster at their gates, they are reexamining
Israelite history to see what went wrong, and in this mental time ma-
chine, they reason that if only Israel had destroyed the nations of
Canaan, history might have been different. So Deuteronomy calls for
the Israelites to immediately destroy all Canaanite cultic paraphernalia,
and refrain from signing treaties or intermarrying with the nations.

Other voices in the Bible may disapprove of marrying the local inhabitants. In the book of Genesis, Rivka said to Isaac, "I am almost dying because of the daughters of Het. If Jacob took one of these daughters of
Het, one of the girls of the land for a wife—why should I live?" But her
aim is a Terahite woman for her son. There was no separation from the
local inhabitants, as Abraham and Isaac established treaties with them,
and Jacob's children married them. Samson's parents expressed their
preference that he would marry a local girl, but they arranged his marriage to the Philistine. By contrast, Deuteronomy's Moses demands total avoidance, warning the Israelites that they have the responsibility to
drive the others out:

◇ *A Warning from Moses (Num. 33:55–56)*
>   If you do not drive out the inhabitants of the land from before
>   you,
>   It will happen that those who remain will be stings in your eyes
>   and thorns in your sides.
>   They will be your enemies on the land in which you live,
>   And it will happen that I will do to you what I planned to do to
>   them.

In reality, Israel did not drive out all the Canaanites. This created a
theological dilemma: since God promised the land, why did God not
drive out all the inhabitants? The answer in the books of Joshua and
Judges is classically biblical: it was all Israel's fault. Joshua didn't win a total conquest because God wanted to see what Israel would do:

◇ *The Test of Faith (Judg. 2:22–23)*

> In order to test Israel through them, whether they were guard-
> ing the way of YHWH to go in them as their fathers did or
> not, YHWH left these nations without chasing them away
> quickly, and didn't give them to Joshua.

At the end of his career, Joshua warns that if Israel fraternizes with
the local peoples, God will continue to let them remain:

◇ *Another Chance (Josh. 23:12–13a)*

> If you turn away and cleave to the rest of these nations, those
> who remain with you, and you intermarry with them and
> come into them and they into you,
> Know very well that YHWH your God will not continue to
> drive these nations away from you.

But as the book of Judges explains, Israel didn't pay heed to the
warning.

◇ *A Warning Unheeded (Judg. 2:1–2)*

> I brought you up from Egypt and brought you to the land which
> I had sworn to your fathers.
> I said, "I will never break my covenant with you. And you
> should not make any covenants with the inhabitants of this
> land: you shall tear down their altars."
> You didn't listen to me.
> What is this that you have done?

God, angry at Israel's failure, decided not to drive the peoples out:

◇ *A Divine Decree (Judg. 2:20–21)*

> Then YHWH got angry at Israel and he said, "Because this na-
> tion has transgressed my covenant, which I commanded
> their fathers, and have not listened to me, I in return will
> not drive out anyone before them from the nations that
> Joshua left when he died."

The remaining people will not only be scourges, as Moses had
warned. They and their gods will be a trap into which Israel will fall.

◇ *A Scourge and a Snare (Judg. 2:3b)*

> So I in return said, "I will not chase them away from you. They
> will be scourges for you and their gods will be a snare."

Falling into this trap will be cataclysmic. Israel, having failed to oust
the previous inhabitants, will be ousted herself:

◇ *Snares and Traps (Josh. 23:13)*

> Know well that God will not continue to drive out these nations
> from before you.
> They will be a snare and a trap to you, a scourge in your sides
> and thorns in your eyes,
> Until you are lost from this good land, which YHWH your God
> has given you.

As long as these other nations remain, they will continue to give Israel the experience of war, and they will test Israel's faithfulness to divine injunctions.

◇ *More Tests and Wars (Judg. 3:1–4)*

> These are the nations that YHWH left in order to test through
> them Israel, all who didn't experience any of the Canaanite
> wars. Only so that the generations of Israelites would
> know, to have them experience war, only those who hadn't
> known it before: the five Philistine kings and all the Canaan-
> ites and Sidonians and Hivites who live in the Lebanon from
> Mount Ba'al-Hermon till the approach to Hamath.
> And they would remain to test Israel through them, to know
> whether they would observe the commandments of
> YHWH which he commanded their fathers through Moses.

"Test" and "failure" are important concerns of the historical books of
the Bible. These books were composed at a time when the Bible's world
was falling apart. The eighth century witnessed an earthquake so massive and devastation so widespread that the prophets Amos, Micah, and
Isaiah draw comparisons to the destruction of Sodom and Gomorrah
and consider the surviving community "a remnant." Ecological disasters
followed—drought and hail and insects—and these were followed by

military horror, when the Assyrians destroyed the Northern Kingdom in 722 B.C.E. and reduced Judah to Jerusalem and the surrounding towns. From that time until the Babylonian destruction of Jerusalem until 589 B.C.E. and beyond into the exile, Israel's historians wrote in the shadow of destruction. Their choices were stark. They could have concluded that Israel's God was weak, and those who did had no reason to continue to worship YHWH. They could have concluded that Israel's God was malevolent and hated Israel, and those thinkers also had no reason to continue to worship YHWH. The biblical authors needed to make sense of Israel's history and doom in a way that would enable them to maintain faith in the power and goodness of God and in God's love for Israel. Their solution was to "blame the victim"; to understand all the catastrophes as chastisement, punishment, and retribution. This would allow them to keep faith in God and to hope for the possibility of better days ahead. With this politico-theological agenda, they looked at Israel's history to determine what went wrong.

To this way of thinking, Israel's immediate failure to eradicate the nations was only the beginning of the long cycle of sin and retribution and repentance that the historians understood to be Israel's history. And primary in this failure was apostasy (worshiping other gods) and marriage to the local women.

◇ First Misstep (Judg. 3:5–6)

> The Israelites lived in the midst of the Canaanite, the Hittite, the Amorite, the Perizzite, the Hivite, and the Jebusite and they took their daughters as wives and gave their own daughters to their sons and worshiped their gods.

Israel's belief that God promised the land to her ancestors is intertwined with her conviction that the original inhabitants of Canaan were wrongdoers. When God took a solemn oath to give Abraham's descendants the land (Gen. 15), God also explained that fulfillment would be postponed for several hundred years because "the iniquity of the Amorites is not yet complete" (Gen. 15:16). Leviticus clarifies what this sin is and how it made the Amorites lose the land. It concludes its list of tabooed acts of incest, idolatry, and sexual perversity with a metaphysical and historical explanation:

◇ *How the Original Inhabitants Lost Their Land (Lev. 18:24–30)*

> Do not pollute yourself with all of these,
> For with all of these, the nations whom I am chasing out before
>   you polluted themselves.
> The land became polluted and I took note of its iniquity,
> And the land vomited out its inhabitants.
> And you—observe my rules and my laws and do not do any of
>   these abominations,
> (Not) the citizen nor the stranger who lives in your midst.
> For the people of the land who were before you did all these,
>   and the land became polluted.
> Let the land not vomit you out as you pollute it, as it vomited
>   out the nation who was before you.
> For whoever will do any of these abominations, those souls
>   who do so will be cut off from their people.
> Observe my discipline not to do these abominable customs,
>   which were done before you, so that you do not become
>   polluted by them. I am YHWH your God.

The message is clear: the peoples of the land performed deeds that polluted both themselves and the land. Israel must be careful not to do the same, for the land vomits out whoever pollutes it. Deuteronomy speaks the language of retribution rather than pollution, but it conveys the same message: the nations do things Israel must not do, and consorting with them will bring Israel to act as they do. These peoples and their behavior are the "Other" by which Israel defines itself.

Israel's alienation from the early inhabitants of the land is also reflected in the ancestral stories. There is no family connection between Israel and these peoples. Israel considered the Edomites and the various Bedouin-like tribes to be descendants of Esau and Ishmael, co-branches of Abraham's own lineage. Genesis also maintains that Abraham's father, Terah, was the ancestor of the Arameans (through Laban) and of the Moabites and Ammonites (through Lot), also members of the original family of the Israelites. But the various branches of the Canaanites have no such connection. Even Genesis 25, which draws more peoples into the family network as descendants of Abraham and his second wife, Keturah, does not provide a familial relationship for any of the seven nations of the land. They are entirely "other" than Israel in blood as well as action, and Israel must shun them.

This distancing from and "otherizing" of the Canaanites disrupts the universalism of the primal history of Genesis, chapters 1–11. It singles out Canaan for venom and opprobrium, placing in Noah's mouth a strange malediction:

◇ *The Curse of Canaan (Gen. 9:25–27)*

> Cursed be Canaan, the servant of servants he will be to his brothers.
> Blessed is YHWH the God of Shem, may Canaan be a servant to him.
> May God be beautiful to Japheth, may he dwell in the tents of Shem, and may Canaan be a servant to him!

Everything about this vituperative blast is strange. It seems so jarringly at odds with the universalism of a story line in which Noah is the ancestor of all the peoples of the earth. Noah's son Ham has humiliated his drunken father, but in retribution Noah singles out only one of Ham's sons, Canaan. He then utters a curse that introduces enmity and subservience into the post-flood world. And he makes it carry through to future generations. This hardly seems like the behavior of a man "righteous in his generation," who walks with God. Perhaps the horrible nature of this anathema is the reason for its inclusion in the Primeval History. The heroes of the flood in Mesopotamian mythology became godlike by being made immortal. But Noah goes downhill after the flood, first becoming drunk, then shamed by his son, and then, as the low point in his career, he pronounces this mean and misdirected curse. The narrator may include such a bizarre episode at the nadir of the story of Noah precisely because he does not approve of otherizing the Canaanites. But whether or not the author approves, the curse shows how widespread the disdain for Canaan was in biblical culture.

The list of Canaan's descendants in the table of nations identifies the group that Israel believes is archetypically accursed.

◇ *The Genealogy of Canaan (Gen. 10:15–19)*

> Canaan begat Sidon his eldest and Het and the Jebusite, the Amorite and the Girgashite, and the Hivite, the Arakite and the Sinite, and the Arvadite, the Zemarite, and the Hamathite.
> Afterward the families of the Canaanite dispersed.
> The boundary of the Canaanite is from Sidon as you come

through Gerar to Gaza to Sodom and Gomorrah and
Admah and Zeboiim and Lasah.

Geography rather than language determined membership in
"Canaan," which includes the Amorites, who speak a West Semitic language, and the Hittites, whose language is Indo-European. It is clearly
politics that decide Canaan's extent. For Canaan here extends beyond
the seven nations of the land to include the Phoenician territory from
Sidon in the Lebanon south through Tyre, all the way to the Philistine
cities south to Gaza, and then across the Negev through Gerar to the five
cities of the plain destroyed in the time of Lot. The list doesn't actually
say that Phoenecians and Philistines are "Canaanites," but it includes
their territory. In the same way, Judg. 3:1–4 identifies this same list of
peoples, "the five Philistine kings and all the Canaanites and Sidonians
and Hivites," as the nations that God left to battle Israel and test its uprightness.

Deuteronomy prohibited marriage with the peoples of the lands, and
the book of Judges incorporated in this forbidden group all the peoples
that Genesis relates were descended from Canaan. Neither list included
the Moabites, Ammonites, and Edomites, for Deuteronomy declared
that these peoples lived in lands that God gave to them. But the book of
Kings goes further than Deuteronomy or Judges in its opposition to foreign wives, for it includes Moabites, Ammonites, and Edomites when it
indicts King Solomon for his many marriages. The passage is intended to
illustrate how right Deuteronomy was to warn about the impact of foreign wives.

◈ Solomon's Foreign Wives (1 Kings 11:1–6)

> King Solomon loved many foreign women, including the
> daughter of Pharaoh: Moabites, Ammonites, Edomites,
> Sidonians, and Hittites from the nations about which God
> said to Israel, "Do not come into them and let them not
> come into you, for surely they will incline your hearts after
> their gods."
> To them Solomon cleaved for love.
> He had seven hundred princess wives and three hundred concu-
> bines and they inclined his heart away.
> It happened in Solomon's old age.
> His wives inclined his heart after other gods.

His heart was not fully with YHWH his God like the heart of
David his father.

Solomon went after the Ashtoreths, the gods of the Sidonians,
and after Milkom, the repulsive one of the Ammonites.

Solomon did evil in YHWH's eyes and didn't go fully after
YHWH like David his father.

At that time Solomon built a high place for Chemosh, the repulsive one of Moab, on the mountain that faces Jerusalem,
and to Molech, the repulsive one of the Ammonites.

He did the same for all his foreign wives, who used to burn in-
cense and offer sacrifices to their gods.

The historical books do not often speak against foreign women
and record some of these marriages matter-of-factly. Many of King
Solomon's wives came to him through dynastic marriages that were
aimed at consolidating international relations. Marrying the daughter of
as great a king as Pharaoh was a mark of Solomon's importance, and the
book of Kings records this marriage with pride (1 Kings 3:1). But in this
one passage, the lesson is very clear: foreign wives lead to foreign worship. The passage goes further than Deuteronomy, demonstrating the
danger of marriage to Egyptians, Moabites, and Ammonites, nations
Deuteronomy does not prohibit. Even Solomon's Ammonite wives (like
the mother of King Rehoboam) could mislead, and even Solomon, who
was noted for his wisdom, could be misled. The result was catastrophic:
Solomon's son lost the greater part of his kingdom.

◇ *The Decree of Division (1 Kings 11:9–13)*

Then YHWH got angry at Solomon, that he had inclined his
heart away from YHWH the God of Israel, who had appeared to him twice.

YHWH had commanded him about this matter, about not going after other gods, and Solomon did not observe what
YHWH commanded.

YHWH said to Solomon, "Because this happened with you, and
you didn't observe my commandment and my rules which I
commanded you, I will certainly tear this kingdom away
from you and give it to your servant. But not in your days
will I do this, for the sake of your father David. I will tear it
from the hand of your son.

"But one concession: I will not tear away the whole kingdom. I will give your son one tribe for the sake of David my servant and for the sake of Jerusalem which I have chosen."

If not for the foreign wives, says this historian, the United Kingdom would have stayed together. The whole history of Israel could have been different, if not for the foreign wives.

Queen Jezebel, or Deuteronomy's
Worst Nightmare

WEALTH AND POWER magnify the effects of the quintessential foreign wife, Jezebel, daughter of the king of Sidon, the northernmost of the Phoenician cities included as "Canaan" in Genesis 10 and Judges 3. As the wife of King Ahab of Northern Israel, she brought her foreign gods and ideas into the heart of Israel.

The book of Kings remembers Ahab primarily for his establishment of the cult of Ba'al in Samaria:

◇ *Judgment on Ahab (1 Kings 16:30–33)*

> Ahab son of Omri did evil in the eyes of YHWH more than all who were before him.
>
> It happened that it was not enough for him to go in the sins of Jeroboam son of Nebat, so he took as wife Jezebel daughter of Ethba'al the king of the Sidonians, and he went and worshiped Ba'al and bowed down to him.
>
> He erected an altar to Ba'al in the temple of Ba'al which he built in Samaria.
>
> Ahab made the asherah and Ahab continued to behave thus and to anger YHWH the God of Israel more than all the kings that came before him.

The book of Kings tells us nothing about Ahab's leadership of a coalition of South Syrian states to victory over the Assyrians. It remembers instead his worship of Ba'al and attributes the states to his marriage to a Sidonian princess. Jezebel herself tried to spread the worship of her gods Ba'al and Asherah, killing the prophets of YHWH and subsidizing Canaanite priests so that the prophet Elijah confronted "four hundred prophets of Ba'al and four hundred and fifty prophets of Asherah who ate at Jezebel's table" (2 Kings 18:19). Even after Elijah defeated them decisively in a dramatic contest on Mount Carmel and roused the people to

kill the prophets of Ba'al, Jezebel did not give up. Instead, she sent word
to Elijah, "Thus may the gods do to me and continue to do if it is not that
by tomorrow I will make your life like one of their lives" (1 Kings 19:2).
The contest was not yet over. Her otherwise estimable piety was a prime
danger, for it magnified the intrusion of a foreign cult into Israel.

The next appearance of Jezebel is in the story of Naboth's vineyard.
Here too she appears as a well-meaning woman who does everything
wrong, this time by trampling on Israelite law.

◇ A Question of Patrimony (1 Kings 21:1–3)

> Naboth the Jezreelite had a vineyard in Jezreel next to the palace
> of Ahab king of Samaria.
> Ahab spoke to Naboth thus, "Give me your vineyard and let it
> be my vegetable garden, for it is near my house. I will give
> you a better vineyard in its stead. If you wish, I will give you
> money at full price."
> Naboth said to Ahab, "God forbid, YHWH himself forbid that I
> should give my fathers' patrimony to you."

Here we have a classic economic issue; the enlargement of estates
where there is no empty land. Many people sold land during Israel's history. The Elijah and Elisha stories interspersed with the tales of this dynasty show that, at the time of Ahab and his sons, people were incurring
debts that they were not able to repay and thus were forced to sell land
to pay off what they owed. Significant rural poverty was accompanied
by the growth of large landholdings, a process (called "latifundization")
that continued in the next (eighth) century, when Amos and Isaiah bitterly attacked those who obtained land in this way. The sale of one's patrimony was all too common in the time of Ahab, but Naboth was not a
debt-ridden poor man. He turned back the encroaching king with a flat
"no," a refusal that he softened by referring to Israel's basic belief that
people should preserve their ancestors' land and the memory that is attached to it.

◇ Jezebel to the Rescue (1 Kings 21:4–7)

> Ahab came home depressed and angry about the fact that
> Naboth the Jezreelite said, "I will not give you my fathers'
> patrimony."
> He lay down on his bed and turned his face and didn't eat.

> Jezebel his wife came to him and said, "Why is your spirit de-
> pressed and you will not eat?"
> And he said to her, "Because I spoke to Naboth the Jezreelite
> and said to him, 'Give me your vineyard for money, or if
> you wish I will give you another vineyard instead of it,' and
> he said, 'I will not give you my vineyard.' "
> Jezebel said to him, "You, now, perform kingship over Israel!
> Arise, eat, and be satisfied! I will give you the vineyard of
> Naboth the Jezreelite."

Ahab has no tradition of "eminent domain" that allows a government
to take any land it wants, but Jezebel sees that a subject stands in the way
of the king's desires, and she will **perform kingship,** acting as she believes kings should act.

◈ *A Show Trial for Treason (1 Kings 21:8–15)*

> She wrote scrolls in Ahab's name, sealed them with his seal, and
> sent the scrolls to the elders and the nobles in his city who
> sat with Naboth.
> She wrote in the letters thus, "Proclaim a fast and seat Naboth at
> the head of the people. Seat two worthless people opposite
> him and let them testify thus, 'you "blessed" God and the
> king,' and take him out and stone him till he dies."
> The men of his city, the elders and the nobles who lived in his
> city, did as Jezebel had sent to them, just as was written in
> the scrolls that she sent to them.
> They called a fast and sat Naboth at the head of the people.
> Two worthless men came and sat opposite him.
> The worthless men accused Naboth thus before the people,
> "Naboth 'blessed' God and the king" and they took him out
> of the city and stoned him and he died.
> They sent to Jezebel thus, "Naboth was stoned and he died."
> As soon as Jezebel heard that Naboth had been stoned and had
> died, Jezebel said to Ahab, "Arise, inherit the vineyard of
> Naboth the Jezreelite who refused to sell it to you, for
> Naboth is not alive, he is dead."

Ahab's predicament, which Jezebel has made her own, is like David's
when he was faced with an inconvenient Uriah; like David, she will not

simply kill a subject without a cover story. David used the cover of warfare. Placing Naboth in a situation in which he will be convicted for
"blessing" the king, a euphemism for cursing the king, is an act of treason. Her plan rests on the widely held convention that the king can con-
fiscate the lands of those executed for treason.

◇ The Prophecy of Doom (1 Kings 21:16–19)

> As soon as Ahab heard that Naboth was dead, Ahab arose to go
> down to the vineyard of Naboth the Jezreelite to inherit it.
> The word of YHWH came to Elijah the Tishbite thus, "Arise
> and go down to meet Ahab king of Israel in Samaria. Look!
> He is in Naboth's vineyard to which he has gone down to in-
> herit. You shall speak to him and say, 'Have you murdered
> and also inherited?' And say to him thus, 'This is what
> YHWH says, "In the place where the dogs licked the blood
> of Naboth, the dogs will also lick your blood." ' "

Jezebel wished to gratify her husband's desire, but the prophet tells
Ahab that he has been doomed to a terrible death. Foreign wives bring
their own ideas about social institutions, and Jezebel has run roughshod
over Israel's cherished traditions. Her vision of kingship is imperial and
imperious, not so different from David's before he learned better. With
this vision, she overrides the Israelite concept that land should remain
within the owner's family, a concept of no interest to her. She also subverts the integrity of the judicial system. Perhaps her view is like that of
Egypt or later Persia: the word of the king is law, and if the king commands, his subjects must obey. But the results of her ideas are abhorrent
to Israel, where divine demands about law and land override royal
wishes.

The house of Ahab began to unravel. Ahab himself died of wounds
incurred fighting at Ramoth-Gilead. His son Jehoram had good intentions. He dismantled Ba'al worship, and seemed to listen more to Elisha
than his predecessors had listened to prophets. But he ruled only twelve
years before Jehu, anointed by a disciple of Elisha, brought the final
doom of the house of Omri in a bloody coup. Having begun his insurrection, Jehu approached Jezreel, where King Jehoram was recuperating
from war wounds. Jehoram and the visiting King Ahaziah of Judah went
to meet him.

◆ Doom Delivered (2 Kings 9:22–26)

> As soon as Jehoram saw Jehu, he said, "Is all well with Jehu?"
>
> He said, "What is 'well' as long as there be your mother Jezebel's many whoredoms and sorceries?"
>
> Jehoram reversed his hands and fled. He said to Ahaziah, "It is deceit, Ahaziah!"
>
> Jehu filled his hand with his bow and struck Jehoram between his arms.
>
> The arrow came out through his heart and he fell in his chariot.
>
> Jehu said to his adjutant Bidqar, "Pick him up and throw him into the portion of field that was Naboth the Jezreelite's. For remember, I and you together were riding together after his father Ahab, and YHWH sent this message to him, 'By oath, I have seen the blood of Naboth and the blood of his sons yesterday,' says YHWH, 'and I will pay you back in this portion,' says YHWH. And now, pick him up and throw him into the portion, as YHWH said."

Jehu accuses Jezebel of "whoredoms and incantations." Jezebel's "whoredoms" are not sexual (as far as we know). They are her acts of worship to her own gods, which from Israel's point of view are *genûnîm*, "whoredoms," acts of faithlessness to YHWH. In the same way, her "witchcrafts" are her prayers to her gods. Jehu's indictment of her loyalty to her home gods is a tip-off that an insurrection is afoot. He kills Jehoram, invoking the death of Naboth as justification for brutality, and then turns to Jezebel.

◆ The Death of Jezebel (2 Kings 9:30–36)

> Jehu entered Jezreel.
>
> Jezebel heard and placed kohl on her eyes, and made her head nice.
>
> She looked out the window.
>
> Jehu was coming in the gate.
>
> She said, "Is all well with Zimri, the killer of his master?"
>
> He looked up at the window and said, "Who is with me, who?"
>
> Two or three eunuchs looked at him.
>
> He said, "Throw her down!"
>
> They threw her down and some of her blood splattered on the wall and on the horses, who trampled her.

> He came and ate and drank and said, "Take care of that ac-
> cursed woman and bury her, for she is the daughter of a
> king."
> They went to bury her and didn't find anything but her skull,
> her feet, and her hands.
> They came back and told him and he said, "It is the word of
> YHWH which he spoke through his servant Elijah the Tish-
> bite, thus, 'In the portion of Jezreel the dogs will eat the
> flesh of Jezebel.' "

The story of her death reveals a woman of courage. Facing the murderer of her husband's family, the queen makes herself up to look her
best and calls Jehu a murderer, comparing him to a long-ago royal assas-
sin who ruled only a week before being assassinated himself. She speaks
with dignity, defiance, and grace. Nevertheless, we readers almost cheer
when her servants throw her out of the window to be eaten by dogs.
Her motives may have been pure, but Jezebel has done everything
wrong. She is not evil herself, but she is the very embodiment of Evil,
and the arch-villain of Israel. Jehu, on the other hand, the fierce usurper
who goes on to massacre all the house of Ahab, plays the part of the
champion of the forces of light, spouting prophecies of God to justify
his barbarisms. Despite his bloodthirstiness, he stands on the side of Israel's native lore. Jezebel, operating on a national scale with her royal
power, did precisely what Deuteronomy feared: she imported her foreign customs into Israel. As the Deuteronomist historian sums up
Ahab's reign (1 Kings 16:31): "Following Jeroboam's sin was not serious
enough for him (Ahab), so he married Jezebel the daughter of Ethba'al
and went and worshiped Ba'al and bowed down to him."

Cozbi

DEUTERONOMY'S WARNING that foreign women will lead Israel astray is dramatically borne out in the desert at Shittim, the site of Israel's catastrophic apostasy with Baʿal-Peʿor. The Bible contains six memories of this event, in Numbers, Deuteronomy, Joshua, Psalms, and Ezekiel, a testimony to its traumatic nature and to its prominence in Israel's memory. Deuteronomy stresses the moral lesson:

◇ *Each Man Destroyed (Deut. 4:3–4)*
> Your own eyes have seen what YHWH did at Baʿal-Peʿor:
> Each man who went after Baʿal-Peʿor, YHWH your God destroyed him from your midst.
> But you who cleave to YHWH your God are all alive today.

To Deuteronomy the issue is simple: the guilty perished, and those who are alive to listen to Moses speak are innocent survivors who can avoid destruction by staying fast to God. But the matter was not so simply laid to rest. The book of Joshua emphasizes the collective nature of sin and punishment: Phineas declares that the transgression of the Israelites at Peʿor still hangs over them, and he warns the tribes of Reuben, Gad, and Manasseh that any sin of theirs will be answered by a punishment of all Israel.

◇ *Ongoing Taint (Josh. 22:16–18)*
> What is this transgression that you transgress against the God of Israel, turning away from following YHWH by building an altar, so that you can rebel today against YHWH?
> Wasn't the sin of Peʿor enough for us, from which we have not been purified till this very day, and there was a plague against the congregation of Israel?

You have turned today from following YHWH, you have rebelled today against YHWH, and tomorrow He will be enraged against the whole congregation of Israel.

Ezekiel's memory is the most catastrophic: because the house of Israel rebelled in the desert, God has vowed that Israel would ultimately
lose possession of the land they had not yet even entered (Ezek.
20:21–26). Even after the exile to Babylon, the sin at Ba'al-Pe'or loomed
large in Israel's memory.

The fullest rememberings also include both a savior and a salvation
and explain a prominent feature of Israel's religious life: the monopoly
of the priesthood by the descendants of Phineas. Psalm 106, a poetic
retelling of Israel's history, recalls the plague at Ba'al-Pe'or and celebrates
how Phineas saved Israel:

◈ *Pe'or, Plague, and Prayer (Ps. 106:28–31)*
They attached themselves to Ba'al-Pe'or and at funerary offer-
ings.
They angered (God) by their misdeeds, and a plague broke out
against them.
Phineas stood up and prayed, and the plague stopped.
It was accounted to him as an act of righteousness for genera-
tions until eternity.

These lines form a mini-version of a classic biblical tale, with a sin,
God's wrath, a savior whose words turn away wrath, an intercessor
whose words turn away wrath, and an eternal reward for the savior. But
what caused Israel to sin? The "backstory" is found in Numbers 25, a
prose recollection of the same event.

Scene 1. The sin of Israel (Num. 25:1–3)
Israel stopped in Shittim and began to be faithless with the
daughters of Moab.
They called the people to their sacrifices; the people ate and
bowed down to their gods.
Israel became attached to Ba'al-Pe'or and God's anger flared at
Israel.

The cataclysm began with a dinner invitation to Israel from the
women of Moab. Perhaps they wanted to be friendly with the people

whom Balaam had tried, but been unable, to curse. Later, after things turned sour, Moses led a war against the Midianites. At that time he suggested another reason for the dinner invitation: "Have you let the women live? They were the ones who acted at the word of Balaam to bring trespass to Israel about the matter of Pe'or and there was a plague in the congregation of Israel" (Num. 31:15–16). In Moses' memory, the women were Midianites; in the story in Numbers 25, the women are Moabites. These are two separate recollections of an event that loomed large in Israel's memory. The event is the same, but the women are of different nationalities. And the backstory of Numbers 25 has its own backstory, as Moses relates a behind-the-scenes view: The invitation was instigated by Balaam, who knew it would cause Israel to sin. And it did, for at the dinner, Israel "broke the faith": it was "faithless" to its obligation to God.

The word for "faithless," or "break the faith," *zanah*, is very important in the Bible's vocabulary. God demands exclusive fidelity: Israel may not worship other gods, which "breaks the faith," or *zanah*. The Levite's concubine was faithless, *watizneh*, when she went home to her father; Israel breaks the faith especially when it turns to other gods, but also when it doesn't fully obey the laws. The book of Numbers requires Israelite men to wear a fringe on their garments so that, seeing it, the wearer "will not go astray after your eyes or heart, as you faithlessly follow them; so that you will remember to do all my commands and be holy to YHWH your God" (Num. 15:39–40). The opposite of *znh* is to be holy; infidelity is anything that gets in the way of holiness.

At Shittim, Israel's faithlessness took the form of eating. The women issued an invitation to dine, and the people ('*am*) came to dine and bowed to Ba'al-Pe'or. Because women issued the invitation, many readers have assumed that only men came to the table. But the "people" included the women, and we may imagine that all of Israel sat down to eat. As Psalm 106 also remembers, Israel partook of a banquet. A meal would seem innocent, but in the ancient world, an animal to be eaten was first offered to the gods, and in Israel, eating meat that had been sacrificed to a god was enough to constitute the act of being faithless. Eating the food of Ba'al-Pe'or attached Israel to Ba'al-Pe'or, and when they came and ate sacrificial offerings, **God's anger flared.**

Later post-biblical tradition remembers the story differently. Even though none of the biblical references has anything to do with sex, by the time of Josephus and Philo, memory is changing. Josephus, who devotes a lot of attention to this story, elaborates on Moses' mention of

Balaam's plan: the Midianites must send out the most beautiful girls to entice the Israelite boys, and then demand that the would-be lovers renounce the god of their fathers to worship the Midianite and Moabite gods (§129–30). Philo is very direct: Balaam states that nothing makes a man fall captive as easily as women's beauty, and suggests that the women titillate the Israelite men, "for coyness titillates . . . and inflames the passions." Then, when the men are in the grip of lust, the women are to have them worship their gods (Vita Mos. I, 295–99). Pseudo-Philo is even more graphic: Balaam suggests that the women of Midian should be naked and adorned with gold and jewels so that the Israelites will fall into their snares. The early Jewish midrash, the *Sifre,* perhaps not so certain that Israelite men can be inflamed by the sight of a woman, has Balaam suggest that the Midianites set up a fair to sell linens. The *Sifre* knows that Israel wants linen. The old woman selling the linen will send the Israelite buyer into the back of the tent, where a young woman will offer hospitality and wine until the man's lust awakens. Then the girl will demand an act of worshiping Pe'or before sex.

Whether the enticement is by nudity or by linen or by wine, the end result is the same: a trade of idol-worship for sex. And sex has remained the dominant memory of the story of Ba'al-Pe'or. It entered Christian sources as they picked up on this version of the story, speaking of "Balaam who taught Balak to put a stumbling block before the sons of Israel, that they might eat food sacrificed to idols and practice immorality" (Rev. 2:14). Even modern scholars have embellished the story with images of orgies and sexual adventures.

As we have seen, *znh,* "be faithless," when applied to a wife means adultery, a sexual act. It is also the root behind *zônah,* the prostitute, the woman who has no chains of fidelity. During the Graeco-Roman period, Hellenistic ideas about beauty and sexual seduction were entering Israel, and many of the biblical stories were retold as tales of seduction. It was perhaps inevitable that a story involving women and sin and using the term *zanah* would be recast as a prime instance of such misbehavior. Whether by food or sex, the women of Moab (or Midian) enticed Israel to sin, and **God's anger flared.**

Israel had awakened God's wrath, at another sinful banquet, around the golden calf. That time the sin was idolatry, not apostasy. No foreign God was involved and the feast was for YHWH, but the worship involved making an idol, a molten object as the focus of worship, and God's anger was inflamed. At that time, God spoke to Moses first: "Let my anger flare and I will destroy them and I will make you a great nation" (Exod. 32:10). Instead, Moses broke the tablets and called for the Levites, who killed three thousand Israelites before Moses went up to offer atonement. Here, too, God speaks to Moses.

Scene 2. To turn away wrath (Num. 25:3–5)

> YHWH said to Moses, "Take all the heads of the people and impale them for YHWH in the sun, and YHWH's anger will turn away from Israel."
>
> Moses said to Israel's leaders, "Each of you kill his people who have attached themselves to Ba'al-Pe'or."

The story doesn't tell us that a plague had broken out before God spoke to Moses. Perhaps God spoke to Moses before the plague, as God did in the episode of the golden calf. If so, Moses was not able to stop it from happening, for many other biblical allusions tell us there was a plague, and in the next scene in this story, the people are weeping before the tent of meeting, suffering the consequences of God's wrath. Moses either failed to avert the plague, or God did not tell him of it beforehand.

God's instruction to Moses to impale the leaders of Israel publicly is not a normal biblical punishment. Why should they die if they were not to blame? God seems to be demanding a punishment of the leaders that would serve as the symbolic slaying of the whole people. This strange request, otherwise unique in the Bible, has been "interpreted" by translating "ringleaders" instead of "heads." But the text clearly says "the heads." The ancient world knew the concept of vicarious punishment of leaders. The Assyrians, for example, had the institution of the "Substitute King." When the astrologers reported signs that a god was angry, steps were taken to protect the monarch: he stepped down from his throne, and a temporary king was appointed who was treated royally for a month and then killed. Thereafter, the true king came back to his throne. In this way, the death of the "king" could assuage the god's anger and the real monarch would remain alive. Greece had such symbolic slaying, though not always of the leader, in the institution of the *pharmakos,* who, by dying, would bear the people's sins away. But to biblical eyes, the execution of innocent leaders for the sins committed by some of their subjects seems strange and immoral. And Moses doesn't do it. Instead, he "relays" an instruction to the officials to find and kill the guilty parties. This was not God's instruction. Moses has modified the divine decree according to his own understanding of justice and the role of the leader.

Would impaling the leaders have averted the plague? Did the leaders execute their own guilty people without effectively stopping the plague? Were the Israelites paralyzed into inaction by the enormity of the punishment? Or did the scene change too quickly for anyone to act? The story never tells us what happened. Deuteronomy records that the guilty died and the innocent lived, so perhaps the officials punished the guilty. Or perhaps the plague spared the innocent. The story abruptly jumps to another event on this terrible day, "on the day of the plague over the matter of Pe'or" (Num. 25:18). Perhaps there were originally two separate stories about Ba'al-Pe'or, and we have the beginning of one and the end of another, or perhaps the story simply elides over details that Israel knew.

Scene 3. Death to the Midianite (Num. 25:6–9)

> Look! Here comes an Israelite man, bringing the Midianite woman close to his brothers in the sight of Moses and the whole congregation of Israel, while they are crying at the entrance to the tent of meeting.
>
> Phineas the son of Elazar son of Aaron saw and arose from among the congregation.
>
> He held a lance in his hand.
>
> He came up behind the Israelite man into the *qubbah* ("alcove") and pierced the two of them, the Israelite and the woman, in her *qubbah*.
>
> The plague lifted from the Israelites.
>
> The dead of the plague were twenty-four thousand.

This new scenario begins as the plague is raging. **While they are crying,** an Israelite shows up with a Midianite, bringing her **close to his brothers in the sight of Moses and the whole congregation of Israel.**

What was this man doing? Post-biblical tradition usually relates that he took her into a tent-chamber for the purpose of sex. This, of course, would have constituted a marriage act in ancient Israel, and Phineas was reacting to Zimri's marrying an outsider. Phineas's act would then be an extreme parallel to the Deuteronomic command that Israel not marry the native inhabitants but exterminate them; in this case the priest exterminates the Israelite who married the native. The same authors who read sex into the Moabite dinner also spin sexual scenarios about Zimri and Cozbi. Josephus relates that Zimri, whom he calls Zambrias, delivered an impassioned speech about the prescription of every aspect of life, about autonomy and about his right to choose his wife. The *Sifre* eroticizes Phineas's actions, describing how God created twelve miracles, such as making the couple's lovemaking last long enough for Phineas to get his spear and skewer them **in flagrante;** making the spear long enough to go through both of them, making Phineas's arm strong enough so that he could hold the couple upon his spear and show Israel what he had done. But enchanting as the image of Zimri and Cozbi skewered in the act may be ("the skewered screw"), it seems remote from the intent of the biblical story. In the first place, Deuteronomy does not demand the death penalty for those who marry native inhabitants. Second, Midianites are not native inhabitants of Canaan, not listed among the seven peoples of the land whom Israel is not allowed to marry. And third, the story does not use the normal biblical words for marriage and sex, "take [a wife]" and "come into her." "Bring close" is not the language of marriage or sexual relations, and the sexual scenario is as much a later allomorph of the story of Zimri and Cozbi as it is of the story of the Moabite dinner.

The story tells us that Zimri took Cozbi into a *qubbah,* and Phineas followed them. *Qubbah* is a unique word found only here. It is probably related to the Arabic *qubbatu,* a type of tent, from which we get the English word "alcove." Early Arabic literature sometimes refers to a tent-shrine called a *qubbah,* something like Israel's "tent of meeting," the *'ôhel mô'ed,* which scholars have dated back to the fifth and even seventh centuries B.C.E. The *qubbah* was staffed by priestesses of high status and used as a divinatory center. The Midianites may have had such a tent, which Zimri set up in the midst of Israel. Zimri was not thinking about sex during a plague, at a time when all the people were weeping at the door to the Tent of Meeting. Desperate to stop the plague, he brought a princess/priestess of Midian to perform acts of prayer and intercession in a Midianite tent-shrine he constructed for the occasion. This second scenario seems probable in the light of the Balak-Balaam story that precedes this one (Num. 22–24), and revolves around curses and blessings. That story uses the unusual word *qabah* eight times, once when the elders of Moab and Midian asked Balaam to curse Israel (*qabah li' ôtô,* Num. 22: 11), six times by Balak and once by Balaam. In Akkadian the word *qabû* means "speak, call"; here it is clearly a technical term for invoking divine power against an enemy. The frequency of this term in this story and its rarity elsewhere in the Bible suggests that *qbh* is a technical Moabite / Midianite term for invoking God. The *qubbah* could then be the place where such invocation of divine power could be enacted. There, at the site of the misdeed, Phineas executes them.

Zimri may have seen no harm in bringing this Midianite princess to add her powers to Israel's in an attempt to stop the plague. She may have been praying to YHWH rather than Baʿal-Peʿor. Just as Balaam of Moab was a prophet of YHWH and blessed Israel with YHWH's power, so too Cozbi of Midian could have been involved in a cult of YHWH. If she prayed to a foreign God, like Baʿal-Peʿor, her acts would clearly be idolatry, and Zimri's would be apostasy. But Zimri might have reasoned that a Midianite ritual to YHWH would be acceptable. Phineas, however, viewed it as harmful foreign worship.

The text never really spells out what Zimri and Cozbi are doing, but Phineas's action is very clear: he kills them. And the plague stops. Phineas has done just the right thing to make God's flaring anger subside. And God rewards him.

Scene 4. Reward for Phineas (Num. 25:10–13)

> YHWH spoke to Moses thus: "Phineas son of Elazar son of Aaron the priest turned back my wrath from the Israelites as he took my zeal for his own in their midst so that I did not destroy the Israelites in my zeal.
>
> "Therefore, say, 'I am giving him my covenant of peace and it will be for him and his seed after him, an eternal covenant of priesthood, for he had zeal for his god; he makes atonement for the Israelites.' "

A covenant of peace seems a strange reward for homicide, but Phineas did bring peace and well-being when he stopped the plague. God was raging in his *qinʾāh*. This word, translated "jealousy" or "zeal," is a master's appropriate reponse to the faithlessness, *znh*, of his subordinate. When the "spirit of jealousy," *ruʾah qinʾāh*, comes over a husband, he can bring his wife to the special oath trial of a suspected adulteress described in Num. 5:11–21. He will not be punished for false accusation even if the trial proves her innocent, for a husband has a privilege to feel righteous indignation / jealousy. God demands the same exclusive fidelity that a husband expects. In the second commandment, God commands, "Do not bow down to (other gods) or worship them, for I the Lord your God am a jealous God, *ʾel qannāʾ*, and punish to the third and fourth generation" (Exod. 20:5). God will respond with the *qinʾāh* of a husband, a *qinʾāh* that can inflame God so the result can be, as here, plague or other devastation. Phineas takes it upon himself to express God's *qin'ah* for him, to be the agent of God's wrath by killing Cozbi and Zimri, and in this way, he turns away God's wrath much as a back-fire stops a raging forest fire. One other biblical character claims to have taken God's *qin'ah* upon himself, Elijah (1 Kings 19:10, 17) and Pseudo-Philo and rabbinic midrash identify Phineas with Elijah.

The seriousness of the event at Ba'al-Pe'or is indicated by the many recollections of it, by the huge number of dead, twenty-four thousand people killed in the plague; by the swiftness of the penalty, and by the reward of eternal priesthood to Phineas. It might seem strange that a story about such a serious event contains so many ambiguities—the difficulty in determining exactly what Zimri and Cozbi did wrong, the lack of clarity as to whether Zimri sinned by consorting with Cozbi sexually or by bringing her in as a cult official, and the telescoping of the dinner with the daughters of Moab with the killing of Zimri and Cozbi. But these very uncertainties convey the eerie and cryptic experience of meeting the ferocious aspect of God. In this way, it resembles another story of terror, the tale of Moses and Zipporah and the "bridegroom of blood," which is also deeply elliptical and enigmatic. But that story made it clear that Moses was extremely fortunate to have a Midianite wife. This story just as clearly conveys the distinct impression that Moabite and Midianite women are a danger to Israel—to its integrity and therefore to its very survival.

Cozbi's name indicates the nature of the confusion and of the danger. Cozbi is related to the Akkadian *kuzbu,* "sexual attractiveness, beauty." But it is also related to the Hebrew root *kzb,* meaning "deceit or falsehood." The two meanings of the name contain the same message as the teaching of Proverbs, "Grace is a falsehood and beauty is futility" (Prov. 31:30). Together they also present Phineas's view of the foreign woman: attractive and deceitful. Phineas gives Cozbi no chance to prove that she is or could be loyal to God. He immediately casts her as deceit itself. He believes that if he allows her to come into Israel for whatever purpose, she will weaken Israel's cohesion and faith and destroy it. The foreign woman will instigate apostasy, the most dangerous act that Israel can perform. At Ba'al-Pe'or the result was twenty-four thousand Israelites dead of the plague. If associating with foreign women continues, it will be the death of Israel.

Phineas's actions have occasioned considerable comment through the ages. His role in stopping the plague placed him in a class with Moses and Aaron as a great model of one who "stood in the breach," and his zeal for God caused him to be identified with Elijah in some rabbinic midrash. During the Maccabean period, he was the model for Mattathias, who also acted with zeal for God when he killed a Jew breaking the commandment and thus sparked the revolt (1 Macc. 2:26, 50–64). But Phineas's act of murder did not always meet with approval. As attitudes toward zealotry and vigilantism changed, later texts stressed the uniqueness of Phineas's deed and the many miracles God performed around the event. These texts did not want people to act like Phineas. But Phineas himself was never in disrepute; his motive for the killing, the protection of Israel, was never questioned. He stood in the breach, as it were, preventing foreign elements from coming into Israel, and preventing the anger of God from breaking out over it.

Hagar, My Other, My Self

THE STORIES of Israel at Baʿal-Peʿor and of Cozbi and Phineas bear the same message about foreign women: Danger! Keep away! The story of Hagar, Sarai, and Abram is far more benevolent. It deals with a different kind of ethnic arithmetic. Rather than the addition of foreign women or their radical subtraction, this story concerns the multiplication of Abraham and the divisions this requires. But it too urges separation.

The Abraham–Sarah cycle is all about multiplication, and the story of Hagar and Sarai that dramatizes it is at the exact center of the sequence. The structure of the cycle emphasizes its importance, for it moves in concentric rings from the *lekh lekha* ("Go!") of the call to Abraham to leave home (Gen. 12) to the *lekh lekha* ("Go!") of the call to Abraham to sacrifice Isaac (Gen. 22). The beginning of Genesis, chapter 12, is about letting go of the past by cutting ties to Abram's father; chapters 22 and 21 are about letting the future go, cutting ties to the sons, and their near death. Moving inward toward the center we find the two disposable-wife stories, chapters 12, Sarai in Egypt, and 20, Sarah in Gerar, in which Abraham cuts his ties to his wife but gets her back. The next ring concerns Lot and Sodom; in Genesis, chapters 13 and 14, Abram separates from Lot, who goes to Sodom; in chapters 18 and 19 Abraham intervenes on Lot's behalf to save Lot and Sodom, and Abraham's son Isaac and Lot's sons Moab and Ben-Ammi are born, separate branches of Terah's family. The innermost ring is about covenants: chapter 15, the covenant among the carcasses, and chapter 17, the covenant of circumcision. And in the middle, between the two covenants, is the story of Sarai and Hagar.

The content of the story has a similar ring structure: two women who revolve around a man, head of the household, who has all the authority. As always in these biblical stories, names count. The man is *ʾab-ram*, "exalted father," the wife is *sarai*, "the princess," and the other woman is *hagar*, which sounds like *haggēr*, "the outsider." The two women are dependent on the man's will, but their shared situation does not bind them together. On the contrary, far from uniting them, oppression turns them against each other. Hagar and Sarai are not allies; they vie for status in the household. Biblical co-wives, even blood sisters like Rachel and Leah, are such rivals that the Hebrew word for "co-wife," *ṣarah*, is also the word for "trouble." The rivalry between Sarai and Hagar is particularly acute and dramatic because all the advantage seems to be Sarai's. Sarai is the full, free wife; Hagar is a slave.

In Islamic tradition, Hagar was not a slave but a princess wed to Abram in a dynastic marriage. So too a Jewish midrash relates that Hagar was a princess in the house of Pharaoh. When Pharaoh saw the wonders that God had performed for Sarai and Abram, he said, "Better for my daughter to be a servant in this house than a princess in any other," and sent her off. But even if she was born a princess, Hagar is a slave in Sarai's household. Justice would demand that Sarai treat Hagar well. When she does not, we are bothered. Several midrashim try to resolve this ethical issue by finding fault with Hagar, by assuming that she must have done something wrong. They explain that Hagar let everybody see the contempt in which she held her mistress, saying, "You think my mistress is righteous? She puts on a righteous face, but clearly God knows that she is not righteous: she has been barren all these years and I got pregnant the first night!" In contrast, readers today tend to be angry at Sarai, to castigate her for being insensitive to the plight of someone for whom she should have felt both compassion and solidarity.

◇ *Act I. The Coming of Ishmael*

Scene 1. A problem and a plan (Gen. 16:1–3)

> Sarai, Abram's wife, had not borne him a child.
> She had an Egyptian slave-woman named Hagar.
> Sarai said to Abram, "Look, please: God has stopped me from giving birth. Come, please, into my slave-woman; perhaps I will be built up through her."
> Abram listened to the voice of Sarai.

Sarai conceives a plan to use her slave as her surrogate. These opening lines emphasize Sarai's initiative. She, the active agent, thinks up the plan, proposes Hagar, and gives her to Abram. Not long ago, readers of this story were shocked and astonished by her plan; now, in an age of surrogate motherhood, it seems like an ordinary, nontechnological version of surrogacy. Evidence from ancient texts show that this arrangement, although not common, was once a regular feature of family relations. Three ancient Near Eastern marriage contracts stipulate that should the bride be barren after a specified number of years, she will give her husband her slave. How she acquired the slave doesn't matter: the slave could be part of the wife's dowry or purchased for this purpose; as long as she is the owner of the slave at the time she gives him to her husband, the slave could be her surrogate. These contracts show that this arrangement was not confined to one place or time within the Mesopotamian legal tradition: one is from 1900 B.C.E. and the Assyrian mining and merchant colonies in central Anatolia (now Turkey), one from Nuzi (in Syria) around 1600 B.C.E., and one from southern Babylonia about 500 B.C.

The best-known example of surrogacy is in the laws of Hammurabi. Paragraph 146 concerns the *nāditu*, a priestess belonging to an order of women who lived together and generally pooled their economic resources. They did not take vows of chastity, and could leave the group life and get married, but they were not supposed to have children. So, say the laws of Hammurabi, if a man marries a *nāditu*, she will give her husband a slave girl to have his child; if she does not, he can take a second wife. Since any second wife would quite likely be a rival to the first wife and even displace her, a woman would prefer to give her husband her own slave as a concubine to forestall such a marriage.

Neither Sarai, who proposes Hagar, nor Abram, who agrees, mentions obtaining the consent of the slave girl. To contemporary readers, such consent seems necessary for the arrangement to be moral. But none of the ancient texts sees any ethical problem with this arrangement. Ancient societies accepted slavery as a regular part of social life. Using another person's body as a surrogate for one's own is part of the fabric of slavery. Just as a slave's muscles can be utilized for the good of the master, so can a slave woman's womb. Sarai plans that Hagar's womb will be the way that Sarai herself will be **built up.** Abram agrees, and Hagar must comply.

So far, everything is according to plan.

Scene 2. The plot thickens (Gen. 15:3–6)

> Sarai the wife of Abram took Hagar the Egyptian, her slave-woman, at the end of ten years that Abram had lived in the land of Canaan.
>
> She gave her to Abram her husband for him as a wife.

He came into Hagar and she conceived.

She saw that she had become pregnant, and her mistress was diminished in her eyes.

Sarai said to Abram, "My wrong is on account of you. I gave my
   slave-woman into your lap. She sees that she is pregnant and
   I am diminished in her eyes. Let YHWH judge between me
   and you."

Abram said to Sarai, "Here: your slave-woman is in your hands.
   Do to her what is good in your eyes."

Sarai abused her.

She fled from her presence.

Something unanticipated happens. Hagar, who was supposed to be a
neutral body being passed from Sarai to Abram, reacts. This "womb
with legs" is a person with her own viewpoint, and her mistress is **diminished in her eyes.** Hagar knows that she has something Sarai
doesn't have, a child in her womb, and this knowledge makes her cease
to consider Sarai's status high above her own. Ancient documents anticipate such a development. The laws of Hammurabi and the contracts
know that once a slave becomes a slave wife, she may not keep acting
like a slave. They differ about what the mistress should do if that happens, and the laws provide that if the slave wife has not yet borne children, her mistress can sell her; if she has, her mistress can demote her to
an ordinary slave (¶147).

Sarai's reaction to her loss of authority is sharp. She indicts Abram,
**"My wrong is on account of you. . . . May YHWH judge between me
and you."** Sarai has a version of what feminists call a "click moment."
She realizes that her own hands are tied. She is wife no. 1, but the pregnant wife no. 2 is gaining on her and there is nothing she can do about it:
when she gave the slave girl to her husband, she relinquished her authority over her. She has lost all leverage. Sarai sees herself at risk, and attacks Abram because he holds all authority in the household.

Sarai's attack has a purpose. She wants something from Abram: the
restoration of her authority over Hagar. Abram understands this, understands that power is the issue, and he restores it to Sarai by giving control of Hagar back to her, in effect turning Hagar back into a simple
slave, **"your slave-woman is in your hands."** Hagar is once again
passed from person to person. Neither Abram nor Sarai ever calls her by
her name. They treat her as a slave, not a person, and to recognize that
she is also a person would get in the way of their plans. So Abram de-

clares, **"your slave-woman is in your hands."** He further adds, with perhaps unconscious irony, **"do to her what is good in your eyes."** The phrase is the verbal equivalent of washing one's hands. The Ephraimite in Gibeah said, "Do to them whatever is good in your eyes" as he offered his daughter and the Levite's concubine to the threatening mob ("The Bad Old Days," page 123). In the face of their certain evil, the phrase sounds evil and immoral. Here too, Abram knows Sarai does not intend kindness to Hagar. She will certainly assert her regained power by dominating Hagar in some way. But Abram indicates that he will not oversee Sarai's actions, will not control them, will not judge them or react to them. She is free to **do to her what is good in your eyes.**

And so it happens. Sarai does what is good for her. Rescued from her own personal abyss, she is going to make sure that Hagar doesn't threaten her again. And so, in her last act in the story, she abuses her, *watteʿannehā*. As we have seen, *ʿinnah* is a key word in biblical language, fraught with allusions we will consider in a moment. But first, we ask: since a slave is oppressed by definition, how do you abuse a slave? What did Sarai do? The story never says. We could spin midrashim of Sarai's beating Hagar or sending her out in freezing rain. But perhaps she simply starts treating her like an ordinary slave. Commanding her to draw water from the well, for example (as suggested by a classic rabbinic midrash), would be a denial of the status that Hagar had achieved by being pregnant, and thus would be considered abuse, oppression, or degradation. Hagar knows that dominance is the issue. She does not want to be under Sarai's authority, and as Sarai acts to protect her turf, Hagar once again reacts. She flees. She leaves Sarai and Abram behind, and the story goes with her to the wilderness.

Scene 3. Angel in the desert (Gen. 16:7–14)

> An angel of YHWH found her by the water spring in the wilderness, by the spring on the way to Shur.
>
> It said, "Hagar, slave-woman of Sarai, where are you coming from and to where are you going?"
>
> She said, "From the presence of Sarai my mistress I am fleeing."
>
> The angel of YHWH said to her, "Return to your mistress and be oppressed under her hand."
>
> The angel of YHWH said to her, "Greatly will I multiply your seed so that it cannot be counted in its multitude."
>
> The angel of YHWH said to her, "Look, you are pregnant, you are going to give birth to a son and you will call his name

> Ishmael, for YHWH has seen your oppression. He will be a
> wild onager of a man, his hand against all, and all hands
> against him, and he will live in the face of his brothers."
>
> She called the name of YHWH who spoke to her, "You are El
> Roi (the God of my seeing)," for she said, "have I also come
> here looking after the one who sees me.
>
> "Therefore one calls the well, 'well of the living one who sees
> me.' Look! It is between Kadesh and Barad."

The wilderness in the south of Israel is a place fraught with angels: here Elijah meets an angel as he goes to Horeb, and Hagar meets one, too. Their dialogue begins with an almost ritual question: **"Hagar, slave-woman of Sarai, where are you coming from and to where are you going?"** The angel addresses her by name, for he knows who she is. She answers simply, **"From the presence of Sarai my mistress I am flee-ing."** It doesn't matter where she is going: the essential fact is that she is fleeing Sarai. The reader feels the pathos of the oppressed slave, but the angel says, **"Return to your mistress and be oppressed under her hand."** Is this the proper way to treat a runaway slave? The angel is act-ing in accord with ancient Near Eastern laws that, like the laws in this country before the Civil War, respected the slaveowner's property rights and required the person who found a runaway slave to return the slave to his or her owner. But biblical law is different: biblical law requires one to help a runaway slave escape and not give him or her back to the owner (Deut. 23:16–17). True, the events took place long before Deuteronomy, but the angel's actions must have shocked an Israelite reader: why should an angel place the laws of property over the freedom of persons?

Hagar's angel is not finished. Angels usually have threefold messages, and this one does, too. The first part, **Return . . . and be oppressed;** the second part, **"Greatly will I multiply your seed so that it cannot be counted"**; the third, **"you are pregnant, and you are going to give birth to a son and you will call his name Ishmael ('God hears'), for God has heard your oppression. He will be a wild onager of a man."** The second address makes Hagar the only woman to receive a divine promise of seed, not through a man but as her own destiny. And the third statement puts Hagar in the company of those few women— Samson's mother, Hannah, and Mary in the New Testament, who re-ceive a divine annunciation of the coming birth. And what a birth! Hagar will have a glorious progeny who can never be exploited or subjected—if she voluntarily goes back to be exploited. And so Hagar goes back. Recognizing the divine power, she neither argues nor avoids the request. But before she gives up her autonomy, she exercises it by naming God according to her own experience. God called Hagar by name, the only character in the story to do so, and Hagar responds, naming God **El Roi, "God of my seeing,"** which can mean both "the God I have seen" and "the God who sees me." Seeing is important to Hagar and to the narrator. When she saw that she was pregnant, her mistress was diminished in her eyes, but Abram told Sarai, **"Do to her what is good in your eyes."** Hagar's vision and Sarai's vision have brought her to this spring, itself a play on the word for "eye." Now the mutual "seeing" between God and Hagar points to a solution. Her own explanation is enigmatic and difficult to understand, but it seems to mean **"Have I also to this place (come) looking after (or seeing the traces) of the one who sees me?"** The name itself is clear: El Roi, "the God of my seeing." The once and future slave leaves her mark upon how people remember God.

Scene 4. The birth (Gen. 16:15–16)
> She gave birth for Abram to a son.
> Abram called the name of his son, whom Hagar had borne, Ishmael.
> Abram was eighty-six years old when Hagar gave birth to Ishmael for Abram.

When Hagar gives birth to Ishmael, Abram names him, giving him the name that the divine messenger has already pronounced: "God listens." El Roi, the God who sees, also listens. Listening, like seeing, is very important in this story: Abram listened to Sarai's voice (Gen. 16:2), the angel told Sarai that God listened to her affliction (16:11), God will tell Abraham (as renamed by God in 17:4), "I have listened to you about Ishmael" (17:20), God tells Abraham to listen to Sarah (21:12), and finally, God will listen to Ishmael's cry (21:17). Ishmael's name emphasizes the God who listens even when we are not aware of God's activity.

Sarai is not involved in Ishmael's birth. Three times the text mentions that Hagar bore the child. Sarai has been displaced, and the son never becomes hers. This is very different from what will happen when Bilhah acts as a surrogate for the barren Rachel. There the surrogacy plan works, the child is considered Rachel's, and Rachel names him Dan, saying "God has vindicated me (*danannî*) and listened to my voice" (Gen. 30:6). But Sarai's treatment of Hagar broke the connection; God listened

to Hagar, and promised Hagar that her child would be hers. Ishmael belongs to Abram and Hagar, promised to each of them in separate annun-
ciations.

This story resonates with other ancestral stories. The narrative gives
one detail in a story generally lacking in specifics: Hagar is an Egyptian
slave. Mention of Egypt takes the reader back to Genesis 12, in which
Sarai is brought into the house of Pharaoh to be a slave concubine and
has to be rescued by God. The reader realizes that Sarai herself is a just-
freed slave. Sarai in Egypt and Hagar in the house of Sarai have similar
histories, and Sarai's oppression of Hagar highlights a disturbing aspect
of human behavior. We like to believe that the experience of suffering
makes us more sympathetic to the suffering of others. It does not.
Sarai's own experience as a slave does not make her more empathic to
the slave in her own home. On the contrary, it makes her want to assert
her dominance and authority so she won't lose it again. As usual, the
biblical narrator does not comment on the actions. It is left to the reader
to note how easily the oppressed can become oppressors. When God
raises high the lowly, how will the newly empowered behave toward
those who lack power and autonomy?

The mention of Egypt also harkens to the future, to the Exodus story
that lies at the basis of Israel's self-understanding. The two words "slave"
and "Egypt" together form the mantra of ancient Israel: "We were
slaves in Egypt and God took us out from there." It is reinforced today
by its recitation at the Passover celebration; it was reinforced in biblical
times at the Feast of the First Fruits described in Deuteronomy 26. At
that time, everybody appeared before God to recite the credo "A starving
Aramean was my father and he went down to Egypt just to stay for a little while, few in number, but we multiplied, and the Egyptians made us
into slaves. And they oppressed us and gave us harsh exploitation and we
cried unto God and God heard our affliction and brought us out of there
with a strong hand and an outstretched arm and with signs and wonders
and brought us to this place and gave us this land, flowing with milk and
honey (Deut. 26:5–9)." Recitation of this narrative impressed slavery and
redemption on the consciousness of every Israelite and later, every Jew.
Law, too, remembers slavery, invoking the memory of their ancestors'
slavery and liberation as justification for laws that demand that Israelites
act against their own economic interest. The redemption from bondage
in Egypt is the paradigm for a key tenet of biblical theology: God is the
overturner of the powerful, and at God's will, the low become high.
That theme became even more important as Israel fell on hard times,

and it took on a new valence, a vector toward the future: as God brought Israel out from Egypt, God will redeem Israel from exile. The narrator does not innocently identify Hagar as an "Egyptian": no coincidence, it is a direct allusion to the central myth of Israel's origins.

Other details of the Hagar story also correspond to Israel's sacred history. Sarai abused and degraded Hagar, *watte ʿannehā*, in the same language by which the old credo in Deuteronomy 26 describes the Egyptian treatment of Israel, *waye ʿannûnû*. Like Hagar, the people of Israel were exploited, oppressed, and degraded in addition to being slaves. And like Hagar, Israel went into slavery knowing that this would be so. The angel's demand that Hagar return and be oppressed, **hit** ʿanî, also echoes the Covenant among the Carcasses in Genesis, chapter 15. There, God intensified the promises to Abram by going through a solemn oath-swearing covenant ceremony. While reciting the promise of progeny and future, God announced that Abram's descendants would be strangers in a land that was not theirs, and that people would enslave and degrade them for four hundred years before God would redeem them. The fulfillment of God's promises will be delayed: all Abram can expect is to die peacefully before the troubles begin.

The parallels between Genesis chapters 15 and 16 are striking. In chapter 15, God tells Abram that God will multiply his progeny, but that his descendants will be degraded slaves and that God will bring them out and give them the land. In chapter 16, God's angel tells Hagar to return to be exploited; afterward she will have a child who cannot be exploited, and God will multiply her progeny. The story of Hagar parallels the story of Israel: she is the archetype.

The exploitation offered both Abram and Hagar points to a disturbing aspect of God's behavior: why does God insist that suffering come before reward? This scenario repeated itself many times in Israel's experience, but nowhere is an explanation given as to why Israel—and Hagar too—have to suffer. The only explanation Abram is given is that the iniquity of the Amorites is not yet full. This makes sense—Israel cannot inherit the land until the Amorites have polluted it so much that (in the words of Leviticus 18) "it will vomit them out" and Israel can come in. But the "iniquity of the Amorites" explains only why Israel has to wait for the land; it says nothing about why they have to be slaves while they wait. The pattern of Hagar and Abram and of later Israel shows that the way to God's reward is through the margins of society and the depths of degradation. Only then, it seems, does God redeem. This pattern offers hope to the oppressed, but it remains as an unexplained aspect of God's behavior in the world.

The close correspondence between Hagar and Israel continues in the denouement of her story, after the birth of Isaac.

◇ Act II. The Leaving of Ishmael (Gen. 21)

Scene 1. At the weaning of Isaac (Gen. 21:8–13)

> The boy grew and was weaned, and Abraham held a huge banquet on the day he weaned Isaac.
>
> Sarah saw the son of Hagar the Egyptian that she had borne for Abraham playing.
>
> She said to Abraham, "Send away this slave-woman with her son, for the son of this servant-woman will not inherit together with my son, with Isaac."
>
> The matter seemed wrong in the eyes of Abraham because it concerned his son.
>
> God said to Abraham, "Let it not seem wrong in your eyes concerning the boy and your servant-woman. Whatever Sarah tells you to do, listen to her, because through Isaac will your seed be called. And the son of this servant-woman, him too I will make into a nation, for he is your seed."

Sarai is central to God's plan and God renames her Sarah, announcing that it was through her that God's covenant with Abraham would be fulfilled (Gen. 17:16–21). But at the weaning ceremony, Sarah sees Ishmael "playing." What the lad was doing, the story doesn't say. The verb for his behavior, ṣḥq, can mean "to play," "to laugh," or "to sport," and can cover a wide range of activity. The Septuagint adds that Ishmael was playing "with her son Isaac," but it also doesn't tell us exactly what he was doing. Whatever it was, in Sarah's eyes it was a threat: her son, after all, is supposed to be the "player," for Isaac, *yiṣḥaq*, meaning "he plays," is from the same root. So, once again, Sarah takes the initiative. Acting to ensure that Isaac will truly inherit the promise that God made to her and Abraham, she asks Abraham to send Hagar and Ishmael away. Abraham is reluctant. Until God informed him that God's covenant would be with Sarah's child, he had been satisfied to have Ishmael as his heir to the covenant (Gen. 17:15–17, 19). Once again, God intervenes to instruct Abraham to listen to Sarah, reminding him that Isaac will carry on Abraham's promised line, and reassuring him that Ishmael will also have an Abrahamic lineage. As a result, Hagar and Ishmael are sent away.

Scene 2. The redemption of Ishmael (Gen. 21:14–21)

> Abraham arose early in the morning.
>
> He took a bread and a skein of water.
>
> He gave (them) to Hagar, placed (them) on her shoulder with the child.
>
> And he sent her away.
>
> She walked wandering in the wilderness of Beersheba.
>
> The water in the skein was finished.
>
> She sent the boy away under one of the bushes.
>
> She went and sat facing the boy, as far away as a bow shot, for she said, "Let me not see the boy's death."
>
> She sat facing the boy and lifted her voice and wept.
>
> God heard the voice of the boy.
>
> The angel of God called to Hagar from the sky and said, "What is it, Hagar? Do not be afraid, for God has heard the voice of the boy as he is there.
>
> "Arise, lift up the boy, and hold your hand on him, for I will make him a great nation."
>
> God opened her eyes and she saw a well of water.
>
> She went and filled the skein of water and gave drink to the boy.
>
> God was with the boy and he grew up.
>
> He lived in the wilderness, and became a bow (and arrow) hunter.
>
> He lived in the wilderness of Paran and his mother took a wife for him from the land of Egypt.

Some readers are horrified at Abraham's cavalier treatment of human beings, and horrified that God orders him to do this. But we should note that in a world in which slavery is accepted, Hagar and Ishmael are not sold: they are freed. Hagar and Ishmael leave Abraham's household as emancipated slaves. Of course, emancipation is not without its problems. Hagar, who found Beer-lahai-roi quite easily when she ran away from Sarai, now wanders in the desert until their water runs out. Ishmael would have died had God not intervened. But God, hearing the boy's voice, gives them water in the wilderness, and once again pronounces a great future that will come from Ishmael. This part of their story is also a forerunner of Israel's story, when the emancipated Israelite slaves wander thirsty in the desert until God provides water (Exo. 15–18). And God awards Ishmael the promise that Israel will be given in the wilderness of Sinai: each is to be a nation with a special destiny. In slavery and in freedom, Hagar is Israel.

The final note in the story reminds us that Ishmael's future is shaped by Hagar's understanding. A single mother, she is both father and mother, completing her parental duties by arranging for his marriage. Abraham has no role in shaping the future of Hagar and her descendants. He has relinquished that right by emancipating them; God has given Hagar that right by treating her as the head of her own family and lineage.

The Hagar story is not the only episode in Genesis that foreshadows the sacred history of Israel. Many of the ancestor tales contain such intimations. The great commentator Nahmanides had a maxim, *ma'aseh 'abôt sîman labbanîm*, "the deed of the ancestors is a sign for the children." The Rabbis understand the adventures of patriarchs in this way, and we may note that some of the experiences of the women in Genesis share this same paradigmatic, archetypal nature. Abraham's descent to Egypt because of famine in Genesis 12 foreshadows the famine-induced descent of Jacob and his family to Egypt at the end of Genesis. However, it is Sarai who most anticipates the fortunes of Israel as she becomes a forced concubine in Pharaoh's harem and then is rescued by God's miraculous intervention. And Hagar anticipates Israel as she lives out the life of an oppressed, covenanted, and eventually emancipated slave in Abraham's household.

The story of Sarai and Hagar is not a story of the conflict between "us" and "other," but between "us" and "another us." Hagar is the type of Israel, she is the redeemed slave, she is "us." And Sarai is both type and mother of Israel, she is both "us" and the one from whom Israel is born. Pitting part of Israel's consciousness against another part, the story creates tension in the mind of the readers. At the heart of the Abraham–Sarah cycle is a story demonstrating that the destiny of the people around Israel is not utterly different from Israel's. Readers often follow the line of Abraham–Isaac–Jacob, viewing the other peoples as branches off the trunk. But the stories themselves show a more complicated sense of history. In their view, the other nations formed in these stories—Moab, Ammon, Ishmael, Edom—have destinies that are closely intertwined with Israel's. By God's grant, Esau and the Edomites inhabit Mount Seir, and the Moabites and Ammonites are settled in their lands. And by God's grant, the Ishmaelites are in everybody's face, untamable and not subservient to the laws of the states in which they live. The ancestral stories of Genesis understand the extreme complexity of history and the difficult nature of covenants with God. They reflect the reality of a world with refugees, political oppression, and famine. They understand the intricacy of a special destiny and the need to maintain the destiny and the specialness of Israel without alienating or demonizing the other peoples. Instead of seeing the Ishmaelites as an unsocialized element within its boundaries or as demonic opponents of God's will or even as people who have to be expelled or tamed, Genesis integrates Ishmael into Israel's self-understanding as its God-approved alter ego. For Ishmael is in many respects the polar opposite of Israel, and a nation that often found itself marginal, exploited, and on the brink of destruction may have appreciated Ishmael's destiny of utter freedom.

The story of Hagar as the archetype of Israel and of the coming and leaving of her son Ishmael depicts the destinies of Israel and Ishmael as parallel and presents a model of separation without denigration. But separation, nonetheless.

Royal Origins
Ruth on the Royal Way

HAGAR LEFT and formed her own lineage. Other women came in and formed the lineages of the Davidic dynasty; these women we may call the "throne mothers" of Judah. Of these, the most prominent was Ruth. She is at the opposite pole of the approval/disapproval spectrum from Cozbi the Midianite, who was killed as soon as she came into Israel. Ruth the Moabite came and became the ancestor of King David.

The book of Ruth begins in "the days when the judges judged," the same era as the stories in the book of Judges. But this period seems very different from the way it looks in the book of Judges. There we encounter tales of warfare, treachery, and terror; in the book of Ruth we see a romantic picture of a peaceable country troubled only by famine. Villains abound in the book of Judges, enemies abound, Israel behaves faithlessly and ignores its obligations to God. There are no villains in the book of Ruth, and all the characters are noteworthy for their mindfulness of God's blessing and for their willingness to demonstrate ḥesed, "loving-kindness," by acting benevolently toward one another beyond the expectations of legal and even moral obligations. Both books record disaster and redemption, but in Judges, vulnerable women are doomed and the nation is saved only when God raises redeemers to rescue Israel from the foreign oppressors. In Ruth, on the other hand, vulnerable women are saved through their own initiative and through the goodwill of a powerful man. God never has to intervene directly, and the union of this good man of Israel and the wonderful foreign woman he helps begins the road to the redeemer.

The differences between these stories are not so visible at the beginning. Like the book of Judges, the book of Ruth starts with disaster and quickly multiplies disaster upon disaster, loss upon loss.

◇ *Naomi and Ruth*

Scene 1. Exile and death (Ruth 1:1–6)

It happened in the days when the judges judged.

There was a famine in the land.

A man went from Bethlehem in Judah to live awhile in the fields of Moab, and his wife and his two sons.

The man's name was Elimelech and the name of his wife was Naomi and the names of his two sons were Mahlon and Kilyon, Ephratites from Bethlehem in Judah.

They came to the fields of Moab and stayed there.

Elimelekh, Naomi's husband, died and she remained, she and her two sons.

They married Moabite women. The name of one was Orpah and the name of the second was Ruth and they lived there around ten years.

The two of them also died, Mahlon and Kilyon.

The woman remained from her two children and her son.

She arose, she and her daughters-in-law, and returned from the fields of Moab, for she had heard in the fields of Moab that YHWH had taken notice of his people to give them food.

When the disasters end, Naomi is the only remnant of her original family. The exile has taken its toll, and the three childless widows head back to Bethlehem.

Scene 2. Return and release (Ruth 1:7–13)

She left the place where she had stayed and her two daughters-in-law with her.

They went along the way to return to Judah.

Naomi said to her two daughters-in-law, "Go, turn back each of you to her mother's house. May YHWH act benevolently to you as you have acted with the dead and with me! May YHWH grant you that you will find a resting-place, each one in her husband's house!"

She kissed them.

The two lifted up their voices and wept.

They said to her, "Indeed we will return with you to your people."

Naomi said, "Turn back, my daughters, why should you come with me? Do I have any more sons in my loins that will be your husbands? Turn back, my daughters, go, for I have become too old to be a man's. And if I thought I had some hope for that—even if I become a man's tonight, and gave birth to sons, would you wait around until they grew up? Should you suffer so in not being married? No, my daughters, even though I am very bitter on your account. But the hand of YHWH has come against me."

As they head toward the land of Judah, Naomi blesses her two daughters-in-law and sets them free to pursue new marriages. She is returning to her former home. They offer to *"return"* with her. But, repeating their language of return, she tells them to **return** ("turn back") to their own former home, to their mothers' houses. From there, they can get married again. There is drama in her speech to them as she explains that she cannot provide more brothers to act as levirs and assure their future. But there is also hyperbole, for even if she were to remarry, new sons of a new father could not be levirs for the old male line. Naomi is speaking as the head of their household. She acts as the "father" in releasing them from their obligations to her, and as a mother in setting them on this path to new marriage, and her repetition of the phrase "my daughters" (*benōtay*, rather than "daughters-in-law," *kalotaô*) emphasizes the spirit in which she sends them off. Naomi is bitter that she will have to lose them too, but they can have lives to lead.

Scene 3. The moment of decision: Ruth's first ḥesed (Ruth 1:14–18)

They lifted up their voices and cried more.

Orpah kissed her mother-in-law.

But Ruth cleaved to her.

She said, "Look! Your sister-in-law is returning to her people and to her God. Return, follow your sister-in-law."

But Ruth said, "Entreat me not to leave you, to return from following you. For wherever you go, I go, and wherever you stay the night, I will stay the night. Your people are my people and your god, my god. Where you die, I will die and there be buried. So shall YHWH do to me, and so continue to do, if indeed death will separate me and you!"

She saw that she was firmly resolved to go with her and stopped speaking to her (about it).

Ruth refuses release. Her statement **"your people are my people and your god, my god"** rings with balanced, poetic phrases. She did not need to invent her lines, for they resonate with the Bible's cadences of covenant and contract. King Jehoshaphat of Judah used this form twice, when Israel's kings invited him to join them in a war, and he answered, "As mine, so yours; as my people, so your people; as my horses, so your horses" (1 Kings 22:4; 2 Kings 3:7). In the book of Chronicles the formula is slightly different, even closer to Ruth's: "As mine, so yours, your people as my people, and with you in war" (2 Chron. 18:3). And Jonathan used this same form to bid David farewell when he fled Saul: "Go in peace, for we have sworn thus in the name of YHWH, 'God will be between me and you, between my seed and your seed forever' " (1 Sam. 20:42).

Ruth's covenant with Naomi is very much like Jonathan's and David's. She recites an oath—**"So shall YHWH do to me, and so continue to do"**—perhaps performing some action, like drawing a hand across her throat, that symbolizes what God will do if she breaks the oath. And she declares their union in the cadences with which such relationships are cemented. Ruth is now joined to Naomi till death and even beyond. She has "adopted" Naomi as her own family, and adopted Naomi's life as her own, turning her back on the possibility of returning to her former life and family. Instead, she "returns" from Moab with Naomi. In effect, Ruth is now Naomi's daughter.

Scene 4. A sad return (Ruth 1:19–22)

> The two of them went till they came to Bethlehem.
> The whole town was abuzz about them.
> The women said, "Is this Naomi?"
> She said to them, "Do not call me Naomi (Pleasant One). Call me 'Marah' (Bitter-Woman), for Shaddai has made things very bitter for me. I went away full and YHWH brought me back empty. Why should you call me Naomi when YHWH has spoken against me, Shaddai has made things bad for me?"
> Naomi returned, and Ruth the Moabite her daughter-in-law with her, the one who turned from the fields of Moab.
> They came to Bethlehem at the beginning of the barley harvest.

The two of them came back. The storyteller emphasizes Ruth's coming and her balanced relationship with Naomi. When Abraham traveled, "he" went, with the verbs in masculine singular, leaving the reader to assume Sarah went along. Even when the story is going to revolve around Sarah, as in the disposable-wife tale, "Abraham went down to Egypt" (Gen. 12:10). In the same way, even though the Levite went on a journey specifically in order to bring back his concubine, when he finally left her father's house, "he got up and went . . . and his concubine with him" (Judg. 19:10). But Ruth is not an appendage; she has come by choice, and the narrator recognizes the importance of her action. So the two of them come back to Bethlehem.

But they do not come back rejoicing. Naomi returns to Bethlehem manless and destitute, and renames herself "bitter-woman." She is very much aware of her misfortune, and God's role in it. The reader doesn't know this; the narrator never gives God's reasons, never names an evil that Naomi's men may have performed. This is strikingly different from the story of Judah and Tamar. There the narrator reports that Judah's sons did evil and God killed them, though Judah himself doesn't know this. Some modern readers of the book of Ruth have assumed that God blamed and punished Elimelekh and his family for leaving the land. But famine drove Abraham from the land, and Jacob; and Elisha the prophet counseled his friend the Ṣhunammite woman to escape famine. Having to leave is a sad thing; it is not a sin. It may be caused by God's wrath, but it is not the cause of it.

God never acts in the book of Ruth. Nevertheless, God is very present in the characters' minds and they perceive God's Providence in the working out of their destiny. Naomi has no doubts: God has decreed her suffering. But she does not really understand God or her own situation. Even if God was the cause of her manlessness, God is not her enemy. And the proof, which she does not yet see, is that manlessness is not emptiness. Naomi has not returned empty; Ruth has chosen to join her and *they came* to Bethlehem.

The narrator tips us off that Naomi has another person who will prove to be of great advantage to her, a mighty relative named Boaz. Ruth and Naomi do not immediately think about him. They have a problem: they have to eat. It is harvesttime, but Naomi cannot suddenly reclaim her dead husband's field from the person who has been working it in her absence. Even if she could ultimately gain the use of the land, the present harvest belongs to the one who planted the barley. Ruth offers a plan:

◇ *Plans and Providence*

Ruth's plan (Ruth 2:1–3)

> Naomi had a kinsman of her husband, a mighty man from
> Elimelekh's family whose name was Boaz.

> Ruth the Moabite said to Naomi, "I will go, if you please, to the
> field and glean among the sheaves after whomever I find fa-
> vor with."
> She said to her, "Go, my daughter."
> She went and came and gleaned in the field after the harvesters.
> And her "happenstance" happened.
> That portion of field belonged to Boaz from Elimelekh's family.

Naomi and Ruth have only one asset: the right of the poor to glean
the dropped stalks that Israelite harvesters are supposed to leave behind
for them. Ruth offers to do this, hoping that someone would look kindly
at her. Providence does more than arrange for this. Ruth gets a "coincidence," *miqreh,* a serendipitous happening that makes one wonder about
causality. Abraham's steward prayed for a *miqreh* when he asked that the
girl who would give his camels water would be the one destined for
Abraham's son. Now Ruth's *miqreh* occurs: the field she chooses happens to belong to Boaz, Naomi's wealthy kinsman, about whom we
have already been alerted. But is Boaz the providential one, or is this
truly just happenstance? Rivka proved herself the choice of Providence
for Abraham's son in three ways: she treated the steward with gracious
benevolence; she belonged to the right family; and her family was God-
fearing. Boaz belongs to the right family. Now it is up to him to show the
rest.

◈ Ruth and Boaz

Boaz's first ḥesed (Ruth 2:4–13)

> Look! Boaz came from Bethlehem and said to the reapers,
> "YHWH be with you," and they said to him, "May YHWH
> bless you!"
> Boaz said to his manservant who stood over the reapers,
> "Whose young woman is this?"
> The manservant who stood over the reapers said, "She is the
> Moabite woman who returned with Naomi from the fields
> of Moab. She said, 'Let me please glean, and let me gather
> among the sheaves after the reapers,' and she has stood
> from the morning until now. This one: she sat only a little in
> the house."
> Boaz said to Ruth, "Do truly hear, my daughter. Do not go to
> glean in another field, and do not pass from this one, and in
> this way you should stick close to my women. Keep your

eyes on the field where they reap and go after them. For indeed I commanded the young men not to touch you. When
you are thirsty, go to the vessels and drink what the young
men draw."

She fell on her face and bowed to the ground and said to him,
"Why have I found favor in your eyes that you give me
recognition and I a stranger?"

Boaz answered, saying, "I have been told of all you did for your
mother-in-law after the death of your man; and you left
your father and mother and your homeland and came to a
people whom you did not know before. May YHWH reward you for your action and may your reward be full from
YHWH the God of Israel, under whose wings you have
come to seek shelter!"

And she said, "I have found favor in your eyes that you have had
compassion on me and have spoken to the heart of your
servant-woman, and I am not even as one of your servant-
women."

Boaz is the providential one in the same three ways as long-ago
Rivka. He comes from Elimelekh's family; he is mindful of God; and he
acts toward Ruth with *ḥesed* (benevolence) that goes beyond the anticipated. She can follow Boaz's women and be the first gleaner in the field,
and she can drink from the water that is drawn for his workers. He
treats her as a member of his own household, and when Ruth asks why
he does so, he expresses his approval of her actions. He recognizes that
in coming to Bethlehem with Naomi, she has become another Abraham, leaving her father and mother and her homeland. In so doing, she
has come into God's territory and protection, and he prays for God to
reward her.

Ruth ends the conversation formally, acknowledging what Boaz has
done.

Boaz's further ḥesed (Ruth 2:14–18)

At the time for eating, Boaz said to her, "Come here and eat
from the food and dip your bread in the vinegar."

She sat next to the harvesters and he gave her parched grain and
she ate and was satisfied and had some left over.

She arose to glean and Boaz commanded his manservants, saying, "Let her glean also among the sheaves; do not scold her.

> And also let fall some from the heaps and leave them and let
> her glean and don't yell at her."
> She gleaned in the field until evening and beat out what she had
> gleaned, and it was about an ephah of barley.
> She hoisted it and came to the town.
> Her mother-in-law saw what she had gleaned.
> And she took out and gave her what she had left after she ate
> her fill.

The characters in the book of Ruth themselves act to fulfill the blessings that they bestow on one another in the name of God. Boaz is no exception. Not only does he treat her as a member of the household, he also instructs his workers to let her glean among the sheaves (rather than waiting until the sheaves have been cut) and also to let her glean among the handfuls of grain, perhaps after the kernels have been separated from the chaff. These are not the appropriate areas for gleaning, and as a result Ruth gleans an ephah of barley, about the amount that a worker could be expected to harvest in a day, but a gleaner could never expect anywhere near as much.

◇ *Providence Acknowledged (Ruth 2:19–23)*

> Her mother-in-law said to her, "Where did you glean today, and
> where did you do this? May the one who recognized you be
> blessed!"
> She told her mother-in-law what she had done with him and she
> said, "The name of the man with whom I did this today is
> Boaz."
> Naomi said to her daughter-in-law, "May he be blessed by
> YHWH, who has not left off acting benevolently with the
> living and the dead."
> Naomi said to her, "The man is our kin, one of our possible redeemers."
> Ruth the Moabite said, "And he really said to me, 'Stick to my
> lads until they have finished all my harvest.' "
> Naomi said to her daughter-in-law Ruth, "Good, my daughter,
> you should really go out with his servant girls and nobody
> will harrass you in another field."
> She stuck to Boaz's servant girls to glean until the end of the
> barley harvest and the wheat harvest, and she returned to
> her mother-in-law.

God's providential arrangement of the meeting does not pass unnoticed. Seeing the amount of barley that Ruth has brought home, Naomi immediately knows something extraordinary has happened, and when she hears Ruth's story, she is overjoyed and acknowledges God's hand in the matter. The blessing is a little enigmatic. Grammatically it can mean "Blessed is he by God because he (Boaz) has not stopped acting benevolently with the living (Naomi and Ruth) and the dead (Elimelekh)." But why should Naomi have thought that Boaz would stop? And when did he start? It is God whom Naomi now recognizes has not stopped his *hesed* for her.

There is another reason to think that Naomi's blessing is for God, for this blessing is yet another feature that the meeting of Boaz and Ruth has in common with the meeting of Abraham's steward and Rivka. When he saw Rivka's behavior and heard who she was, the steward said, "Blessed be YHWH the God of my lord Abraham who has not left off his acting benevolently and faithfully with my master" (Gen. 24:27). Naomi's acknowledgment of God's role, **"May he be blessed by YHWH, who has not left off acting benevolently with the living and the dead,"** is a variation on what may have been a formulaic blessing that the people of ancient Israel pronounced to identify Providence. It is particularly poignant coming from Naomi's lips, for she returned to Bethlehem convinced that God had brought her evil. She has immediately recognized the change of her fortune, and knows that the turn will also be good for her dead husband, Elimelekh.

So Ruth continues to glean in Boaz's fields, even living with his workers for the seven weeks of harvest before she returns to Naomi. It is now Naomi's turn to act. She had once blessed Ruth and Orpah, **"May YHWH grant you that you will find a resting-place, each one in her husband's house!"** She now takes action to make that happen.

◇ *Plans and Providence*

Naomi's plan and Ruth's further hesed (Ruth 3:1–11)

> Naomi her mother-in-law said to her, "My daughter, indeed I seek for you a resting-place that will be good for you. And now, indeed, Boaz, our kinsman, with whose servant girls you have been—Look! He is threshing barley in the threshing floor tonight. You should bathe and anoint yourself with oil and put on your dress and go down to the threshing floor. Do not reveal yourself to anyone until he has finished

eating and drinking. And when he lies down, you will know the place in which he is lying and you will come and uncover at his nether regions and lie down. He will tell you what you should do."

She said to her, "Everything that you have said, that I will do."

She went down to the threshing floor and did according to everything her mother-in-law commanded.

Boaz ate and drank and was satisfied and he came to lie down at the edge of the grain heap.

She came stealthily and uncovered at his nether regions and lay down.

It happened at midnight.

The man trembled and started, and look! A woman is lying at his nether regions.

He said, "Who are you?"

She said, "I am Ruth your servant. May you spread your cloak over your servant, for you are a redeemer."

He said, "Blessed are you by YHWH, my daughter, your latest act of benevolence is better than your earlier one, that you have not gone after the young men, poor or rich! Now, my daughter, do not fear! Everything that you say I will do for you, for the whole gate of my people know that you are a valiant woman."

The meeting of Ruth and Boaz is God's ḥesed, says Naomi, good for all of them, including the dead. Naomi sees her opportunity to find Ruth the "resting-place" that she had once wished for her, in the arms of a husband. But she does not feel that she can approach Boaz directly. Perhaps widows did not have the right to negotiate marriage contracts; or perhaps Israel had a dowry system in addition to bride-price, and being destitute, she could not provide it. So she sets out to be Providence's helper by devising a strange plot. Ruth is to prepare herself as if for a wedding, and lie at the man's legs in the middle of the night. The outline of Naomi's plan is clear, but one part is deeply enigmatic, possibly playing on double entendres. Ruth is to "uncover"—what? The phrase for uncovering the sexual parts is *glh 'rwah*, but there is no *'rw* here. The phrase *galah kanap* appears twice in the Bible (Deut. 23:1; 27:20) in the sense of "uncover under the robe." But here *galah* is followed by *margelōtāv*, itself a word that appears only one other time in the Bible. It may be possible to understand *margelotav* as a rare form of *regel*, "leg," so that Ruth would uncover his legs, and euphemistically, even his genitals. But more probably, *margelotav* is the same formation as *mereshitav*. Since *mereshitav* from *ro'sh* means "at the head," so too *margelōtāv*, from *regel*, means "at the feet." But, in that case, what is Ruth uncovering "at his feet"? There are only two possibilities: she is uncovering him, or herself, and the narrator may be playing with the reader by not making the scene absolutely clear.

But it is clear that Naomi is sending Ruth to do something which is totally inappropriate behavior for a woman, and which can lead to scandal and even to abuse. Prostitutes might come to the threshing floor in the middle of the night, but not proper women, and if Ruth were to be seen, the gossips would be busy. Moreover, if Boaz took advantage of her, what recourse would she have? Who would believe that a woman who came to the threshing floor was raped? Naomi's plan presumes that Boaz will prove trustworthy and will continue to act in the spirit of benevolent *hesed* that he has shown so far. And her plan demands enormous trust from Ruth, who must truly believe that Naomi wants only good for her, and is not using her for prostitution; and she must also share Naomi's faith in Boaz. But Ruth agrees to do whatever Naomi suggests.

Their trust is not misplaced. Boaz awakens trembling—who could be there? It could even be a succubus at his legs, a female demon come to steal his seed, and he looks to see if it is indeed a woman. When he asks who she is, Ruth answers. Thus far Naomi's plan. Naomi left the rest to Boaz, **"He will tell you what you should do."** But Ruth goes further: she tells Boaz what to do, asking him to spread his cloak over her, an act of betrothal. She also makes it clear why she has asked this of him, reminding him that he is a *go'el*, a family member entitled to redeem their property. Boaz recognizes that she is acting in loyalty to Naomi and to Elimelekh's family and blesses her for pursuing this path, declaring that this *hesed* of coming to him is even greater than her first *hesed* of coming back with Naomi. After all, the family has no legal claim on Ruth. Since there was no one to be a levir and create a son for Ruth and an heir for Elimelekh, Naomi formally set her free to marry any man she wishes. She has come to offer herself to Boaz, who as the *go'el*, the redeemer, will be able to reacquire Elimelekh's field from whoever now has it, and will have first right of purchase if Naomi then sells it. In this way, Elimelekh's family will be able to continue even though he had no offspring to be his heir. Boaz recognizes that Ruth's approach to him arises from her loyalty to Elimelekh's family, which goes far beyond any possible expectation. It is a true *ḥesed* and he blesses her for it.

Now Boaz has a plan.

◈ Plans and Providence

Boaz's plan (Ruth 3:12–18)

"Now, even though I am indeed a redeemer, there is also a redeemer closer than I.

"Stay the night and in the morning, if he will redeem you, good,
let him redeem you. If he will not wish to redeem you, I will
redeem you. By the life of God! Lie here till the morning."

She lay at his legs till morning.

She arose before one man could recognize another.

He said, "Let it not be known that a woman came to the threshing floor."

He said, "Bring your shawl that you wear, and hold it."

She held it and he measured six of barley, put it on her, and they
came to town.

She came to her mother-in-law.

She said, "Who are you, my daughter?"

She told her everything that the man had done to her.

She said, "He gave me these six of barley, for he said, 'Do not
come empty to your mother-in-law.' "

She said, "Stay, my daughter, until you know how the matter
falls out. The man will not be quiet; he will finish the matter
today."

There is one major drawback to Naomi's plan: there is another kinsman who, being more closely related, has a prior right to redeem the
land. Boaz must eliminate him from the picture before he can join himself and the land to Ruth and Naomi. But in the meantime, he asks her
to stay the night. Does he sleep with her? The text does not tell us, but it
does indicate that the answer is important. When Naomi sees Ruth, she
asks, **"Who are you?"** Even though it is still too dark to clearly distinguish faces, Naomi would know it is Ruth returning, especially as she
adds **"my daughter."** the question is pointed: Are you just Ruth, my
widowed daughter, or are you Ruth, the betrothed of Boaz? Ruth tells
her what has happened, that her situation is still ambiguous, but then
presents her with the barley, which in context is a form of bride-price or
betrothal present. So they wait.

◇ *Law and Ḥesed (Ruth 4:1–8)*

> Boaz went up to the gate and sat there, and look! The redeemer
> about whom Boaz spoke passed by. He said, "Turn aside
> and sit here, Mr. Whoever-you-are," and he turned and sat.
>
> He took ten men from the town elders and said, "Sit here," and
> they sat.
>
> He said to the redeemer, "The portion of field that belongs to
> our brother Elimelekh, Naomi is selling, who returned
> from the fields of Moab. I said, 'I will tell you thus, "Buy it in
> front of those sitting here and in front of the elders of my
> people."' If you will redeem it, redeem it, and if you will
> not redeem it, tell me and I will know, for there is no one
> but you to redeem and I after you."
>
> He said, "I will redeem."
>
> Boaz said, "On the day that you acquire the field from Naomi
> and from Ruth the Moabite, you have acquired the dead
> man's widow to erect the name of the dead on his inherited
> portion."
>
> The redeemer said, "I cannot redeem for me lest I destroy my
> own inheritance. You redeem my redemption for me, for I
> cannot redeem."
>
> (Once, in Israel, they did thus for redemption or sale, to execute
> the matter: a man took off his shoe and gave it to the other
> and that was the testimony.)
>
> The redeemer said to Boaz, "Acquire it for yourself," and took
> off his shoe.

Boaz's statement is very intricate, and the legal situation regarding
this land is complex. There are several possibilities. Elimelekh might
have sold his land to buy food before the famine caused him to leave for
the fields of Moab. A redeemer might be expected to buy back the land,
but the right to do so is usually activated when the original purchaser
tries to resell. In this case, Naomi would be selling not land but "land futures," the right to redeem the land at some future time. Elimelekh
might simply have left the land behind and someone else worked it in his
absence. Now, after the harvest, Naomi might be in a position to reclaim
that land. According to our understanding of biblical law, a widow
would have the right to live on the land, not to sell it. However, we have

only glimpses of biblical law, and it might be that a widow could sell. A redeemer would have the right and obligation of first purchase. As Jeremiah's cousin told him, "Yours is the rule of redemption to buy" (Jer. 32:7) when he asked Jeremiah to buy his fields. The relative buys land (or buys it back from another purchaser) in order to keep land in the family. The land would be his, and he would add it to his own patrimony, but he may have been expected to use the usufruct to support the widow. Perhaps the elders understood the situation better than we do, but since this is a stratagem by Boaz to outmaneuver his kinsman, they may also have been confused.

The confusion does not lessen when the relative declares his willingness to redeem. Boaz then informs him that when he acquires the land, someone will also acquire the widow Ruth for the purpose of perpetuating the lineage on its land. The written text (the Ketiv) says, "I have acquired": Boaz, who has already betrothed Ruth, will engender a child who will lay claim to this land. This would mean that the kinsman would buy land of which the usufruct would support Naomi, and then the land itself would go to Boaz's child rather than to the kinsman. The Masoretic reading (the Qere) reads, "You have acquired." On the day the redeemer buys the land, he obligates himself to beget a child. Either way, the result is the same: the redeemer who acquires the land or land future will have it only in trust for a child who will inherit it, and he will not be able to add the land to his own patrimony. He will use his own money to redeem the land, he will use the produce to support two women, and eventually the land will pass to someone who is not his legal heir. This he cannot afford to do, and he formally relinquishes his right to Boaz, who publicly announces his betrothal and intentions.

Boaz's statement does not sound quite right. Why should a kinsman have to marry Ruth in order to buy the land for the family? A redeemer is not a levir. A levir marries his brother's childless widow only to beget a son for his dead brother who will inherit the land. When there is no levir, a redeemer who keeps the land in the family is not required to acquire the widow with the land, nor is the redeemer required to create an heir for that land. Boaz is not presenting an accurate legal scenario, but his speech is not mere flimflam. Ruth, although a daughter-in-law rather than a daughter, with no blood ties to Elimelekh, nevertheless bears within her the potential to provide an heir for the line of Elimelekh because she is serving as a daughter to Naomi. The oath that she took to Naomi created a permanent daughtership between them, and as the daughter, she will carry on the name by remaining with the land and marrying her relative. Ruth has already indicated her willingness to raise a child for the dead man's line. From a moral standpoint, to take the land and ignore the woman who stands ready to bear an heir is to kill Elimelekh and his son: Mahlon's last hope for the perpetuation of their name. According to the code of ḥesed by which Ruth and Boaz are operating, everyone is to go beyond the requirements of the law. As we read the Ketiv, Boaz is fathering the eventual heir, and the redeemer will take the financial loss. As we read the Qere, the kinsman should go beyond his legal obligation—redeem the land and, by taking Ruth, create an heir who will then take Elimelekh's field away from him. The kinsman does not argue with Boaz. He does not dispute the moral obligation to support Naomi or beget an heir. But he cannot afford it, and he bows out.

Ruth and Boaz marry.

◇ Happy Endings, Happy Beginnings (Ruth 4:9–17)

> Boaz said to the elders and all the people, "You are witnesses today that I have acquired everything that belonged to Elimelekh and to Kilyon and Mahlon from Naomi. And also Ruth the Moabite, Mahlon's wife, I have acquired as a wife to erect the name of the dead on his inherited portion. May the name of the dead not be cut off from his brothers and from the gate of his place. You are witnesses today."
>
> All the people in the gate and the elders said, "We are witnesses. May YHWH make the woman coming into your home like Rachel and like Leah, the two of whom built the house of Israel. Do valiantly in Ephrat and call the name in Bethlehem. May your house be like the house of Peretz whom Tamar bore to Judah, from the seed that YHWH will give you from this young woman."
>
> Boaz took Ruth and she became his wife.
>
> He came into her and YHWH granted her pregnancy and she gave birth to a son.
>
> The women said to Naomi, "Blessed be YHWH who didn't leave you without a redeemer today. May his name be called in Israel. May he be a life renewer for you and support you in your old age. For your daughter-in-law who loves you is better for you than seven sons."
>
> Naomi took the baby and laid him to her lap and she became his nursemaid.

> The neighbor women called his name thus, "A child is born to
>   Naomi."
> They called his name Obed.
> He was the father of Jesse the father of David.

The statement of Boaz and the townspeople's blessings show the two
different aspects of the birth of the child. Boaz calls everyone to witness
that **"Ruth the Moabite, Mahlon's wife, I have acquired as a wife to
erect the name of the dead on his inherited portion"** and ends with a
rousing **"May the name of the dead not be cut off . . . "** But the townspeople witnessing the event bless him: **"May your house be like the
house of Peretz whom Tamar bore to Judah, from the seed that
YHWH will give you from this young woman."** The child should be
not only Elimelekh and Mahlon's descendant; he is also Boaz's son, and
the line begins with him. In the same way, Tamar's child was considered
to be not Er's but Judah's, and the reckoning of the line of Boaz begins
with Peretz himself. The genealogy at the end of the book of Ruth bears
this out, tracing the men from Peretz through Boaz to King David.

The women add yet another blessing, one that stresses the importance of the child to Naomi's future. She now is assured of a secure
place in a family structure. In one birth, Ruth has provided Boaz with a
descendant, Elimelekh with a memory, Naomi with renewal, and Israel
with the grandfather of kings. But then, like Tamar, the mother of
Peretz, Ruth disappears: all the women name the child, and Ruth as-
cends into the pantheon of throne mother.

This charming narrative of gracious family behavior discusses important issues about Israel's destiny. In many ways, it reverses the Dinah
story, another "family" narrative about Israel, its land and its neighbors.
Dinah went out to see the "daughters of the land." Her attempt ended
in a disaster, but her dream of a relationship with other women comes
true with the friendship of Naomi and Ruth. The closeness between
them, the *hesed* and the trust they show each other, the initiative and
boldness that each brings out in the other, pave the way for their own
happiness, the perpetuation of Elimelekh's lineage on its land, and the
birth of King David.

The story ostensibly concerns the tale of one particular family, a very
important family, the royal family of Judah. But the names of the characters indicate that its theme goes far beyond their fate. Naomi herself
draws attention to the significance of these names by declaring as she returns to Bethlehem that she should no longer be called Naomi, but

Marah ("Bitter-Woman One"), for God has embittered her life by killing her men. The father forced to leave the land is named Elimelekh, "My God-is-King"; the sons who die are Mahlon, "Disease," and Kilion, "Destruction"; the daughter-in-law who turns away is Orpah, "Back-of-neck": Ruth, who stays with Naomi, is "Sprinkle" or "Dewy," the fertility-giving moisture; and the kinsman whom Ruth marries is Boaz, "He-who-has-Might." When we retell the story using names translated into English, we get a vivid picture of its significance for Israel:

Once, many years ago, famine drove My-God-is-King and Pleasant-One from Bethlehem in the land of Judah to the land of Moab. There My-God-is-King died. His two sons Disease and Destruction married local women, but after a while, they too died, leaving only Pleasant-One and her two daughters-in-law. When they heard that there was food in Bethlehem, they set out to return. On the way, Pleasant-One released her two daughters-in-law and sent them back to begin new lives. Back-of-neck tearfully turned and left, but Dewy stayed with her mother-in-law, now no longer Pleasant-One but Bitter-Woman, for God had killed her men. In Bethlehem, they turned to their kinsman He-who-has-Might. First God, then Pleasant-Woman, then Dewy, and then He-who-has-Might planned to bring them together, and finally He-who-has-Might married Dewy and from this union came He-who-Serves, the grandfather of Beloved.

Read this way, the story is an allegory for Israel's destiny, beginning with her bereavement and ending with her joy. Pleasant-Woman is Jerusalem/Judah, so often personified as a woman, the most lovely of women. Elimelekh is the king of Israel or the institution of kingship; the dead sons are the many dead children of Israel. When Pleasant-Woman comes back to the land, "Dewy" the Moabite comes with her, and by mating with the remaining strength in the land (He-who-has-Might), she revitalizes Israel. The combined efforts of these gracious three, all of whom act with ḥesed toward one another, make possible the rebirth of the lineage. And so **"A child is born to Pleasant-Woman,"** from whom came Beloved [*"and a redeemer comes to Zion"*].

Beloved is David, the founder of the dynasty that ruled Judah until its destruction. David himself may have told this story of his ancestry in order to show his "legitimate" claim to Moab. But the book of Ruth is not the story as David told it. The language in which Naomi describes her bitter state, her affliction by God, and also God's continuing loving-kindness toward her, reflects the lament and prophecy language of a later period. The book of Ruth deals with leaving and then returning to the land of Israel, which could refer to the descent to Egypt and the Exodus from there. But the book also revolves around leaving family property and then reacquiring it. This is a concern of a much later period, the return to Zion after the Babylonian exile. The people who remained in the land occupied the fields of those who were banished, and when the exiles returned, conflicts must inevitably have arisen. The book of Ruth assumes that property should rightly belong to the original owners.

The book of Ruth addresses two other major questions that the return from Babylon presented: What should be the relationship between those who returned and those who came with them, wives for instance, who had joined them in Babylon and had not originally come from Judah? And what should be the relationship of the Israelites who were in exile with those who remained in Judah during those two generations? These questions came to a head when Ezra, backed by the power of the Persian throne, declared that only those who had returned from Babylon, the *golah,* were to be considered the true Israel, the true Jews. He convinced the men of the community to separate themselves from their foreign wives and from the "peoples of the land," which included the Judeans who had not experienced the Babylonian exile. According to the covenant the men made with Ezra, those who did not renounce their wives would no longer be considered members of the community.

The decision to divorce their wives and to separate from the "peoples of the land" came amid serious dispute in Israel, and important prophetic voices express differing views. Isaiah emphasizes that the foreigners who have attached themselves to God and Israel will *not* be separated out, but will be most welcome at the temple (Isa. 55:6–7). And even Malachi, who indicts Israelites for marrying the "daughter of a foreign god," is against the idea of divorcing the foreign wives, upset at people ignoring the marriage covenant and abandoning the "wife of their youth" (Mal. 2:14–16). To these voices, the women who come back to Israel with those returning from exile are to be considered part of the community.

The telling of the Ruth and Naomi story in the paradigmatic, even allegorical fashion of the book of Ruth should best be seen in the context of these issues. On all of them, the book's views could not be more radically different from those of Ezra and Nehemiah. In the book of Ruth, after all, all three communities—the kinsman in the land (Boaz), the returning Israelite (Naomi), and the returning Moabite wife of an Israelite (Ruth)—are all faithful to the name and memory of the old king, and it is the cooperation among all three that leads to the continuation of the line of those who stayed in the land and those who had gone into exile. In this way, the ancestry story and the genealogy of the great king of Israel's past point the way toward the nation's glorious future.

Royal Origins
The Moabite

THE BOOK OF RUTH repeatedly identifies Ruth as a Moabite. This is no innocent detail. It was Moabite women who invited Israel to attend the feast that resulted in Israel's calamitous attachment to Ba'al-Pe'or (Num. 25). Those women and Ruth are polar opposites. The friendship of the Moabite women at Shittim brought death; the friendship of Ruth the Moabite leads to new life. The women at Shittim incited Israel to faithlessness; Ruth the Moabite is the very model of fidelity.

This parallelism is not coincidental. The story about Ba'al-Pe'or may originally have been a story about Midianite women, whom Moses held responsible (Num. 31:15–16). Even the story in Numbers 25 shifts abruptly from the Moabite women to the assassination of the Midianite princess Cozbi. Perhaps "Moabite women" appear in Numbers 25 as an artistic device that accomplishes what Midianite women could not: a symmetrical antithesis to the positive image of Ruth.

Moab and Ammon occupy a special position in Israel's worldview. The two nations bordered on Israel, and the Moabite language was very close to Hebrew. Their history was one of conflict. Moabites conquered Israel toward the beginning of the period of the book of Judges and ruled until Ehud led an insurrection. David conquered Moab and amalgamated Moab into Israel, where it stayed until King Mesha of Moab achieved independence. In the mind of Israel, Moab is the best and the worst of the foreign nations. The book of Numbers relates how Balak, king of Moab, wanting to destroy Israel, sent the prophet Balaam to curse it; and how the power of God changed Balaam's curses into blessings. Similarly, as we have seen, Numbers 25 indicts Moab for the sin of Ba'al-Pe'or. Numbers 31 connects the two stories as Moses indicts the Midianite women and Balaam for inciting them: "Have you let the women live? They were the ones who acted at the word of Balaam to bring trespass to Israel about the matter of Pe'or and there was a plague in the congregation of Israel" (Num. 31:15–16). Post-biblical traditions explain that when Balaam could not curse Israel, he tried to destroy it by suggesting the dinner invitation that resulted in Israel's sin.

Deuteronomy also expresses profound ambivalence toward Moab, declaring that God gave the children of Lot their own lands, never calling for their extermination (Deut. 2:9–11, 18–23). Nevertheless, says Deuteronomy, Moab and Israel must be separate: "The Moabite and Ammonite shall not come into the congregation of YHWH. Even in the tenth generation he shall not come into the congregation of YHWH forever" (Deut. 23:4). Grandchildren of Edomites and Egyptians can enter the congregation; but Moabites and Ammonites never can, for Moab and Ammon did not offer Israel water and drink during their desert wanderings, and hired Balaam to curse them (Deut. 23:7).

But this separation proved difficult to maintain. The "Moabite women" in Numbers and "Ruth the Moabite" may be polar opposites on the disapproval-approval, disaster-delight, demonic-angelic scale, but they have more in common than might seem apparent. In both stories, the women want to be connected to Israel. The women invite Israel to dinner; Ruth accompanies Naomi to Bethlehem and later goes to Boaz during the night. They take the initiative, and the Israelites respond. Numbers is the worst-case scenario: Israel responds by embracing their God. Ruth is the best-case scenario: Naomi brings Ruth "under the wings of God" (Ruth 2:12), and Boaz brings her into Israel's family structure.

The Moabite women in the Bible are assertive and friendly, characteristics that can be seen in the mothers of the Moabite and Ammonite peoples, the daughters of Lot. As the tale is told in Genesis, Lot and his daughters went to stay in a cave in the hills after the destruction of Sodom and Gomorrah.

◇ *The Daughters of Lot (Gen. 19:30–38)*

> Lot came up from Zoar and settled on the mountain, his two daughters with him, for he was afraid to stay in Zoar.
> He lived in a cave, he and his two daughters.
> The elder daughter said to the younger, "Our father is old, and there is no man in the land to come into us in the way of the whole world. Come, let us give him wine to drink and we will lie with him, and we will cause seed to live from our father."
> They gave their father wine that night, and the elder came and lay with her father.
> He was not aware when she lay down or when she got up.

On the next day, the elder said to the younger, "Now I have lain
with my father last night. Let us give him wine to drink
tonight too and you come and lie with him and we will
cause seed to live from our father."
They gave their father wine to drink that night too.
The younger got up and lay with him.
And he was not aware when she lay down or when she rose up.

The two daughters of Lot became pregnant from their father.
The elder gave birth to a son and she called his name Moab.
He was the father of Moab till this day.
The younger also gave birth to a son and she called his name
Ben-Ammi.
He is the father of the Ammonites till this day.

Early modern biblical scholars often considered this story an ethnic
slur on Moabites and Ammonites. According to their reading, the sons'
very names, Moab (from *me-'ab,* "from the father") and Ammon (from
ben-'ammi, "the son of my kin"), identify them as children of incest,
mamzerîm. Since biblical law prohibits marriage between Israelites and
mamzerîm, some scholars have maintained that the birth story of Moab
and Ammon can explain the prohibition against their entry into the congregation. But such a negative interpretation of the story piles assumption upon assumption. Even though we are horrified by incest, as was
biblical Israel, the story does not impute any bad motive to the daughters of Lot. Contemporary readers may be angry at Lot for having been
so willing to throw his daughters out to the mercy of the aggressive, vo-
racious people of Sodom, but the story does not suggest that the daughters themselves were either angry at him or seeking revenge. On the
contrary, the story explicitly declares their motive, an interior view not
common in biblical literature. It does so to provide them with the no-
blest of motives: believing that there are no men left in the world, **"we
will cause seed to live from our father."** The daughters of Lot did not
save humanity by acquiring their father's seed, but they did preserve the
line of Lot. Without their act, Lot would have had no posterity. Lot's
daughters presented their father with sons after all his older sons had
been killed. They gave him his lineage, who are the Moabites and Ammonites.

In ancient Israel, the preservation of a man's lineage was always important; the preservation of a noble lineage was even more so. Lot,

Abraham's nephew, was the grandson of Terah, the father of Abraham, the one who first set out from Mesopotamia. By descending from Lot and his daughters, the Moabites and Ammonites descend from a double issue of a noble trunk. In the ancestry of Moab and Ammon, the fourth generation from Terah (Lot's daughters) mated with the third generation (Lot), just as in the ancestry of Israel, the fourth generation from Terah (Rivka) mated with the third (Isaac).

The fact that the Terahite descent of Moab and Ammon results from incest does not make it shameful. The Pharaohs of Egypt came from brother–sister incest in each generation. This did not make the person of Pharaoh less exalted in the eyes of the Egyptians, but rather more holy, for the sacred, even divine, seed of Pharaoh was not diluted by any mere human lineage. In the same way, incest among the progenitors of a people indicates the purest of lineage. The sons whom Lot's daughters provide for him are doubly his seed and thereby a double continuation of the line of Terah.

Ancestors, gods, and gods-on-earth are special beings, marked in their specialness by their breaking of the taboos, including the one against incest, that restrain ordinary people. Breaking the taboos doesn't shame them; it heightens their sacredness. It also emphasizes their otherness, for ordinary people are expected to refrain scrupulously from incest. The prohibition of sex between parent and child may be the closest thing we have to a universal social law. Most scholarly attention has focused on the prohibition of mother–son incest, which has been called the primal taboo. To Freud, this was a significant part of personality formation. It is the "Law of the Father" that prohibits the child from completing his Oedipal fantasies on pain of castration. Foucault made this "prime law" the basis for culture's construction of both sex and gender. There continues to be serious discussion of how culture arrives at this rule, and the impact of culture on this rule itself.

Far less attention has been given to father–daughter incest, even though it is more prevalent. In regard to mother–son incest, society's desire to keep the lines of family discrete and unconfused unites with male concerns about a man's exclusive rights over his woman's sexuality and his anxiety about being superseded by younger men. The desire for discrete family lines also drives the prohibition of father–daughter incest, though here the social interest is not reinforced by male anxieties over being superseded. On the contrary, this prohibition is at odds with the concept of the rights of the paterfamilias to autonomy and authority in his own household, and to control the lives and bodies of his children.

The father–daughter incest taboo involves a vital paradox: the father has complete rights over his daughter's sexuality, but he is not allowed to use it; he has only the right to forbid its use by anyone other than the man he chooses. A father is not supposed to have sexual relations with his daughter even in a social structure in which he has the power and authority to sell her into slavery or kill her as a sacrifice. If the contention of sociobiology is correct, that genes have a strong drive to reproduce, then the father–daughter incest taboo contains another major self-contradiction, for even though a man desires to reproduce, he must deny himself the use of the sexually nubile girl in his household; even if he has no sons, he himself cannot produce a son in his daughter's body.

The literary result of all these contradictions is that legal corpora are squeamish about reinforcing this taboo, though they never eradicate it. The biblical laws prohibit father–daughter incest in the general prohibition against a man sleeping with his own flesh (Lev. 18:6), but they do not reinforce it by detailing it explicitly, a notable omission in a whole list of specific incest taboos enumerated in this section of Leviticus. In the laws of Hammurabi, a mother and son convicted of incest are to be burned to death; but a father and daughter so convicted are banished. The laws do not want to undermine the freedom of a father's action by punishing him for his actions within his family. At the same time, they cannot condone or permit the incest. As a result, they do not allow father and daughter to live in society. The squeamishness of ancient laws to reinforce the taboo has been matched by the political reluctance of societies to intervene in family affairs and to punish sexually abusive fathers. Father–daughter incest is infinitely more common than the mother–son incest that receives most theoretical attention.

But the act of the daughters of Lot was a very special type of incest. In almost all other cases of father–daughter incest, the father initiates the sexual encounter, abusing his position of power. But Lot did not do this. Not only did they initiate the act by getting him drunk; he did not pursue them when he was inebriated, nor even participate in the action. The story makes it clear that they got him so drunk that **He was not aware when she lay down or when she got up.** He was completely unconscious, siring sons through his daughters while remaining completely guilt-free. Such a begetting through one's daughter without actively committing incest could be almost the fulfillment of a male wish-fantasy.

Modern readers suspect that Lot may not have been totally unconscious, a possibility suggested by another ancient tale of father–daughter incest, Ovid's story of Myrrha and her father, Cinyras. Myrrha was obsessed with her father and, knowing that incest with him was forbidden in her country, became suicidal in her lovesickness till her old nurse devised a plan. At the festival of Ceres, when married women left the marital bed, Cinyras became drunk. The nurse told him about a girl who loved him, and brought Myrrha in the darkness. Cinyras slept with her, and Ovid comments, "He might have called her daughter, knowing how young she was; she might have answered, dear father, so the names were right and proper to suit the guilty deed." She then returned to him again and again until he called for lights. Seeing his daughter, Cinyras drew his sword, and Myrrha fled, wandering in the Sabaean land till she turned into a myrrh tree and the tree gave birth to Adonis. Lot was no Cinyras; he had no idea he was having sexual relations. His daughters' goal was children rather than sexual intimacy, and Lot intended nothing.

But could conception have been possible if he was unconscious? It is almost axiomatic in our culture that "men can't be raped," that if they don't take action at some point, sexual congress is impossible. But Genesis is interested in seed, not in sex. And the ancients believed that a woman could obtain seed from an unconscious, even dead, male. In the ancient Egyptian myth of Isis and Osiris, Osiris's jealous brother Seth killed him, sealed him in a coffin, and threw it into the Nile. Isis, Osiris's sister and wife, found him and "raised the weary one's inertness [his phallus], received the seed, bore the heir," who was Horus, Osiris reincarnate. This conquest of death was one of the great acts of Isis, and Egyptian art often depicts her in the form of a winged woman or a hawk, hovering over Osiris's penis or his inert body.

The story of Isis and Osiris contributes to the glory of them, and served as the founding myth of the important cult of Osiris/Horus as the mediator between life and death. Yet another ancient story tells of conception from a father and his daughter without "normal" incestuous relations between them. A medieval rabbinic fantasy, the *Aleph-Bet of Ben Sira*, relates the conception of the great sage Ben Sira, whose parents were the prophet Jeremiah and his own daughter. Jeremiah came upon a group of evil Ephraimites masturbating into the public pool. Fearing that he would inform on them, they would not let go of him until he too masturbated into the pool. When Jeremiah's daughter came to bathe sometime later, she encountered the sperm of Jeremiah in the pool and became pregnant. Every single point in this totally and patently nonhistorical story is contradicted by Scripture, for Jeremiah lived over a hundred years after the Ephraimites were exiled to Assyria, and he complains that he had to sit alone and unmarried. This fantastic, mythic story draws on two ancient ideas: that sperm might survive in bathwater and impregnate a woman without sex, and that extraordinary conception is a sign of greatness. In a similar mythical scenario, the Persian Zoroaster was conceived from sperm that had long lain dormant in a river.

Stories of extraordinary conceptions bring honor to the father, the son, and the mother. Zoroaster and Ben Sira and even Adonis are marked as special at the very moment of conception. In the same way, the Moabites are marked for a special destiny. The action of the daughters of Lot was an act of love and faithfulness to their father and to the need to give life an honorable, even heroic act. In the ancestor stories of Genesis, in which God explicitly controls the opening and closing of wombs, the pregnancy of the daughters of Lot and the birth of Ammon and Moab are a reward for their extraordinary actions.

This story is not intended to be a discussion of father–daughter incest. It is at once the memory of the highly unusual actions of the daughters of Lot, and a sign of the behavior of their descendants. For the unnamed mother of Moab and her much later descendant Ruth have much in common. Ruth, of course, does not commit incest: the incestuous relationship between the progenitors of a people is not a paradigm to be repeated in the real world of actual families. But she does aggressively pursue Boaz, and comes to his bed in the middle of the night. Like her foremother, Ruth does not consider herself bound by conventional mores when an important issue is at stake. Both women are faced with the problem of begetting children when they have no husbands, and both opt to search for a solution within the family, so that the house to which they are attached would survive. Ruth's story is like a less intense echo of the Moab story. Her situation is not as dire, and her act is not as drastic, but she and the daughters of Lot share a common thrust. When the posterity of their house is in peril, these women act unconventionally, even contra-conventionally, to preserve it. Subverting one cultural norm, conventional sexual mores, they reinforce and support an even more primal principle, paternal lineage.

Royal Origins
Tamar

AT THE WEDDING of Ruth and Boaz, the townspeople bless him with the wish that "the woman who is coming into your house" should "be like Rachel and Leah, the two who built the House of Israel" and that "your house be like the house of Peretz whom Tamar bore to Judah, from the seed that God gives you from this girl." Ruth will be the agent of the continuation of this lineage, a line drawn, in the last sentences of the book, from Peretz to Boaz and on to King David. A woman also began this line: Tamar, the mother of Peretz. Without Tamar, there would have been no Peretz and no Boaz; without Ruth, no Obed and thus no King David. Their stories have many similarities, most of which are shared by the story of Lot's daughters: the continuation of a lineage, a departure from home, widowed women, and the birth of a child. And they relate how the determined and apparently questionable actions of a widow made this crucial continuity possible. Tamar and Ruth share their loyalty, their assertiveness, and their ingenuity, qualities shared by Ruth's own distant ancestress, the mother of Moab, and perhaps also by Judah's mother, Leah, who traded with Rachel for a night with their mutual husband, Jacob.

The story of the house of Judah begins abruptly, just after Joseph has been sold into slavery, partially at Judah's instigation.

◈ *Act I. The Beginning of the House of Judah (Gen. 38:1–7)*

It happened at that time.
Judah went away from his brothers.
He headed for an Adullamite man named Hirah.
There Judah saw the daughter of a Canaanite man named Shua.
He took her and came into her.
She conceived and gave birth to a boy and he called his name Er.
She conceived again and gave birth to a boy and she called his name Onan.

> She did it again and gave birth to a son and she called his name
> Shelah. It was in Kezib that she bore him.
> Judah took a wife for his eldest, Er, and her name was Tamar.

The story tells us when Judah departed: **It happened at that time.** In the structure of Genesis, this means right after the sale of Joseph. But the story never reveals the reason he left. His reason for leaving home is not important to the story, but his destination is: **He headed for an Adullamite man named Hirah,** who will appear later on as Judah's friend. Judah, like Dinah, seeks contact with the local inhabitants; unlike her, he successfully forges a lasting relationship: **Judah saw the daughter of a Canaanite man named Shua. He took her and came into her.** Having left his paternal home, Judah is out of his father's care and supervision. Like his father before him, he can choose his woman and negotiate his own marriage. And like Jacob, he will be the father of the most significant part of his father's lineage, at least in the eyes of the Judeans who transmitted the story.

Judah's wife is identified as the daughter of a Canaanite, and commentators both ancient and modern have assumed that his troubles stemmed from his marriage to a Canaanite. But the story itself contradicts such an assumption: it does not comment negatively about the marriage, nor tell us that it displeased God. On the contrary, the union was blessed with three sons. In the ancestor stories of Genesis, in which God actively opens and closes the wombs of women, three sons can hardly be a mark of divine disapproval. In this story, moreover, when God is displeased with a character's actions, God intervenes to kill the perpetrator. But Judah has no problems until after his sons marry. Furthermore, perhaps to forestall the assumptions that readers nevertheless continue to make, the narrator explicitly states that Judah's sons died because of their own actions.

Shua is a Canaanite and Hirah is an Adullamite. Judah is indeed connecting with the other inhabitants of the land. And like all Jacob's sons, he must marry an outsider. Who else can they marry? Isaac and Jacob were "endogamous"—they married women from their own family. But the family of Jacob and that of Laban have separated, and the two men have sworn a nonaggression pact (Gen. 31). So any woman whom Judah weds will be an outsider until after they are married.

Quickly we learn about the development of Judah's family. Er is born and then Onan and Shelah. Judah takes Tamar to be the wife of Er. The story pointedly tells us nothing about where Tamar came from or who her father was. She could have been a Canaanite or an Aramean; she could have come from Mesopotamia (as the later Testament of Judah relates); she could even have been the daughter of one of Judah's brothers, though it is hard to believe that the narrator would not relate that. Her origin doesn't matter, for she now acquires a new identity: she is Judah's daughter-in-law.

Her name matters, for like names in so many biblical stories, it reveals the issue of the story. *Tamar* is the date palm tree, a tree that can bear copious and precious fruit. But the fertility of the date palm is not assured; it must be pollinated by direct human action. The name Tamar hints that this new daughter-in-law has the *potential* to bear, but her fertility will be endangered. The plot will determine whether she disappears (as did Tamar, the daughter of David) or becomes the ancestress of a precious hero.

The equally expressive names of the sons present the triple crisis of the story. Tamar, the potential fruit-bearer, is mated first to Er and then to Onan. Their names also indicate the directions in which they could have gone. Er, whose name could have meant "the energetic one" (from *ʿûr*, "arise, be awake"), instead does evil *(raʿ)* and becomes "the one who has no issue" (from *ʿrr*, "be barren"). Onan, whose name could have meant "vigor" (from *ʾwn*, "manliness, vigor"), becomes instead "nothingness" (from *ʾawen*, "nothing"). The name of the third son, Shelah, could indicate that he should be her next mate, from *šelah*, "hers," but the story tells us that he was born in Kezib, from *kzb*, "false."

Things have gone quickly and smoothly for Judah's family until this point, but matters suddenly take a dramatic turn with the death of Er.

◇ *Act II. Disaster to the House of Judah (Gen. 38:7–11)*

> Er, Judah's eldest, was evil in YHWH's eyes and YHWH killed him.
>
> Judah said to Onan: "Come into your brother's wife, perform the levirate act, and raise up seed for your brother."
>
> Onan knew that the seed would not be for him and it happened that as he came to his brother's wife, he ejaculated on the earth without giving seed for his brother. What he did was evil in YHWH's eyes, and He killed him too.
>
> Judah said to Tamar his daughter-in-law, "Sit as a widow in your father's house until Shelah my son grows up," for he thought, "Lest he too die like his brothers."
>
> Tamar went and sat in her father's house.

The death of Er presents the first critical juncture of the story. How will Tamar's fertility be actualized and Judah's line continue when she, like Ruth and Naomi, is a widow? As we have seen, ancient Near Eastern and biblical laws provide a solution in the institution of the levirate. A levir provides an heir for his childless dead brother by inseminating his brother's widow. He acts as his brother's surrogate and incest taboos are suspended. Judah's firstborn son has died childless, so he gives Tamar to Onan, the next son. But Onan is not willing to act to his own economic detriment. As the elder surviving son, he stands to inherit two-thirds of Judah's estate. If he provides an heir for his brother, that child will inherit his dead "father's" portion. Since Er was the eldest, his son would inherit half of the estate, and Onan would be left with only a quarter. Onan is not willing to lose five-twelfths of the estate, and **ejaculated on the earth** in *coitus interruptus*. For this offense, he too is killed by God. His "levirate" action, his calculations, and his life have all come to nothing.

With the death of Onan, Judah's crisis deepens, as does Tamar's. There is just one son left, and Judah fears that this one will also die if he gives Tamar to him. Not only have we seen that Onan didn't perform the levirate; in an act unusual for biblical storytelling, the narrator lets us know why he did not and why God killed him and Er. The uncommon presentation of the characters' motives puts us, the readers, in the know, setting up a dramatic irony, for Judah does not know any of this. Judah, in his ignorance, has come up with his own theory: Tamar is responsible. In the book of Ruth, the narrator tells us nothing, but Naomi reasons that God has killed her family. Here, the narrative tells us, but Judah does not suspect God's role. Instead, he thinks Tamar may be a lethal woman. This belief in the "killer wife" also shows up in the apocryphal book of Tobit, where Sarah's bridegrooms die, killed by a jealous demon (Tob. 3:7–9 and 8:9–11). Judah's belief that his remaining son will die if he mates with Tamar prevents him from treating Tamar as she deserves. The readers, who know what happened, also know that Judah is mistaken, and thus Judah seems more foolish than evil in his mistreatment of Tamar. At the same time, it shows that a man with both power and lack of understanding becomes an oppressor.

Levirate rules presented Judah with several options, to some extent determined by Shelah's age. According to the Middle Assyrian law, any surviving brother over ten years old should perform the levirate (MAL ¶33). If Shelah is over ten, Judah should give Tamar to him; though she may have to wait for the consummation until Shelah is older. Judah proposes to do precisely this, but deceitfully, since he does not intend to risk his son's life and his own posterity by mating him with Tamar. If Shelah is under ten years old, Judah can ask her to wait for Shelah, or he can perform the levirate himself. At the very least, since he does not want to perform the levirate or have Shelah do so, he should release her from his family just as Naomi, who had no surviving sons, released Ruth. As a true widow, she would still have a chance to make a new life (the date palm could still become fertile), and Judah could marry Shelah to someone else who would give him grandchildren. But Judah is not honest about his intentions, and so he wrongs Tamar.

His command that she "live as a widow in your father's house" is a contradiction in terms, for the very definition of "widow" is that she has no man controlling her and is, for better or worse, "free." But "widow" Tamar is not free; she is back under her father's supervision and in her father-in-law's jurisdiction. She cannot create her own destiny, but must stay bound to Judah or be subject to severe punishment, even death. Later, when Judah believes that she has been faithless, he will be ready to burn her. By leaving her to be a "widow in her father's house," Judah binds her perpetually to his family without intending to provide her a secure future.

This could be the end of Tamar's potential, for it would seem that she can do nothing. If the story ended with her hidden away in her father's house, she would be just another victim in one more story that shows a man treating his woman as expendable to save his own life. Tamar would have joined Jephthah's daughter and the concubine as another woman victimized by the mistaken power of their heads of household in the Bible's vision of the "bad old days" before the state, when each man had absolute control over his household. But Tamar's story is not yet over.

◇ *Act III. Tamar's Trick (Gen. 38:12–19)*

> The days grew many.
> Bat-Shua, Judah's wife, died.
> Judah was consoled and he went to his sheep-shearers, he and
>   his friend Hirah the Adulamite, to Timnah.
> Thus was told to Tamar: "Look! Your father-in-law is going up
>   to Timnah to shear his sheep."
> She took off her widow's garments, she covered herself with a
>   scarf and was concealed.

> She sat at "The Eye-Opener" [Petah 'Eynayim] on the Timnah road, for she saw that Shelah had grown and she hadn't been given to him as a wife.
>
> Judah saw her and thought her a prostitute, for she had covered her face.
>
> He headed toward her on the road and said, "Let's do this: I will come into you," for he did not know that she was his daughter-in-law.
>
> She said, "What will you give me if you come into me?"
>
> He said, "I will send a goat from the flock."
>
> She said, "If you give me a pledge until you send it."
>
> He said, "What pledge should I give you?"
>
> She said, "Your seal, your cord, and your staff that is in your hand."
>
> He gave it to her, he came into her, and she conceived by him.
>
> She arose, she went away,
>
> She took her scarf off and wore her widow's clothes.

Once Tamar realizes that Judah will not give her to Shelah, she knows that she herself must act to protect her future. She must trick Judah into performing the levirate himself. Tamar ceases to be a victim and takes her destiny into her own hands. When she hears that Judah is celebrating the sheep-shearing in Timnah, she sees her opportunity to act. The celebrating should put Judah in a party mood and awaken his libido. Since his wife is dead, he will not be hurrying home. He might be ready for some sexual action, and if Tamar plays out the scenario properly, she may satisfy both their desires. She places herself where Judah cannot fail to come, on the road from Timnah at a place called, with considerable irony, **petah 'êynayim,** "the opening of the eyes."

Once again, the narrator shows us a character's motives. We should not be scandalized by Tamar's actions, because we know her reasons. Biblical authors rarely do this, but the stories about Lot's daughters, Ruth, and Tamar all tell us why these women act unconventionally. Now Tamar **saw that Shelah had grown and she hadn't been given to him as a wife.** She will be trapped for life if she doesn't do something. But Judah did not sleep with her when Onan died, and she has no reason to suppose that she can either convince or entice him to do so now. His fear of her has already prevented him from approaching her, so she must hide her identity. Tamar takes dramatic action, removing her widow's garments and wrapping herself in a veil. When Judah sees her sitting by the road, he assumes she is a prostitute. The veil does not signal this, for ancient texts indicate that prostitutes were not usually veiled. Proverbs 7 refers to the bold appearance of the prostitute, and the veil is married woman's garb in the book of Judith (Jdt. 10:2, 16:9). The Middle Assyrian laws allow only married women to veil themselves, specifically prohibiting prostitutes from doing so (MAL ¶40). This makes sense, for if prostitutes could wear veils, any woman could be one without fear of being recognized. This is what Tamar does. Using her veil as an anti-recognition strategy, sitting at the "opening of the eyes," she draws a veil across Judah's eyes and prevents him from seeing her identity. He assumes that she is a prostitute because only a "street-walker" would be hanging around in the open roadway! The narrator once again stresses Judah's lack of knowledge: he did not recognize his daughter-in-law. By this device, the narrator shows us Judah sleeping with Tamar while telling us that he is certainly not guilty of desiring his own daughter-in-law. He sees a woman sitting in the street. Such a woman would be considered approachable, and Judah approaches.

There is irony in Tamar's pretending to be a prostitute. She becomes anonymous in the same way that prostitutes are anonymous. And she masquerades as precisely the kind of woman whose behavior male control prevents wives and daughters from emulating. The essence of the prostitute is that she is outside the constraints of family life. No one restricts access to her, or protects it by the threat of retribution. Men can sleep with her without weakening the social system that forbids married women to say yes to anyone but their husbands. Women who are attached to family structures and nevertheless act as if they were without constraints will be punished for breaking their bonds. They are liable to be called "whores," in a pejorative rather than a technical sense, and their action called "harlotry" even when it is not sex for hire.

This dual valuation of free, unconstrained female sexual activity is reflected in biblical Hebrew as well as in English. The Hebrew term zônah, "prostitute," is a participle of the very word znh that is often (mis)translated as "to go whoring." A wife or daughter who misbehaves sexually (or any other way) is said to be znh (faithless); but a prostitute, zônah, is one who always acts without constraint. Designated whores, outside the family structure, are not punished, and men are not condemned for sleeping with them. After all, that is the purpose of the institution. A man can therefore freely proposition a woman whom he takes to be a whore. But if she is not a whore, he affronts those who protect and control her. Even if she is willing, the men of her family may be outraged, and they, like Dinah's brothers, may not let him get away with treating their woman *kezonah,* "like a prostitute."

There are other women who were outside the ancient family structure and, we believe, had control over their own sexuality. The *qedēšāh,* normally translated "hierodule," was a woman attached to the temple rather than to a family. These women have long been assumed to be "sacred prostitutes," but considerable contemporary scholarship demonstrates that there is no reason for this belief. There were other chores that they could do: in the only biblical passage that offers a glimpse of their activity, they weave garments for the asherah. The *qadištu*-priestess in Mesopotamia was involved in childbirth and probably other matters relating to female biology. The great similarity between the *qedēšāh* and the *zônah* (at least in male eyes) is that the *qedēšāh* is outside the family system and thereby approachable for sexual encounter or arrangement. The great difference is that, while both have the right to say yes, only the *qedēšāh,* who has other functions, may have the economic freedom to say no.

Divorcing a wife sets her free. Given the economic constraints on most women, the assumption is that she will remarry as soon as possible; until then (as far as we know) she is a "free agent," able to negotiate her own way. Widowhood, on the other hand, does not always confer this freedom. A widow with children is still part of her deceased husband's family and lives in that household. A new marriage would be arranged by her late husband's family, possibly by her own sons. A childless widow is reattached by means of the levirate, and Near Eastern law makes it clear that if no one performs the act, the woman is (truly) "a widow" and should be released. Later biblical state law provides a formal public ritual by which a widow can initiate this release (Deut. 25:2–10). But in the ancestor stories of Genesis, long before the biblical state, the authority is Judah's, and he has not released Tamar. Denied a role in Judah's family, she is nevertheless bound by its constraints. Should she act otherwise, she will be punished as an unauthorized "whore."

So, sitting at "the eye-opening," Tamar is playing a dangerous game. She must close Judah's eyes in the present, or else he won't sleep with her, but she must provide a way to open them in the future, or she will be in serious trouble. So when he propositions her, she acts like a prostitute. In three "he said, she said" exchanges, she negotiates the payment of a kid and asks for his staff, his cord, and his seal—the equivalent of his credit card—as a token or pledge of the payment that he will send her. Judah leaves them willingly, for he has no need to hide his actions.

◇   *Act IV. A Debt of Honor (Gen. 38:20–23)*

> Judah sent a goat by means of his friend Hirah the Adullamite to retrieve his pledge from the woman.
> He didn't find her.
> He asked the people of her place thus, "Where is the *qedeshah*? The one of Eynayim on the road?"
> They said, "There was no *qedeshah* there."
> He returned to Judah and said, "I didn't find her, and the local people said, 'There was no *qedeshah* there.' "
> Judah said, "Take it from her lest we become a mockery. Look, I sent this goat and I didn't find her."

Judah, being an honorable man, sends his friend Hirah to pay the woman. But Tamar has disappeared back into her widowhood, and Hirah looks in vain for a *"qedēšāh"* (whom Judah could be paying for any number of services) rather than for a "prostitute," who was clearly hired for sexual favors. Even though it was not illegal to sleep with a prostitute, it appears that Judah nevertheless preferred to keep it quiet. Men may authorize prostitutes to serve their needs, but individually, they prefer not to seem too needy. Judah would like better that people not know exactly what he was trying to pay the woman for. His care for his reputation also makes him stop Hirah from continuing his inquiries. Judah's concern not to seem needy or foolish shows that he cares deeply about the way he is perceived by others.

◇   *Act V. Disgrace and Denouement (Gen. 38:24–26)*

> It happened after three months had passed.
> Thus was told to Judah, "Tamar your daughter-in-law has been faithless and what's more, look! She is pregnant from faithless acts."
> Judah said, "Take her out and let her be burned!"
> She was being brought out, and she sent to her father-in-law thus: "By the man to whom these belong I am pregnant."
> She said, "Recognize, please, to whom this seal and cord and staff belong."

Judah recognized and said, "She has been more righteous than I,
   that for this I did not give her to Shelah my son."
He did not continue to know her carnally.

Tamar has read Judah (and her whole society) correctly. When her
pregnancy begins to show, Judah is told, **"Tamar your daughter-in-law
has been faithless and what's more, look! She is pregnant from faithless acts."** To the people carrying the tale, her pregnancy is both proof
and reminder that Tamar has acted in defiance of her obligation to Judah. Judah's status, his very honor, is endangered. Her faithlessness
brings no less shame to him than adultery brings to a husband and a
nonvirgin daughter brings to her father. Pregnancy takes the shame
even further, giving it an undeniable reality and the prospect of a perpetual reminder. The man who worried that people would mock him for
trying to pay someone who disappeared is now faced with the ridicule
he would endure if a daughter-in-law could get away with thinking so
little of his authority that she conceived a child with a man of another
household! And so, Judah acts to restore his honor and status: **"Take her
out and let her be burned!"** Her execution will be a public confirmation
of the forbidden and treasonable nature of her offense, and of his own
"honorable" action in enforcing her obedience. And it will clearly show
who is in charge.

Tamar now seems totally unable to do anything to save herself. The
grammar of the sentences underscores the power dynamics. Judah
speaks in imperatives, while Tamar's action is described with a rare form
in Hebrew grammar, the passive participle, **She was being brought out.**
But Tamar is not as powerless as it seems, for she has anticipated the entire scenario. She sends Judah's staff and seal to him with word that she
is pregnant by their owner. This time she uses an imperative, though
softened with a plea, **"Recognize, please!"** Judah does recognize the objects, and this transforms everything. He had seen his sons die, and had
not recognized God's justice; he had seen Tamar and had not perceived
her right to have a life; he had seen the veiled Tamar and had not known
her. But now he recognizes the staff and seal, and understands all that he
had failed to see before. He stops the proceedings, declaring, **"She has
been more righteous than I, that for this I did give her to Shelah my
son."** The "for this" is the pregnancy. Judah's recognition that he is the
father exonerates Tamar, for the man she has slept with is an appropriate
levir, her own father-in-law. She has operated unconventionally, but

within the constraints of her role as a childless widow. Judah failed to have Shelah impregnate her, but now she has caused him to impregnate her himself. She is therefore more righteous, in her commitment to continuing the line through the levirate, than Judah has been.

"She is more righteous than I" is the most probable translation of *ṣadeqah mimmennî*. There is another possibility: "She is righteous. It is from me." The "it" implied would be the baby. According to this translation, Judah "acquits" her in his role as the family's judge, and then gives the reason: the child is his. There would be no stigma in this. Even though, normally, a father-in-law/daughter-in-law union is an incestuous act, the incest provision is suspended for the levirate. The father is the son's surrogate just as a brother-levir can be his brother's surrogate and sleep with his sister-in-law, also an incestuous act under normal circumstances. The gossiping public would realize that a pregnancy by Judah validated Tamar's innocence.

Once the widow is pregnant, the levirate is over. The laws do not specify that the woman should continue to be the wife of the levir. Sleeping with a daughter-in-law becomes an incestuous act, and the story hastens to assure us that Judah never slept with Tamar again.

◈ *The Birth of the Bold (Gen. 38:27–30)*

> It happened at the time that she gave birth.
> Look! Twins in her womb!
> And as she was birthing, one gave a hand.
> The midwife took it and tied a scarlet thread onto his hand, to say, "This one came out first."
> And as he turned his hand back, look! His brother came out.
> She said, "How have you broken through your breach?"
> And he called his name Peretz.
> And afterward his brother came out who had the scarlet on his hand.
> And he called his name Zerah.

Judah applauds Tamar's action and God rewards it. Her boldness, initiative, and willingness to defy society's expectations have enabled God to provide Judah with two new sons after the death of his first two sons. By continuing to consider herself a member of Judah's family and insisting on securing her own future within its parameters, she has made it possible for that family to thrive and develop into a major tribe and eventually the Judean state. The story marks the significance of this birth of twins with the language that heralded the birth of Jacob and Esau, **Look! Twins in her womb!** But as she is birthing, Tamar's role in Israel's history ends. She will act no more. Midwives mark and witness the children's arrival, and "he," almost certainly Judah, names them. The attention of the story and its readers passes from Tamar to her sons and to the father who names them, claiming his role in their lives.

Tamar passes from the scene, but her impact continues. One of the twins is even bolder than Jacob. Jacob, the second born, came out holding on to his brother's heels, and spent the first part of his life trying to supplant him. Peretz supplants his brother even before he leaves the womb. He shows the key characteristic of his mother, breaking through constraints and creating the breach (*pereṣ*) through which he is born. But the birth of Peretz is not Tamar's only effect and achievement. Despite the story's keen interest in the lineage of Judah, it does not relate the life of Peretz or follow his descendants, and we realize his unique significance only when another bold, unconventional, and loyal woman, Ruth, intervenes to make his lineage lead eventually to the Davidic dynasty. In the more immediate context, Genesis continues with the story of Joseph and Judah. And in this story we realize that the woman who transformed the history of the kingdom of Judah also transformed Judah himself. Judah, whom his mother named in thanksgiving (from *wdh*, "give thanks"), becomes the one who has acknowledged (from *wdh*, "confess, acknowledge") that Tamar was the righteous one. This acknowledgment changes him, and he begins to act more like Tamar. He had left his brothers before he married Batshua, but the rest of Genesis shows him back in Jacob's family. He had betrayed Joseph out of jealousy, but he henceforth acts out of loyalty to his brother Benjamin and his father, and is willing to stand up to the Egyptians in order to ensure their safety. The very words echo the story of Tamar, for he who had given his staff as pledge to Tamar turns himself into a pledge for the safety of Benjamin (Gen. 43:9; 44:32–34).

Ruth and Tamar have much in common with Dinah. Like the former, she looks for friendship with women beyond ethnic boundaries. Like the latter, she engages in sexual activity not arranged by the paterfamilias. Like Tamar, her sexual action endangers her father's honor, but his honor is restored. But there are several crucial differences that make Dinah almost their polar opposite. On the simplest level, Dinah goes out of the Israelite family, Tamar and Ruth come in. The five mothers of what becomes the most prominent family in Judah have different points of origin. The daughters of Lot come from inside the nuclear family; Leah

comes from the next level of extended family; Tamar is from somewhere outside, and Ruth begins outside Israel and then is a widow in Israel. With the exception of the daughters of Lot, whose actions are
forbidden in normal circumstances, all women come into a family from
outside it. Whoever their progenitors are, they leave their birth family
and enter the family of their father-in-law. They lose their earlier identity
as young girls and adopt a new one. Dinah attempts to do this before an
official marriage has been arranged for her. The marriages of Leah,
Tamar, and Ruth give them their adult identities as members of their
husbands' households. They wholeheartedly embrace their new identity, and when they are widowed, Tamar and Ruth act to maintain it. It is
this commitment that transforms their apparently subversive actions
into underpinnings of their family. Dinah's out-of-control move has the
potential to destroy the patrilineal structure; Tamar and Ruth reinforce
it. These differences produce distinctly different results. Dinah has no future; Tamar and Ruth occupy prominent positions in the royal lineage of
Israel.

Tamar has much in common with Judah's foremothers: Sarah, Rivka,
and Leah. Sarah, like Tamar, was given away (to Pharaoh and Abimelech) when Abraham wrongly perceived a threat to his own life; like
Tamar, she took action to bear a child by arranging the surrogacy of Hagar. Tamar turned herself into a second Rivka when she veiled herself as
Rivka once veiled herself at the sight of Sarah's son, Isaac (Gen. 24:66);
she disguised herself as Rivka disguised her son Jacob (Gen. 27:14–16);
and she became the mother of twins. Leah disguised herself, pretending
to be Rachel in order to marry Jacob. Later, after Jacob rejected her, she
actively managed to sleep with him through "hiring" his sexual services
by using mandrakes; the result was the birth of Issachar, and later Zebu-
lun (Gen. 30:16–20). Thus, the great-grandmother, the grandmother, and
the mother of Judah overcame vulnerability and powerlessness to give
birth to and determine the success of the grandfather and father of Judah and of Judah himself. Tamar continues this pattern to the next generation. They all were prepared to risk scandal, humiliation, ostracism,
or death to have children with their families. They all were assertive and
proactive, and each of them engaged in unconventional sexual activity
to accomplish their purpose. And the same is certainly true of the other
mothers of David's line, the daughters of Lot and Ruth.

Taken by themselves, incest, adultery, and licentious behavior are
subversive acts that could destroy the social order. In most contexts,
such behavior is an indication of the loss of male control over female

sexuality, and it can destroy the patriarchal system. However, in the context of the faithfulness of these women to their family and to its men, the loss of male control was actually a good thing; it enabled women to act in ways that served the family structure and enabled it to survive. The characteristics of family loyalty, wits, determination, unconventionality, and agressiveness that Tamar and Ruth brought into their family will characterize the Judean monarchy to which these women gave birth.

The Royal Way

THE DAUGHTERS of Lot, Leah, Tamar, and Ruth produce the lines of the kings of Judah, which stretch from Terah to Lot to his elder daughter, and from her son Moab to Ruth; and on the other side from Terah to Abraham to Judah and Tamar; from Tamar's son Peretz to Boaz; and from Boaz and Ruth to David. Lot had a second daughter, and her line extends from her son Ben-Ammi to the Ammonites, and from the Ammonites to Na'amah, the Ammonite wife of King Solomon and the mother of Rehoboam (1 Kings 14:21). All the future kings of Judah came from Rehoboam and Na'amah.

David's connection to Moab is not limited to his great-grandmother Ruth. He had sent his parents there for protection during his outlaw years, and then conquered Moab near the beginning of his reign. Solomon's story resonates with the story of Tamar and Judah. Judah was Jacob's fourth son, Peretz was Judah's fourth son, and after Absalom and Amnon were killed, Solomon was the fourth living son whose name the Bible remembers. Peretz pushed his way past Zerah to become the firstborn and heir to the line, just as Solomon pushed past Adonijah to become his father's royal successor. In addition, the names of the characters in the two stories bear a strange resemblance to the stories of David and Solomon. Peretz, "breakthrough," is a word frequently associated with the story of David, who named Ba'al Peratzim saying, "The Lord broke through (*paraṣ*) my enemies as water breaks through a dam" (2 Sam. 5:20–22) and named Peretz Uzzah, where the Lord "broke through against Uzzah" (2 Sam. 6:8). Obed, Ruth's son, is also the name of one of David's inner guard (Chron. 11:47); Tamar is the name of David's daughter. Bathshua, named Judah's wife in Gen. 38:12 and in Chronicles, is also the name by which Chronicles knows David's wife Bathsheba, Solomon's mother. More remotely, Naomi sounds like Na'amah, mother of Rehoboam, and comes from the same verbal root, and the name Hirah, Judah's friend, sounds somewhat like the name of King Hiram of Tyre, who befriended David and Solomon. Are these all coincidences? Or are they sly hidden allusions by the storytellers?

David has much in common with Ruth and Tamar. As a young boy, he left his parental home to become a member of Saul's household. Like Ruth, he married into his new family and formed a close relationship with a family member of the same gender, for David and Jonathan and Ruth and Naomi are the Bible's closest same-sex friendships. Then David, like Tamar, had to leave his household when the paterfamilias became frightened of him. David, like Tamar, disguised himself as needed. And both David and Tamar proved their righteousness by showing their paterfamilias something that belonged to them. Tamar sent Judah his staff and seal, saying "recognize," and when Judah recognized them, he said, "She is more righteous than I" (Gen. 38:25–26). David showed Saul a piece of the robe that David had cut while Saul was sleeping, saying, "See . . . and know that I didn't kill you" (1 Sam. 24:11), to which Saul responded, "You are more righteous than I" (1 Sam. 24:17). And David and Tamar came back in triumph, Tamar to the house of Judah, and David to the kingship.

David as ruler subverted some of the major traditions of Israel. He danced and sacrificed before the ark, merging the roles of priest and king. He began an aggressive campaign of expansion, enlarging the territory of Israel beyond its traditional boundaries. He manipulated the death of one of his trusted inner guards. But in all of his excesses, he remained faithful to his belief that God made promises to him and to his lineage. David's belief in the importance of the lineage principle colored the decisions that he made as judge and leader. When the Wise Woman of Tekoa told him the parable of her son who murdered his only brother, David was prepared to override the demand of her family that he execute the killer, in order to keep their father's line going. His love of his own lineage led him to lay aside his responsibilities as political and judicial authority, ignoring his son Amnon's rape of David's own daughter, refusing to acknowledge the threat Absalom presented, and continuing to mourn him even after he was killed in his war of rebellion. Royal concern for the birth and safety of an heir echoes the concern of Ruth and Tamar to have sons for their dead husband's family.

There is another woman crucial to the development of Judean kingship: Bathsheba. The pivotal story of David and Bathsheba is both the height of David's assertion of power and the means by which he learned

that there are limits to that power. It shows a David willing to break Israel's most sacred laws—those against adultery and murder—and a
David willing to acknowledge his mistake, repent, and learn from it.

David also has much in common with Judah, for his behavior vis-à-vis
Bathsheba echoes Judah's treatment of Tamar in Genesis 38. Both men
used their power to manipulate those under their control. Both violated
family norms—David by mating with Bathsheba, Judah by not mating
with Tamar. Both exercised their power over life and death, Judah first
condemning Tamar to a living death and later ordering her execution,
and David sending Uriah to the most dangerous spot in the battle. And
both acknowledged that they did wrong. David is like a larger-than-life
version of Judah, whose wrongs go one step further than Judah's. His violation of the norm against adultery is more serious than Judah's violation of levirate rules. He actually commits administrative assassination
by arranging Uriah's death; Judah only commands an execution that
does not take place.

At first glance, Bathsheba does not seem to have much in common
with the other mothers of this dynasty. She seems to be entirely passive.
David sees her and takes her, and the only words she speaks are her announcement of her pregnancy. It is hard to imagine her in the company
of the determined and proactive Tamar, or serving as a model for aggressive and subversive behavior on behalf of principle. But Bathsheba
very much belongs in this company. The pregnancy of both women precipitates male action: they each use the emphatic "I," *'anoki*, to emphasize their situation: *harah 'anôkî* says Bathsheba, announcing her
pregnancy. By the man to whom these things belong *harah 'anôkî*, says
Tamar as she sends Judah his pledge. At the beginning of her story,
Tamar too was the silent object of male action. Judah took her for his
son, gave her to another son, and sent her away to her father's house. It
is only later that she begins to act for her own benefit and the benefit of
Judah's house. So too over a longer span of time, Bathsheba develops
into a player, acting to become the queen mother and have her son en-
throned as the heir. Bathsheba determines the destiny of Solomon in the
grand manner of Sarah and Rivka. And, like them, she has the divine
word on her side, for Bathsheba worked with the prophet Nathan, who
bore God's word to David. By the end of her story, Bathsheba, like
Tamar, has seen her child, like Peretz, become the breakthrough son and
heir.

Bathsheba shares another trait with Tamar: we are not sure where

she came from. Her father's names, Ammiel or Eliam, could be good
Hebrew names, but they could also be slight Hebrew modifications of
Aramean, Canaanite, or Moabite names. By the time we meet her, she is
the wife of Uriah the Hittite, but nevertheless she lives near the palace.
And she is married, so when she comes into the family and bears David a
son, she follows the same trajectory as Tamar and Ruth, from "beyond
the pale" into its center.

We can easily understand why the ancestry of kings should be full of
unconventional people and subversive actions. Kings, after all, are not
noted for their eagerness to conform to social mores. We can also see
why the subversive actions that they admire are dedicated to preserving
the lineage of the royal family, the dynastic succession. In the worldview
of kings, support of the royal line is essential.

It is somewhat harder to understand why the Israelite kings were so
welcoming of foreign wives, even in Israel, where the rights and obligations of kings were not as different from those of commoners as they
were elsewhere in the ancient world. Even in Israel, the kings were different from the rest of the populace, marked off by God's special
covenant with David. By logical extension, we could expect a rigorous
three-part division: the king, "us," and "them." But this does not happen. On the contrary, the kings of Israel welcomed foreigners at court
and in the harem. The Deuteronomist historian, eager to find reasons
for the downfall of the state, faults them for this; the book of Chronicles, on the other hand, does not.

There are several reasons for the kings' attitude. First, they themselves are outside the normative group, either above it in the pyramid of
power, or at its economic or judicial center. They are thus less committed to the historical sociological factors that bind the society together.
Indeed, they may view some of these factors, such as local or tribal allegiances, as rivals to their own power. Second, kings also tend to see the
state in territorial terms: whatever territory the central government controls directly is part of the state by definition. From the view of the
throne, annexing additional territory does not weaken the boundaries of
the state; it simply expands them. The royal concept of national identity
is similarly political: whomever the king rules are his people. Adding
more people enlarges the circle at the center of which the king sits. Of
course, conquered peoples do not always see it this way. They may retain their independent sense of identity until such time as they revolt.
But until that happens, the king will view all the people in his territory as

his subjects. And third, kings seek to maximize their alliances with the major powers of their day and with their neighbors, and marriage is a powerful alliance-builder.

Kings are notoriously willing to ignore or subvert traditional social institutions, but there is one that they uphold vigorously: the inherited privilege of their own family is the source of their power, and so the key loyalty that they demand of their wives, whether foreign-born or native-born, is a commitment to continue the royal line. The stories told of the "mothers" of the dynasty—the daughters of Lot, Tamar, Ruth, and Bathsheba—portray them all as actively accepting this commitment.

These stories are an effective counterpoint to the more negative opinion of foreign wives. Outsiders can indeed have a positive role in Israel's destiny. The dynastic mothers demonstrate steadfast allegiance to their adopted identities. Once married, they are not foreign wives, *nāšîm nokriyyôt;* whatever their origin, they are mothers of Israel.

Outsider Women
Exile and Ezra

WHEN JERUSALEM was destroyed, the kings were dethroned, the leadership was sent into exile, the people were scattered, and new people arrived in the land of Israel. At this time, at least some of Israel's thinkers began to view foreign women as the very symbol of apostasy and faithlessness. Before the exile, the horror stories of Ba'al-Pe'or, Jezebel, and Solomon's wives showed a concern that these foreign women would lead the people to idolatry. During the exile, the prophet Ezekiel sounded a new note. In his version of the "marital metaphor" for the relationship of God and Israel, he attributed the wantonness of Jerusalem to her particular ancestry. In a vituperative and graphic diatribe (Ezekiel 16), he declared that Jerusalem began life as the outcast, exposed child of a Canaanite father and a Hittite mother, that God adopted her as his ward and betrothed her at puberty. But her origin was the cause of Jerusalem's later wantonness (and God's retaliatory devastation). It was a family trait.

◇ *Like Mother, Like Daughter (Ezek. 16:44–48)*

> "Look! Everyone who pronounces upon you will say this proverb, 'Like mother, like daughter.'
>
> "You are the daughter of your mother, who spurned her husband and sons.
>
> "And you are the sister of your sisters, who spurned their husbands and children.
>
> "Your mother was Hittite and your father Amorite.
>
> "Your big sister is Samaria and her daughters, she who sits on your left, and your sister who is smaller than you is Sodom, and her daughters.
>
> "Did you not walk in their ways and do their abominations?
>
> "In just a little while you were becoming more corrupt than they in all your ways.

> "As I live!" says Lord YHWH, "your sister Sodom did not do, nor
> her daughters, as you and your daughters have done."

Jerusalem has done abominations, and Ezekiel links them to the proverbial evil of Sodom and to the evil of Samaria, which had been proved by her destruction. These "sisters" are a standard of evil, which, Ezekiel proclaims, Jerusalem has overtaken. The link carries the message, spelled out in the proverb, that a city's evil is "inherited" from its parentage and most especially from the Hittite mother. Even though Jerusalem had been outside the Canaanite milieu since infancy, had even been nurtured by God, her "genetic" nature remained, so that her behavior was "Like mother, like daughter." Ezekiel's portrayal of Jerusalem's misbehavior carried a clear message to human society: even though a girl may leave her birth family, her birth family never leaves her. To take a foreign wife—even one raised in Israel—is to bring the outsider into your home.

Matters came to a head in the Persian period. There was no king to represent the unity of the people, and opinion was divided as to whether monarchy had been a good thing for Israel. The book of Kings catalogues the many times that the kings sinned and led Israel astray, and blames them for the destruction of Jerusalem. The book of Chronicles is in favor of kingship, portraying David and Solomon as great leaders, omitting the stories (Bathsheba–Uriah and Tamar and Amnon) with which the book of Samuel undermines the reader's faith in the monarchy and the story (Solomon's wives) in which the book of Kings indicts him for his foreign marriages. It is probably no coincidence that the book of Chronicles was not worried about intermarriage, carries no cautionary comments or tales about foreign wives, and records mixed marriages matter-of-factly without any particular notice.

This difference of opinion erupted into conflict at the time of Ezra. Leaders of the community come before Ezra to complain of foreign marriages in all strata of the community.

◇ *The Holy Seed (Ezra 9:1–3)*

> When these matters were concluded, the leaders approached
> me thus, "The people Israel, the priests and the Levites,
> have not separated themselves from the peoples of the
> lands according to the abominations of the Canaanite, the
> Hittite, the Perizzite, the Jebusite, the Ammonite, Moabite,
> Egyptian, and Edomite ('dmy!). For they have married their

daughters for wives for themselves and their sons and they have mixed the holy seed with the peoples of the lands. And their leaders and magistrates were first in this transgression."

When I heard this matter, I tore my garment and my robe.

I tore out bunches of my hair and beard and I sat appalled.

The complaining "leaders" are clearly not the total leadership of the people, since they claim that leaders led the offense. The substance of their complaint is not apostasy. They object to these marriages not because they might lead to apostasy, but simply because they are marriages to other peoples. Their objection is not strictly legal. Only the first four peoples, the Canaanites, Hittites, Perizzites, and Jebusites were forbidden by Deuteronomy, and they disappeared long before the period of Deuteronomy, and certainly by the Persian period. The complainants begin with them to give an aura of legitimacy to their objections to the others, Israel's neighbors, who were not forbidden by pre-exilic texts. These marriages are characterized as a particular kind of offense, a *ma'al*, a trespass against boundaries, particularly of the holy. Those who have joined with the peoples of the lands have not only trespassed national boundaries, they have transgressed the key boundary between holy and profane because, to these leaders, Israel is a "holy seed."

The term "seed" is not extraordinary: it is one of the many ways in which Israel is depicted as a plant or a vine. The idea of Israel as a seed became more prominent as land and king became less secure markers of the nation's identities. The Bible's later writers speak of God choosing the seed of Abraham (Isa. 41:8); and of the house of Jacob (Ezek. 20:5). They declare that the seed had gone bad (Jer. 2:21; Isa. 57:4; first in Isa. 1:4), that God will reject the seed (2 Kings 17:20), and that God will return the seed of the house of Israel (Jer. 23:8), of Abraham, Isaac, and Jacob (Jer. 33:26), of Israel (Isa. 45:25), and that God will maintain covenant with it (Isa. 59:21; 61:8–9; cf. Jer. 31:36).

Those complaining to Ezra speak not just of "seed," but "holy seed." Such language begins to appear in connection with restoration and for an eschatological future. The seed has ceased to be the purely descriptive seed of Abraham, of Jacob, of Israel, and Israel has become very special seed: "seed that the Lord has blessed" (Isa. 61:8–9), "seed blessed by God" (Isa. 65:23), "seed of peace (Zech. 8:12), "seed of God" (Mal. 2:15), and the "holy seed" in Ezra.

The holy seed first appears in Isaiah, in connection with his hope for a new beginning after the destruction he was convinced would come. He likened the destruction to the felling of an oak and a terebinth, which leaves stumps behind from which the trees can regrow. In just this way, says Isaiah, a holy seed will grow from the stump of Israel (Isa. 6:13). He envisions an open Israel in which strangers join with the house of Jacob (Isa. 14:3). But Ezra's complainers have a more priestly view of seed and holiness: a genetic lineage, and state, whose borders are tightly controlled. For them, the problem posed by intermarriage is neither apostasy nor abomination; it is adulteration.

Ezra responds with a public demonstration of grief that attracts others who are worried about this grand transgression. He proclaims a "prayer" that is actually a diatribe.

◇ Ezra's Prayer (Ezra 9:3–9)

When I heard this matter, I tore my clothes and my cloak and plucked the hair of my head and my beard and sat desolate.

To me gathered all those who trembled at the word of the God of Israel about the great transgression and I sat desolate until the evening sacrifice.

"My God, I am shamed and humiliated to lift, my God, my face to you.

"For our sins are great, higher than our head, our guilt great up to the sky.

"Since the days of our fathers we have been in great guilt to this very day.

"And because of our sins, we have been given, we and our kings and our priests, into the hand of the kings of the nations, into sword and exile, and are in ridicule and shame to this day.

"Now, for a moment, YHWH our God has extended grace to leave us a remnant and give us a stake in his holy place, to enlighten our eyes has our God (done this) and to give us a little renewal from our servitude.

"For we are slaves and God has not abandoned us in our servitude, and he has given us benevolence before the kings of Persia to give us renewal to erect our temple, to rebuild our ruins, and to give us a fence around Judah and Jerusalem.

"And now, what can we say, our God, after all this, for we have abandoned your commands, which you commanded by the hand of your servants the prophets, thus, 'The land which you are coming to inherit is outcast in the quarantine of the peoples of the lands for the abominations with which they filled her from edge to edge in their pollution. And now, do not give your daughters to their sons and do not take their daughters for your sons. Do not seek their welfare or good forever, so that you may be strong and eat of the good of the land and give it as inheritance to your sons forever.'

"After all that had come upon us because of our evil deeds and our great guilt—indeed, you, our God, kept back some of our punishment and left us this remnant—shall we go back to violating your commandments and marrying these nations of abominations? Would you not get angry until destruction so that there would be no remnant, no survival?"

Ezra's prayer is penitential in tone and Deuteronomic in its theology. Like Moses, Joshua, and Samuel, he reminds the people of their many transgressions, and accuses them of continuing the old pattern of violation even in the moment of new beginning. The prayer is ostensibly addressed to God, but it doesn't ask for God's mercy. Its purpose is to move the people to change their ways by reminding them what trouble comes from sin and then naming Israel's new sin: disobeying God's command to keep away "from the peoples in the land to which you are coming to inherit it." All the recent troubles of Israel are the result of its transgressions, and the first order of these is intermarriage with the local inhabitants. Like Israel's classic Deuteronomic covenant-renewal oration, Ezra's "prayer" moves the people to tears and leads them to promise to mend their ways:

◇ *našîm nokriyyôt (Ezra 10:2–5).*

Secaniah son of Yehiel of the family of Elam spoke to Ezra:

"We have trespassed against our God.

"We have brought into our homes foreign wives from the peoples of the land.

"But there is hope for Israel about this.

"Now let us make a covenant to our God to expel all the wives and their offspring at the advice of my lord and those who quake at the command of God. Let it be done as the Torah. Arise, for this matter is yours to do.

"We are with you, be strong and do it."

Then Ezra arose and adjured the leaders of the priests, Levites, and all Israel to do this and they took an oath.

The momentum of this response leads Ezra to action. First he fasted "because of the transgression of the *gôlah* (formerly exiled) community." And then he called for an assembly:

◈   *The Assembly (Ezra 10:7–14)*

They sent a proclamation through Judah and Jerusalem to all the members of the *golah* to gather at Jerusalem: "Everyone who will not come for three days at the advice of the leaders and officers will be excommunicated, with all his possessions, and he will be separated from the assembly of the *golah*."

All the men of Judah, Benjamin, and Jerusalem assembled at the third day, which was the ninth month, the twenty-fifth day of the month, onto the street of the temple, shivering at this matter and the rains. Ezra the priest arose and said to them:

"You have transgressed: you have settled foreign wives, adding to Israel's guilt. Now give thanks to YHWH the God of your fathers and do his will. Separate from the peoples of the land and the foreign wives."

The whole assembly spoke in a loud voice, "It is true, we must do as you have said. But the people are many, and it is the rainy season, and we have no strength to stand outside, and the work will take more than one or two days because many of us have sinned in this matter. Let the leaders of the congregation and all of those in our cities who have foreign wives come at appointed times with the elders of each city and its judges to turn away God's anger from us about this matter."

The people then make arrangements to appear, and from the first day of the tenth month until the first day of the first month, they assemble and repudiate their wives.

The combination of peroration and penitence gives the whole passage a heavily Deuteronomic tone. Both leaders and people have learned well the lessons of the Deuteronomistic historical books. The term "foreign wives," *našîm nokriyyôt*, reinforces the lesson, for it appears only in Ezra, where it emerges seven times, in Nehemiah, and in the historian's verdict on Solomon in 1 Kings 11:1.

The pious tone induces the reader to see the whole event as an occasion of sin and repentance and to miss the radical nature of the affair. The "peoples of the land" that Deuteronomy forbids are the long-gone Canaanites. It never forbade Israel to make treaties or marry the Moabites, Ammonites, Egyptianites, and Edomites; they were simply to be kept separate, not allowed to "enter the congregation of YHWH" (Deut. 23:4). The prophets heralded the return from Babylon as a "new Exodus," a parallel to the departure from Egypt that would rival that exodus. But the peoples of the land to which they came back were not the original inhabitants. Most of them were the descendants of those Judeans who were not exiled to Babylon, who stayed on, as peasants usually do, or ran away to Egypt and then drifted back. Ezra's list of nations combined the abominated nations from Deuteronomy with those that Deuteronomy says "may not enter the congregation of Israel." He then invoked the authority of God's original commandment to prohibit marriage to the entire list. In this way, he created a new reality: he read out of the community everyone who did not go through the Babylonian exile. Theological language leads to new sociological fact.

Encouraged by his initial group of "tremblers," Ezra puts his new definition of Israel into effect by inviting to his assembly all the male members of the *gôlah*. The very term indicates that they were the ones who had returned from the exile, *galût*. The other Judean and Israelite men were not invited: they are just part of the "peoples of the land." At the assembly he convinces the returnees that their new wives are latter-day Canaanites, and breaks up their marriages.

Ezra is concerned with foreign wives in particular. Female returnees who married the "peoples of the land" have already joined those people, and to Ezra they are not part of Israel. But the women that the male returnees have married are adulterating the *gôlah*, which Ezra considers a "holy seed." They have to be expelled together with their children, a deviation from the normal divorce pattern of the ancient world in which the woman left and the children, who were their father's lineage and posterity, stayed with him. Ezra does not want these children, even though their fathers were of the "pure seed." The reason may very well be economic; indeed the division of the community into the *gôlah* and the "peoples of the land" may very well reflect struggles over who owned the land that the people abandoned when they went into exile, land that had been worked in the interim by those who remained. But he never mentions such causes, speaking only the theological language of Deuteronomic law, the pollution language of Leviticus, and the ontological polarity of "holy seed" and "foreign women." As with any politician, we are tempted to ask whether Ezra was using theological language to justify economically motivated actions or whether he truly believed he was defending the "holy seed" from adulteration. But whatever his motives, his argument was successful, and the community of former exiles expelled its wives.

Ezra's actions were not universally applauded. The prophet Malachi objected to this mass divorce. His language is obscure, but he clearly objects to rejecting the wife of one's youth in order to seek "the seed of God" (Mal. 2:15). The book of Ruth is not at all ambiguous about this issue. Reciting it in the days of Ezra was a direct rebuttal of Ezra's idea that foreign wives dilute the holy seed. But the real refutation of Ezra came from the people, who continued to marry foreign women.

Nehemiah also complains about this practice, for other reasons:

◇ Nehemiah's Turn (Neh. 13:23–28)

> In those days too I saw Jews who had settled Ashdodite, Ammonite, and Moabite women.
>
> Their children spoke half Ashdodite and did not know how to speak Judean as the language of each people.
>
> I contended with them and cursed them and hit people from among them and plucked their hair and adjured them by God "not to give your daughters to their sons and not to take from their daughters to your sons and to you. For because of these, Solomon the king of Israel sinned. In all the nations there never was a king like him, and beloved of his God. God made him king over all Israel. Even him the foreign wives caused to sin. Shall we listen to you to do this great evil to transgress against our God to settle foreign wives?"
>
> I chased out from among them one of the sons of the high priest Yehoiyada ben Elyashuv who was the son-in-law of Sanballat the Haronite.

Nehemiah mentions the corruption of language and reminds the people that foreign wives enticed even the great Solomon to sin. But he too uses the new pollution language as he states that he "purified" the priests and

Levites from the foreign element (Neh. 13:30). The marriage problem never went away, and Jewish men kept marrying local women. The Maccabeans passed laws, but they too could not prevent the behavior, and the rabbis provided conversion procedures so that foreign women cease to be foreign before Jews marry them.

Individual foreign women continue to enter Israel, but the idea of the foreign woman as a source of danger to the community did not disappear. It reached almost mythological status in the figure of the "foreign" or "strange" woman (*'iššah zarah, 'išša nokriyah*) in the book of Proverbs, chapters 1–9. This woman is outside the pale, by origin or by behavior. Sometimes she is clearly an adulteress, strange to the man's family; sometimes she breaks cultic rules; and sometimes she is a foreigner. All these are ways in which a woman can be strange, or "go strange." As in the English word "outlandish," the one from out-the-land is also out-the-customs of the land. And the one who disregards the mores of the land, like the adulteress, is deemed an outsider woman.

This association of the foreign woman with all kinds of otherness makes her the very symbol of the "Other." The next step will be to see all women, even Israelite women who behave themselves, as somehow "other," and Hellenism will bring that step to Israel.

Part Four

VOICE

BIBLICAL BOOKS convey their messages both by their contents and by the arrangement of those contents. The editors, or "redactors," of Genesis arrange the Abraham story into a tight cycle that goes from "Go!" in chapter 12 to "Go!" in chapter 22 (see the discussion above, pp. 225). The editors of the Pentateuch set the stories of Israel as two parallel groups, one in Exodus and one in Numbers, and the juxtaposition of these stories illuminates Israel's ideas about faith, loyalty, and leadership. The editors of the historical books arrange two parallel groups of victim stories, in Judges and Second Samuel, to offer both a justification for and a critique of monarchy. They also create another group of stories, in which the voice of God operates through female oracles. From Judges to Kings, a woman arises at each critical juncture of Israel's history to proclaim the future. These are the stories about "voice."

Oracles of the Conquest of Canaan
Rahab and Deborah

THE FIRST SAVIOR-WOMAN in Israel's new land is also its first oracle. The Canaanite prostitute Rahab, under orders from the king of Jericho to hand over the Israelites in her house, hides them on her roof and sends the king's men looking for them in the wrong direction. Then she goes up to the roof and says to the Israelites:

◇ *A Declaration of Faith (Josh. 2:9–11)*

> "I know that YHWH has given you this land
> And that dread of you has fallen upon us,
> And that all the inhabitants of the land have melted before you.
> For we have heard how YHWH dried up the waters of the Red
>   Sea before you when you went out of Egypt,
> And what you did to the kings of the Amorites on the other side
>   of the Jordan to Sihon and to Og, that you utterly destroyed
>   them.
> We heard and our hearts melted;
> No man has spirit before you,
> For YHWH your God is God in heaven above and on the earth
>   below."

This is a formal declaration, beginning with **"I know,"** and ending with her affirmation, **"YHWH your God is God in heaven above and on the earth below."** She speaks in the pattern of other statements of faith, using the "I know" with which Moses' father-in-law Jethro declared after the Exodus, "Now I know that the Lord is greater than all gods" (Exod. 18:11). After Elisha cured the Syrian captain Naaman from leprosy, Naaman affirmed, "For I know that there is no such God in all the land" (2 Kings 5:15). As Jethro was convinced by the Exodus, and Naaman by being cured of leprosy, Rahab has been brought to her affirmation by the knowledge of God's miracles. Like the Gibeonites who come after her, she has heard about God's great deeds (Josh. 9:9–10), and she even quotes the very verses of the Song of the Sea that predicts how hearing the word of God's actions will cause dread to fall upon the inhabitants and make their hearts melt (Exod. 15:14–16). Rahab is the first of the nations to be convinced that God is indeed **God in heaven above and on the earth below.**

Rahab goes beyond a faith declaration as she reveals that she knows what God is about to do: **"I know that YHWH has given you this land."** Israel has not yet crossed the Jordan, but Rahab knows it will take over Canaan. These words of prediction spoken by a Canaanite prostitute convince the spies. They recognize the truth and do not suffer the fear that plagued the emissaries whom Moses had sent out a generation before. And they bring her message back to Joshua. The first prophet after Moses to announce to Israel the paths of her history, Rahab becomes the first oracle of Israel's destiny.

There is a connection here between women and prediction, a connection that converges once more when the conquest of Canaan is completed.

The action begins suddenly with an introduction of Deborah.

✧ Deborah, Prophet and Judge (Judg. 4:4–5)

> Deborah the prophet-woman, Lapidot-woman—she judged Israel at that time.
>
> She would sit under "Deborah's Palm Tree" between Ramah and Beth-El on Mount Ephraim, and the Israelites went up to her for judgment.

Unlike Rahab, the outsider's outsider, Deborah was an insider's insider, a public leader, active in the public arena as part of her normal life.

✧ The Call (Judg. 4:6–10)

> She sent and called for Barak ben Abinoam from Qedesh-Naftali.
>
> She said to him, "Did not YHWH God of Israel command: 'Go and pull toward
>
> " 'Mount Tabor and take with you ten thousand men from the men of Naphtali and Zebulun. I will draw Sisera the head of Yabin's army and his chariotry and masses to Wadi Kishon and I will give him into your hand.' "
>
> Barak said to her, "If you go with me, I will go. If you will not go with me, I will not go."

> She said, "I will indeed go with you, especially since you will get
> no glory on the way you are going, for into the hand of a
> woman YHWH will deliver Sisera."
> Deborah rose and went with Barak to Qedesh.
> Barak mustered Zebulun and Naphtali to Qedesh.
> Ten thousand men went up at his feet, and Deborah went up
> with him.

Deborah's summons to Barak in our story hints at a previous call to him: **"Did not YHWH God of Israel command?"** Now Deborah calls him as a prophet, an envoy of God, as part of the important role prophets in the ancient Near East played in battle. As discussed above (page 48), prophets mustered and inspired the troops, and also declared the correct, auspicious time to begin the battle.

Deborah delivers an oracle before they even leave for the battle, telling Barak that he will not achieve glory, for God will deliver Sisera into the hand of a woman. Like the reader, Barak surely interprets this to mean that Deborah will bring the victory, but her speech, like all oracles', is cryptic, and it is only later that we learn yet another woman will enter the fray.

◇ *The Battle (Judg. 4:12–16)*

> Sisera mustered all his chariotry, nine hundred iron chariots,
> and all his people from Harosheth-Hagoyim to Wadi
> Kishon.
> Deborah said to Barak, "Arise, for this is the day that YHWH
> gives Sisera into your hand. Indeed YHWH goes out before
> you?"
> Barak quickly descended from Mount Tabor and ten thousand
> men after him.
> YHWH distressed Sisera and all the chariotry and all the camp
> by the sword before Barak, and Sisera descended from his
> chariot and fled on foot.
> Barak chased the chariots and the camp to Harosheth-Hagoyim
> and fell on Sisera's camp with the sword. None remained.

Deborah the prophet announces the victory, **God will deliver Sisera,** and reassures God's presence in that place, **"Indeed YHWH goes out before you,"** and in that time, **"Arise, for this is the day."** She herself does not go down to the battlefield. Like Moses, she is not a military commander. She stays on Mount Tabor; she inspires and predicts and celebrates in song. Her weapon is the word, and her very name is an anagram of "she spoke" (*dibberah*).

Deborah and Rahab are the literary bookends that surround the conquest of Canaan, which is nestled inside the greater section, about "Israel in the land of Israel" that occupies Joshua-Judges-1 and 2 Samuel—1 and 2 Kings); and that history is itself bracketed by Rahab and the prophet Huldah.

Oracles of Saul
Hannah and the Witch of Endor

THE CONQUEST was achieved, but the social order established by Israel deteriorated until it imploded in the catastrophes at the end of the book of Judges. It was time for dramatic change, the inauguration of kingship, which culminated in the reign of King David. The advent of the monarchy was the next great turning point in Israel's history, and this too was announced by a woman, Hannah. Unlike Deborah and Huldah, she was not a prophet. On the contrary, she was a "normal" woman, whose peaceful story comes after the end of the book of Judges. The Hebrew Bible places the book of Samuel, the next historical book, right after the book of Judges. The Greek Bible (the Septuagint) places the book of Ruth (which takes place "when the judges judged") after Judges and before Samuel. The first few chapters of Samuel and the book of Ruth have a lot in common. Each story culminates in a birth that will lead to the kingship, and each is a peaceful idyll in which good people live their lives in a world very different from the violence portrayed at the end of Judges. The domestic settings suggest that the monarchy will be good for ordinary people; the fact that the stories involve Ephratites hints from where the monarchy will come; and the very tranquillity of the stories suggests the internal peace that Israel hoped the monarchy would bring.

◇ *The House of Elkanah (1 Sam. 1:1–8)*

> There was a man from Ramatayim-tsofim from Mount Ephraim whose name was Elkanah son of Yeroham b. Elihu b. Tohu b. Tsuf the Ephratite.
> He had two wives.
> The name of one was Hannah and the name of the second Peninah.
> Peninah had children, but Hannah did not have children.

The man came up from his town every year to worship and sacrifice to YHWH of hosts at Shiloh.

There the two worthless men Hophni and Pinhas were priests
for YHWH.

On the day, Elkanah sacrificed and gave Peninah his wife and all
her sons and daughters portions.

To Hannah he gave a parallel portion, for Hannah he loved, and
God had closed her womb.

Her co-wife would anger her so that she would cry aloud, for
God had closed her womb.

And so it would happen every year when she went up to the
house of YHWH: thus she would get angry and thus she
would not eat.

Elkanah her husband said to her, "Hannah, why are you crying
and why are you not eating? Why are you sad? Am I not better to you than ten sons?"

The story begins with a classic biblical dysfunction. The woman who
will give birth is childless—like Sarai, Rivka, and Rachel, hints the story,
this barren woman will give birth to a great hero chosen by God. Her
childlessness causes friction in the family, as there was between Rachel
and Leah, and Sarai and Hagar, co-wives set up by society and language
to be rivals for the husband's favor. But there is no real contest: even
though Peninah has many children, **Hannah he loved.** Elkanah shows
his love for Hannah by giving her a disproportionate share of the sacrificial animal, perhaps even a share equal to all of Peninah's family combined.

Peninah's reaction is interesting. It seems that she never gets used to
the obvious favoritism, for every year, when they come up on their pilgrimage, Peninah provokes Hannah to anger **so that she would cry
aloud** about the fact that God had closed her womb. What she said we
do not know, as we do not know how Hagar "disrespected" Sarai. But it
must have been a severe provocation to make Hannah cry loudly. Moreover, did Peninah behave this way all the time, or only **every year when
she went up to the house of YHWH?** Such behavior could not endear
Peninah to Elkanah or change his behavior, and we must wonder why
she would do this. Perhaps she was angry that her children were slighted
in order to give Hannah such a large portion. Or perhaps she had another reason, intimated by the phrase **so that she would cry aloud.**

Should we simply translate "so that she cried aloud"? The word *har͑imah*, "she made her cry aloud," could support either translation, but the words "so that," *ba ͑abûr* usually imply purpose. Is the word implying that Peninah was purposely trying to get Hannah to express her frustration aloud? Perhaps picking up this clue, a rabbinic midrash explains that Peninah wanted to help Hannah; she made her angry so she would not accept childlessness as her fate and would cry aloud so that God would hear her affliction. If this was truly Peninah's purpose, millennia of tradition owe her an apology, and the story has two more parallels to the story of Ruth. It too would have no villains, only people trying to be kind to one another. And the two births, of Samuel and of Obed, the son of Ruth, would be the result of women showing solidarity with one another in ways that the society does not anticipate. If this was truly Peninah's purpose, it worked. Hannah refused to eat (from depression or fasting) and prayed for a child.

Elkanah doesn't understand. Knowing that co-wives are rivals, he reassures Hannah. Moreover, knowing that childless women are in a terrible predicament, he declares, **Am I not better to you than ten sons?** He seems blind to his own wife's emotions. But he is not totally obtuse. There is really nothing he can do. He cannot give Hannah a child. He cannot give Hannah control over Peninah as Abram gave Sarai control over Hagar, because Peninah is not a slave wife. He reassures her of his love. Furthermore, since a childless woman could be in a precarious position if he died, he intimates that he is taking care of her, providing for her as Ruth provided for Naomi, which the neighbors acclaimed, "for she is better for you than seven sons" (Ruth 4:15). But Hannah's desire for a child goes beyond a wish for status or security. Elkanah's lack of understanding only highlights her true wishes. What did she answer him? The narrator doesn't tell, for Elkanah's understanding is not the issue. Hannah's true answer is in her actions.

◇ *Hannah at the Sanctuary (1 Sam. 1:10–18)*

> Hannah arose after she had eaten in Shiloh and after drinking.
> Eli the priest was sitting on a chair next to the doorposts of the sanctuary of YHWH.
> She was bitter and she prayed to God and she wept.
> She vowed a vow and said, "YHWH of hosts, if you see the affliction of your servant and remember me and do not forget your servant, and give your servant a human seed, I will

give him to YHWH all the days of his life. A razor will not
come on his head."

As she was praying much before YHWH, Eli was watching her
mouth.

Hannah was speaking to her heart, only her lips were moving,
and her voice was not heard, and Eli thought her drunk.

Eli said to her, "How long will you be drunk? Take away your
wine."

Hannah spoke up and said, "No, my lord, I am a woman in difficult spirit and have not drunk wine or strong drink. I am
spilling out my soul before YHWH. Do not consider your
servant as a worthless one, for it is because of the greatness
of my complaint and my anger that I have spoken till now."

Eli spoke and said, "Go in peace and the God of Israel will give
the request that you requested from him."

She said, "May your servant find favor in your eyes."

The woman went on her way and ate and her face was no
longer (sad).

The family has come for a *zebaḥ*, a sacrifice that the worshipers eat in
communion with God. Eating in this context is a religious obligation,
and so we are told that Hannah ate and drank. She then goes to the sanctuary to offer prayers. Did she believe that God would hear her prayers
better from there? Pilgrims may believe that God hears prayers everywhere. Nevertheless, they go to sites that they consider sacred in order
to intensify their prayers, using the sanctity of the place to boost
the powers of their own prayers. And so Hannah stays a long time at the
sanctuary in her personal prayer.

Was it unusual for women to come to offer their own prayers? The
story doesn't hint that there was any irregularity involved. Eli doesn't try
to chase her away or tell her that women belong in the home. It is the intensity of her prayers and their long duration that attract his attention,
and the fact that he cannot make out what she is saying. Eli may have become accustomed to the sight of drunkenness associated with these pilgrimage feasts. Moreover, he may have expected women in distress to
make a loud noise, to cry out or to ululate like mourners. Instead, she is
praying silently. The story does not tell us why, nor does it tell us what
she said. Her prayer was private, and the text leaves it that way. Only one
part of the prayer has public importance: the promise of the child to

God. And this vow is spelled out: the child would be given right back to God in service, and marked for that service by the long hair that distinguished a Nazirite.

Later readers were keenly interested in Hannah's prayer: what could she have said to make God give her a child? Rabbinic authors suggest what her arguments might have been. She argued that her womb should not be created for nothing; she argued that God commanded procreation; she argued that Israel was supposed to teach its children the Torah, so there had to be children. Hannah to them is a master petitioner, a model of persuasive argumentation. They also considered her the very model of the importance of the silent prayers they introduced at the center of the worship service.

When Hannah explains her plight, Eli promises that she will have a child. How he knew this, the story does not say. But so it happened.

◇ *The Birth of Samuel (1 Sam. 1:19–23)*

> They arose early in the morning and bowed down before YHWH and turned and came to their house in Ramah.
> Elkanah knew his wife Hannah and YHWH remembered her.
> It happened with the turn of the year that Hannah conceived and bore a son and called his name Samuel, "For I requested him from YHWH."
> The man Elkanah went up with his whole household to offer the annual sacrifice to YHWH and his vow.
> Hannah did not go up, for she said to her husband, "Until I wean the child and I bring him and he will be seen before the face of YHWH and will live there forever."
> Elkanah her man said to her, "Do what is good in your eyes. Sit until you wean him, for God fulfilled his word."
> The woman sat and nursed her son until she weaned him.

This child is Hannah's. She has prayed for it, she has been promised it, and when the boy is born, she takes control. There is no question here of the father asserting dominance over the child: she herself names the child. The man who is better to her than ten sons shows it by giving her control over him: **"Do what is good in your eyes."** Elkanah may not have quite understood his wife's utter determination to have a son, but he does understand that God promised the son and kept the promise, and he does understand the obligation of vows. The man who goes with his household to fulfill his own vow will honor his wife's vow. Hannah has dedicated the child to God, and he will not make any claims on the boy to prevent her from carrying out her vow.

And so she does. After the weaning, Hannah brings Samuel to the sanctuary:

◇   *The Dedication of Samuel (1 Sam. 1:24–28)*

> She brought him up with her when she weaned him with a three-year-old steer* and an ephah of flour and a skein of wine, and brought him to the sanctuary of YHWH in Shiloh. And the boy was a boy.
> They slaughtered the steer and brought the boy to Eli.
> She said, "By me, my lord, by your life, my lord, I am the woman who stood here with you to pray to YHWH. For this boy I prayed and YHWH gave me my request, which I requested from him. And I for my part am devoting him to YHWH. All the days he will be he is devoted to YHWH."
> And they bowed down there to God.

Hannah stays central to the story as she is the one to bring him up and she brings the offerings. It doesn't matter whether Elkanah came with her, or Elkanah and Peninah and all their children. The story never says that they don't come, and the plural verb "they slaughtered" sounds as though others were there. It would have been appropriate for the whole family to come. But the initiative and the control were Hannah's, and she is the one who gives the dedication speech. Her speech emphasizes the requested nature of this child. When she named him, she called him Samuel, and she declared, **"for I requested him from YHWH."** This is not an explanation of the name Samuel, which means "name of God," but an exposition of the major theme of his birth, that God answered her request. This is the language that Eli had used when he announced the birth **"will give the request that you requested from him,"** and she returns to this theme at his dedication, "YHWH gave me my **request, which I requested from him."** She then plays on the verb for "request," *š'l*, stating, **"I . . . am devoting him to YHWH,"** *hišʾiltîhû*, and dramatically declaring, **"he is devoted to YHWH,"** *hûʾ šaʾûl*. But *hûʾ šaʾûl* can also mean "he is Saul," and the naming sounds suspiciously like an explanation of the name of Saul.

---

*Emendation: see notes.

Why would the storyteller go to such elaborate lengths to explain the name Saul? It is tempting to conclude that the story was originally told as a birth narrative about Saul, but was later displaced to Samuel, perhaps when Saul's kingship went into disfavor. Many readers have proposed this idea, but it seems bizarre that editors would simply displace a birth narrative. More likely, all this play on Saul's name is a deliberate narrative technique, for the notion of "request" and the answering of request, the central theme of the birth of Samuel, is also the climax of Samuel's life, his crowning achievement, and the concern of the book of Samuel. As Samuel grew old, the people made a major request of him, and he answered "the requesting people," *hā ʿām haššōʾalîm* (1 Sam. 8:10). The people asked for a king, and when Samuel crowned a king, he declared, "Now, here is the king you have chosen, the king you requested (*šěʾiltem*), and look! God is giving a king over you" (1 Sam. 12:13). That king was Saul, and he was crowned by the boy who was requested from and then devoted to God. Hannah's request for a son and God's granting of it foreshadow the way the people request a king and God grants their request; the plays on Saul's name intimate the one who will be given in request.

Hannah foreshadows the kingship. She also proclaims its advent, for after devoting the boy, she recites a psalm:

◇ *The Exalted Horn (1 Sam. 2:1–10)*

> My heart rejoices in YHWH, my horn is exalted in YHWH.
>
> My mouth is wide open toward my enemies, for I rejoice in your salvation.
>
> There is no holy one like YHWH. Indeed, there is no one except you, and no rock like our God.
>
> Do not speak so much (from) on high, on high; let not arrogance come from your lips.
>
> For YHWH is a god of knowledge, and by him schemes are weighed.
>
> The bow of the heroes is unbroken; and those who have failed take strength.
>
> Those who have been satisfied hire themselves out for food, but the ones who hunger can stop (hiring themselves?) forever.
>
> The barren woman gives birth to seven, but she of many sons is bereft.
>
> YHWH kills and brings life, brings (people) down to Sheʾol and raises them up.

YHWH dispossesses and enriches, brings low and exalts.

He raises the poor man from the dust, brings up the destitute from the ashes.

To seat him with the nobles, lead them to a seat of honor.

For the foundations of the earth are YHWH's, and he placed the inhabited world upon them.

He guards the feet of his devotees, but the wicked fall silent in the dark.

Not by strength does a man become mighty.

YHWH—his rivals are terrified, he thunders over them from the heavens.

YHWH judges the ends of the earth,

He gives strength to his king, exalts the horn of his anointed one.

This psalm does not seem like a poem that Hannah would have composed for the occasion of her weaning of Samuel and presentation to the temple. Much in this psalm seems alien to her situation. Enemies, arrogant speeches, heroes, and bowmen evoke a realm far from the domestic life of Hannah, her co-wife, and Elkanah. If Hannah could read, she might have chosen one from a repertory of psalms at the sanctuary. But not this one, which talks about the king, God's anointed. Most probably, the storyteller chose an appropriate psalm to place in Hannah's mouth. And it is appropriate, for it talks about the joy and exaltation of the speaker, the barren woman becoming the mother of many and the lowly being exalted. The psalm's significance goes beyond Hannah's personal situation, for it has a particular significance at the opening of the book of Samuel. It relates the key themes of the whole book. God reverses fortunes, **YHWH dispossesses and enriches, brings low and exalts.** God will exalt someone from the poor (first Samuel, then Saul and then David), and he will bring the exalted down (also Saul). And the poem concludes with the essential message of the books of Samuel: **He gives strength to his king, exalts the horn of his anointed one.** As Hannah recites this psalm, she identifies her exaltation with the king's, and she also announces the coming of kingship to Israel.

The coming of the monarchy is the subject of the books of Samuel. It was a long and involved process that began with Samuel and did not reach completion until the appointment of Solomon, the first king to inherit his throne. Poems frame the story as the song of Hannah resonates in the longer Thanksgiving song of David in 2 Samuel 22 (= Psalm 18).

The two songs are not identical, for only Hannah's song talks about giving birth, and only David's song presents an elaborate metaphorical depiction of distress as drowning. But the other themes of Hannah's song echo in David's. Both are about the "horn," the might of the king (1 Sam. 2:1 and 10; 2 Sam. 22:3) and salvation from enemies (1 Sam. 2:1 and 2 Sam. 22:4). Both songs call God a rock (1 Sam. 2:2 and 2 Sam. 22:32) and celebrate God's giving strength (1 Sam. 2:4 and 2 Sam. 22:40). Both refer to She'ol (1 Sam. 2:6 and 2 Sam. 22:6) and to God thundering from heaven (1 Sam. 2:10 and 2 Sam. 22:14). And both songs end with the close relationship between God and his anointed, the king (1 Sam. 2:10 and 2 Sam. 22:51). Together these two songs underscore the themes of the books of Samuel, the glory of David's kingship. With hindsight, one can also see a pointed allusion to David in Hannah's song, for her warning to the enemies, not to speak so much so haughtily (*lit* "multiply speaking 'high, high' ") corresponds to the height of the two main enemies of the young David: Goliath and Saul. The song of Hannah is a poetic overture and the song of David an intermezzo, a celebration before the story of the rest of Israel's history.

But before there was David, there was Samuel the anointer, and there was Saul, who turned out to be only an interim king who died without being able to found a dynasty. Other literary frames (*"inclusios"*) highlight the self-contained nature of Saul's rule. The first frame is war. As the story opens, the Philistines mass at Aphek and inflict a terrible defeat on Israel at Eben Ezer which kills Eli's two sons and Eli himself and puts an end both to the old priesthood and to Israel's system of government by "judges" (1 Sam. 4). At the end of the book of Samuel, the Philistines again mass at Aphek (1 Sam. 28) and again defeat Israel, at Mount Gilboa, killing Saul and his sons and ending this first abortive Israelite kingship (1 Sam. 30). And the other frame is the oracle. Both the coming of Saul and his demise were major turning points in Israel's history, and like the story of other periods of Israel's history, his reign is bracketed by women oracles. Hannah has another counterpart, the necromancer of Endor.

The Necromancer at Endor

AT FIRST SIGHT, this woman appears to be unlike any other in the historical books. The master of an outlawed craft, she seems so far beyond Israel's horizons as to be unable to play any part in its history. But the necromancer is a true counterpart to Hannah; their different natures themselves symbolize the life and reign of Saul. Like the simple woman who "announced" his kingship, Saul was the smallest of the smallest of the rural population, and his reign remained simple and non-"majestic." But like the necromancer who declared his end, Saul's reign ended illicit and rejected. Moreover, it was Saul himself who made her craft illegal, and (the book of Samuel emphasizes) it was he who caused his kingship to be rejected by God.

Though different in nature, Hannah and the necromancer have much in common. They act in ways that would not be predicted by cultural stereotypes: Hannah takes the initiative in prayer and proves wiser than Eli, and the necromancer conjures for Saul and then consoles him. Even more significantly, they both fill their oracular function through words that are not their own, one with a psalm and the other by channeling the dead Samuel.

◇ The Necromancer (1 Sam. 28:5–8)

> Saul saw the Philistines' encampment. He was afraid and his heart trembled greatly.
>
> Saul inquired of YHWH and YHWH didn't answer him, not by dreams, not by Urim and not by prophets.
>
> Saul said to his servants, "Seek for me a necromancer woman, and I will go to her and ask through her."
>
> His servants said, "Look! There is a necromancer woman in Endor."

It was not unusual for leaders to consult an oracle before battle. Moses instructed Joshua to do so (Num. 27:21), and King Ahab consulted four hundred prophets (1 Kings 22). Saul has an extra incentive: he is afraid. And his fear is intensified when he can get no word through the official divinatory channels. So he goes outside the legitimate system to inquire by a form of oracle that he himself had outlawed, necromancy by use of an *'ōb*, a technology for communication with the dead.

◇ *The Necromancy (1 Sam. 28:8–19)*

> Saul disguised himself, wearing other clothes.
>
> He went, and two of his men with him and they came to the woman at night.
>
> He said to her, "Divine for me, please, with the *'ōb* and bring up for me the one I will tell you."
>
> The woman said to him, "Look! You know what Saul did, that he cut off the *'ōb* and the familiars from the land. Why are you ensnaring my life to cause my death?"
>
> Saul adjured her by YHWH, saying, "By the life of YHWH, no punishment will fall upon you about this matter."
>
> The woman said, "Who should I bring up for you?"
>
> He said, "Bring up Samuel for me."
>
> The woman saw Samuel and she cried out very loudly.
>
> The woman said to Saul, "Why did you lie to me, for you are Saul?"
>
> The king said to her, "Do not fear, what did you see?"
>
> The woman said to Saul, "I saw the divine coming up from the earth."
>
> He said to her, "What did he look like?"
>
> She said, "An old man is coming up and he is wrapped in a cloak."
>
> And Saul knew that it was Samuel, and he bowed low on the ground and lay prostrate.
>
> Samuel said to Saul, "Why have you disturbed me, bringing me up?"
>
> Saul said, "I am very distressed, and the Philistines are fighting me, and God has left me and doesn't answer me anymore even by prophets or by dreams, and I have called you to tell me what to do."
>
> Samuel said, "Why did you make inquiry of me when YHWH has left you and is with your adversary? And YHWH will do for him as he said through me, and YHWH has torn the kingdom from your hand and will give it to your neighbor,

to David. As you did not listen to the voice of YHWH and didn't perform his wrath against Amalek, therefore this matter YHWH has done to you this day. And YHWH will also give Israel with you into the hand of the Philistines. And tomorrow you and your sons are with me. The camp of Israel also YHWH will give into the hand of the Philistines."

The story doesn't tell us how the necromancer conjured Samuel. That is left as the secrets of the trade, and it is only through comparative studies that we conclude that the *'ôb* might be a pit or trench that the necromancer filled with blood or animal parts or possibly a skull filled with the same. In *The Odyssey* Circe sends Odysseus to the very gate of Hades to consult the great sage Tiresias. She gives him explicit directions to dig a pit, to pour libations, and to let the blood of animals stream into the pit so that the shades will swarm up (Odyssey 10:504–40). The very word for the necromancer's trench, *kosmos* (in Greek), may be a loan from the Semitic word *qsm*, "conjure," the verb with which Saul initiates the necromancy. Mesopotamian parallels suggest that the *'ôb* may have been a skull, perhaps a plastered skull with which the woman poured libations.

Whatever the necromancer does, it works. Even though she is reluctant to risk her life by breaking the law, she succeeds in raising a "divine being," *'elohîm*, a spirit. At this point, she does not know what otherworldly being is approaching her: it could be a demon, an angel, or a ghost. But somehow, seeing this spirit, she knows who Saul is: perhaps the spirit immediately told her. She describes him to Saul, who cannot see him, but when she describes him, **"An old man is coming up and he is wrapped in a cloak,"** Saul knows that it is Samuel and she sees immediately that her client is Saul.

The necromancer now channels the words of Samuel's ghost, a speech that predicts Saul's death. Samuel is not happy at being brought up: the dead do not like to be disturbed. Saul has once again angered him. If ever there was a slight chance of a good outcome for Saul, it is gone, and the book of Chronicles declares this necromancy the final straw. Samuel repeats his old denunciations and pronounces Saul's doom with the authority of YHWH, whose name he invokes seven times. He refers to Saul's failure to destroy Amalek, and recalls the message he gave Saul at that time: God has torn the kingdom from Saul and given it to his neighbor (1 Sam. 15:28), and Samuel now identifies that neighbor as David. Samuel does not repeat the lesson to kings in his earlier speech: Then, when he told Saul that he had not listened to God's word, he added, "Rebellion is as the sin of magic" (1 Sam. 15:23). Now he declares that Saul did not listen to God's word as he stands conjured by an act of real rather than metaphorical magic. The very act of necromancy is mute testimony that Samuel's earlier words have come to pass.

Samuel does not do the one thing that Saul asks of him: he does not tell Saul what to do. This omission echoes in the words he does say: Saul's fate is sealed and there is nothing he can do. Saul is devastated. He lies there defeated as the necromancer approaches him.

◈ The Necromancer's Hospitality (1 Sam. 28:20–25)

> Saul hurriedly fell to his full length on the ground and was very frightened by the words of Samuel.
> He had no strength, for he hadn't eaten food all that day and all that night.
> The woman came to Saul and saw that he was shocked.
> She said, "Look, your servant listened to you, I placed my life in my hand and listened to the words you spoke to me. And now, please, listen to your servant. I will place before you a round of bread and eat! You will have strength when you go on your way."
> He refused and said, "I will not eat."
> His servants and the woman importuned him and he listened to them.
> He got up from the ground and he sat on the bed.
> The woman had a fatted calf in the house.
> She hurried and slaughtered it.
> She took flour and kneaded it and baked unleavened bread.
> She served Saul and his servants.
> They ate, they arose, and they went on that night.

Saul has reached the end of his strength. He has been fasting, either because of depression or to petition God. And now an amazingly flattering portrait emerges of a woman who was, after all, involved in an outlawed activity. She, unlike Samuel, will give him something concrete to do: he can at least eat. Twice she calls herself "your servant," a term often used by women in petition, as she reminds him that **"I placed my life in my hand."** But her petition is not for herself. She wants only to convince him to eat: **"I will place before you a piece of bread."** She reminds him that his job is not finished, that he needs his strength **"when you go on your way,"** perhaps an allusion to his final acts as he goes to his fate. And she won't take no for an answer. She and Saul's servants keep urging him until he agrees to eat.

The necromancer becomes the very model of Israelite hospitality. Like Abraham, she offers *a pat leḥem,* a "round" of bread (Gen. 18:5), but then provides meat, giving her guest what might be her only fatted calf. Like Abraham, she *hurries* (Gen. 18:6) to prepare the meal, and as with Abraham, the details of bread baking are recorded to show that the bread is prepared absolutely fresh and new for the visitors (though in Genesis, Abraham can tell Sarah to prepare the bread, Gen. 18:6). Her meal marks a fitting end to Saul's kingship. At the beginning of Samuel's career, Hannah and Elkanah slaughtered an ox when they brought their son to Eli, and Hannah offered thanksgiving that included the prediction of monarchy (1 Sam. 1:25). At the beginning of Saul's career, Samuel entertained him at a festive meal and announced that he would be king (1 Sam. 9:19–24). Now, at the end of Saul's reign, the necromancer is the counterpart to both Hannah and Samuel, and her meal resonates with theirs.

This is not an evil woman. Quite the contrary, the necromancer is presented as good and generous. Her ability to communicate with spirits does not make her evil. Her craft is outlawed because it is an uncontrollable and ungovernable access to divine knowledge. But it is effective, and it can be benevolent. Like the more legitimate prophets, the necromancer is a channel for contact with divine power, and she shares her benevolence with other oracle women such as Rahab, Abigail, and even Huldah, who desire the good of the men to whom they speak. The necromancer has the terrible task of channeling an announcement of doom, but she can at least give Saul the courage and strength to face it.

Abigail

WHILE SAUL was still king, David formed a private army with which he protected the southern flank of Israel (and of Philistia) from the enemies approaching out of the south. Right after Samuel dies, the story introduces one of the men whose flocks David protected:

◇ *Nabal and Abigail (1 Sam. 25:2–4)*

> There was a man at Maon whose affairs were in Carmel.
> The man was very wealthy and had three thousand sheep and
>   one thousand goats.
> It happened while he was shearing his sheep in the Carmel.
> The name of the man was Nabal.
> The name of his wife was Abigail.
> The woman was of goodly intelligence and beautiful in looks.
> The man was hard and evil were his deeds.
> He was a Calebite.

This simple narration introduces the two characters David will meet. One is known only as "the boor," Nabal. His very name tips off the way he will act; as Isaiah declares, "for a boor will speak boorishly and his heart will do iniquity" (Isa. 32:6). His wife, by contrast, is described as both smart and beautiful. She is not called "wise," *ḥakamah,* because the two "wise women" who appear in David's story, the wise women of Abel and of Tekoa, seem to have had professional positions. Abigail is simply a landowner's wife, without any particular authority. Her significance will come from her own characteristics. The narrator is not neutral: the reader has no doubt as to who is the villain in this story: the fool will be further named a "worthless one" by both his servants and his wife.

The narrator adds one more detail: Nabal is a Calebite, a man (perhaps the leader) of the clan that was so prominent in the time of the conquest. The written text (Ketib) puns: *kelibbô*, "as his heart," a declaration of Nabal's essential lawlessness: he does whatever he pleases. "As his heart" has immediate relevance to Nabal's conduct in the story; "the Calebite" has more significance toward David's ultimate destiny, to which the end of the story returns.

◇ *Request, Refusal, and Reaction (1 Sam. 25:4–13)*

> David in the wilderness heard that Nabal was shearing his sheep.
>
> David sent ten lads.
>
> David said to his lads, "Go up to the Carmel. Come to Nabal and greet him for me. Say, 'Thus for life and to you, peace and to your house, peace and to all that is yours, peace. Now, I have heard that they are shearing for you. Now, your shepherds were with us and nobody caused them abuse and nothing went missing all the days that they were in the Carmel. Ask your lads and they will tell you. Let my lads find favor in your eyes, for we have come on a holiday. Give, please, whatever you please to our servants and your son David.' "
>
> David's lads came and spoke to Nabal in just this way in the name of David and they rested.
>
> Nabal spoke to David's servants, saying, "Who is David? Who is the son of Jesse? Today, many are the servants who are breaking out each from before his master. Should I take my bread and my water and my meat that I slaughtered for my shearers and give it to men from I know not where?"
>
> David's men turned on their way and returned. They came and told him all of these matters.
>
> David said to his men, "Gird on your sword."
>
> Each man girded on his sword, and David also girded on his sword.
>
> There went after him about four hundred men and two hundred remained with the gear.

David approaches in the most gentle and proper manner possible. He has instructed his men to be subservient, addressing Nabal as one would a superior and stressing the good that David wishes him and which he has in fact brought to him through his protection. Nabal, on the other hand, speaks coarsely. "Fine talk does not become a boor," says the proverb (Prov. 17:7). Nabal insults David, comparing him to an old servant who has rebelled against his master. His speech is not stupid. It is even clever, playing on the name of David's ancestor Peretz (the "breaker-out") and his grandfather's name, Obed (the "servant"). But his actions are profoundly boorish. As Isaiah tells us, a boor will not give food to the hungry and drink to the thirsty (Isa. 32:6), and Nabal refuses to share the shearing-feast with David's men.

David may have been diplomatic and self-abasing in his message. But he reacts to Nabal's response the way someone running a protection racket during Prohibition would have reacted: he is ready to punish Nabal for his refusal. The stage is set for disaster.

⟡ *Abigail to the Rescue (1 Sam. 25:14–23)*

> To Abigail the wife of Nabal one of the lads spoke, saying,
>
> "Look, David sent messengers from the wilderness to greet our master and he swooped down at them. The men were very good to us. We didn't fail and we didn't lose anything all the days we went around with them when we were in the field. They were a wall for us both night and day all the days we were with them herding the sheep.
>
> "And now, know and see what you will do, for evil has been decided against our master and all his house and he is a worthless man as he spoke to him."
>
> Abigail hurried and took two hundred (units) of bread and two wineskeins and five dressed sheep and five seah of parched grain and one omer of raisins and two hundred fig cakes and placed them on donkeys.
>
> She said to her servants, "Pass before me; I am coming behind you."
>
> To her husband she said nothing.
>
> It happened that she was riding on the ass and going down the hidden side of the mountain.
>
> Look! David and his men are going down toward her and she meets them.
>
> David said, "For a lie, I guarded all that that one has in the wilderness and nothing was lost from anything he has, and he has returned me evil for good. Thus shall God do to the enemies of David and thus shall he continue, if I should

> leave from all of his any who piss against the wall till morn-
> ing light."
> Abigail saw David. She hurried and descended from the ass, she
> fell on her face toward David and bowed down to the
> ground.

Nabal's words were more prescient than he anticipated, for his own
servants now join the "many servants who break out against their master." They turn to Abigail with their problem, and she immediately
knows what to do: she too will go against her husband's express wishes
and bring an offering to David.

Abigail knows her situation. She alone must turn away the anger of
someone who marches toward her with four hundred armed men. She
faces in reality the situation that Jacob imagined he faced when he came
back from Mesopotamia and knew that he had to confront Esau. Like
David, Esau came to meet Jacob with four hundred men (Gen. 33:1);
Esau too had been wronged, his blessing stolen from him as David feels
his payment was stolen from him. Unlike David, Esau was not angry and
intended Jacob no harm, but Jacob didn't know that. Jacob prepared an
enormous offering for his brother, much larger than Abigail's, sending
the gifts before him explicitly to appease and atone for the wrong he had
done him (Gen. 32:13–22). Abigail's offering suits her own situation: she
will feed David's men in place of her boorish husband.

Meeting David, Abigail begins to speak.

◆ As His Name, So Is He (1 Sam. 25:24–27)

> She fell at his feet and said, "My lord, let the sin be upon me. Let
> your servant-woman speak to your ear and listen to the
> words of your servant-woman:
> "Let not my lord pay attention to this worthless man.
> "Nabal is his name and as his name, so is he.
> "His name is Nabal and *nebalah* (outrage) is with him.
> "I, your servant, did not see my lord's lads whom you sent.
> "And now, my lord—by the life of YHWH and by your life,
> YHWH has indeed prevented you from coming into blood-
> guilt, has rescued you.
> "And now, may all your enemies who seek my lord's evil be like
> Nabal.
> "And now, may this gift which your servant has brought to my
> lord be given to the lads who go at my lord's feet."

Abigail knows that she doesn't have the luxury of time. The story emphasizes three times that **she hurried** to get here. Now she will have to get her point across quickly. David has stopped his advance to talk to her, but she cannot expect infinite patience from this general on the warpath. She must choose her words carefully. Her speech is a masterpiece of biblical rhetoric. In very few words, Abigail rescues her household from David, she prevents David from committing a sin, and she ensures her own future (**"you will remember your servant,"** 1 Sam. 25:31). She begins by emphasizing her submission and lesser status. She may be the wife of a wealthy landowner and David a fugitive brigand, but she is a woman with a few servants, and he is the sword-bearing leader of four hundred armed men. The time calls for a rhetoric of humility, and she submits, falling on her face, calling David "my lord" (thirteen times in her speech) and herself "your servant" (five times). Jacob, going before Esau, used the same tactic, calling him "my lord" (Gen. 32:4, 18; 33:13–14) and himself "your servant" (Gen. 32:18, 20; 33:5). But Abigail next does something that Jacob does not do: she takes all guilt upon herself. Jacob knows that he already bears the guilt for Esau's anticipated anger. There can be no more guilt for making peace. Abigail makes it clear that she does not share Nabal's guilt in refusing payment to David's men. She does not specify what guilt she offers to bear; possibly it is the guilt that might come from an oath not fulfilled. Taking on the guilt is the rhetoric of persuading women. Rivka told Jacob that if he would listen to her, she would accept upon herself any curse that Isaac might utter (Gen. 27:13). The Wise Woman of Tekoa assured David that she would accept any guilt that might occur from the sparing of her son, and David's throne would be clear of guilt (2 Sam. 14:9). Petitioning women hasten to assure the men they seek to persuade that granting them their wish will bring the men no harm.

Abigail knows that she has to convince David she is not acting as Nabal's emissary, so she begins by insulting her husband. The insult strategy is familiar in Israel's history. For example, the midwives in Egypt called the Hebrew women "animals," *ḥayyôt*, to protect themselves. In the same way, Abigail distances herself from Nabal by declaring him a boor, and creates a bond between herself and David.

This bond generates ethical demands. It distinguishes between the boor (*nabal*) who commits outrages (*nebalah*) and the man who would never commit a *nebalah* such as slaughtering an innocent household. Abigail herself took no part in Nabal's rejection of David. Far from it, she reveals herself as God's emissary. In the first of three "And now" clauses, she avows that God is acting to prevent David's bloodguilt. She is so certain of God's actions that she can reveal them under oath, implying that she herself is acting as God's agent. In her second "And now" clause, she expresses her wish that all David's enemies be as easily thwarted as Nabal, and in her third "And now," she offers her own gift to David's men, which, like Jacob offering his gifts to Esau (Gen. 33:11), she calls a *berakah,* a gift-in-blessing.

Abigail then turns to announcing David's destiny and, in particular, his destiny from YHWH, whom she calls by name five times and "your god" once.

◇   *Prince over Israel (1 Sam. 25:28–31)*

"Forgive the sin of your servant:

"YHWH will indeed make a trustworthy house for my lord, for my lord is fighting the wars of YHWH, and no evil will ever be found with you.

"Should a man arise to pursue you and seek your life, the life of my lord will be tied in the tied (book) of the living with your God YHWH, and he will hurl away the life of your enemy with a slingshot.

"It will be when YHWH will do for my lord all that he has spoken about you for good, and will command you to be the prince over Israel—let this not be a snare or a stumbling block to my lord's heart, that he should spill blood without reason, and my lord will save himself.

"YHWH will be good to my lord, and you will remember your servant."

Just as Abigail placed herself on David's side in his battle with Nabal, so she places herself on his side in the larger battle. David is not only running for his life, he is **fighting the wars of YHWH,** as Saul himself commanded him to do (1 Sam. 18:5). But he is now in a fight with Saul, **the man who arises to pursue you and seek your life.** Abigail subtly alludes to David's confrontation with Saul in the previous chapter (1 Sam. 24). Saul had unwittingly left himself vulnerable to David's attack, but David refrained from killing him, declaring as his reason that "I will not set forth my hand against my lord, for he is YHWH's anointed" (1 Sam. 24:6). David cut off a piece of his robe in order to prove to Saul that he could have killed him, and tells him "there is no evil in me" (1 Sam. 24:12–13). But now, the same David who refrained from killing Saul wants to kill Nabal: Nabal is not God's anointed! Abigail has to show him that just as being favored over the boor means David cannot himself act as a boor, so too fighting the wars of YHWH means that David must not commit any evil. David must not kill Nabal and his innocent household. Spilling blood would be a stumbling block, and Abigail convinces David to *save himself* from this error.

Abigail assures David that God will build him a posterity (**"a trustworthy house"**). Eli had not achieved it (1 Sam. 2:35), nor would Saul. God will protect David from his enemies, she declares, and end the life of Saul, for God has appointed David the prince over Israel. Abigail is not the first person to tell David he will be king. Saul has just told him that he knows he will be king (1 Sam. 24:20), but Abigail gives him his proper title, *nāgîd,* "prince." David understands her message:

◇ *Message Received and Acknowledged (1 Sam. 25:32–35)*

> David said to Abigail:
> "Blessed is YHWH the God of Israel who sent you today to meet me.
> "Blessed is your sense and blessed are you, for you have kept me back today from coming into bloodguilt and my hand has saved me.
> "For by the life of YHWH God of Israel who saved me from doing evil to myself, if you had not hurried and come to meet me, indeed there would not have been left to Nabal by morning's light any who piss against the wall."
> And David took from her hand that which she had brought him.
> He said to her, "Go in peace to your house. See, I have listened to your word and accepted your appearance."

David understands the promises in Abigail's speech. In the next chapter, when Saul again falls into David's power, David repeats his determination to respect the sanctity of God's anointed. He states to Abishai, "Who has sent his hand against the anointed of God and been free from punishment?" (1 Sam. 26:9). David has also internalized Abigail's lesson, and he repeats it to Abishai in solemn avowal, "By the life of YHWH, indeed YHWH will strike him or his day will come and he will die, or he will go down in battle and be extinguished" (1 Sam. 26:10). He has fully internalized Abigail's prediction that **"YHWH will hurl away the life of your enemy."**

Abigail predicts that God **"will command (David) to be the prince**

over Israel." With almost the same words, King David tells Michal, "God chose me over your father and all his household to command me to be prince over the people of God" (2 Sam. 6:21). Abigail's threefold prophesy is repeated by Nathan when he declares to David the king that YHWH commanded David to be *nagîd* (2 Sam. 7:8) and cleared away his enemies (7:9), and Nathan reiterates the promise of a faithful house (7:16).

The narrator tells us David **"accepts [Abigail's] appearance,"** using the language of acceptance that Jacob requested from Esau (Gen. 32:21). She leaves, but there is an epilogue to their encounter:

◇ *To Wife! (1 Sam. 25:36–43)*

> Abigail came to Nabal.
> He was having a feast in his house like a royal feast.
> The heart of Nabal was joyous and he was very drunk.
> She didn't tell him anything small or big till morning light.
> It happened in the morning when the wine left Nabal, his wife told him these things.
> His heart died within him and he became like stone.
> After ten days, God struck Nabal and he died.
> David heard that Nabal died and he said, "Blessed be YHWH who pursued the case of my shaming by Nabal. He kept his servant from evil and YHWH turned Nabal's evil on his head."
> David sent and spoke to Abigail to take her to him as a wife.
> The servants of David came to Abigail to the Carmel and spoke to her thus, "David has sent us to you to take you as his wife."
> She arose and bowed down to the ground, and she said, "Here is your servant, as a servant to wash the feet of the servants of my lord."
> Abigail hurried and arose and rode on her donkey and five of her maidservants who went at her feet and she went after the messengers of David and became his wife.
> And David took Ahinoam from Jezreel and the two of them became his wives.

Abigail's words are coming to pass. God does indeed hurl away at least one enemy of David, killing Nabal off with a stroke as he realizes how close he came to disaster. And David does remember Abigail, making her his wife.

David now has a proven prophet in his house. In another world this wise woman could have become his trusted adviser and perhaps his official seer. But Abigail, having appeared to predict David's destiny and ensure it, disappears into his household and is not heard of again. David's prophet Nathan, and those who serve the kings after David, are all men. It is only toward the very end of the monarchy that another woman arises to be the bridge to a new pattern of Israel's relationship with God. This oracle of the end and the beginning is Huldah.

Huldah

UNLIKE PRIESTS, generals, judges, and governors, a prophet does not have to be appointed by superiors, and a prophet's status does not depend on advancement within a hierarchy or on completion of a course of study. As Amos and again Jeremiah inform us, God tells the prophet to speak. Prophecy is a "gift of the Spirit," offered to whomever God wills, and societies can accept women as recipients of the gift and value them as prophets even as they deny women roles in the official hierarchies of religion and polity. Toward the end of Israel's history, King Josiah sent his men to see a female prophet, Huldah, to validate the discovery of a scroll in the Temple that called for Israel to behave in ways it had not been observing.

◇   *The Book and the Charge (2 Kings 22:12–14)*

> "Go inquire of YHWH on my behalf and on behalf of the people and on behalf of all of Judah about the words of this book which was found.
>
> "For great is the wrath of YHWH which has been kindled against us because our fathers did not listen to the words of this book to act according to everything that was written concerning us."
>
> Hilkiah the priest and Ahiqam and Achbor and Shaphan and Asaia went to Huldah the prophet, the wife of Shalem ben Tikva ben Harhas, the wardrobe keeper, who was living in Jerusalem in the royal quarter.
>
> They spoke to her.

The narrator in 2 Kings shows no astonishment that the "prophet-in-residence" was a woman. The author of the book of Chronicles also is not amazed by this. Chronicles relates that the prophet Azariah encouraged King Asa to extend his reform to all of Israel (2 Chron. 15:1–7); the prophet Jehu encouraged King Jehoshaphat to renew the reform that he had begun but appeared to abandon (2 Chron. 17:7–9); in the same way, Huldah will encourage Josiah to broaden the reform that he began when he sent his men to repair the Temple. Huldah the female prophet is treated no differently than Azariah or Jehu.

Scholars have sometimes wondered why the king's men did not go to Jeremiah, whose writings attest to his greatness as a prophet. But Huldah did not represent some opposite pole to Jeremiah; unlike those whom Jeremiah calls "false prophets," both Huldah's message and terminology are exceedingly close. However, a king could choose his prophets. Years before, King Ahab of Israel told Amaziah of Judah that he rarely consulted Micaiah, since Micaiah always gave him bad news. Jeremiah often spoke ill of the government, so perhaps Josiah did not like him. The king's men already knew what Jeremiah was likely to say, and perhaps they hoped that Huldah would have better news for them. But she didn't.

There may be another reason for the king to have sent his men to Huldah rather than to Jeremiah. In ancient Assyria, King Esarhaddon received omens that he should start rebuilding Babylon, which his own father had destroyed at the command (he believed) of the gods. The new omens seem to contradict the old decree, and Esarhaddon sought to validate them by calling in specialists who could pose questions of the divine. Such inquiry may have been Huldah's normal role. Jeremiah, on the other hand, was not attached to the court and did not request omens for a royal client.

The issue presented to Huldah is serious, for the book found in the Temple not only demanded cultic practices that had not been performed by the court; it predicted destruction if its dictates were not observed. Huldah does not speak about the book itself, but about the destruction it predicts, a destruction that she corroborates:

◇ The End Is Nigh (2 Kings 22:15–20)

> She said to them, "Thus says YHWH the God of Israel, 'Speak to the man who sent you to me,' Thus says YHWH: 'Look! I am bringing evil upon this place and on its inhabitants, all the matters that are in the book, which the king of Judah has read.
>
> 'Because they left me and offered incense to other gods so that they anger me with all the works of their hands, my rage has been kindled against this place and will not be snuffed.' "

"To the king of Judah who sent you to inquire of YHWH, to
   him you should say this: 'Thus says YHWH the God of Israel: "The matters which you have heard—because your
   heart is soft and you surrendered to YHWH when you
   heard what I said about this place and about its inhabitants,
   to be a desolation and a curse, you tore your clothes and
   cried before me—I for my part have also heard," says
   YHWH.
"Therefore I will gather you to your fathers and you will be
   gathered to your tombs in peace and your eyes will not see
   the evil which I am bringing on this place." ' "
They returned the word to the king.

Huldah knows that the book is authentic. She validates its applicabil-
ity to her time rather than its origin or authorship. She verifies that God
will bring all the matters that are in the book, the predictions of doom in
the curses of Deuteronomy, so that this place and its inhabitants will be
a desolation and a curse. For Josiah, she adds a special message: **"Your
eyes will not see the evil which I am bringing on this place."** The king
might have interpreted her words as an indication that Israel's doom
would be delayed till after his death. But oracles are cryptic, and Huldah's prophecy was borne out by Josiah's early death, before the coming
doom.

Huldah is a pivotal figure. The last prophet in the Deuteronomic history, she provides closure to the period of the occupation of the land (introduced by Rahab), to the monarchy (proclaimed by Hannah), and to
the throne of David (proclaimed by Abigail). But she marks not only an
end. She is also the beginning of the new phase of biblical interpretation
that becomes ever more important in Israel. Like the many interpreters
who came after her, Huldah is a link, a triangulation point between herself, the words of the Book, and the world around her. She recognizes
her own society in the dictates of the Book and in its failure to observe
those prescriptions, and she applies the Book's own curses to her own
day. The king and his emissaries give her this authority on the basis of
her own qualifications as prophet. Later, Israel, no longer inquiring of
prophets, rested its interpretative behavior on the authority of the Book
itself.

Woman as Voice

THE HISTORICAL BOOKS present six female oracles: Rahab, Deborah, Hannah, Abigail, Huldah, and the necromancer. Together these women outline the history of Israel, punctuating it with reminders that this history was shaped and foretold by God. The Pentateuch too knows of a connection between women and oracles, for the matriarchs Sarah and Rivka are privy to divine knowledge. Sarah seems to know God's wishes, for God echoes her voice, telling Abraham to listen to her (Gen. 21:12). Rivka's connection is more explicit, for Rivka, rather than Isaac, receives an oracle about the destiny of her children and later acts to bring it to pass. The Pentateuch also preserves traces of what appear to have been far more extensive traditions about the prophet Miriam, one of the three leaders of Israel when they left Egypt.

The oracles do not preach, castigate, or reprove. That is the job of the court prophets who admonish the Israelite kings, and of the classical literary prophets, who concentrate on the sins or failings of Israel. And none of these women are intercessory figures like Samuel, Moses, and Abraham, who prayed to God for the people or for their individual clients. They are not "prophets" in that fuller sense of the word, but they convey the will of God.

The oracles appear at all Israel's turning points, presenting by their existence and by their messages the direction in which Israel will move. It is a quintessential outsider, the Canaanite prostitute Rahab, who announces the conquest of Canaan and Israel's life in the land. She, the outsider, declares that Israel will come from the outside into the land, and then herself comes into the midst of Israel. An insider's insider, Deborah, pronounces the end of the battles of conquest. The beginning of the next stage, Saul's kingship, is announced by a marginal woman, the peasant Hannah, who speaks words that are not her own; the end of his reign is pronounced by another such, the necromancer, who also speaks words that are not her own. They are appropriate frames for

Saul's kingship, which was never quite consolidated and was always somewhat marginal. David's reign is pronounced by the wife of a wealthy landowner, who sides with him over her husband much as Israel sides with David over Saul. Abigail ultimately becomes David's wife, as does Israel. And the end of it all, of the Davidic dynasty and the tenure in the land, is pronounced by Huldah, like Deborah, a professional prophet. She, an insider, predicts that Israel cannot remain inside the land.

It is not surprising to find Deborah and Huldah accepted as *nebi'ôt*, professional prophets. Unlike priests, kings, judges, or administrators, prophets were not born to their role or appointed by a hierarchy. There were cadres of professional prophets, but there were also lone mavericks, called by the spirit of God. A woman whose predictions came true might be sought after for further oracular pronouncements, perhaps to predict the future and perhaps to declare cause or find evidence in a legal case. The other women, Rahab, Hannah, and Abigail, are pressed into service as "onetime" prophets to both mark and participate in the making of Israel's history. Without Rahab, the spies would not have returned her words of certainty and the Israelites might not have been so willing to cross the Jordan. Without Hannah, Samuel would not have been born and there might have been nobody able to oversee the transition to kingship without massive civil disruption. Without Abigail, David would have killed Nabal's household and might never have been made king of Israel. These women, like Sarah and Rivka before them, actively participate in the destiny that they are privileged to know and pronounce.

Even if the appearance of these women is a literary device, and especially if this is so, why do the writers place them at these junctures, and why does the audience accept their appearance and divine foreknowledge? Is there something about women that makes them particularly appropriate for this role?

One could, of course, adopt a "romantic femininist" explanation of women's powers. People who wish to exclude women from formal religious hierarchies and ritual requirements often suggest that women do not need to be ordained, do not need spiritual discipline, because they are naturally attuned to the divine. The rhythms of the menstrual cycle and the creative power of childbearing, says this line of argument, bring them into harmony with cosmic processes, and their involvement in child-rearing enhances their empathic powers. By following this argument to a logical conclusion, we could arrive at a phenomenology of women's intuitive communion with God and their mediation of divine destiny to those in power. But this argument, appealing though it may be as a corrective to some of the more negative things that male religious authorities have said about women, does not match the historical reality that an oracle can be a postmenopausal wise woman or very young and virginal, like the Delphic oracle. This romantic feminist argument also flies in the face of our own reality, which includes dense women and intuitive, empathic men. Nor is there any reason to suspect that the biblical historians had any such essentialist notion about the inherent divine wisdom of women.

The appearance of these prescient women can be understood in part as rising from the same cultural factors that created the goddesses of wisdom and the biblical Lady Wisdom of Proverbs 1–9. This wisdom of "woman" in cultures that often excluded real women from the scholarly realm results from a combination of historical/cultural and biographical/psychological factors. Historically, women often performed such technologically sophisticated tasks as transforming grain into bread, wool into cloth, and herbs into medicine while men were out digging canals, felling forests, removing rocks from fields, and terracing hills. Biographically, women have always been the chief child-minders and therefore loom large in the psyche of children as the all-knowing, all-powerful "goddess of the nursery." Such partially subconscious recollections can give rise to a fear of women but at the same time contribute to a sense that women are mistresses of occult and esoteric knowledge.

Women are the agents of social transformation who prepare children to enter human society. Beyond this, women guard the thresholds and death. They are the portals through which all people come into this world, often becoming ritually "outside" as they give birth, when they menstruate, and again when they tend the dying. Many of their occupations were consciously belittled by the men of Israel; and the fact that women were in a tabooed state during menstruation and after childbirth shows that these events were seen as powerful and to some extent otherworldly. Women negotiate the boundary between the this-worldly and the otherworldly far more often than men, and are frequently the way that men approach this boundary, through birth and through sexual intercourse.

Several other aspects of women's social situation contribute to their association with divine knowledge. Women, like prophets in general, stood outside the power system. Their class might make them figures of privilege, like the Shunammite, but they did not have many established niches in the power structure. This considerable disadvantage conveys several important advantages. First, people who are close to a power structure are often enmeshed in it and can see only their own position clearly; but those who stand on the periphery frequently gain the advantage of distance. Second, women had to master many different semiotic systems. Like any other peripheral group, they had to learn the mainstream language and behavior and, at the same time, know the protocols and language of women's social relationships with one another. Moreover, women in biblical Israel were liminal persons. They had to know the customs and behavior modes of their birth family and then master another set of customs and behavior when they married. If widowed or divorced, they would learn yet a third. Such multiple systems multiply perspectives, and this may explain "women's intuition."

Women could occupy the same social space as Israel's male prophets, who also stood outside the hierarchic power system. The prophets are often shown in the company of women. Mothers turned to them when their children were sick, often traveling to find them. Women could also go on pilgrimages to the prophets on Sabbath and holidays. Prophets would often stay with women, poor ones like the widow of Zarephat, and rich ones like the Shunammite. Women and prophets could also work together, as Bathsheba did with Nathan to secure the throne for her son Solomon.

Women appeared as oracles throughout the ancient world, from the Delphic oracle of early Greece to the Sibyls of the Graeco-Roman period. In Israel, where God often works through the marginal and brings the peripheral to the center, women appeared as the harbingers of history. Their role in the historical books is the counterpart of the "angels" of the book of Genesis: messengers sent by God to alert those to whom God's attention has turned.

Part Five

READING
THE WOMEN
OF THE BIBLE

Women of Metaphor, Metaphors of Women

THE WOMEN who appear in biblical stories are often striking characters, distinct personalities who have gone beyond the confines of the tales in which they appear to become important figures in our cultural memory. At the same time, these women are not fleshed-out individuals. Many of them appear in only one story, and that story tells us only those facts that serve the writer's agenda. The Bible tells us nothing of their backgrounds, nothing of their future, nothing of their thoughts; solely their actions in a particular context. The striking incompleteness of these portraits has sometimes proved frustrating and infuriating. Many contemporary women feel that this fragmentary presentation exploits and abuses the characters; they want the narrators to care about the lives and thoughts of the women about whom they write. But these partial images have also been a spur to literary and poetic imagination. Readers of the Bible, millennia past and present, have brought these characters out of the confines of the narrative, adding personality traits and personal history in an ongoing process of midrash and story.

The Bible's lack of interest in the individuality of its characters is not limited to the women. Only a few males—Abraham, Moses, David, Elijah, Elisha—have anything resembling a biography in the Bible. Most men, like the women, appear at a given moment and then disappear, sometimes to reappear in a later episode, but in some cases never to appear again. Incomplete portrayals do in fact serve the purpose of the narrators, whose concern is the destiny of the people of Israel, and who choose and shape their stories for national political reasons. Plot and character are all subordinate to the larger concerns. Their stories are important for what they indicate about Israel's society, history, and destiny, the individuals for what they contribute to an understanding of these issues.

The narrators understand a profound lesson that we keep rediscovering anew: *the personal is political*. The events of a person's life are not determined solely by his or her personal characteristics and motives. People may choose how they act from their own perspective and for their own purposes, but their intentions do not assure results. "Life is not fair," as we say. The intersection of an individual with the structures and institutions of his or her society often determines the outcome of that person's acts as much as his or her desires or personal agenda do. Biblical authors tell us about individual women and men precisely at the moment when their stories illuminate the social structure, political events, and cultural patterns of the day. To these authors, their characters (apart, perhaps, from the grand "historical" figures) are as much archetypes as they are individuals, and the specific plots of their stories are simultaneously unique to their lives and paradigms for all the similar events that could have taken place in the history of Israel. The stories are about individuals, and yet when they are read with reference to one another, they do not seem to be about their characters at all.

The paradigmatic nature of the ancestor stories of Genesis has long been recognized. The development of the family of Abraham into the nation of Israel is both history and parable. The stories shape Israel's memory, creating and reinforcing a sense of family central to Israel's sense of who it is and how it operates in the world. But they also serve as archetypes of Israel's destiny. The deeds of the ancestors and the events of their lives contain intimations of Israel's future. Rabbinic writers understood this, particularly in regard to the tales in which the forefathers had to leave the land. The medieval commentator Nahmanides coined a maxim, Ma'asê abot Sîmān labbānîm, "the deeds of the fathers are signs for the children"; thus the temporary descents of the patriarchs to Egypt as seen as foreshadowings of Israel's enslavement and emancipation from Egypt. The stories of the matriarchs share this paradigmatic quality, though the rabbis took no note of it. Hagar's slavery, emancipation, and annunciation manifest the pattern of Israel's own slavery, emancipation, and covenant. Sarah's sojourn as a slave in Pharaoh's house and later in Gerar foreshadows Israel's slavery in Egypt and her second captivity in Babylon. Rivka's captivity in Gerar reinforces the hint that there will be more than one captivity for Israel. And the Dinah story demonstrates the intricate difficulties of Israel's destiny among the nations, focusing on the essential question of how Israel should form alliances and how it should grow. The family of the ancestors is Israel in embryo.

The many stories about marriage to outsiders dramatize the boundary issues that marriage presents. Marriage is always a threshold action. Its liminal nature is evident when we consider that a girl entering a marriage had to transform herself in two ways: from a girl to a woman and from a subordinate member of one family to a still subordinate member of another. The change was so radical that it could be described symbolically as the "death" of the child.

Marriage was also a crisis for both families. The girl's birth family formed an alliance with another family, a relationship that could be instrumental in determining its future destiny. The boy's family, for its part, opened its boundaries to an "Other," to someone who was coming from outside the family into its very heart as the bearer and caretaker of its future children. What ideas would this outsider import? What customs? What beliefs? Marriage is fraught with the danger of change, and this danger is at the heart of the dispute over non-Israelite women. Incest laws demand that women come from outside the family, defining all who might be living within the extended family as forbidden. But how far outside is too far? Where does difference become too great to tolerate? Ancient Israel's reality was that it lived amid other peoples, and that other peoples lived in its midst. Crucial national issues of survival and self-definition were raised every time a woman was "taken in marriage." The biblical stories about marriages to outside women and their consequences were the natural vehicle with which Israel expressed and explored the dimensions of this perennial issue.

The paradigmatic nature of the stories about victors and victims is not as self-evident, until we realize that the victor stories follow the paradigm of Israel's central sacred story: the lowly are raised, the marginal come to the center, the poor boy makes good. Little Israel, like its heroes and heroines, triumphs by the will of God, and the heroines demonstrate Israel's faithful action. The God-fearing defiant women of the Exodus, and also Rahab, are models of how Israel should behave in adversity and the reward they can expect. Yael the apparently powerless tent-dweller is the archetype of those who conquer their powerful adversaries by faith and determination. Later, when once again there was no king, Esther became the model for the behavior and salvation of Jews in the diaspora, and Judith, like the much earlier Yael, rose to destroy the enemy of Israel. The women who were saviors of Israel, like the boy David who slew Goliath, all demonstrate the ability of the small and marginal to win by their will and the power of God.

The victims are also images of the Israel that is small and vulnerable, a potential and actual victim of more powerful nations. The Bible often portrays Israel as a woman. In the famous "marital metaphor," the prophets refer to Israel, or Jerusalem, as the wife of God, receiving Israel's relationship to God on the model of hierarchical marriage, with unequal partners, that was familiar to them. Husbands provided for their wives, but they also controlled them, scrutinizing, judging, and punishing their behavior. The prophets show us a patriarchal marriage gone awry. Once, Jeremiah tells us, this was a wonderful romance, and Israel was supremely faithful to God. And in the future, Deutero-Isaiah predicts, the marriage will be glorious. But in the present, things are not so good: Israel is first a wayward, then a punished and rejected, wife. Hosea indicted Israel for infidelity to God with her "lovers," which included the empires that surrounded her: Egypt, Babylonia, and Assyria. Hosea saw Israel as a woman in a world of men, looking to great nations (her "lovers") for help and protection. Thus did he and other prophets use the metaphor of marriage to express their view of Israel as dependent and vulnerable, yet valued.

The image of Israel as a woman also lies at the heart of the poetry of lament, in the metaphor of *bat* or *betûlat yisrael*, "Daughter" or "Young Maiden Israel," or *bat ṣiyyôn*, "Daughter Jerusalem (or Jerusalem-girl)." *Bat yisrael* first appears in the eighth century, in the writings of Amos, the first of the literary prophets. In the midst of a serious castigation of Israel, Amos foretells the utter destruction of the country. As soon as he mentions the coming ruination, he changes tone and begins to mourn. At the moment of destruction, his anger is dissipated and he grieves for the victim. He switches to the classic rhythm of lament (*qînah*) and evokes a mournful image, *naflah lôʾ tôsîf qûm betûlat yisrael*, "Maiden Israel has fallen and rises no more" (Amos 5:2). The essence of pathos is conveyed by a devastated young woman. Two centuries later, Jeremiah returned to this image. Maiden Zion "sighs and spreads out her hands—'Woe is me, for my soul is weary before those who slay'" (Jer. 4:31)—in one of the many passages of enormous sorrow over the ruin of *bat ṣiyyôn* and *bat ʿammi*, "my maiden-people." The book of Lamentations also uses this image of a mourning woman in its distress over the destruction of Jerusalem: "My eyes have filled with tears, my innards are in turmoil, my liver has flowed to the ground because of the destruction of my maiden-people" (Lam. 2:11).

The stories about women who are victims and the metaphors of "maid Zion" both build on the same fundamental image of woman as victim, a type of narrative symbolism in which the fate of the daughter of Jephthah, the concubine in Gibeah, and Tamar, the daughter of David, represent the fate of all young women victimized by the men of their families. The narrator underscores the paradigmatic nature of the stories of Jephthah's daughter and the Levite's concubine by not preserving the women's names. Their fate is the fate of others.

Woman as victim is an enduring image in Western civilization, able to capture both female vulnerability and the response of readers and viewers to tales of tragedy. On the one hand, a young woman is a figure of intimacy and attraction. Men and women both love the image of a young woman, innocent and yet full of the promise of life and fertility. At the same time, the young woman is vulnerable and powerless, kept that way by the very society that feels so sorry about her victimization. The combination creates a powerful emotional stew that makes the ruined young woman an enduring symbol of pathos, the most tragic victim figure the biblical poet can image.

Israel's understanding of herself as potentially small and marginal also provided the metaphorical context for the stories about women who were oracles. Of these, only Deborah and Huldah had official positions, and only Deborah had any power in the politico-judicial sphere. Their marginality made it possible for God to speak to them, for they were not tied up in the power struggles of their day, not blinded by an interest in the status quo. The Bible also considered Israel as a whole the medium of God's will and message to the world.

As victor, as victim, as vulnerable, and as vehicle for the divine, Israel saw herself as the "woman" of the world. Ironically, it was the nation's own patriarchal social system and the Bible's unusual approach to it that created this metaphorical self-understanding. Men were the only participants in the public hierarchies of politics, law, and cult, and only they held economic power. The Bible did not question these inequities or justify them by positing an inherent inferiority or weakness of women. The Bible understands the role of women in society and history, but its anthropology is gender-neutral, or at the very least gender-blind. There is no essential difference between men and women. Men are not more assertive, more intellectual, more rational, or more strong-willed. Women are positioned differently because that is the way things are, not because their weakness or passivity requires their subordination. The social inferiority of women may be "explained" by the myth of the Garden of Eden, but it is never justified by gynophobic or misogynist stereotypes. Being a woman put one in a powerless class (a class to which most men also belonged) and made one dependent on the men in her family. Gender matters, but neither humanity nor Israel revolves essentially or ontologically on a sexual axis. The dualisms that really count are between the Divine and the human (male *and* female) and between Israel and the other nations.

The disjunction between women's social inferiority and their ontological parity with men formed a creative tension that enabled biblical thinkers to see the similarity between the social situation of women within Israel and the social situation of Israel in the world. Weaker than the empires, vulnerable to them and ultimately their victim, Israel never considered herself inferior to the nations. Knowing that weakness and even subordination do not imply inferiority, Israel could see herself in the savior-victors who can rise to victory, in the daughter-victims in their texts of terror, and in the oracle-women in their knowledge of God. Israel can glory in the stories of women victors and empathize with the victims. And Israel can present God speaking through marginal women oracles as God speaks through Israel. The stories about women in the Bible are a powerful vehicle by which Israel can understand its own place in the universe.

The Later Adventures of
Biblical Women

THE WRITTEN TEXT is just a frozen moment in time. Authors built on earlier versions of the stories, written and oral, and crafted their own literary creations to express their issues. At a certain date, the text of these stories was "fixed" or "frozen," and successive storytellers no longer changed the written word. But the stories did not freeze along with the written word. The carefully crafted ambiguity of biblical stories provided them with elasticity. When combined with the importance of storytelling to provide paradigms and to persuade, this elasticity ensured an ongoing evolution. New generations could see their own issues in these stories and could discuss these later issues by expanding and retelling the stories much as the biblical authors discussed their issues by recording and creating them. As new conceptions of women and society evolved in Israel, later readers of the Bible could "flesh out" the faintly defined individuals in these stories in ways that matched their own conceptions. They developed a literature to be read along with the frozen biblical text. Two major forms developed: "parallel bibles," which retell biblical stories with numerous elaborations, and exegetical midrash, which provide multiple interpretations of stories, verses, and even words. By these means, the later readers resolved ambiguities, filled in gaps, expanded the narratives, and introduced their own concerns.

The conquest of Israel by Alexander the Great led to a confrontation with Greek culture. Hellenism had an enormous impact on Israel, even on those who did not rush to adopt it. Sexuality and gender became major concerns, and new Greek-influenced ideas about gender led to the first misogynist statement in the Hebrew Bible, the lament of Ecclesiastes that a woman is "more bitter than death; she is all traps, her hands are fetters and her heart is snares" (Eccles. 7:26). The later "sequel" to Ecclesiastes, the Wisdom of Ben Sirah (Ecclesiasticus), has very strong opinions about the nature of woman—few favorable—as do other Jewish and Christian works from the Graeco-Roman period.

These writings evince a heightened sense of the "dangers of women," and their ability to use beauty and sexual attraction as weapons against men. The figure of Judith puts this new concern in the most positive light. Judith is an unquestioned heroine, but when she sets out to save Israel, she girds herself in the armor of womanhood: she has her hair done, puts on makeup, attires herself glamorously, and goes out in her beauty to confront the enemy general. Her strategy succeeds, for he is so taken with her beauty that he drinks himself into a stupor and falls down drunk, at which point she takes his sword and cuts off his head. A great heroine, indeed, but the story carries a subliminal message: Beware the beauty of women! This idea also comes to the fore in the apocryphal stories of the "Watchers," Hellenistic retellings of the story of the sons of God and the daughters of humankind from Gen. 6:1–4. And under the influence of this new awareness of sexuality as weapon, many of the women of the Bible were reconceived. Abigail became a vamp, the Moabite women paraded nude, and the familiar image of Delilah as a grand seductress took shape. In these new interpretations, Yael defeats Sisera by exhausting him sexually, Delilah frustrates Samson by withdrawing at the critical moment, the Israelites have orgies with the Moabite women, Judah is lured into marriage by a Canaanite woman, the sin of Onan becomes "Onanism" (coitus interruptus) rather than denial of the levirate, and the unnamed sin of Er is sexualized as a refusal to have normal sex, or even sex at all, with Tamar. In this new light, the story of the Garden of Eden is retold as a tale of lust and carnal knowledge. And Joseph is glorified as the "righteous one," the ṣaddîq, for his fortitude in resisting the advances of Potiphar's wife.

Ethnicity and intermarriage were great issues in Second Temple literature. Marriage to foreign women became a hot topic during the restoration period, when Ezra engineered mass divorces from the "women of the land" and extended the biblical prohibition against intermarriage with the nations of Canaan to include all women who were not part of the gôlah, the group that came back from Babylon. Ezra's view was contested. The prophet Malachi, who did not approve of foreign wives, nevertheless objected to the mass divorces, and the book of Ruth probably reached its final form as a polemic against Ezra's policies. On the opposite side, the tale of the engagement of Rivka probably reached its final form in this period and seems designed to reinforce the ideas of marrying within one's (extended) family. The issue also comes to the fore in the development of the Dinah story, which is often retold in Hellenistic Jewish texts.

The Dinah story took on particular interest at this time because of the long, complicated relationship of Israel to the people of the northern area, ultimately known as the Samaritans. Relations with the northern territory had been strained since the schism under Jeroboam, but after the Assyrian conquest of North Israel, and the exile of its leadership, King Hezekiah of Judah invited the non-exiled population to come rejoin the cult of Jerusalem. The Assyrians settled a foreign people in the north and the newcomers adopted the Israelite religion, but not with enough stringency or exclusivity to satisfy the Deuteronomistic movement. The Israelites who came back from Babylon intermarried with these northerners, but Ezra eliminated those marriages along with marriages to the other peoples of the land. In the polemic at this time, the lines of opinion about accepting the Samaritans as Jews converge with the lines of opinion about intermarriage in general. The book of Chronicles seems inclined to accept the Samaritans, as it accepted intermarriage. Ezra's camp vehemently opposed both. The frequent reference to "the land" in Genesis 34 may in fact be a trace that this battle left in the biblical text itself.

Post-biblical Israel continued to relate Genesis 34 in light of relations with the Samaritans, particularly after the wars of expansion of the Hasmonean ruler John Hyrcanus, during which he destroyed Shechem and forcibly circumcised the Idumeans. The Hellenistic retellings of the Dinah story are unanimous in their approval of Simeon and Levi's destruction of Shechem. Only the circumcision ruse was at all controversial, with one manuscript of the Testament of Levi claiming that Levi argued against the circumcision, the Epic of Theodotus relating that Jacob favored it, and most accounts simply omitting the circumcision. The retellings have no qualms about the slaughter of Shechem, and they remove the story's moral ambiguity by including reference to a divine command for vengeance, a guardian angel to aid in victory, and even a magical sword made in heaven. Most versions vilify the Shechemites for what they did to Dinah, for pagan immorality, and for a Sodom-like lack of hospitality to strangers. They even accuse the Shechemites of attempting to defile Sarah, an episode that Genesis attributes to the Philistines at Gerar. The book of Jubilees represents a second approach. Rather than vilify the Shechemites, Jubilees includes a long diatribe against intermarriage. In this climate, Theodotus and, later, Josephus relate that Dinah went to Shechem to attend a festival and to see the city or its treasures. After all, her desire for relations with the "daughters of the land" might encourage interrelations with the gentiles. Similarly, it would not do for Dinah to fall in love with a gentile, and several texts, most notably Targum Pseudo-Jonathan and Pseudo-Philo, state emphatically that she was raped. In this way, Dinah has done no wrong, the vengeance of the brothers has strong provocation and everyone in the ancestral family stays free from fault.

Many of the same concerns about sexuality, ethnicity, and zeal show up in the later history of the story of Ba'al-Pe'or. Maccabees presents Phineas as a great hero and as the model for Mattathias (1 Macc. 2:26); the book of Ben Sirah considers him the third most powerful intercessor in Israel's history. Josephus and Jewish Midrash both expand the story. They pick up Moses' accusation in Numbers 31 that Balaam incited the Moabites to entice Israel and include elaborate versions of Balaam's plan. In Josephus's version, Balaam realized that sex was the weakness of Israelite men, and told the Moabites to send their most beautiful women to captivate them. Then, when passion was at its height, the women were to withdraw, claiming that as long as the Israelites stayed faithful to their laws, they would not be faithful to them, the Moabites. They were then to demand that the Israelite men accept their belief and sacrifice to many gods. In this way, Balaam reasoned, sexuality could lead to apostasy. The plan worked, and Zambrias succumbed, consorting with the Midianite priestess and devoting himself to a cult of her liking. When Moses called an assembly to discuss his apostasy, Zambrias delivered a frontal attack on Moses and on Israelite law, presenting arguments against the uniqueness of Israel and its lack of autonomy that must have been the arguments Josephus typically heard from the apostates of his day. When Moses, having no answer, dissolved the meeting, Phineas killed Zambrias.

The Midrash Sifrei, the Tannaitic Midrash to Numbers, has a somewhat different scenario, one concerned less with the danger of female beauty but no less with intermarriage. Rabbinic texts read the biblical rule that denied Ammonites and Moabites the right to participate in the cult ("enter the congregation of the Lord") as a proscription of intermarriage. In addition, Targum Pseudo-Jonathan translated the law of Leviticus 18:23, "Do not give your seed to Molech," originally a prohibition of child sacrifice, as "You shall not have intercourse with a non-Jewish woman and give her your seed and make her pregnant for the benefit of other worship." Rabbinic texts, concerned about intermarriage, often interpret the Molech rule in this way. Judaism adopted a matrilineality rule for Jewish identity in the Roman period. Biblical law considered both family and group identity to flow along patrilineal lines, but the new principle declared that the child of a non-Jewish mother was not Jewish. This made intermarriage with foreign women even more dangerous to Israel, and Rabbinic retellings of the episode of Zimri and Cozbi reflected their perception of this threat.

The Rabbinic texts do not put as much stress on the seductive powers of beauty as the Hellenistic Jewish authors do. Josephus, Philo, and Pseudo-Philo expect the beauty of the Moabite women to attract the Israelite men. In the Sifrei, Israel is entrapped through its liking for linen. Balaam suggests that the Midianites set up a market booth displaying linen, with an old woman to tend it. Since she does not present a sexual temptation, the Israelites will enter the booth. When the unsuspecting Israelite goes inside the stall, a young woman is to offer hospitality. Everything is to seem harmless till the third day. Then the young woman is to offer drink to the man and entice him sexually, and then, when he is drunk and aroused, she will demand that he abandon the law and sacrifice to her gods. This tale of gradual entrapment stresses that encounters with foreign women are dangerous, even ordinary commercial transactions. Harmless though they may seem, they are a conduit to sexual relations, intermarriage, and apostasy.

The Sifrei, the Targum Pseudo-Jonathan, and the Babylonian Talmud all show considerable interest in the punishment by Phineas of Zimri. The Mishnah contains a law, probably originally passed in the Hasmonean court, that "If one stole a service vessel, or cursed with an incantation, or has sexual intercourse with an 'Aramean' women, zealots accost him" (Sanhedrin 9, 6). Another Talmudic reference to this rule cites the woman as "Cuthean," (literally Samaritan), but most say "Aramean." In this context, both "Aramean" and "Cuthean" mean "foreign woman." The Mishnaic word for "zealots," *qannā'im*, is the same word that the Bible uses (in its verb form) to describe the action of Phineas. "Zeal" was considered a heroic attribute in the Hellenistic world. Later, however, the rabbis did not want to encourage zealotry, with its threat of lynching and vigilantism. The Jerusalem Talmud states unequivocally that the Mishnaic law allowing zealots to confront one who intermarried did not correspond to the "will of the sages," and the Babylonian Talmud declared that sages who were asked to permit a zealot's actions could not do so. The Sifrei tames Phineas's vigilante action by relating that he was carrying out the decision of the assembly to kill the miscreants. Moreover, he was able to kill Zimri and Cozbi only because God intervened to help with six miracles; the Targum and Bavli add six more. God made Phineas strong enough, made the spear long enough, made Zimri's sexual prowess last long enough so that Phineas would confront the couple in flagrante, and the spear penetrated the two of them in a way that demonstrated to all just what was happening and why Phineas acted. Moreover, these sources underscore the fact that Phineas was allowed to kill Zimri and Cozbi only because he caught them during the sex act. The same restriction applies to other vigilantes: they cannot kill in any other circumstances. Since Phineas required several miracles to carry out the punishment, it is unlikely that anyone else will be able to duplicate his feat. By means of the many miracles, Phineas could remain a hero in Rabbinic eyes without becoming a paradigm for vigilante justice. Intermarriage, moreover, can be seen as such a danger that God would intervene to stop it clearly and publicly.

Strong disapproval of intermarriage also colored Second Temple retellings of the story of Judah and Tamar. Early texts emphasize that Tamar was not a Canaanite. They give her a glorious ancestry, as the descendant of Noah's son Shem, and even as from the seed of Terah. Judah may have married a Canaanite, seduced (according to the Testaments) by beauty, wine, and wealth, but Tamar, the mother of the tribe of Judah, was from the home family.

Another principle of Second Temple and Jewish Midrash that influenced the later retellings of the story of Judah and Tamar was their desire to see the ancestors as perfect role models. Pseudo-Philo exalts Tamar as the model of fidelity in adversity. Rabbinic texts point to her unwillingness to embarrass Judah in public, and stress that she sent his staff and seal to him in private. Most Jewish texts pay more attention to Judah. In their desire to valorize him, they are faced with the fact that he married a Canaanite woman. Hellenistic texts consider this marriage an act of wrongdoing. Wine, zeal, and lust, explains Judah in his Testament, made him lose the classic Hellenistic battle for control. These apocryphal texts minimize Judah's later errors. Bat-Shua is the cause of all the disasters: she would not allow Er to sleep with Tamar because Tamar was not Canaanite, and she refused to allow Shelah to marry Tamar. Some Rabbinic texts have a different view of the problem. Targum Jonathan, which translates Lev. 18:21 (the Molech rule) as "Do not have intercourse with a gentile woman . . . ," chooses denial, translating the words "Canaanite man," whose daughter Judah marries, as "tradesman," a rare but attested meaning of the word "Canaanite." Medieval Jewish interpreters follow the same path. A Talmudic passage makes the reason for this reading clear: after the injunctions of Abraham and Isaac, Judah certainly would not have married a Canaanite! The desire to see

Judah as righteous causes the Midrash Breshit Rabbah to relate that God sent the angel of temptation to interest Judah in the disguised Tamar. If not for the angel, implies this midrash, Judah would not have approached Tamar, and so the man's reputation is above charges of sexual license.

Even those traditions that consider Judah at fault for intermarriage or incest exonerate Tamar. Her actions are all part of God's plan, and she is never blamed. But she is not the center of her own story, which the rabbis read as Judah's redemption. These sources pay particular attention to Judah's public confession, which redeems him and gives him the right to be the ancestor of the kings of Israel. The Talmud sees him as a model of those who are willing to endure public humiliation in order to sanctify God. One passage explains that as his reward, all four letters of God's name (YHWH) are found in his name, which is spelled *yhwdh*.

The later texts understand this brief confession, *ṣadeqah mimmennî* (usually translated as "She is more righteous than I"), in a way that valorizes both Judah and Tamar. Targum Pseudo-Jonathan translates, "She is righteous. By me she is pregnant." In the Babylonian Talmud, Judah rules, "She is righteous," and a heavenly voice declares "from me" (Makkot 23b). Another text has the Holy Spirit declaring, "She is innocent," and Judah saying, "from me." Judah and Tamar can thus be perfect ancestors and archetypes of Israel.

Israel's prohibition of intermarriage was somewhat tempered by its normalization of the conversion process. This was a tripartite ritual: the convert accepted the yoke of heaven, underwent circumcision (if male), and was immersed in a body of water. But the questions remained: Was conversion a good thing? Should people be encouraged to convert? In the context of this discourse, Rahab emerged as one of the great heroines of post-biblical Jewish and Christian tradition, a prime example of the righteous convert. God returned her love and rewarded her (and the Gibeonites) despite their Canaanite origin. Rahab is often associated with Ruth and with Jethro. She was Joshua's convert, as Jethro was Moses'. Both came to join Israel because God granted "light" to Israel. Their coming proves that when Israel does good, righteous people come to join her, and speaks well also of their home nation, for God will remember their conversion to the merit of the people from whom they came.

Rahab is also a model of repentance. One strain of Jewish exegesis, found in the Talmud and an early midrash, considered her an innkeeper rather than a prostitute. But another strain informs us that Rahab was ten years old when Israel left Egypt, was a prostitute while Israel wandered in the desert, and converted at the age of fifty. Her salvation from such a beginning proves how powerful repentance can be. It is even greater than prayer, for Moses prayed unsuccessfully to be allowed to enter the land, while Rahab was rewarded for her repentance by being saved from the Canaanites. A Rabbinic legend relates that King Hezekiah addressed his own prayer facing Rahab's wall, saying, "She saved two, and you saved so many of hers, so I, whose fathers converted so many, all the more so should you save my life."

And Rahab is revered as the progenitress of both prophets and priests. One passage explains that her honor was so great that Israel made light of Ezekiel and Jeremiah because they were not known as her descendants, so Scripture had to ascribe them to her. Rahab becomes almost superhuman in Rabbinic legend, which considered her one of the four great beauties of the Bible, the others being Yael, Michal, and Abigail. In an "after-dinner" story in the Babylonian Talmud, a rabbi declares that one need only recite the name "Rahab, Rahab" to come to climax. When his comrade responds that he himself had said "Rahab, Rahab" with no such result, the first responds that it works only for those who know her, a hint perhaps that some believed Rahab, about whom the Bible says she lives "in the midst of Israel till this very day," never died.

The other foreign women who became saviors are also valorized, Yael, for example. As often happens in post-biblical retellings, a stream of tradition sexualizes her story, emphasizing her beauty and interpreting the seven verbs of the fall of Sisera as seven ejaculations of Sisera. But she is not condemned; her act was "sin for Torah," done to weaken Sisera so that she could kill him. Another stream states unequivocally that Sisera never touched Yael.

Two midrashim attest to the great importance the Rabbis attributed to Yael's act. In Exodus Rabbah, her deed is associated with Jethro's: Jethro the Midianite "received the savior who was fleeing from the enemy," and Yael the Kenite received "the enemy who was fleeing from the savior." In Breshit Rabbah, Yael is "most blessed of women who live in tents," greater than the women of the wilderness generation or even than the matriarchs, because "they gave birth and sustained the world, but what would it have helped them—without her they would have been lost!" Medieval exegetes continued to emphasize Yael's cunning and her eagerness to help God, and declared that she was a judge and savior even before she killed Sisera.

As cultural ideas about the proper roles for women changed, so did the interpretation of the ancient stories, and the new interpretations were often presented as arguments either for change or for the status quo. The story of Dinah was used as an opportunity to discourage the freedom of women. Given this social background, the great twelfth-century Jewish commentator known as Rashi calls Dinah a *yaṣ' anît*, the Hebrew equivalent of *wāṣitum*, "goer-outer," "gadabout," with the same connotation. In the same spirit, the Renaissance Christian commentator Tyndale states, "Dinah goeth but forth alone, and how great myscheve and troble followed," and Calvin makes the lesson explicit: by this story "Fathers are taught to keep their daughters under narrow watch." The question of women in public office focused on such figures as Deborah. The Rabbis found Deborah problematic, and declared that her arrogance in holding public office, and Huldah's long after her, was the reason they both were given vile names: Deborah, "the bee," and Huldah, "the weasel." By contrast, Aquinas approved of Deborah and used her as proof that women *should* be allowed to study and teach. The Bible was integral to the Christian debate over women's ability to preach, with Paul's demand for the silence of women serving one side of the debate, and biblical women themselves, the other.

Changing theology as well as changing social mores brought dramatic alterations to the story of Israel's heroines. Early Christian exegesis held Rahab up as a model of whatever virtue the writers considered paramount. In the Epistle of James, she was justified by her works, when she saved the spies (Jas. 2:25); in the Epistle to the Hebrews, her faith is emphasized, and she is classed with Abraham and Moses as those who gave up their earlier lives because of it. The author of I Clement (written around 95 C.E.) sees her as the model of both faith and hospitality and, in addition, recognizes her as a prophet (chapter 12). The Gospel of Matthew lists her as one of the foremothers of Jesus, the ancestress of Boaz.

During the later development of Christian theology, something strange happened to all the women in the ancestry of Christ. As "grace" became ever more important in the history of salvation, and redemption from sin a central issue, Christ's mission to a sinful world and for redemption of sin colored the way that all his foremothers were viewed. A tradition grew, espoused by Jerome and endorsed by Aquinas, that Christ came into the world not only for sinners but through them. All of the erstwhile heroines in his lineage were examined and found to be flawed: Rahab as a prostitute, Tamar for incest with her father-in-law, Bathsheba by adultery, Ruth as a foreigner. Rahab's profession became the most important element of her story, and the scarlet cord that saved her family was seen as a symbol of the blood of Christ that saves the unrighteous. As Aquinas explains, the geneaology includes "only those whom Scripture censures, so that he who came for the sake of sinners, by being born of sinners, might blot out all sin" (Summa Theologica, v. 5. p. 3 Q. 31).

The later life of these stories is complex and fascinating, and often quite revealing of the societies that read them. In the Reformation, Calvin highlights the power of faith to redeem. To him, for example, Rahab's prostitution is important, for it shows that "those who are hardly allowed a place among the profane and the reprobate, are by faith introduced into the company of angels" (Calvin, *Commentary on Hebrews* 11:31). Luther highlights the actions and ingenuity of Tamar, whom he considers a *"mirabilis mulier"* (wonder-woman) who forced Judah to obey God's command. Moreover, Luther identifies her as a Canaanite, and he considers this foreignness integral to the story, declaring its lesson to be that a Canaanite woman was the mother of the whole tribe of Judah.

The contemporary adventures of these stories is particularly fascinating. With our heightened awareness of women's issues, the women of the Bible have gained far more prominence than they had in the past few hundred years. Feminist thinkers valorize them, sometimes pointing out what should have been obvious, for example that Tamar is as important to the story of Genesis 38 as is Judah, that Jephthah's daughter's faith is equal to his, that her willingness to be sacrificed is like the much exalted martyr's faith of Isaac and Jesus. The feminist thinkers have rediscovered less patriarchal readings of the written story, and they have often explicitly changed the focus of the story to reflect the perspective of the female characters. The women of the Bible have become paragons of strength, initiative, and cunning, or paradigmatic sufferers of the woes and terrors of their sex. At the same time, however, the increased focus on them has produced a backlash. Their initiative is denounced: Rivka becomes a manipulator, Sarah an oppressor, Tamar a sneak. The heroines are castigated for their very heroic acts: Rahab is suspected of aggrandizing herself by secretly telling the king about the presence of the spies so that she could save them; Yael is faulted for adultery and for violating norms of hospitality by killing her guest. Women are accused of "asking for it": the concubine brought everything about by being faithless to her husband, Bathsheba was a femme fatale who set out to entice the king. Even David's daughter Tamar, the quintessential victim, has been attacked. This negativity parallels other indications of contemporary anti-feminism and shows that the fear of women, long an undercurrent in Western thinking, has not been eradicated. This antipathy does not originate in the Bible, but it continues to influence the way the Bible is read.

The elastic, complex, ambiguous stories continue to provoke readers to interpret them in ways that dramatically illustrate their own agendas. They also challenge us today to read the stories in a way that sanctifies both the Bible and its readers.

Mirrors and Voices
Reading These Stories Today

In the Words of Long Ago

There is more to Bible stories than meets the eye, much more than we dream of when we teach these stories to our children. Woman stories, ancestor stories, primeval stories, prophetic stories are layered and nuanced to discuss important issues. From their beginning and throughout their transmission, they have been means to express our ideas about community, identity, and spirituality. Once we understand this, they can continue to be so today.

There is much we can learn from stories formulated in a time so different from our own. Precisely because the background of these stories is so archaic and different, we sometimes can see things that the familiarity of our own times and institutions obscures. It is far easier to perceive oppression in the customs of others or of times gone by than it is to notice and name it when it is built into social interactions that we take for granted. The presence of slavery and patriarchy in the Bible is very disturbing to those of us who consider such social institutions moral evils. A century and a half ago, there were those who quoted the Bible in support of maintaining slavery; today, groups who still believe in male dominance quote the Bible to prove their views. In some circumstances it seems that the Bible is on trial, accused of supporting and even inventing oppressive structures. There is nothing about biblical religion that requires patriarchy, nothing that demands slavery or economic oppression, and nothing that prevents them. The Bible did not invent these systems, nor did it transform them. First Judaism and ultimately the Christian world eventually abolished slavery, and the contemporary Western world seems to be in the process of dismantling patriarchy. Perhaps future generations will solve the problem of poverty. They may also perceive additional social problems, unnoticed both by the biblical world and by our own, which they will then seek to erase. Biblical religion was able to accommodate to later social transformations. It may even have paved the way for them by its own tradition of self-critique and its demand for ethical primacy. Promoting new ethical awareness and greater moral sensibility is a major aim of studying the Bible.

Ancient stories possess a great advantage. The rapid succession of news and happenings in today's world rapidly supplants in our consciousness even the most horrific of contemporary events. We do not often think any more about the mass rapes in Bosnia and what they tell us about sexuality and aggression. We are surprised, yet again, to see this act revealed once more as a tool of ethnic violence, this time in Rwanda. And the images from Rwanda are fading from our memories as airplanes crash, embassies explode, football players get their just desserts, elections go on, and hundreds of millions mourn the death of celebrities. But the rape of Tamar and the bloody attack on the anonymous concubine keep confronting us. They are part of Scripture, a literature that tradition mandates us to read and reread. As a result, the treatment of one nameless girl in Gibeah and its violent aftermath can reveal the connection of sexual violence and war in a way that the millions of crimes in Bosnia and Rwanda do not. Because the story in Judges remains to be reread, it can show that rape is the surface tip of violence in society, a revelation of resentments harbored and rage building. It can demonstrate that when the act is treated as an occasional individual aberration or as an extreme manifestation of sexual desire, then the violence and rage that fueled the act will continue to build and will result in more rape, in murder, in bombings, revolution, and terror.

Tradition sometimes infantilizes biblical stories, simplifying them "for the masses" into simple morality tales. When we do not try to force them into a simple voice, and when we do not try to make all of them say the same univocal thing, then these complex and symbolic stories can illuminate dilemmas that are still before us, problems that continue to occupy us today. We have not solved the issue of perfect order, the question of how to govern ourselves so that we can become a holy society. The stories about the daughter-victims remind us that no society can be considered just that does not protect its most vulnerable; that no form of government that does not control violence and intimidation among its citizens can be considered admirable. The stories are subversive, for they can make us question the perfection of our own society, in which violence is still used in interpersonal relations. The stories about victim women also show us the difficulties inherent in proclaiming "family values" to be the ultimate social institution. The family, without a doubt, is the major unit of socialization, organization, and identity in

society. But the family is an inherently hierarchical arrangement between people of widely divergent economic, physical, and political
power. Today, more economic and judicial rights for women are reducing the power disparities between husband and wife. But the wide gap
between parents and children remains as an essential, almost definitive
element in family life. In a good family, this vulnerability of children
generates feelings of compassion and responsibility in the parents. But
not in all families. In some families, parents feel privilege and proprietary rights more than concern and obligation. In these families, there
has to be some protection for the children. The texts of terror in the
book of Judges stand as powerful testimony to the potential results of
unchecked and unregulated power in heads of families and caution us
against withdrawing too much in the name of restoring "dignity" or "integrity" to the family.

We have also not solved the problem of maintaining and celebrating
group identity without reinforcing estrangement and enmity between
groups. Maintaining boundaries by coercion can create resentment and
friction within the group; maintaining them by "otherizing" all others
can create hostility between groups. And yet if boundaries totally collapse and we all become "one people," we will be alienated and divorced
from our separate traditions. We may also wind up alienated from a totality so large, homogenized, and amorphous that it offers no sense of
identity or continuity, no appreciation of historical purpose or continuation of ancient vectors and goals. The biblical stories of marriage to foreign women and of the destinies of Dinah and Judah are important
vehicles for exploring the advantages and dangers of openness and the
difficulty of maintaining identity without exclusivity. They also demonstrate the relationship between a strong sense of center and a worry
about boundaries.

Reading biblical stories gives us a forum to open up these questions,
to see the continuity of our modern dilemmas with ancient issues, and
to prevent us from reaching facile solutions, particularly solutions based
on a partial reading of only one biblical text that we emphasize over
others.

Grace and Critique

For those who wish to remain grounded in the faith communities that
focus on the Bible, it is important to realize that biblical stories about
victims are not misogynist and that the boundary stories are not simply

chauvinist or xenophobic. Understanding that these stories are frequently told as critiques of the social situations that they portray rather than in approval of them can lead us to applaud rather than deplore their inclusion in Scripture. Contemporary readers can read with a "hermeneutics of grace," a method of interpretation that recognizes the basic decency and well-meaning character of the biblical authors. But we should not congratulate ourselves too much or let the hermeneutics of grace totally supplant the critical modes of interpretation by which we continue to reexamine our traditions even as we preserve them. The Bible's metaphorical uses of women in stories and images are built on a reality in which women were powerless and vulnerable. Widows cannot epitomize the destitute when they are able to inherit land and have the economic means, training, and access to livelihood necessary for self-sufficiency. Women symbolize victimization only when they are so vulnerable that they continue to be victimized. They cease to represent the margins of society the moment they achieve power at the center. If we tell the biblical stories about women without taking note of the social system that gives them symbolic value, and naming its inequities, then we unwittingly help to perpetuate the skewed system that the Bible assumes. We need to expose the social underpinning of these stories as we tell them. Then the revealed substructure can illuminate the workings of the system within which the stories operate and cast the light of comparison or contrast on our own. The stories, together with an exposition of their social reality, present a structure much like the exposed pipes and conduits of Paris's Centre Georges Pompidou. This structure is revelatory, for it shows how everything fits together to form a working whole; it shows the relationships between the individual and the collective, between the personal and the political, and between the symbols and the unconscious attitudes that fuel the symbolism.

Mirrors

There is an enormous difference between the Bible's assumption that women are socially dependent and vulnerable and today's more egalitarian ideas. There have been many changes in the last two and a half millennia—technological, sociopolitical, biological, and ideological innovations that have contributed to this change of consciousness. But this difference does not make the biblical stories irrelevant. Once acknowledged, it allows us to hold up these stories as a mirror to our own social reality to see if our real situation conforms more to our own perception of the way things ought to be or to the stories' assumptions and the way things used to be. When we use these stories as a mirror, it becomes clear that in many respects, the more things change, the more they have stayed the same:

1. The widow is no longer the epitome of destitution, but our contemporary analog is the poor single mother who is unable to tend to her children and provide for them at the same time.

2. The abuse and battery of women in all strata of our society, from welfare mothers through "soccer moms," society matrons, and celebrity wives, says something about where power continues to reside, and speaks to the poisonous social demand that men be powerful and show their power somewhere, if not in the world, then at least in their home.

3. The constantly shocking abuse of children testifies to a home situation in which parents still reign unchecked, one in which they can treat their children as chattel and demonstrate their power over them with actual (if not legal) impunity.

4. The many instances of rape, both the rape of strangers and the "date rape" of noncompliant women, is a tear in our own social fabric, a glimpse at the rage and resentment barely beneath the surface of those who fear that they are losing their control and privilege.

All these contemporary "aberrations" show that our world is not as categorically different from the ancient world as we would like to believe. The stories do speak to issues in our society. When there is nothing in reality that corresponds to the biblical victim stories, then these stories (in their revealed state) will have done their job and the old metaphors will cease to have their power.

In the meantime—keep on listening. You never know where the word of God will speak. It may come from a Canaanite prostitute or a recognized oracle, a state official or an outlawed witch. The word of God appears where it will, and it is up to us to hear and recognize what we are hearing.

NOTES

Introduction

xv **What . . . do women want?** This is Freud's famous question, highly revealing of a mind-set that categorizes all women as "other" and then stereotypes them. For a full discussion of the results of looking in the Hebrew Bible with this question in mind, see Tikva Frymer-Kensky, *In the Wake of the Goddesses: Women, Culture and the Biblical Transformation of Pagan Myth* (New York: Free Press, 1993).

xviii **"texts of terror"** This term comes from Phyllis Trible, *Texts of Terror: Literary-Feminist Readings of Biblical Narratives,* Overtures to Biblical Theology (Philadelphia: Fortress Press, 1984). It has become a code word for this type of story.

xxv **"depatriarchalizing"** This is another term first used by Phyllis Trible, "Depatriarchalizing in Biblical Interpretation," *Journal of the American Academy of Religion* 41 (1973): 30–48.

The Hand That Rocks the Cradle: The Rivka Stories

5 **the important role that women could play** For an anthropological study of the power of women in such patriarchal households, see Jill Dubisch, "Introduction," and E. Friedl, "The Position of Women: Appearance and Reality," in *Gender and Power in Rural Greece,* ed. Jill Dubisch (Princeton: Princeton University Press, 1986), 42–52; and Susan Rogers, "Female Forms of Power and the Myth of Male Dominance," *American Ethnologist* 2 (1975): 727–56.

For this issue in the Hebrew Bible, see JoAnn Hackett, "In the Days of Jael: Reclaiming the History of Women in Ancient Israel," in *Immaculate and Powerful: The Female in Sacred Image and Social Reality,* ed. Clarissa Atkinson, Constance Buchanan, and Margaret Miles (Boston: Beacon Press, 1985), 15–38; Carol Meyers, *Discovering Eve: Ancient Israelite Women in Context* (Oxford: Oxford University Press, 1988); and T. R. Hobbs, "Man, Woman and Hospitality—2 Kings 4:8–36," *Biblical Theology Bulletin* 23 (1993): 91–100.

5 **coming right after the binding of Isaac** Meir Sternberg (*The Poetics of Biblical Narrative: Ideological Literature and the Drama of Reading* [Bloomington: Indiana University Press, 1985], 129–36) shows the structural analogy of the Isaac and Ishmael stories. Ishmael's story contains his late birth, mortal danger averted by divine intervention, and marriage to a compatriot of his Egyptian mother. The reader expects the same three parts for Isaac, and therefore something of his marriage "is now due by compositional logic."

6 **The placement of this birth notice** Lieve Teugels cites a rabbinic midrash that,

while Abraham was standing on Mount Moriah, "they came to tell him that the wife of his son was born (" 'A Strong Woman, Who Can Find?' A Study of Characterization in Genesis 24, with Some Perspectives on the General Presentation of Isaac and Rebekah in the Genesis Narratives," *Journal for the Study of the Old Testament* 63 [1994]: 89–104). Teugels also cites Benno Jacob's commentary on Genesis (*Das erste Buch der Torah*, 505), in which he stresses the relationship between this birth announcement and the death of Sarah at the beginning of the next chapter: Rebekkah will be Sarah's replacement, and is born before her death.

6 **Act I. The Marriage of Rivka** For studies of Genesis 24, important commentaries are E. A. Speiser, *Genesis*, Anchor Bible 1 (Garden City, N.Y.: Doubleday, 1964); Claus Westermann, *Genesis 12–36: A Commentary*, trans. John Scullion (Minneapolis: Augsburg, 1985); Victor P. Hamilton, *The Book of Genesis 1–17* and *The Book of Genesis 18–50*, The New International Commentary on the Old Testament (Grand Rapids: Eerdmans, 1990, 1995); Nahum Sarna, *Genesis*, Jewish Publication Society Torah Commentary (Philadelphia: JPS, 1989). Independent studies are Susanne Gillmayr-Bucher, "The Woman of Their Dreams: The Image of Rebekah in Genesis 24," in *The World of Genesis: Persons, Places, Perspectives*, ed. Philip Davies and David Clines, JSOT suppl. 257 (Sheffield: Sheffield Academic Press, 1998), 90–101; Andrew Schein, "The Test of Rebecca," *Tradition* 31 (1996/97): 28–33; Lieve Teugels, "The Anonymous Matchmaker: An Enquiry into the Characterization of the Servant of Abraham in Genesis 24," *JSOT* (1995): 13–23; Teugels, "A Strong Woman"; C. Turiot, "Le marriage d'Isaac (Gen. 24). Un texte a lire aujourd'hui," *Sémiotique et Bible* 51 (1988): 22–35; M. Sternberg, "The Wooing of Rebekah," in *The Poetics of Biblical Narrative*, Indiana Studies in Biblical Literature (Bloomington: University of Indiana Press, 1985), 131–52; Kenneth Aitken, "The Wooing of Rebekkah: A Study in the Development of the Tradition," *JSOT* 30 (1984): 3–23; Wolfgang Roth, "The Wooing of Rebekah: A Tradition-Critical Study of Genesis 24," *Catholic Biblical Quarterly* 34 (1972): 177–87.

Alexander Rofé's very important article ("An Enquiry into the Betrothal of Rebekah," in *Die Hebräische Bible und ihre zweifache Nachgeschicte: Festschrift für Rolf Rendtorff*, ed. Erhard Blum, Christian Macholz, and Ekkehard Stegemann [Neukirchen-Vluyn: Neukirchener Verlag, 1990], 27–30) deals with the dating of this story and argues convincingly that it comes from a late postexilic era. Aitken argues for a long oral history ("Wooing of Rebekkah"), as does Westermann (*Genesis 12–36*); Rofé rejects even that ("An Enquiry"). Since the form of the story as we have it has late expressions, it seems certain that the story is at least revised in the later period. I agree with Rofé that the story as we have it is part of the polemic of the Ezra–Nehemiah period, for which see the discussion in the chapter on Ruth, pp. 238–56.

8 **ideal woman** See the discussions by Gillmayr-Bucher ("The Woman of Their Dreams") and Teugels ("A Strong Woman"). Teugels adds that Rivka has the right descent; that she is a virgin, and then, at the end of the story, when she veils herself, that she also has appropriate humility. "Virgin" is Teugel's value, and Schein's ("The Test"). The Hebrew *betulah* means only the appropriate age for a bride.

9 **Chastity** See discussion by Tikva Frymer-Kensky, "Virginity in the Bible," in *Gender and Law in the Hebrew Bible and the Ancient Near East*, ed. Tikva Frymer-Kensky, Victor Matthews, and Bernard Levinson, JSOT supp. 262 (Sheffield: Sheffield Academic Press, 1998): 79–96.

9 **She is also very strong** Teugels ("A Strong Woman") contrasts the strong, active Rebekkah with the absent, passive Isaac. Isaac is the bearer, precious vessel, or incarnation of the promise, and Rebekkah is the divinely sent helper responsible for the proper transmission to the next generation. He notes that Rivka is characterized by her actions, Isaac by nonspeech and nonaction, and the servant by speech.

10 **mother's house** For functions of the mother, see initially Carol Meyers, " 'To Her Mother's House': Considering a Counterpart to the Israelite *bêt ʾab*," in *The Bible and the Politics of Exegesis: Essays in Honor of Norman K. Gottwald on His Sixty-fifth Birthday*, ed. David Jobling, Peggy Day, and Gerald Sheppard (Cleveland, Ohio: Pilgrim Press, 1991), 39–51.

11 **"spin" on the matter** Teugels ("The Anonymous Matchmaker") considers the distortions in the envoy's account to be close to intimidation. In a similar vein, Schein ("The Test") argues that the envoy had done his research, that he had prayed for help, that he found the girl and then spun it all to make it look like divine inevitability. Susanne Gillmayr-Bucher ("The Woman of Their Dreams") identifies his use of the term *naʿarah* with his dream of the ideal wife as someone who will help, will anticipate wishes and fulfill them gladly. The term appears again in vv. 55 and 57 (*nʿr* ketib) when she is asked whether she will go. The one who filled the servant's wishes now agrees to become the wife.

13 **"We will call the girl . . ."** Susanne Gillmayr-Bucher draws attention to the terms. They call the *naʿarah*—the one who has fulfilled the servant's desires—and ask her for the one thing that will make her an *ʾiššah*.

13 **second Abraham** Commentators have remarked on the absence of information about Isaac and how that emphasizes Rebekkah's courage. Mary Donavan Turner considers her a "hero" who follows Abraham ("Rebekah: Ancestor of Faith," *Lexington Theological Quarterly* 20[1985]: 42–50); Teugels ("A Strong Woman") stresses her "unconditional faith."

14 **in the same language** See the discussion by Sternberg (*The Poetics*).

14 **her family's blessing** Many commentators have noted that this blessing is the same as the blessing given to Abraham in Gen. 22:17. Mary Donovan Turner ("Rebekah: Ancestor of Faith"), noting that *yaraš* is used for Abraham, Rivka, and then Jacob, concludes that these three are the ancestors of this promise.

15 **Abraham's servant, who represented him** Teugels points out that the family treats him as if he were Abraham, calling him "blessed" (as God blessed Abraham) and "master" ("anonymous").

15 **autonomous person** Gillmayr-Bucher points out that going out after the servant is the first verb of Rivka's action that is not a response to some other anticipatory verb. In this case she gets up and leaves, and then the servant takes her.

15 **veils herself** Teugels speaks about her humility as yet another desirable characteristic of a wife; however, he assumes that "what is fit and predestined from a 'divine' point of view does not appear so from a 'human point of view' " ("A Strong Woman," 103). But, says the story, "he loved her."

15 **The Assyrian laws** MAL A, 40, 41.

15 **could be disposable** See the discussion on pp. 91–92.

16 **she goes directly to inquire of YHWH** On the birth oracle, see Sharon Pace Jeansome, "Genesis 25:23—The Use of Poetry in the Rebekkah Narratives," in *The Psalms and Other Studies on the Old Testament Presented to Joseph I. Hunt*, ed. Jack Knight and Lawrence Sinclair (Nashotah, Wis.: Nashotah House Seminary, 1990), 145–52. Jeansome points out that the use of poetry draws attention to the oracle as the guide to what follows.

16 **sibling rivalry** On this issue, see Susan Niditch, *Underdogs and Tricksters: A Prelude to Biblical Folklore* (New York: Harper & Row, 1987); Dan W. Forsyth, "Sibilant Rivalry, Aesthetic Sensibility and Social Structure in Genesis," *Ethos* 19 (1991): 453–510; Everett Fox, "Stalking the Younger Brother: Some Models for Understanding a Biblical Motif," *JSOT* 60 (1993): 45–68; and Frederick Greenspahn, *When Brothers Dwell Together: The Preeminence of Younger Siblings in the Hebrew Bible* (New York: Oxford University Press, 1994).

16 **The birth of the twins** Yael Feldman (" 'And Rebecca loved Jacob' but Freud did not," *Jewish Studies Quarterly* 1 [1993]: 72–88), points out that twins enable the story to circumvent the triangularity of family dynamics, normally a fundamental presupposition of classical psychoanalysis. This "squaring the triangle" neatly distributes loyalties, allowing dyadic parent-child bonding.

17 **Mesopotamian collections of oracles** See the Namburbi oracles published by Richard Caplice ("Namburbi Texts in the British Museum," *Orientalia* 34 [1965]: 105–31; "Further Namburbi Notes," *Orientalia* 42 [1973]: 508–17). For the ritual of the substitute king, see initially Marti Nissinen, *References to Prophecy in Neo-Assyrian Sources*, State Archives of Assyria Studies 7 (Helsinki: Helsinki University Press, 1998).

17 **time to transfer the family heritage** For recent studies of this passage, see William Propp, "Pulling the Goat Hair over Isaac's Eyes," *Bible Review* 14 (1998): 20; Benjamin Goodnick, "Jacob's Deception of His Father," *Jewish Bible Quarterly* 22 (1994): 237–40; Joseph Rackman, "Was Isaac Deceived?" *Judaism* 43 (1994): 37–45; Adrien Bledstein, "Binder, Trickster, Heel and Hairy-Man: Rereading Genesis 27 as a Trickster Tale Told by a Woman," in *A Feminist Companion to Genesis*, ed. Athalya Brenner (Sheffield: Sheffield Academic Press, 1993).

18 **Rivka is faced with a problem** Westermann compares Rivka's rising up against the privilege of the firstborn to Hagar rising up against Sarai's oppression.

18 **Nuzi** See the discussion by Speiser, *Genesis*, Anchor Bible.

18 **going to ensure that the omen of Jacob's destiny will be fulfilled** As Mary Donovan Turner points out, the story never explicitly tells us that Rivka acted because of the oracle or because of "a fierce overprotectiveness of Jacob," and this ambiguity has caused commentators to either praise or condemn Rivka (Turner, "Rebekah: Ancestor of Faith").

18 **more likely to care for her in her old age** So Fewell and Gunn, who also observe that her knowledge that God has chosen Jacob lets her manipulate Isaac's authority (David Nolan Fewell and David Gunn, *Gender, Power and Promise: The Subject of the Bible's First Story* [Nashville: Abingdon Press, 1993]. Naomi Steinberg similarly points both to the oracle that determined her favoritism and to the idea that the

loyalty she will receive from Jacob will ensure her own place ("Gender Roles in Rebekkah Cycle," *Union Seminary Quarterly Bulletin,* 39 [1984]: 175–88).

18 **knowledge of sheep breeding** See Propp ("Pulling the Goat Hair").

18 **Abigail and the Wise Woman of Tekoa** See the discussion on pp. 58–63.

18 **take upon themselves the consequences of the acts** According to Turner, this offer shows Rivka passing a test as difficult as Abraham's binding of Isaac.

19 **trickery** See Richard A. Freund, "Lying and Deception in the Biblical and Post-Biblical Judaic Tradition," *Scandinavian Journal of the Old Testament* (1991): 45–61; and O. Horn Prouser, "The Truth About Women and Lying," *JSOT* 61 (1994): 15–28. The fact that Rebecca is a woman trickster has resulted in considerable debate, beginning with Esther Fuchs, "Who is Hiding the Truth? Deceptive Women and Biblical Androcentrism," in *Feminist Perspectives on Biblical Scholarship,* ed. Adela Yarbro Collins, SBL Centennial Publications 10 (Chico, Calif.: Scholars, 1985): 137–44; see also Ann W. Engar, "Old Testament Women as Tricksters," in *Mappings of the Biblical Terrain: The Bible as Text,* ed. Vincent L. Tollers and John Maier (Lewisburg, Pa.: Bucknell University Press, 1990): 143–57, who points out that the trickery of these women involves intelligence, in that the woman understands the needs of family or people and faith, since the trickery is blessed by God and brings about his will. Rebekkah consciously forms herself as God's instrument.

19 **The story never tells us that Rivka must use deception** Esther Fuchs ("Who Is Hiding the Truth?") believes that the lack of explicit explanation perpetuates androcentric reading of text and stereotypes women as untrustworthy. But the biblical readers would not have reacted in this way.

19 **valued cunning in the underdog** They told stories about the ancestor Jacob as the trickster who tricks and then gets tricked. Isaac tricked Abimelech, Jacob tricked Isaac, Laban tricked Jacob (by giving him Leah instead of Rachel), Rachel tricked Laban (with the teraphim). In another chain of trickery, Jacob tricked Isaac, Jacob's sons tricked him (when they sold Joseph), Joseph tricked Jacob's sons (with the cup).

19 **Early interpreters** Turner ("Rebekah: Ancestor of Faith") demonstrates how early Jewish Midrash and Christian interpreters, such as Ambrose and Origen, praised Rivka, as did Luther and Calvin. Bible scholars of the nineteenth and twentieth centuries, on the other hand, condemned her strongly for her deceit of Isaac. I would add that it was not only her trick but her proactivity and independence of opinion from Isaac that upset these scholars, whose own ideal of womanhood was much more passive and innocent. For more or less contemporary condemnations of Rivka, see Gary Rendsburg ("Notes on Genesis XXXV," *Vetus Testamentum* 34 [1984]: 361–66), who claims that the biblical note that Rivka's nurse died is a way of pointedly ignoring Rivka's own destiny, and is therefore a clue to let readers conclude that Scripture is unhappy with her actions. Contrary to his title, Donald Sharp ("In Defense of Rebecca?", *Biblical Theology Bulletin* 10 [1980]: 164–68) concludes that Rivka's actions "can be viewed as pure selfishness" but suggests that the depiction of Esau as hairy and undomesticated is Jacob's implicit defense for Rebecca. Christine Garside Allen ("Who Was Rebekah? On Me Be the Curse, My Son!" in *Beyond Androcentrism: New Essays on Women and Re-*

ligion, ed. Rita M. Gross [Missoula, Mont.: Scholars Press, 1977], 183–216) strikes home as she asks whether the male commentators consider that the most serious error that Rebekah committed was deceiving her husband.

19 **divine guidance** See Kenneth Aitken, "The Wooing of Rebekka," *JSOT* 30 (1984): 3–23.

20 **Did Isaac know?** Bledstein and Rackman both claim that he did. Jacob makes mistakes. Goodnick ("Jacob's Deception of His Father") points out that Jacob lost his cool and addressed his father with an imperative, *qum,* "arise," whereas Esau uses the more polite *yaqum,* "let (my father) arise." He suggests that Jacob was stressed by the deceit. Propp ("Pulling the Goat Hair") suggests that Isaac's first question, "Who are you, my son," is like Naomi's question to Ruth, "Who are you, my daughter," which both mean "How did you fare?" and that Esau would have responded by reporting on the hunting. Since Jacob answers literally, Isaac's suspicions were aroused.

22 **guilt-producing rhetoric** See Tikva Frymer-Kensky, *In the Wake of the Goddesses.*

22 **Recent anthropological fieldwork** See Jill Dubisch, ed., *Gender and Power,* in the first note on this chapter.

Saviors of the Exodus

For important early studies of these stories, see Moshe Greenberg, *Understanding Exodus* (New York: Behrman House, 1969); Uriel Cassuto, *Peruš al Sefer Shmot* (Jerusalem: Magnes, 1959). For commentaries, see Brevard Childs, *The Book of Exodus* (Philadelphia: Westminster, 1974); Benno Jacob, *The Second Book of the Bible: Exodus,* trans. Walter Jacob (Hoboken: Ktav, 1992); and William Propp, *Exodus 1–18* (New York: Doubleday, 1999).

24 **the midwives** C. Isbell, "Exodus 1–2 in the Context of Exodus 1–14: Story Lines and Key Words," in *Art and Meaning: Rhetoric in Biblical Literature,* ed. David J. A. Clines, David M. Gunn, and Alan J. Hauser, JSOT supp. 19 (Sheffield: JSOT, 1982), 44–53; Renita Weems, "The Hebrew Women Are Not Like the Egyptian Women: The Ideology of Race, Gender and Sexual Reproduction in Exodus 1," *Semeia* 39 (1992): 25–34; Thomas Römer, "Les Sages-femmes du Pharaon (Exode 1/15–20)," *Études théologiques et religieuses* 69 (1994): 265–70.

24 **Hebrew midwives** Römer argues that logic demands that they were Egyptians, since they clearly also assisted at Egyptian births ("Sages-femmes du Pharaon"). However, higher-class women may use lower-class midwives, as whites used black midwives in the American South. But lower-class women do not generally have midwives from the upper classes.

25 **Pharaoh is no fool** Pharoah is often read as a fool by modern authors. But his logic works within his own perspective. His error that oppression can defeat the "Other" has been repeated often in history. Dismissing Pharaoh as a fool draws attention away from an indictment of this error. But this error certainly prevents Pharaoh from being the embodiment of divine wisdom.

25 **Shifrah** The Septuagint renders this Sephora, giving her the same name as Zipporah, wife of Moses.

25 **Pu'ah** Römer suggests that the name, related to Ugaritic *pġt,* "young girl," reinforces the idea that the story is written as a prelude to the story of the daughters ("Sages-femmes du Pharaon").

25 **Fearing God** Römer argues that "fearing God" is attributed to foreigners, as in Gen. 20:8 and Jon. 1:10, 17, and that these texts are late, reflecting Israel's diaspora experience of other nations fearing God (ibid.). However, the term is also applied to Israel, as in Genesis 22. Significantly, it is often associated with admonitions to Israel to "do good" or "refrain from evil." (See discussion in Tikva Frymer-Kensky, "The Akedah: A View from the Bible," in *Beginning Anew: A Woman's Companion to the High Holy Days,* ed. Gail Twersky Reimer and Judith A. Kates [New York: Touchstone Books, 1997]). The phrase cannot indicate either the nationality of the midwives or the date of the text.

25 **they refuse to obey immoral orders** Rose Salberg Kam suggests that they are obedient to "an inner law of nurturing life that they place above mere human commands" (*Their Stories, Our Stories: Women of the Bible* (New York: Continuum, 1995), 82.

25 **they trick Pharaoh** As Weems points out, this is the conventional weapon of the powerless. In this weapon of deception, the "truth" is not defined by the powerful, and the underclass can shape it according to their own reality ("Hebrew Women"). Kam points out that this tale is designed to enable Pharaoh to save face (*Their Stories, Our Stories*).

26 **denigration of Israel is ludicrous** Weems ("Hebrew Women") goes a step further, holding that the narrator exposes Egyptian hegemony over the Hebrew people as farce. But I am prevented from reading it as farce by the fact that Pharaoh's response results in the death of babies.

26 **God rewards them** Many exegetes have suggested that this verse is a later addition; Römer suggests that the previous verse is ("Sages-femmes du Pharaon"). But there is no reason to consider the verses repetitive: one talks about the result for Israel—increase in population; the second about the result for midwives—an established posterity. Mention of a posterity is also a clue that they have now exited the story. Römer also suggests that the entire story never existed independently but was an elaboration of the story that went from enslavement directly to the order to throw the boys in the Nile, thus forming a prelude to the Exodus (ibid.).

26 **throw the boy children into the Nile** As noted by Benno Jacob (*Second Book of the Bible*) and then by Exum ("You Shall Let"), Pharaoh forgets to specify Hebrew boy children. Exum suggests that the demand to kill male infants foreshadows the final plague, the killing of the firstborn.

26 **tells them to let the daughters live** As noted already by Phyllis Trible, had Pharaoh realized the effectiveness of women in thwarting his decree, he would have better commanded the female infants to be killed ("Depatriarchalizing in Biblical Interpretation," *Journal of the American Academy of Religion* 41 [1973]: 30–48).

26 **the daughters** Early studies of this story are by Moshe Greenberg, *Understanding Exodus;* and J. S. Ackerman, "The Literary Context of the Moses Birth Story (Exodus 1–2)," in *Literary Interpretations of Biblical Narratives,* ed. K. R. R. Louis, J. S. Ackerman, and T. S. Warshaw (Nashville: Abingdon Press, 1974), 74–119. More re-

cently, see J. Cheryl Exum, "You Shall Let Every Daughter Live: A Study of Exodus 1:8–2:10," *Semeia* 28 (1983): 63–82; Exum, "Second Thoughts About Secondary Characters: Women in Exodus 1:8–2:10," in *A Feminist Companion to Exodus and Deuteronomy,* ed. Athalya Brenner (Sheffield: Sheffield Academic Press, 1994), 75–87; J. Siebert-Hommes, "Twelve Women in Exodus 1 and 2: The Role of Daughters and Sons in the Stories Concerning Moses," in idem., 62–74 (originally in *Amsterdamse Cahiers voor Exegese en Bijbelse Theologie* 12 [1988]: 47–58).

26 **gave birth to a son** Exum notes the irony that without Moses there would be no story, but without the initiative of the women there would be no Moses ("You Shall Let").

26 **His sister** Exum notes that the sister deserves as much credit for saving the baby as the mother or the princess (ibid.).

26 **and took** For this understanding, see Cassuto (*Peruš al Sefer Shmot*).

28 **Moshe** Exum remarks on the "irony which results from the allusion to Moses' role in the Exodus" ("You Shall Let"), but I do not understand foreshadowing allusions as irony. For fuller discussion of the name, see Jacob, *Second Book of the Bible*.

28 **"draws out" Israel** See Isa. 63:11.

28 **triad of daughters** Exum ("You Shall Let") rightly rejects Ackerman's suggestion ("Literary Context") that the variation Moshe/*mashuy* is meant to be a mistake that pokes fun at a foolish princess.

28 **"Bithya"** Josephus names her Thermuthis (Antiquities 2.224) and Jubilees calls her Tarmut (47:5). Artapanus, according to Eusebius (Praep. Ev. 9:27), calls her Merris.

28 **Three subversive daughters** J. Siebert-Hommes notes that there were twelve daughters ("Twelve Women"). I do not see why three women acting together render women less powerful than one savior would have been, as Exum contends in "Second Thoughts."

28 **have foiled the plans of men** In "Second Thoughts," Exum rejects reading with the text even though the portrayal of women is affirmative. It is certainly true that the text shows us only the ideas about women of the "(probably male) narrators," but it is the text we are investigating here rather than a historical or social reality that may or may not lie behind the text. Exum suggests that according recognition to women as national heroes is a strategy of patriarchy to reward women for complicity. The Hebrew Bible text gives no evidence that it sees life as a battle between the sexes, or that it consciously assumes that sexual politics are necessary to keep women in line. Should we say that portraying men as heroes keeps them in line? After all, most men do not have power, either. A society that is to function without constant punitive measures of violent social control has to create a climate in which people are encouraged to act for the public good. Recognition of heroism is one such mechanism.

29 **The Wife** For important early studies, see G. Vermes, "Baptism and Jewish Exegesis: New Light from Ancient Sources," *New Testament Studies* 4 (1957–58): 308–29; and Vermes, "Circumcision and Exodus IV 24–26: Prelude to a Theology of Baptism," in his *Scripture and Tradition in Judaism: Haggadic Studies,* 2d rev. ed., Studia post-Biblica 4 (Leiden: Brill, 1973). More recent studies include C. Houtman, "Exodus 4:24–26 and Its Interpretation," *Journal of the Northwest Semitic Languages* 11 (1983): 178–92; Lawrence Kaplan, " 'And the Lord Sought to Kill Him'

(Exodus 4:24): Yet Once Again," *Hebrew Annual Review* 5 (1981): 65–74; Bernard Robinson, "Zipporah to the Rescue: A Contextual Study of Exodus 4:24–26," *Vetus Testamentum* 36 (1986): 447–62; William Propp, "The Origins of Infant Circumcision in Israel," *Hebrew Annual Review* 11 (1987): 355–70; Ilana Pardes, "Zipporah and the Struggle for Deliverance," in her *Countertraditions in the Bible: A Feminist Approach* (Cambridge: Harvard University Press, 1992), 79–97; Thomas Römer, "De l'archaïque au subversif: le cas d'Exode 4/24–26," *Études théologiques et religieuses* 69 (1994): 1–11; G. W. Ashby, "The Bloody Bridegroom: The Interpretation of Exodus 4:24–26," *The Expository Times* 106 (1995): 203–5; Terry John Lehane, "Zipporah and the Passover," *Jewish Bible Quarterly* 24 (1996): 46–50; William Propp, "That Bloody Bridegroom (Exodus 4:24–26)," *Vetus Testamentum* 43 (1993): 495–518.

29 **which son** Jewish commentary often considers it to be Eliezer, the younger son, but Robinson argues that it must be the firstborn Gershom, the only one whose birth has been mentioned and the firstborn. This would make the firstborn of Egypt liable for the Pharaoh's mistreatment of God's firstborn, Israel, and Gershom to suffer for the "sin of his father Moses" in first refusing to serve ("Zipporah to the Rescue"). This parallelism would work only if God attacked Gershom, not Moses, which Robinson does not suggest but is possible.

29 **probably Moses** So understood by the Targums, cf. Shmot Rabbah 1:33, 5:8, for discussion see also TJ Nedarim 3, 9.

29 **"seeking to kill"** For this idiom, see Jer. 26:21, *biqqeš hamîtô*.

29 **narrator leaves this ambiguous** For this, see Greenberg, *Understanding Exodus;* and Stephen Geller, "The Struggle at the Jabbok: The Uses of Enigma in Biblical Narrative," *Journal of the Ancient Near East Society* 14 (1984): 37–60, reprinted in Geller, *Sacred Enigmas: Literary Religion in the Hebrew Bible* (London: Routledge, 1996).

29 **noncircumcision of his son** For a collection of early sources giving this reason, see Vermes, "Baptism and Jewish Exegesis." Cassuto suggests that the son (whom he considers the older) had not been circumcised since travelers were not circumcised, and Moses considered himself a traveler in Midian. For this reason, he claims, the generation of the wandering in the desert was not circumcised (*Peruš al Sefer Shmot*).

29 **Some scholars** See Ashby (op. cit.) and Robinson ("Zipporah to the Rescue").

30 **doing God's bidding** A variant of the idea that the attack is related to Moses' initial refusal to go to Egypt concentrates on the psychology of Moses, seeing the attack as what Buber called an "event of the night," the sudden collapse of the newly certain one shared by other religious founders. For Martin Buber, *Moses* (London: Phaidon, 1946), 209, n. 54, see Sherry Shulewitz ("Zipporah's Role").

30 **bloodguilt** See Propp, "Bloody Bridegroom." Propp suggests that Moses' flight to Midian would have been seen as a murderer's quest for asylum. Now returning home with unexpiated bloodguilt prompts the attack.

30 **dangerous ordeal** On this, see the authors cited by Robinson ("Zipporah to the Rescue"). Robinson is "sure" that this was not the original import of the story but that it nevertheless has this element now. For details of the parallels to the Jabbok story, see Römer ("De l'archaïque au subversif"); and Stephen Geller, "The Struggle at the Jabbok."

30 **circumcises their son** For some reason, Ashby is uncertain whether Zipporah circumcises Moses or Gershom ("Bloody Bridegroom"). Perhaps they are influenced by Wellhausen's idea that the son's circumcision was vicarious for the others and Gressman's emendation to make Moses the one circumcised. For a discussion of this theory, see Robinson ("Zipporah to the Rescue").

30 **blood of the firstborn** See Lehane, "Zipporah and the Passover." Cassuto suggests that, as the firstborn suffers for the deeds of his father, so here, a few drops of blood from the son protect the father (*Peruš al Sefer Shmot*).

30 **Joshua circumcised Israel** The parallels are noted by Robert Alter, who points out that the word *baderek*, "on the way," is used in both stories (*The World of Biblical Literature* [New York: Basic Books, 1992], 117–21).

30 **Traditional rituals** Ashby ("Bloody Bridegroom") points out that until recently, the Paschal Candle had to be lit "from the flint," though the flint in a cigarette lighter was all right.

30 **"bridegroom in blood"** Robinson has Zipporah saying "son-in-law by virtue of blood"; that by touching the foreskin to Moses, she has circumcised him symbolically and thus has become Moses' father-in-law ("Zipporah to the Rescue"). Bill Propp suggests that Zipporah's statement, "for me," indicates she has acted as the *hoten*, the circumciser ("Origins of Infant Circumcision").

31 *Hatan* See discussion in E. Kutsch, *htn*, in *Theological Dictionary of the Old Testament*, ed. G. Johannes Bottenweck and Helmer Ringgren, trans. John T. Willis (Grand Rapids: Eerdmans, 1977); T. G. Mitchel, "The Meaning of the Noun *htn* in the Old Testament," *Vetus Testamentum* 19 (1969): 93–112; and Ruth and Erhard Blum, "Zippora und ihr hatan dammim," in *Die hebräische Bible und ihre zweifache Nachgeschichte: Festschrift für Rolf Rendtorff zum 65. Geburtstag*, ed. Erhard Blum, Christian Macholz, and Ekkehard Stegemann (Neukirchen-Vluyn: Neukirchener Verlag, 1990), 41–54.

31 **blood-sealed covenant** See discussion by Cassuto (*Peruš al Sefer Shmot*) and by Blum and Blum ("Zippora"). Benno Jacob suggests that every circumcision renews the marital bond (*Second Book of the Bible*).

31 *damim* Propp ("That Bloody Bridegroom"), following Gisela Schneemann, ("Die Deutung und Bedeutung der Beschneidung nach Exod. 4:24–26," *Theologische Literaturzeitung* 105 [1980]: 794), "a bridegroom who has shed blood." Seeing the attack, Zipporah has realized that Moses had committed murder. She then improvises a blood expiation for him, symbolically circumcising him by touching the bloody foreskin to his genitalia. Propp suggests that the original sense of *damim* is the blood of circumcision, later on developing the sense of bloodguilt. Noting the connection of circumcision to puberty and marriage, Propp remarks on the similarity of the story to ritual ordeals undergone by men at puberty, at a time in which many cultures also circumcise them (ibid.).

31 **protective value of circumcision** For this aspect of circumcision, see Propp ("Origins of Infant Circumcision").

31 **almost incantatory words** Shulewitz believes that Zipporah turns to incantatory ritual in her role as culture bearer, and that the narrative brings out woman's role in the transmission of culture ("Zipporah's Role").

31 **Isis** For the presentation of Isis in relation to Zipporah, see Pardes ("Zipporah and the Struggle"). The connection with Anat and Ishtar and the animals is my own.

32 **narrator of the last line** This "gloss" makes it likely that this is an old story. The antiquity of the story does not mean that Römer ("De l'archaïque au subversif") is wrong in considering part of the discussion on foreign women. The inclusion of a story so frightening and so difficult to understand in the final editing of the text may have been to make a statement about a savior foreign woman. It also makes a statement about experience of the frightening aspect of God, with which survivors of the destructions of Israel and Judah would have been familiar.

32 **identifying Zipporah's statement with *mulôt*** Blum and Blum understand the narrator as saying "in reference to the cutting," meaning that the blood here was not in connection with defloration but by cutting. However, they believe the issue is that Zipporah and her son are now joining Israel ("Zippora").

32 **prevent a killing** Römer points to the use of *hymt* in both stories, in 1:16 and 4:24. Römer emphasizes that the savior and, by extension, the people, owe their lives to foreign women. He considers this text exilic rather than archaic, part of the discussion of foreign women ("De l'archaïque au subversif"). But since the mother of Moses is prominent in the intermediate story, we should modify this to say women in general. This may not make this any less "subversive" (Römer's term, ibid.) from the way the Bible is usually read.

The Guardian at the Door: Rahab

Studies: Robert Culley, "Stories of the Conquest: Joshua 2, 6, 7, 8," *Hebrew Annual Review* 8 (1984): 25–44; Phyllis Bird, "The Harlot as Heroine: Narrative Art and Social Presupposition in Three Old Testament Texts," *Semeia* 46 (1989): 119–39; Magnus Ottosson, "Rahab and the Spies," in *Dumu-é-dub-ba-a: Studies in Honor of Åke Sjöberg*, ed. Hermann Behrens, Darlene Loding, and Martha Roth (Philadelphia: Babylonian Section, University Museum, 1989), 419–27; Yair Zakovitch, "Humor and Theology or the Successful Failure of Israelite Intelligence: A Literary-Folkloric Approach to Joshua 2," in *Text and Tradition: The Hebrew Bible and Folklore*, ed. Susan Niditch (Atlanta: Scholars Press, 1990), 75–98; Frank M. Cross, "Reply to Zakovitch," idem., 99–106; Bernard Mehlman, "Rahab as a Model of Human Redemption," in *"Open Thou Mine Eyes . . . ": Essays on Aggadah and Judaica Presented to Rabbi William G. Braude on his Eightieth Birthday and Dedicated to His Memory*, ed. Herman J. Blumberg et al. (Hoboken: Ktav, 1992), 193–207; L. Daniel Hawk, "Strange Houseguests: Rahab, Lot and the Dynamics of Deliverance," in *Reading Between Texts: Intertextuality and the Hebrew Bible*, ed. Danna Nolan Fewell (Louisville: Westminster/John Knox, 1992), 89–97; and Tikva Frymer-Kensky, "Reading Rahab," in *Tehillah le-Moshe: Biblical and Judaic Studies in Honor of Moshe Greenberg*, ed. Mordechai Cogan, Barry Eichler, and Jeffrey Tigay (Winona Lake, Ind.: Eisenbrauns, 1997), 57–68. For commentary treatments, see J. Alberto Soggin, *Joshua: A Commentary*, Old Testament Library (London: SCM, 1972); and Robert Boling, *Joshua: A New Translation with Notes and Commentary*, Anchor Bible 6 (Garden City, N.Y.: Doubleday, 1982).

35 **two ordinary men** For this comparison, see Robert Culley ("Stories of the Conquest") and Yair Zakovitch ("Humor and Theology"). Zakovitch overplays the ordinariness of the men, whom he considers "first-class bunglers" (ibid.).

35 **Whatever their reason** Ottosson suggests that the men went to Rahab's house because she was associated with them, either because she was originally a no-madic woman or because she belonged to social circles ("Rahab and the Spies").

35 **the king finds out** Zakovitch is very unkind, suggesting that she herself told the king ("Humor and Theology," 85). There is no basis for this in the text.

37 **first of the inhabitants of the land** See Gordon Mitchell, "Together in the Land: A Reading of the Book of Joshua," *Journal for the Study of the Old Testament* 134 (1993): 152–90.

37 **vocabulary of Israel's holy war** Dennis McCarthy, "Some Holy War Vocabulary in Joshua 2," *Catholic Bible Commentary* 33 (1971): 228–30.

37 **the Song of the Sea** The connection was noted by the rabbis in the Mekhilta *Shi-rata* 9. Zakovitch notes that Rahab reverses the order of the two sentences, as is the rule in biblical quotations ("Humor and Theology," 89).

37 **Deuteronomic form of covenants** See K. M. Campbell, "Rahab's Covenant," *Vetus Testamentum* 22 (1972): 243–45.

38 **conquest of Bethel** The importance of this analogy is noted by Boling (*Joshua*).

38 **Abimelech proposes a treaty** The parallel is noted by Ottosson ("Rahab and the Spies").

39 **the destruction of Sodom and Gomorrah** For a reading of these two texts to-gether, see L. Daniel Hawk ("Strange Houseguests"). To his parallels, I would add that both stories took place in the same geographical plane. Hawk concludes that Rahab comes out much better than Lot.

40 **Deut. 7:2** See also Deut. 20:17. For discussion, see "To the Barricades," pp. 199–208.

41 **break the rule of the ḥerem** For discussions of this issue, see Lyle Eslinger, *Into the Hands of the Living God* (Sheffield: Almond, 1989), 24–25. Robert Polzin consid-ers the whole story to be a meditation on the issues of justice and mercy (*Moses and the Deuteronomist: A Literary Study of the Deuteronomic History* [Bloomington: Indiana University Press, 1993]). Polzin's argument requires him to make Rahab deserving of extermination and undeserving of being saved. This is very uncon-vincing.

42 **ḥerem is not an absolute** See Mitchell ("Together in the Land").

43 **those who were convinced by the reports of God's might** See Lawson Stone, "Ethical and Apologetic Tendencies in the Redaction of the Book of Joshua," *Catholic Biblical Quarterly* 53 (1991): 25–36.

44 **wide-open door** In this spirit, Lyle Eslinger states that Rahab is a whore because she is the door "left open by the divine whoremonger, through which the Is-raelites are led to stray, 'a-whoring after other Gods' " (*Into the Hands of the Living God,* 46).

44 **the prostitute** For this aspect of the story, see Phyllis Bird ("The Harlot as Heroine").

Warriors by Weapon and Word: Deborah and Yael

DEBORAH

There is a prodigious amount of literature on both the story and the song. The stan-dard commentary treatments are Robert Boling, *Judges,* Anchor Bible 6A (Garden

City, N.Y.: Doubleday, 1975); and J. Alberto Soggin, *Judges: A Commentary*, 2d ed., Old Testament Library (London: SCM, 1987). The historical situation has been studied by (among others) Heinz-Dieter Neef, "Deboraerzählung und Deboralied: Beobachtungen zum Verhältnis von Jdc. IV und V," *Vetus Testamentum* 44 (1994): 47–60; David Schloen, "Caravans, Kenites, and *Casus belli:* Enmity and Alliance in the Song of Deborah," *Catholic Biblical Quarterly* 55 (1993): 18–38; Lawrence Stager, "The Song of Deborah: Why Some Tribes Answered the Call and Others Did Not," *Biblical Archaeology Review* 15, no. 1 (1989): 51–64; and Stager, "Archaeology, Ecology, and Social History: Background Themes to the Song of Deborah," *Congress Volume: Jerusalem, 1986,* ed. John A. Emerton (Leiden: Brill, 1988), 221–34.

The literary structure of the story has been given careful scrutiny and mapping by Yairah Amit, "Judges 4: Its Contents and Form," *Journal for the Study of the Old Testament* 39 (1987): 89–11; and by Stephen Hanselman, "Narrative Theory, Ideology and Transformation in Judges 4," in *Anti-Covenant: Counter-reading Women's Lives in the Hebrew Bible,* ed. Mieke Bal (Nashville: Abingdon Press), 95–111, who believes that the structure accentuates the role of the women. Athalya Brenner compares the structure of the story and the song and finds that the poem, which includes Sisera's mother, also shows Yael mediating between the two mothers ("A Triangle and a Rhombus in Narrative Structure: A Proposed Integrative Reading of Judges IV and V," *Vetus Testamentum* 40 [1990]: 131–38).

Another approach to this story has focused on the ferocity of women who appear in these stories. P. C. Craigie ("Deborah and Anat: A Study in Poetic Imagery [Judges 5]," *Zeitschrift für die alttestamentliche Wissenschaft* 90 [1978]: 374–81) and Jane Rasmussen ("Deborah the Woman Warrior," in *Anti-Covenant,* 80–95) point to the Canaanite Goddess Anat; J. Glen Taylor points to the two ferocious Ugaritic goddesses, Anat and Astarte, and suggests that their image lies behind Deborah and Yael ("The Song of Deborah and Two Canaanite Goddesses," *JSOT* 23 [1982]: 99–108). The most detailed study along these lines is by Susan Ackerman, who points out that the closeness of Anat and Baal in Ugaritic mythology is a good parallel to the close partnership between Deborah and God. Ackerman admits that Anat is far more bellicose than Deborah, who is not an Israelite form of Anat but only "in the vein of Anat" (*Warrior, Dancer, Seductress, Queen: Women in Judges and Biblical Israel* [New York: Doubleday, 1998]).

Yet another type of writing about Deborah depicts reactions to the very concept of a woman judge or woman warrior. Jane Shaw depicts how two popular writers deal with this issue ("Constructions of Women in Readings of the Story of Deborah," in *Anti-Covenant,* 113–32). More recent discussions of these issues are by Alice Ogden Bellis, "The Jael Enigma," *Daughters of Sarah* 21 (1995): 19–21; Carol Blessing, "Judge, Prophet, Mother: Learning from Deborah," idem., 34–37; Priscilla Denham, "It's Hard to Sing a Song of Deborah," in *Spinning a Sacred Yarn: Women Speak from the Pulpit,* ed. Ann Greenawalt Abernethy, Carole Carlson, and Patricia Carque (New York: Pilgrim Press, 1982), 58–64.

45　**story and song** Baruch Halpern maintains that the story is an interpretation of the much older poem ("The Resourceful Israelite Historian: The Song of Deborah and Israelite Historiography," *Harvard Theological Review* 76 [1983]: 379–401). On the other hand, K. Lawson Younger surveys the literature of the ancient Near

East and concludes that important events are always preserved in both prose and poetic form. Younger reverses the order in which people normally read, stating that the song seems to presume a knowledge of the narrative ("Heads! Tails! Or the Whole Coin? Contextual Method & Intertextual Analysis: Judges 4 and 5," in *The Biblical Canon in Comparative Perspective: Scripture in Context IV,* ed. K. Lawson Younger, W. W. Hallo, and B. F. Batto, Ancient Near Eastern Texts and Studies 11 (Lewiston, N.Y.: Edward Mellen, 1991), 109–46.

46 **judged Israel** Daniel Block concludes that her role was as representative of God, that she was outside the town receiving the pleas of the people on God's behalf. Her judging is thus an aspect of her prophecy ("Deborah Among the Judges: The Perspective of the Hebrew Historian," in *Faith, Tradition, and History: Old Testament Historiography in Its Near Eastern Context,* ed. Allan R. Millard, James H. Hoffmeier, and David W. Baker [Winona Lake, Ind.: Eisenbrauns, 1994], 229–53).

47 **introduces a new tense** Ellen van Wolde points to the change in grammatical formation. The beginning of the story has two nominal clauses and then the participial until verse 5b, and concludes that the coming up for justice begins the foregrounded action ("Deborah and Ya'el in Judges 4," in *On Reading Prophetic Texts: Gender-Specific and Related Studies in Memory of Fokkelien van Dijk-Hemmes,* ed. Bob Becking and Meindert Dijkstra [Leiden: Brill, 1996], 283–95).

47 **"Awake, awake"** JoAnn Hackett reads this typical call to arms as the poet calling on Deborah to get the battle going ("In the Days of Jael: Reclaiming the History of Women in Ancient Israel," in *Immaculate and Powerful: The Female in Sacred Image and Social Reality,* ed. Clarissa Atkinson, Constance Buchanan, and Margaret Miles [Boston: Beacon Press, 1985], 15–38). However, the poet clearly places the summons in the mouth of the people.

48 **prophetic initiation of battle** See James Ackerman, "Prophecy and Warfare in Early Israel: A Study of the Deborah-Barak Story," *Bulletin of the American Schools of Oriental Research* 220 (1975): 5–13. Ackerman relates the story of Barak and Deborah to the study of Holy War by M. Weippert, " 'Heiliger Krieg' in Israel und Assyrien: Kritische Anmerkungen zu Gerhard von Rads Konzept des 'Heiliger Krieg im alten Israel,' " *ZAW* 84 (1972): 460–93; and the study of nagid by W. Richter, "Die nagid-formel: ein Beitrag zur Erhellung des nagid-Problems," *Biblische Zeitschrift* 9 (1965): 71–84.

48 **reluctant to go** James Ackerman compares this "go!" with the "go!" of God's call to Moses (Exod. 3:10, 16) and to Gideon (Judg. 6:14) and to Samuel about Saul (1 Sam. 9:16). Each of these episodes also involves a demurral, by Moses, Gideon, and Saul, as well as an assurance that God is with the one being charged. Deborah thus plays the role of an envoy of God ("Prophecy and Warfare").

48 **insists that Deborah go with him** Danna Fewell suggests that Barak is testing Deborah, that if she will stake her life on this message, so will he ("Judges," in *The Women's Bible Commentary,* ed. Carol A. Newsome and Sharon H. Ringe [Louisville: Westminster, 1992], 67–77).

48 **bothered by Barak's reluctance** Meir Sternberg is typical of this attitude when he claims that Deborah's presence tarnishes Barak's glory (Meir Sternberg, *The Poetics of Biblical Narrative: Ideological Literature and the Drama of Reading* [Bloomington: Indiana University Press, 1985]). Recognizing that most readers consider

Barak less than a man, Sakenfeld suggests that the text be used to make us consider why violence should be acceptable for men (Katharine Doob Sakenfeld, "Deborah, Jael, and Sisera's Mother: Reading the Scriptures in Cross-Cultural Context," in *Women, Gender and Christian Community,* ed. Jane Dempsey Douglass and James F. Kay [Louisville: Westminster/John Knox Press, 1997], 13–22.)

48 **tarnishes his glory** For a discussion of this attitude, see Sakenfeld, "Deborah, Jael, and Sisera's Mother: Reading the Scriptures in Cross-Cultural Context" and Gale Yee, "By the Hand of a Woman: The Metaphor of the Woman Warrior in Judges 4," *Semeia* 61 (1993): 99–132, 185–237; for an extreme example, see Meir Sternberg, who says that Barak "plays the woman" and that Deborah's presence tarnishes Barak's glory (*The Poetics of Biblical Narrative.*)

48 **Esarhaddon oracle** Translated by Simo Parpola, *Assyrian Prophecies,* State Archives of Assyria 9 (Helsinki: Helsinki University Press, 1997), lxxiii. For further information on prophets and wars, see Marti Nissinen, *References to Prophecy in Neo-Assyrian Sources,* State Archives of Assyria Studies 7 (The NeoAssyrian Text Corpus Project, University of Helsinki, 1998).

48 **"Israel's chariot and cavalry"** 2 Kings 2:12; 13:14. The Midianite prophet Balaam is also consulted by his king, and the kings of Israel and Judah call out the prophets to decide whether to go to battle with Aram in 1 Kings 22.

48 **troubled by the presence** See Priscilla Dunham, "It's Hard to Sing the Song of Deborah" by contrast. Jane Rasmussen believes that the original story was entirely about Deborah as warrior in a woman's goddess cult, but here God is the real warrior (Jane Rasmussen, "Deborah the Woman Warrior," in *Anti-Covenant,* 80–95). Perhaps Anat the woman warrior influenced the description of Deborah, but the Song seems to have been written fairly close to the events depicted, perhaps even by Deborah, and there is no reason to doubt the historicity of these characters.

48 **women in war** See Danna Nolan Fewell and David Gunn, "Controlling Perspectives: Women, Men, and the Authority of Violence in Judges 4–5," *Journal of the American Academy of Religion* 58 (1990): 389–411. Similar attitudes are expressed by Carol Blessing, "Judge, Prophet, Mother: Learning from Deborah," *Daughters of Sarah* 21 (1995): 34–37; and by Sakenfeld ("Deborah, Jael, and Sisera's Mother") and Yee ("By the Hand of a Woman"). Mieke Bal demonstrates how much more trouble readers have with killing by women (*Murder and Difference: Gender, Genre, and Scholarship on Sisera's Death* [Bloomington: Indiana University Press, 1988]).

48 **"Enmerkar"** For the epic, see Thorkild Jacobsen, ed. and trans., *The Harps That Once: Sumerian Poetry in Translation* (New Haven: Yale University Press, 1987), 275–319. The woman sage appears in lines 587 ff.

48 **the Assyrian prophets** See H. B. Huffmon, "Ancient Near Eastern Prophecy," *Anchor Bible Dictionary,* vol. 5 (New York: Doubleday, 1992), 73–83; Simo Parpola, *Assyrian Prophecies,* State Archives of Assyria 9 (Helsinki: Helsinki University Press, 1997); and Marti Nissinen, *References to Prophecy in Neo-Assyrian Sources,* State Archives of Assyria Studies 7 (Helsinki: Helsinki University Press, 1998).

50 **"mother in Israel"** See Claudia Camp ("The Wise Women of 2 Samuel: A Role Model for Women in Early Israel?" *Catholic Biblical Quarterly* 43 [1981]: 14–29). Cheryl Exum describes the mother as one who liberates from oppression and en-

sures well-being ("Mother in Israel: A Familiar Figure Reconsidered," in *Feminist Interpretation of the Bible,* ed. Letty Russell [Philadelphia: Westminster, 1985], 73–85).

50 **Ashurbanipal** The text is translated by Robert Biggs, in *Ancient Near Eastern Texts Relating to the Old Testament,* 3d ed., James Pritchard, ed. (Princeton: Princeton University Press, 1969), 606. I thank my student Elizabeth Hopp-Peters for this reference.

50 **Atossa** See Aeschylus, *Perseus,* lines 159–214.

50 **awaiting the return of her son** O'Connor gives details of women at the window in classic sources and the ancient Near East and concludes that the primary association of window-watching is expectation or waiting.

50 **opposite poles** For the juxtaposition, see Michael O'Connor, "The Women in the Book of Judges," *Hebrew Annual Review* 10 (1986): 277–93. Fokkelien van Dijk-Hemmes points out that Yael is the mediator between the "good" mother and the "bad" mother by being a "good" mother for Israelites and a "bad" mother for Sisera ("Mothers and a Mediator in the Song of Deborah," in *A Feminist Companion to Judges,* ed. Athalya Brenner [Sheffield: Sheffield Academic Press, 1993], 110–14).

51 **like the queen bee** See Bernhard Asen, "Deborah, Barak and Bees: *Api mellifera,* Apiculture and Judges 4–5," *ZAW* 109 (1997): 514–33. Yael would be the new queen bee who opens her sting chamber (tent) and copulates (peg) with Sisera. Asen's explanation of Barak's name as a remembrance of a tree struck by lightning, in which sacred bees resided, is less successful.

YAEL

51 **the hollow of his head** The word *raqqah* is usually translated "temple." The root, however, indicates something empty or hollow. Danna Fewell and David Gunn envision the peg driven through the mouth (*Gender, Power and Promise* [Nashville: Abingdon Press, 1993]); Ellen van Wolde, associating the verb with *rqq* II, "spit," suggests the throat ("Ya'el in Judges 4," *ZAW* 107 [1995]: 240–46).

52 **sexual allusion** This has been noted by Yair Zakovitch ("Sisseras Tod," *ZAW* 93 [1981]: 364–74); Athalya Brenner ("Who's Afraid of Feminist Criticism? Who's Afraid of Biblical Humour? The Case of Obtuse Foreign Rulers in the Hebrew Bible," *JSOT* 63 [1994]: 38–55); and Susan Niditch ("Eroticism and Death in the Tale of Jael," in *Gender and Difference in Ancient Israel,* ed. Peggy Day [Minneapolis: Fortress Press, 1989], 43–57). Zakovitch suggests that the later story eliminated the sexual overtones ("Sisseras Tod"); Walter Houston argues that sexuality is suspected only because of the story of Judith ("Murder and Midrash: The Prose Appropriation of Poetic Material in the Hebrew Bible [Part II]," *ZAW* 109 [1997]: 534–48.

53 **her husband's ally** Mieke Bal has pointed out that what she calls the "anthropological code" would not necessarily assure the wife's loyalty ("Murder and Difference: Uncanny Sites in an Uncanny World," *Literature and Theology* 5 [1991]: 1–10), whereas Fewell and Gunn assert that it would have ("Controlling Perspectives").

53 **priestly functionary** This is the theory of Susan Ackerman ("Jael as a Cultic Functionary," in *Warrior, Dancer, Seductress, Queen*).

53 **expectations of hospitality** Victor Matthews shows that the story presents the

events in such a way that all the hospitality protocols are systematically violated ("Hospitality and Hostility in Judges 4," *Biblical Theology Bulletin* 21 [1991]: 13–21).

53 *sûrah* For this suggestion see Yairah Amit, *The Book of Judges: The Art of Editing*, trans. Jonathan Chipman (Leiden: Brill, 1999).

55 **shame Barak** For discussion of this aspect of the woman warrior, see Gale Yee, "By the Hand of a Woman." Yee maintains that the woman warrior is liminal because she is neither the stereotypical male nor female, and her very liminality means that her significance depends on the gender ideology of the interpreter.

55 **Judith** The most extensive comparison between the two is by Sidnie White, "In the Steps of Jael and Deborah: Judith as Heroine," in *No One Spoke Ill of Her: Essays on Judith*, ed. James VanderKam (Atlanta: Scholars Press, 1992), 5–16. Houston suggests that Judith influenced Pseudo-Philo's retelling of Yael ("Murder and Midrash").

55 **time for an old-fashioned savior** For the emergence of women precisely at such junctures, see Hackett ("In the Days of Jael") and below, pp. 58–63.

56 **ideas that came into Israel from the Greek world** For these issues, see Tikva Frymer-Kensky, *In the Wake of the Goddesses*.

56 **Elizabeth Cady Stanton** The Woman's Bible. Pt. 2: Comments on the Old and New Testament from Joshua to Revelation (New York: European Publishing Co., 1898) 20. Alice Bellis, who cites Stanton, notes that even though violence is rarely justified, extraordinary circumstances call for extraordinary action, and women are not barred from such calls to action ("The Jael Enigma," 19–20).

56 **the salvation of Israel** Yairah Amit demonstrates how the structure of the story highlights that Yael is activated by God, who is controlling the whole event (*Judges*). Hackett ("In the Days of Jael") argues that it is part of "holy war" battles that they are won not by the human participants but by YHWH, and refers to YHWH's routing of Sisera's troops (Judg. 4:15) or by the stars and the torrent (Judg. 5:20–21). Daniel Block argues that this "theological dimension" influences the portrayal of Deborah from the beginning ("Deborah Among the Judges").

56 **the Aqhat epic** Many commentators have noted the similarities of this text with the story of Yael (see most recently Susan Ackerman, *Warrior, Dancer, Seductress, Queen*). The differences are equally obvious. The text is fragmentary, and we do not know how Aqhat got into a tent, so we do not know if he was somehow invited as Yael invited Sisera.

56 **fear . . . for the woman inside** Alice Ogden Bellis suggests that if her story is one of "self-defense there is nothing to denounce, nor is there a hero to celebrate" (*Helpmates, Harlots, and Heroes: Women's Stories in the Hebrew Bible* [Louisville: Westminster/John Knox, 1994], 123). But the text doesn't care.

56 **rape** In this vein, Katherine Sakenfeld suggests that the story can be read as a protest against rape, especially in war ("Deborah, Jael and Sisera's Mother").

57 **through God's prophet Deborah** Houston suggests that the mention of "treaty" in verse 11 hides a plot worked out by Deborah and Yael ("Murder and Midrash").

57 **Was she loyal to Israel** On this see Schloen, "Caravans, Kenites, and *Casus belli*." Hannelis Schulte suggests that Yael may even have been an Israelite ("Richter 5: Das Debora-Lied: Versuch einer Deutung," in *Die Hebräische Bibel und ihre zweifache Nachgeschicte*, 177–91).

57 **those chasing the general** Thus Fewell and Gunn suggests that she realized
which way the wind was blowing. Danna Nolan Fewell and David M. Gunn,
"Controlling Perspectives: Women, Men, and the Authority of Violence in
Judges 4–5," *Journal of the American Academy of Religion* 58 (1990), p. 389–411.

A Wise Woman of Power

For discussions, see J. P. Fokkelman, *King David* (Assen: Van Gorcum and Co., 1981);
Claudia Camp, "The Wise Women of 2 Samuel: A Role Model for Women in Early Israel?" *Catholic Biblical Quarterly* 43 (1981); 14–29; Marcia Geyer, "Stopping the Juggernaut: A Close Reading of 2 Samuel 20:13–22," *United Seminary Quarterly Review* 41
(1986); 33–42; Robert Gordon, "The Variable Wisdom of Abel: The MT and Versions
at 2 Samuel 20:18–19," *Vetus Testamentum* 43 (1993): 215–26. For commentary treatment,
see P. Kyle McCarter, *Second Samuel*, Anchor Bible 9 (Garden City, N.Y.: Doubleday,
1984), 425–32.

58 **the voice of the besieged** On this see Geyer, "Stopping the Juggernaut."

59 **Abimelech . . . died an ignoble death** For studies of this story, see T. A. Boo-
gart, "Stone for Stone: Retribution in the Story of Abimelech and Shechem,"
Journal for the Study of the Old Testament 32 (1985): 45–56. As the title shows, Boog-
art sees direct retribution between the seventy sons of Jerubbaal, lying on a
stone, whom Abimelech slew, and "Abimelech lying on or near the bloody stone
that had crushed his skull." We can extend his insight further: Abimelech destroys his home by killing his brothers; the home, in the person of a woman, kills
him.

59 **"Listen to the words"** Fokkelman relates this to prophetic introductions, high-
lighting the significance of what is coming, and notes that the woman has control of the discussion (*King David*). Geyer prefers to translate "the words," *dibrei*,
as "complaint" and relate them to the *dabar* of Joab's answer in v. 21, which she
understands as his denial of her assertion ("Stopping the Juggernaut"). Camp
notes the confrontation of the chief of the Assyrian army with Hezekiah's representatives in 2 Kings 18:17–36. The women have authority similar to that of
prophets and military leaders. Camp assumes that one develops such wisdom-
based authority with age ("Wise Women of 2 Samuel").

59 **'Let them inquire at Abel'** McCarter (*Second Samuel*) prefers to read with the
Septuagint, translating "Let them inquire at Abel and Dan whether that which
the architects of Israel ordained has been carried out," and reading the Hebrew
ubdn for *wšm*, taking *htmw* as *hatammû*, "have they concluded?" or "have they per-
fected?" instead of *hētammû*, and then reading *'asr samn*, "which we placed," instead of *'anoki šlmy*. The Greek seems more of an attempt to simplify or modify
the Hebrew than an original version. Moreover, McCarter's translation completely eliminates the specialness of both Abel and the Wise Woman. For
McCarter, the whole purpose of the "wise woman" is to reverse the effect of the
first "wise woman" (of Tekoa). The Wise Woman of Tekoa convinced David to
subordinate the needs of the public to one man (Absalom, on McCarter's reading); now the Wise Woman of Abel arranges to subordinate one man (Sheba) for
the needs of the public. McCarter's translation also doesn't explain why Abel is a

"mother-city." Simply being exemplary would not give it this status. For a discussion of the merits of the Septuagint "translation," see the next note.

60 **'and then they will conclude'** Robert Gordon ("Variable Wisdom of Abel") has demonstrated that the Greek translation is in fact a double translation, and reconstructs the original Septuagint as reflecting an original Hebrew *š'l yš' lw b'bl wbdn htmw 'šr šmw 'mwny yśr'l*, substantially as McCarter (*Second Samuel*), so that the Jerusalem Bible translates "Let them ask in Abel and in Dan if all is over with what Israel's faithful ones have laid down." In support of McCarter's "carried out," Gordon adduces Josh. 4:10, where *tom* means "was carried out."

60 **a center for judgment** Geyer relates this to Deut. 19:18–19, which speaks of the inquiry of witnesses (using the verb *daraš*), and believes the proverb is a synecdoche referring to cross-examination to stand for legal proceedings in general ("Stopping the Juggernaut"). Geyer is certainly right that the proverb refers to legal proceedings instead of general wisdom, but in the light of Deut. 17:8–9, a synecdoche from witness examination is not required.

61 **peacemakers of the faithful of Israel** In McCarter's reading (*Second Samuel*), the peacemakers disappear into "which they placed" and the faithful, *'emûnê*, become the *'amônê*, the "architects" or "founding fathers." But did Israel have a story about founding fathers and their rules?

61 **She has made the decision** Gordon assumes that the "I" refers to the city, as in 1 Sam. 5:10 the city of Ekron says "to kill me" ("Variable Wisdom of Abel"). But the city is not talking, the Wise Woman is, and the "I" must refer to her.

63 **political power** Camp argues that the use of proverbs, i.e., of traditional wisdom, is the source of this authority. Her use of the proverbial "Let them inquire" is meant to indicate the inappropriateness of attacking such a city ("Wise Women of 2 Samuel").

The Shunammite

Studies: Alexander Rofé, *The Prophetical Stories: The Narratives about the Prophets in the Hebrew Bible, Their Literary Types and History*, trans. from the Hebrew 1982 edition (Jerusalem: Magnes, 1988), 27–33; Burke Long, "The Shunammite Woman: In the Shadow of the Prophet," *Bible Review* 7 (1991): 13–42; T. R. Hobbs, "Man, Woman and Hospitality—2 Kings 4:8–36," *Biblical Theology Bulletin* 23 (1993): 91–100; Claudia Camp, "1 and 2 Kings," in *The Women's Bible Commentary*, ed. Carol Newsome and Sharon Ringe (Louisville: Westminster/John Knox, 1991), 96–109; M. E. Shields, "Subverting a Man of God, Elevating a Woman: Role and Power Reversals in 2 Kings 4," *Journal for the Study of the Old Testament* 58 (1993): 59–69; Burke Long, "A Figure at the Gate: Readers, Reading and Biblical Theologians," in *Canon, Theology and Old Testament Interpretation: Essays in Honor of Brevard S. Childs*, ed. Gene Tucker, David Petersen, and Robert Wilson (Philadelphia: Fortress Press, 1988), 166–86.

64 **Elisha cycle of stories** For these, see Tamis Renteria, "The Elijah/Elisha Stories: A Socio-Cultural Analysis of Prophets and People in Ninth-Century B.C.E. Israel," in *Elijah and Elisha in Socioliterary Perspective*, ed. Robert Coote (Atlanta: Scholars Press, 1992), 75–156; and J. A. Todd, "The Pre-Deuteronomistic Elisha Cycle," in idem., 1–36.

64 **not remembered by name** Burke Long ("The Shunammite Woman") assumes that namelessness means powerlessness and refers to Tamar's being called "this woman." But Amnon calls Tamar "that" (not "this") woman as a dismissive and belittling term. The Shunammite is neither dismissed nor belittled.

65 **Prophets are known to repay kindness** Todd ("Pre-Deuteronomistic Elisha Cycle") suspects Elisha's motives. He believes that Elisha feels some discomfort because he is in a woman's domain and therefore wants to play the power broker within a patron–client system, thereby putting the woman in his debt. He bases his suspicion on the rules of hospitality, for which see M. Herzfeld, " 'As in Your Own House': Hospitality, Ethnography and the Stereotype of Mediterranean Society," in *Honor and Shame and the Unity of the Mediterranean*, ed. David Gilmore (Washington, D.C.: American Anthropological Association, 1987), 75–89; and Victor Matthews, "Hospitality and Hostility in Judges 4," *Biblical Theology Bulletin* 21 (1991): 13–21.

67 **His lack of understanding** Camp speaks of the "insensitive" husband whose power she usurps ("1 and 2 Kings"). Hobbs, however, notes that the strong actions are not done in opposition to her husband, for women normally have power in the household ("Man, Woman and Hospitality").

67 **power in their own households** Hobbs underscores this point ("Man, Woman and Hospitality"), and cites the studies by E. Friedl, "The Position of Women: Appearance and Reality," in *Gender and Power in Rural Greece*, ed. Jill Dubisch (Princeton: Princeton University Press, 1986), 42–52; and Susan Rogers, "Female Forms of Power and the Myth of Male Dominance," *American Ethnologist* 2 (1975): 727–56.

68 **posture of subservience** Long picks up the lack of her subservience but attributes it to her "pressing her advantage against a prophet whose status has been diminished by ignorance" ("The Shunammite Woman," 17). But there does not seem to be a contest of power going on. If he had been diminished, she would not have believed in his miraculous powers.

69 **"By the life . . ."** Hobbs, who concentrates on protocols of hospitality that are clearly not being observed here, considers that the Shunammite shamed Elisha and sees in the similarities of the Shunammite's words to Elisha's declarations to Elijah "no small touch of irony" ("Man, Woman and Hospitality," 96).

69 **The Shunammite was right** Once again, Burke Long sees a contest, calling the Shunammite a victor because she forced a change in Elisha ("The Shunammite Woman"). Camp has a similarly adversarial view of the "usurpation" of her husband's power ("1 and 2 Kings"). She is a savior-victor, but not at Elisha's expense. Burke Long is right that in the later readings of this story, Elisha is valorized and her ability to persuade him (Long uses the word "manipulate") is forgotten ("The Shunammite Woman"). Renteria sees the story as emphasizing that followers of the prophet would be cared for, thus empowering resistance to the monarchy ("The Elijah/Elisha Stories").

72 **"to our brother Elimelekh"** It is noteworthy that, even though Naomi is not given title to the land, she is prepared to sell it or to sell the right of redemption for it. See comments on Ruth.

72 **The land is hers** On the inheritance of land, Osgood, "Women and the Inheritance of Land." Osgood argues that "sale" was never allowed, since land was in-

alienable and "buy" and "sell" must refer to the use. In each generation, similarly, what was transferred in inheritance is the right of each *bêt 'ab* to a usufruct portion of *mišpaḥah* land. Modern anthropology would show that it is not only male, but the control of land was regulated and kept within the lineage to which it had been given. Osgood maintains that even if the head of the *bêt 'ab* died the land remained at the disposal of his widow and/or any children. This is significant with regard to Naomi and Ruth, who still had rights to Elimelech's land. But the Shunammite goes one further: the land is regarded as hers, an appellation that would be most appropriate if she had inherited it (or the disposal of it) from her father rather than from her husband.

72 **Owning her own land** On these issues, see S. Joy Osgood, "Women and the Inheritance of Land in Early Israel," in *Women in the Biblical Tradition*, ed. George Brooke (Lewiston, N.Y.: Edwin Mellen, 1992), 29–52.

Villains

DELILAH

For studies with bibliography, see Alice Bach, *Women, Seduction and Betrayal in Biblical Narrative* (Cambridge: Cambridge University Press, 1997); John Vickery, "In Strange Ways: The Story of Samson," in *Images of Man and God: Old Testament Short Stories in Literary Focus*, ed. Burke Long (Sheffield: Almond, 1981), 58–73; J. Cheryl Exum, "Aspects of Symmetry and Balance in the Samson Saga," *Journal for the Study of the Old Testament* 19 (1981): 3–20; Exum, "The Theological Dimension of the Samson Saga," *Vetus Testamentum* 33 (1983): 30–45; Exum, "Desire and Danger: The Drama of Betrayal in Judges and Judith," in *Anti-Covenant: Counter-Reading Women's Lives in the Hebrew Bible*, ed. Mieke Bal (JSOT supp. 81; Sheffield: Almond, 1989), 65–77; Robert Alter, "Samson Without Folklore," in *Text and Tradition: The Hebrew Bible and Folklore*, ed. Susan Niditch (Atlanta: Scholars Press, 1990), 49–56; David Bynum, "Samson as a Biblical φήρ ὀρεσκώος," in idem., 57–73.

77 **the annunciation** On this, see Adele Reinhartz, "Samson's Mother: An Unnamed Protagonist," *JSOT* 55 (1992): 25–37. Reinhartz explains that the anonymity of the mother focuses attention on the angel.

78 **population was mixed** Yigael Yadin suggests the similarity of Danite and Philistine ideas ("And Dan, Why Did He Remain in Ships?" *Australian Journal of Biblical Archaeology* 1 [1968]: 9–23; reprinted under this title in vol. 1 of the series, Publications of the Henri Frankfort Foundation [Amsterdam: Adolf M. Hakkert, 1973]).

79 *pattî* See the discussion in Tikva Frymer-Kensky, *In the Wake of the Goddesses: Women, Culture and the Biblical Transformation of Pagan Myth* (New York: Fawcett Columbine, 1992), 260, n. 103. The enticement involved in *pattî* is verbal rather than sexual.

79 **a lot less sexy** In Betsy Merideth's otherwise excellent analysis ("Desire and Danger: The Drama of Betrayal," in *Anti-Covenant*, 63–78), she is misled by the standard reading of the story to assert that Delilah, like the later Judith, uses sexual wiles.

79 **later retellings** One of the more interesting readings is by Mieke Bal, "Delilah Decomposed: Samson's Talking Cure and the Rhetoric of Subjectivity," in *Lethal*

Love: Feminist Readings of Biblical Love Stories (Bloomington: Indiana University Press, 1987), 37–67. Bal analyzes how popular culture and religious education turn Delilah into a paradigmatic case of woman's wickedness, and teach the myth that a strong man will be a seduced by a woman and then betrayed. All the popular texts she chooses make this judgment. For more on the retellings, see Alice Bach, *Women, Seduction and Betrayal*. Bal shows how this is the basic assumption of all the popular retellings she analyzes, and she turns this sexual charge on its head in her own reading, suggesting a highly psychologizing interpretation of the story as symbolic of male maturation and fear. Bal is aware that her reading is not intended by the narrator.

82 **Samson has been here before** Robert Alter suggests that Samson is in the grip of a "repetition compulsion," which is signaled through the story by the word *paʿam*, "time." He likes playing with fire, literally in the story and idiomatically. In Alter's words, he likes "taking honey where lions wait to pounce" ("Samson Without Folklore," 51).

83 **lions and honey** For this parallel, see Othniel Margalith, "Parallels of Samson's Stories with Stories of Aegean Sea People" (in Hebrew), *Beth Mikra* 27 (1966): 122–30.

83 **miraculous hair** See the discussion by Margalith, "Samson's Riddle and Samson's Magic Locks," *Vetus Testamentum* 36 (1986): 225–34, who brings the parallel Greek sources to this legend. Margalith suggests that the story of Joshua and the sun over Ayalon, as well as that of Jonah and the whale, also have Greek parallels.

83 **Herakles** See Pausanias 10.29.7; Hyginus 32–36. The parallels are discussed by David Bynum ("Samson as a Biblical φήρ ὀρεσκῷος"), who also notes similarities to the stories of the Centaurs, wild semi-men, and other wild men.

84 **"bizarro-universe" image of Yael** Merideth concentrates on the relation to the Judith story. In both stories, the woman is the agent of the man's destruction. Judith the heroine and Delilah the villain are distinguished not so much by their actions but by the side they are on ("Desire and Danger"). Merideth is right in asserting that the story is less about how Delilah will betray Samson and more about how far Samson's pride and pretensions to immortality will carry him to disaster. Merideth's own argument should be carried a step further: it is the very myth of seductive, betraying women that causes Delilah to be seen as a sexual temptress rather than someone paid to persuade Samson to reveal his secret.

ATHALIAH

For studies see: Nadav Na'aman, "Royal Inscriptions and the Histories of Joash and Ahaz, Kings of Judah," *Vetus Testamentum* 48 (1998): 333–49; Patricia Dutcher-Walls, *Narrative Art, Political Rhetoric: The Case of Athaliah and Joash* (JSOT supp. 209 (Sheffield: Sheffield Academic Press, 1996); Lloyd M. Barré, *The Rhetoric of Political Persuasion. The Narrative Artistry and Political Intentions of 2 Kings 9–11*, Catholic Biblical Quarterly Monograph Series 210, Washington, D.C., 1988. For commentary, see Mordechai Cogan and Hayyim Tadmor, *II Kings*, Anchor Bible (Garden City, N.Y.: Doubleday, 1988).

85 **"Daughter of Ahab"** For Athaliah as daughter of Omri, see H. J. Katzenstein, "Who Were the Parents of Athaliah?" *Israel Exploration Journal* 5 (1955): 194–97.

85 **What would Athaliah stand to gain** Carol Smith suggests that Athaliah may have been looking for stability rather than fighting Yahwism. She does not explain how the killings would increase stability. Nevertheless, it needs to be emphasized that there is no hint of religious battles against Yahwism in the reign of Athaliah. I see no reason to assume that women, even queens, worshiped foreign deities unless the text tells us that they do.

85 **queen-mother** There is considerable dispute on the exact status of the queen-mother. Five major articles have been devoted to the topic, Neils-Erik Andreasen, "The Role of the Queen Mother in Israelite Society," *Catholic Biblical Quarterly* 45 (1983): 179–94; Zafira Ben-Barak, "The Status and Right of the Gebira," *Journal of Biblical Literature* 110 (1991): 23–34; Susan Ackerman, "The Queen Mother and the Cult in Ancient Israel," *JBL* 112 (1993): 385–401; Ktziah Spanier, "The Queen Mother in the Judaean Royal Court: Maacah—A Case Study," in *A Feminist Companion to Samuel and Kings* (Sheffield: Sheffield Academic Press, 1994), 186–95; and Carol Smith, " 'Queenship' in Israel? The Cases of Bathsheba, Jezebel and Athaliah," in *King and Messiah in Israel and the Ancient Near East: Proceedings of the Oxford Old Testament Seminar,* ed. John Day, JSOT supp. 270 (Sheffield: Sheffield Academic Press, 1998), 142–62. Andreason presented an argument that the queen-mother had an official role during her husband's reign. Ben-Barak, who collected the evidence for Near Eastern queen-mothers as well as biblical queen-mothers concluded that the paucity of prominent ones indicated that the force of personality of these powerful women, rather than the specifics of their position, made them so prominent. Typically, she concludes, these women would assert themselves in the matter of the accession of their sons to the throne. Spanier, however, believes the queen-mother was an important person in the court, and Smith understands that there had to be some position for the queen-mothers to yield influence, but holds that this position was the queen rather than queen-mother. Ackerman considers the position of the Hittite *tawananna,* studied by Bin-Nun Shoshanna (*The Tawananna in the Hittite Kingdom* [Heidelberg: Heidelberg University, 1975]). Bin-Nun argued that the title referred to a religious functionary. As a parallel, Ackerman speculates that the queen-mother's job was to devote herself to the cult of Asherah within the king's court. Ackerman believes that the queen-mother was the earthly counterpart of Asherah, and her political power and rule in the accession of her son stems from this. Asa deposed his mother Ma'acah from the position of queen-mother because she made an asherah, but there is no hint that Athaliah indulged in this cult.

86 **Sammuramat** For these and other such queens, see Ben-Barak, "Status and Right," and the bibliography she cites.

86 **Jehu would actively try to incite the people** Ben-Barak considers her assumption to the throne "an act of desperation," declaring it an "entirely understandable" fear that the "God-fearing people of Judah" would kill her (ibid., 28).

88 **ever indicts Athaliah as a Ba'al worshiper** Modern commentators assume that she built the Ba'al temple, and Susan Ackerman suggests that she was a worshiper of Asherah ("Queen Mother and the Cult"). In this they are preceded by the Chronicler.

88 **Chronicles** Jacob Myers calls her an *adjutrix diaboli* (devil's helper) in Chronicles,

much more than in Kings *(II Chronicles,* Anchor Bible [Garden City, N.Y.: Double-day, 1965], 126).

The Disposable Wife

There is an enormous bibliography written about all aspects of this story. For general studies, see Robert Polzin, "The Ancestress of Israel in Danger," *Semeia* 3 (1975): 81–89; John Ronning, "The Naming of Isaac: The Role of the Wife/Sister Episodes in the Redaction of Genesis," *Westminster Theological Journal* 53 (1991): 1–27; Mark E. Biddle, "The 'Endangered Ancestress' and Blessing for the Nations," *Journal of Biblical Literature* 109 (1990): 599–611; Ilona Rashkow, "Intertextuality, Transference and the Reader in/of Genesis 12 and 20," in *Reading Between Texts: Intertextuality and the Hebrew Bible,* ed. Danna Nolan Fewell (Louisville: Westminster/John Knox, 1992), 57–73; J. Cheryl Exum, "Who's Afraid of the 'Endangered Ancestress,' " in *The New Literary Criticism and the Hebrew Bible,* ed. Cheryl Exum and David Clines, JSOT supp. 143 (Sheffield: JSOT, 1993), 91–113; the article is reprinted in Exum, *Fragmented Women: Feminist (Sub)versions of Biblical Narratives* (Valley Forge: Trinity, 1993), 148–69; Barry Eichler, "On Reading Genesis 12:10–20," in *Tehillah le-Moshe: Biblical and Judaic Studies in Honor of Moshe Greenberg,* ed. Mordechai Cogan, Barry Eichler, and Jeffrey Tigay (Winona Lake, Ind.: Wisenbrauns, 1997), 23–38; and Fokkelien van Dijk-Hemmes, "Sarai's Exile: A Gender-Motivated Reading of Genesis 12:10–13:2," in *A Feminist Companion to Genesis* (Sheffield: Sheffield Academic Press, 1993), 222–34.

93 **thrice-told wife-sister masquerade** The fact that the story is told twice has pre-occupied modern scholars. With the development of "higher" or source criti-cism and modern biblical scholarship, scholars viewed the clear similarities between the stories in Genesis 12, 20, and 26 as clear evidence of separate sources, often assigning 12 and 26 to J and 20 to E (see, for example, E. A. Speiser, *Genesis,* Anchor Bible 1 ([Garden City, N.Y.: Doubleday, 1964]). Further under-standing of the development of biblical traditions focused attention on the rela-tionship between these stories, and most scholars began to believe that Genesis 12 was the original version (still assigned to J, but originally an oral tradition), that 20 was a later literary reflection concerned with moral issues, and 26 a liter-ary composition to show that Isaac's life paralleled Abraham's. Thus J. van Seters takes Genesis 12 to be "early Yahwist," 20 as "Elohist," and 26 as "late Yahwist" *(Abraham in History and Tradition* [New Haven: Yale University Press, 1975], 167–91); Claus Westerman takes Genesis 12 as J and the other two as individual stories not part of a "source" *(Genesis 12–36: A Commentary* [Minneapolis: Augs-burg, 1985]); and George Coats, using genre analysis, comes to a similar conclu-sion ("A Threat to the Host," in *Saga, Legend, Tale, Novella, Fable: Narrative Forms in Old Testament Literature* [George Coats, ed.; JSOT supp. 35; Sheffield: JSOT, 1985], 71–81). R. D. Alexander takes a parallel approach, considering oral develop-ment of the three stories rather than literary variation, and suggests that the sto-ries might have been modified in light of each other at the time of their incorporation into Genesis ("Are the Wife/Sister Incidents of Genesis Literary Compositional Variants?" *Vetus Testamentum* 42 [1992]: 145–53).

However the three stories developed, all three were redacted into the final form of the book of Genesis, and the question arises why they were all included and how they relate to one another. Susan Niditch, in her study of the image of the trickster, maintains that the different types of storytellers in ancient Israel, such as popular, courtly, and preacherly, were responsible for the different versions. She describes Genesis 12 as an "economical" and traditional telling; Genesis 20 is "baroque-rhetorical," less traditional, interested in the status quo, and possibly told in a court setting during a healthy monarchic period; and Genesis 26 is an "anthological" telling, paying little attention to the trick and concentrating on how the underdog improves his status (*Underdogs and Tricksters: A Prelude to Biblical Folklore* [San Francisco: Harper & Row, 1987], 23–69). Pamela Tamarkin Reis, interested in why all three are preserved, suggests that not only do the stories foreshadow the descent into Egypt and the exodus with Egyptian wealth, but Genesis 20 and 26 explain why the Israelites did not go through the land of the Philistines. Reis goes further, claiming that Genesis 20 also adumbrates the capture of the ark by the Philistines in 1 Samuel 4–5, and Genesis 26 the bringing of the ark to Jerusalem in 2 Samuel 6:16–23 ("Take My Wife, Please: On the Utility of the Wife/Sister Motif," *Judaism* 41 [1992]: 306–15). Her explanations, however, rest on several dubious assumptions: one, that the Philistines would have borne a grudge for centuries; and second, that the Bible identified the word of God as the "wife" of Israel, an identification commonplace in Judaism from Ben Sira on but one not found in the Bible, which operates with a metaphor of Israel as the wife of God.

J. Cheryl Exum ("Who's Afraid?"), using a psychoanalytical approach, argues that all three versions are necessary to the working out of one aspect of the tale, the unacknowledged male sexual fantasy of one's wife being taken by another man. Retelling them serves the same function of repetition as in Freud's "repetition-compulsion," in which one works out a neurosis by repeating it, in order to offer a "semiotic cure" for it. In Genesis 12, the "primal" story, the Pharaoh (a narrative "superego") actually takes the woman; in Genesis 20, God offers moral law so that he does not touch her; by 26 the moral code is internalized, the woman's desired and feared sexuality no longer poses a threat, and she is not taken. The patriarch can now rest secure.

93 **will not hesitate to kill him** There is indeed evidence that adultery was considered the "great sin" in the ancient Near Eastern world. For adultery in general, see Raymond Westbrook, "Adultery in Ancient Near Eastern Law," *Revue Biblique* 97 (1990): 542–80. For Egypt in particular, see C. J. Eyre, "Crime and Adultery in Ancient Egypt," *Journal of Egyptian Archaeology* 70 (1984): 92–105; and for Ugarit see W. L. Moran, "The Scandal of the Great Sin at Ugarit," *Journal of Near Eastern Studies* 18 (1959): 280–81.

94 **"sexual hospitality"** For this theory, see Julian Pitt-Rivers, *The Fate of Shechem or the Politics of Sex* (Cambridge: Cambridge University Press, 1977). A variant of this is suggested by James Hoffmeier, who presents evidence of diplomatic marriages arranged with daughters and suggests that, since the patriarchs had no daughters or sisters, they had to deceitfully present their wives as sisters in order to ingratiate themselves with the host kings ("The Wives' Tale of Genesis 12, 20 and 26 and the Covenants at Beer-Sheba," *Tyndale Bulletin* 43 [1992]: 81–99).

94 **protection against Sarai's violation** Eichler, "On Reading Genesis 12:10–20."

94 **"wife-sister"** This connection was first suggested by E. A. Speiser, "The Wife-Sister Motif in the Patriarchal Narratives," originally in *Biblical and Oriental Studies*, ed. A. Altmann (Cambridge: Harvard University Press, 1963), 15–28; reprinted in *Oriental and Biblical Studies: Collected Writings of E. A. Speiser* (Philadelphia: University of Pennsylvania Press, 1967), 62–82. It is included in his popular Anchor Bible *Genesis*. Doubt, however, was cast by Sam Greengus ("Sisterhood Adoption at Nuzi and the 'Wife-Sister' in Genesis," *Hebrew Union College Annual* 46 [1975]: 5–31); and the contracts were reviewed by B. Eichler, "Another Look at the Nuzi Sistership Contracts," in *Essays on the Ancient Near East in Memory of Jacob Joel Finkelstein*, ed. Maria de Jong Ellis, Memoirs of the Connecticut Academy of Arts and Sciences 19 (Hamden, Conn.: Archon Books, 1977), 45–59, who demonstrated that the wife-sister arrangement was an indication of severe socioeconomic pressure rather than superior status.

94 **a story about Abram** There is no point in debating whether Sarai was a "tacit accomplice" (Niditch, *Underdogs and Tricksters*) or an object (Ilona Rashkow and Sharon Jeansonne, *The Women of Genesis: From Sarah to Potiphar's Wife* [Minneapolis: Fortress Press, 1990]). In these stories, says Ilona Rashkow, "one can oxymoronically hear echoes of female voicelessness and its attendant sexual danger of violence" ("Intertextuality, Transference," 62). In this she recognizes the thematic similarity to the stories of Lot's daughters, to Hagar and the concubine: a man willing to sacrifice a female ostensibly important to him, and the sacrifice usually involves sex. As Exum points out, the male fantasy that created all the characters in the story, including Sarai, is not interested in the woman's point of view; however, since it imagines Sarai in the first place, it imagines her as complicit ("Who's Afraid?").

96 **Abraham would not have taken her back** For a collection of sources from the Genesis Apocryphon, Philo, Josephus, and rabbinic literature, which express this attitude, see Moshe Weinfeld, "Sarah in Abimelech's Palace (Genesis 20)—Against the Background of Assyrian Law and the Genesis Apocryphon," in *Mélanges bibliques et orientaux en l'honneur de Monsieur Mathias Delcor*, ed. A. Caquot et al.; *Alter Orient und Altes Testament* 25 (Neukirchen-Vluyn: Neukirchener Verlag, 1985), 433–34. Modern scholars also agree with this idea, as John Ronning suggests that Genesis 12 must be dependent on Genesis 20, i.e., that the author assumed the reader would get the answer for God's intervention from the later story ("The Naming of Isaac").

96 **Isaac was Abraham's child** Rabbinic midrash reports gossip about Isaac's paternity. [See tanhuma, *toledot* 1.]

96 **"she is my sister"** In later biblical law, such a marriage would clearly be incestuous, and later writers were bothered by the implications that Abraham and Sarah were in fact related. On this question, see Reuven Firestone, "Prophethood, Marriageable Consanguinity and Text: The Problem of Abraham and Sarah's Kinship Relationship and the Response of Jewish and Islamic Exegesis," *Jewish Quarterly Review* 83 (1993): 331–47.

97 **Abraham has done nothing wrong** Robinson and Eichler trace the development of a critique of Abraham. Robinson cites the Manichaean Faustus in his anti-Christian argument, and Eichler cites Nahmanides as the first Jewish author

to condemn Abraham and suggests that the medieval Jewish exegetical sensitivity to this issue was a response to Nahmanides.

Daddy's Daughters

99 **as Abraham almost killed Isaac** According to Carol Delaney, the actions of Abraham began this right of fathers (*Abraham on Trial: The Social Legacy of Biblical Myth* [Princeton: Princeton University Press, 1998]). The Abraham story certainly exemplifies this right, but it is not new to Israel, as the abundant evidence for child sacrifice in Phoenecia and early Greece illustrates.

99 **even over her parents** In this way, Rebecca and Leah were willing to leave Laban and go with Jacob (Gen. 31:14–15), and Michal helped David escape from her father Saul (1 Sam. 19:12–18).

100 **the book of Judges** In addition to the standard commentaries, see Yairah Amit, *The Book of Judges: The Art of Editing,* trans. Jonathan Chipman (Leiden: Brill, 1999); and Gale Yee, *Judges and Method: New Approaches in Biblical Studies* (Minneapolis: Fortress Press, 1995). For a concentration on the women in the book of Judges, see Michael O'Connor, "The Women in the Book of Judges," *Hebrew Annual Review* 10 (1987): 277–93; J. Cheryl Exum, "Feminist Criticism: Whose Interests Are Being Served?" in *Judges and Method* (Minneapolis: Fortress Press, 1995), 65–90; Danna Nolan Fewell, "Judges," in *The Woman's Bible Commentary,* ed. Carol A. Newsome and Sharon H. Ringe (Louisville: Westminster, 1992), 67–77; and Susan Ackerman, *Warrior, Dancer, Seductress, Queen: Women in Judges and Biblical Israel* (New York: Doubleday, 1998).

100 **put aside their reservations** Part of the artistry of the book of Judges is to present the arguments against kingship (like Jotham's fable, Judg. 9:7–15) and a parody of premature kingship (Abimelech, Judg. 9:22–57), while manipulating the reader's emotions to want kingship. In this way, the book hints that the historical solution will in itself not work.

Father-right Awry: Jephthah and His Daughter

102 **The story of Jephthah's daughter** For a literary analysis, see the excellent close reading of this story by Phyllis Trible, *Texts of Terror: Literary-Feminist Readings of Biblical Narratives, Overtures to Biblical Theory* (Philadelphia: Fortress Press, 1984), 93–116. For the classic text-traditional type of study, see Wolfgang Richter, "Die Überlieferungen um Jephtah" (Ri 10, 17–12, 6), *Biblica* 47 (1966): 485–556.

102 **son of a . . . prostitute** Trible calls birth from a prostitute an "irredeemable flaw" (*Texts of Terror*); and Mieke Bal declares it a negative note (*Death and Dissymetry: The Politics of Coherence in the Book of Judges* [Chicago: University of Chicago Press, 1988]). But, as Phyllis Bird has shown, the prostitute does not always have a negative image in the Bible ("The Harlot as Heroine: Narrative Art and Social Presupposition in Three Old Testament Texts," *Semeia* 46 [1989]: 119–39, reprinted in *Missing Persons and Mistaken Identities: Women and Gender in Ancient Israel* [Minneapolis: Fortress Press, 1997], 197–218). The Mesopotamian laws show that birth from a prostitute does not entail a stigma: it does, however,

set Jephthah up to become a victim. The Near Eastern material has been discussed by Isaac Mendelsohn, "The Disinheritance of Jephthah in the Light of Paragraph 27 of the Lipit-Ishtar Code," *Israel Exploration Journal* 4 (1953): 116–19; and in David Marcus, "The Legal Dispute Between Jephthah and the Elders," *Hebrew Annual Review* 12 (1990): 105–14. Mendelsohn and Marcus suggest that perhaps local custom allowed such de-legitimization. My own feeling is that it did not allow it, but they did it anyway, wronging him.

103 **Jephthah has been wronged** Danna Nolan Fewell and David Gunn, arguing from the structure of the story, see that the narrator considers Jephthah a victim of abuse, deprived of family and community *(Gender, Power and Promise: The Subject of the Bible's First Story* [Nashville: Abingdon Press, 1993]). To them, this tale lets the reader see Jephthah craving for acceptance and makes his vow tragic, and also indicates that he is destined to repeat the sorrow of his youth.

104 **The language of their negotiation** The records that survive are in Akkadian, but the Hebrew words here are exact translations: *śanē*, "hate, reject" (Akk. *zēru*); *gerreš*, "eject" (Akk. *tarādu*); and *mēšib*, "restore" (Akk. *turru*). For these, see David Marcus, "The Legal Dispute Between Jephthah and the Elders." Marcus brings forward an example from a Nuzi adoption contract, in which a father wants to reinstate a son he had disinherited. The verb used is the Akkadian equivalent of "you return me" ("The Bargaining Between Jephthah and the Elders [Judges 11:4–11])," *Journal of the Ancient Near East Society* 19 [1989]: 95–100). Marcus, as Mendelsohn before him ("The Disinheritance of Jephthah"), assumes that the elders of Gilead must have overseen a legal proceeding in which they permitted the de-legitimization. However, since Gilead is the name of both father and region, it is most likely that the "elders of Gilead" are Jephthah's brothers themselves.

104 **ancient Near Eastern gods** The most recent translation of Enuma Elish is by Benjamin Foster, *From Distant Days: Myths, Tales and Poetry of Ancient Mesopotamia* (Bethesda, Md.: CDL Press, 1995); for the Ugaritic, see Michael Coogan, *Stories from Ancient Canaan* (Philadelphia: Westminster/John Knox, 1978). There have been numerous studies of YHWH and the sea; see initially John Levenson, *Creation and the Persistence of Evil* (Princeton: Princeton University Press, 1994).

104 ***all his words*** J. Cheryl Exum points out the importance of words in this story. The brother's speech exiles Jephthah, and their later speech brings him back. In combat, words don't succeed; in his vow, words go out of control, and his last word in the story, "Go," severs family integrity. Exum associates all the words with *mispah*, which resonates with the crucial verb *paṣîtî*; as Jephthah says, "I have opened (my mouth) to God" ("On Judges 11," in *A Feminist Companion to Judges*, ed. Athalya Brenner [Sheffield: Sheffield Academic Press, 1993], 131–45). We might add that the interweaving of words and events and the preponderance of speech-acts in this story certainly fit a tale, one of whose messages is the significance of words as vows.

106 **Jephthah vowed a vow** Phyllis Trible judges the vow an act of unfaithfulness that seeks to manipulate God *(Texts of Terror)*. In a similar vein, Fewell and Gunn feel that he is bargaining despite the spirit of God, that he is desperate to succeed and to belong. They suggest that the purpose may have been to enthuse the

troops, in which case the vow was public (*Gender, Power and Promise*). In Israel's context, where oaths and vows are part of the fabric of belief, making such a vow might have been almost de rigeur. It is certainly a link in the process of preparing for battle (Magnus Ottosson, *Gilead: Tradition and History,* Coniectanea Biblica Old Testament Series 3 [Lund: Gleerup, 1969], 58–177). It is worth noting that none of the vows in the book of Judges turn out well, so perhaps the vows are part of the problematic of pre-state society and part of the subtle polemic of the book of Judges. As soon as there is a king, he overrides his ill-thought vow.

106 **a strange promise** The particularities of the vow have occasioned a great deal of comment. It was foolish (Trible, *Texts of Terror*) and stupid (Ottosson, *Gilead*), like Saul's vow (J. Cheryl Exum, "The Tragic Vision and Biblical Narrative: The Case of Jephthah," in *Signs and Wonders: Biblical Texts in Literary Focus*, ed. Exum, [Decatur, Ga.: Society of Biblical Literature, 1989], 59–83; and W. Lee Humphries, "The Story of Jephthah and the Tragic Vision: A Response to J. Cheryl Exum ['The Tragic Vision and Biblical Narrative']," in *Signs and Wonders,* 85–96). The vow, moreover, is intentionally ambiguous. David Marcus claims that all four of these vows have a direction correlation between the condition and the promise (*Jephthah and His Vow* [Lubbock: Texas Tech University Press, 1986]). But there is no such direct connection between Absalom's return and a sacrifice.

106 **"the one who comes out of the doors"** Opinion has always been divided as to whom Jephthah intended to sacrifice. Some, like Heinz-Dieter Neef, assume that he would have known human sacrifice was illegal ("Jephta und seine Tochter, Jdc. XI: 29–40," *Vetus Testamentum* 49 [1999]: 206–17). On the other hand, most scholars reject the idea that he intended an animal, since it would not have been an important enough sacrifice (see, for example, Pamela Tamarkin Reis, "Spoiled Child: A Fresh Look at Jephthah's Daughter," *Prooftexts* 17 [1997]: 279–98). Beth Gerstein holds that he had to kill his daughter to move from father to public father/patriarch, but there is no evidence for this ("A Ritual Processed: A Look at Judges 11:40," in *Anti-Covenant: Counter-Reading Women's Lives in the Hebrew Bible,* ed. Mieke Bal, *JSOT* supp. 81 [Sheffield: Almond, 1989]: 175–94). Most scholars try to avoid the implication that Jephthah actually intended to kill someone. It is unlikely to be an animal, for as Ottosson points out in Josh. 2:19, "whoever comes forth" is clearly a person, so it must be so here (*Gilead*). On the other hand, it should be noted that Idomeneus said *res,* "(the first) thing." The masculine form of "comes forth" might mean that Jephthah expected a male, but he must have known the custom of women coming out to greet victors, as the women of Israel came out to greet David and Saul (1 Sam. 18:6). Marcus (*Jephthah*) and Reis ("Spoiled Child") suggest that he intended to consecrate rather than kill, and Marcus points to the fact that a sacrifice was offered in conjunction with Samuel's consecration. Reis's suggestion that Jephthah intended to consecrate and redeem a slave seems anachronistic.

107 **Idomeneus** The story of Idomeneus is related by Servius (III 121 and XI 264). Walter Baumgartner also brings examples from folklore ("Jephtas Gelübde (Judg. 11:30–40)," *Archiv für Religionswissenschaft* 18 [1915]: 240–49, cited by Marcus, *Jephthah*, 28).

107 **General Meander** See William W. Goodwin, *Plutarch's Morals,* vol. 5 (Boston:

Boston, Little, and Brown, 1870), 488. These stories, and other partial parallels, are discussed by Marcus, *Jephthah,* 40–41.

107 **the girl emerged** Fewell and Gunn believe that people knew of this public vow and stayed inside, but Jephthah's daughter decided to make sure no one else was the victim of the reckless oath: "Her voluntary action passes judgement on her father's willingness to bargain for glory with the life of another" (*Gender, Power and Promise,* 127; and Fewell, "Judges"). Arguing along similar lines, Reis has a radically different reaction. She too believes that Jephthah's daughter knew about the vow, but came out anyway because "daddy's girl" assumed her father could fix anything. Moreover, since the vow is about consecration rather than death, Reis considers Jephthah's daughter a "daddy's girl" who subconsciously chooses to stay unmarried ("Spoiled Child"). Reis's account of this episode robs Jephthah's daughter of her heroism and makes it difficult to see why she should have become the occasion for an annual ritual. Mieke Bal takes a different tack, as she suggests that this act is a dramatic example of the belief that women are the open door, the leak in the system ("The Architecture of Unhomeliness," in *Death and Dissymmetry,* 169–231).

108 **He has no other issue** The Hebrew has *'ên lô mimmenû,* but the Masoretes suggest (*sevirin,*) reading it *mimmenâ,* "apart from her."

108 **daughters of Zelophehad** See discussion pp. 72–73.

108 **the Wise Woman of Tekoa** See 2 Sam. 14 and discussion, pp. 000–000.

108 **"you have really brought me to my knees"** The Hif'il of *kara'* is used in depictions of war, where God is usually the subject (2 Sam. 22:40; Ps. 17:13; 18:40; 78:31).

108 **"bring trouble to me"** *'akar* describes the effect on Jacob of Shimon and Levi's raid on Shechem (Gen. 34:30); on Israel of taking from the *herem* at Jericho (Josh. 6:18; 7:25); of Saul's oath (1 Sam. 14:29); and of Ahab's acts (1 Kings 18:17, 18).

109 **He doesn't ask** Reis notes that this is the only dialogue in which Jephthah doesn't ask "why," but her explanation rests on her assumption that the daughter is acting improperly, and that "Jephthah's daughter has been, and is continuing to be, spoiled" ("Spoiled Child," 285).

109 **his sense of horror and tragedy** Fewell and Gunn, who hold that the vow was public, detect a note of exasperation: she should have stayed inside—didn't she know better? And Fewell notes that his speech is a classic case of blaming the victim ("Judges"). He seems to be accusing her of collaborating with his enemies, says Esther Fuchs, and yet on another level, it is "a pointed expression of grief and helplessness" ("Marginalization, Ambiguity, Silencing: The Story of Jephthah's Daughter," *Journal of Feminist Studies in Religion* 5 [1989]: 36–45).

110 **a tragic figure** Gila Ramras-Rauch compares the story to Greek tragedy: his cry is an *anagnorisis,* a full realization by the tragic hero who considers himself the measure of all things; in turn, his tragic flaw, *hamartia,* is the hubris that caused him to become the leader ("Fathers and Daughters: Two Biblical Narratives," in *Mappings of the Biblical Terrain: The Bible as Text,* ed. Vincent Tollers and John Maier [Lewisburg, Pa.: Bucknell University Press, 1990], 158–69). Exum also sees it as a tragic moment, for Jephthah is unwittingly responsible for taking the life and it is against his will ("The Tragic Vision and Biblical Narrative"). Humphreys objects to calling it "tragic," not because of lack of pathos but because Jephthah is not great enough ("A Response"). But, as Exum says, the tragedy is in the ac-

tion and the silence of God. One does not need a great hero, neither does he have to have hubris. The *hamartia* in Jephthah's case was his act of making the vow. But surely every parent in such a circumstance has a right to be called "tragic."

110 **the loss of his only child** The mourning for an only child is particularly intense, the *'ebel yahîd* of Jer. 6:26; Amos 8:10; cf 2 Sam. 14:2 f.

110 **She shares piety** Evaluating the daughter's acceptance of the sacrifice has been a major issue for contemporary readers. Some, accepting the ideas of Pseudo-Philo, stress that the sacrifice is hers, not her father's (Cynthia Baker, "Pseudo-Philo and the Transformation of Jephthah's Daughter," in *Anti-Covenant*, 195–209; and Pieter Willem van der Horst, "Deborah and Seila in Pseudo-Philo's 'Liber Antiquitatum Biblicarum,' " in *Messiah and Christos: Studies in the Jewish Origins of Christianity; Presented to David Flusser on the Occasion of His Seventy-fifth Birthday*, ed. Ithamar Gruenwald, Shaul Shaked, and Gedaliahu A. G. Stroumsa, Texte und Studien zum antiken Judentum 32 [Tübingen: Mohr, 1992], 111–17). Contemporary feminist readers have a very different attitude. To Exum, she speaks against herself, keeping paternal authority unchallenged. She does her daughter's duty, and since she does not resist, she absolves him of responsibility. As such, the story serves phallocentric interests. Peggy Day calls Jephthah's daughter the archetype of female adolescence, resolving a moral dilemma by ignoring her own well-being ("From the Child Is Born the Woman: The Story of Jephthah's Daughter," in *Gender and Difference in Ancient Israel*, ed. Peggy Day [Minneapolis: Fortress Press, 1989], 58–74). Fewell and Gunn, who believe that she stepped forward on purpose, have her taking control of the vow to deliver a lesson on recklessness (*Gender, Power and Promise*). As Fewell points out, rather than reading innocent submission, one might hear a "tone of ironic judgement" ("Judges," 71). I prefer the third option: piety and courage.

110 **Philo of Byblos** He is preserved in Eusebius, *Propter Evangelium*. For text and discussion, see Howard A. Aldridge and Robert A. Oden, Jr., *Philo of Byblos, the Phoenecian History, Introduction, Critical Text, Translation Notes* (CBQ monograph series 9 [Catholic Biblical Association, Washington, D.C., 1981]).

110 **Iphigenia** The first sustained treatment is by Peggy Day, who brings the different versions of the Iphigenia version to bear on the issue ("From the Child"). Thomas Römer includes a fuller treatment of one particular version, Euripides' *Iphigenia in Aulis*, first performed in 405. Quoting from the translation in A. S. Way, *Euripides in Four Volumes* (London, 1916), Römer shows the various parallels of Iphigenia greeting her father first (lines 631–32), accepting her own glorious death (lines 1375–76), and telling the maidens to sing so that her name would be remembered (1490–96). To Römer, Iphigenia dies ("Why Would the Deuteronomists Tell About the Sacrifice of Jephthah's Daughter?" *JSOT* 77 [1998]: 27–38, citing W. Stockert, *Euripides, Iphigenie in Aulis* [Vienna: Vorlag der österreichischen Akademie der Wissenschaften, 1992], 79–81). Römer concludes that the story of Jephthah's daughter is a direct copy from Euripides, put into the Jephthah section by a late Israelite author who wanted to introduce irony and skepticism about the intervention of God, thus sacrificing the Deuteronomistic "ideology of divine pedagogics." However, there is nothing intrusive about this story in its present location. On the contrary, its position in Judges is vital to an understanding of Judges. If there is any literary dependence, it is more likely to have gone the

other way, for Iphigenia's "O mother, let me run ahead of you! Do not be angry at me if I am first to clasp my father against my heart" (lines 631–32) is more significant in the Jephthah story than in *Iphigenia in Aulis*. Nor is there any reason to suspect a late composition. On the contrary, the connection with a ritual probably indicates its antiquity in Israel. The close parallels to the Greeks may possibly be a result of cultural interchange, but it would have happened far earlier. For further information about child sacrifice in Greece, see P. Bonnechere, *Le sacrifice humain en Grèce ancienne* (Athens: Centre International d'Étude de la Religion Grecque Antique, 1994).

111 **child cemetery of Carthage** Pozo Moro and the Tophets (child cemeteries) are discussed most recently by Jon Levenson, *The Death and Resurrection of the Beloved Son: The Transformation of Child Sacrifice in Judaism and Christianity* (New Haven: Yale University Press, 1995).

111 **"descend upon the hills"** In the Sinai traditions, God goes down on the mountain (Exod. 19:18–20). Römer therefore suggests that the phrase here is an ironic allusion ("Why Would the Deuteronomists Tell?"). Reis, who doesn't like Jephthah's daughter, suggests that she is going down spiritually to weep before other gods, but there is no hint of this ("Spoiled Child"). For the literal meaning, see Sakae Shibayama, "Notes on Yārad and ʿAlāh: Hints on Translating," *Journal of Bible and Religion* 34 (1966): 358–62. The key point is leaving her father. Gerstein suggests that she wants to see herself as independent and powerful ("A Ritual Processed"), Fewell and Gunn that she rejects him (*Gender, Power and Promise*) and prefers to spend her last day with friends rather than with him. David M. Gunn and Danna Nolan Fewell, *Narrative in the Hebrew Bible* (New York: Oxford University Press, 1993).

112 **Jephthah never killed her at all** Most scholars believe that she was killed, but ever since Radak there has been a strong sentiment that she became a perpetual virgin. Marcus presents the evidence that makes it possible that she was dedicated as a celibate rather than killed (*Jephthah and His Vow*).

112 **death of Isaac** For a discussion of these variations see Shalom Spiegel, *The Last Trial: On the Legends and Lore of the Command to Abraham to Offer Isaac as a Sacrifice: The Akedah* (Woodstock, Vt.: Jewish Lights, 1993); and Levenson, *Death and Resurrection*.

113 **a rule in Israel** The word *ḥôq* is literally "a rule." It occurs in a similar context in 2 Chron. 35:25, where *ḥôq ʿal yisrael*, "rule on Israel," refers to commemoration of the dead king Josiah. In both these contexts, the reference is clearly to a ritual.

113 *letannôt* The term may have Northern associations (Judg. 5:11; Hosea 8:10).

113 **death-and-transformation** For this motif in Greece see K. Dowden, *Death and the Maiden: Girl's Initiation in Greek Mythology* (London: Routledge, 1989). For this understanding of the Israelite ritual, see Peggy Day, "From the Child."

114 **"women's mysteries"** Scholars have speculated on idolatrous origins for such a ritual. Since it was in the hills, Ottosson argues that it was originally an Anat cult (*Gilead*). He doesn't explain why Anat's cult would have been mountain-oriented, but perhaps it is because Anat's partner Baʿal was at home on Mount Saphon. Reis envisions a monthly assembly for idolatrous worship, probably connected to the moon, a kind of "pagan precursor to Rosh Hodesh" ("Spoiled

Child"). The story, however, gives us no reason to assume that the daughter's assembly or the annual ritual was idolatrous in any way.

115 **But not so the narrator** For a summary and discussion, see Tikva Frymer-Kensky, "The Akedah: The View from the Bible," *Beginning Anew: A Woman's Companion to the High Holy Days*, ed. Gail Twersky Reimer and Judith A. Kates (New York: Touchstone Books, 1997).

115 **ambiguities** Esther Fuchs is concerned that the ambiguity justifies the behavior and erases the daughter ("Marginalization, Ambiguity, Silencing: The Story of Jephthah's Daughter," *Journal for the Study of Religion* 5 [1989]: 36–45). Despite all the ambiguities, however, the story presents the sacrifice as a tragic event. Gerstein suggests that the narrator uses permanently liminalized woman as a critique of men's activities ("A Ritual Processed"); and Fewell and Gunn ask, "Are the death of the daughter, silence of God and absence of people signs of something amiss in the promise?" (*Gender, Power and Promise*).

116 **civil war** For this connection see Alice A. Keefe, "Rapes of Women/Wars of Men," *Semeia* 61 (1993): 79–97.

The Bad Old Days: Concubine and Chaos

CONCUBINE

For various literary approaches to this story, see P. M. Arnold, *Gibeah in Israelite History and Tradition* (Ann Arbor: Ann Arbor University Microfilms, 1987), 125–69. However, the classic treatment is that of Phyllis Trible, *Texts of Terror: Literary-Feminist Readings of Biblical Publication*, Overtures to Biblical Theology (Philadelphia: Fortress Press, 1984), 65–87.

118 **"there was no king"** For discussion see Robert Wilson ("Israel's Judicial System in the Preexilic Period," *Jewish Quarterly Review* 74 [1983]: 229–48), who points out that without central authority, the legal system depends on consensus. Wilson maintains that Saul had an uneasy mix of incipient royal judiciary and the traditional, while David became judge.

118 **Ruth . . . Judges** In addition, Warren Austin Gage points out that both anticipate the coming of monarchy and both have a relation to Bethlehem ("Ruth Upon the Threshing Floor and the Sin of Gibeah: A Biblical-Theological Study," *Westminster Theological Journal* 51 [1989]: 369–75).

118 *pilegesh* This word comes from Hittite; its exact meaning is unknown but seems to be some sort of secondary wife. For discussion see Chaim Rabin, "The Origin of the Hebrew word pilegesh," *Journal of Jewish Studies* 25 (1974): 353–64. They are both nameless. Don Michael Hudson understands namelessness as a literary technique that indicates loss of wholeness. There are five functions of anonymity: (1) minor role; (2) speed of action; (3) to highlight characters; (4) to universalize characters and events; and (5) to parallel loss of personhood. These chapters identify the last two usages ("Living in a Land of Epithets: Anonymity in Judges 19–21," *Journal for the Study of the Old Testament* 62 [1994]: 49–66). In opposition to Mieke Bal, who gives her a name, Beth (*Death and Dissymetry: The Politics of Coherence in the Hebrew Bible* [Chicago: University of Chicago Press, 1988]),

and J. Cheryl Exum, who calls her Bath-sheber ("Raped by the Pen," in *Fragmented Women: Feminist (Sub)versions of Biblical Narratives* [JSOT supp. 163; Valley Forge: Trinity Press International, 1993], 170–201), Hudson claims that naming is a violation that enervates the narrator's exposé that every concubine could be murdered. One should read anonymity with marginalizing to allow portrayal of what happens to women ("Living in a Land of Epithets").

120 **"she was faithless"** The Septuagint translates "became angry," clearly an interpretation, but one that sees the lack of sexual infidelity in this story. Koala Jones-Warsaw suggests a scenario in which her husband had accused her of not being a virgin ("Toward a Womanist Hermeneutic: A Reading of Judges 19–21," in *A Feminist Companion to Judges*, Athalya Brenner, ed. [JSOT Sheffield, 1993], 172–86). Highly inventive, this has no trace in the text. Exum considers that leaving her husband places her beyond their protection, and therefore what happened to her (failure to be protected) is a punishment for her actions ("Raped by the Pen"). Exum seems much harsher than the text itself.

120 **joy and great hospitality** Trible calls this the "master reconciliation" (*Texts of Terror*); and Victor Matthews shows how all the rules of hospitality are observed in this encounter, in contrast to the later episode when they are all broken ("Hospitality and Hostility in Genesis 19 and Judges 19," *Biblical Theology Bulletin* 22 [1992]: 3–11). Nevertheless, Koala Jones-Warsaw maintains that the father-in-law's extension of hospitality was a means to restrict the Levite's movements ("Towards a Womanist Hermeneutic"), and Peggy Kamuf likens the Levite's taking of the girl to the rape of the Shiloh women ("Author of Crime," in *A Feminist Companion to Judges*, 197–207).

121 **he has succeeded in his mission** It is hard to see why Exum thinks the girl should be punished, or rather that she thinks the men of the Bible think she ought to be punished ("Raped by the Pen"), when the biblical story uses the language of reconciliation, not punishment.

121 **As night begins to fall** Weston Fields points out the importance of night as danger. The "virtual race against the sun" is an appropriate introduction to the story of inhospitality ("The Motif 'Night as Danger' Associated with Three Biblical Destruction Narratives," in *Sha'arei Talmon: Studies in the Bible, Qumran and the Ancient Near East Presented to Shemaryahu Talmon*, ed. Michael Fishbane and Emanuel Tov [Winona Lake, Ind.: Eisenbrauns, 1992], 17–32).

122 **hospitality** See Julian Pitt-Rivers, "The Stranger, the Guest and the Hostile Host: Introduction to the Laws of Hospitality," in *Contributions to Mediterranean Sociology: Mediterranean Rural Communities and Social Change: Acts of the Mediterranean Sociological Conference, July, 1963*, ed. J. G. Peristiany (Paris and The Hague: Mouton, 1963), 14–30; Michael Herzfeld, " 'As In Your Own House': Hospitality, Ethnography and the Stereotype of Mediterranean Society," in *Honor and Shame and the Unity of the Mediterranean*, ed. David D. Gilmore (Washington, D.C.: American Anthropological Association, 1987), 75–89; Christoph Auffarth, "Protecting Strangers: Establishing a Fundamental Value in the Religions of the Ancient Near East and Ancient Greece," *Numen* 39 (1992): 193–216; and Jean Jacques Glassner, "L'hospitalité en Mésopotamie ancienne: aspect de la question de l'étranger," *Zeitschrift für Assyriologie und Vorderasiatische Archäologie* 80 (1990): 60–75. Auffarth shows how the *Odyssey* contains numerous tests of righteousness as to

how people treat the widow (Penelope), the orphan (Telemachus), and the wanderer (Odysseus). For studies of this chapter of Judges in the light of hospitality rules, see Susan Niditch, "The 'Sodomite' Theme in Judges 19–20: Family, Community, and Social Disintegration," *Catholic Biblical Quarterly* 44 (1981): 365–76; Stewart Lasine, "Guest and Host in Judges 19: Lot's Hospitality in an Inverted World," *JSOT* 29 (1984): 37–59; and Victor Matthews, "Hospitality and Hostility." A very different view is expressed by Exum ("Raped by the Pen"), who believes that talk about hospitality displaces the real purpose of the text, which is to give women a lesson in the consequences of sexual independence. Homosexuality is also not an issue: the threat to rape the man deflects from this lesson, and homosexual rape would leave the woman unpunished. Significantly, the story never uses the language of punishment.

123 **Could he . . . offer hospitality** According to Matthews ("Hospitality and Hostility"), this is an egregious error in hospitality and a sign of the disasters to come.

123 **he has enough provisions** According to Matthews (ibid.), this is the second inversion of the hospitality rules; the Levite is setting himself up as a rival rather than lowering himself to accept the hospitality of his host. But possibly he just wants to make it clear that, unlike many travelers, he is not a beggar.

123 **his maidservant** The Levite actually says "your maidservant." Trible suggests that using the term ʾamāh, "maidservant," instead of saying "my servants and your servants," offers her as bait (*Texts of Terror*). But it is hard to know in which context ʾamah has sexual connotations. It is noteworthy that he does not say either "my wife" or "my concubine," but he may be using the polite language of hospitality codes. And ʾamāh is the Hebrew for *pilegesh*.

123 **second miscalculation** Matthews declares that this violation of hospitality is a sign of the disaster to come. Moreover, the Levite compounds the violation: he creates rivalry by declaring that he has everything they need ("Hospitality and Hostility"). But perhaps he only wants to show that, unlike most travelers, he was not in need of charity.

124 **Sodom** The relationship of Judges 19 to the story of Sodom in Genesis 19 has long been noted, and a full list of both correspondences and divergences can be found in H. W. Jüngling, *Richter 19: Ein Plädoyer für das Königtum: stilistische Analyse der Tendenzerzählung Ri 19, 1–30a; 21, 25,* Analecta Biblica 84 (Rome: Pontifical Biblical Institute, 1981). Jüngling concludes that the divergences show no literary dependence. Others, like Robert C. Culley (*Studies in the Structure of Hebrew Narrative* [Philadelphia: Fortress Press, 1976]), maintain that it is impossible to determine which came first. Niditch agrees with Culley but nevertheless opts for the primacy of the Judges story ("The 'Sodomite' Theme"), whereas others, like Daniel Block, argue for the primacy of the Genesis story ("Echo Narrative Technique in Hebrew Literature: A Study in Judges 19," *Westminster Theological Journal* 52 [1990]: 325–41). Lasine declares the relationship a "one-sided literary dependence," asserting that the reader can read Genesis 19 without Judges 19, but not the other way around, since the purpose of the similarity is to "make the reader aware of the topsy-turvy nature of the 'hospitality' in Gibeah" ("Guest and Host," 39). Block's idea is that the similarities show the "Canaanization of Israelite society," that they have sunk to the level of those they were to destroy ("Echo Narrative"). But this assumes that Sodom represents Canaan, and

Benjamin all Israel, neither of which assumption seems warranted by the text. Fields believes that the story places the men of Gibeah into the same category as the Sodomites, who are already a byword for homosexual relations ("The Motif 'Night as Danger' "). But Jewish tradition never thought of the Sodomites as homosexual, and the term "sodomy" has not always meant homosexuality even in the West. Keefe believes that the association with Sodom "defames" Saul's birthplace ("Rapes of Women/Wars of Men," *Semeia* 61 [1993]: 79–97).

124   **no homosexuality** Readers of this story have paid disproportionate attention to the question of homosexuality. When Josephus relates the story (Antiquities 5.141–49), he claims that the men ask for the woman, not for the traveler; and this version was preferred by Saint Ambrose. Niditch, who understands that violent sex represents societal disintegration, nevertheless holds that homosexuality adds a negative feature, and that homosexual rape is a double potent symbol, whereas rape itself would be less problematic ("The 'Sodomite' Theme"). Fields suggests that the men of Gibeah were "so bent on homosexual relations that they would forcibly take a stranger and abuse him" ("The Motif 'Night as Danger,' " 29). In a similar vein, Geoffrey Miller believes the story in Genesis 19 provides two insults: lack of hospitality and deviant, depraved lust, and chapter 20 adds that they were left-handed ("Verbal Feud in the Hebrew Bible: Judges 3:12–30 and 19–21," *Journal of Near Eastern Studies* 55 [1996]: 105–17). This concentration on homosexuality seems backward: one might say that the men were so bent on abusing a stranger that they would have had homosexual relations with him. But even this is not appropriate, for male rape is not "homosexual relations." As Ken Stone points out, homosexual relations in these societies is a metaphor for male-male power, and sexual submission is a feminine role ("Gender and Homosexuality in Judges 19: Subject-Honor, Object-Shame?" *JSOT* 67 [1995]: 87–107).

124   **male rape no less so** Adopting what he calls a "queering approach," Michael Carden seeks to detoxify the language of contemporary discussion of this story by removing the term "homosexual rape" ("Homophobia and Rape in Sodom and Gibeah: A Response to Ken Stone," *JSOT* 82 [1999]: 83–96). The reason for male rape is a result of "patriarchal compulsory heterosexuality associated with misogyny, phallocentrism and homosexual panic." See on this point Richie McMullen, *Male Rape: Breaking Silence on the Last Taboo* (London: Gay Men's Press, 1990). The penetrator is masculine, but the penetration defines the other as "queer."

124   **the traveler's concubine** Offering the concubine has occasioned much comment. Trible claims that the rules of hospitality protect only males (*Texts of Terror*). Lasine, on the other hand, thinks that the Ephraimite became inhospitable by "callously" offering her to the crowd, and that his action "copies and inverts" Lot's hospitality ("Guest and Host"). Matthews, however, recalls that the Levite called her his *'amah* when he introduced her (v. 19), which Matthews translates "maidservant." Matthews suggests that since a wife could expect protection, the traveler's declaration that she was his "maidservant" allowed him to offer her ("Hospitality and Hostility"). This, he claims, gave the Ephraimite permission to treat her as a servant rather than as a wife. *'Amah,* however, is the Hebrew word

for *pilegesh*. And as the wife-sister stories show, even wives could not necessarily expect protection when their husbands saw themselves in danger.

125 **"whatever is good in your eyes"** The irony may be built into the very expression. In 1 Sam. 11, the story of the rescue of Jabesh-Gilead, the elders pretend that they will surrender by saying "tomorrow we will come out and you will do to us what is good in your eyes" (11:10).

125 **sends his concubine out** As Trible points out, the narrator indicates the hurried nature of his action by omitting the object "her" (ibid.). Matthews points out that the guest has saved the host, and "the irony of this reversal climaxes the narrative" ("Hospitality and Hostility"). The actual rape, murder, dismemberment, mayhem, and more murder seem less climactic to him, though he does admit that "a sense of disgust lingers" over the violence done to the concubine.

Here the narrative diverges dramatically from the parallel story about Sodom. Lasine believes the author intends the readers to make the comparison ("Guest and Host," 39); Matthews points out that "clearly the solution provided by Lot's guests is preferable to the Levite's" ("Hospitality and Hostility," 10). This attitude may show an overconcern with one particular form of wrong (inhospitality) and too little to the form of wrong the hospitality tries to avert, violence to stranger-men.

125 **Heads of household** Robert Wilson notes that the paterfamilias had "virtually absolute" control. He suggests that the Deuteronomistic historian influenced the story ("Israel's Judicial System"), which would fit in the light of Deuteronomy's consistent limiting of such paterfamilial authority (see discussion below, pp. 170–74).

125 **to save their own lives** He does not offer to sacrifice himself. As Trible points out (*Texts of Terror*), the use of innocent women is constant.

125 **coin of the realm** Claude Lévi-Strauss discusses women as the medium of exchange in *The Elementary Structures of Kinship*, rev. ed.; trans. James Harle Bell, ed. John Richard von Sturmer and Rodney Needham (Boston: Beacon Press, 1969).

125 **the bloody fields** The term "bloody fields" is Michael Carden's ("Homophobia and Rape").

126 **dishonored him** Drawing on the anthropology of honor, Ken Stone remarks that they challenge his honor through his woman, inflicting dishonor through sexuality ("Gender and Homosexuality").

127 **on the threshold** Alice Bach suggests other readings for her lying on the doorstep: that she has been broken so that the final boundary, the door, could hold firm, or that she herself is the boundary that stopped the mob from committing rape ("Rereading the Body Politic: Women and Violence in Judges 21," *Biblical Interpretation* 6 [1998]: 1–19). Yet another is suggested by Victor Matthews, who points to the legal significance of doors and suggests that she was trying to elicit justice from her husband and community ("Hospitality and Hostility"; and "Entrance Ways and Threshing Floors: Legally Significant Sites in the Ancient Near East," *Fides et Historia* 19 [1987]: 25–40).

127 **no solicitude** To Lasine, the incongruity between her struggle and his indifference is almost too great for the reader to feel outrage ("Guest and Host," 45), but many readers, particularly women, have indeed felt this outrage. To Lasine, "The

reader is forced to view this scene with detachment, which in turn prevents the reader from indulging in 'tragic pity' for the plight of the concubine" (ibid.). La-sine's "reader" is certainly very different from those of us readers who never reach this "detachment," and Keefe describes her powerful emotional response ("Rapes of Women/Wars of Men").

127 **slings her on his ass** To those who see this story as humorous, this is the height of its humor. Lasine sees in the death of the concubine such a comic scene, even though we cannot laugh: the Levite's actions are so bizarre that they burst the category of tragic villainy ("Guest and Host").

127 **speculate** To Robert Polzin, this ambiguity is "perhaps the most outrageous thing of all" (*Moses and the Deuteronomist: A Literary Study of the Deuteronomic History, Part 1* [New York: Seabury, 1980], 200). Mieke Bal suggests that to say he found her dead gives the woman a premature death. There are two moments of murder: by multiple rape and publication of her body, a "semiotics of mis-seeing" ("A Body of Writing: Judges 19," in *A Feminist Companion to Judges* [1993], 208–30).

127 ***ma'akelet*** Trible points out that this word appears only one other time: it is the knife that Abraham raised to kill Isaac. The Binding of Isaac is another story that involves the power of the patriarch. As in the Sodom story, God's intervention saved the patriarch's children.

128 **torn shreds of the social fabric** To Exum, the dismemberment reenacts the rape and comes from a fear of woman's sexuality ("Raped by the Pen"). By con-trast, Alicia Keefe points out that the violated body is a metonym for social dis-ruption because the community of Israel is expressed through language of the female body. Woman's sexuality is a sign for cohesion and continuity, and viola-tion is the disruption. Rape itself is a trope for dissolution of community, possi-bly because agrarian culture had a reverence for the materiality of life ("Rapes of Women/Wars of Men"). Even though the torn body is a sign of dissolution, Peggy Kamuf points out that the dispersed body of a girl without voice is a writ-ten contract which all the brothers sign against one of their own ("Author of Crime," 13).

129 **they were going to kill him** To Niditch, the Levite's claim that they would kill him shows that he is uncomfortable about the nature of the attack, and his fail-ure to protect ("The 'Sodomite' Theme"). Bach makes the claim that if the Levite had been raped, he would have been too humiliated to relate his story ("Rereading the Body Politic"). But how does she know this? Doubting that the rape of one woman could initiate a war, Bach suggests that the narrator of Judges has inverted the story so as "to protect the men of Israel from the spectre of sodomy." In similar fashion, Bach explains the Levite's claim by declaring that shame and horror at sodomy were equivalent to death (ibid.).

130 ***benê beliya'al*** Niditch suggests that this is holy war and this is the situation of the holy war: base fellows in one city have broken the code of behavior ("The 'Sodomite' Theme"). On holy war, see further Niditch, *War in the Hebrew Bible: A Study in the Ethics of Violence* (Oxford: Oxford University Press, 1993). The story does not make clear whether all the men of the city were worthless, or just some of them. But even if only some attacked initially, the failure to protect the girl renders the whole town culpable.

130 **the Greek story of Paktyas** Herodotus 1. 153–61. The story is related by Auffarth ("Protecting Strangers").

131 **the old tribal confederation** Niditch refers to Josh. 22:10–34, where the league worked peace ("The 'Sodomite' Theme").

133 **rape and murder of all the women** They are forced to identify with the criminal they have punished (Kamuf, "Author of Crime"), and they reenact what they claim to abhor (Trible, *Texts of Terror*).

134 **to rescue Jabesh-Gilead** So too Lasine, who points out that the story is not exe-cration of Saul but of Levites and all other Israelites ("Guest and Host"). For the opposite view, see Trible, who points out that Jabesh-Gilead and Gibeah under-cut Saul (*Texts of Terror*); Block ("Echo Narrative"); and especially Yairah Amith, who details all the correspondences that, she believes, make up a "hidden polemic" against Saul (*Hidden Polemics in Biblical Narrative*, trans. from the He-brew by Jonathan Chipman [Leiden: Brill, 2000]), 178–89; earlier, Amith, "Litera-ture in the Service of Politics: Studies in Judges 19–21," in *Politics and Theopolitics in the Bible and Postbiblical Literature*, ed. H. Graf Reventlow, Yair Hoffman, and Ben Uffenheimer, JSOT supp. 171 (Sheffield: JSOT, 1994).

136 **Shiloh** Bach declares her intention to read "against the grain of the writers' inten-tion to narrate the carrying off of women as wives for the men of Benjamin as necessary and natural" ("Rereading the Body Politic"). Bach is reacting to those views that present this as sort of a justified holy war situation, such as Moshe Weinfeld, "Divine Intervention in War in Ancient Israel and the Ancient Near East," in *History, Historiography and Interpretation*, ed. Hayyim Tadmor and Moshe Weinfeld (Jerusalem: Magness, 1982), and other older writings on holy war. But there is no more hint of approval in the biblical text here than anywhere else in these chapters, and feminists have understood that the abduction is "the supreme violation" (Trible's term in *Texts of Terror*). Kamuf suggests that it is nearly a rep-etition of the Levite's carrying her off from her father's home ("Author of Crime"). This would give a nice symmetry with the rape of Jabesh-Gilead paral-leling the rape of the concubine, and the abduction of the Shiloh women parallel-ing the abduction of the girl from her father's house. But the first scene does not read like abduction and seems halcyon in contrast to the rest of the story.

136 **These are violent terms** As Bach notes, "ambush" is a term from warfare; she associates it with the idea of "heroic rape" that she identifies in classical litera-ture. The two words used together in Psalm 10 evoke a lion in lurch. Bach evokes images of the mass rape in Bosnia, especially of the forced impregnation of Mus-lim women, so that the reader will have these in mind while reading about the rape of the women at Shiloh ("Rereading the Body Politic"). My own feeling is that the rape of the women in Bosnia has almost been forgotten by the populace by now, only a few years after Bach wrote, and it is reading about the Shiloh women that can bring the suffering of the Bosnian women to life, rather than the reverse.

137 **there was no king** The canon brings us Hannah, who was well treated and leads the way to the monarchy. The Greek Bible first gives us Ruth, full of goodwill and female hospitality. As Keefe points out, all the rape stories have lack of gover-nance as a common thread, a failure of paternal or royal power to respond to the rape ("Rapes of Women/Wars of Men").

"Off with His Head": David, Uriah, and Bathsheba

DAVID, URIAH, AND BATHSHEBA

A solid commentary treatment of this story can be found in P. Kyle McCarter, Jr., *Second Samuel,* Anchor Bible (Garden City, N.Y.: Doubleday, 1984), 277–310. There have been several excellent close readings of this story, by Phyllis Trible, *Texts of Terror: Literary-Feminist Readings of Biblical Narratives,* Overtures to Biblical Theology (Philadephia: Fortress Press, 1984), and Meir Sternberg, "Gaps, Ambiguity and the Reading Process," in *The Poetics of Biblical Narrative: Ideological Literature and the Drama of Reading* (Bloomington: Indiana University Press, 1985), 186–228.

143 **at the turn of the year** The most likely translation is "springtime," as Josephus relates it (Antiquities 7.129), but it may be that *tšuvat haššanah* should be translated "as the year returns," i.e., "one year after the kings went out," one year after the kings of the Arameans joined the Ammonites (2 Sam. 10) or "one year after the envoys went out," referring to the episode of the Ammonite treatment of David's envoys related in 2 Sam. 10:2. McCarter, who opts for a year after the kings marched out in 2 Sam. 10:6, states that it probably was spring, time of love and war (*Second Samuel*), but the text doesn't say so.

143 **ironic backdrop** Menahem Perry and Meir Sternberg, "The King Through Ironic Eyes: Biblical Narrative and the Literary Reading Process [in the David and Bathsheba story]," *Poetics Today* 7 (1986): 275–322, and Meir Sternberg (*Poetics*) concentrate on the ironic tone of much of this story. For reactions see Gale Yee, " 'Fraught with Background': Literary Ambiguity in 2 Samuel 11," *Interpretation* 42 (1988): 240–53. Yee details the many ambiguities in what she calls this "skeletal narrative," but suggests an explanation beyond irony: by making the interpreters decide on detail and motivation, the author makes the readers consider the moral issues at each point.

144 **Whatever his reasons** Readers who disapprove see irony. Others suggest that he might be too old, or even that he was trying to avoid the demoralization that his death might bring the troops (Moshe Garsiel, "The Story of David and Bathsheba: A Different Approach," *Catholic Biblical Quarterly* 55 [1993]: 244–62).

144 **turning point** David Gunn suggests that the king is on the point of security, and the Ammonite war offers him the crown of empire. But the trappings of kingship germinate the failure ("In Security: The David of Biblical Narrative," in *Signs and Wonders: Biblical Texts in Literary Focus,* ed. J. Cheryl Exum [Decatur, Ga.: Society of Biblical Literature, 1989], 133–51).

144 **goes for a walk** Randall Bailey (*David in Love and War: The Pursuit of Power in 2 Samuel 10–12,* JSOT supp. 75 [Sheffield: Sheffield Academic Press, 1990]) sees in the use of the term *hthlk* another hint at displeasure, since the same verb is used to characterize the way David's band moved around protecting farmers during his Robin Hood days (1 Sam. 23:13; 30:26–31). Carol Fontaine sees here a wisdom motif, explaining that David abandons Prov. 6:22, which adjures you to be mindful of your father's commandments when you walk around and when you lie down ("The Bearing of Wisdom in the Shape of 2 Samuel 11–12," *Journal for the Study of*

the Old Testament 34 [1986]: 61–77). It does seem that the author may be making an ironic allusion to this kind of a wisdom proverb.

144 **male gaze** This position of looking at Bathsheba angers some recent critics. J. Cheryl Exum contends that it turns us all into voyeurs. Moreover, says Exum, the male looks and feels desire. Women readers, she explains, are "invited to the phallic power of the gaze," but the female looks from the male perspective, accepting the concept of women as a source of temptation, which is an indictment of women. However, since David should be at war, what we see indicts him, and so the narrator lets the reader gaze without embarrassment ("Bathsheba Plotted Shot and Painted," *Semeia* 74 [1996]: 47–73). George G. Nicol objects to this characterization of the gaze, since the story does not linger erotically on her ("The Alleged Rape of Bathsheba: Some Observations on Ambiguity in Biblical Narrative," *JSOT* 73 [1997]: 43–54).

144 **Is she naked?** Readers generally assume that she is, but the text is silent. Medieval illustrations showed her naked, but during the Renaissance she began to get dressed. For a study of her representation through the ages, see David M. Gunn, "Bathsheba Goes Bathing in Hollywood: Words, Images and Social Locations," *Semeia* 74 (1996): 75–102.

144 **suspicious of Bathsheba** Mieke Bal reports that most people have a vague recollection that Bathsheba was somehow responsible (*Reading "Rembrant": Beyond the Word-Image Opposition: The Northrop Frye Lectures in Literary Theory* [Cambridge: Cambridge University Press, 1991], 225). Eduard Reuss may have been the first to suggest that Bathsheba must have known David could see her (*Das Alte Testament* [Braunschweig: C. A. Schwetschke und Sohn, 1892–1894], cited by Matthias Augustin, "Die Inbesitznahme der schönen Frau aus der unterschiedlichen Sicht der Schwachen und der Mächtigen," *Biblische Zeitschrift* 27 [1983]: 145–54). Perhaps contemporary readers are influenced by the 1951 film *David and Bathsheba*, in which Bathsheba confesses that she planned the whole thing (see Gunn, "Bathsheba Goes Bathing"; and Exum, "Bathsheba Plotted Shot and Painted"). Some scholars conclude that she did it because she wanted to improve her status (Bailey, *David in Love and War*) or was preparing for a sacred marriage rite, or she wanted a child she was unlikely to get from Uriah (Mia Diamond, "Who Seduced Whom? The Story of David and Bathsheba," *Mosaic* 12 [1992]: 22–31). The writer has no interest in Bathsheba's thoughts or motives. As Adele Berlin points out, she is basically a plot device, what Berlin calls an "agent," a nonperson ("Characterization in Biblical Narrative: David's Wives," *JSOT* 23 [1982]: 69–85). Exum claims that the story's lack of interest in Bathsheba's thoughts is not innocent, for the omission makes her ambiguous and therefore vulnerable to commentators. Exum considers this such violence that she calls it rape, stating "Bathsheba's rape is semiotic—it occurs not in the story but by means of story" ("Bathsheba Plotted Shot and Painted"). To this I cannot agree. The Bible author almost always writes enigmatically. David's thoughts are also not expressed. The condemnations of Bathsheba come from the readers' own projections and fears rather than from any hints in the text. *Honî soit qui mal y pense*: the scheming, manipulative Bathsheba comes from a set of gender stereotypes essentially alien to the biblical author.

145 **gets his answer** It is not clear who said "Isn't that Bathsheba?" It is possible that there was someone else on the roof who now speaks, or that the envoys he sent to inquire came back with the answer but express their answer as a rhetorical question out of deference to the king. Most of the English translations assume this, adding words of clarification: "The man said" (NIV); "And one said" (RSV); "And someone said" (NKJV and McCarter, *Second Samuel*); or shading the verb, as in NJPS, "he reports." But the Hebrew does not indicate another subject, saying only "and says" (so Young's literal translation, "and saith"), and most likely the speaker is David, who thinks he recognized her.

146 **Eliam** The connection of Bathsheba's father with Ahitophel's son is made by the Talmud, *Sanhedrin* 69b, 101a.

146 **adultery** This is the only story about adultery in the Bible, and it is certainly not typical. For the legal issues, see Raymond Westbrook, "Adultery in Ancient Near Eastern Law," *Revue Biblique* 97 (1990): 542–80; and Arnold A. Anderson, "Law in Old Israel: Laws Concerning Adultery," in *Law and Religion: Essays on the Place of the Law in Israel and Early Christianity,* ed. Barnabas Lindars (Cambridge: James & Clark Co., 1988), 13–19, 161–62.

146 **Is there anything a king cannot do?** David has already slept with other men's wives. He took Michal back from her second husband, Paltiel (2 Sam. 3:13–15). Even more significantly, one of his early wives was Ahinoam (1 Sam. 25:43), and there is only one other mention of Ahinoam: as Saul's wife (1 Sam. 14:50). It seems likely that they are the same. When God says He gave David his master's women (2 Sam. 12:8), this may be an allusion to David's marrying Ahinoam. For the special circumstance of Michal, who was originally David's, see Zafira Ben-Barak, "The Legal Background to the Restoration of Michal to David," in *Studies in the Historical Books of the Old Testament,* ed. J. A. Emerton, supp. to *Vetus Testamentum* 30 (Leiden: Brill, 1979), 15–29, reprinted in *Telling Queen Michal's Story: An Experiment in Comparative Interpretation,* ed. David J. A. Clines and Tamara C. Eskenazi, JSOT supp. 119 (Sheffield: JSOT, 1991), 74–90.

146 **Bathsheba's reactions** The issue of Bathsheba's willingness has preoccupied a number of scholars. Meir Sternberg speaks of Bathsheba's infidelity (*Poetics*), but Alice Bach points out that suggestions of rape make some readers uncomfortable ("Signs of the Flesh: Observations on Characterization in the Bible," *Semeia* 63 [1993]: 61–79). Exum claims that "he took" could hint at force ("Bathsheba Plotted Shot and Painted"), but Nicol points out that "ambiguity is the spice of biblical narrative, and the text has no potential for rape" ("Alleged Rape"). Diamond, of course, assumes that Bathsheba initiated everything, claiming that she was longing for a child, which Uriah was unlikely to give her ("Who Seduced Whom?").

146 **he took** J. P. Fokkelman points to moral brutality (*Narrative Art and Poetry in the Books of Samuel,* vol. 1 of *King David [2 Sam. 9–20; 1 Kings 1–2]* [Assen, Netherlands: Van Gorcum, 1981]); Exum to possible force ("Bathsheba Plotted Shot and Painted"). Regina Schwartz notes the connection of military and sexual conquests, showing the progression from taking Abigail with unbloodied hands (her husband the Fool died) to taking Michal, not so cleanly (her husband follows weeping as David asserts his prior claim), to taking Bathsheba by killing her husband and thus becoming the greedy Fool himself. As she states, the consequence

of stealing another's wife is the murder of a loyal servant ("The Histories of David: Biblical Scholarship and Biblical Stories," in *"Not in Heaven": Coherence and Complexity in Biblical Narrative,* ed. Jason P. Rosenblatt and Joseph C. Sitterson [Bloomington: Indiana University Press, 1991], 192–210, 252–54). For more on taking women, see Tod Linafelt, "Taking Women in Samuel: Readers/Responses/Responsibility," in *Reading Between Texts: Intertexuality and the Hebrew Bible,* ed. Danna Fewell (Louisville: Westminster/John Knox, 1992), 99–113.

146 **these little verbs** Nicol ("Alleged Rape") and William Willimon ("A Peculiarly Christian Account of Sin," *Theology Today* 50 [1993]: 220–28) take the quick verbs to indicate how quickly David acted, while Sternberg claims that the narrator is pretending that there is a natural and ordinary chain of events (*Poetics*).

146 **She was purifying herself** Bailey (*David in Love and War*) and Diamond ("Who Seduced Whom?") see her as intending pregnancy and timing the event: Garsiel ("Story of David and Bathsheba") suggests everyone who saw her bathing would know that she was not yet pregnant. Perry and Sternberg ("The King Through Ironic Eyes") want the reader to infer David's paternity, but they and Sternberg (*Poetics*) also claim that the text wants to show that David was not guilty of transgressing the laws of Niddah, then twists that to condemn him by paternity.

148 *parthenoi* Giulia Sissa, *Greek Virginity,* trans. Arthur Goldhammer, Revealing Antiquity 3 (Cambridge: Harvard University Press, 1990).

149 **(Rahab and Deborah and Delilah and Jezebel)** Rahab (Josh. 2:21); Deborah (Judg. 4:6); Delilah (Judg. 16:18); Jezebel (1 Kings 19:2; 21:8). "Sending" is a mark of authority.

150 **cuckold** For a study of the reactions of husbands in European literature, with emphasis both on cuckolds and on honor issues, see Alison Sinclair, *The Deceived Husband: A Kleinian Approach to the Literature of Infidelity* (Oxford: Clarendon, 1993).

150 **how unsuspecting he is** This has been the subject of considerable debate. Fokkelman (*Narrative Art and Poetry*) and Exum ("Bathsheba Plotted Shot and Painted") maintain that Uriah knew nothing; Garsiel ("Story of David and Bathsheba") that he doesn't know at first but finds out that first night. Sternberg (*Poetics*) gives the arguments for each deduction, explaining that the author juggles both the suspicious and the naïve Uriah, never quite letting the reader know.

150 **state of sexual contamination** Bailey refers to 1 Sam. 21:5 as a taboo on sex (*David in Love and War*), but the result of having sex is not being able to eat from the consecrated food, not execution! Even Deut. 23:10–14, which provides for the removal of impurities from a war camp, never says anything about not having sex outside the camp. And certainly nothing about saying hello to your wife.

150 *masat hammelek* The standard translations concentrate on the meaning of gift (RSV, NIV, NJPS, YLT) or specifically of food (KJV, NKJV). But McCarter translates "he marched out with the weapons-bearers," reconstructing 4Q Sam.[a] as [*wyṣʾ*] *ʾwryh b [nśy hklym]* and considering this the original text (*Second Samuel*). Bailey, who also reads in this way, sees a really invidious plot. To him, these are the ones who are to signal the king, who is trying to entrap Uriah, to get him to sleep with Bathsheba in violation of the soldier's oath, to catch him in the act so he could be charged with putting the army in jeopardy (*David in Love and War*). But we do not know that there was a soldier's oath, or that sleeping with your

wife on furlough was a capital crime. Bailey's David is really horrible, always intending to kill Uriah.

151 **why he did not go home** David Marcus calls this a "brilliant coup" on his part ("David the Deceiver and David the Dupe," *Prooftexts* 6 [1986]: 163–71). But maybe not so brilliant, since it got him killed.

151 **"lives in a shack"** Perhaps, as Perry and Sternberg suggest ("The King Through Ironic Eyes"), a subtle thrust at the king in his palace. The reader may also remember that just a few chapters ago (in 2 Sam. 7:2), David himself was concerned that he lived in a palace and the ark only in tents.

151 **a man of piety** Uriah the Hittite speaks as one who worships YHWH, as we should expect from someone in David's inner circle. His very name is Hebrew, "Yah is my light." Perhaps it is not a birth name but a renaming in the faith. N. Wyatt has a different suggestion, that the name is Jebusite and means "Yah is ewar," meaning "Yah is a Hurrian divine title." He identifies him with Araunah the Jebusite, from whom David bought the threshing-floor that became the temple site, and suggests that Araunah should be identified with 'rwnh, the king, the last Jebusite king (2 Sam. 24:23). Acquiring Bathsheba would be like taking over the king's role here too (" 'Araunah the Jebusite' and the Throne of David," *Studia Theologica* 39 [1985]: 39–53).

151 **Uriah's speech** Garsiel points out the impertinence and irony ("Story of David and Bathsheba"), and Marcus, arguing from patterns of retribution, labels his behavior that of an offended husband countering David's attempt to pin paternity on him ("David the Deceiver and David the Dupe").

152 **form of oath** The oath, explains Exum, shows the courage and self-sacrifice of a soldier. Since David can make no headway with a principled man, Uriah must disappear ("Bathsheba Plotted Shot and Painted"). Garsiel explains that the oath is not solidarity with comrades, for he has been feasting. It is a restrained protest of an officer caught between duty and rage ("Story of David and Bathsheba").

152 **Abraham once feared** In Augustin's words, "Abraham's fear became a blood reality for Uriah" ("Die Inbesitznahme der schönen Frau").

153 **even women dropping millstones** Joab's mention of the women at Thebez has opened the door for contemporary writers to see lethal women in this story. As Sternberg calls it, David is also a "Warrior King laid low by a woman" (*Poetics*). To Joseph Blenkinsopp, Bathsheba is an example of the woman who brings death ("Theme and Motif in the Succession History [2 Sam. 11:2 ff] and the Yahwist Corpus," supp. to *Vetus Testamentum* 15 [1965]: 44–57). Carol Fontaine refers to the "feminine shadow of death hovering over Uriah at the gate of Rabbah, all because of his failure to stand father to David's child ("Bearing of Wisdom"). Cheryl Exum notes this tendency, also expressed by David Gunn ("Bathsheba Goes Bathing"). To Exum these writers are expressing and reinscribing the text's androcentric ideology ("Raped by the Pen"). But the actual story never hints that Bathsheba is a femme fatale. At most, perhaps Alice Ogden Bellis is right to suggest that Joab could not afford to directly express his anger about David's strategy and the death of an innocent man, so he directed it against an "intuitively appropriate scapegoat, women in general," the classic case of blaming the victim (*Helpmates, Harlots, and Heroes: Women's Stories in the Hebrew Bible* [Louisville: Westminster/John Knox, 1994]). There is a huge difference between the Bible's

idea that the violation of women is a harbinger of war and violence, and these readers' "understanding" that the woman herself caused it.

153 **"harvesting" the wives of other men** Jon Levenson and Baruch Halpern suggest that this is a domestic version of dynastic marriages, solidifying contacts with various important groups in Israel ("The Political Import of David's Marriages," *Journal of Biblical Literature* 99 [1980]: 507–18).

154 **conventional wisdom** I can see no reason for Regina Schwartz's argument that Bathsheba is compared to an animal because polluting someone's woman, like slaughtering his lamb, is a violation of property rights ("Adultery in the House of David: The Metanarrative of Biblical Scholarship and the Narratives of the Bible," *Semeia* 54 [1991]: 35–56). Fewell and Gunn argue that since David made a meal out of Bathsheba the lamb, YHWH will take David's concubines as a meal for Absalom and give David's daughter as a meal for Amnon (*Gender, Power and Promise*). But Nathan never says this, nor does the narrator of the rape of Tamar, who never suggests YHWH orchestrated the action.

155 **Bathsheba is the poor man** My student and colleague Susan McGarry first drew my attention to this interpretation, which the conventional teachings had blinded me to. J. W. Wisselius, arguing that Uriah is a *ger* and therefore was weaker than Bathsheba, who had important family connections, reaches the same conclusion ("Joab's Death and the Central Theme of the Succession Narrative [2 Sam. 9–1 Kings 2]," *Vetus Testamentum* 40 [1990]: 336–51). Tod Linafelt, who points out that the verb "take" occurs seven times in 2 Sam. 12:1–15, also says the worst crime was taking Uriah from Bathsheba ("Taking Women").

156 **Solomon** Carol Fontaine makes the interesting point that David has chosen folly, but Solomon chooses wisdom, which finally redeems David ("Bearing of Wisdom").

156 **fourfold indemnity** The Septuagint reads "sevenfold," which is the punishment mentioned for theft in Prov. 6:31, and Peter Coxon sees this as an allusion to Bath-Sheba, since *šebaʿ* means "seven" ("A Note on Bathsheba in 2 Sam. 12:1–6," *Biblica* 62 [1981]: 247–50). The Septuagint reading may be influenced by this similarity.

156 **dark side of kingship** As Regina Schwartz notes, the story is very ambivalent about power ("Adultery in the House of David")

156 **kingship will not solve Israel's problems** Significantly, the book of Chronicles, which maintains its faith in kingship, does not record this story.

Trauma and Tragedy: The Betrayals of Tamar

This story has received a great deal of attention as a superb piece of literature, and several have concentrated on explicating the literary artistry by which the author draws us into the story: George Ridout, "The Rape of Tamar: A Rhetorical Analysis of 2 Sam. 13:1–22," in *Rhetorical Criticism: Essays in Honor of James Muilenburg*, ed. Jared Jackson and Martin Kessler (Pittsburgh: Pickwick, 1974), 75–84; Shimeon Bar-Efrat, "The Narrative of Amnon and Tamar," in *Narrative Art in the Bible* (Sheffield: Almond, 1989); J. P. Fokkelman, "2 Sam. 13: 'Chips Off the Old Block,' " in *King David (2 Sam. 9–20; 1 Kings 1–2)*, vol. 1 of *Narrative Art and Poetry in the Books of Samuel* (Assen, Netherlands: van Gorcum, 1981), 99–125; Phyllis Trible, "Tamar: The Royal Rape of Wisdom," in *Texts of Terror: Literary-Feminist Readings of Biblical Narratives*, Overtures to

Biblical Theology (Philadelphia: Fortress Press, 1984), 37–64; Jenny Smith, "The Discourse Structure of the Rape of Tamar (2 Samuel 13:1–22)," *Vox Evangelica* 20 (1990): 21–42. Everyone agrees that the story is structured as a chiasm whose introduction and conclusion concern Absalom and whose central act is the rape and the dramatic shift from love to hate in vv. 14–15, but Ridout's chiasm completely overlooks Absalom's betrayal of Tamar.

157 **Absalom** As many scholars have noted, the story starts and ends with Absalom: it is a tale of Absalom's destiny, of which Tamar's story is only a part. However, as Gerald Hammond points out, matters go too far when the New English Bible titles the section "Absalom's Rebellion and Other Conflicts" and the Revised English Bible titles it "Conflict in David's Family" ("Michal, Tamar, Abigail and What Bathsheba Said: Notes Towards a Really Inclusive Translation of the Bible," in *Women in the Biblical Tradition*, ed. George Brooke, Studies in Women and Religion 31 [Lewiston, N.Y.: Edwin Mellen, 1992], 53–70). Even a scholar like William H. C. Propp calls it "a tale of King David's ill-starred family and a treatise on problematic issues in the Israelite kinship system" ("Kinship in 2 Samuel 13," *Catholic Biblical Quarterly* 55 [1993]: 39–53). It is, foremost, a story about rape.

157 **Amnon** G. R. H. Wright calls attention to the meaning of this name from the root *'mn,* "true, faithful." Since Tamar is the palm tree, he associates the story with Dumuzi (literally "true-son") and Inanna, mistress of the palm tree. The use of cakes in the story and the death of Amnon at a sheep-shearing all point to this Dumuzi story, in which the "faithful shepherd is condemned to death by Inanna." But to see this, Wright has to ignore the plot, reducing the relations to: "A beautiful virgin in the event is deadly and a man is cut off while feasting at the sheepfolds" ("Dumuzi at the Court of David," *Numen* 27 [1981]: 54–63). What happened to the rape? Strained as it is, Wright's discussion does point to the tragic irony of the name Amnon.

158 **Jonadab, with a plan** The text does not indicate that Jonadab predicted a rape; he only envisions them being alone. Perhaps he believes that the king would let them marry! His disapproval becomes clear two years later, when he does not attend Amnon's sheep-shearing party.

158 **the** *biryah* For this interpretation, see Adrien Janis Bledstein, "Was Habbirya a Healing Ritual Performed by a Woman in King David's House?," *Biblical Research* 37 (1992): 15–31. As a princess, claims Bledstein, Tamar would have been educated in the healing arts along with other marks of culture.

159 **heart cakes** The term refers to either therapeutic function (they "enhearten") or shape. Cakes are used in the worship of the "queen of heaven" in Jer. 7:18 and 44:19, but these are called *kawânim,* like the Akkadian *kawânu,* not "heart cakes."8 Fokkelman points out that there are two—thus alluding to sexual overtones (*Narrative Art and Poetry*). Moreover, the word that means to knead the heart cakes ("enhearten" them) also refers to charm by love in the Song of Songs (4:9).

160 **Dinah, daughter of Leah** This story clearly has parallels to the Dinah story, which, however, is "outside" and is not so clearly about rape. Some scholars have suggested that the stories have the same authorship and are bookends in the same composition, what David Noel Freedman calls "Super-J" ("Dinah and

Shechem Tamar and Amnon," *Austin Seminary Bulletin,* Faculty Edition 105 [1990]: 51–63). They are, however, contrastive in that only this one is umambiguously rape and there is a big difference between the hate of Amnon and the love of Shechem.

160 **half sister** The laws of Leviticus (18:9, 11; 20:17) and Deuteronomy (27:22), and the prophet Ezekiel (22:11) forbid such marriage. Propp argues that the narrator alludes to the illegality by "overusing" the terms "brother" and "sister" ("Kinship in 2 Samuel 13"). Strangely enough, the love poetry of both Mesopotamia and Israel use "brother" and "sister" as terms for endearment. Possibly narcissistic longings to marry oneself result both in incestuous longing for the sister, as closest to oneself, and in seeing the beloved as the sibling, the one closest to self. For incest in general, see Athalya Brenner, "On Incest," in *A Feminist Companion to Exodus-Deuteronomy,* ed. Athalya Brenner (Sheffield: Sheffield Academic Press, 1994), 113–38.

161 *nebalāh* In addition to the Dinah story, the word is used to describe Achan's act of taking an object from Jericho, which was anathema (Josh. 7:15), the proposed rape of strangers and the rape of the concubine (Judg. 19:23; 20:6), not remaining chaste as an unmarried daughter (Deut. 22:21), and adultery (Jer. 29:23). For some reason, McCarter (*Second Samuel,* Anchor Bible [Garden City, N.Y.: Doubleday, 1984]) and Smith ("Discourse Structure") associate this with "descending to the level of the Canaanite," but the Bible never explicitly associates *nebalāh* with non-Israel.

161 **"whither would I go?"** McCarter describes an Egyptian stele of defeated kings crying "Where shall I go?" (*Second Samuel*).

161 **"with my shame?"** Ḥerpāh, "shame," technically does not involve guilt. Lyn Bechtel demonstrates that when, in Psalm 89, the king of Israel complains of being shamed, the cause is not any behavior on his part but the fact that God abandoned him ("The Perception of Shame Within the Divine-Human Relationship," in *Uncovering Ancient Stones,* ed. Lewis Hopfe [Winona Lake, Ind.: Eisenbrauns, 1994], 79–92). So too mistreatment by Amnon causes shame through no fault of Tamar. Nevertheless, Tracy Hansen, who identifies with Tamar, notes that a child who is sexually abused may both blame herself for not being able to avoid the abuse and internalize the way she was treated, and thereby grow up with a very negative view of herself as worthless ("My Name Is Tamar," *Theology* 95 [1992]: 370–76).

161 **"you will be one of the outrageous boors"** Tamar has no power to change events: but she can unmask them, thus letting the reader see clearly the behavior of the men in power. On this point see Fokkelien van Dijk-Hemmes, "Tamar and the Limits of Patriarchy: Between Rape and Seduction (2 Samuel 13 and Genesis 38)," in *Anti-Covenant: Counter-Reading Women's Lives in the Hebrew Bible,* ed. Mieke Bal, JSOT supp. 81 (Sheffield: Almond, 1989), 135–56.

162 **Davidic gene heritage** Royalty, like mythical ancestors, is often endogamous. For the Egyptian practice, see A. Erman, *Life in Ancient Egypt* (London: Macmillan, 1894), 153–54. Propp cites a Phoenecian example: Eshmunazor II of Sidon was son of King Tabnit and his wife Immi-ashtart, both of whom were the children of Eshmunazor I (KAI 14:13–15, cited by Propp, "Kinship in 2 Samuel 13," 44, n. 19).

163 **Amnon hated her** Fokkelman claims that Amnon's act of violence reveals him as someone incapable of contact. Tamar is a witness, and to see her again would be a repeated "extremely shameful unmasking and intolerable confrontation with his own shortcomings as a person" (*Narrative Art and Poetry*, 108).

164 **"worse than the other evil"** Propp ("Kinship in 2 Samuel 13"), as R. A. Carlson before him (*David the Chosen King: A Traditio-Historical Approach to the Second Book of Samuel,* trans. Eric J. Sharpe and Stanley Rudman [Stockholm: Almqvist & Wiksell, 1964]), notes the parallel to Deut. 22:28–29 in which a seducer or rapist is never allowed to divorce the woman. The verb for "send away" in our story is the same word translated "divorce" in legal contexts. Tamar herself suggests marriage both before and after the rape.

164 **servant** The servants are sent away to let Amnon be alone with Tamar; here the servant reappears to send Tamar away. The two appearances of "servants" are the frame for the rape itself.

166 **"crying out"** Interestingly, Fokkelman states "the noise of the tearing sounds via the alliteration of *qof* and *ʿayin* is converted into the sound of the voice of Tamar" (*Narrative Art and Poetry*), without noting how much stronger this would be true if the verb were *qarʾah* instead of *ṣaʿaqah*.

166 **enmeshed in family relations** Bar-Ephrat points out that not only are there five words of familial relationship, but they are arranged Absalom/Amnon/Tamar/Amnon/Absalom and the possessive suffixes are 3rd, 2nd, 1st, 2nd, and 3rd. Tamar is truly trapped in the middle (*Narrative Art in the Bible*, 234 ff.).

167 **And now, my sister, hush** Scholars like Propp, asking what fraternity has to do with silence ("Kinship in 2 Samuel 13"), completely miss the second betrayal of Tamar when they assume that Absalom is telling her not to hope for an incestuous marriage. Fokkelman suggests that Absalom wants to take the law into his own hands. Only in a footnote, where he notes the many repetitions of "brother" in Absalom's speech, does Fokkelman remark on the emphasis on family solidarity, but states there is "obviously" no appeal to family solidarity which would be a "misplaced blunder" to ask of a violated woman (*Narrative Art and Poetry*). But it is asked all the time of women abused by family members: far from a "blunder," it is an act of oppression. For victims of domestic abuse, see Joyce Ann Mercer, "Legal and Theological Justice for Abused Adolescent Girls," *Journal of Law and Religion* 9 (1992): 451–69. For this aspect of the Tamar story, see Pamela Cooper-White, *The Cry of Tamar: Violence Against Women and the Church's Response* (Minneapolis: Ausburg Fortress, 1995).

167 **he betrays her** Male commentators do not seem to notice this betrayal, either omitting this passage from consideration (as does Ridout, "The Rape of Tamar") or putting a positive spin on it, as in Fokkelman's suggestion that he wants to spare Tamar the misery and humiliation involved in a lawsuit (*Narrative Art and Poetry*). Perhaps out of unwillingness to see the evil in this betrayal, even female commentators have offered favorable interpretations of Absalom's actions. Trible "redeems" him by showing that he positions himself as her advocate (*Texts of Terror*), and Tracy Hansen finds consolation in the fact that Absalom offers Tamar a home ("My Name Is Tamar"). But Smith notes that the words without action are the beginnings of the negative evaluation of Absalom to come ("Discourse Structure").

168 **He did not punish Amnon** Lev. 18:29 prescribes both death and eradication of lineage. Propp, however, has a strange suggestion: that "perhaps" David should have executed Tamar as well as Amnon, since she did not object to marriage ("Kinship in 2 Samuel 13"). The biblical author, however, makes the forcing of Tamar clear and explicit, and scholarly talk of punishing her for incest is tantamount to yet a third betrayal of Tamar. It is perhaps this type of accusation that Tamar is worried about.

168 **David's pattern to do nothing** Gerald Hammond prefers the standard Masoretic version, explaining that David's power is severely curbed as the sons maneuver for power through the abuse of David's women. David did Amnon's bidding at the beginning of the story, now he can do nothing ("Michal, Tamar, Abigail and What Bathsheba Said").

The Dinah Affair

180 **Mothers in the ancient Near East** For functions of the mother, see initially Carol Meyers, " 'To Her Mother's House': Considering a Counterpart to the Israelite *bêt 'ab,*" *The Bible and the Politics of Exegesis* (Cleveland: Pilgrim Press, 1991), 39–51.

180 **the land** Some scholars have connected this motif with Israel's attitudes toward the indigenous populations. See Stephen Geller, "The Sack of Shechem: The Use of Typology in Biblical Covenant," *Prooftexts* 10 (1990): 1–15. Some post-biblical retellings of the story took the occasion for diatribes against the long-gone Canaanites.

181 **laws of Hammurabi** For translation, see Martha Roth, *Law Collections from Mesopotamia and Asia Minor* (Atlanta: Scholars Press, 1994).

181 **streetwalkers** For the Mesopotamian references see Tikva Frymer-Kensky, *Motherprayer* (New York: Putnam, 1995).

181 **Tyndale . . . Calvin** Quoted from Ilona N. Rashkow, *Upon the Dark Places: Antisemitism and Sexism in English Renaissance Biblical Translation* (Sheffield: Almond Press, 1990), 97. Rashkow analyzes how the renaissance translators "fill in the gaps" to make ambiguous meanings clear.

181 **never tells us clearly that Shechem raped her** The Jerusalem Targum adds *be'anûsa* "by force, in rape," an addition added by other translations, including the NJPS "took her by force." Throughout the millennia, commentators have explained this story as a rape. Recently, however, some scholars have favored a non-rape interpretation. See in particular Ita Sheres, *Dinah's Rebellion: A Biblical Parable for Our Time* (New York: Crossroad, 1990); Tikva Frymer-Kensky, "The Bible and Women's Studies," in *Feminist Perspectives on Jewish Studies* (New Haven: Yale University Press, 1994), 16–39; Lyn Bechtel, "What if Dinah Is Not Raped? (Genesis 34)," *Journal for the Study of the Old Testament* 62 (1994): 19–36; Victor H. Matthews, Bernard M. Levinson, and Tikva Frymer-Kensky, "Virginity in the Bible," in *Gender and Law in the Hebrew Bible and the Ancient Near East* (Sheffield: Sheffield Academic Press, 1998), 79–96. A list of contemporary scholars on each side of the debate is provided by Paul Noble, "A 'Balanced' Reading of the Rape of Dinah: Some Exegetical and Methodological Observations," *Biblical Interpretation* 4 (1996): 173–204. Most recently Suzanne Scholz has analyzed the

way that rape has been "marginalized" (her term) and presented a close reading of the story as a rape plot (Suzanne Sholz, *Rape Plots: A Feminist Cultural Study of Genesis 34* [New York: Peter Lang, 2000] .

181 **ambiguity upon enigma** The enigmatic nature of this story has made it the occasion for a very interesting methodological exchange between Meir Sternberg and Danna Fewell and David Gunn. Sternberg presented an analysis of this story in "Delicate Balance in the Rape of Dinah" (in *The Poetics of Biblical Narrative: Ideological Literature and the Drama of Reading* [Bloomington: Indiana University Press, 1987], 445–76), in which he argued that the gaps are artfully arranged so that a reader can fill them in only one way. This causes the reader not only to reach a certain conclusion but to feel personal ownership of the conclusion that he or she has been manipulated to reach. Danna Nolan Fewell and David Gunn wrote a response to Sternberg's argument in which they claimed that the reader did not have to fill the gaps in a predetermined way, and used their own reading of Genesis 34 as a demonstration that a different reading was in fact possible ("Tipping the Balance: Sternberg's Reader and the Rape of Dinah," *Journal of Biblical Literature* 110 [1991]: 193–211). Meir Sternberg then wrote a rebuttal to their article ("Biblical Poetics and Sexual Politics: From Reading to Counter-reading," *Journal of Biblical Literature* 111 [1992]: 463–88) in which he made a distinction between reading with and counter to the text. However, Sternberg's rebuttal seems unpersuasive: an alternative reading can be counter to traditional interpretations of the text without being counter to the text's own intentions. Paul Noble then wrote a point-by-point comparison of the two positions at each point in the narrative, and claimed that ideological convictions can be held in check by sound exegetical method (Noble, "A 'Balanced' Reading of The Rape of Dinah: Some Exegetical and Methodological Observations," *Biblical Interpretation* 4 [1996]: 99–205).

In the less than decade since this exchange, readers have become more attuned to the artful ambiguity of biblical texts. On this, see David Tracey, *Plurality and Ambiguity: Hermeneutics, Religion, Hope* (Chicago: University of Chicago Press, 1994), and Steven Geller, *Sacred Enigmas: Literary Religion in the Hebrew Bible* (London: Routledge, 1996).

183 ʿ**innah** For a study of the word order, see Lyn Bechtel, "What if Dinah Is Not Raped?" *JSOT* 62 (1994): 19–36. The explanation is my own.

183 *betûlah* For a discussion of this word, see Gordon Wenham "*betulah*, a girl of Marriageable Age," *Vetus Testamentum* 22 (1972): 236–348.

184 *parthenos* For Greece, see initially Michel Foucault, *The Use of Pleasure*, vol. 2 of *The History of Sexuality*, English trans. by Robert Hurley (New York: Vintage, 1986), and Giulia Sissa, *Greek Virginity*, trans. Arthur Goldhammer (Cambridge: Harvard University Press, 1990).

185 **noteworthy attempts by anthropologists** This is the key problem with Carol Delaney's focus on the ideology of "monogenesis," i.e., the Aristotelian notion that the entire embryo is contained in the sperm. Her argument that monogenesis and monotheism led to the establishment of total patriarchy and its desire to control women ignores the fact that patriarchy came long before Aristotle and long before monotheism. Monogenesis was only one of several biological models in ancient Greek medicine. It became the dominant scientific belief precisely

because it fit patriarchal ideals. (Carol Delaney, "Seeds of Honor, Fields of Shame," in *Honor and Shame and the Unity of the Mediterranean,* ed. David Gilmore, Publications of the American Anthropological Association 22 [1987].)

Jane Schneider's thesis that the pan-Mediterranean preoccupation with female chastity arose in the absence of effective state control also suffers from this problem. When kin groups compete over land and other scarce resources, she argues, women are a key resource, and guarding access to this resource both symbolizes the family's ability to protect its material boundaries and reinforces intrafamilial cooperation in the face of potentially disruptive external forces. The valuation of virginity was an established social institution long before the period of the deterioration of state control with which she deals, but the idea of guarding access illuminates some of the control issues involved. (Jane Schneider, "Of Vigilance & Virgins," *Ethnology* 10 [1971]: 1–24.)

An influential article by Sherry Ortner pointed to the emergence of the state as the source of the virginity ideal. The state's increasing stratification in kinship forms encouraged the emergence of the family as an administrative unity with absolute authority vested in the father. In this patriarchy, women are legal minors subject to male control. Once again, Ortner's chronology is off: the absolute authority of the father comes before the establishment of the state; in fact (as we see in Israel), it is the major aspect of governance until the state supersedes its authority. Ortner herself realized the historical myopia of her first analysis after her studies in Polynesia demonstrated that hierarchical social organization preceded state formation and economic intensification. In a more recent work, Ortner explains that hierarchy itself creates this demand for virginity. The status of a person in a hierarchical society is based first on hierarchical position and second on gender within the rank. Thus, at the highest rank, the social organization unites males and females with common interests and tends toward (though it doesn't reach) gender equality. Women also get their share of the family property: in patrilineal exogamous systems women are dowered, in cognatic endogamous systems they inherit. The unexpected kick is that even though marriage is less important in the latter system, both systems nevertheless place great importance on guarding a girl's virginity. Ortner therefore concludes that the stratification itself, by elevating women's position within each stratum, creates the high cultural value of virginity. Noting that "Virginity in its cultural contexts [is] an expression and cultivation of the overall higher 'value' of women in such systems," Ortner suggests the reason is that "virginity downplays the uniquely feminine capacity to be penetrated and to give birth to children." The two articles are Ortner, "The Virgin and the State," *Feminist Studies* 4 (1978): 19–33; and Ortner, "Gender and Sexuality in Hierarchical Societies," in *Sexual Meanings: The Cultural Construction of Gender and Sexuality,* ed. Sherry Ortner and Harriet Whitehead (New York: Cambridge University Press, 1981), 351–409; quotations are from p. 401.

There is some truth in each of these interpretations. Women have sometimes been treated as a resource of wealth and barter. The state and its religious institutions have often formally legitimated, enforced and symbolically justified chastity codes by providing different laws and punishments for female and male sexuality, and by allowing "crimes of honor" that condone by minimal sentencing any homicides committed to avenge the sexual transgression of a female relative. But there are still many questions unanswered. The higher status virginity supposedly confers on women may be true for lifetime virgins in Christian culture, but does not conform to the lived experience of most women. And the economic value of women does not explain the vehemence with which trespasses are often pursued.

Alice Shlegel's study ("Status, Property and the Value on Virginity," *American Ethnologist* 18 [1991]: 719–34) has serious flaws that make it untenable. In the most recent study of virginity, Schlegel uses the index of cultures and notes that the only societies that do not value virginity are those with subsistence technologies, small communities, absence of stratification, matrilineal descent, matrilocal marriage, absence of belief in high gods, no bride-wealth, little or no property exchange at marriage, and ascribed rather than achieved status. She therefore suggests that those societies where young men seek to ally with powerful families value virginity because by ensuring the virginity of families, the bride's family prevents young men from claiming girls by making them pregnant. When abortion is freely available, she adds, virginity is less valued. But historians know of societies, like biblical society, in which bride-wealth is clearly combined with the valuation of virginity. Schlegel's flaw lies in the very methodology of cross-cultural techniques. She recognizes that there are six gradations of attitude toward premarital sexuality: expected, tolerated, mildly disapproved but not punished, mildly disapproved and lightly punished, disallowed except with groom, and strongly disapproved. However, in order to code her computer search, she takes the first three as "virginity not valued" and the last three as "virginity valued." This simplifies far too much. Moreover, there are societies (like contemporary Saudi Arabia) that do more than strongly disapprove, that kill the girl and/or her lover. There are also societies (early and medieval Christianity) whose valuation of virginity was so high that it became the bedrock demonstration of faith. In addition, it is simply not true that virginity is not valued where abortion is available: laws from the ancient and classical world clearly assume the option of abortion or exposure.

185 **"Prime Rule"** For discussion of gender and Foucault's theory of the primal law, see Judith Butler, *Gender Trouble: Feminism and the Subversion of Identity* (New York: Routledge, 1990).

185 **chastity codes** This phenomenon has been studied particularly in the societies around the Mediterranean, because chastity codes are universal through that area. But the same patterns have been discerned in very widespread areas. The classic study is by J. G. Peristiany, *Honor and Shame: The Values of Mediterranean Society* (London: Weidenfeld & Nicolson, 1966). More recently, see David Gilmore, "Introduction" to David Gilmore, ed. *Honor and Shame and the Unity of the Mediterranean*, Publications of the American Anthropological Association 22 (1987): 2–21; Maureen Giovannini, "Female Chastity Codes in the Circum-Mediterranean: Comparative Perspectives," ibid., 61–74; and Anton Blok, "Rams and Billy-Goats: A Key to the Mediterranean Code of Honour," *Man* 16 (1991): 427–40.

185 **when a girl hits puberty** For discussion, see Karen Erickson Paige and Jeffrey M. Paige, *The Politics of Reproductive Ritual* (Berkeley: University of California Press, 1981), and Lucy Mair, *Marriage* (London: Scholars Press, 1977), chapter 10.

186　**In the ancient Near East** See the Sumerian Exercise tablet 7–8: Assyria MAL 55 in Roth op.cit.

186　**A love poem from ancient Sumer** This is Love poem Dumuzi-Inanna H, critical edition by Yitschak Tsefati, *Love Songs in Sumerian Literature—Critical Edition of the Dumuzi-Inanna Songs* (Ph.D. diss., Tel Aviv: Bar-Ilan University, 1985), 209–17; English translation of this poem has been published by Thorkild Jacobsen, *The Harps That Once: Sumerian Poetry in Translation* (New Haven: Yale University Press, 1987), 10–12. Tsefati has now been published in English, *Love Songs in Sumerian Literature* (Tel Aviv: Bar-Ilan University Press, 1998).

186　**"The Marriage of Sud"** Translation by Thorkild Jacobsen, *The Harps,* 167–80.

187　*stuprum* See Angeliki Laiou, "Sex, Consent and Coercion in Byzantium," in *Consent and Coercion to Sex and Marriage in Ancient and Medieval Societies,* ed. Angeliki Laiou (Washington, D.C.: Dumbarton Oaks Research Library, 1993), 109–220, and Diana Moses, "Livy's Lucretian and the Validity of Coerced Consent in Roman Law," ibid., 39–82.

188　**"Law of the Slandered Bride"** See Tikva Frymer-Kensky, "Deuteronomy," in *The Women's Bible Commentary,* ed. Carol Newsom and Sharon H. Ringe (Westminster/John Knox, 1982).

188　**Shechem's true feelings** Attempts to divide sources between the rape and Shechem's love (as in Yair Zakovitch, "Assimilation in Biblical Narratives," in *Empirical Models for Biblical Criticism,* ed. Jeffrey Tigay [Philadelphia; University of Pennsylvania Press, 1985]), 175–96, have as their only basis the unlikelihood of true love after a rape. Without a rape, there is no reason to do this.

188　*Dabaq* Further uses include Solomon cleaving to his wives in love (1 Kings 11:2) and Israel loving God (Ps. 119:31, Deut. 13:5, and Josh. 23:8, and with *nefeš,* Ps. 63:9); and the psalmist in depression is stuck in the mud, Ps. 119:25. In all these contexts, in addition to those in which love is not the subject, the connotation is permanent attachment.

189　*dibber ʾel libbah* The other party may be alienated, as the concubine who has run from the Levite, Israel who has been rejected by God, the destroyed Jerusalem, and David's men who have seen him grieve excessively over Absalom the enemy with whom they have just been at war. Or the other party's position might be insecure, like Joseph's brothers after the death of Jacob, or Ruth as a poor outsider-gleaner in Boaz's fields, or the people of Jerusalem during the siege of Sennacherib.

189　**This has puzzled many readers** To Sternberg, his reaction is "conspicuous by its absence"; Fewell and Gunn declare it justified while the brothers are away. Since the story tells us very little about his motivations, or about Hamor's, it is easy to construct variant scenarios for each character. The only characters whose motivations are spelled out are Shechem's (after the fact) and the brothers', who are aggrieved and angry.

190　**Hamor** Hamor has not been treated kindly by some contemporary readers who believe that Shechem raped Dinah. Meir Sternberg (op. cit.) accuses him of "brazen disregard of antecedents" when he offers marriage without mentioning rape and considers Dinah's presence in Hamor's house clear proof that she was kidnapped and therefore an indictment of his sincerity in negotiations. In this (unaware) feat of creative gap-filling he is followed by Robert Alter, *Genesis.*

192 **their custom of circumcision** The Bible never labels the Canaanites "uncircumcised," a perjorative it uses for the Philistines. This may be an indication that they
were in fact circumcised. Yairah Amit points out that the issue of circumcision
concerned the population of the north after the exile, peoples brought in by the
Assyrians. She therefore suggests that the issue of circumcision is a hidden reference to marriage with Samaritans, meant as a hidden polemic against the diplomatic dignitaries of the Samaritans in the time of Ezra and Nehemiah, attested
in Neh. 13:28. (Amit, "The Hidden Polemic over Those 'Who dwell in Samaria,' "
in *Hidden Polemics in Biblical Narrative,* trans. Jonathan Chipman [Leiden: Brill,
2000], 189–220).

192 **They are angry** Scholarly attitude toward the brothers' behavior has varied directly with their opinion as to whether Dinah was raped. Sternberg feels the text
justifies the brothers; Bechtel casts the brothers as the villains; the Renaissance
translators blamed the brothers. Rashkow believes the brothers destroyed Dinah's life (Ilona Rashkow, *The Phallacy of Genesis: A Feminist-Psychological Approach* [Louisville: Westminster, 1993], 106). Understanding the social behavior of
the brothers (see next note) does not imply a justification of their behavior, just
as understanding what Dinah did wrong from the viewpoint of her society does
not condone that viewpoint.

194 **revenge raid** See discussion by Julian Pitt-Rivers, *The Fate of Shechem or the Politics of Sex* (Cambridge: Cambridge University Press, 1977). As he explains, female
honor undefended doesn't exist, and in its absence male honor cannot be transmitted. Clinton Bailey looks for an explanation in Bedouin culture. Since women
go outside with livestock, only fear of vengeance keeps others from attacking
them (Clinton Bailey, "How Desert Culture Helps Us Understand the Bible,"
Bible Review 7 [1991]: 15–21 and 38).

194 **took Dinah . . . and went out** Meir Sternberg (op. cit.) and Michael Caspi take
this verse as evidence that Dinah was being held captive in Shechem's house
("The Story of the Rape of Dinah: The Narrator and the Reader," *Hebrew Studies*
26 [1981]: 25–45).

195 **plundered the city** Clinton Bailey relates that in the case of murder, the avenging parties may kill but not plunder; to avenge a rape, however, they can plunder
up to seven days. Since consent is not an issue in the destruction of honor, the
brothers' plundering would be understandable according to Bedouin even if Dinah had run off with Prince Charming. Suzanne Scholz, who sees everything as
stemming from rape, states "everybody is implicated in the oppressive and violent behavior of rape—'a novel idea' " (*Rape Plots,* 165).

195 **punished the whole city** Stephen Geller suggests that the slaughter reflects a relentless hatred of Canaanites and that the true crime was the invitation to peaceful relations, to which the whole city had agreed. (Stephen Geller, "The Sack of
Shechem: The Use of Typology in Biblical Covenant Religion," *Prooftexts* 10
[1990], 1–15). He suggests that the story is included in Genesis to offset the otherwise friendly relations that the Canaanites have enjoyed with the neighbors.

195 **"few in number"** Amit ("The Hidden Polemic") points out that "few in number," *metê mispār,* appears in seventh-century and later literature: Deut. 4:27; Jer.
44:28; Ps. 105:12, 1 Chron. 16:19. This is one of her signs that the issue in the story
as we have it is not the long-gone Canaanite occupants of Shechem but the occu-

pants of Samaria. It is certainly true that post-biblical authors such as Theodotus retold this story with the Samaritans in mind. (See John Collins, "The Epic of Theodotus and the Hellenism of the Hasmoneans," *Harvard Theological Review* 73 [1980]: 91–104.)

196 **"Shall he treat our sister as a whore?"** To those who see rape, the idea of bride-price seems like payment, turning the event into intercourse-for-hire. (See, for example, Scholz, *Rape Plots*.)

196 **On his deathbed** For analysis see Stanley Gewirtz, "Simeon and Levi in 'The Blessing of Jacob' (Gen. 49:5–7)," *Hebrew Union College Annual* 52 (1981): 93–128.

198 **retold often in Hellenistic literature** Discussions by Collins, op. cit.; S. R. Pummer, "Genesis 34 in the Jewish Writings of the Hellenistic and Roman Periods," *Harvard Theological Review* 75 (1982): 177–88; James Kugel, "The Story of Dinah in the *Testament of Levi*," *Harvard Theological Review* 85 (1992): 1–34; Tjitze Baarda, "The Shechem Episode in the Testament of Levi: A Comparison with Other Traditions," in *Sacred History and Sacred Texts in Early Judaism: A Symposium in Honor of A. S. van der Woude*, ed. J. N. Bremmer and F. Garlia Martinez (Kampen, The Netherlands: Pharos, 1992), 11–73; and Angela Standhartinger, " 'Um zu Sehen Die Töchter des Landes' Die Perspective Dinas in der Jüsiach-Hellenistischen Diskussion üm Gen. 34," in *Religious Propaganda and Missionary Competition in the New Testament World: Essays Honoring Dieter Georgi* (Leiden: Brill, 1994), 89–116.

To the Barricades: Views Against the Other

200 *ḥerem* See Susan Niditch, *War in the Hebrew Bible: A Study in the Ethics of Violence* (Oxford: Oxford University Press, 1995).

203 **"iniquity of the Amorites"** For this concept of pollution, see Tikva Frymer-Kensky, "Pollution, Purification and Purgation," in *The Word of the Lord Shall Go Forth: Essays in Honor of David Noel Freedman in Celebration of His Sixtieth Birthday*, ed. Carol L. Meyers and Michael O'Connor (Winona Lake, Ind.: Eisenbrauns, 1983). Robert Cohen sees this iniquity as a classical foundational "other" whose evil helps define Israel's good. "Before Israel: The Canaanites as Other in Biblical Tradition," in *The Other in Jewish Thought and History: Constructions of Jewish Culture and Identity*, ed. Laurence Silberstein and Robert Cohn (New York: New York University Press, 1994), 74–89.

204 **"otherizing" of the Canaanites** See Robert Cohen, *The Other;* also see Delbert Hillers, "Analyzing the Abominable: Our Understanding of Canaanite Religion," *Jewish Quarterly Review* 75 (1985): 253–69.

207 **do not often speak against foreign women** Burns considers this Jezebel and Ataliah and this historical experience with royal wives to be the origin of antipathy to foreign wives in general (John Barclay Burns, "Solomon's Egyptian Horses and Exotic Wives," *Foundations and Facets Forum* 7 [1991]: 29–44). However, Burns's suggestion that this antipathy is "prominent" in the Deuteronomistic history is not warranted.

207 **the daughter of as great a king as Pharaoh** See Shaye Cohen, "Solomon and the Daughter of Pharaoh: Intermarriage, Conversion and the Impurity of Women," *Journal of the Ancient Near East Society* 16 (1984): 23–37. Because the passage does not explicitly say that he worshiped the god of Pharaoh's daughter, and

because other passages are proud of this marriage, Cohen suggests that Pharaoh's daughter here in 1 Kings 11 is a gloss. Michael Fishbane goes further, suggesting that 1 Kings 11:1–4 is all written in the early post-exilic period (*Biblical Interpretation in Ancient Israel* [New York: Oxford University Press, 1985]). Knoppers, on the other hand, holds for the unity of the passage (Gary Knoppers, "Sex, Religion and Politics: The Deuteronomist on Intermarriage," *Hebrew Annual Review* 14 [1994]: 121–41).

207 **nations Deuteronomy does not prohibit** Post-biblical legal developments interpret Deut. 23:4's prohibition of allowing Moabites and Ammonites to enter the congregation as a prohibition of intermarriage with them, but this is not the original sense of the passage. Rabbinic law, moreover, interprets Deut. 23:4 to forbid the conversion of or marriage to Moabite and Ammonite men, not women.

Queen Jezebel, or Deuteronomy's Worst Nightmare

209 **foreign wife** For this view of Jezebel, see J. Alberto Soggin, "Jezebel, oder die fremde Frau," in *Mélanges Henri Cazelles,* ed. M. Carrez, J. Doré, and P. Grelot, Alter Orient and Altes Testament 212 (Paris: Desclée, 1981), 453–59; and Alexander Rofé, "The Vineyard of Naboth: The Origin and Message of the Story," *Vetus Testamentum* 38 (1988): 89–104, who believes the story was composed during the debate over foreign wives in the time of Ezra and Nehemiah. See also Else Holt, " '. . . Urged on by his Wife Jezebel': A Literary Reading of 1 Kings 18 in Context," *Scandinavian Journal of the Old Testament* 9 (1995): 83–96, who notes a new attitude in her death; and Tina Pippin, "Jezebel Re-Vamped," *Semeia:* 69–70: (1995): 221–33. Phyllis Trible awards the Deuteronomist the prize for polarized thinking ("Exegesis for Storytellers and Other Strangers," *Journal of Biblical Literature* 114 [1995]: 3–19.

210 **kill the prophets of Ba'al** Holt depicts this as elimination of scapegoats, according to René Girard's theories in *Violence and the Sacred,* trans. P. Gregory (Baltimore: Johns Hopkins University Press, 1977).

210 **Her otherwise estimable piety** Some readers take her fidelity as more than devotion and see Jezebel as modeled after goddesses (Peter Ackroyd, "Goddesses, Women and Jezebel," in *Images of Women in Antiquity,* ed. A. Cameron and A. Kuhrt, [Detroit: Wayne State University Press, 1983], 245–59) and as playing the role of Asherah in the court cult (Susan Ackerman, "The Queen Mother and the Cult in Ancient Israel," *Journal of Biblical Literature* 112 [1993]: 385–401). Ackerman attributes this to Judean rather than Phoenecian practices. There is, of course, no evidence of an official court cult of Asherah.

210 **Naboth's vineyard** See the studies by Frank Andersen, "Socio-Juridical Background of the Nabot Incident," *Journal of Biblical Literature* 85 (1966): 46–57; K. Baltzer, "Naboths Wienberg (1. Kon 21). Der Konflikt zwischen israelitischem und Kanaanäischem Bodenrecht," *Wort und Dienst* NF 8 (1965): 73–88; Robert Martin-Achard, "La vigne de Naboth (1 Rois 21) d'après des études récentes," *Études Théologiques et Religieuses* 66 (1991): 1–16; and Marsha White, "Naboth's Vineyard and Jehu's Coup: The Legitimation of a Dynastic Extermination," *Vetus Testamentum* 44 (1994): 66–76.

211 **Ahab's predicament . . . is like David's** For a comparison of the two stories, see White, who notes that the only major difference between them is precisely the role of Jezebel inciting her passive husband. White believes that this story is modeled after that of Bathsheba. She believes that the letter Jezebel sends is artificially modeled after David's letter. But Jezebel does not incite Ahab to act; she herself acts, and the letter is the way she clandestinely arranges the law.

212 **His son Jehoram** Ahab's son Ahaziah was succeeded by his other son Jehoram after only two years.

213 **The Death of Jezebel** See Sol Otto Eissfeldt, "Aphrodite Parakyptusa," *Göttingische gelehrte Anzeigen* 220 (1968): 302–309; Saul Olyan, "2 Kings 9:31—Jehu as Zimri," *Harvard Theological Review* 78 (1985): 203–7; Ackroyd, who considers this a heroic death ("Goddesses, Women and Jezebel"); Simon Parker, "Jezebel's Reception of Jehu," *Maᶜarav* 1 (1978): 67–78; and Holt (" ' . . . Urged on by his Wife Jezebel' "). Both Holt and Ackroyd hold that, as the antagonist to the YHWH-warrior Jehu, Jezebel is Asherah. But where Ackroyd speaks of heroism, Parker sees seduction, and Holt interprets "Is it peace, Zimri, murderer of your master?" as an attempt at seduction, which I cannot see. But Holt does catch the double guilt, for the cult of Asherah and the vineyard of Naboth that turn Ahab from YHWH. To Holt, Jezebel is the truly guilty scapegoat in the Girardian universe.

Cozbi

217 **post-biblical tradition** See initially Dorothy Sly, "Changes in the Perception of the Offense in Numbers 25:1," *Proceedings in the Eastern Great Lakes and Midwest Biblical Society* 11(1991): 200–9.

217 **Josephus** *Antiquitates Judaicae* IV 6, 6–12, §126–151. I rely on the translation of H. St. J. Thackeray and Ralph Marcus in the Loeb Classical Library (Cambridge, Ma.: Harvard University Press, 1956) (nine volumes). For a study of Josephus's version, see W. C. Van Unnik, "Josephus's Account of the Story of Israel's Sin with Alien Women in the Country of Midian (Num. 25:1 f)," in *Travels in the World of the O.T.: Studies Presented to M. A. Beek,* ed. H. van Voss et al. (Assen: van Gorcum, 1974): 241–61.

218 **Philo** Translations from *On the Life of Moses,* Loeb Classical Library Philo. vol. 6 (Cambridge: Harvard University Press, 1966) 274–595. Sly lists the other references in Philo: Moses 195–305; Virtues 34–46; Spec 55–57.

218 **Graeco-Roman** For a discussion of this process, see Tikva Frymer-Kensky, "Gifts of the Greeks," in *In the Wake of the Goddesses: Women, Culture and the Biblical Transformation of Pagan Myth* (New York: Free Press, 1993), 203–12.

218 *zanah* See Phyllis Bird, " 'To Play the Harlot: An Inquiry into an Old Testament Metaphor,' " now in Bird, *Missing Persons and Mistaken Identities* (Minneapolis: Fortress Press, 1997): 219–38. Bird holds that the root meaning of the verb is sexual, but shows that most of the uses have nothing to do with sex.

219 **Moses has modified the divine decree** See Frymer-Kensky, "Revelation Revealed" (forthcoming) for other occasions in which Moses modified the revelation.

221 *The qubbah* The early studies of ancient Tent Shrines are by Julian Morgenstern, "The Ark, the Ephod and the Tent of Meeting," *Hebrew Union College Annual* 17

(1942–43), 153–266 and 18 (1944), 152. F. M. Cross "The Priestly Tabernacle," in *The Biblical Archaeologist Reader I*, ed. David N. Freedman and G. E. Wright (Garden City, N.Y., 1961), 202, n. 32, who dates them back to seventh century B.C.E.

222 **Phineas executes them** Reif suggests Phineas slayed Cozbi because of the implicit cultic infidelity involved in bringing a foreign priestess to help with the plague (S. C. Reif, "What Enraged Phineas—A Study of Numbers 25:8," *Journal of Biblical Literature* 20 [1971]: 200–206. Harriet Lutzky considers another possibility, that killing the priestess was a symbolic slaying of the deity the priestess represented (Harriet C. Lutzky, "The Name 'Cozbi' [Numbers XXV 15:18]," *Vetus Testamentum* 47 [1991]: 546–48). This, however, assumes that it was not YHWH.

223 **Cozbi** Lutzky, following Mosis, thinks of two separate verbs, *kzb* I, "to lie" and *kzb* II, "voluptuousness, sexual attractiveness." Mosis *("kzb,"* in *Theological Dictionary of the Old Testament* 7, ed. G. J. Botterweck et al. [Grand Rapids, 1995], 104–21) suggests that the interpretations of the crime as sexual may have come from the meaning of Akkadian *kuzbu* as sexual attractiveness. She also points out the connection with Ishtar and Ashera, and suggests that the name may have evoked Astarte.

Hagar, My Other, My Self

225 **Hagar** For a close reading of this story see Phyllis Trible, "The Desolation of Rejection," in *Texts of Terror: Literary Feminist Readings of Biblical Narratives* (Philadelphia: Fortress Press, 1984), 9–35. For analyses, see Tikva Frymer-Kensky, "Hagar," in *Talking About Genesis: A Resource Guide* (New York: Doubleday, 1996), 94–97; and Hemchand Gossai, "A Voice Crying in the Wilderness," in *Power and Marginality in the Abraham Narrative* (Lanham, Md.: University Press of America, 1995), 1–23. For an analysis of the traditional source-critical approach, see T. D. Alexander, "The Hagar Traditions in Genesis XVI and XXI," in J. A. Emerton, ed., *Studies in the Pentateuch Journal for the Study of the Old Testament*, supp. XLI (Leiden: Brill, 1990), 131–48. Alexander concludes that the two chapters are sufficiently different to indicate that they are not simply variant accounts and that chapter 21 relies on the reader's knowing Genesis 16. For commentaries see Claus Westermann, *Genesis 12–36: A Commentary*, trans. John Scullion (Minneapolis: Augsburg, 1985); and Victor P. Hamilton, *The Book of Genesis 1–17* and *The Book of Genesis 18–50*, the New International Commentary on the Old Testament (Grand Rapids: Eerdmans, 1990, 1995). For Paul's later use of this story see Elizabeth Castelli, "Allegories of Hagar: Reading Galatians 4:21–31 with Postmodern Feminist Eyes," in *The New Literary Criticism and the New Testament*, ed. Edgar Mcknight and Elizabeth Malbon (Valley Forge, Pa.: Trinity Press International, 1994), 228–50, and literature cited there.

225 **chapters . . . 21** For an interesting analysis of this chapter see Hugh White, "The Initiation Legend of Ishmael," *Zeitschrift für die alttestamentliche Wissenschaft* 87 (1975): 267–306.

225 **names count** The true etymology of Hagar is best related to Arabic *hajara*, "to move around," but some have suggested an Egyptian title of the eighteenth dynasty, *hkrt njswt*, "the jewel of the king" (Manfred Görg, "Hagar, die Ägypterin,"

Biblische Notizen 33 [1986]: 17–20). The sound of the name would certainly suggest the *hagger*, the outsider who lives in the midst of Israel. For this suggestion, see already Ina Petermann, "Schick die Fremde in die Wüste!" in *(Anti)-Rassistische Irritationem: Biblische Texte und interkulturelle Zusammenarbeit* (Berlin: Alektor, 1994), 137–50, who notes also that Israel is reminded that they too were *ger*'s in the land of Egypt. Another connection is with Arabic *haġarum*, "stone," as the name for the area in the south of Israel. Targum Onkeles locates the spring to which she ran on the way to *hgr*', a translation of Shur with Arabic = stone, and may be the southern border country. See G. I. Davies, "Hagar El-Heġra and the location of Mount Sinai," *Vetus Testamentum* 22 (1972): 152–63.

226 **Hagar was a princess in the house of Pharaoh** See Midrash Genesis Rabbah 45:1.

226 **to be angry at Sarai** Typical is Louis Leloir, "Hagar the Egyptian's Flight to the Desert: A Biblical Spirituality of the Desert," in *Monastic Studies 16 in Honour of Dom Jean LeClerq* (Montreal: The Benedictine Priory, 1985), 92–110, who says, "A free woman and more intelligent than her maid . . . we see the start of the biblical tradition of female jealousy." None of these statements, of course, have any place in the text.

226 **her slave as her surrogate** John Waters objects to this translation, saying that neither Genesis 16 nor 20 uses the regular word for slave ("Who Was Hagar?" in Cain Felder, ed., *Stony the Road We Trod: African American Biblical Interpretation* [Minneapolis: Fortress Press, 1991], 187–205). But the Bible never uses the word ʿ*ebed* in the feminine, using only ʾ*amāh* and *šipḥāh*. Characterizing her as a slave is not racist: in the Bible mind, on the contrary, it emphasizes her similarity to the later Israelites.

227 **Ancient societies accepted slavery** As Gossai remarks *(Power and Marginality,* 1–23), it is troublesome that people debate the morality of the surrogacy arrangement without ever considering slavery, so that "the greater violence is overlooked."

228 **a person with her own viewpoint** Hagar is often viewed as a heroine by contemporary readers who see her as the triply oppressed, by status, race, and sex, who resisted Sarai (Elsa Tamez, "The Woman Who Complicated the History of Salvation," English trans. Betsy Yaeger, in *New Eyes for Reading: Biblical and Theological Reflections by Women from the Third World*, ed. John Pobee and Barbel von Wartenberg-Potter [Geneva: World Council of Churches, 1986], 129–39). She has become the emblem of African-American women who have shared this triple oppression (Dolores Williams, *Sisters in the Wilderness: The Challenge of Womanist God-Talk* [Maryknoll, N.Y.: Orbis, 1993], 245; Renita Weems, "A Mistress, A Maid and No Mercy," in *Just a Sister Away: A Womanist Vision of Women's Relationships in the Bible* [San Diego: LuraMedia, 1988], 1–19; Weems, "Do You See What I See? Diversity in Interpretation," *Church & Society* 82 [1991]: 28–43); and Katy Taylor, "From Lavender to Purple: A Feminist Reading of Hagar and Celie in the Light of Womanism," *Theology* 97 [1994]: 352–62). Taylor speaks of Hagar's "womanist qualities of contrariness and courage," but as Weems points out, we are all just a paycheck away from being Hagar. John L. Thompson discusses positive comments about Hagar in the history of interpretation, in "Hagar: Test, Terror and

Tradition," *Perspectives* 10 (1995): 16–19, and less positive views in "Hagar, Victim or Villain? Three Sixteenth-Century Views," *Catholic Biblical Quarterly* 59 (1997) 213–33.

228 **cease to consider Sarai's status high** It is interesting to contrast Trible's categorization of the situation, "hierarchical blinders disappear" (*Texts of Terror*, 12) to J. Gerald Janzen's "Hagar's attitude arises in the context of a struggle between social classes, she displays a consciousness defined by that struggle. . . . conceiving its own enlargement only as a function of the diminution of the other" ("Hagar in Paul's Eyes and in the Eyes of Yahweh [Genesis 16]: A Study in Horizons," *Horizons in Biblical Theology* 13 [1991]: 1–22, quote from p. 6). Typically, the simple-sounding biblical lines do not tell us which assumption about Hagar's attitude is correct.

228 **"My wrong is on account of you"** *ḥamasî ʿalēka* is ambiguous. It can mean "the wrong (that has been done to me) is on your head" or "the wrong (that I am about to do) is on your head." Danna Nolan Fewell and David Gunn opt for the latter reading, claiming that she is angry to the point of doing violence, and whatever she does will be Abram's fault ("Keeping the Promise," in *Gender, Power and Promise: The Subject of the Bible's First Story* [Nashville: Abingdon, 1993], 39–55). My reading has the support of the Targum, which interjects an accounting in which Sarai relates what she has done for Abram. J. Gerald Janzen points out that Hagar has in fact wronged Sarai by her behavior, whatever it was (*Abraham and All the Families of the Earth: A Commentary on the Book of Genesis 12–50*, International Theological Commentary [Grand Rapids: Eerdmans, 1993]).

228 **Sarai sees herself at risk** Gossai believes it inconceivable that a slave-woman could be a challenge and threat "to the established power reflected in the persons of Sarai and Abram" (*Power and Marginality*, 8). But as the disposable-wife episode shows, and Sarai now realizes, Sarai has no established power. In the same way, Gossai sees Abram's response as more of a reminder than permission. But, in fact, Abram is restoring to Sarai the reflected authority of a first wife.

229 *watteʿannehā* For the connection of this verb to the Egypt experience and to Abraham, see Janzen, who says these two parallels invite the reader to compare the treatment of this maid with Egypt's treatments of the Hebrews (*Abraham and All the Families of the Earth*). Trible alludes to the "suffering servant" (*Texts of Terror*, 8, 28).

229 **classic rabbinic midrash** Genesis Rabbah 45:6 relates that she made her do servile work even though Abram objected.

229 **by the water spring** Janzen notes the prominence of well episodes in Israel's ancestral stories and it is remarkable that the first focuses on an Egyptian. He remarks that the story of Hagar and her descendants in Gen. 16:9–12 parallels in miniature the story of Abram and his descendants in Gen. 15:13–16 (*Abraham and All the Families of the Earth*).

229 **wilderness . . . Shur** Aramaic *shura* means "wall," and Shur might refer to the wall of fortifications that the Egyptians built along the Suez isthmus to keep out Asiatics. Hagar is on the Shur road, which may or may not mean that she is headed for Egypt. She does not say she is going to Egypt when the angel asks her.

229 **The angel of YHWH** Hamilton (*Genesis*) notes the connection with Elijah in 1 Kings 19.

230 **"Ishmael . . . for God has heard your oppression"** Usually, God sees affliction (Gen. 29:32; Exod. 3:7; Exod. 4:31; Deut. 26:7) and hears the outcry (Exod. 3:7; Deut. 26:7). In particular, God gave pregnancy to Leah because he saw her affliction (Gen. 29:32), and Hannah prays for the same (Gen. 1:11). But listening is so important in this story that the name is an amalgam of the two expressions, to see affliction and to hear outcry.

230 **divine annunciation** Like the address to the mother of Samson (Judg. 13:3–4, 7) and Isaiah's announcing Immanuel (Isa. 7:14–17), the annunciation has four elements, not all of which need be present: (1) announcing of pregnancy, whether known already or not; (2) proclamation of birth; (3) giving of name prior to birth; and (4) announcing of special role and destiny.

230 **his hand against all** As Margaret Poteet points out, it will be the Ishmaelites who will buy Joseph and sell him into slavery ("Literary Unity in the Patriarchal Narratives" [Ph.D. diss., University of Oklahoma, 1990]).

231 **naming God** Trible talks about Hagar daring to name the deity (*Texts of Terror*, 17–18, 28). Scott Holland reads the text together with another encounter in the wilderness, Moses and the burning bush, in which God states, "I have seen the affliction of my people." In that case, Moses asks for the name, whereas Hagar names God ("Hagar and the God-Who-Sees": Reflections on Genesis 16:3–13," *Conrad Grebel Review* 11 [1993]: 165–68).

231 **Seeing is important to Hagar** Devora Steinmetz notes the importance of ʿayin, and points out that not only "spring" (ʿêyn hammayyim) but also the word for "degrade, abuse," ʿinnah, plays on this word. But Steinmetz considers Hagar "blind," rejecting both the suffering of her past and God's promise of her future. She interprets Hagar's silence to the angel's first statement a rejection; but Hagar knows that angels speak in triplicate, and she waits for the angel to finish. Steinmetz also emphasizes Abraham's blindness, not seeing what he should do until God intervenes (*From Father to Son: Kinship, Conflict and Continuity in Genesis* [Louisville: Westminster/John Knox, 1991], 72–85).

231 **"Have I also to this place"** Reading like Th. Booij, "Hagar's words in Genesis XVI 13a," *Vetus Testamentum* 30 (1980): 1–7, "Would I have gone here indeed looking for him that looks after me." Verse 13 presents grammatical and textual differences. Wellhausen suggested a textual emendation. It has been widely accepted to read halôm as Elohim and add weḥ ây, thus: "Have I not seen God [and am alive] after my seeing." This would thus refer to the idea that looking upon God means death, for which see Judg. 6:22–23, in which Gideon says, "Woe, for I have seen an angel of the Lord face to face" and has to be reassured; and Judg. 13:21–23, in which Manoah also needs assurances that he will not die as a result of seeing the angel. Abraham Ahuviah takes ʾaharē, "after," as standing in for penê, "face, before," since the narrator is reluctant to talk about seeing the face of God. Thus, "Have I really seen the face of the one who sees me?" ("The Angel of the Lord Found Her by a Spring of Water in the Wilderness [Genesis 16:7(!)]," *Beth Mikra* 136 [1994]: 71–72; Hebrew). But Hagar sounds triumphant rather than anxious. Horst Seebass reads halom as lehayyim, "Was it not for life (that I have seen)?" ("Zum Text von Gen. 16:3b," *Vetus Testamentum* 21 [1971]: 254–56). Other suggestions are by Hamilton and Janzen (see their commentaries), "Have I really seen the back of him who sees me?," referring to Exodus 33:23, "You cannot see my

face . . . you will see my back"; and similarly Trible, "Have I even here seen after the one who sees me?" (*Texts of Terror*, 18). These do not account for *halom*, which cannot mean "here" or "really" but "to here," which is the reason for the proposed emendations. Seebass and Hugh White have collected attempts to solve this difficulty (Seebass, "Zum Text von Gen. 16:3b," 254–56; White, "The Initiation Legend of Ishmael," 267–306).

231 **El Roi** The pointing of the Masoretic text indicates a noun, "my seeer" or a participle with suffix, "my seeing." N. Wyatt suggests that this may simply be an old participle of a verb with the final weak consonant *h/y*, meaning "El who sees," one of the suggestions made by Rashi. Wyatt notes that it might also be connected to the difficult next sentence, in which Hagar stresses that she has seen ("The Meaning of *El Roi* and the Mythological Dimension in Genesis 16," *Scandinavian Journal of the Old Testament* 8 [1994]: 141–51). Wyatt speculates that there may have been an old cult around Beer-Sheba, connected to the Ugaritic myth of the birth of El's twins (KTU 1, 12) and the Greek birth of the Dioscuroi. Beyond the birth and the twoness, I have trouble seeing the connection.

232 **Egyptian slave** Iaian M. Duguid presents an interesting angle when he mentions the turn to Hagar as another example of Israel's turn to Egyptian fertility, otherwise shown by going there during famines ("Hagar the Egyptian: A Note on the Allure of Egypt in the Abraham Cycle," *Westminster Theological Journal* 56 [1994]: 419–21).

232 **Sarai's own experience** As Danna Fewell states in her midrash on this story, "Exclusion would beget exclusion, Hagar feared" ("Changing the Subject: Retelling the Story of Hagar the Egyptian," in *Genesis: A Feminist Companion to the Bible*, ed. Athalya Brenner. Second series [Sheffield: Sheffield Academic Press, 1998], 182–94).

233 **be oppressed** Janzen points to the "middle voice" construction of *hit`anî*, which is neither victor nor victim but undergoes the action of the other by its own choosing (*Abraham and All the Families of the Earth*, 11).

234 **What the lad was doing** For a discussion of the many translations that have been proposed and their emotional connotations, see Gerald Kendrick, "Selected Translation Problems in Genesis," *The Bible Translator* 4 (1990): 425–27.

235 **horrified at Abraham's cavalier treatment** By contrast, Steinmetz is angered that Abraham "loses sight of his destiny" and has to be instructed what to do (*From Father to Son*, 72). As usual, the biblical story contains no valuation, though clearly it holds that Abraham had to send Ishmael away once God commanded it. The parallel with the binding of Isaac is clear.

235 **horrified that God orders him** As are Fewell and Gunn, who conclude that "God shows himself to be a god of good and evil" (*Gender, Power and Promise*, 51). Similar is John Waters's "Is Yahweh immune from moral judgement?" ("Who was Hagar?," 200). Fewell and Gunn claim, rightly, that Hagar and Ishmael inhabit the margins of the text, but it is, after all, Jacob's text, and the Ishmaelites would have their own text, written or oral. As Walter Brueggemann notes, the text does not force us to choose, making clear that God is well inclined toward Ishmael, and Ishmael's promise is considerable (Brueggemann, "Genesis," in *Interpretation: A Bible Commentary for Teaching and Preaching* [Atlanta: John Knox Press, 1982]).

235 **Hagar . . . now wanders in the desert** Trible remarks that "Hagar knows not exodus, but exile" (*Texts of Terror*, 23). But Israel's exodus also felt like exile until they arrived at Sinai, and perhaps even after, until they arrived in the land.

Royal Origins: Ruth on the Royal Way

There have been numerous commentaries written on the book of Ruth. The most notable in English are Tod Linafelt, *Ruth*, Berith Olam: Studies in Hebrew Narrative & Poetry (Collegeville, Minn.: The Liturgical Press, 1999); Kiersten Nielsen, *Ruth: A Commentary* (Louisville: Westminster/John Knox, 1997); Jack Sasson, *Ruth: A New Translation with a Philological Commentary and a Formalist-Folklorist Interpretation* (Baltimore: Johns Hopkins University Press, 1989; Robert Hubbard, Jr., *The Book of Ruth*, New International Commentary on the Old Testament (Grand Rapids: Eerdsman, 1988); Edward Campbell, *Ruth: A New Translation with Introduction, Notes and Commentary,* Anchor Bible (Garden City, N.Y.: Doubleday, 1975). My own commentary, written for the Jewish Publication Society Commentary series, should be forthcoming soon. Of note also are two anthologies: *Reading Ruth: Contemporary Women Reclaim a Sacred Story,* ed. Judith Kates and Gail Reimer (New York: Ballantine, 1994); *A Feminist Companion to Ruth,* ed. Athalya Brenner (Sheffield: Sheffield Academic Press, 1993).

240 **the spirit in which she sends them** Fewell and Gunn note the similarity with Judah's sending Tamar away. They conclude from this that Naomi blames the Moabite women as dangerous and sends them for that reason, veiling her suspicions with "polite rhetoric" (Danna Fewell and David Gunn, *Compromising Redemption: Relating Characters in the Book of Ruth* [Louisville: Westminster/John Knox, 1990]: 72–74. This would go entirely against the grain of the book of Ruth. Moreover, Naomi's action of release is correct; Judah's is not.

243 **miqreh** The many similarities between the story of Ruth's and Rivka's betrothal are mentioned throughout. Abraham Rofé dates the Rivka story to this same period on linguistic grounds. ("An Enquiry into the Betrothal of Rebekah," in *Die Hebräische Bible und ihr zweifache Nachgeschicte: Festschrift für Rolf Rendtorff,* ed. Erhard Blum, Christian Macholz, and Ekkehard Stagemann (Neukirchen-Vluyn: Neukirchener Verlag, 1990): 27–30. Rofé concludes that the story of Rivka suits the ideology of Ezra and Nehemiah "as against the notables of Judea, who relied on the precedent of Ruth and Boaz, the exclusivist party buttressed its position with the example of Abraham" (p. 37).

248 **a succubus** For this see Jack Sasson, *Ruth.*

248 **there was no one to be a levir** Attempts to understand the story in terms of levirate are doomed to failure. Ancient Near Eastern law does not carry levirate throughout the extended family. There comes a point at which the childless widow is declared free ("a widow," as the Middle Assyrian laws say) and can go where she wishes. Moreover, Naomi has specifically freed Ruth. This is no place to go into intricate discussions of the law and the plans. The story is ambiguous enough to have kept commentators guessing. I give my best reconstruction here; for details of legal analysis on each point, see my forthcoming commentary to Ruth.

254 ***"and a redeemer comes to Zion"*** For the phrase, see Isa. 59:20.

255 **reflects the lament and prophecy language of a later period** See key expressions like "bitter," which appears in *wehî mār lāh* in Lam. 1:4 and *hēmar šaddai lî* in Ruth 1:21; "God afflicted" in Lam. 3:33 and Ruth 1:21; similarly, God still has *ḥesed* in Lam. 3:22, 32, and Ruth 2:22.

Royal Origins: The Moabite

258 **the daughters of Lot** The most comprehensive study is by Zeev Weissman, "Ethnology, Etiology, Genealogy and Historiography in the story of Lot and his daughters (Genesis 19:30–38)," in *Sha'arei Talmon: Studies in the Bible, Qumran and the Ancient Near East Presented to Shemaryahu Talmon*, ed. Michael Fishbane and Emanuel Tov (Winona Lake, Ind.: Eisenbrauns, 1992), 43*–52* (in Hebrew). For a feminist analysis, see Elke Seifert, "Lot und seine Tochter: eine Hermeneutik des Verdachts," in *Feministische hermeneutik und erstes Testament* (Stuttgart: Kohlhammer, 1994), 48–66. And for a comparative study see Warren Kliewer, "The Daughters of Lot: Legend and Fabliau," *The Illiff Review* 25 (1968): 1–28.

259 **ethnic slur** August Dillman, Genesis English translation by William B. Stevenson (Edinburgh, Scotland, 1897), 113. Driver quotes others but declares himself more moderate (*Deuteronomy*, p. 203). This opinion is still voiced by many readers of this story.

260 **Egypt** See Walter Scheidel, "Incest Revisited: Three Notes on the Demography of Sibling Marriage in Roman Egypt," *Bulletin of the American Society of Papyrologists* 32 (1995): 143–55.

260 **the one against incest** The classic study of incest is Otto Rank, *The Incest Theme in Literature and Legend: Fundamentals of a Psychology of Literary Creation*, trans. G. Richter (Baltimore: Johns Hopkins University Press, 1912). For a discussion of Freud and Foucault, see Judith Butler, *Gender Trouble: Feminism and the Subversion of Identity*, 10th anniversary ed. (New York: Routledge, September 1999; 1st ed., 1989).

260 **father–daughter incest** As Rashkow notes, the story of Lot's daughters has a lot more to do with most clinical incest than does the story of Oedipus (the phallacy of Genesis). Stories about father–daughter incest appear in Stith Thompson, *Motif Index of Folk Literature*, 6 vols., rev. and enl. ed. (Bloomington: Indiana University Press, 1989), as T411.

261 **The biblical laws** See Jonathan Ziskind, "Legal Rules on Incest in the Ancient Near East," *Revue internationale des droits de l'antiquité* 35 (1988): 79–109. For father–daughter incest, see Ilona Rashkow, *The Phallacy of Geneis: A Feminist-Psychoanalytic Approach* (Louisville: Westminster, 1993), 65–94; and Ilona Rashkow, "Daddy-Dearest and the 'Invisible Spirit of Wine,' " in *Genesis: A Feminist Companion to the Bible*, Second Series, ed. Athalya Brenner (Sheffield: Sheffield Academic Press, 1998), 82–107.

261 **this section of Leviticus** For a discussion see S. F. Bigger, "The Family Laws of Leviticus 18 in Their Setting," *Journal of Biblical Literature* 98 (1979): 187–93; Jonathan Ziskind, "The Missing Daughter in Leviticus xviii," *Vetus Testamentum* 46 (1996): 125–30; and Tirzah Meacham, "The Missing Daughter: Leviticus 18–20," *Zeitschrift für die alttestamentliche Wissenschaft* 109 (1997): 254–59.

262 **Ovid's story of Myrrha and her father, Cinyras** Cited from *Electronic Version of*

Metamorphoses, by Ovid, trans. Rolfe Humphries (Stanford: Academic Text Service of Stanford University), 243–451.

262 **Isis and Osiris** See Miriam Lichtheim, *Ancient Egyptian Literature, a Book of Readings* (Berkeley: University of California Press, 1975).

262 *Aleph-Bet of Ben Sira* For this story in English, see *Rabbinic Fantasies: Imaginative Narratives from Classical Hebrew Literature,* ed. David Stern and Mark Jay Mirsky (Philadelphia: Jewish Publication Society, June 1990).

263 **faithfulness to their father** Fewell and Gunn point out that it is no wonder girls so marginalized should construct their own remaining value in terms of their ability to give life. They are rewarded with sons, and it is ironic that their story supplants the others: they are the survivors of the destruction (*Gender, Power and Promise*). But Fewell and Gunn are hesitant to praise them, since praise so easily becomes blame (and indeed others have blamed the girls), and incest is almost always the act of the father. The question of praise or blame has occupied readers. Rabbinic readers believed their actions were ultimately vindicated by the birth of Ruth the Moabite and Naamah the Ammonite (Rehoboam's mother). Zeev Weissman, however, connects the story with the prohibition of Moabites from "entering the congregation," since bastard children of incest would be taboo. He points to the sequence of laws in Deuteronomy 23, since they start (in Hebrew) with not uncovering the father's robe (23:1; English 22:30), continue with the prohibition of castrated people from "entering the congregation" (23:2, Eng. 23:1), then the bastard (23:3, Eng. 23:2), and then the Moabite and Ammonite (23:4, Eng. 23:3). But Deuteronomy itself connects the prohibition of the Moabites and Ammonites to their behavior in the desert, not to any putative bastardy, and the story in Genesis has no hint of censure.

Royal Origins: Tamar

For analysis, see the foundational article by Susan Niditch, "The Wronged Woman Righted: An Analysis of Genesis 38," *Harvard Theological Review* 72 (1979): 143–49; Johanna Bos, "Out of the Shadows: Genesis 38; Judges 4:17–22; Ruth 3," in *Reasoning with the Foxes: Female Wit in a World of Male Power,* ed. Cheryl Exum and Johanna Bos (*Semeia* 42 [1988]), 37–67; and Ellen van Wolde, "Texts in Dialogue with Texts: Intertextuality in the Ruth and Tamar Dialogues," *Biblical Interpretation* 5 (1997): 1–28. For a discussion of various theories about the sources and early development of the story, see J. A. Emerton, "Some Problems in Gen. XXXVIII," *Vetus Testamentum* 25 (1985): 338–61. For commentaries see E. A. Speiser, *Genesis,* Anchor Bible 1 (Garden City, N.Y.: Doubleday, 1964); Claus Westermann, *Genesis 37–50;* by John Scullion (Minneapolis: Augsburg, 1986); and Victor Hamilton, *Genesis 18–50, New International Commentary on the Old Testament* (Grand Rapids, Mich.: Eerdmans, 1995).

264 **just after Joseph has been sold** The relationship between the two stories has occupied commentators since at least the fifth century Midrash Breshit Rabbah (85:2). For recent writings on this topic see Judah Goldin, "Youngest Son, or Where Does Genesis 38 Belong?", *Journal of Biblical Literature* 96 (1977): 27–44; Mieke Bal, "One Woman, Many Men and the Dialectic of Chronology," in *Lethal Love: Feminist Literary Readings of Biblical Love Stories* (Bloomington, Ind.: Indiana

University Press, 1987), 89–103; Aaron Wildavsky, "Survival Must Not Be Gained Through Sin: The Moral of the Joseph Stories Prefigured Through Judah and Tamar," *Journal for the Study of the Old Testament* 62 (1994): 37–48; and Peter Lockwood, "Tamar's Place in the Joseph Cycle," *Lutheran Theological Journal* 26 (1992): 35–43. Goldin emphasizes the line of narration that first shows why Reuben, the firstborn, cannot be the chief heir, then Simeon and Levi (Gen. 34) and thus the reader want to see if it will be Judah or Joseph. Mieke Bal suggests the parallel is to the Potiphar's wife episode, and is placed to warn the reader not to conclude too easily that women are lethal. Wildavsky believes that the story of Judah and Tamar teaches leaders they cannot save their people by violating the moral law; Tamar, by making Judah fulfill his duties as levir, fulfills her obligation under the law and teaches Judah that his fears should not have made him violate the commandment (of levirate). Lockwood considers Genesis 39 a miniature version of the Joseph cycle, exposing the faults of the ancestors and urging them to make peace with their foes. As Lockwood notes, the true parallel to Joseph is not Judah but Tamar: both are threatened, driven from their home, and force their victimizers to acknowledge wrongdoing and to mend their ways.

264 **he called his name Er** J. Alberto Soggin suggests that the "he named" of v. 3 (Er) and v. 29 and 30 (Peretz and Uzzah) is a grammatical error ("Judah and Tamar (Genesis 38)," in *Of Prophets' Visions and the Wisdom of Sages: Essays in Honour of R. Norman Whybray on his Seventieth Birthday*, ed. Heather McKay and David Clines, JSOT supp. 162 (Sheffield: Sheffield Academic Press, 1993), 281–87. But this story is very careful about male/female forms, which alternate a lot in this text. We as readers should take the "he names" seriously: Judah directs the naming of his firstborn son and later the naming of Tamar's children.

265 **commentators both ancient and modern** The Testament of Judah (10–13) and the book of Jubilees (chapter 41) blame the death of Er and Onan on Judah's marriage to a Canaanite. Among modern commentators, Calum Carmichael blames Judah's role in selling Joseph into slavery and more in having his "half Israelite half Canaanite sons" mate with Tamar: to him the law of *kilayim* (plowing with two seeds, Deut. 22:9–11) is a commentary on this story ("Forbidden Mixtures," *Vetus Testamentum* 32 [1982]: 395–415). Along similar lines see Edmund Leach, "The Legitimacy of Solomon: Some Structural Aspects of Old Testament History," reprinted in *Genesis as Myth and Other Essays* (London: Jonathan Cape, 1969), 25–83; 113–17.

265 **where Tamar came from** By contrast to the Canaanite hypothesis for Tamar's origin, Edmund Leach builds his analysis on the assumption that Tamar was a pure Israelite ("The Legitimacy of Solomon"), thus giving Judah "pure-blooded descendants," while his original sons were all tainted. Leach's argument is also based on his assumption that pure-bloodedness had any relevance for the Judean monarchy. See the excellent refutation by J. A. Emerton, "An Examination of a Recent Structuralist Interpretation of Genesis XXXVIII," *Vetus Testamentum* 26 (1986): 79–98.

267 **dramatic irony, for Judah does not know** See Jean Louis Ska, "L'ironie de Tamar," *Zeitschrift für die alttestamentliche Wissenschaft* 100 (1988): 261–63, who discusses the way the motivation clauses (introduced by *ki*) establish a complicity between author and reader.

267 **Naomi reasons that God has killed her family** Ellen van Wolde points out that in Genesis 38 the narrative refers to YHWH's killing; in the book of Ruth, Naomi does so ("Texts in Dialogue"). The intertextual contrast itself sets up an irony: even though Naomi did not know, she understood, and Judah did not.

267 **"killer wife"** For a discussion of this theory, see Mordechai Friedman, "Tamar, A Symbol of Life: The 'Killer Wife' Superstition in the Bible and Jewish Tradition," *Association of Jewish Studies Review* 15 (1990): 23–61. Friedman remarks that the attribution of demonic forces to women is absent in the Bible except in this story. He posits a stage in the development of the sources in which the sons died for this reason, and suggests that the story we have is purposely debunking the idea. If so, it failed, for the idea comes back with full force in rabbinic literature.

267 **more foolish** To Johanna Bos, the men are "wrongheaded irresponsible bunglers who don't see straight." She attributes this to a gynocentric bias in the story ("Out of the Shadows"). At the same time, the aims of the story are clearly patriarchal and androcentric: continuing the line. This gynocentric-within-androcentric combination makes sense in the Bible's gender system, which sees no difference in the nature or goals of men and women. On this, see Frymer-Kensky, *In the Wake of the Goddesses: Women, Culture, and the Biblical Transformation of Pagan Myth* (New York: Maxwell Macmillan International, 1992); and this book, pp. 337–38.

268 **he can perform the levirate himself** See Hittite Laws 193 and MAL 33. On the levirate, see Eryl W. Davies, "Inheritance Rights and the Hebrew Levirate Marriage," *Vetus Testamentum* 31 (1981): 138–44 and 257–68; and Raymond Westbrook, in *Property and Family in Biblical Law* (Sheffield: JSOT, 1991).

268 **so he wrongs Tamar** Wildavsky considers the major point of the story to be that Judah should not let his fear prevent him from observing the law ("Survival Must Not be Gained Through Sin"). But the issue is not only "law": Tamar is put in an untenable position. In her intertextual study, van Wolde does not see that there is more difference between Naomi's sending Ruth and Orpah back to their mother's house and Judah's sending Tamar back to her father's ("Texts in Dialogue"). The difference is not simply male/female speech but the freedom of the women. For more on how Tamar was wronged, see Niditch, "The Wronged Woman Righted."

268 **she can do nothing** Bos points out that Tamar has been a passive figure and is now a passive bystander, and it seems that Judah will remain the center of the story ("Out of the Shadows").

268 **by the mistaken power** Of course, the story still shows this, a fact picked up by Carol Smith, who suggests that Genesis 38 raises the question of whether the "patently unsuitable" Judah should have that kind of power over another person ("The Story of Tamar: A Power-filled Challenge to the Structures of Power," in *Women in the Biblical Tradition*, ed. George Brooke, *Studies in Women and Religion* 31 [Lewiston, N.Y.: Edwin Mellen, 1992], 16–28). Given the fact that these stories are transmitted after the monarchy took away such power from heads-of-household, I do not think it raises the question; rather it answers it with yet another no. Smith does note that Genesis 39 suggests that maybe the old ways were not so desirable if you were not male and powerful.

269 **"the opening of the eyes"** The Revised Version reads "The Gate of Enaim," a reading adopted also by van Wolde (ibid.). For *petaḥ* as the city gate, see 1 Kings

17:10, where *petah haʿir* refers to the entrance to the small town of Zarephat where a widow was gathering wood; and 1 Chron. 21:9, in which the Ammonites came out and fought *petah haʿir*. Both these passages must refer to outside a gate or other entrance. For a discussion of the ancient reading, "crossroads," see J. A. Emerton, "Some Problems." This reading is adopted by Soggin ("Judah and Tamar"). It doesn't matter if it was a gate, a crossroads, or a regular road. Women who would be sitting there would be assumed to be "public women."

269 **shows us a character's motives** Van Wolde points to the double *ki:* "for she says that" as a sign that the narrator is involved in her awareness, guiding the reader to agree with Tamar ("Texts in Dialogue").

269 **Tamar takes dramatic action** Bos notes that the piling up of the verbs in verse 24 "highlights the contrast" with her former passive state ("Out of the Shadows"). Smith suggests that Tamar had other options, such as entering her father-in-law's bed, in the manner of Ruth, or perhaps legal action ("The Story of Tamar"). But Judah had already rejected her because of his fear and would be unlikely to take her in, and as for legal action, the victim stories show that in the "bad old days," parties unlawfully exiled from their home (like Jephthah) really had no legal recourse against the men in power in their households.

270 **wrapping herself in a veil** Reading *wattekus* in the Puʿal or *wattitekas* in the hitpaʿel, as in the veiling of Rivka (Gen. 24:66), rather than the Masoretic *qal*. This lapse is best explained as either a Masoretic change of vowels or a scribal loss of one *tav* rather than a sign that Hebrew was not current at the origin of the text (so Soggin, "Judah and Tamar," who also sees a Graecism in "pledge"; see the note to "token . . . of the payment," p. 423).

270 **once again stresses Judah's lack of knowledge** Morimura Nobuko stresses the importance to the text of exonerating Judah but feels that "there is an air of blaming Tamar for deceiving Judah." She further believes that when Judah admits that Tamar was right, "the one who has the last word is the winner" ("The Story of Tamar: A Feminist Interpretation of Genesis 38," *Japan Christian Review* 59 [1993]: 55–67). I do not believe that the story operates on a zero-sum mentality: on the contrary, once Tamar has righted the wrong done her, everyone gains: Tamar, an assured place in life and posterity, and Judah, two new sons.

270 **prostitutes** See Phyllis Bird, "The Harlot as Heroine: Narrative Art and Social Presupposition in Three Old Testament Texts," in *Missing Persons and Mistaken Identities* (Minneapolis: Fortress Press, 1997), 197–218.

271 **qedēšah** See Mayer Gruber, "Hebrew *Qedēšah* and her Canaanite and Akkadian Cognates," *Ugarit-Forschungen* 18 (1986): 133–48; and Joan Goodnick Westenholz, "Tamar, *Qedeša, Qadištu* and Sacred Prostitution in Mesopotamia," *Harvard Theological Review* 82 (1989): 245–65. Bird is certainly right in her contention that a *qedēšah* is not a whore ("Harlot as Heroine").

271 **"sacred prostitutes"** See the discussion in Tikva Frymer-Kensky, *In the Wake of the Goddesses,* and literature cited there. Bernhard Luther, who admits that "it seems out of the question" that there were professional sacred prostitutes, nevertheless perpetuates the old idea (based solely on Herodotus 1:199 on Babylonia) that each girl was prostituted once to be consecrated to the divinity, and suggests that Judah did not understand cult prostitution and therefore confused a whore with a *qedēšah* ("The Novella of Judah and Tamar and Other Israelite Novellas,"

in *Narrative and Novella in Samuel: Studies by Hugo Gressman and Other Scholars 1906–1923*, trans. David Orten, ed. David Gunn [Sheffield: Almond, 1991], 89–118). But the Canaanite literature discovered since Luther wrote does not show any evidence of sexual initiation of girls by prostitution.

271 **public ritual** See Calum Carmichael, "A Ceremonial Crux: Removing a Man's Sandal as a Female Gesture of Contempt," *Journal of Biblical Literature* 96 (1977): 321–36.

272 **token . . . of the payment** Speiser (*Genesis*) derived the Hebrew word ʿerabôn from the Old Assyrian *erubātu*, with the same meaning. Soggin considers this a rare word and therefore improbable and suggests that it is a "Graecism" from ἀρραβών, "pledge", well known from the Pauline Epistles (J. Alberto Soggin, "Judah and Tamar"). This would have great significance for the dating of the text. However, *erubātu* comes from the common root *erēbu*, "enter" (Hebrew ʿrb), and it is likely that this verb is the origin of *erubātu*, ʿerabôn and ἀρραβών. The Hebrew verb ʿrb occurs in the sense of "give as pledge, stand security" in Gen. 43:9; 44:32, in both cases of which Judah gives himself as pledge for Benjamin, and in Prov. 6:1, 11:15; 14:10, 20:16, 19; 27:13.

272 **"let her be burned"** Many commentators have noted that burning is not the pre-scribed punishment for adultery in the Bible. Since a priest's daughter is to be burned, and *qedēšāh* appears in this story, Michael Astour suggests that there was an earlier stage of this story in which Tamar was a hierodule who got pregnant (which, he argues, they were not supposed to do) and was going to be burned, when she turned into a palm tree from which Peretz burst forth, much as Ovid's Myrrha turned into a myrrh tree and Adonis burst forth from her (Michael Astour, "Tamar the Hierodule: An Essay in the Method of Vestigial Motifs," *Journal of Biblical Literature* 85 [1966]: 185–96). Such a speculative story is so remote from the present plot that nothing would connect it but the names of Tamar and Peretz. Burning is not confined to a priest's family: Lev. 20:14 prescribes it for a man who sleeps with a woman and her mother. But that is not really the point: this story is set in a time before the giving of the Sinaitic laws that spell out Is-rael's punishments; it is also set in a time before the consolidation of the state that would have had its fixed procedures. In the ancestral period, Judah the paterfamilias-judge could pronounce both verdict and sentence in a legal case, and in our story there are not even any judicial proceedings: Judah the paterfamilias-ruler determines what will happen to the members of his family.

273 **"righteous"** An interesting disparity exists between those who argue that the righteousness of Tamar consisted in observing the law, like David Banon ("Ex-egèse biblique et philosophie," *Études Théologiques et Religieuses* 66 [1991]: 489–504), and those who maintain the story demonstrates that righteousness and justice are more important than literal law (Carol Smith and Thomas Krüger, "Genesis 38—Ein 'Lehrstück' alttestamentlicher Ethik," in *Konsequente Traditions-geschichte: Festschrift für Klaus Baltzer zum 65. Geburtstag*, ed. Rüdiger Bartlemus, Thomas Krüger, and Helmut Utzscneider [Universitärsverlag Freiburg Schwiez and Göttingen: Vanderhoeck & Ruprect, 1993], 205–26). The laws that they sug-gest are being (a) upheld or (b) undermined are the levirate law, the incest taboo, and cultic prostitution. Krüger and Smith also realize that intermarriage is under consideration, and the negative stance challenged.

274 **never slept with Tamar again** Van Wolde points to the Hebrew "he did not know her": once his eyes have been opened, no other knowledge is needed. Tamar, who sat at the gate of the eyes, is the eye-opener ("Texts in Dialogue").

274 **Judah applauds Tamar's action and God rewards it** Bos and Fuchs have remarked on the awarding of a "throne of motherhood" that safeguards patriarchal institutions (see Esther Fuchs, "The Literary Characterization of Mothers and Sexual Politics in the Hebrew Bible," in *Feminist Perspectives on Biblical Scholarship,* ed. Adela Yarbro Collins [Chico, Calif.: Scholars, 1995], 117–36).

275 **Ruth and Tamar** For earlier comparisons of these two, see Westermann, *Genesis;* Danna Nowell Fewell and David Gunn, *Compromising Redemption: Reading Characters in the Book of Ruth,* Literary Currents in Biblical Interpretation (Louisville: Westminster, 1990); and Athalya Brenner, "Naomi and Ruth," in *A Feminist Companion to Ruth* (Sheffield: Sheffield Academic Press, 1993); and Soggin, "Judah and Tamar."

275 **the daughters of Lot** Smith recognizes the similarity in which the unusual sexual behavior provides the desired result without the direct intervention of God. Smith notes the similarity to the other women of Genesis who are also childless, Sarah, Rivka, and Rachel, though in their case, since their barrenness is the issue, God intervenes directly. Smith considers the closest parallel to Tamar to be Rivka, because of the birth of twins ("The Story of Tamar"). It is also worth noting the parallel to Leah, who masqueraded as Rachel and who first "hired" Jacob's sexual services by using mandrakes.

The Royal Way

278 **the names of the characters** For some of them see Gary Rendsburg, "David and his Circle in Genesis XXXVIII," *Vetus Testamentum* 36 (1986): 438–46.

Outsider Women: Exile and Ezra

283 **Ezekiel 16** For a comprehensive analysis of this chapter, see Moshe Greenberg, *Ezekiel 1–20,* Anchor Bible 22 (Garden City, N.Y.: Doubleday, 1983). For a study of its gender ideology, see Carol J. Dempsey, "The 'Whore' of Ezekiel 16: The Impact and Ramifications of Gender-Specific Metaphors in Light of Biblical Law and Divine Judgment" in *Gender and Law in the Hebrew Bible and the Ancient Near East,* Victor Matthews, Bernard Levinson, and Tikva Frymer-Kinsky, eds. *JSOT Supplement* 206 (Sheffield: Sheffield Academic Press, 1998), 57–58.

284 **book of Kings** For details of the passages that condemn the kings, see Lyle M. Eslinger, "Through the Fire," in *Into the Hands of the Living God, Journal for the Study of the Old Testament* Supplements 84 (Sheffield: Sheffield Academic Press, 1989). The explicit passages in which the kings provoked God by causing Israel to sin are: 1 Kings 14:16; 15:26, 30; 16:2, 25, 30; 21:22; 22:51–3; 2 Kings 3:2–3; 10:29–31; 13:3, 11; 14:24; 15:9, 18, 24, 30; 16:2–3, 25, 30; 17:1–6; 21:22; 22:51–53. Only 17:7 ff. declares "Israel sinned," and even there the specific offenses named are illustrated in the narratives as kingly events.

284 **book of Chronicles** For the ideology of the book and its matter-of-fact way of treating intermarriage, see Sara Japhet, *First and Second Chronicles: A Commentary*

(Louisville: Westminster/John Knox, 1993), and *The Ideology of the Book of Chronicles and Its Place in Biblical Thought* (Frankfurt am Main: Peter Lang, 1989).

284 **Edomite** Reading with the Septuagint and 1 Esdras 9:36. It is tempting to preserve the Masoretic texts' "Amorite" and see it as a code for the old Judeans, but Amorite/Edomite is an easy scribal substitution.

285 **"holy seed"** For the new concept of holiness, see James Kugel ("The Holiness of Israel and the Land in Second Temple Times," in *Texts, Temples and Traditions: A Tribute to Menahem Haran*, ed. Michael Fox [Winona Lake, Ind.: Eisenbrauns, 1996], 21–32), who demonstrates the ongoing development of the "holiness" concept in post-biblical writings.

289 **"peoples of the land"** See the discussion by Sara Japhet, "People and Land in the Restoration Period," in *Das Land Israel in biblischen Zeit: Jerusalem Symposium 1981*, ed. George Strecker (Göttingen: Vandenhoeck & Ruprecht, 1982), 103–25. Japhet refers to this as an "early midrash." For particular discussion of this midrash, see Yehezkel Kaufman (*toledot ha'emuna hayisraelit* [Jerusalem 1972] IV 293; Michael Fishbane, *Biblical Interpretation in Ancient Israel* (New York: Oxford University Press, 1985); and Sara Japhet, "Law and 'the Law' in Ezra Nehemiah," *Proceedings of the Ninth World Congress of Jewish Studies* (Jerusalem: Magnes, 1988), 99–115. See also the genealogy of Sheshan in 1 Chron. 2:34–41 discussed by Sara Japhet, "The Israelite Legal and Social Reality as Reflected in Chronicles: A Case Study," in *Sha'arei Talmon: Studies in the Bible, Qumran and the Ancient Near East Presented to Shemaryahu Talmon*, ed. Michael Fishbane and Emanuel Tov (Winona Lake, Ind.: Eisenbrauns, 1992), 79–91.

289 **"enter the congregation"** In Judaism this term means to "join the people" and is a term for intermarriage, but in Deuteronomy it means to "enter the sacred precincts." The rabbis, who understand marriage, forbid only Moabite men, using Ruth as a way to permit wives from Moab and Amnon here.

289 **"new Exodus"** See the discussion by Michael Fishbane, "The Exodus Motif," in *Biblical Text and Texture: A Literary Reading of Selected Texts* (Oxford: Oneworld, 1998), 121–39.

289 **Ezra is concerned with foreign wives** Tamara Eskanazi and Elanore P. Judd ("Marriage to a Stranger in Ezra 9–10," *Second Temple Studies 2: Temple and Community in the Persian Period*, ed. Tamara Eskenazi and Kent Richards, JSOT supp. 175 [Sheffield: JSOT, 1994], 266–85) place the event in the context of immigrant communities seeking to establish boundaries. They point out that Ezra arrives late: earlier returnees considered the Judaeans appropriate partners. Tamara Eskanazi ("Out from the Shadows: Biblical Women in the Postexilic Era," *JSOT*, [1992]: 25–43) draws on the specifics of women's position in documents from Elephantine to conclude that Jewish women could inherit land and argues that the fear of mixed marriages makes the most economic sense if women could inherit in Judah at this time, a conclusion with which Harold Washington concurs ("The Strange Woman of Proverbs 1–9 and Post-Exilic Judaean Society," in *Second Temple Studies 2*, 217–42). Daniel Smith-Christopher ("The Mixed Marriage Crisis in Ezra 9–10 and Nehemiah 13: A Study of the Sociology of the Post-Exilic Jewish Community," *Second Temple Studies 2*, 243–61) considers that the original returnees may have married the local wives precisely because they brought land as dowries. He also notes that since the Persian empire encouraged intermarriage,

the breakup was an act of political defiance. In contrast, Washington holds that the Persians demanded each group maintain its ethnic identity.

289 **Ezra does not want these children** This makes obvious sense if the purpose of the regulation is to keep land within the previously exiled community. Harold Washington ("The Strange Woman") points out that membership in the civic-temple community was determined by descent within the paternal estate, and real property was distributed according to lineage.

289 **struggles over who owned the land** Ezekiel mentions that those left behind in Judah claim that the land was given to them, and says it will be returned to the exiled (Ezek. 11:15). According to Peter Ackroyd (*Exile and Restoration: A Study of Hebrew Thought of the Sixth Century B.C.* [London: SCM, 1968]), only about 10 percent of the people went into exile, but I do not know how he arrives at that exact figure.

290 **Malachi** See, with reservation, Beth Glazier-Macdonald, "Intermarriage, Divorce and the Bat-'el Nekar: Insights into Mal. 2:10–18," *Journal of Biblical Literature* 106 (1987): 603–11. To me it seems most probable that the "wives of your youth" whom Malachi does not want people to divorce are wives acquired in Babylon whom the returnees have left behind.

291 **"strange" woman . . . in the book of Proverbs** See Claudia Camp, "What's So Strange About the Strange Woman?" in *The Bible and the Politics of Exegesis: Essays in Honor of Norman K. Gottwald on his Sixty-fifth Birthday*, ed. David Jobling, Peggy Day, and Gerald Sheppard (Cleveland: Pilgrim Press, 1991), 17–31; and Joseph Blenkinsopp, "The Social Context of the 'Outsider Woman' in Proverbs 1–9," *Biblica* 72 (1991): 457–73. They differ primarily on dating; Blenkinsopp dates Proverbs 1–9 to the time of Ezra-Nehemiah, and Camp to a century later.

291 **Hellenism** For this, see Tikva Frymer-Kensky, "Gifts of the Greeks," in *In the Wake of the Goddesses*.

Oracles of the Conquest of Canaan: Rahab and Deborah

RAHAB

For earlier studies see Robert Culley, "Stories of the Conquest: Joshua 2, 6, 7 and 8," *Hebrew Annual Review* 8 (1984): 25–44; 8 (1984): 25–44; *Immaculate and Powerful: The Female in Sacred Image and Social Reality*, ed. Clarissa W. Atkinson, Constance H. Buchanan, and Margaret R. Miles (Boston: Beacon, 1985); Phyllis Bird, "The Harlot as Heroine: Narrative Art and Social Presupposition in Three Old Testament Texts," *Semeia* 46 (1989): 119–39; Yair Zakovitch, "Humor and Theology or the Successful Failure of Israelite Intelligence: A Literary-Folkloric Approach to Joshua 2," in *Text and Tradition: The Hebrew Bible and Folklore*, ed. Susan Niditch (Atlanta: Scholars, 1990), 75–90, and Frank Cross, "Reply to Zakovitch," ibid., 99–106; Tikva Frymer-Kensky, "Reading Rahab," in *Tehillah le-Moshe: Biblical and Judaic Studies in Honor of Moshe Greenberg*, ed. Mordechai Cogan, Barry Eichler, and Jeffrey Tigay (Winona Lake, Ind.: Eisenbrauns, 1997), 57–67.

298 **quotes the very verses of the Song of the Sea** The connection was noted by ancient rabbis in Mekhilta Shirata 9. As Zakovitch notes, biblical quotations reverse the order of the original.

298 **Rahab is the first of the nations** See Gordon Mitchell, "Together in the Land: A Reading of the Book of Joshua," *Journal for the Study of the Old Testament* 134 (1993): 152–90.

DEBORAH

Studies on the history include: Baruch Halpern, "The Resourceful Israelite Historian: The Song of Deborah and Israelite Historiography," *Harvard Theological Review* 76 (1983): 379–401; Lawrence Stager, "Archaeology, Ecology, and Social History: Background Themes to the Song of Deborah," Congress vol. (Leiden: E. J. Brill, 1988), 221–34; Nadav Na'aman, "Literary and Topographical Notes on the Battle of Kishon (Judges IV–V)," *Vetus Testamentum* 40 (1990): 423–36; J. David Schloen, "Caravans, Kenites, and Casus belli: Enmity and Alliance in the Song of Deborah," *Catholic Biblical Quarterly* 55 (1993): 18–38.

   Philological, exegetical, and literary studies: Heinz-Dieter Neef, "Der Sieg Deboras und Baraks über Sisera: Exegetische beobachtungen zum aufbau und werden von Jdc. 4:1–24," *Zeitschrift für die Alttestamentliche Wissenschaft* 101 (1989): 28–49; Peter Ackroyd, "Composition of the Song of Deborah [Judges 5:2]," *Vetus Testamentum* 2 (1952): 160–62; Joseph Blenkinsopp, "Ballad Style and Psalm Style in the Song of Deborah: A Discussion," *Biblica* 42 (1961): 61–76; Morris Seale, "Deborah's Ode and the Ancient Arabian Qasida," *Journal of Biblical Literature* 81 (1962): 343–47; Peter C. Craigie, "Song of Deborah and the Epic of Tukulti-Ninurta," *Journal of Biblical Literature* 88 (1969): 253–65; Craigie, "Some Further Notes on the Song of Deborah," *Vetus Testamentum* 22 (1972): 349–53; Alexander Globe, "Literary Structure and Unity of the Song of Deborah," *Journal of Biblical Literature* 93 (1974): 493–512; D. F. Murray, *Studies in the Historical Books of the Old Testament* (Leiden: Brill, 1979), 155–89; Jan P. Fokkelman, "The Song of Deborah and Barak: Its Prosodic Levels and Structure," in *Pomegranates and Golden Bells: Studies in Biblical, Jewish, and Near Eastern Ritual, Law, and Literature in Honor of Jacob Milgrom*, ed. David P. Wright, David Noel Freedman, and Avi Hurvitz. (Winona Lake, Ind.: Eisenbrauns, 1995), 595–628.

   Ideational and feminist studies: Jürgen Kegler, "Debora: Erwägungen zur Politischen Funktion einer Frau in einer patriarchalischen Gesellschaft," *Traditionen der Befreiung* (Munich: Kaiser, 1980), 37–59; Priscilla Denham, "It's Hard to Sing a Song of Deborah" (Judges 4:1–24), in *Spinning a Sacred Yarn: Women Speak from the Pulpit* (New York, N.Y.: Pilgrim Press, 1982), 58–64; Barnabas Lindars, "Deborah's Song: Women in the Old Testament," *Bulletin of the John Rylands University Library of Manchester* 65 (1983): 158–75; JoAnn Hackett, "In the Days of Jael: Reclaiming the History of Women in Ancient Israel," in *Immaculate and Powerful* (Boston: Beacon Press, 1985), 15–38; J. Cheryl Exum, " 'Mother in Israel': A Familiar Story Reconsidered," in *Feminist Interpretation of the Bible*, Letty Russel, ed. (Philadelphia: Westminster, 1985), 73–85; Yairah Amit, "Judges 4: Its Content and Form," *Journal for the Study of the Old Testament* 39 (1987): 89–111; Guy Couturier, "Débora, une autorité politico-religiuse aux origines d'Israël," *Sciences Religieuse* (Studies in Religion) 18 (1989): 213–28; Danna Nolan Fewell, "Controlling Perspectives: Women, Men and the Authority of Violence in Judges 4–5," *Journal of the American Academy of Religion* 58 (1990): 389–411; Fokkelien van Dijk-Hemmes, "Mothers and a Mediator in the Song of Deborah," in *A Feminist Companion to Judges*, ed. Athalya Brenner (Sheffield: *JSOT*, 1993), 110–14; Daniel Block, "Deborah Among the Judges: The Perspective of the Hebrew Historian," in *Faith*,

Tradition, and History: Old Testament Historiography in its Near Eastern Context, ed. A. R. Millard, James Hoffmeier, and David Baker (Winona Lake, Ind.: Eisenbrauns, 1994), 229–53: Ellen van Wolde, "Deborah and Yaʿel in Judges 4," in *On Reading Prophetic Texts: Gender Specific and Related Studies in Memory of Fokkelien van Dijk-Hemmes*, ed. Bob Becking and Meindert Dijkstra (Leiden: E. J. Brill, 1996), 283–95.

298 **the Israelites went up to her for judgment** Van Wolde points out that "she would sit" in the *qôtel* form is background information. Then in 5b "the people went" is in the *vayiqtol*, which she considers "foregrounding" (Ellen van Wolde, "Deborah and Yaʿel in Judges 4").

299 **into the hand of a woman** Barnabas Lindars suggests that the whole purpose of the story is to intrigue the readers with this idea and delay their knowledge of Yael until later ("Deborah's Song: Women in the Old Testament [Judges 4–5]," *Bulletin of the John Rylands University Library of Manchester* 65 [1983]: 158–75). Lindars may press the centrality of this theme a little too much, but it is a good corrective to the many commentators, such as J. Alberto Soggin (*Judges: A Commentary* (Philadelphia: Westminster Press, 1991), who marginalize the women. On this, see Stephen Hanselman ("Narrative Theory, Ideology and Transformation" in Judges 4 in *Anti-Covenant*, Mieke Bal, ed. (Sheffield, Almond Press, 1989), pp. 95–120.

299 **yet another woman** See S. D. Goitein, "Women as Creators of Biblical Genres," *Prooftexts* 8 (1988): 1–33.

300 **an anagram of "she spoke"** See Ellen van Wolde, "Deborah and Yaʿel in Judges 4." Her explanation of the name Barak is less convincing: the lightning that Deborah fires up with her words.

Oracles of Saul: Hannah and the Witch of Endor

For studies see Walter Brueggemann, "I Samuel 1: A Sense of Beginning," *Zeitschrift für Alttestamentliches Wissenschaft* 102 (1990): 33–48; Randall Bailey, "The Redemption of YHWH: A Literary Critical Function of the Songs of Hannah and David," *Biblical Interpretation* 3 (1995): 213–31; Carol Meyers, "The Hannah Narrative in Feminist Perspective," in *Go to the Land I Will Show You: Studies in Honor of Dwight W. Young*, ed. Joseph Coleson and Victor Matthews (Winona Lake, Ind.: Eisenbrauns, 1996), 117–26. The literary nature of the story has been analyzed by Robert Polzin, *Samuel and the Deuteronomist: A Literary Study of the Deuteronomic History, Part 2, I Samuel* (Bloomington: Indiana University Press, 1989). For standard commentary information, see Hans Hertzberg, *I & II Samuel: A Commentary*, Old Testament Library (Philadelphia: Westminster, 1976), and Kyle McCarter, *I Samuel*, Anchor Bible (Garden City, N.Y.: Doubleday, 1980).

303 **Elkanah doesn't understand** See the discussion by David Silber, "Kingship, Samuel and the Story of Hannah," *Tradition* 23 (1988): 64–75, and Yairah Amit, "Judges 4: Its Content and Form," *Vetus Testamentum* 40 (1990): 4–20.

304 **"A razor will not come on his head"** The Septuagint has a longer version, containing the full Nazirite vow, "He will be a Nazirite. . . . He will not drink wine or

strong drink and a razor will not come on his head." Arguing from the fragmentary 4Q Sam.ᵃ *wyyn wškr*, McCarter argues that the original Hebrew text must have included "And wine and strong drink he will not drink." There are many minor differences in this text between the Greek and Hebrew manuscripts. I have translated the Hebrew. For a complete textual list of these variants, see McCarter. I note only a few. The Greek and Hebrew texts actually differ in more than details. Stanley Waters shows that they have different attitudes toward some of the themes of the story (Waters, "Hannah & Anna: The Greek and Hebrew Texts of 1 Sam. 1," *JBL* 107 (1988): 385–412. Both Peninah and Hannah are more prominent in the Hebrew.

304 **"in difficult spirit"** Reading with the Hebrew, rather than "unfortunate," as McCarter reads with the Greek.

304 **and ate** The Greek says "and she came to the chamber and ate." But they were on pilgrimage and had no chamber.

304 **no longer (sad)** For the translator's addition, see Job 9:27: "I will give up my (sad) face and be cheerful."

305 **she herself names the child** Meyers points out that this is indicative of control and brings other aspects of Hannah's dominance: her name is mentioned fourteen times, and she is the subject of verbs three times more often than she is the object. Moreover, only she appears in all the dialogues in this story.

306 **The story never says they don't come** The longer Septuagint makes it clear that Elkanah also came, that he brought the sacrifice, and they slaughtered it together. Meyers believes that the Septuagint has expanded the text to make it clear that they observed the cultic behavior of the time of the Septuagint, but at this early period, women had a greater cultic role.

306 **requested** For a study of the parallels involved in this word, see Polzin, who also incorporates the theme of her supposed drunkenness, suggesting that the text wishes to hint at both error and drunken mistakenness in the request for kingship.

307 **Hannah foreshadows** Silbers suggests the story and the psalm actually foreshadow Saul's downfall as well as his coming. The coat that she brings Samuel every year (as recorded in 1 Sam. 3) is the very coat that Saul ripped and that symbolized the kingship.

308 **a poem that Hannah would have composed** This is a unanimous opinion; see Hertzberg, McCarter, and Bailey. Bailey stresses that only "the childless wife has borne seven" is related to Hannah.

308 **an appropriate psalm** It is made even more appropriate by the Septuagint, which expands verse 9 to read "He gives what is vowed to the one making a vow and blesses the years of the righteous." For this as expansion and for the textual history of the psalm and its variants, see Theodore Lewis, "The Textual History of the Song of Hannah: Samuel II: 1–10," *Vetus Testamentum* 44 (1994): 18–46.

308 **significance at the opening of the book of Samuel** Brevard Child suggests that this opening psalm and David's Thanksgiving psalm at the end establish a dominant messianic perspective. Brueggemann connects also the prose passages that begin and end the book of Samuel, which show together that Israel's historical process is "bonded" by God. Bailey, however, points out that the subject of the

poems is YHWH as the agent of change. He believes that the songs offer reassurance even though the stories framed by the songs do not show YHWH raising the poor or being the deliverer for the sacrificed priests of Nob (1 Sam. 22) or for Tamar (2 Sam. 13). Since the stories might cause the readers to doubt God, the poems reassure them.

309 **The two songs** Polzin presents a complete list of the parallels between the two songs, and notes the significance of "Tall, tall," (high, high).

The Necromancer at Endor

For studies see W. A. M. Beuken, "1 Samuel 28: The Prophet as 'Hammer of Witches,'" *Journal for the Study of the Old Testament* 6 (1978): 3–17; David Gunn, *The Fate of King Saul*, JSOT supp. 14 (Sheffield: *JSOT*, 1980); Michael O'Connor, "The Necromancer's Dinner and the Lightness of Ruth" (paper presented at conference on "The Hebrew Bible: Sacred Text and Literature" at the Center for Judaic Studies at Wayne State University, Detroit, Mich., Nov. 1, 1988, with thanks to Michael O'Connor for giving me the manuscript); Uriel Simon, "A Balanced Story: The Stern Prophet and the Kind Witch," *Prooftexts* 8 (1988): 159–71; Mordechai Cogan, "The Road to En-dor," in *Pomegranates and Golden Bells: Studies in Biblical, Jewish and Near Eastern Ritual, Law and Literature in Honor of Jacob Milgrom*, ed. David Wright, David Noel Freedman, and Avi Hurvitz (Winona Lake, Ind.: Eisenbrauns, 1995), 319–26: (with caution) Pamela Tamarkin Reis, "Eating the Blood: Saul and the Witch of Endor," *JSOT* 73 (1997): 3–23; and Susan Pigoff, "I Samuel 28—Saul and the *Not* So Wicked Witch of Endor," *Review and Expositor* 95 (1998): 435–44. Peter Miscall presents an analysis of this story in *1 Samuel: A Literary Reading* (Bloomington: Indiana University Press, 1986), 167–82. For standard commentary information, see Hans Hertzberg, *I & II Samuel: A Commentary*, Old Testament Library (Philadelphia: Westminster, 1976), and Kyle McCarter, *I Samuel*, Anchor Bible (Garden City, N.Y.: Doubleday, 1980). For later treatment of this story, see K. A. D. Smelik, "The Witch of Endor: I Samuel 28 in Rabbinic and Christian Exegesis till 800 A.D.," *Vigiliae Christianae* 33 (1977): 160–79.

310 **counterpart to Hannah** Michael O'Connor notes the relationship between the two. Both women take charge, and the necromancer's telling the king to shut up and eat is like Hannah's telling Eli to shut up and let her pray. To O'Connor, their relationship indicates that the public expression of women's religion, orthodox (Hannah) or unorthodox, would have no place in the new monarchic culture.

311 **no word through the official divinatory channels** Mordechai Cogan suggests that the priests would not use the Urim and Thummim for him because he slaughtered the eighty-five priests at Nob (1 Sam. 22:18–19). Cogan presents examples of Near Eastern kings using multiple means of divination and also of the "righteous sufferer" in the wisdom poem "I will praise the lord of wisdom," *Ludlul bēl nēmeqi*, who complains that he tries all means of divine communication to no avail ("The Road to En-dor").

311 **"with your adversary"** The Hebrew *ʿārēka* could be a scribal error for *ṣārēka*, or an Aramaism. The Septuagint reads *rēʿēka*, "your companion."

312 *ʾôb* For a discussion, see Harry Hoffner, "Second Millennium Antecedents to the

Hebrew *'ôb,"* *Journal of Biblical Literature* 86 (1967): 385–401. For comparative material for the classics, see Michael O'Connor; for Mesopotamia, see Irving Finkel, "Necromancy in Ancient Mesopotamia," *Archiv für Orientforschung* 29–30 (1983–84): 1–17.

312 **Circe** It is worth noting that Tiresias mentions dangers to come, but it is Circe who tells Odysseus how to overcome them. On this see Judith Yarnall, *Transformations of Circe: The History of an Enchantress* (Urbana: University of Illinois Press, 1994).

312 **may be a loan from the Semitic word qsm** This suggestion is from O'Connor, who notes that the trench can also be called a *megaron* or *bothron*. The Latin word for the trench, *mundus*, may be a translation from the more ordinary use of the word *kosmos*. Alternatively, the trench may be called "world," since it is the connector of this world to the netherworld.

312 **skull** Finkel presents examples of the use of skulls. He cites a ritual in which a dog's skull is used to pour a libation to dispel a ghost, but suggests that the major purpose of the skull was for ventriloquism.

312 **a "divine being"** This is the only time that *'elōhīm* refers to a ghost, but at this point the necromancer does not know the identity of the numinous being approaching her.

312 **now channels the words** Pigoff calls the "witch" a "prophetic mediator," pointing to the questions that Saul asks, "What do you see?" (v. 13) and "What is his form?" (v. 14), as evidence that Saul does not see, and therefore logically does not hear (Pigoff, "I Samuel 28").

312 **to be disturbed** For the danger in disturbing the dead, see William W. Hallo, "Disturbing the Dead," in *Minhah le-Nahum: Biblical and Other Studies Presented to Nahum M. Sarna in Honour of his 70th Birthday,* ed. Marc Brettler and Michael Fishbane, JSOT supp. 154 (Sheffield: Sheffield Academic Press, 1993), 183–92. The term could be used for tomb disturbance. Hallo points out that the term *rgz,* used here, is also used in Phoenecian inscriptions. Simon, looking for a reason for Samuel's lack of compassion, suggests that Samuel may have been personally injured by having his spirit raised.

312 **his old denunciations** Miscall points out that Samuel's speech condenses the entire narrative of 1 Sam. 16–27 into the fulfillment of his denunciation in 1 Sam. 13:13–14 and 1 Sam. 15:22–29.

313 **"your servant"** In Simon's excellent discussion of her speech, he suggests that this appellation restores royal dignity to Saul. He is certainly right that the term elevates the man to whom the woman is speaking. We should note, however, that when Abigail comes to petition David during his outlaw year, she also calls herself "your servant," using both *'amah* and *šiphah* (1 Sam. 25:24, 27). Polzin makes the point that *'amah* functions in the Deuteronomistic history to refer to the woman involved in establishing and legitimating David as king (Robert Polzin, *David and the Deuteronomist: A Literary Study of the Deuteronomic History, Part 3: 2 Samuel* (Bloomington: Indiana University Press, 1992). Pigoff makes the same point about *šiphah.* Ruth addresses Boaz in a similar manner (Ruth 2:13), for this is the language with which a woman petitions a man who is not her husband.

314 **goes to his fate** Miscall refers to the use of *derek,* "way," to mean goal, journey, or mission in 1 Sam. 9:6, 8, and 1 Sam. 15:18–20.

314 **her only fatted calf** Simon suggests that she is like the poor man in Nathan's parable, unlike Abraham, who had many animals. As usual, Pamela Tamarkin Reis offers a very different interpretation ("Eating the Blood"). Assuming that a response of eager hospitality would be bizarre, she claims that the witch is maneuvering him. Looking for evil, she sees the word for *zebah,* "slaughter" of the calf, an indication that she did not cook it, that she had Saul eat blood and thus brought him into compact with her, dooming him but saving her life. But *zebah* is the appropriate term, since meat was not to be eaten without appropriate offering to God, and the story does not bear out Reis's interpretation.

314 **her meal resonates with theirs** Pigoff noted the relationship of Samuel's feast with the meal "catered by a witch—the prophetic mediator of Samuel's word of doom" ("1 Sam. 28," 440).

314 **effective** Cogan suggests that the very reliability of such practices made them dangerous, and cites a Hebrew article by Yehezkel Kaufman, "Concerning the Story of the Necromancer," in his *Mikivshonah shel ha-yetsira ha-miqra'it* (Tel Aviv: Dvir, 1966). Cogan notes that this story, which is very old, shows an aversion to such necromancy long before Deuteronomy.

Abigail

For earlier studies see Jon Levenson, "I Sam. 25 as Literature and as History," *Catholic Biblical Quarterly* 40 (1978): 11–28; Natan Klaus, "Ne'um Abigail" (Abigail's Speech), *Beth Mikra;* Robert Polzin, "Providential Delays (2 Sam. 24:1–26:25)," in *Samuel and the Deuteronomist: A Literary Study of the Deuteronomic History, Part 2* (Bloomington: Indiana University Press, 1989), 205–15; Moshe Garsiel, "Wit, Words and a Woman: I Samuel 25," in *On Humour and the Comic in the Hebrew Bible,* ed. Yehuda Radday and Athalya Brenner (Sheffield: Almond, 1990), 163–68; and Alice Bach, *The Pleasure of her Text: Feminist Readings of Biblical and Historical Texts* (Philadelphia: Trinity Press International, 1990), 25–44. See also the treatment in Kyle McCarter, *Samuel I,* Anchor Bible (Garden City, N.Y.: Doubleday, 1980).

315 **two "wise women"** See Claudia Camp, "The Wise Women of 2 Samuel: A Role Model for Women in Early Israel?," *Catholic Biblical Quarterly* 43 (1981): 14–29, and above, pp. 58–63 .

320 **the tied (book) of the living** The verb *ṣarar* means "to tie," and N. H. Tur-Sinai explained that the "tying-up" of the living, which also appears in Job 14:17, is the same as the "book of the living" referred to in Ps. 60:29 (N. H. Tur-Sinai, *The Book of Job: A New Commentary,* rev. ed. [Jerusalem: Kiryath Sefer, 1967]). At the golden calf episode, Moses asks that if God would not forgive the people's sin, God should erase him from "the book you have written" and God replied that the one who sinned "I will erase from my book" (Exod. 32, 32–33). Keeping the document tied prevents names from falling out accidentally.

321 **nāgîd** Levenson suggests it was her good sense rather than prophecy that made her know David would be king. But the God-centered nature of her language, and the frequent repetition of God's name, make it more likely that she speaks

from prophecy. Her function as oracle would not be affected by the source of her inspiration.

322 **Nabal died** Polzin points out that Nabal's death is "proleptic" of Saul's.

Huldah

For studies, see Duane Christensen, "Huldah and the Men of Anathoth: Women in Leadership in the Deuteronomic History," *Society of Biblical Literature Seminar Papers, 1984*, 399–404; Lowell K. Handy, "The Role of Huldah in Josiah's Cult Reform," *Zeitschrift für Alttestamentliches Wissenschaft* 106 (1994): 40–53; Diana Edelman, "Huldah the Prophet of Yahweh or Asherah?" in *A Feminist Companion to Samuel and Kings*, ed. Athalya Brenner (Sheffield: Sheffield Academic Press, 1994), 231–50; David A. Glatt-Gilad, "The Role of Huldah's Prophecy in the Chronicler's Portrayal of Josiah's Reform," *Biblica* 77 (1996): 16–31.

324 **Chronicles** For this, see David Glatt-Gilad, "The Role of Huldah's Prophecy."

325 **Jeremiah** Edelman brings the many verbal parallels between Huldah and Jeremiah. Her own conclusion, however, that Josiah sent his men to Huldah as prophetess of Asherah, the intercessor goddess, is improbable. Even in the inscriptions that bless in the name of YHWH and his Asherah, the active party whose blessing is invoked is YHWH, and the verb is in the masculine singular.

325 **King Esarhaddon** The Mesopotamian parallels are brought by Handy, "The Role of Huldah."

326 **biblical interpretation** Claudia Camp remarks on Huldah's claiming authority over the text and over the people's history in interpreting their situation (Camp, "Female Voice, Written Word: Women and Authority in Hebrew Scripture," in *Embodied Love: Sensuality and Relationship as Feminist Values*, ed. Paula M. Cooey, Sharon A. Farmer, and Mary Ellen Ross (San Francisco: Harper & Row, 1987).

The Later Adventures of Biblical Women

Some of the post-biblical traditions of biblical stories (primarily Second Temple sources) have been collected by James Kugel, *Traditions of the Bible: A Guide to the Bible as It Was at the Start of the Common Era* (Cambridge: Harvard University Press, 1999). Classic rabbinic sources have been collected in Hebrew in the multivolume *Torah Šelemah: A Talmudic-Midrashic Encyclopedia of the Five Books of Moses*, ed. Menahem Kasher (in progress from the Torah Shelemah Institute, Jerusalem, 1992–present). In English, the classic source for Jewish traditions is Louis Ginsberg, *Legends of the Jews* (Philadelphia: Jewish Publication Society, 1911). Early Christian sources can be searched on CD-ROMs of the church fathers.

340 **Garden of Eden** See Bernard Prusak, "Women: Seductive Siren and Source of Sin? Pseudepigraphical Myth and Christian Origins," in *Religion and Sexism*, ed. Rosemary Reuther (New York: Simon & Schuster, 1974), 89–116.

340 **retold** For discussion with examples, see "Gifts of the Greeks," in Tikva Frymer-Kensky, *In the Wake of the Goddesses: Women, Culture and the Biblical Transformation of Pagan Myth* (New York: Free Press, 1993), 202–12, 276–81.

340 **Joseph . . . the ṣaddîq** For these stories see James Kugel, *In Potiphar's House: The Interpretive Life of Biblical Texts* (Cambridge: Harvard University Press, 1994), and Shalom Goldman, *The Wiles of Women/The Wiles of Men: Joseph and Potiphar's Wife in Ancient Near Eastern, Jewish, and Islamic Folklore* (Albany: State University of New York Press, 1993).

340 **the tale of the engagement of Rivka** For a discussion of this aspect of the Rivka story, see Alexander Rofé, "An Enquiry into the Betrothal of Rebekah," in *Die Hebräische Bible und ihr zweifache Nachgeschicte: Festschrift für Rolf Rendtorff,* ed. Erhard Blum, Christian Macholz, and Ekkehard Stagemann (Neukirchen-Vluyn: Neukirchener Verlag, 1990), 27–30. Rofé presents convincing linguistic evidence for late vocabulary and syntax and persuasive argument for the lateness of some of the underlying assumptions of the story. He argues that the whole story was written to inculcate the ideas about no intermarriage and no leaving the land, ideas vitally important during the Second Temple period. However, there is no reason to assume that the story itself does not rest on earlier versions, written or oral.

341 **trace that this battle left** For a discussion of the hidden polemic, see Yairah Amit, "The Hidden Polemic over Those 'Who dwell in Samaria,' " in *Hidden Polemics in Biblical Narrative,* trans. Jonathan Chipman (Leiden: Brill, 2000), 189–220; and see notes to Dinah chapter.

341 **Post-biblical Israel** John Collins, "The Epic of Theodotus and the Hellenism of the Hasmoneans," *Harvard Theological Review* 73 (1980): 91–104; Stanley Gewirtz, "Simeon and Levi in 'the Blessing of Jacob' (Gen. 49: 5–7)," *Hebrew Union College Annual* 52 (1981): 93–128; Reinhard Pummer, "Genesis 34 in the Jewish Writings of the Hellenistic and Roman Periods," *Harvard Theological Review* 75 (1982): 177–88; James Kugel, "The Story of Dinah in the *Testament of Levi,*" *Harvard Theological Review* 85 (1992): 1–34; Tjitze Baarda, "The Shechem Episode in the Testament of Levi: A Comparison with Other Traditions," in *Sacred History and Sacred Texts in Early Judaism: A Symposium in Honor of A. S. van der Woude,* ed. J. N. Bremmer and F. Garlia Martinez (Kampen, The Netherlands: Pharos, 1992), 11–73; and Angela Standhartinger, " 'Um zu Sehen Die Töchter des Landes' Die Perspective Dinas in der Jüsiach-Hellenistischen Diskussion üm Gen. 34," in *Religious Propaganda and Missionary Competition in the New Testament World: Essays Honoring Dieter Georgi* (Leiden: Brill, 1994), 89–116.

341 **Josephus** *Antiquitates Judaicae* IV 6, 6–12, §126–51. I rely on the translation of H. St. J. Thackeray and Ralph Marcus in the Loeb Classical Library. For a study of Josephus's version, see W. C. Van Unnik, "Josephus's Account of the Story of Israel's Sin with Alien Women in the Country of Midian (Num. 25:1f)," in *Travels in the World of the O.T.: Studies Presented to M. A. Beek,* ed. H. van Voss et al. (Assen: van Gorcum, 1974), 241–61, and William Klassen, "Jesus and Phineas: A Rejected Role Model," *Society of Biblical Literature Seminar Papers* (1986), 490–500.

342 **Pseudo-Philo** See Dorothy Sly, "Changes in the Perception of the Offense in Numbers 25:1," *Proceedings in the Eastern Great Lakes and Midwest Biblical Society* 11 (1991): 200–209. Sly lists the other references in Philo: Moses 195–305; Virtues 34–46; Spec 55–57. Translation from *Life of Moses,* Loeb Classical Library.

344 **Phineas required several miracles** For the slightly variant lists, see BT Sanhedrin 82b and Numbers Rabbah 20–25.

344 **Judah and Tamar** See the study by Esther Menn, "Judah and Tamar (Genesis 38)," in *Ancient Jewish Exegesis: Studies in Literary Form and Hermeneutics*, supplements to the *Journal for the Study of Judaic Studies* 51 (Leiden: Brill, 1997).

344 **Tamar . . . descendant of . . . Shem** Pseudo-Jonathan 38:6, Genesis Rabbah 85:10, Numbers Rabbah 13:4.

345 **Judah's public confession** See C. E. Hayes, "The Midrashic Career of the Confession of Judah (Genesis 38:26), Parts 1 and 2," *Vetus Testamentum* 45 (1995): 52–81.

345 **Rahab . . . righteous convert** Song of Songs Rabbah 27:4.

345 **associated with Ruth** Midrash Ruth Zutra 1, 1.

345 **with Jethro** Song of Songs Rabbah 1:22; Numbers Rabbah 3:2.

345 **Joshua's convert** See Otsar hamidrashim *yitbarech* 3.

345 **to the merit of the people from whom they came** Talmud Jerusalmi, Rosh Hashanah 57b.

345 **innkeeper** Sifrei Numbers 88, 5; Targum (ad loc).

345 **Rahab was ten years old . . . converted at fifty.** Mekhilta de Rabbi Ishmael *yitro* 1.5.

346 **Moses prayed unsuccessfully** Tanna debei Eliyahu Zutra 22.1.

346 **Hezekiah . . . prayer** JT Sanhedrin 10, 28, 3:2; BT Berakhot 4, 8b Kohelet Rabbah 5, 5:1.

346 **revered as the progenitress of both prophets and kings** Sifrei *beha'alotka* 20; Ruth Rabbah 1:2; Job Zutra 1, 34; Peskita de Rav Kahana 13, 5.

346 **Ezekiel and Jeremiah** Pesikta de Rav Kahana 13, 12.

346 **four great beauties** Megilla 16a Otsar Midrashim *hupat Eliyahyu* 5.

346 **"Rahab, Rahab"** Ta'anit 5b, Megillah 16a.

347 **Renaissance Christian commentator Tyndale** See Ilona N. Rashkow, *Upon the Dark Places: Antisemitism and Sexism in English Renaissance Biblical Translation* (Sheffield: Sheffield Academic Press, 1990), p. 97.

INDEX

About the Author

Tikva Frymer-Kensky is a professor of Hebrew Bible at the Divinity School at the University of Chicago. She is the author of many works of biblical scholarship and spirituality, including *In the Wake of the Goddesses: Women, Culture and the Biblical Transformation of Pagan Myth* and *Motherprayer: The Pregnant Woman's Spiritual Companion*. She lives in New York City and Chicago.

A Note on the Type

This book was set in Monotype Dante, a typeface designed by Giovanni Mardersteig (1892–1977). Conceived as a private type for the Officina Bodoni in Verona, Italy, Dante was originally cut only for hand composition by Charles Malin, the famous Parisian punch cutter, between 1946 and 1952. Its first use was in an edition of Boccaccio's *Trattatello in laude di Dante* that appeared in 1954. The Monotype Corporation's version of Dante followed in 1957. Although modeled on the Aldine type used for Pietro Cardinal Bembo's treatise De Aetna in 1495, Dante is a thoroughly modern interpretation of the venerable face.

Composed by Digital Composition, Berryville, Virginia
Printed and bound by Berryville Graphics,
Berryville, Virginia
Designed by Anthea Lingeman